FOUNDATION PRESS

CRIMINAL PROCEDURE

STORIES

Edited By

CAROL S. STEIKER

Professor of Law
Harvard Law School

FOUNDATION PRESS

2006

THOMSON
—★—™
WEST

© 2006 By FOUNDATION PRESS
   395 Hudson Street
   New York, NY 10014
   Phone Toll Free 1–877–888–1330
   Fax (212) 367–6799
   foundation-press.com
Printed in the United States of America

ISBN–13: 978–1–58778–983–0
ISBN–10: 1–58778–983–3

 TEXT IS PRINTED ON 10% POST CONSUMER RECYCLED PAPER

CRIMINAL PROCEDURE STORIES

FOUNDATION PRESS

CRIMINAL PROCEDURE STORIES

*

INTRODUCTION

Carol S. Steiker

CRIMINAL PROCEDURE STORIES: INTRODUCTION

The United States is unique in the world in the degree to which its criminal processes—both police practices and adjudication—are governed by federal constitutional law. Constitutional litigation that episodically and unpredictably reshapes the structure of criminal justice systems throughout the nation stands in sharp contrast to other modes of criminal justice reform, such as legislation, specialized commissions, or administrative oversight. Whether this emphasis on constitutional regulation provides important safeguards or whether it is nuts (simply no way to run a railroad)—or perhaps both—is an interesting question, which the chapters that follow help in various ways to answer. But, at a minimum, this arrangement assures that the development of American criminal procedure is driven by stories, by the individual Supreme Court cases that have left a lasting imprint on the doctrines that manage the interactions between citizens and law enforcement agents and that structure the adjudicative process.

Perhaps more so than cases in any other legal category, criminal procedure cases make great stories—which is why so many variations on these issues find their way into movies and television shows. This book hosts an extraordinarily colorful cast of characters, ranging from the Damon Runyon-esque character of Charlie Katz,[1] to the Tony Soprano-esque character of "Fat Tony" Salerno,[2] to the Hoffa-esque and Kennedy-esque characters of Jimmy Hoffa and Bobby Kennedy themselves, squaring off over the Kennedy Justice Department's prosecution of Hoffa for jury tampering.[3] The crimes at issue in these cases range from the sort of serious violent crimes, such as murder and rape, that one might expect to drive important developments in constitutional doctrine, to the more surprising, oddball offenses. Who would have thought that the pornographic pencil doodle seized by the police from Dollree Mapp would lead to the incorporation of the Fourth Amendment exclusionary rule,[4] or that Paul Hayes' bad check to the Pic Pac grocery store would launch a thousand pleas?[5]

---

[1] *See* Katz v. United States, 389 U.S. 347 (1967).

[2] *See* Salerno v. United States, 479 U.S. 1026 (1987).

[3] *See* Hoffa v. United States, 385 U.S. 293 (1966).

[4] *See* Mapp v. Ohio, 367 U.S. 643, 668 (1961) (Douglas, J., concurring).

[5] *See* Bordenkircher v. Hayes, 434 U.S. 357 (1978) (approving the constitutionality of plea bargaining in a case involving the passing of a forged check for $88.30).

The stories I have chosen for inclusion in this volume span roughly equally the divide between police practices and adjudication, and they include many of the cases that will be found in any Criminal Procedure syllabus (*Mapp*[6] and *Miranda*[7] for police practices, and *Brady*[8] and *Batson*[9] for adjudication). When I have included cases that are less universally studied (*Powell*,[10] *Brignoni-Ponce*,[11] and *Mistretta*,[12] for example), it is because they allow the consideration of themes (the history of racial discrimination in the administration of criminal justice in the South, the limits on the use of racial profiling as a tool of law enforcement, and the constitutional status of the Federal Sentencing Guidelines) that are central to understanding the development of American criminal procedure.

Close consideration of the stories behind these cases—the individuals, the social and political worlds in which their criminal prosecutions arose, the provenance of their legal claims, the Supreme Court's internal struggles to resolve the claims, and the human and doctrinal repercussions of the Court's decisions—offers many rewards. Of course, it is intriguing and entertaining. Teachers of criminal procedure have long relied upon the intrinsic, voyeuristic thrill of studying cops-and-robbers and courtroom drama, and they will not be disappointed by the vivid details unearthed in these tales (John Brady's journey from death row to a law-abiding life outside of prison; the prosecutor who named his dog "Batson" after his most famous case). But consideration of these stories as a unit also yields powerful and perhaps surprising insights that go beyond mere narrative enrichment.

The most striking theme that emerges from the stories behind the cases—far more than the opinions themselves suggest—is the intersection of the criminal procedure revolution and the struggle for racial equality, especially in the South. It is no accident that the story of

[6] Mapp v. Ohio, 367 U.S. 643 (1961) (incorporating the 4th Amendment exclusionary rule).

[7] Miranda v. Arizona, 384 U.S. 436 (1966) (requiring the administration of warnings to permit the introduction of statements taken by law enforcement agents during custodial interrogation).

[8] Brady v. Maryland, 373 U.S. 83 (1963) (requiring prosecutors to disclose to the defense all material exculpatory evidence).

[9] Batson v. Kentucky, 476 U.S. 79 (1986) (changing the rules for proving discriminatory intent in the use of peremptory strikes during jury selection).

[10] Powell v. Alabama, 287 U.S. 45 (1932) (reversing the capital convictions of the "Scottsboro Boys" for violation of their Sixth Amendment right to counsel).

[11] United States v. Brignoni-Ponce, 422 U.S. 873 (1975) (allowing roving border patrol agents to use Mexican ancestry as a factor, but not the sole factor, in deciding whether to stop and question motorists).

[12] Mistretta v. United States, 488 U.S. 361 (1989) (upholding the constitutionality of the Sentencing Reform Act of 1984, which established the Federal Sentencing Commission and led to the promulgation of the Federal Sentencing Guidelines).

the "Scottsboro boys" appears first in this volume and is depicted on its cover, as the Scottsboro case represents the Supreme Court's first, early foray into the constitutionalization of state criminal procedure in a self-conscious effort to check abuses of the criminal justice process engendered by pervasive racial subordination. The Scottsboro case is almost a caricature of Southern justice run amok: flimsy charges of rape brought against black men by white women lead to quick convictions and death sentences with a minimum of legal process. But other cases that are less frequently recognized as "race" cases reveal themselves to be crucibles of similar struggles.

Perhaps the best example is *Duncan v. Louisiana*,[13] the case that incorporated the right to trial by jury. The opinion is often taught as a case about the abstract value of juries, excerpted to showcase quotes about the advantages and disadvantages of lay decision-making in criminal cases. But the story behind Duncan's prosecution (and the prosecution of his *lawyer*, as well) reveals just how common it was for the criminal justice system to be wielded as a weapon against civil rights organizers during the civil rights movement of the 1950s and '60s. Local law enforcers in the South used the criminal justice system in their communities very much as dictators use their armies—to intimidate dissenters with threatened and actual violence sanctioned by law. Although the *Duncan* Court makes little mention of race or Southern-style criminal justice, the context could not have been lost on the Supreme Court in the flashpoint year of 1968. And while the Court was surprisingly reluctant to discuss race in many of its key criminal procedure decisions of the 1960s, it emphasized again and again the theme of "equality" for criminal defendants. For example, the need for equality of poor or uneducated defendants vis-à-vis wealthier or more sophisticated defendants was central to the *Miranda* Court, just as equality of defendants in general vis-à-vis the prosecution was a major theme sounded by the *Brady* Court.

It is interesting to speculate why discussion of criminal procedure as a tool of racial equality is so absent from the formal decisions of the Court during the criminal procedure revolution of the 1960s. Perhaps the Court's decision to regulate the criminal process by incorporation of the criminal procedure provisions of the Bill of Rights through the Due Process Clause seemed to preclude overt reference to issues of racial justice, which the Court tended to address under the rubric of Equal Protection. Perhaps incorporation felt more universal and "colorblind," or less controversial and "political," than overtly race-based rulings, given the divisive politics of the time. But it is impossible to read the *Duncan* story and conclude that racial justice could be anywhere but just beneath the surface of the Court's concerns.

[13] 391 U.S. 145 (1968).

The *Duncan* story points up another subterranean issue that evaded direct treatment from the Court but could not have escaped its notice: the harshness of much criminal punishment in relation to the offenses at issue. Gary Duncan himself faced a potential two–year sentence—and actually received two months and stiff fine—for what at most constituted a slap at the arm of another teenager. Paul Hayes faced life in prison for forging an $88 check for groceries. And the Federal Sentencing Guidelines in general were widely decried for their overall severity and for constricting judicial discretion to allow for leniency. But *Duncan*, *Bordenkircher*, and *Mistretta* were all cases—as the title of this volume declares—about criminal *procedure*, not about the substantive criminal law. The same Court the ushered in a so-called "revolution" in constitutional criminal procedure was far more reluctant to undertake any potent constitutional regulation of criminal justice outcomes, despite the potential power of the Eighth Amendment's prohibition of "excessive fines" and "cruel and unusual punishments." As a result, some of the Court's decisions seem oddly out-of-tune with the concerns of the day. *Mistretta* is a case in point: did anyone really think that the primary defect of the Sentencing Guidelines was that they violated constitutional separation of powers by giving the judiciary *too much* power?

But tone-deafness is not the worst defect of the Court's emphasis on procedure over substance in its constitutional regulation of criminal justice. The most significant cost of the Court's neglect of criminal justice outcomes is the unchecked rise of the American prison population with its concomitant increased racial disparate impact, as Bill Stuntz elaborates in his chapter on *Bordenkircher* and plea-bargaining. It is a profound irony that the Warren Court, famous for its concerns about racial justice, equality, and the rights of criminal defendants, failed to prevent—indeed, failed to even try to prevent—the tidal surge of mass incarceration, overwhelmingly of poor and minority defendants, during the last quarter of the twentieth century.

Indeed, re-reading the landmark cases of the infamously "soft on crime" Warren Court, especially in light of the next several decades of legal developments, suggests that the Court hardly deserves the blame for handcuffing the police that its detractors asserted, with their "Impeach Earl Warren" bumper stickers that helped elect Richard Nixon to the presidency in 1968. Or, from the opposite political perspective, the Warren Court's criminal procedure revolution looks a lot less revolutionary in assuring the rights of criminal defendants when viewed through the rear-view mirror thirty or forty years later. In particular, Chief Justice Warren's careful, almost tortured, opinion in *Terry v. Ohio*,[14] approving brief warrantless intrusions on less than probable

---

[14] 392 U.S. 11 (1968).

cause, ultimately legitimized a wide variety of other such intrusions, as Justice Douglas predicted at the time of the *Terry* decision and reiterated in a stinging rebuke in the Court's first racial profiling case less than a decade later.[15] Similarly, the Court's opinion approving the use of an undercover informant in Jimmy Hoffa's case, which relied crucially on an "assumption of risk" theory first developed by Justice Brennan, has had broad repercussions in legitimizing a wide variety of intrusive law enforcement tactics, as elaborated by Tracey Maclin in his chapter on the *Hoffa* case.

Even the primary treasures (or targets, depending on one's point of view) of the Warren Court's revolution—*Mapp, Gideon, Brady, Miranda*—have generally failed in important respects to deliver on their ringing promises. This failure is due not merely to intentional abandonment of the Warren Court's commitments resulting from the changing membership of the Court over time (though of course, such changes were important). Rather, the absence of effective remedies undermines rights, however broadly they may be asserted, as David Cole and Stephanos Bibas elaborate in their discussions, respectively, of *Gideon* and *Brady*. Conversely, the creation of extremely powerful or drastic remedies has a natural tendency to lead to the limitation of whatever right is at stake, as Yale Kamisar and Pam Karlan demonstrate in their treatments, respectively, of *Mapp* and *Batson*. As a result, many of the great pronouncements of rights in constitutional criminal procedure have had more symbolic than concrete significance, a theme that is developed most explicitly by Mike Klarman's rich history of Scottsboro and Steve Schulhofer's evaluation of *Miranda*.

But before we write off the criminal procedure "revolution" as just so much overblown hype, it is striking to see in these pages how doctrines long thought virtually lifeless can be rejuvenated in a different context or a different day. For example, the right to a jury trial, incorporated by *Duncan* and rendered virtually obsolete by the system of plea-bargaining approved in *Bordenkircher*, came back with a vengeance in the line of cases flowing from *Apprendi v. New Jersey*,[16] which eventually led to the invalidation of the Federal Sentencing Guidelines and various state sentencing schemes as well, as discussed by Kate Stith in the *Mistretta* chapter. In an even more startling turn-around, the Supreme Court has wielded the extremely deferential standard for evaluating claims that a criminal defendant received "ineffective assistance of counsel"[17] to overturn three capital convictions in the past five years, a development

---

[15] *See* United States v. Brignoni-Ponce, 422 U.S. 873, 888 (1975) (Douglas, J., concurring) ("The fears I voiced in *Terry* about the weakening of the Fourth Amendment have regrettably been borne out by subsequent events."). Justice Douglas' views are discussed both by John Barrett in his *Terry* chapter and by Bernard Harcourt in his chapter on *Brignoni-Ponce* and racial profiling.

[16] 530 U.S. 466 (2000).

[17] *See* Strickland v. Washington, 466 U.S. 668 (1984).

that introduces a ray of hope into David Cole's otherwise bleak assessment of the right to counsel in his chapter on *Gideon* and *Strickland*. Pam Karlan's chapter on *Batson*, too, concludes with consideration of the Supreme Court's recent invalidation of a Texas man's capital conviction because of a pattern of race-based peremptory strikes by the prosecution.

Moreover, even when it is not reinvigorating old doctrines to generate surprising outcomes, the Court continually returns to its prior work to seek tools for crafting new solutions to new problems. In the classic tradition of common-law development, nothing is ever wasted; even when the Court is scanning the horizon into the future, it always has one eye simultaneously looking back over its shoulder. David Sklansky describes how Justice Scalia, when faced with the challenge of limiting "the power of technology to shrink the realm of guaranteed privacy,"[18] returned to and reconciled with the Court's much-maligned approach in *Katz* more than three decades earlier, when the technology at issue was much cruder and less pervasive. Dan Richman demonstrates how the Court's struggle with the validity of preventive detention in the context of the pre-trial confinement of mobster Anthony Salerno set the terms of discussion for the even bigger and more vexing problem of non-criminal preventive detention of suspects in the post-9/11 "war on terrorism."

The nature of Fourth Amendment limits on the use of emerging technology and the scope of constitutional limits on law enforcement techniques in the war on terrorism are only two of many important unanswered questions that will become pressing in the immediate future. The invalidation of sentencing guidelines in federal and some state courts will no doubt lead to legislation that will require further constitutional consideration by the Court. The permissibility of racial profiling in its many possible incarnations is overdue for consideration by the high Court. And the future dimensions or even life of controversial doctrines like *Mapp* and *Miranda* always remain in question, especially as the new Roberts Court takes shape. Whatever new chapters will be written on these issues, however, there can be little doubt that the story starts with the stories considered here.

When I first started this project, the most striking challenge was narrowing the cases to a manageable number. There seemed to be so many stories that needed to be told, so many legal developments that should have been included, so many thoughtful debates that have framed the issues. But now, looking back on the completed project, what strikes me is how little law there really is, how much has not yet happened, how much we do not know. This multitude of unanswered questions is, of course, one of the great frustrations of our system of regulating the criminal process through constitutional adjudication. But it is also one of the great and exciting challenges of our system for students, lawyers, judges, and scholars. I hope that the work done here in faithfully preserving these stories and reflecting on their significance helps in some small way to advance this common task.

---

[18] Kyllo v. United States, 533 U.S. 27, 34 (2001).

1

Powell v. Alabama: The Supreme Court Confronts "Legal Lynchings"

Michael J. Klarman[*]

A Fateful Train Ride

The freight train left Chattanooga for Memphis at 10:20 A.M. on March 25, 1931. Thirty minutes after it had pulled out of Stevenson, Alabama, the station master saw a group of white hoboes walking along the train tracks toward the station. They told him that several black youths had thrown them off the train after a fight. The station master telephoned ahead to the next stop, Scottsboro, but the train had already passed through. It was finally stopped at Paint Rock, where a sheriff's posse discovered nine black youngsters and, to everyone's surprise, two young white women dressed in men's overalls.[1]

The nine blacks, known to history as the Scottsboro Boys, ranged in age from 13 to 20. Five of them were from Georgia, though they claimed not to know one another. The other four were from Chattanooga, and they did know one another. All of the nine were vagrants, and most were illiterate.

Twenty minutes after the train was stopped, one of the women, Ruby Bates, called over a posse member and told him that she and her companion, Victoria Price, had been gang raped by the blacks. The boys were immediately arrested and taken to the Scottsboro jail. As the sheriff sent the women to two local doctors for medical examinations, news of the alleged attacks spread. By day's end, a crowd of several

---

[*] I am grateful to Carol Steiker and Bill Stuntz for comments on an earlier draft and to Jessica King, James McKinley, Gabe Mendel, Asieh Narriman, Sheri Shepherd, and Sarah Teich for research assistance. The wonderful reference librarians at the University of Virginia School of Law provided invaluable assistance in researching this article; I owe special thanks to Cathy Palombi. Anyone working on Scottsboro must acknowledge the extraordinary contributions to our understanding of this episode made by Dan Carter and James Goodman.

[1] Dan T. Carter, *Scottsboro: A Tragedy of the American South* (rev. ed. 1979), 3–5; James Goodman, *Stories of Scottsboro* (1994), 1–4.

hundred had gathered outside of the jail, demanding that the "niggers" be turned over for lynching. Sheriff M.L. Wann pleaded with the mob to allow the law to take its course and threatened to shoot anyone who rushed the jail. He also telephoned the governor for assistance, and by 11:00 PM, twenty-five armed guardsmen were on their way to Scotts-boro. To ensure the boys' safety, they were moved to a sturdier jail in nearby Etowah. The local circuit judge, Alfred E. Hawkins, convened a special session of the grand jury to indict the boys; local citizens complained of the five-day delay. One local newspaper remarked, "It is best for the county that these things be disposed of in a speedy manner as it gives no excuse for people taking the law into their own hands."[2]

A decade or two earlier, black men charged with raping white women under similar circumstances might well have been executed without trial. Lynchings in the South peaked in the late 1880s and early 1890s, when well over a hundred were reported annually and in some years over two hundred. Most lynchings were linked to allegations of crime—usually murder or rape, though occasionally the alleged "of-fense" was as minor as breach of racial etiquette or general uppityness. Prior to World War I, lynchings typically enjoyed the support of local communities; efforts to prosecute even known lynchers were rare, and convictions were virtually nonexistent.[3]

By 1930, however, the annual number of reported lynchings had declined dramatically—from 187.5 in the 1890s to 16.8 in the second half of the 1920s. This decline was attributable to many factors, including the threat that federal anti-lynching legislation would be enacted, the dimin-ishing insularity of the South, more professional law enforcement, and better education. But the decline in lynchings probably also depended on their replacement with speedy trials that reliably produced guilty ver-dicts, death sentences, and rapid executions. Some jurisdictions actually enacted laws designed to prevent lynchings by providing for special terms of court to convene within days of alleged rapes and other incendiary crimes. In many instances, law enforcement officers explicitly promised prospective lynch mobs that black defendants would be quickly tried and executed if the mob desisted, and prosecutors appealed to juries to convict in order to reward mobs for good behavior and thus encourage similar restraint in the future.[4]

In such cases, guilt or innocence often mattered little. As one white southerner candidly remarked in 1933, "If a white woman is prepared to

---

[2] Carter, 6–17 (quotation at 17); Goodman, 21–22; *New York Times* (hereafter, *NYT*), 25 March 1931, p. 21.

[3] Carter, 105; Michael J. Klarman, *From Jim Crow to Civil Rights: The Supreme Court and the Struggle for Racial Equality* (2004), 118–19.

[4] Klarman, 119.

swear that a Negro either raped or attempted to rape her, we see to it that the Negro is executed." Prevailing racial norms did not permit white jurors to believe a black man's word over that of a white woman; prevailing gender norms did not allow defense counsel to closely interrogate a white woman about allegations involving sex. As one contemporary southern newspaper observed, the honor of a white woman was more important than the life of a black man. And because most southern white men believed that black males secretly lusted after "their" women, they generally found such rape allegations credible. Congressman George Huddleston of Birmingham, whom the NAACP initially approached to represent the Scottsboro boys on appeal, repulsed the overtures, observing that they "had been found riding on the same freight car with two white women, and that's enough for me!" White people in Scottsboro told an investigator from the American Civil Liberties Union (ACLU) that "we white people just couldn't afford to let these niggers off because of the effect it would have on other niggers."[5]

The Scottsboro boys received precisely the sort of "justice" that often prevailed in trials that substituted for lynchings. Both local newspapers treated the defendants as obviously guilty even before the trial. The hometown newspaper of the alleged victims, the Huntsville *Daily Times*, described the rapes as "the most atrocious ever recorded in this part of the country, a wholesale debauching of society." Judge Hawkins tried to assign all seven members of the Scottsboro bar to represent the defendants, but all but one of them declined. That one was Milo Moody, nearly seventy years old and later described by one investigator as "a doddering, extremely unreliable, senile individual who is losing whatever ability he once had."[6]

The trials began on April 6, just twelve days after the train incident. A crowd estimated at five to ten thousand gathered outside the courthouse, which was protected by national guardsmen wielding machine guns. Hawkins appointed as trial counsel a Tennessee lawyer, Stephen R. Roddy, who had been sent to Scottsboro by the defendants' families to look after their interests. Roddy was an alcoholic, and one observer reported that "he could scarcely walk straight" that morning. When Roddy objected to his appointment on the grounds that he was unpre-

---

[5] Klarman, 118 ("white woman"); "Excerpts from a Confidential Report on the Scottsboro Cases", 7 May 1931, Papers of the National Association for the Advancement of Colored People (August Meier, ed., University Publications of America, 1982, microfilm edition) (hereafter, "NAACP"), part 6, reel 2, frames 893–94 (Huddleston); H. Ransdell, "Report on the Scottsboro Case" (27 May 1931) (hereafter, "Ransdell Report"), *ibid.*, reel 3, frames 150–80, p. 26/frame 175 ("white people"); Carter, 133–35.

[6] Carter, 13, 17–18, 20 (Huntsville *Daily Times*); "Memorandum on visit to National Office, May 18, 1931, of Mrs. Hollace Ransdall [sic]," 19 May 1931, NAACP, part 6, reel 3, frame 27 ("doddering"); Goodman, 26.

pared and unfamiliar with Alabama law, Hawkins appointed Moody, the local septuagenarian, to assist him. Roddy was permitted less than half an hour with his clients before the trial began. Defense counsel moved for a change of venue based on the inflammatory newspaper coverage and the attempted lynching of the defendants. But Sheriff Wann now denied that the defendants had been threatened, and Judge Hawkins denied the motion.[7]

The state sought the death penalty against eight of the nine defendants—all but the one who was identified as being only thirteen years old. The nine were tried in four groups, beginning with Clarence Norris and Charley Weems. Victoria Price was the main prosecution witness, and she testified that the black youths had thrown the white boys off the train and then gang raped her and Bates. According to one second-hand account, Price testified "with such gusto, snap and wise-cracks, that the courtroom was often in a roar of laughter." Judge Hawkins blocked defense counsels' efforts to elicit admissions that the women were prostitutes and that they had had sexual intercourse with boyfriends the night before the train incident, which would have explained the semen found in their vaginas during medical examinations. Testimony given by the examining doctors raised serious doubts as to whether the girls had been raped: They were not hysterical when examined, nor had they incurred any serious physical injuries. Moreover, Price had so little semen in her vagina that a sequential rape by six men, as alleged, was highly improbable. And the sperm found in the women was non-motile, which virtually ruled out the possibility of intercourse within the preceding few hours. The two women also provided inconsistent accounts of various details of the incident, such as whether they had spoken with the white boys on the train and how long the interracial fracas had lasted. One man present when the train was stopped testified that he had not heard Price make any rape allegations. However, the admission by Norris on cross-examination that the women had been raped by all of the other eight defendants, though not by him, severely undercut his defense. (It later came out that Sheriff Wann had warned Norris that he would be killed if he did not admit that the girls had been raped.) Defense counsel prodded the illiterate and confused Norris to change his story, but he held firm. The defense called no witnesses and made no closing argument.[8]

While the jury deliberated on the fate of Norris and Weems, the trial of Haywood Patterson began. When the first jury returned to the courtroom to announce guilty verdicts and death sentences, crowds in and out of the courthouse erupted with delight. According to defense

---

[7] Carter, 19–24 (quotation at 22).

[8] Carter, 24–35; Ransdell Report, *supra* note 5, at p. 7 (Price quotation).

lawyer Roddy, "[i]nstantly, a wild and thunderous roar went up from the audience and was heard by those in the Court House yard where thousands took up the demonstration and carried it on for fifteen or twenty minutes." Even though Patterson's jury heard this commotion, Judge Hawkins refused to declare a mistrial.[9]

The prosecution's case grew stronger with each trial, as previously unhelpful witnesses were dropped, and the alleged victims improved their stories with practice. Patterson contradicted himself on the witness stand within five minutes as to whether he had seen the girls being raped or indeed had seen them at all. Several of the other defendants testified inconsistently as well; one confirmed that the girls had been raped, while others denied even having seen the girls on the train. After less than twenty-five minutes of deliberation, the jury convicted Patterson and sentenced him to death.[10]

Five of the defendants were prosecuted together in a third trial. The state's case against them was even weaker because these defendants did not incriminate each other on cross-examination, the women were less certain in identifying them, and one of the defendants was nearly blind and another had such a severe case of venereal disease that raping a woman would have been very difficult. The jury nonetheless returned five more death sentences. Judge Hawkins declared a mistrial in the case of the last defendant, Roy Wright, when the jury could not agree on whether to sentence the 13–year-old to life imprisonment or death—a sentence the prosecution had not even sought. None of the four trials lasted more than a few hours.[11]

Representation on Appeal

The Communist party quickly realized the potential for propaganda and fund-raising afforded by the Scottsboro episode, which it saw as the Sacco and Vanzetti case of the 1930s. Communists denounced the trials as "legal lynchings" and assailed the "parasite landlords and capitalist classes of the South." Less radical voices also protested this "barbarous penalty" imposed on eight black youngsters. By contrast, the National Association for the Advancement of Colored People (NAACP), generally reluctant to intervene in criminal cases unless reasonably certain that the defendants were innocent, was slow to act. This enabled the Interna-

---

[9] Carter, 35–38; "To the Friends and Relatives of the Nine Negro Boys Charged with Rape, in Jackson County, Alabama," 11 Apr. 1931, NAACP, part 6, reel 2, frames 624–27 (quotation at p. 4/frame 627).

[10] Carter, 38–43; Goodman, 14–15.

[11] Carter, 42–48.

tional Labor Defense (ILD), the legal arm of the Communist party, to secure the defendants' consent to its representing them.[12]

Stung by criticism from supporters for its dilatory response and finding that "public interest is so deep that we cannot afford not to be in the case," NAACP leaders aggressively challenged the ILD for control of the boys' appeals. The NAACP convinced some black leaders in Chatta-nooga that communist involvement would be a millstone around the boys' necks, and the defendants were persuaded to retract their consent to ILD representation. The ILD responded by publicly attacking the NAACP as "bourgeois reformists" and "secret allies of the lynchers" who would help "lead the boys to the electric chair." The communists believed that the boys could be saved only by mass protest, not appeals to the ruling class. They ridiculed the NAACP for its willingness to "kiss the rope that hangs their brothers, if only the rope is blessed by a ruling class judge," and they accused the association generally of ignoring the interests of the black masses.[13]

In response, the NAACP warned that communists were using the case for their own advantage and that their incendiary rhetoric would harm the boys' chances of winning reversal on appeal or gubernatorial commutation. Walter White, general secretary of the NAACP, told the mother of one of the boys, Eugene Williams, that "the odds against her son were terrific at best—that when Red prejudice was added to Black, she would practically insure her boy's execution by remaining tied up with the Communists." White even accused the communists of calculat-ing that "the boys dead will be worth more for propaganda purposes than alive." By contrast, the NAACP's strategy was to hire an eminent white lawyer from the South who would avoid publicity and try to win reversal or commutation on narrow legal grounds.[14]

NAACP leaders were torn between wanting not to jeopardize the boys' chances of winning the support of moderate whites in the South and wishing not to alienate its more radical members who favored vocally condemning the white South for its willingness to execute the boys on dubious evidence. By distancing itself from the ILD, the NAACP

---

[12] Carter, 48–60 (quotations at 49–50); Goodman, 7–8, 25–29.

[13] Walter White to Bob & Herbert, 3 May 1931, NAACP, part 6, reel 2, frames 825–31 ("so deep" at p. 5/frame 829); Carter, 61–68 (other quotations). *See also* Roy Wilkins to White, 7 May 1931, NAACP, part 6, reel 2, frames 889–90; William Patterson to NAACP, 30 June 1933, *ibid.*, frames 459–72.

[14] White to Bob & Herbert, *supra* note 13, at p. 2/frame 826 ("red prejudice"); "Murder from Afar," *Philadelphia Tribune*, 27 Aug. 1931, NAACP, part 6, reel 8, frame 351; Carter, 69–72. *See also* Walter White to "Lud" (Ludwell Denny), 29 Apr. 1931, NAACP, part 6, reel 2, frames 748–49; White to Roy Wilkins, 13 May 1931, *ibid.*, frames 973–75.

alienated many blacks, who saw little reason to repudiate the communists' assistance, which they saw as "sincere and whole hearted." The editor of one black newspaper observed that the NAACP had "outlived its usefulness if it now feels that fighting the spread of communism is more important than fighting white southerners who will lynch, massacre, and slaughter and expect to get away with it." Another black editor accused the NAACP of having "an Uncle Tom attitude in this case." Yet Walter White was convinced that it would be "suicidal" for the NAACP "to be tied up in any way with that outfit of lunatics (the communists)." Most black newspaper editors saw the battle between the NAACP and the ILD as "deplorable" and a "sad spectacle," and one observed that "we have too few friends to have the quarrel as to which we shall lend a helping hand in any given case."[15]

After months of repeatedly changing their minds over the choice of legal representative, by the end of 1931 all of the boys had settled on the ILD, partly because of the NAACP's occasionally condescending attitude toward them and their parents. For example, one NAACP official, William Pickens, referred to some of the boys' parents as "the densest and dumbest animals it has yet been my privilege to meet"—a statement that the ILD ensured the parents heard about. The communists also sent small monthly checks to the boys' families and treated the parents with kindness and respect.[16]

In a last effort to win back control of the cases, the NAACP persuaded Clarence Darrow to participate in the appeals. Not wishing to be perceived as rejecting assistance from the nation's most eminent criminal defense lawyer, the ILD professed eagerness to have Darrow's help. But the organization insisted that Darrow sever his connections with the NAACP and take orders from the ILD, which prompted Darrow and the association to withdraw from the case. One black newspaper predicted that the consequence of Darrow's withdrawal "is almost surely to be murder in Scottsboro" and that the boys' "innocent blood will be a crimson stain on the [ILD]."[17]

---

[15] Carter, 69 ("sincere and whole hearted," quoting Florida *Sentinel*); White to Bob & Herbert, *supra* note 13, at p. 4/frame 828 ("lunatics"); "The Conservative NAACP," *Black Dispatch*, 14 May 1931, NAACP, part 6, reel 8, frame 118 ("Uncle Tom"); "This We Regret," *California News*, 7 Jan. 1932, *ibid.*, frame 469 ("deplorable"); "An Offensive Defense," *Carolina Times*, 9 Jan. 1932, *ibid.*, frame 507 ("sad spectacle"); "The Reds at Scottsboro," *Baltimore Afro–American*, 9 Jan. 1932, *ibid.*, frame 489 ("too few friends"); Carter, 85–90.

[16] William Pickens to White, 6 June 1931, NAACP, Part 6, reel 3, frames 355–57; Carter, 90–96.

[17] "Murder in Scottsboro," *Philadelphia Tribune*, 7 Jan. 1932, NAACP, part 6, reel 8, frame 464; Carter, 97–103; Goodman, 37–38.

Because communists generally viewed courts as simply "instruments of ... class oppression," they did not place much faith in litigation. Rather, they favored "revolutionary mass action outside of courts and bourgeois legislative bodies." Communists believed that the Scottsboro cases could educate the masses and increase party membership, especially among blacks. Throughout the spring and summer of 1931, communists organized large demonstrations in the North—often featuring the boys' mothers—to protest the boys' treatment and to petition Governor Benjamin Meeks Miller of Alabama and President Herbert Hoover for redress. In Dresden, Germany, communists threw rocks through the windows of the American consulate and condemned the "bloody lynching of our Negro co-workers"—a scene repeated elsewhere in Europe that summer. Even in Tallapoosa County, Alabama, communists used the "Scottsboro lynch verdict" to organize black sharecroppers into a union demanding higher wages and the release of the boys; whites responded with violence and murder.[18]

By the summer of 1931, Governor Miller was receiving thousands of abusive letters from around the world. One typical protest condemned "the brutal slave drivers of Alabama acting through a Ku Klux Klan judge and jury inflamed by race hatred ... to send nine innocent children to the electric chair." ILD attacks on white Alabamians as "lynchers" were reprinted in local newspapers, increasing resentment toward the Scottsboro boys. Local whites grew more defensive, insisting that the boys had been given "as fair a trial as they could have gotten in any court in the world." The Commission on Interracial Cooperation, which often supported the appeals of southern blacks convicted in obviously unfair trials, refused to support the Scottsboro defendants because of hostile public opinion. The governor's secretary explained that Scottsboro had become "a white elephant" for Miller and that the ILD's inflammatory statements had "tied his hands." One white constituent warned the governor not to let any "threat or demand from dirty yankees or damn communists from the North and throughout the world ... sway you." Judge Hawkins confided to defense lawyer Roddy that he did not "really think the boys should be put to death, but ... the Communists are more of an issue than are the FACTS of the case." One white Alabamian captured the view of many, observing that "I might have been for acquittin' them at the first trial, but now after all this stink's been raised, we've got to hang 'em."[19]

---

[18] Carter, 121–30, 138–146 (quotations), 167; *NYT*, 1 July 1931, p. 9; *NYT*, 18 July 1931, p. 30. *See also Daily Worker*, 20 Jan. 1932, NAACP, part 6, reel 8, frame 532.

[19] Carter, 112 ("as fair a trial"), 119 (Hawkins), 136 ("acquittin'"), 136 note 90 ("dirty yankees"), 145 ("slave drivers"), 153; Pickens to White, 1 June 1931, NAACP, part 6, reel 3, frame 252 ("white elephant"); Pickens to White, *supra* note 16, p. 1/frame 355 (Pickens noting what Roddy reported Hawkins as saying).

Alabama Supreme Court

It was in this climate that the cases were appealed to the Alabama supreme court. In recent decades, state supreme courts in the South had become somewhat more protective of the procedural rights of black criminal defendants, frequently reversing convictions, even in cases of murder or rape, on grounds such as prejudicial racial statements by prosecutors, the refusal of trial judges to change venue or grant defense counsel adequate time to prepare, and the use of coerced confessions. To be sure, criminal justice for southern blacks remained unequal: Blacks still could not serve on southern juries; black lawyers could not command fair hearings in southern courtrooms; black witnesses were treated as less credible than white witnesses; and the death penalty was never imposed on white rapists or on men who raped black women. Still, some progress had been made. Yet in explosive cases that generated criticism from outside of the South or that were otherwise perceived to threaten white supremacy, southern courts regressed in their treatment of black defendants.[20]

Alabama whites were especially incensed by criticism over Scottsboro because they felt they deserved praise for avoiding a lynching. The Scottsboro *Progressive Age* complimented local citizens for their "patience and chivalry" after the alleged rapes, and the Chattanooga *Daily Times* praised them for setting "the rest of the South an impressive example in self-restraint." A Georgia newspaper warned that appealing the convictions of black men for raping white women was "playing with fire"; a hasty trial was preferable to a lynching and indeed was "a first step, and a very important one." Many southern newspapers predicted a resurgence in lynchings if outsiders persisted in criticizing trials such as those at Scottsboro.[21]

When the Scottsboro appeal reached the state supreme court, its justices were said to be seething with anger at the protests and threats directed at them. The Communist party newspaper, the *Daily Worker*, had called the court an "instrument of the Wall Street Imperialists," which would surely affirm the boys' convictions. Chief Justice John C. Anderson publicly criticized such statements, which he said had been made with "the evident intent to bulldoze this court," and he insisted that the justices "will not be intimidated."[22]

---

[20] Klarman, 130–31.

[21] Carter, 105–16 ("chivalry" at 105, "impressive example" at 106); Washington (Georgia) *Forum*, 25 June 1931, *quoted in* Anne S. Emanuel, "Lynching and the Law in Georgia, circa 1931: A Chapter in the Legal Career of Judge Elbert Tuttle," 5 *William & Mary Bill of Rights Journal* (winter 1996): 215, 246 note 161 ("first step"). *See also* "The Steffens–Dreiser Nonsense," unidentified newspaper (probably the *Montgomery Advertiser*), 22 May 1931, NAACP, part 6, reel 8, frame 134.

[22] Carter, 156 (first two quotations); "Defers New Action in Scottsboro Case," *NYT*, 8 Nov. 1932, p. 13 (third quotation); Goodman, 49.

In their appeal, the ILD lawyers raised the issues of race discrimination in jury selection and the inadequacy of defense counsel, but they emphasized the unfairness of the trials and especially the mob's influence on the juries. In reply, the state attorney general denied that "a curious mob" had influenced the outcome of the trials. The headline in the *Montgomery Advertiser*'s report of the oral argument observed, "Negro Partisans 'Dictate' Course to High Court."[23]

The Alabama supreme court had previously reversed convictions in similar cases of mob domination. Other southern courts in less publicized cases had reversed convictions when defense counsel had been appointed even *a couple of days* before trial. Yet on March 24, 1932, the Alabama supreme court voted six to one to uphold the death sentences of seven of the defendants (the court granted a new trial to Eugene Williams because he had been a juvenile—thirteen years old—at the time of conviction). The court emphasized that the speed of the trials was "highly desirable" because it instilled greater respect for the law and that the presence of national guardsmen surrounding the courthouse gave "notice to everybody that the strong arm of the state was there to assure the accused a lawful trial." The court also ruled sufficient the appointment of counsel on the morning of trial. In a letter to the NAACP's Walter White, Chief Justice Anderson, the sole dissenter, explained that the communists "had been very imprudent and injected a lot of irrelevant bunk into the controversy and instead of helping it possibly injured these defendants." Anderson, who much preferred that "these defendants be tried under different circumstances," regretted that his colleagues had not been "above permitting outside influence to prejudice these defendants." (As a reward for his efforts, Anderson received a telegram from an ILD branch assailing him as a "traitor to the masses" for his willingness to abide by the majority's decision).[24]

The *Montgomery Advertiser* opined that the court's ruling "should satisfy all reasonable persons" that the Scottsboro boys had received fair trials. Yet several other Alabama newspapers regretted that the court had not granted a new trial to allay doubts regarding the defendants' guilt. The *Birmingham Age-Herald* observed, "the fact remains that there was an element of mob feeling in the air," and the *Birmingham News* insisted there was "ground for divergence of opinions regarding these cases." Moderate whites in Alabama blamed the ruling on communist efforts at intimidation, which they suspected the state jurists had "leaned unconsciously backwards" to resist. A black newspaper similarly

---

[23] Carter, 156–58.

[24] Powell v. State, 141 So. 201, 211, 213 (1932); Chief Justice John C. Anderson to Walter White, 25 Apr. 1932, NAACP, part 6, reel 5, frame 792; Carter, 159–60, 170 note 98 ("traitor"); Klarman, 131–32.

concluded, "it is possible that the highest legal tribunal in Alabama affirmed these death sentences because it did no[t] want to appear as being swayed, cowed or bluffed by a group of radicals." Communists thought the ruling revealed the "highest courts working hand in glove with owners of America against [the] working class."[25]

The *Daily Worker* predicted that review by the U.S. Supreme Court—just another "capitalist court"—would be a "mere gesture aimed at facilitating the legal lynching of these children." A black newspaper in the North professed greater faith in the high court, reasoning that "America, grasping for the moral leadership of the world, cannot afford to set the example of staging a legal lynching." The liberal *Nation* agreed that the boys' prospects were "very bright" because "the conscience of the world will be profoundly shocked" if the Court affirmed their convictions and thus "encourag[ed] legal lynchings in the South."[26]

The U.S. Supreme Court

In 1932 the U.S. Supreme Court was hardly the champion of racial equality that it would one day become in popular mythology. Around 1900, the Court had sustained the constitutionality of laws mandating racial segregation and disfranchising blacks, leading the fledging NAACP to conclude in 1915 that the Court "has virtually declared that the colored man has no civil rights." To be sure, the Court in the second decade of the twentieth century struck down residential segregation ordinances, certain laws that promoted peonage (compulsory labor to discharge debts), and the grandfather clause (a device insulating illiterate whites from the disfranchising effect of literacy tests). But in 1927 the Court strongly implied that state-mandated racial segregation in public schools was constitutionally permissible, and in 1935 the Court would unanimously sustain the exclusion of blacks from Democratic primaries—the only elections that mattered in the one-party South. In 1932, virtually nobody thought of the Court as a heroic defender of the rights of racial minorities.[27]

---

[25] Carter, 159 ("all reasonable persons"; "in the air"; "unconsciously backward"); "The Affirmation of the Scottsboro Cases," *Birmingham News*, 25 March 1932, NAACP, part 6, reel 8, frame 586; "The Scottsboro Appeal," *San Antonio Inquirer*, 8 Apr. 1932, *ibid.*, frame 631 ("cowed," excerpting editorial from the Houston *Defender*, 2 Apr. 1932); "Backs Conviction of Seven Negroes," *NYT*, 25 March, 1932, p. 6 ("hand in glove"). *See also* "Scottsboro Boys Doomed," *Savannah Tribune*, 14 Apr. 1932, NAACP, part 6, reel 8, frame 651.

[26] Carter, 160 (*Daily Worker*); *Iowa Bystander*, undated (but probably around 30 Jan. 1932), NAACP, part 6, reel 8, frame 562 ("legal lynching"); "The Scottsboro Case," *Nation*, 12 Oct. 1932, p. 320.

[27] *Crisis*, 9 (Apr. 1915): 293; Klarman, chapters 1–3.

Nor had the Court yet taken substantial strides toward protecting the procedural rights of criminal defendants in state courts. Prior to *Moore v. Dempsey* in 1923, the Court had reversed state criminal convictions on federal constitutional grounds in only a handful of cases involving race discrimination in jury selection.[28] In other cases, the Court had denied that the Fourteenth Amendment converted the procedural protections of the federal Bill of Rights into safeguards against *state* governments and had narrowly construed the Due Process Clause of that amendment, which does explicitly constrain the states.[29]

Moore v. Dempsey was the progenitor of modern American criminal procedure. The case arose from an infamous racial massacre in Phillips County, Arkansas, in 1919. Black tenant farmers and sharecroppers had tried to organize a union and to hire white lawyers to sue planters for peonage practices. Local whites cracked down with a vengeance. When whites shot into a church where black unionists were meeting, blacks returned the gunfire. A white man was killed, and mayhem quickly ensued. Marauding whites, supported by federal troops ostensibly dispatched to quell the disturbance, went on a rampage, tracking down blacks throughout the countryside and killing dozens of them. Many other blacks were tortured into making incriminating statements. Seventy-nine blacks, and no whites, were prosecuted and convicted for their actions during this "race riot," and twelve received the death penalty. The trials of those twelve lasted only an hour or two each, and the juries, from which blacks had been systematically excluded, deliberated for only a few minutes. Huge mobs of angry whites surrounded the courthouse, menacing the defendants and the jurors and threatening a lynching. Six of the defendants appealed their death sentences to the Supreme Court, arguing that mob-dominated trials violate the Due Process Clause of the Fourteenth Amendment. By a vote of seven to two, the Supreme Court agreed, reversed the convictions, and ordered a federal district judge to conduct a hearing on whether the defendants' trial had been influenced by the mob.[30]

---

[28] *See* Rogers v. Alabama, 192 U.S. 226 (1904); Carter v. Texas, 177 U.S. 442 (1900); Neal v. Delaware, 103 U.S. 370, 397 (1881); Strauder v. West Virginia, 100 U.S. 303 (1880).

[29] Twining v. New Jersey, 211 U.S. 78 (1908) (rejecting application of the Fifth Amendment's protection against self-incrimination to the states and denying that the Fourteenth Amendment's Due Process Clause bars a prosecutor from commenting on the refusal of a criminal defendant to take the witness stand); Maxwell v. Dow, 176 U.S. 581 (1900) (holding that use of an 8–person jury in a noncapital criminal case does not violate due process); Hurtado v. California, 110 U.S. 516 (1884) (holding that the Due Process Clause of the Fifth Amendment does not guarantee that criminal prosecutions by the states must proceed by grand jury indictment).

[30] Richard C. Cortner, *A Mob Intent on Death: The NAACP and the Arkansas Riot Cases* (1988), 7–23; Klarman, 98, 120–23.

Moore offered some hope that the Scottsboro defendants might find justice in the Supreme Court. Their lawyers raised three constitutional claims in their appeal: mob domination of the trials in violation of the Due Process Clause; intentional exclusion of blacks from the grand and petit juries in violation of the Equal Protection Clause; and denial of the right to counsel in violation of the Due Process Clause. On the day of the oral argument, extra police officers patrolled the Supreme Court building and grounds; the plaza facing the Capitol was cleared; and elaborate preparations were made to preempt the mass communist demonstrations that had been promised. Mary Mooney, mother of the imprisoned California labor leader Tom Mooney (who had been wrongfully convicted for the Preparedness Day bombing in San Francisco in 1916), attended the Court session, noting her interest in seeing that other mothers' sons received justice. Several of Alabama's congressmen also attended the argument, as did an unusually large number of blacks.[31]

A few weeks later, the Court reversed the defendants' convictions on the ground that the right to counsel had been denied, and it declined to reach the other two issues. Perhaps the justices chose the basis for decision that they deemed least controversial. Reversing the defendants' convictions because of mob domination would have required extending *Moore,* as the Scottsboro trials were not quite so farcical as those of the Phillips County defendants: The Scottsboro boys received a genuine defense; their trials lasted for several hours (not forty-five minutes); the juries trying them deliberated more than the five minutes in *Moore*; their cases did not raise the broader implications of the Phillips County race riot; and they had not been tortured into confessing. For the Court to have reversed the Scottsboro convictions on the basis of *Moore* might have required basic changes in Jim Crow justice. Similarly, to invalidate their convictions because of race discrimination in jury selection would have been far more provocative to white southerners because preserving white supremacy in the courtroom required excluding blacks from juries. By contrast, overturning the convictions because the defendants had been denied the right to counsel was unlikely to affect the outcome of any retrials or Jim Crow justice in general.[32]

Prior to *Powell*, the Court had never ruled that due process requires the states to provide counsel to indigent defendants in capital cases, but neither had it rejected that position. Every state court confronting that issue had required the government to appoint counsel in such circumstances. To be sure, Powell had received a court-appointed lawyer. He made two arguments as to why this appointment failed to satisfy federal

---

[31] Brief of Petitioners, *Powell v. Alabama*, 3–4, 34–62; "Guarded High Court Hears the Negro Pleas," *NYT*, 11 Oct. 1932, p. 19.

[32] Klarman, 123–24.

constitutional standards. First, the state had not afforded him adequate opportunity to hire counsel of his own choice. Second, the court appointment was inadequate because it had been made the morning of the trial, and thus defense counsel was denied an adequate opportunity to consult clients, interview witnesses, and prepare a defense.[33]

The Alabama court had deemed this last-minute appointment of counsel sufficient to satisfy the state constitutional requirement of a court-appointed lawyer in capital cases. In general, the U.S. Supreme Court has no authority to review state court interpretations of state law. Thus, for the Court to reverse Powell's conviction, it would have to construe the Due Process Clause of the Fourteenth Amendment to require the assistance of counsel in capital cases. American constitutional history reveals that the justices are least reluctant to expand constitutional rights when doing so involves holding a few renegade states to the norm already espoused by the vast majority. As of 1932, not a single state had rejected the right of indigent defendants in capital cases to state-appointed counsel. Indeed, one reason that state courts had not yet considered whether the Due Process Clause of the Fourteenth Amendment guaranteed such a right is that all of them confronting the issue had interpreted their state constitutions to do so.

Once the justices determined that due process required the appointment of counsel for indigent capital defendants, reversing Powell's conviction was easy. First, Powell had been denied the opportunity to hire a lawyer of his own choice. Second, to most disinterested observers, the trial judge's appointment of counsel had been obviously inadequate. At the trials, although defense counsel did cross-examine prosecution witnesses, they made only a feeble effort to change the trial venue, presented neither opening nor closing arguments, and called none of their own witnesses other than the defendants, some of whom implicated each other in a desperate effort to avoid the death penalty. The Scottsboro trials may not have been quite the sham affair under review in *Moore*, yet most lawyers would have considered obviously inadequate the representation afforded to the defendants.[34]

Moreover, the trial record revealed a high probability that the boys were innocent—a circumstance likely to be significant to Supreme Court justices reviewing their convictions, even if technically irrelevant to the merits of their appeal. Because criminal procedure safeguards often shield the guilty from punishment, they are usually controversial, and the justices are probably more inclined to identify new rights in cases where defendants have a strong claim of innocence. As we have seen, the medical evidence introduced at the Scottsboro trials raised serious

---

[33] Brief for Petitioners, *Powell v. Alabama*, at 36–62; Klarman, 124–25.

[34] Brief for Petitioners, *Powell v. Alabama*, 9–14, 51–59; Klarman, 125.

doubts as to whether any rape had occurred, and the accusers had provided inconsistent testimony. Moreover, the women possessed a clear motive for fabrication: avoiding a possible Mann Act prosecution for traveling across state lines for immoral purposes (prostitution).

Many newspapers, even in parts of the South, applauded the high court's decision in *Powell*. The *Richmond Times–Dispatch* went so far as to say that the ruling "will be welcomed throughout the country, with the possible exception of Alabama." The *New York Times* likewise hailed the ruling, which it said "ought to abate the rancor of extreme radicals, while confirming the faith of the American people in the soundness of their institutions and especially in the integrity of their courts." Professor Felix Frankfurter of the Harvard Law School called the decision "a notable chapter in the history of liberty" and observed that the same Court that had recently served the interests of property owners was now protecting "illiterate" and "vagrant" blacks from oppression. A black newspaper proclaimed the ruling "a great stroke in the name of justice," and the NAACP saw it as a "vindication" of its view that victories for racial justice "are best won by strictly legal means." By contrast, the *Daily Worker* condemned *Powell* for instructing Alabama authorities on "how 'properly' to carry through such lynch schemes." The liberal lawyer Morris Ernst likewise assailed the decision as "empty and meaningless" and "cunningly uncourageous" because it disregarded those issues of "deep social significance" and left the defendants in "horrid shape" for a retrial, which was likely to feature a half-hearted lawyer "who will saunter ... before a white jury while mobs outside sing anthems and shout for hangings."[35]

On Remand

The Court's ruling seemed to make Alabama whites even more defensive. After the initial trials, some of them had doubted whether the defendants had been treated fairly. However, after what the *Birmingham Post* called the high court's "stinging rebuke" of the state supreme court, anyone publicly expressing doubts about the defendants' guilt or the fairness of their trials was courting physical danger. White Alabami-

---

[35] "The Scottsboro Case," *Richmond Times–Dispatch*, 9 Nov. 1932, p. 10; "The Scottsboro Case," *NYT*, 8 Nov. 1932, p. 13 ("rancor"); *NYT*, 13 Nov. 1932, sect. 3, pp. 1–2 (Frankfurter quote); "The Scottsboro Mob Justice," *Indianapolis Recorder*, 12 Nov. 1932, NAACP, part 6, reel 8, frame 784 ("great stroke"); *Baltimore Afro–American*, 19 Nov. 1932, *ibid.*, frame 794 (NAACP quote); Carter, 163–65 (quoting New York *Daily Worker*, 8 Nov. 1932, at p. 163); Morris Ernst, "Dissenting Opinion," *Nation*, vol. 135 (1932), p. 559. *See also* "The Scottsboro Case," *New York Herald–Tribune*, 8 Nov. 1932, p. 20; "The Scottsboro Case," *Baltimore Sun*, 9 Nov. 1932, p. 10 (noting that the decision is "in conformity with the principles of fair dealing and will awaken approving echoes in every part of the nation"); "Righteously Remanded," *Richmond News Leader*, 8 Nov. 1932, p. 8 (noting that "hysteria was responsible for conviction" and expressing approval of the result).

ans also greatly resented northern newspaper accounts that portrayed them as barefooted, tobacco-chewing illiterates. Judge Hawkins opined with regard to the retrials that "[t]he presence of troops will be more imperative now than ever."[36]

The ILD asked Samuel Leibowitz, a Jewish lawyer from New York who was one of the nation's leading criminal defense attorneys, to represent the defendants at their new trials. Leibowitz agreed to serve without fee in exchange for a promise of independence in orchestrating the defense and a commitment from the ILD to lower its public profile regarding Scottsboro. Upon arriving in Alabama, Leibowitz sought to distance the case from the communist issue and professed no intention to tell Alabamians how to run their affairs.[37]

Before the retrials began, one of the ILD lawyers moved for a change of venue, which was granted—to Decatur, Alabama, fifty miles west of Scottsboro. Nearly all whites there were already convinced of the defendants' guilt. A large crowd attended the first of the retrials, though the threat of violence that pervaded the original proceedings was initially absent. The Scottsboro episode had attracted so much national attention that representatives of several New York newspapers and the wire services were in attendance.[38]

Leibowitz moved to quash the original indictments on the ground that no blacks had served on grand juries in Jackson County since Reconstruction, even though they were nearly ten percent of the county's population. Summoned to testify, the county's jury commissioners denied that blacks were excluded because of their race. Leibowitz also called as witnesses several blacks from Jackson County to demonstrate that they satisfied the statutory jury-selection standard of "integrity, good character, and sound judgment." The prosecutor tried to humiliate and intimidate these black witnesses, but they held up well under cross-examination, and Leibowitz established that they were as well qualified as many whites to serve as jurors. Nevertheless, Judge James Edwin Horton overruled the motion to quash the indictments.[39]

Leibowitz then challenged the jury-selection system in Morgan County, site of the new trials. He called as witnesses ten prominent blacks from the county to demonstrate their qualifications to serve as

---

[36] Carter, 113, 179–81 ("presence of troops" at 181), 189–90 ("stinging rebuke" at 190); *Birmingham News*, 25 March 1932; *NYT*, 12 March 1933, p. 27.

[37] Carter, 181–85; Goodman, 118–19.

[38] Carter, 183–84, 190–92; Goodman, 118; "Fight for Negroes Opens in Alabama," *NYT*, 28 March 1933, p. 6.

[39] Carter, 194–99; Goodman, 120–23.

jurors. These educated and refined blacks, most of whom held college degrees, made impressive witnesses.[40]

When Leibowitz had demanded that the prosecutor refer to black witnesses with courtesy titles, courtroom spectators had been merely puzzled, but when he questioned the honesty of county jury commissioners, they grew visibly angry. A crowd of 200 young men gathered in town to "protest[] against the manner in which Mr. Leibowitz has examined the state's witnesses." After Judge Horton rejected the defense's challenge to jury selection, he admonished courtroom spectators about the death threats being made against Leibowitz on Decatur streets and warned that he would order the national guardsmen to shoot to kill if any effort was made to harm the defendants.[41]

The prosecution's strategy at Patterson's retrial was to have Victoria Price testify as graphically as possible about the rapes. Leibowitz's cross-examination was brutal, as he tried to demonstrate that Price was a prostitute and that her account of what happened on the train was riddled with contradictions. Price proved a feisty witness who yielded no ground, although Leibowitz was able to elicit from her some contradictory statements. Any damage he did to Price's credibility, however, came at the cost of alienating courtroom whites, who were outraged at this attack on the chastity and honesty of a southern white woman. One courtroom spectator whispered to another, "It'll be a wonder if ever he leaves town alive," and two hundred angry local residents gathered to protest the manner in which Leibowitz had cross-examined Price. Judge Horton responded by strongly defending the rule of law, denouncing the "mob spirit," and insisting that he would defend the lives of the defendants and anyone else involved in the case.[42]

Doctor R.R. Bridges testified that all of the sperm found in Price's vagina was non-motile, which should have been conclusive exculpatory evidence, given that the alleged rapes had occurred only ninety minutes before the medical examination. A second doctor, Marvin Lynch, privately confessed to Judge Horton that he had never believed that the young women had been raped. But Lynch rejected Horton's exhortations to state this view publicly, explaining that "[i]f I testified for those boys I'd never be able to go back into Jackson County." The defendant's medical expert, Dr. Edward A. Reisman, testified that a woman raped sequentially by six men could not possibly have in her vagina only the small traces of semen found in the medical examination of Price. Reisman also

---

[40] Carter, 199–201; Goodman, 123–24.

[41] Carter, 198, 201–03; "Warning by Judge at Alabama Trial," *NYT*, 6 Apr. 1933, p. 13 (quotation); "Negro Defense Gets Test of Juror List," *NYT*, 31 March 1933, p. 9.

[42] Carter, 204–13, 223–24 (quotations); Goodman, 125–27.

declared that women who had just been raped could not have appeared as calm and collected as Price and Bates had been. One local resident was unimpressed by this testimony: "When a nigger has expert witnesses, we have a right to ask who is paying for them."[43]

The star witness for the defense was Ruby Bates, who made a dramatic entrance and testified that no rapes had occurred. However, her credibility was necessarily compromised by the blatant contradictions with her testimony in the original trials. The prosecutor further impeached her credibility by suggesting that she had been paid to testify—an allegation that apparently convinced most locals. In closing arguments, one prosecutor referred to the "fancy New York clothes" worn by Bates and, pointing at the Jewish defense attorneys (Leibowitz and Joseph Brodsky of the ILD), appealed to the jury to prove that Alabama justice could not be bought "with Jew money from New York." Another prosecutor told the jury, "If you acquit this Negro, put a garland of roses around his neck, give him a supper and send him to New York City," where "Dr. Harry Fosdick [the liberal Protestant minister from New York who had provided support for Bates] [will] dress him up in a high hat and morning coat, gray-striped trousers and spats."[44]

Even if this had been a run-of-the-mill, black-on-white rape case, it would have been difficult for a jury of southern whites to have acquitted Patterson. But Scottsboro was no ordinary case. With communists attacking white Alabamians as lynchers, and Leibowitz assailing white jury commissioners as liars, an acquittal was out of the question. The trial had ceased to be about determining Patterson's guilt or innocence and had become instead a challenge to southern white supremacy. With the issue framed this way, the jury took just five minutes to convict (though one juror held out against the death penalty for hours before finally capitulating). Leibowitz called the result "a triumph of bigotry," and the *Chicago Defender*, one of the leading black newspapers in the country, denounced the trial "as a mockery, a pretension of justice and a crime against our national honor." New York newspapers professed "shock" at the verdict, while some southern newspapers blamed any unfairness on outside agitation, which Alabama whites naturally resented.[45]

---

[43] Carter, 213–16 (first quotation at 215), 227–28 ("nigger" at 228); Goodman, 127–28, 175–76.

[44] Carter, 231–40 ("New York clothes" and "Jew money" at 235; Fosdick quote at 237); Goodman, 131–34; "New York Attacked in Scottsboro Trial," *NYT*, 8 Apr. 1933, p. 30.

[45] Carter, 239–42; *Chicago Defender*, 15 Apr. 1933, p. 14 (quoting Leibowitz); Editorial, "The Decatur Verdict," *NYT*, 10 Apr. 1933, p. 12; "A Blow to Justice," *New York Herald Tribune*, 10 Apr. 1933, p. 14. *See also* " 'Sorry,' " *Meridian* (Mississippi) *Star*, 11 Apr. 1933,

The day Patterson was convicted, twenty thousand blacks in New York City signed a petition promising to join a protest march later that spring in Washington, D.C. Huge crowds gathered in New York to hear Ruby Bates proclaim herself a victim of the oppression of the Scottsboro ruling class and to hear Leibowitz denigrate Alabama whites as "bigots whose mouths are slits in their faces, whose eyes pop out like a frog's, whose chins drip tobacco juice, bewhiskered and filthy." The New York press faithfully reported such comments, which were then widely re-printed in Alabama newspapers, making Leibowitz even more anathema to southern whites. One Alabama journal retorted, "the New York Jew says there is no such thing as a fair trial in Alabama. It seems to this paper . . . [that] this recent recruit from Russia is a poor sort of chap to try to blight the good name of Alabama."[46]

After pronouncing sentence on Patterson, Judge Horton delayed the other retrials because Leibowitz's statements to the press were a "mill-stone around the necks of the defendants." Meanwhile, some southern newspapers outside of Alabama for the first time declared the boys innocent. Douglas Southall Freeman, editor of the *Richmond News Leader*, observed that "[t]he men are being sentenced to death primarily because they are black" and because of the " 'unwritten law' that when a white woman accuses . . . a Negro he must prove his innocence." Josephus Daniels, editor of the *Raleigh News and Observer*, called the verdict "shocking" and "outrageous." The *Chattanooga News* declared that one could not "conceive of a civilized community taking human lives on the strength of this miserable affair." By contrast, newspapers in the Deep South tended to defend the fairness of the trials.[47]

In Alabama, the few whites who continued to raise doubts were forcefully suppressed. A sociology professor at Birmingham Southern University who was sympathetic to the boys was denied an extension of his contract. Rabbi Benjamin Goldstein, another supporter, was forced to resign from his temple in Montgomery and then to leave the state; his congregants worried that the rabbi's controversial stand on Scottsboro would unleash a wave of antisemitism. One observer noted that many

---

p. 4 (calling the trial "fair-square" and denouncing Leibowitz's charge of bigotry as "without a shred of fact or evidence").

[46] Carter, 243–50 ("bigots" at 244; "Jew" at 245); "Negro Protest Paraders Battle Police for Hour," *New York Herald Tribune*, 11 Apr. 1933, p. 32.

[47] Carter, 246–47 ("millstone" at 246), 252–54; "South Split over the Scottsboro Verdict," *Literary Digest*, 115 (Apr. 22, 1933), p. 4 (newspaper quotes); "A Shocking Verdict," *Raleigh News & Observer*, 10 Apr. 1933, p. 4; "A Suggestion to the South," *Raleigh News & Observer*, 11 Apr. 1933, p. 4 ("outrageous"); Goodman, 153. *See also* " 'Justice' in Alabama," *Richmond Times–Dispatch*, 12 Apr. 1933, p. 6 (calling it "incon-ceivable that the jury should have brought in a verdict of guilty" and calling Patterson probably innocent).

whites conceded the defendants' probable innocence but nonetheless insisted, "[i]f we let Negroes get by with this case, no white woman will be safe in the South." Many moderates apparently hoped that the governor would commute the sentences to life imprisonment, apparently deeming this an acceptable compromise for black men falsely accused of raping white women.[48]

In June 1933 Judge Horton, whom Leibowitz had called "one of the finest jurists I have ever met," granted the defense motion for a new trial, explaining that he found the evidence against Patterson unconvincing. Horton secretly hoped that his action would forestall further prosecutions of the defendants.[49]

The *Birmingham Post* applauded Horton's decision and declared the defendants probably innocent, but it was the only newspaper in the state to do so. Some prominent whites in Alabama, including the president of the state bar association, also endorsed Horton's ruling, but the predominant reaction in the state was hostile. Tom Heflin, a former U.S. senator from Alabama, declared that Horton's ruling was "putting wicked thoughts in the minds of lawless negro men and greatly increasing the danger to the white women of Alabama." The state attorney general who had helped prosecute the case, Thomas E. Knight, Jr., sought to have the judge—whom one critic derided as having "no more backbone than in an angle worm"—removed from the case. The following year, Horton, who had faced no opposition when he stood for election six years earlier, was defeated for reelection. By contrast, Knight was elected lieutenant governor.[50]

The Scottsboro retrials resumed in November 1933. Recent developments raised doubts as to whether the defendants and their lawyers could be protected from mob violence. That summer in Tuscaloosa, three ILD lawyers defending blacks charged with raping and killing a white woman had been turned over by deputy sheriffs to a firing squad, and two of them were killed. In September, an elderly black man accused of raping a mentally retarded white woman—even the police found the allegation incredible—was lynched. The local newspaper blamed the ILD for spreading communist propaganda among "our contented Negro population," while the *Montgomery Advertiser* attributed the lynchings to "hotheads who ... fear[ed] that outside interference would block the

---

[48] Carter, 253–62 (quotation at 261). Cf. Sandra Day O'Connor, *Thurgood Marshall: The Influence of a Raconteur*, 44 *Stan. L. Rev.* 1217, 1220 (1992) (recollecting Thurgood Marshall observing, in connection with a 1930s case from Virginia in which a black man was convicted of murdering two white women, "You know something is wrong with the government's case when a Negro only gets life for murdering a white woman").

[49] Carter, 239, 264–70; Goodman, 173–82.

[50] Carter, 270–73 (quotation at 271–72).

course of justice." Yet, with Birmingham newspapers noting an "extremely grave" probability of a massacre, Judge W.W. Callahan declined to request militia protection for the trials, and the governor sent none. Callahan also denied the defense motion for a change of venue, despite sworn statements in affidavits submitted by ILD investigators that a national guardsman had conceded he and his colleagues would offer only token resistance to a lynching attempt and that local whites had admitted they would conceal their belief that the boys should be executed in order to get on the jury.[51]

Before the new trials began, the jury commissioners in Jackson County altered the jury lists by adding the names of several blacks. At a preliminary hearing, a defense handwriting expert testified that the names of most or perhaps all of the blacks had been fraudulently added after the lists had been initially compiled. Despite this uncontradicted testimony, Judge Callahan invoked the presumption that jury commissioners had acted lawfully and rejected the defense motion to quash the indictments.[52]

At Patterson's retrial, Judge Callahan refused to permit Leibowitz to question Victoria Price about whether she had had sexual intercourse the night before the train trip, and he nearly ruled Leibowitz in contempt when the lawyer persisted in trying to get such evidence before the jury. Callahan repeatedly rescued Price when she became bogged down in contradictions and denied Leibowitz the opportunity to undermine the credibility of prosecution witnesses. Intimidated by death threats and recovering from surgery in a New York hospital, Ruby Bates refused to return to Alabama to testify. The prosecution used against Patterson his earlier admission that he had seen some of the black youths raping the women. Yet the prosecutor's most effective point may have been the question he posed to jurors in his closing argument: Did they really wish to believe the defendant's account, which essentially charged their neighbors in Scottsboro with doing "a lot of awful things over there"? Callahan instructed the jury that "there is a very strong presumption under the law that [a white woman charging rape] would not and did not yield voluntarily to intercourse with ... a Negro" and that this was true "whether she be the most despised, ignorant and abandoned woman of the community, or the spotless virgin and daughter of a prominent home of luxury and learning." He glowered at Leibowitz while instructing the jury to ignore any of defense counsel's intimations

---

[51] Carter, 276–80 (newspaper quotations at 277); *NYT*, 20 Nov. 1933, p. 1 ("extremely grave"); "Lynchings Feared in Scottsboro Case," *NYT*, 10 Nov. 1933, p. 7; "Plans to Lynch the Scottsboro Boy Exposed by Detectives," *Washington Sentinel*, 25 Nov. 1933, NAACP, part 6, reel 9, frame 262. *See also* Roy Wilkins, Memorandum on the Scottsboro Case, 3 Nov. 1933, *ibid.*, reel 2, frames 516–17.

[52] Carter, 281–84; "Jury Roll Upheld in Alabama Case," *NYT*, 26 Nov. 1933, p. 1.

regarding Price's prior sexual history, then forgot—before Leibowitz reminded him—to give the jury the instruction form for rendering a verdict of acquittal, an oversight the significance of which the jury was unlikely to miss. The jury convicted Patterson and sentenced him to death, and then a second jury did the same in the retrial of Clarence Norris. Leibowitz left the courtroom under heavy guard because of death threats.[53]

On appeal, both defendants challenged their convictions on the ground of race discrimination in jury selection. Precedents of the U.S. Supreme Court from around 1900 made it very difficult to prove such discrimination. The Alabama supreme court rejected Norris's claim on the basis of these precedents. The court refused to presume discrimination by the jury commissioners, denied any affirmative duty to place blacks on juries, and deferred to the commissioners' denials of race discrimination. With regard to the appellant's claim that Callahan's administration of the trial was reversible error, the Alabama jurists found only that "on one or two occasions [he had] manifested slight impatience." The court did not even reach the merits of Patterson's appeal because of an arguable failure to comply with Alabama's rules of appellate procedure. The flaw was highly technical: Patterson's claim was untimely only if the ninety-day period in which to file a bill of exceptions commenced at the date of judgment rather than the date of sentencing and if his new-trial motion, which would have tolled the ninety-day period, was nugatory because filed after expiration of the trial court's term. (And even then, the bill of exceptions had been filed late only because of a plane crash.) Technical though it was, this procedural gaffe placed Patterson's life in jeopardy. The Alabama supreme court refused to consider the merits of his jury-discrimination claim, which apparently meant that the U.S. Supreme Court could not do so either, even though Patterson's appeal rested on precisely the same ground as Norris's.[54]

The U.S. Supreme Court—Again

Late in 1934, two ILD attorneys were caught trying to bribe Victoria Price to change her story. An infuriated Leibowitz declared that the ILD had "assassinated the Scottsboro boys with that sort of business," and

---

[53] Carter, 285–303 ("awful things" at 294, Callahan charge at 297); Goodman, 227–29; *California Eagle*, 24 Nov. 1933, NAACP, part 6, reel 9, frame 253; "Accuser Renames Scottsboro Negro," *NYT*, 28 Nov. 1933, p. 11; "Scottsboro Case Given to the Jury Which is Locked Up," *NYT*, 1 Dec. 1933, p. 1; "Judge Tells Alabama Jury How to Find Negro Guilty," *New York Herald Tribune*, 1 Dec. 1933, p. 1; "Scottsboro Negro is Convicted Again," *NYT*, 7 Dec. 1933, p. 16.

[54] Carter, 303–08; Klarman, 127–28; Goodman, 238; Patterson v. State, 229 Ala. 270, 273, 156 So. 567 (1934); Norris v. State, 156 So. 556, 564 (Ala. 1934).

he threatened to withdraw from the case unless the communists did so. The *Daily Worker* responded by accusing Leibowitz of joining forces with the "Alabama lynch rulers," and the ILD tried to fire him on the pretense that he was inexperienced in constitutional appeals. But Leibowitz convinced Patterson, Norris, and their parents to stick with him. As in 1931, however, a subsequent visit from ILD lawyers promptly convinced the boys and their families to change their minds. Another unseemly battle for control of the case ensued—this time between Leibowitz and the ILD. Only after the boys had switched back and forth numerous times was a compromise finally reached: Leibowitz represented Norris in the Supreme Court, while the lawyers hired by the ILD represented Patterson.[55]

Norris's appeal focused on race discrimination in jury selection. Alabama responded by invoking *Thomas v. Texas* (1909), which held that federal courts must defer to state court findings of fact on that issue. During Leibowitz's argument, Chief Justice Charles Evans Hughes interrupted to ask if the lawyer could prove his allegation that the names of blacks had been forged on the jury rolls. Leibowitz said that he could, and in a moment of high drama, the justices examined the jury rolls of Jackson County through magnifying glasses—apparently the first time they had ever engaged in independent evidence-gathering in appellate proceedings.[56]

Six weeks later, the justices overturned Norris's conviction—the first time in decades the Court had overturned a criminal conviction on the ground of race discrimination in jury selection. To be sure, *Norris* created no new substantive constitutional law; since *Strauder v. West Virginia* in 1880, the Court had consistently construed the Equal Protection Clause to bar race discrimination in jury selection. However, *Norris* did alter the critical rules governing how such claims were to be proved; for over a generation, these rules had doomed to failure virtually all such claims. The justices now reinvigorated the long-dormant dicta of *Neal v. Delaware* (1881), which approved inferring intentional discrimination from the lengthy absence of blacks from jury service. If, under such circumstances, the state was not obliged to go beyond simply denying the existence of race discrimination, then the constitutional safeguard "would be but a vain and illusory requirement." Further, *Norris* held, when an alleged constitutional violation turned on disputed facts, the

---

[55] Carter, 308–19 (quotations at 311, 312); Goodman, 238–43; "Held as 'Bribers' in Scottsboro Case," *NYT*, 2 Oct. 1934, p. 7; "Leibowitz Ousts Communists in Scottsboro Case," *New York Herald Tribune*, 11 Oct. 1934, NAACP, part 6, reel 9, frames 468–69; "Negroes Pick Leibowitz," *NYT*, 21 Oct. 1934, p. 28; "Norris Picks Leibowitz in Final Action," (New York) *Amsterdam News*, 17 Feb. 1935, NAACP, part 6, reel 9, frame 532.

[56] Carter, 319–20; *NYT*, 16 Feb. 1935, p. 2; *NYT*, 19 Feb. 1935, p. 42; Thomas v. Texas, 212 U.S. 278 (1909); Norris v. State, 294 U.S. 587, 593 note 1 (1935).

federal courts must find those facts for themselves, not simply defer to state findings.[57]

Norris was an appealing case for the justices to reconsider the rules governing proof of race discrimination in jury selection for two reasons. First, not only had blacks been absent for decades from juries in these Alabama counties, but local court officers had been caught in an embarrassing lie, the only plausible explanation for which was the desire to cover up the intentional exclusion of blacks from juries. Second, by 1935 the innocence of the Scottsboro boys, in the words of one northern journal, had "long been established before the bar of public opinion." Most Americans apparently found Ruby Bates's recantation more persuasive evidence of the defendants' innocence than had the Morgan County jury. Even many southern newspapers "rejoiced" in the Court's decision reversing Norris's conviction because, as one of them put it, "[t]he conscience of the nation and the world is convinced that the seven Negroes are not guilty of the crime of which they were charged."[58]

The reversal of Norris's conviction need not necessarily have helped Patterson because of the alleged procedural flaw in his appeal. Yet the justices, after acknowledging Alabama's right to dismiss federal claims not raised in compliance with its own appellate-procedure rules, nonetheless remanded Patterson's case to the state court to reconsider in light of *Norris*. As justification for this unprecedented move, the justices professed themselves unwilling to believe that Alabama judges would have condemned Patterson to death because of procedural flaws in his appeal had they foreseen that the Supreme Court would soon invalidate the jury-selection procedures used in his case.[59]

---

[57] *Norris*, 294 U.S. at 598 (quotation); Neal v. Delaware, 103 U.S. 370, 391, 397 (1881); Benno C. Schmidt, Jr., "Juries, Jurisdiction, and Race Discrimination: The Lost Promise of *Strauder v. West Virginia*," 61 *Texas Law Review* (May 1983): 1401, 1476–83; Klarman, 39–43, 125–28; Carter, 322–24.

[58] "Scottsboro—What Now?," *New Republic*, 82 (17 Apr. 1935), pp. 270–71 (first quotation); "Where the Stars Fell," *Raleigh News & Observer*, 3 Apr. 1935, p. 4 ("conscience of the nation"); "The South and Scottsboro Ruling," *Literary Digest*, 13 Apr. 1935, p. 10 ("rejoiced" in *Norfolk Virginia–Pilot* and *Richmond Times Dispatch*); Carter, 326; Goodman, 148–49; "Justice for Negroes," *NYT*, 2 Apr. 1935, p. 20 (noting that the case "has become a public symbol of the mischief that may be wrought when prejudice is allowed to invade the place dedicated to impartial justice"); "The Scottsboro Decision," *New York Herald Tribune*, 2 Apr. 1935, p. 18 (predicting "[t]here will be relief that a gross miscarriage of justice has again been averted"); "The Scottsboro Decision," *Washington Post*, 3 Apr. 1935, p. 8 (observing that "[f]rom the beginning the atmosphere of these cases has been that of a miscarriage of justice"); *id.*, "Comment on the Scottsboro Ruling"; "New Scottsboro Opinion," *Baltimore Sun*, 3 Apr. 1935, p. 12.

[59] "Comment," 35 *Columbia Law Review* (1935), 941–2; "Justice for Negroes," *NYT*, 2 Apr. 1935, p. 20; "Scottsboro—What Now?," *New Republic*, 82 (17 Apr. 1935), 271; Patterson v. Alabama, 294 U.S. 600 (1935).

Subsequent History

The ILD regarded its victory in the high court as "another proof of the might of mass pressure and mass protest." By contrast, Leibowitz saw it as a "triumph for American justice and . . . an answer to all those subversive elements who seek to engender hatred against our form of government." The *New York Times* similarly declared that the decision "shows that the highest court in the land is anxious to secure and protect the rights of the humblest citizens."[60]

Governor D. Bibb Graves of Alabama proclaimed that the Court's decisions were the "supreme law of the land" and that "we must put the names of Negroes in jury boxes in every county." He even mailed a copy of the rulings to all circuit judges in the state with instructions to comply. Newspapers outside of the South applauded the governor's stance, but in the Deep South the reaction was different. The Charleston *News and Courier* declared that putting blacks on juries was "out of the question" because it "would revolutionize Southern jurisprudence and demoralize Southern civilization." Thus, the Supreme Court decision "can and probably will be evaded." Because the Fourteenth Amendment had been "imposed on the South when it was bound hand and foot and gagged, . . . [it] is not binding upon [the] honor or morals" of the South.[61]

The Court's second round of Scottsboro reversals did not, as some had hoped, deter Alabama from trying again. Leibowitz tried to persuade Governor Graves to block further prosecutions, but the Court's interventions had only further inflamed public opinion in Alabama. The state's high court faithfully quashed the indictments but clarified that this would not prevent retrials, and Lieutenant Governor Knight immediately announced that the cases would "be prosecuted to their conclusion."[62]

---

[60] Carter, 324–25 (quotations); "Justice for Negroes," *NYT*, p. 20 ("humblest citizens"). *See also NYT*, 2 Apr. 1935, p. 15; "The Scottsboro Ruling," *Washington Post*, 7 Apr. 1935, p. B7 (quoting the *Philadelphia Inquirer*, which called *Norris* "conclusive proof that the highest court in the land is determined that substantial justice shall be accorded to all citizens").

[61] Carter, 325–29 (Graves at 325); "A 'One Big State' Decision," *Charleston News & Courier*, 3 April 1935, p. 4 ("revolutionize"); "The Realities," *Charleston News & Courier*, 5 Apr. 1935, p. 4–A ("honor and morals"); "The South and Scottsboro Ruling," *Literary Digest*, 13 Apr. 1935, p. 10; "Graves Orders Negro Jurors for Alabama," *New York Herald Tribune*, 6 Apr. 1935, p. 30; "Negroes in the Courts," *NYT*, 7 Apr. 1935, p.E8 (declaring that the governor "deserves the approbation of the country"). *See also* "The Greater Menace," *Charleston New & Courier*, 11 Apr. 1935, p. 4 (predicting that "there will be no general compliance 'in spirit' with the court's decision" or with the governor's order).

[62] Carter, 328–29; "Scottsboro Case to be Reopened," *NYT*, 3 Apr. 1935, p. 7 (quotation).

Meanwhile, organizations supporting the Scottsboro defense effort were beginning to quell their intramural divisions. After the Communist International in 1935 decided to support a popular front with liberal organizations against the "towering menace of fascism," the ILD ceased attacking NAACP leaders as "capitalist lackeys" and agreed to share control of the Scottsboro retrials. The ILD, the NAACP, the ACLU, and other organizations now formed the Scottsboro Defense Committee (SDC), which orchestrated the defense for the next round of trials, relegated Leibowitz to the background, and enlisted a respected white lawyer from the South to do most of the courtroom work. For the first time, some Alabama moderates were willing to form a state Scottsboro committee, but they wanted the ILD muzzled and they resisted affiliating with Leibowitz, whose ILD connections and intemperate remarks had thoroughly alienated white Alabamians. Even if these conditions were satisfied, most of these moderates refused to commit themselves publicly on the defendants' guilt or innocence, and some of them insisted that the boys accept compromise prison sentences. The Alabama Scottsboro Fair Trial Committee that they formed accomplished little—most notably, failing in efforts to secure a new trial judge and prosecutor.[63]

Late in 1935, a new grand jury in Jackson County, consisting of thirteen whites and one black, returned another indictment against all nine of the defendants. (Alabama law required a two-thirds majority for a grand jury to return an indictment, making it easy to nullify a token black presence.) Early in 1936, Patterson was retried. Twelve blacks appeared on the 100–person venire from which his jury was drawn, but actually getting blacks to serve was another matter. Seven of the prospective black jurors were excused at their own request—"looking anything but regretful" as they left the courthouse, according to one newspaper reporter. The prosecutor used peremptory challenges to strike the other five blacks from the jury. Many whites on the venire admitted that they believed blacks were inferior, but Judge Callahan refused to strike them for that reason.[64]

At the trial, the state concocted new evidence against Patterson, producing a prison guard who testified to a supposed confession he had made. Although the defense demonstrated that it was almost certainly a fabrication, Callahan admitted the confession into evidence. He also obstructed defense counsel at every turn, failed to disguise his irritability with them, and glared at Patterson while defining the crime of rape. One prosecutor informed jurors of their duty to "protect the fair womanhood

---

[63] Carter, 330–38 (quotations at 331), 352–59.

[64] Carter, 338–41 (quotation at 341); Goodman, 253–55; "Scottsboro Jury Includes Negro," *New York Post*, 13 Nov. 1935, NAACP, part 6, reel 9, frame 588.

of this great State" and reminded them that after returning a verdict they would have to go home and face their neighbors.[65]

Observers were shocked when the jury imposed only a 75–year prison sentence on Patterson. A Birmingham newspaper called this "probably the first time in the history of the South that a Negro has been convicted of a charge of rape upon a white woman and has been given less than a death sentence." The jury foreman reported that he had been convinced of Patterson's innocence, but his colleagues had felt that an acquittal would effectively banish them from their communities; the lengthy prison sentence was a compromise.[66]

Soon after Patterson's conviction, three of the Scottsboro defendants—Norris, Powell, and Roy Wright—were in a car returning them to the Birmingham jail when Powell slashed a sheriff with a knife. Whether he had been provoked was disputed, though the stabbing was not. Powell was then shot in the head, though not fatally. Northern newspapers tended to doubt the veracity of the sheriff's account that the shooting was in self-defense.[67]

By 1936, Alabama officials, reflecting growing public weariness over the Scottsboro episode, began hinting at a compromise on sentences less than death. The SDC was reluctant to have the boys plead guilty to crimes they had not committed, but some members worried that the grounds for federal appeals were disappearing and that refusing to compromise could lead to more death sentences. A deal was negotiated under which some of the defendants would be released immediately, while others would be prosecuted only for assault and receive sentences of less than five years in prison. By the summer of 1937, editorial opinion in Alabama both supported and predicted a compromise solution. But Judge Callahan blocked it, insisting that the defendants be retried in his courtroom.[68]

Norris went on trial again in Decatur in the summer of 1937, and the jury returned another death sentence. Enlightened public opinion, as reflected in newspaper editorials urging a compromise, apparently went unrepresented on Morgan County juries. The prosecutor now hinted that with the convictions of the two "ringleaders of the crime"—Patterson and Norris—the state was prepared to compromise. Andy Wright was

---

[65] Carter, 341–46 (quotation at 345); Goodman, 255–57; "Scottsboro Case Goes to Jury," *NYT*, 23 Jan. 1936, p. 1.

[66] Carter, 347–48; Goodman, 257–58.

[67] Carter, 348–51; Goodman, 258–61; "Scottsboro Negro Shot Trying Break As He Stabs Guard," *NYT*, 25 Jan. 1936, p. 1; "Alabama Must Answer," *New York Post*, 25 Jan. 1936, NAACP, part 6, reel 9, frame 608.

[68] Carter, 362–66; Goodman, 291–93.

the next defendant to be retried, and the state did not even seek the death penalty. The prosecutor delivered an impassioned attack on New York City, and the jury imposed a ninety-nine year sentence. Next, Charley Weems was reprosecuted, convicted, and sentenced to seventy-five years in prison. The state then dropped the rape charges against Powell and charged him only with assaulting the deputy sheriff; he pled guilty and received a twenty-year sentence. The state abandoned its cases against the other four defendants—the two youngest and the two most physically disabled at the time of the alleged rapes—and they were released. One observer wryly noted that this resolution left Alabama in the "anomalous position of providing only 50 per cent protection for the 'flower of southern womanhood.' "[69]

Newspapers outside of Alabama treated the dropping of charges against the four as a virtual admission that all of the defendants were innocent. Later in 1937, the Supreme Court, having exhausted plausible grounds under the federal constitution for reversing the Scottsboro convictions, declined to review Patterson's seventy-five-year sentence. The justices probably believed the boys were innocent, but that was not, unfortunately, a sufficient basis for reversing their convictions.[70]

With judicial appeals evaporating, the SDC focused on securing a gubernatorial pardon. Governor Graves agreed that Alabama could not justifiably continue to imprison some of the boys on evidence deemed insufficient to hold the others. Late in 1937, he told the boys' representatives that he would release them before his term expired. In the summer of 1938, after the Alabama supreme court had affirmed the death sentence of Norris and the prison sentences of the others, Graves commuted Norris's sentence to life imprisonment. Major Alabama newspapers now supported clemency for the remaining prisoners, but the governor had a last-minute change of heart and reneged on his promise to free them.[71]

Walter White then went to the White House to ask Eleanor Roosevelt to urge the president to intervene. President Roosevelt wrote to Graves, a political supporter, and urged him to pardon the remaining Scottsboro prisoners. But the governor had tested the political waters and concluded that releasing them would finish him politically. This pattern of negotiated compromise followed by repudiation was repeated

---

[69] Carter, 369–77 ("ringleaders" at 371; "anomalous position" at 376); Goodman, 302–08; "Scottsboro Case Ends as 4 Go Free; 2 More Get Prison," *NYT*, 25 July 1937, p. 1.

[70] Carter, 377–79. *See also* "New Scottsboro Opinion," *Baltimore Sun*, 3 Apr. 1935, p. 12 (noting after *Norris* that "[i]t is a pretty fair suspicion ... that the learned justices acted as they did because they don't believe the Scottsboro boys are guilty").

[71] Carter, 379–91; Goodman, 313–17; Chalmers to Gov. Graves, 19 Dec. 1938, NAACP, part 6, reel 2, frames 283–88.

several times over the next eleven years. Members of the parole board feared that if they recommended release, "some candidate may seize upon it as an issue and endeavor to discredit the whole parole and probation system." Finally, in 1943–1944, three more of the Scottsboro prisoners were released; but two of them promptly violated the terms of their parole by heading North in search of better employment opportunities, and the prison board threw them back in jail. The last of the Scottsboro prisoners, Andy Wright, was not freed until 1950. The nine Scottsboro boys together spent more than 100 years in prison. Not until 1976 had the racial attitudes of whites in Alabama changed sufficiently for Governor George Wallace to issue an unconditional pardon to Norris, which effectively acknowledged his innocence.[72]

Long-term Ramifications

The Court's interventions probably saved the Scottsboro boys from execution, though not from years of wrongful incarceration. What were the broader consequences of these decisions for black criminal defendants in the South?

Justice George Sutherland wrote a narrow opinion in *Powell*; not only did it cover only capital cases, but it was ostensibly limited to the circumstances of the Scottsboro boys—"the ignorance and illiteracy of the defendants, their youth, the circumstances of public hostility, the imprisonment and close surveillance of the defendants by the military forces ..." In 1942 the Court in *Betts v. Brady* refused to extend *Powell* to all indigent felony defendants. However, several subsequent decisions held that under certain circumstances, such as a defendant's youth or low intelligence, state-appointed counsel was constitutionally required in felony prosecutions. Most of these cases involved white defendants from northern states. The facts were generally less egregious than those in *Powell*, and the justices usually divided.[73]

Despite these extensions of *Powell*, the justices said almost nothing about the *quality* of defense representation that the Constitution required. The one partial exception was *Avery v. Alabama* in 1940, where the Court ruled that an appointment three days before a capital murder trial began was permissible unless the defendant could show prejudice resulting from the short preparation period. Thus, despite *Powell* and its progeny, southern blacks could be woefully underrepresented without there being a constitutional violation. And so they were. Because the value of most constitutional rights depends on having competent lawyers

---

[72] Carter, 391–426 (quotation at 406); Eleanor Roosevelt to Walter White, 10 Dec. 1938, NAACP, part 6, reel 2, frame 277.

[73] *Powell*, 287 U.S. at 71; Betts v. Brady, 316 U.S. 455 (1942); Klarman, 230 (citing and discussing other cases).

to raise them, southern blacks benefitted little from those rights to which they were entitled.[74]

Most black criminal defendants in the South could not afford to hire their own lawyers, and thus their fates rested upon court-appointed counsel. The NAACP financed a few cases its lawyers considered likely to succeed. But the association rarely got involved in criminal litigation until after trial; it had limited funds for such cases, and it did not regard itself as a legal aid bureau. Thus, the NAACP's involvement was limited to cases where "there is injustice because of race or color, and where there is a possibility of establishing a precedent for the benefit of Negroes in general." These restrictive ground rules led the association to reject many cases of obvious racial injustice.[75]

Even the rare black defendant who could afford to hire a lawyer could not be certain that he was getting his money's worth. Very few black lawyers practiced in the South in the 1930s or 1940s. The number in Mississippi declined from twenty-one in 1910 to three in 1940, and the number in South Carolina fell from seventeen to five. Outside of major cities, there were essentially none. Furthermore, the few black lawyers who did exist were a distinct liability in most Jim Crow courtrooms, both because of the racial prejudice of white judges and jurors and because of the inferior legal training most of them had received (being barred from southern law schools).[76]

Yet at least most black lawyers, one might assume, would have faithfully pursued the best interests of their clients. Black defendants never knew what they were getting with white lawyers. To be sure, some white lawyers proved genuinely committed to serving their clients' interests and pursued cases without adequate compensation while risking reprisals for defending unpopular causes. But most white lawyers shared the prejudices of their communities, assumed their clients deserved whatever sentences they received, and barely went through the legal motions in order to collect a fee.[77]

Willie Francis, a sixteen-year-old black who was sentenced to death in Louisiana for murdering a white man, was victimized by this sort of inept lawyering. Francis achieved national prominence in 1946–1947 when Louisiana sought to execute him "by installments" after the electric chair malfunctioned during the initial execution attempt. At trial, Francis's two court-appointed lawyers had failed to challenge the

---

[74] Avery v. Alabama, 308 U.S. 444 (1940); Klarman, 230–31, 271.

[75] Thurgood Marshall to John Henry Joseph, 10 July 1941, NAACP, part 8, series B, reel 7, frame 426.

[76] Klarman, 156, 271.

[77] Klarman, 271–72.

all-white jury or to file a change-of-venue motion, even though Francis had been transferred to another county's jail to protect him from threatened mob violence. Defense counsel also failed to object to Francis's possibly coerced confession, which was the only direct evidence linking him to the crime. His lawyers made no opening argument, called no witnesses, and neglected to inform the jury that the police had "lost" the alleged murder weapon. Then they failed even to appeal Francis's conviction, thus forfeiting any valid constitutional claims he may have had. Francis may have been innocent of murder, yet no appellate court ever scrutinized his trial record. His case was unique, however, not because of this inept lawyering—which was all too common in the trials of indigent southern blacks—but because of the bungled execution attempt. In 1947 the U.S. Supreme Court, by a five-to-four vote, rejected Francis's claim that a second execution attempt would constitute cruel and unusual punishment or violate due process. The justices did not even consider whether his trial representation had been adequate.[78]

White lawyers risked severe social sanctions for defending black clients too vigorously when local communities were demanding blood. Most chose not to do so. Sonny Dobbs, a black man charged with murdering a white man in Atalla County, Mississippi, in 1946, was defended by court-appointed whites, whom the NAACP thought did an excellent job under the circumstances. Still, they "lived in Mississippi and wanted to stay here" and thus dared not take the steps that were essential to an effective defense, such as demanding a change of venue or challenging race discrimination in jury selection. White lawyers who refused to capitulate to such pressure found their legal practices crippled and sometimes suffered physical violence. Joseph Murray, who in 1939–1940 ably represented two blacks from McCormick, South Carolina, who were probably falsely accused of murder, reported that he had "incurred the ill will of so many people here that I am now unable to secure any practice and it looks as if I might have to move to some other place and begin over to try and again build up a practice." Stanley Belden, a white ACLU lawyer who ably represented a black man facing possibly trumped-up murder charges in Hugo, Oklahoma, in 1941, saw his legal practice ruined and was forced to leave the state.[79]

Southern courts refused to extend *Powell* to require effective representation of indigent defendants. The justices had ruled that appointment of counsel on the morning of trial was inadequate, so southern judges would appoint lawyers a few days before trial. Black defendants whose lives were in jeopardy were routinely provided lawyers so near to

---

[78] Arthur S. Miller & Jeffrey H. Bowman, *Death by Installments: The Ordeal of Willie Francis*. (1988), 23–27; Klarman, 272.

[79] Klarman, 272–73.

trial that no serious investigation of facts or preparation of trial strategy
was possible. In the most explosive cases, moreover, court-appointed
lawyers were strongly discouraged from seeking continuances by threats
to lynch their clients. Lawyers who persevered against such pressure
generally saw their motions for continuances denied anyway, or else
judges granted much shorter delays than they had sought.[80]

Placing blacks on southern juries probably would have benefitted
black defendants more than ensuring adequate representation of defense
counsel. This is why contemporary observers believed the jury-discrimination claim of the Scottsboro defendants was more significant than
their right-to-counsel argument. Yet, in practice, *Norris* had little impact
on black jury service in the South.

Southern newspapers predicted that *Norris* would be easily circumvented. The Jackson (Mississippi) *Daily News* deemed the decision only a
minor nuisance because lawyers would have to invest time in evading it.
In states such as Mississippi and South Carolina, where jury service was
linked to voter registration, *Norris* made little if any difference because
blacks remained almost universally disfranchised in the 1930s. *Norris*
also left open the possibility of using jury-selection schemes that vested
enormous discretion in the hands of (white) jury commissioners. Proving
race discrimination in the administration of such schemes was difficult,
especially because state courts still made the initial factual determinations.[81]

Southern whites correctly concluded that *Norris* could be circumvented by placing the names of a few blacks on the jury rolls. Such
blacks were often superannuated, dead, disabled, or departed, and they
never appeared in numbers approximating the percentage of a county's
black population. Even those blacks making it onto the rolls were rarely
called for service, and if they were, they could often be intimidated.
When a black college president in Texas refused to be excused from jury
service in 1938, white hoodlums removed him from the jury room and
threw him head first down the steps of a Dallas courthouse. Moreover,
the presence of an occasional black on a grand jury was easily nullified
by rules requiring less than unanimity for an indictment. The even-more
occasional black called for service on trial juries could be excluded
through challenges for cause, over which trial judges exercised enormous

---

[80] Klarman, 273.

[81] Carter, 326–28; Klarman, 154; *Survey*, 71 (May 1935) 144; *Birmingham News*, 5
Apr. 1935, p. 8; *Charleston News and Courier*, 13 Apr. 1935, p. 4. *See also Birmingham
News*, 30 Apr. 1935, p. 1, *reproduced in* Rayford W. Logan, ed., *The Attitude of the Southern
White Press Toward Negro Suffrage, 1932–1940* (1940), 2 (noting that after *Norris* a bill
was introduced into the Alabama senate that would have limited jury service to registered
voters); "Alabama Undeterred," *Pittsburgh Courier*, 27 Apr. 1935, p. 12 (same).

discretion, or through prosecutors' peremptory challenges, the number of which some states increased after *Norris*.[82]

The most that *Norris* seems to have accomplished was to place a single black on an occasional jury in large cities of the peripheral South. In the deep South and in rural areas throughout the region, exclusion of blacks from juries remained the rule. In a Louisiana case that reached the Supreme Court in 1939, a rural parish with a black population of nearly fifty percent had "complied" with *Norris* by placing the names of three blacks, one of whom was dead, on a jury venire of 300. A study conducted in 1940 found that the vast majority of rural counties in the deep South "have made no pretense of putting Negroes on jury lists, much less calling or using them in trials."[83]

Because southern states reformed their jury-selection practices so little after *Norris*, the justices continued to find easy cases for reversing convictions because of race discrimination in jury selection. By the late 1940s, they were growing frustrated at the inefficacy of their decisions, but they still declined to take the steps necessary actually to place blacks on southern juries. The Court refused to condemn the practices of limiting jury service to registered voters and of conferring virtually unfettered discretion over jury selection to commissioners. The Court did not even flatly prohibit the insidious practice of commissioners limiting prospective jurors to their personal acquaintances—meaning white people. In *Akins v. Texas* in 1945, the Court inexplicably deferred to a state court's finding that there had been no race discrimination in jury selection despite the testimony of all three jury commissioners that they had refused to permit more than one black to sit on Akins's grand jury. The justices declined even to hear a case contesting the constitutionality of prosecutors using peremptory challenges to exclude blacks from juries because of their race. As a result, southern juries remained almost entirely white for another generation. Every one of the fifteen black men executed by the *border state* of Kentucky between 1940 and 1962 had been convicted of a crime against a white person by an all-white jury.[84]

The famous Martinsville Seven case illustrates how the exclusion of blacks from jury service invited racial injustice. Seven young black men were charged with raping a white woman in the southside region of Virginia in 1949. The woman had indisputably been raped, and all seven defendants had indisputably engaged in forcible intercourse with her or

---

[82] Klarman, 154.

[83] Pierre v. Louisiana, 306 U.S. 354 (1939); Klarman, 154–55.

[84] Akins v. Texas, 325 U.S. 398 (1945); People v. Roxborough, 12 N.W. 2d 466 (Mich. 1943), *cert. denied*, 323 U.S. 749 (1944); George C. Wright, "By the Book: The Legal Executions of Kentucky Blacks," in W. Fitzhugh Brundage, ed., *Under Sentence of Death: Lynchings in the South* (1997), 266.

been present as accomplices. No lynch mob attempted to execute the defendants, and the trial was conducted in a mob-free atmosphere. The defendants were not beaten into confessing. The trials did not occur until five months after the crime, and defense counsel was appointed four months before trial. Both the judge and the prosecutor avoided references at trial to the defendants' race. Three blacks sat on the grand jury that indicted the defendants, and blacks appeared in each of the jury pools for the six separate trials. Although black newspapers and some radical journalists compared these proceedings to those at Scottsboro twenty years earlier, the dissimilarities are actually more striking: The Martinsville Seven had real trials with real lawyers that were conducted with relative dispassion before a fair judge.[85]

Yet the trials, convictions, and executions of the Martinsville Seven were fundamentally unjust for two reasons having to do with race. First, although blacks were in the jury pools for all of the defendants' trials, every one of the seventy-two jurors who tried and convicted them was white. Blacks were excluded from the juries because of their opposition to the death penalty or through the prosecutors' use of peremptory challenges. Second, every one of the 45 death sentences imposed for rape or attempted rape in Virginia between 1908 and 1950 involved a black man and a white woman. (Similarly, between 1925 and 1950, Florida executed thirty-three blacks and only one white for rape, and in its entire history Mississippi had executed no whites for rape.)[86]

Thus, although the Martinsville Seven enjoyed ostensibly fair trials, their fate ultimately depended on their race. In rape cases in Virginia, only blacks who assaulted whites ever received the death penalty, and only white jurors adjudicated their guilt and imposed sentence. Oliver Hill, a black lawyer from Richmond who helped represent the Martinsville Seven, concluded that white Virginians knew that "we don't need to lynch the niggers. We can try them and then hang them." Virginia executed the Martinsville Seven in February 1951—the largest mass execution or lynching for rape in American history.[87]

Black jurors probably would have benefitted black defendants in other cases as well, assuming their independent judgment could have been guaranteed (quite possibly an unwarranted assumption in the South of this era). Odell Waller was another black Virginian whose death sentence attracted national attention. He was a sharecropper convicted of murdering a white farmer, Oscar Davis, in Pittsylvania County,

---

[85] Eric W. Rise, *The Martinsville Seven: Race, Rape, and Capital Punishment* (1995), chapters 1–2, especially pp. 53–54; Klarman, 278.

[86] Rise, 85, 102, 126, 156–57; Klarman, 279.

[87] Rise, 3, 93.

Virginia, in 1940. Waller had undeniably killed Davis, but he had a plausible self-defense claim. The two men had an unpleasant history, including Davis's mutilation of Waller's dog. Immediately before Davis's death, they had quarreled over the distribution of crop shares. Waller claimed that Davis was known to carry a gun and that he was reaching for it when Waller shot him. The all-white jury rejected Waller's self-defense claim. How could having blacks on Waller's jury—and one-third of Pittsylvania County's population was black—not have made a difference? When the race of the defendant and decedent were reversed in another sharecropper homicide case in Pittsylvania County around the same time, the all-white jury deliberated just fifteen minutes before acquitting the defendant, apparently crediting his self-defense claim. Yet Governor Colgate Darden repulsed entreaties to commute Waller's death sentence, and he was executed in 1942.[88]

Because most white men in the South presumed that sex between a black man and a white woman was rape, black defendants who pleaded consent as a defense to charges of raping white women had essentially no chance before all-white juries. Even black defendants who pled mistaken identity might have benefitted from having blacks on their juries. In 1935, a white Birmingham physician was quoted as saying that if a black man raped a white woman, "an example and a spectacle of punishment" was necessary. "If possible get the right Negro and string him up. String up one or two of his nearest relatives, at the same time. And if the right one can't be found, take some other Negro." It seems safe to assume that all black jurors would have disagreed with that sentiment.[89]

Why *Powell* and *Norris* Were So Inefficacious

One reason decisions such as *Powell* and *Norris* had so little impact is that southern black defendants could not ordinarily appeal their sentences. State appellate and federal judges were more likely than state trial judges to vindicate the constitutional rights of southern blacks, because they were better educated, more professionalized, and more independent of local opinion that often proved hostile to the rights. Yet cases of black criminal defendants usually did not proceed beyond trial courts, mainly because state provision of counsel to indigents did not generally extend to appeals, but also because procedural defaults frequently insulated trial error from appellate review.[90]

---

[88] Richard B. Sherman, *The Case of Odell Waller and Virginia Justice 1940–1942* (1992), 1–14, 25–31, 99–115, 123–28, 155–65; Waller v. Virginia, 16 S.E. 2d 808 (1941), *cert. denied*, 316 U.S. 679 (1942); Klarman, 379–80.

[89] Virginius Dabney, *Below the Potomac: A Book About The New South* (1942), 189–90.

[90] For this and the following paragraphs, *see* Klarman, 155–58. *See also* "When Negro Convicts Kill," *Charleston News & Courier*, 9 Apr. 1935, p. 4 (noting that "negroes will not

The criminal procedure cases that reached the Supreme Court did so only because of outside financial assistance. Incidents such as the race riot in Phillips County, Arkansas, and the alleged rapes and ensuing trials at Scottsboro captured national attention. Because the criminal trials deriving from these incidents revealed Jim Crow at its worst, they provided outstanding fund-raising opportunities for the NAACP and the ILD, respectively. However, the NAACP took relatively few criminal cases, and the association was absent from most of the rural South and thus could not intervene in cases when it would have done the most good—when the trial record was being created. Thus, in run-of-the-mill criminal cases, indigent black defendants were represented not by elite legal talent hired by these organizations, but by court-appointed lawyers, who could not invariably be counted upon to aggressively defend their clients' rights because of the "personal odium" that attached to those challenging "the venerable system."[91]

Furthermore, enlistment of competent counsel on appeal frequently came too late to do defendants much good, as inept or careless lawyering at trial produced procedural defaults that insulated constitutional violations from appellate review. The issue of race discrimination in jury selection was procedurally defaulted in both *Moore* and *Powell* and very nearly so in *Patterson*. In *Brown v. Mississippi* (1936), the landmark decision holding that criminal convictions based on coerced confessions violated due process, the issue nearly failed to gain a hearing in the Supreme Court because defense counsel had challenged the voluntariness of the confessions at the wrong point of the trial. Until the Supreme Court in the 1960s changed the rules regarding federal court deference to state procedural defaults, many valid federal constitutional claims were denied a hearing in any appellate court.[92]

The ruthlessness of the Jim Crow system made it difficult for lawyers to compile the sort of trial record necessary for effective appellate review. Fear of economic and physical reprisals deterred all but the most intrepid blacks from signing affidavits supporting a change in trial venue. When Walter White of the NAACP traveled to Phillips County to investigate the facts in *Moore*, he was nearly lynched. One of the blacks whom Leibowitz had called to testify at the hearing challenging race discrimination in jury selection in Morgan County had a cross burnt on his front yard for "stepping out of line." Rigorous cross-examination of

---

get their cases into the supreme court unless some agency or society shall put up the money to hire lawyers . . . and pay the expenses of the appeal").

[91] Klarman, 459 (quotation).

[92] Brown v. Mississippi, 297 U.S. 278 (1936); Powell v. State, 141 So. 201, 210 (Ala. 1932).

white witnesses, especially women in rape cases, not only alienated white jurors but also jeopardized the safety of defense counsel.[93]

Finally, public officials in the South had little direct incentive to abide by the constitutional rights of black defendants because civil and criminal sanctions for violations were generally unavailable. After *Screws v. United States* in 1945, it was far from certain whether the justices would permit the imposition of federal criminal liability even on sheriffs who beat defendants into confessing. Nor was it clear in the 1940s that courts would construe federal civil rights statutes to authorize the imposition of monetary liability on public officers who contravened state law as well as the federal constitution; and every state required the appointment of counsel for indigent capital defendants and forbade race discrimination in jury selection.[94]

For all these reasons—the inability of most southern black defendants to afford counsel, the relative absence of alternative sources of legal assistance such as the NAACP, the difficulty of maneuvering around state procedural default rules, the obstacles to compiling a favorable trial record, and the absence of effective sanctions against rights violators—few criminal cases like *Powell* and *Norris* reached the Court. As one black newspaper observed after *Powell*, "Out of the thousands of cases where Negroes are convicted without fair trials, few ever reach the Supreme Court, and even if they do the results are rarely altered . . . We are afraid it will take more than decisions of the Supreme Court to rectify the flagrant evils of our judicial system."[95]

Intangible Benefits of Litigation

Litigation in defense of the rights of southern blacks may have been more important for its intangible effects: convincing blacks that the racial status quo was malleable, educating them about their rights, helping to mobilize protest, and instructing northern whites about Jim Crow conditions. A social movement for civil rights faced intimidating obstacles in the South. One of the most formidable was simply convincing blacks that the status quo of racial subordination was contingent rather than inevitable. As Walter White observed, the NAACP's greatest difficulty was "getting over to the masses of our folks the significance of these fights."[96]

---

[93] Carter, 201 note 21 (quotation).

[94] Screws v. United States, 325 U.S. 91 (1945); Klarman, 270–71.

[95] "The Scottsboro Case," *Chicago Bee*, 20 Nov. 1932, NAACP, part 6, reel 8, frame 797.

[96] For this and the following paragraphs, *see* Klarman, 162–67 (quotation at 163), 284–86.

In theory, black protest could have assumed a variety of forms: migration, violent revolt, political mobilization, economic pressure, street demonstrations, or litigation. In practice, however, options were limited. Violent protest would have been suicidal, given overwhelming white physical power and the will to use it. Political protest was unavailable to southern blacks, who remained almost universally disfranchised. Few southern blacks commanded sufficient financial resources to leverage social change through economic pressure. Street demonstrations, which proved so effective in the 1960s, were not yet a realistic option; the South was still too violent, segregation and disfranchisement too deeply entrenched, and the threat of national intervention too remote. Black leaders observed, no doubt correctly, that a Gandhian strategy of non-violent protest in the South would have led to "an unprecedented massacre of defenseless black men and women." Only two protest options were realistically available to southern blacks: migration and litigation. Millions pursued the former; many fewer chose the latter.[97]

Most civil rights leaders appreciated the limited potential of litigation to transform race relations given prevailing mores and conditions. Charles Houston, the principal legal strategist of the NAACP in the 1930s, recognized that law "has certain definite limitations when it comes to changing the mores of a community," because "[i]t is too much to expect the court to go against the established and crystallized social customs." Yet even if litigation could not "bring on a social revolution," as Ralph Bunche observed, it could advance long-term objectives. Litigation educated blacks about their rights and inspired them to challenge the racial status quo. The NAACP's national office wrote letters to southern blacks explaining their rights and the obligation of whites to respect them. Some black communities in the South felt so hopeless and isolated that for the national office merely to make inquiries on their behalf would "do a lot of good." A memorandum by Houston declared that a principal objective of litigation should be "to arouse and strengthen the will of local communities to demand and fight for their rights."[98]

Houston and Thurgood Marshall thought that organizing local communities in support of litigation was nearly as important as winning lawsuits. They frequently made speeches at mass rallies while visiting southern communities for court appearances. "On occasion," a recent

---

[97] Klarman, 163.

[98] Charles H. Houson & Leon A. Ransom, "The Crawford Case," *Nation*, 139 (4 July 1934): 18–19 ("certain definite limitations"); Genna Rae McNeil, *Groundwork: Charles Hamilton Houston and the Struggle for Civil Rights* (1983), 135 ("crystallized social customs"); Ralph J. Bunche, *The Political Status of the Negro in the Age of FDR* (Dewey W. Grantham, ed. 1973), 108 ("social revolution"); J. Rice Perkins to Walter White, 7 May 1935, NAACP, part 3, series A, reel 4, frame 367 ("do a lot of good"); Charles H. Houston, memorandum, 26 Oct. 1934, *ibid.*, reel 1, frames 859–60 ("arouse and strengthen").

biographer writes, Marshall "appears to have been brought to town nominally to work on pending litigation but actually to rally the troops." Because of the need "to back up our legal efforts with the required public support and social force," Houston referred to himself as "not only lawyer but evangelist and stump speaker." Because cases such as Scottsboro demonstrated to blacks the importance of binding together in self-defense, they provided unparalleled fund-raising and branch-building opportunities for the NAACP. As one black editorialist observed, "[w]hatever else happens in the Scottsboro case, . . . [i]t has given us one of the greatest chances for consolidated action we have had since emancipation."[99]

Litigation also provided southern black communities with salutary examples of the accomplishments and courage of black Americans. Watching a skilled black lawyer subject a white sheriff to a grueling cross-examination educated and inspired southern blacks, who virtually never witnessed such scenes of blacks confronting whites on an equal footing. Bold and capable performances by black lawyers in southern courtrooms seemed to contravene the very premises of white supremacy. Marshall explained this dynamic in connection with a criminal trial in Hugo, Oklahoma, in 1941, where no black lawyer had ever before appeared in the courtroom. Marshall and his white co-counsel, Stanley Belden of the ACLU, had agreed that Marshall would cross-examine all of the police officers, "because we figured they would resent being questioned by a Negro and would get angry and this would help us. It worked perfect. They all became angry at the idea of a Negro pushing them into tight corners and making their lies so obvious." Marshall continued: "Boy, did I like that—and did the Negroes in the courtroom like it. . . . You can't imagine what it means to those people down there who have been pushed around for years to know that there is an organization that will help them. They are really ready to do their part now. They are ready for anything."[100]

Litigation may also have raised the salience of the race issue for whites. Houston observed that "[t]he truth is there are millions of white people who have no real knowledge of the Negro's problems and who never give the Negro a serious thought." As Bunche noted, "[c]ourt decisions, favorable or unfavorable, serve to dramatize the plight of the race more effectively than any other recourse; their propaganda and educative value is great." Criminal cases may have afforded the best educational opportunities, as they revealed Jim Crow at its worst—

---

[99] Mark V. Tushnet, *Making Civil Rights Law: Thurgood Marshall and the Supreme Court, 1936–1961* (1994), 30; McNeil, 145 ("evangelist"); William N. Jones, "Day by Day," *Baltimore Afro–American*, 22 Apr. 1933, p. 6 ("greatest chances").

[100] Klarman, 285 (quotations).

southern blacks, possibly or certainly innocent of the crimes charged, being railroaded to the death penalty through farcical trials. As one black newspaper observed, "No single event touching the Negro question in this country has been forced into the conscience, the life and the public opinion of the American people as has the Scottsboro case."[101]

Finally, litigation, when successful, provided blacks with one of their few reasons for optimism before World War II. As one black leader observed in 1935, even if court victories produced little concrete change, at least they "keep open the door of hope to the Negro." Roscoe Dunjee, the NAACP's principal agent in Oklahoma, noted after one such court victory, "It is just such rifts in the dark clouds of prejudice which cause black folks to know that a better day is coming by and by."[102]

Intangible Harms of Litigation Victories

Rulings such as *Powell* and *Norris* may have produced intangible harms as well as benefits. By 1950 or so, lynchings were nearly obsolete in the South, and legal lynchings had been tempered and confined to narrower portions of the Deep South. Yet nowhere in the South did blacks serve as jurors in inflammatory cases of alleged black-on-white crime. All-white juries applied unwritten substantive liability rules decreeing that only black men could be executed for raping white women and only whites were permitted to kill other whites in self-defense. Criminal justice outside of the rural Deep South may have acquired a veneer of legitimacy by the 1940s. The justices could find no constitutional error in cases such as those of the Martinsville Seven or that of Odell Waller because the trials had ostensibly been fair. Yet black men were still being executed under circumstances where whites almost surely would not have been.[103]

Given this state of affairs, one may wonder whether the Court's criminal procedure interventions were not insidious. In landmark decisions protecting the rights of southern black defendants, the justices employed some of their boldest rhetoric about the high court's heroic role in defending unpopular minorities from majoritarian oppression. For example, in *Chambers v. Florida* (1940), which extended *Brown v. Mississippi*'s bar on coerced confessions to cover interrogation practices other than physical violence, the Court proudly proclaimed the obligation of judges to "stand against any winds that blow as havens of refuge for those who might otherwise suffer because they are helpless, weak,

---

[101] Klarman, 166 (Houston and Bunche quotes); "Group of National Negro Leaders Will Attack All Segregation and Injustice," *Richmond Planet*, 4 March 1933, NAACP, part 6, reel 8, frame 810.

[102] Klarman, 167 (quotations).

[103] For this and the following paragraphs, *see* Klarman, 282–84.

outnumbered or because they are non-conforming victims of prejudice and public excitement." Newspapers reported the decision in banner headlines such as, "Justices Rededicate Themselves as a Haven of Refuge for all Non–Conforming Victims of Public Prejudice." A glowing editorial in the *Nation* quoted some of the Court's rhetoric and basked in the happy ending of *Chambers*: Americans should "be proud" because the Court had freed "obscure and humble" black men who implicated no larger political or economic concerns.[104]

Yet *Chambers* apparently had little effect on southern sheriffs, who continued to coerce confessions from black suspects. Nor, as we have seen, did rulings such as *Powell* and *Norris* significantly alter Jim Crow justice. Were blacks clearly better off because of rulings that had little practical consequence for southern criminal justice but that enabled the Court to trumpet the vigilant defense that judges offered against racial prejudice in law? Before the Court's interventions, at least everyone could see mob-dominated trials for what they were—farcical substitutes for lynchings. After such rulings, however, casual observers might have been misled into believing, along with the *New York Times*, that "the High Court stands on guard with flaming sword over the rights of every one of us."[105]

Blacks could be excused if they demurred from such sentiments. Even in states such as Virginia, where the formal requirements of due process were more attentively observed, blacks did not sit on juries in racially explosive cases, and all-white juries applied informal liability rules that discriminated against blacks. In the postwar period the justices had opportunities to redress these problems. Defendants appealed cases to the Court that attacked the racially motivated use of peremptory challenges by prosecutors and racial disparities in the administration of the death penalty. The justices refused even to grant review. Not until the 1970s would the Court invalidate the discriminatory administration of the death penalty, and not until the 1980s would it forbid the race-conscious use of peremptory challenges. Yet the rhetoric of *Chambers* suggests that the justices believed they had already taken enormous strides toward eliminating race discrimination from southern criminal justice. They had not. Their accomplishments were fairly trivial—more a change in form than in substance. To the extent that the justices and their admirers were deluded into thinking otherwise, these criminal procedure rulings may have caused actual harm to the interests of southern blacks.

The Court's denial of review technically does not indicate approval of the lower court's decision (though it may imply this, given the

---

[104] Chambers v. Florida, 309 U.S. 227, 241 (1940); Klarman, 282 (other quotations).

[105] "Due Process," *NYT*, 12 March 1940, p. 22.

justices' self-proclaimed role as heroic defender of minority rights). Yet this Court did not simply fail to intervene against certain racial inequalities in the criminal justice system of the South; it actually affirmed unjust convictions. In *Akins v. Texas* in 1945, each of the jury commissioners had admitted his intention to limit the number of blacks per grand jury to one, yet somehow the justices found the record unclear on this point. Moreover, Akins had an especially appealing case for reversal of his murder conviction because his self-defense claim almost certainly would have prevailed had he been white. Yet the justices affirmed his death sentence. *Lyons v. Oklahoma* in 1944 was the most compelling coerced confession case since *Brown v. Mississippi*; the record contained convincing testimony by several whites that Lyons, a black man, had been savagely beaten with a blackjack for several hours in an effort to obtain his confession. Lyons, too, had a strong claim of innocence. Yet the justices decided to defer to the jury's determination that Lyons's second confession, obtained just twelve hours after his brutal beatings had ended, was voluntary. For anyone convinced by the *Chambers* rhetoric, the force of the claims by Lyons and Akins that they had been unjustly treated was necessarily diminished. A Court serving as a "haven[] of refuge for ... [the] helpless, weak, ... or ... non-conforming victims of prejudice" would surely have intervened on behalf of these defendants had their claims been meritorious. But their claims *were* meritorious. By affirming their convictions, the Court probably helped legitimize the unjust treatment of black criminal defendants.[106]

CONCLUSION

It was no accident that modern American criminal procedure was born in cases involving southern black defendants. For the Supreme Court to begin monitoring the state criminal process required a departure from 150 years' worth of tradition and legal precedent grounded in federalism concerns. The justices were not prepared to take that step in cases of marginal unfairness, but only where the trial had been a complete sham. Such legal travesties occurred most frequently in the South in cases involving black defendants charged with interracial rape or murder.

The state-imposed death penalty in such cases was little more than a formalization of the lynching process. The purpose of a mob-dominated trial was simply to avoid a lynching, and the purpose of a lynching was as much to ensure black subordination as to punish guilt. The southern appellate courts and the U.S. Supreme Court applied different paradigms when reviewing such trials. Southern courts saw praiseworthy progress in the mere avoidance of lynchings. By contrast, Supreme Court justices

---

[106] Lyons v. Oklahoma, 322 U.S. 596 (1944).

expected criminal trials to be about adjudicating guilt or innocence, not simply preempting a lynching.

The trials in such cases were so egregiously unfair that national public opinion probably endorsed the Court's interventions. Even within the South, these rulings had many supporters, as they simply bound southern states to behavioral norms that they usually had embraced on their own. Thus, these early criminal procedure rulings probably do not represent the sort of countermajoritarian judicial decision making one often associates with landmark decisions such as *Mapp v. Ohio* or *Miranda v. Arizona*; it is more accurate to see them as the Court imposing a national consensus on recalcitrant outliers. Indeed, southern state courts themselves might have rectified the obvious injustices had the circumstances been slightly different. In the early decades of the twentieth century, southern courts had become more committed to procedural fairness, even in cases involving black defendants charged with serious interracial crimes. Yet in cases that generated outside criticism of the South or that were perceived to pose broader challenges to white supremacy, southern appellate courts regressed. Cases that might otherwise not have reached the U.S. Supreme Court slipped through the state system uncorrected and provided the occasion for landmark criminal procedure rulings.[107]

Considered against the backdrop of the Court's other contemporaneous race decisions, these early criminal procedure rulings demonstrate that not all Jim Crow measures were of a piece. During this era, the Court unanimously affirmed the constitutionality of public school segregation, the white primary, and the poll tax. The justices apparently thought it one thing to segregate and disfranchise blacks, quite another to execute possibly innocent blacks after farcical trials.[108]

Finally, evaluating the consequences of decisions such as *Powell* and *Norris* is complicated. The Court probably saved the lives of the Scottsboro boys, but it could not protect them from unjust prison sentences. The more the Court intervened on their behalf, the more determined white Alabamians seemed to punish them. Thus, despite two Supreme Court victories, the Scottsboro boys each served from five to twenty years in prison for crimes they did not commit.

In terms of broader effects, the rulings proved disappointing. The quality of defense representation for indigent southern blacks did not significantly improve as a result of *Powell*, and few if any blacks sat on southern juries as a result of *Norris*. To be sure, the litigation producing

---

[107] Miranda v. Arizona, 384 U.S. 436 (1966); Mapp v. Ohio, 367 U.S. 643 (1961).

[108] Breedlove v. Suttles, 302 U.S. 277 (1937) (poll tax); Grovey v. Townsend, 295 U.S. 45 (1935) (white primary); Gong Lum v. Rice, 275 U.S. 78 (1927) (public school segregation).

these and other decisions may have had intangible benefits for the civil rights movement: teaching blacks about their rights, convincing them that racial change was possible, helping to organize them, and educating whites about the atrocities of Jim Crow. But by implying that the Court had effected meaningful changes in the southern criminal justice system when in fact it had not, Supreme Court victories may also have harmed southern blacks.

2

Mapp v. Ohio: The First Shot Fired in the Warren Court's Criminal Procedure "Revolution"

Yale Kamisar*

Although Earl Warren ascended to the Supreme Court in 1953, when we speak of the Warren Court's "revolution" in American criminal procedure we really mean the movement that got underway half-way through the Chief Justice's sixteen-year reign. It was the 1961 case of *Mapp v. Ohio*,[1] overruling *Wolf v. Colorado*[2] and holding that the state courts had to exclude illegally seized evidence as a matter of federal constitutional law, that is generally regarded as having launched the so-called criminal procedure revolution.[3]

---

* Shortly after this chapter went to press, I received a copy of the manuscript for Carolyn Long's *Mapp v. Ohio: The Origin and Development of the Exclusionary Rule* (University Press of Kansas, 2006). This is a lively, informative and insightful account—and the most comprehensive account I have ever read—of *Mapp v. Ohio* and its aftermath. I would have referred to it at various places if it had been available when I wrote my chapter.

[1] 367 U.S. 643 (1961).

[2] 338 U.S. 25 (1949).

[3] *See, e.g.*, Stephen J. Schulhofer, *The Constitution and the Police: Individual Rights and Law Enforcement*, 66 Wash.U.L.Q. 11, 12 (1988), observing that in the field of criminal procedure "the 'real Warren Court'" emerged with the decision in *Mapp*. Some might argue that the Warren Court's revolution in criminal procedure commenced with Griffin v. Illinois, 351 U.S. 12 (1956), establishing an indigent criminal defendant's right to a free transcript on appeal, at least under certain circumstances. *Griffin* did foreshadow some of the cases handed down by the later Warren Court, but "it was only some years after this decision that a majority of the Court consistently took positions now regarded as characteristic of the Warren Court." Francis A. Allen, *The Judicial Quest for Penal Justice: The Warren Court and the Criminal Cases*, 1975 U.Ill.L.F. 518, 519 note 4.

The Obscenity Case that Wasn't

However, anyone who had read the briefs in the *Mapp* case or heard the oral argument in the Supreme Court would have thought that it was an obscenity case. The principal issue seemed to be whether an Ohio statute criminalizing the mere possession or control of obscene material, under which Dollree Mapp was convicted and sentenced to prison, violated the First and Fourteenth Amendments.[4] *Mapp* is not only the most famous search and seizure case in American history, but might also be called the stealth search and seizure case.

When the Supreme Court granted review in *Gideon*,[5] the famous right to counsel case, it asked the lawyers to discuss whether the Court's holding in *Betts v. Brady*[6] should be reconsidered.[7] As a result, many assumed that that twenty-year-old precedent would be overturned. (And it was.)[8] When the Court granted review in *Miranda* and three companion cases,[9] most Court-watchers expected the Court to dispel the uncertainty and confusion generated by *Escobedo v. Illinois*[10] (a case decided two years earlier), and to hand down a momentous decision in the police interrogation-confessions area. (And it did.) But *Mapp* was not preceded by advance publicity or discussion. The ruling must have come as a surprise to almost everyone—including Ms. Mapp's own lawyer.

As the Court pointed out during the oral argument,[11] Ms. Mapp's brief did not even cite *Wolf v. Colorado*, the precedent *Mapp* was to

---

[4] *See* text at notes 16–32, 47–50 *infra*.

[5] Gideon v. Wainwright, 372 U.S. 335 (1963). *Gideon* is the subject of a separate chapter in this volume.

[6] 316 U.S. 455 (1942). Under the *Betts* rule, or the "special circumstances" rule, an indigent defendant charged with a serious non-capital offense such as armed robbery had to represent himself unless there were special circumstances, *e.g.*, the defendant was mentally deficient or the case was unusually complicated.

[7] *See Gideon*, 372 U.S. at 338.

[8] *Gideon* established a "flat" or "automatic" right to appointed counsel in all felony cases. Argersinger v. Hamlin, 407 U.S. 25 (1972), held that absent a valid waiver, no person may be *incarcerated* for any offense, whether classified as petty, misdemeanor or felony, unless represented by counsel.

[9] The "*Miranda* opinion," 384 U.S. 436 (1966), was actually an opinion in four cases: Miranda v. Arizona, California v. Stewart, Vignera v. New York and Westover v. United States. *Miranda* is the subject of a separate chapter in this volume.

[10] 378 U.S. 478 (1964). For a summary of the wide disagreement over the meaning of *Escobedo*—and over what it ought to mean—*see* YALE KAMISAR, POLICE INTERROGATIONS AND CONFESSIONS: ESSAYS IN LAW AND POLICY 161–62 (1980).

[11] *See* 55 LANDMARK BRIEFS AND ARGUMENTS OF THE UNITED STATES: CONSTITUTIONAL LAW 1164 (Philip Kurland & Gerhard Casper eds. 1975) (hereinafter Landmark Briefs & Arguments). It should be noted that the ACLU which had filed an *amicus* brief in the case, did ask the

overrule.[12] Moreover, when asked by one of the Justices whether "you're asking us to overrule *Wolf* against *Colorado*,"[13] the lawyer replied: "No, I don't believe we are."[14]

The *Mapp* case arose as follows:[15]

Dollree Mapp, a 28–year old black woman, and her daughter by a former marriage lived on the top floor of a two-family dwelling. One day, three Cleveland police officers arrived at the dwelling pursuant to information that (1) a suspect in a recent bombing was hiding out there; and (2) a large amount of "policy paraphernalia" was hidden in the house. The police knocked on the door and demanded entrance. However, after calling her lawyer, Miss Mapp refused to admit the police without a search warrant.

Court to "re-examine" *Wolf*. But the ACLU only devoted one paragraph of its 21–page brief to the issue, *see id*. at 1154, and one commentator aptly described it as "sort of an 'oh, by the way'" paragraph. LUCAS A. POWE, JR., THE WARREN COURT AND AMERICAN POLITICS 196 (2000).

[12] At one point in his brief, Miss Mapp's lawyer did make an effort to bring his case within the doctrine of the infamous "stomach pumping" case, Rochin v. California, 342 U.S. 165 (1952), maintaining that the police action in *Mapp*, like the police behavior in *Rochin*, was "conduct that shocks the conscience." *See* Landmark Briefs & Arguments 1103. But the brief made no attempt to deal with, and did not even cite, Irvine v. California, 347 U.S. 128, 133 (1954), which took the position that *Rochin* was not really a search and seizure case, but one that turned on police "coercion"—"applied by a physical assault upon [the defendant's] person to compel submission to the use of a stomach pump." The failure to mention *Irvine* is quite surprising because, to quote the U.S. Supreme Court, "the [Ohio Supreme Court] found determinative the fact that the evidence had not been taken 'from defendant's person by the use of brutal or offensive physical force against defendant.'" 367 U.S. at 645.

At one point in the oral argument, in response to a direct question, Ms. Mapp's lawyer did say he thought his case "comes within the doctrine of the *Rochin* case," but when asked to specify "[w]hat particular facts" brought it within *Rochin*, he could only reply: "I can't say definitely.... I'm very sorry, but I don't have all of the facts in the case, just the conclusion that I came to on that." Landmark Briefs & Arguments 1200.

[13] *Id*. at 1165. Although the Justice who asked this question is not identified, it was probably Justice Frankfurter, the author of the majority opinion in *Wolf*. Because the lawyer had referred to him by name, we know that Frankfurter had asked the same question a few moments earlier, without getting a direct answer. *See id*. at 1164.

[14] No doubt troubled by his colleague's wrong response, or lack of response, to the question whether he was asking the Court to overrule *Wolf*, Bernard Berkman, the ACLU lawyer who followed Ms. Mapp's lawyer to the podium, told the Court at the outset that he *was* asking the Court to "reconsider" *Wolf*. *See id*. at 1170. But he devoted virtually all of his time to a discussion of the Ohio obscenity statute.

[15] This summary of the facts is based primarily on the account set forth in the *Mapp* opinion, 367 U.S. at 644–45. *See also* the discussion in Francis A. Allen, *Federalism and the Fourth Amendment: A Requiem for Wolf*, 1961 Sup. Ct. Rev. 20–21.

The police called for reinforcements. Several hours later, when at least four more officers had arrived on the scene, the police again sought entrance. When Miss Mapp did not come to the door immediately, the police gained admittance by breaking open one of the back doors. A short time later, Miss Mapp's attorney arrived, but the police did not allow him to enter the house or to see his client.

In the meantime, inside the house, Miss Mapp demanded to see a search warrant. One officer held up a piece of paper which was said to be a warrant. Miss Mapp grabbed the paper and put it in her blouse. A struggle broke out, in the course of which the police recovered the paper. In light of what the police called Ms. Mapp's "belligerent" behavior in seizing and trying to hold on to the "search warrant," the police handcuffed her.

(At the trial, no search warrant was produced by the prosecution. Nor was this failure ever explained. According to the Ohio Supreme Court, "considerable doubt" existed as to whether "there ever was any warrant for the search of defendant's home.")

After being handcuffed, Miss Mapp was forcibly taken upstairs to her bedroom where the dressers, the closet and some suitcases were searched. The search soon spread to the rest of the second floor (including the living room and Mapp's daughter's bedroom), and then to the basement (where a trunk found there was searched). The widespread search turned up a few "obscene" pamphlets (a far cry from the kind of porn material one hears about today) for which Miss Mapp was ultimately convicted and sentenced to prison. (She claimed she was simply storing the materials for a former roommate.)

Some twenty years after the decision in *Mapp*, Justice Potter Stewart, by this time a retired Supreme Court Justice, disclosed the following:

> At the conference following [the oral argument in *Mapp*], a majority of the Justices agreed that the Ohio statute violated the *first* and fourteenth amendments. Justice Tom Clark was assigned the job of writing the opinion of the Court. What transpired in the month following our conference on the case is really a matter of speculation on my part, but I have always suspected that the members of the soon-to-be *Mapp* majority had met in what I affectionately call a "rump caucus" to discuss a different basis for their decision. But regardless of how they reached their decision, five Justices of the Court concluded that the *fourth* and fourteenth amendments required that evidence seized in an illegal search be excluded from state trials as well as federal ones. *Wolf* was to be overruled.[16]

---

[16] Potter Stewart, *The Road to Mapp v. Ohio and Beyond: The Origins, Development and Future of the Exclusionary Rule in Search-and-Seizure Cases*, 83 Colum. L. Rev. 1365, 1368 (1983) (second emphasis added).

A "rump caucus" did take place, but it is unclear which Justices participated in it or how many there were.

According to one account, Justice Tom Clark played a key role in transforming *Mapp* from an obscenity case to a search and seizure case.[17] Although many considered Clark a police-prosecution oriented Justice,[18] his experience as a young lawyer with blatant violations of the Fourth Amendment had made him a keen student of the law of search and seizure.[19] As Clark observed, a decade after he had retired from the Court:

> I myself think that the fourth amendment is the most valuable of all the amendments because it does not matter what you have—if you have all the money in the world—unless you have the safety of your home and the privacy of your mind and heart, you have nothing. *Nothing*. Someone can take it away, regardless of what you have.[20]

Moreover, Justice Clark had been greatly troubled by the "empty gesture" approach to the protection against unreasonable search and seizure the Court had taken in the *Wolf* case.[21] Although Clark had concurred in the result in *Irvine*, a case which upheld the admissibility of evidence produced by admittedly flagrant state police violations of the Fourth Amendment,[22] he had noted at the outset of his concurring opinion that "[h]ad [he] been here when *Wolf* was decided," he would

---

According to BERNARD SCHWARTZ, SUPER CHIEF 392 (1983) (hereinafter Schwartz), "[t]he conference discussion and vote was summed up by Harlan in a letter to Clark." Justice Harlan wrote, *id.* at 392–93:

> I would have supposed that the Court would have little difficulty in agreeing (as indeed I thought the whole Court had) that a state prohibition against mere knowing possession of obscene material, without any requirement of a showing that such possession was with a purpose to disseminate the offensive matter, contravenes the Fourteenth Amendment, in that such a statute impermissibly deters freedom of belief and expression, if indeed it is not tantamount to an effort at "thought control."

[17] *See* Schwartz, *supra* note 16, at 393.

[18] This was largely a result of Clark's sharp dissents in Jencks v. United States, 353 U.S. 657 (1957) and Miranda v. Arizona, 384 U.S. 436 (1996). *See generally* Note, *Justice Tom C. Clark's Unconditional Approach to Individual Rights in the Courtroom*, 64 Tex. L. Rev. 421 (1985).

[19] *See* Paul R. Baier, *Justice Clark, the Voice of the Past, and the Exclusionary Rule*, 64 Tex. L. Rev. 415, 417, 419 (1985).

[20] Tom C. Clark, *Some Notes on the Continuing Life of the Fourth Amendment*, 5 Am. J. Crim. L. 275, 276 (1977) (based on an April, 1977 lecture delivered at the University of Texas Law School).

[21] *See* Baier, *supra* note 19, at 419.

[22] *See* the discussion of Irvine v. California, 347 U.S. 128 (1954), in the text at notes 126–48.

have imposed the exclusionary rule on the states.[23] And he had ended his *Irvine* concurrence with the thought that "[p]erhaps strict adherence to the tenor of [*Wolf*] may produce needed converts for its extinction."[24]

According to one account, no sooner had Clark left the conference room, where he had agreed to write the opinion of the Court overturning Mapp's conviction on First Amendment grounds, than he turned to Justices Black and Brennan, who were standing in the elevator with him, and asked: "[W]ouldn't this be a good case to apply the exclusionary rule and do what *Wolf* didn't do?"[25] According to this account, "[i]n his discussion with Brennan and Clark, [Justice Black] showed willingness to agree to a decision overruling Wolf.... though he indicated that he still had difficulty in doing it on Fourth Amendment grounds alone."[26]

However, one of Chief Justice Warren's biographers tells a different story. According to him, Chief Justice Warren and Justice Brennan agreed with Justice Douglas, the only *Wolf* dissenter still on the Court, that *Wolf* should be overruled, and they did so quite early. But because nobody else supported this position at the time, the vote in conference was to overturn Mapp's conviction on First Amendment grounds.[27]

When Clark changed his mind shortly after the conference, the foursome still needed a fifth vote to topple *Wolf*. The best bet was Hugo Black. According to this account, Chief Justice Warren and Justices Douglas and Brennan (but not Clark) then visited Justice Black in his chambers and persuaded him to join them.[28]

The author of a recent biography of Hugo Black is the only one I could find who specifically stated that *both* Clark's meeting in the elevator with Black and Brennan *and* the Warren–Douglas–Brennan meeting with Black in the latter's chambers took place.[29] In any event, it seems to be undisputed that Justice Douglas was the first to throw out the idea that *Wolf* should be overruled[30] and that Black was the last to join the anti-*Wolf* group.

---

[23] 347 U.S. at 138.

[24] *Id.* at 139.

[25] *See* Schwartz, *supra* note 16, at 393.

[26] *Id.* Concurring in the judgment in *Wolf*, Justice Black had "agree[d] with what appears to be a plain implication of the Court's opinion that the federal exclusionary rule is not a command of the Fourth Amendment but is a judicially created rule of evidence which Congress might negate." 338 U.S. at 39–40.

[27] *See* Ed Cray, Chief Justice: A Biography of Earl Warren 374 (1997).

[28] *See id.* at 375.

[29] *See* Roger K. Newman, Hugo Black: A Biography 555–56 (1994).

[30] *See id.* at 555; Powe, *supra* note 11, at 196; Schwartz, *supra* note 16, at 393.

Before learning that Justice Clark had changed his mind in favor of deciding the *Mapp* case on search and seizure grounds, Justice Douglas had prepared a draft opinion "apply[ing] the Fourth Amendment with full force to the states, making the exclusionary rule part and parcel of the constitutional guarantee."[31] (Douglas's draft opinion was never circulated because of Clark's change of mind just after the conference.)[32]

Getting and holding Justice Black's vote was no small feat. For, as noted earlier,[33] concurring in *Wolf*, Black had taken the position that the exclusionary rule was not a command of the Fourth Amendment itself, but merely a judicially created rule of evidence. Twelve years later, he was "still not persuaded that the Fourth Amendment, standing alone, would be enough to [exclude evidence] seized from [a defendant] in violation of its commands,"[34] but by this time he had found what he considered the true basis for the exclusionary rule:

> Reflection on the problem . . . has led me to conclude that when the Fourth Amendment's ban against unreasonable searches and seizures is considered together with the Fifth Amendment's ban against compelled self-incrimination, a constitutional basis emerges which not only justifies but actually requires the exclusionary rule.[35]

One passage in Justice Clark's *Mapp* opinion seems to support Justice Black's view of the search and seizure exclusionary rule. It talks about the " 'intimate relation' " between the Fourth and Fifth Amendments and how the two Amendments "express 'supplementing phases of the same constitutional purpose—to maintain inviolate large areas of personal privacy.' "[36] Did Justice Clark really believe this or, anxious to keep Black on board, did Clark write this in order to humor Black? Many years later, Justice Clark recalled:

> Finally, in 1961 we got the five [votes] to overrule *Wolf.* . . . I had to convince Justice Black. He did not want to swallow the fourth amendment; he wanted to bring in the fifth. And so we sat down and worked in the fourth and had the fourth and fifth mentioned together. If you still do not understand it, I do not either! But we overruled *Wolf* . . .[37]

---

[31] *See* Schwartz, *supra* note 16, at 393.

[32] *Id.*

[33] *See* note 26 *supra*.

[34] 367 U.S. at 661 (Black, J. concurring in *Mapp*).

[35] *Id.* at 662.

[36] *See* 367 U.S. at 656–57.

[37] *See* Clark, *supra* note 20, at 279.

Professor Lucas Powe, a commentator who rarely uses strong words, calls Justice Black's rationale for the search and seizure exclusionary rule "preposterous."[38] Black's theory does leave much to be desired, but Powe goes too far.

The famous *Boyd* case[39] viewed the compulsory production of incriminating papers as the equivalent of an unreasonable search and seizure and the use of evidence obtained in violation of the Fourth Amendment as a form of compulsory self-incrimination.[40] Moreover, in his celebrated dissent in the *Olmstead* case,[41] Justice Louis Brandeis maintained that the use in a criminal prosecution of facts ascertained by a violation of the Fourth Amendment "must be deemed a violation of the Fifth."[42]

Nevertheless, Justice Black's theory of the exclusionary rule is badly flawed and, so far as I know, nobody subscribes to it today.

First of all, at the time of *Mapp* the prevailing view had long been that the physical evidence typically excluded in search and seizure cases, *e.g.*, drugs and weapons, was beyond the scope of the protection provided by the Self–Incrimination Clause.[43] The Clause was said only to furnish protection against "testimonial compulsion."[44]

Second, although Justice Black may have believed that the privilege against self-incrimination was "incorporated" by the Fourteenth Amend-

---

[38] *See* Powe, *supra* note 11, at 196–97.

[39] Boyd v. United States, 116 U.S. 616 (1886).

[40] *See id.* at 630–35. *See also* Agnello v. United States, 269 U.S. 20, 33–34 (1925).

[41] Olmstead v. United States, 277 U.S. 438 (1928).

[42] *See id.* at 478–79.

[43] *See* FRED E. INBAU, SELF-INCRIMINATION: WHAT CAN AN ACCUSED PERSON BE COMPELLED TO DO, 3–8, 87 (1950); CHARLES T. MCCORMICK, EVIDENCE 263–66 (1st ed. 1954); EDMOND MORGAN, BASIC PROBLEMS OF EVIDENCE 140–42 (1957); 8 JOHN HENRY WIGMORE, EVIDENCE §§ 2263, 2265 (3d ed. 1940). Moreover, as pointed out in Allen, *supra* note 15, at 25–26, "a Fifth Amendment theory of the exclusionary rule can probably not be justified either by historical or analytical considerations." *See also* Yale Kamisar, *Wolf and Lustig Ten Years Later: Illegal State Evidence in State and Federal Courts*, 43 Minn.L.Rev. 1083, 1088–90 (1959); Jack B. Weinstein, *Local Responsibility for Improvement of Search and Seizure Practices*, 34 Rocky Mt. L. Rev. 150, 160–61 (1962).

[44] Since the discussion in *Mapp*, the Court has made this even more clear. In Schmerber v. California, 383 U.S. 757 (1966), upholding the taking of a blood sample from an intoxicated driver, over his objection, the Court observed that the privilege "protects an accused only from being compelled to testify against himself, or otherwise provide the State with evidence of a testimonial or communicative nature and that the withdrawal of blood and use of the analysis in question does not involve compulsion to these ends." *Id.* at 761. United States v. Wade, 388 U.S. 2218 (1967), held that requiring a defendant to appear in a lineup and to utter the words "put the money in the bag" does not violate the privilege. *See generally* 2 WAYNE R. LAFAVE, JEROLD H. ISRAEL & NANCY J. KING, CRIMINAL PROCEDURE § 7.2 (2d ed. 1999).

ment and binding on the states, a majority of the Court did not.[45] It was not until 1964 that the Court held that the Fifth Amendment's privilege against self-incrimination was to be "enforced against the States under the Fourteenth Amendment according to the same standards that protect those personal rights against federal encroachment."[46]

Justice Clark probably would not have needed Justice Black's vote nor have had to put up with Black's Fifth Amendment theory of the exclusionary rule if—instead of "simply 'reach[ing] out' to overrule *Wolf*"[47]—the Court had ordered reargument of the case and directed the lawyers to reexamine *Wolf*. If this step had been taken, Justice Stewart, who had been "shocked" by the Court's transformation of *Mapp* into a search and seizure case,[48] most likely would have voted to overrule *Wolf* the second time around. As he stated in a public lecture some years after he had retired from the Court:

> I believed then [at the time of *Mapp*], and I believe now, that the exclusionary rule *is* constitutionally required, not as a "right" explicitly incorporated in the fourth amendment's prohibitions, but as a remedy necessary to ensure that those prohibitions are observed in fact. Thus, although I did not join in the Court's opinion in the *Mapp* case—because it decided an issue that was not before the Court—I agree with its conclusion that the exclusionary rule *is* necessary to keep the right of privacy secured by the fourth amendment from "remain[ing] an empty promise."[49]

Justice Clark's response to the dissenters' charge that the overruling of *Wolf* was not properly before the Court is not convincing: "Although appellant . . . did not insist that *Wolf* be overruled [that is a gross understatement], the *amicus curiae* . . . did urge the Court to overrule *Wolf* [that is an overstatement of considerable proportions]."[50]

---

[45] *See* Twining v. New Jersey, 211 U.S. 78 (1908); Adamson v. California, 332 U.S. 46 (1947). Both cases were overruled in Malloy v. Hogan, discussed in the next sentence.

[46] Malloy v. Hogan, 378 U.S. 1, 10 (1964).

[47] 367 U.S. at 674 (Harlan, J., dissenting).

[48] *See* Stewart, *supra* note 16, at 1368:

I was shocked when Justice Clark's proposed Court opinion reached my desk. I immediately wrote him a note expressing my surprise and questioning the wisdom of overruling an important doctrine in a case in which the issue was not briefed, argued or discussed by the state courts, by the parties' counsel or at our conference following the oral argument. After my shock subsided, I wrote a brief memorandum concurring in the judgment on first and fourteenth amendment grounds, and agreeing with Justice Harlan's dissent that the issue which the majority decided was not properly before the Court.

[49] *Id.* at 1389.

[50] 367 U.S. at 646 note 3.

Justice Douglas tried to brush off the dissenters' protests with what one commentator5[51] called "light-hearted assurances" that the Justices already knew all the arguments for and against the exclusionary rule.5[52] I share the view that the better course would have been to order the reargument of the case directed to the issue of the *Wolf* rule.[53] Nevertheless, there is *something* to be said for Douglas's view. After all, as Judge (later Justice) Benjamin Cardozo observed *more than three decades before* the *Mapp* case was decided (in a portion of his famous *Defore* opinion that very few law professors have ever taken seriously): "To what [has been] written [about the exclusionary rule] little of value can be added."[54]

Let us now take a look at some of what had been written about the exclusionary rule prior to *Mapp*.

Historical Perspective: The Rules Governing the Admissibility of Illegally Seized Evidence Prior to Mapp

1.   The *Weeks* Case and the Federal Exclusionary Rule

The 1914 *Weeks* case[55] established the federal exclusionary rule. Although this must surprise many readers of Burger Court and Rehnquist Court search and seizure opinions, nowhere in *Weeks* is the exclusionary rule called a "remedy" nor is there any discussion, or even mention, of the effectiveness of the exclusionary rule versus the effectiveness of alternatives such as tort remedies or internal self-discipline.[56]

---

[51] Allen, *supra* note 15, at 22–23.

[52] *See* 367 U.S. at 671 (Douglas, J., concurring):

[S]ubject to the sound discretion of a court, all arguments must at last come to a halt. This is especially so as to an issue about which this Court said last year that "The arguments of its antagonists and of its proponents have been so many times marshaled as to require no lengthy elaboration here." *Elkins v. United States*, [364 U.S. 206, 216 (1960)].

[53] Allen, *supra* note 15, at 22.

[54] People v. Defore, 242 N.Y. 13, 21, 150 N.E. 585, 587 (1926). Of course, in this very opinion, Judge Cardozo proceeded to write some of the most famous lines ever written on the subject. If the case against the exclusionary rule had to be reduced to one or two sound bites, it would be hard to do better than to quote from Cardozo's opinion, *id.* at 587, 588:

[According to the search and seizure exclusionary rule], [t]he criminal is to go free because the constable has blundered.

* * *

[If this court adopted the exclusionary rule], the pettiest peace officer would have it in his power, through overzeal or indiscretion, to confer immunity upon an offender for crimes the most flagitious.

[55] Weeks v. United States, 232 U.S. 383 (1914).

[56] Indeed the *Weeks* rule or federal exclusionary rule was never called an "exclusionary rule" until several decades after *Weeks* was decided. *See* Yale Kamisar, *Does (Did) (Should)*

As Francis Allen has pointed out, the *Weeks* opinion "contains no language that expressly justifies the [exclusionary] rule by reference to a supposed deterrent effect on police officials."[57]

Nor is the notion of deterrence expressed for the next thirty-five years—in the long interim between *Weeks* and *Wolf*. No doubt the Court that decided *Weeks* and the Court that adhered to its doctrine in subsequent decades expected, or at least hoped, that law enforcement officials would not be so ignorant of, or indifferent to, the search and seizure rules worked out in the courts as to be unaffected by them, but there is no suggestion in *Weeks* or the search and seizure cases decided during the next thiry-five years that the exclusionary rule's *survival* depended on proof that it was significantly affecting police behavior.

In excluding private papers seized from an illegal search of defendant's home, a unanimous *Weeks* Court, per Justice Day, took the position that if a federal official "acted without sanction of law" in conducting a search, a court should not—by admitting the evidence seized by the official—"affirm" or "sanction" the search or seizure *after* the event:

> The United States Marshall . . . acted without sanction of law . . . and under color of his office undertook to make a search of private papers in direct violation of the constitutional prohibition against such action. . . . To sanction such proceedings would be to affirm by judicial decision a manifest neglect if not an open defiance of the prohibitions of the Constitution, intended for the protection of the people against such unauthorized action.[58]

Moreover, as Justice Brennan observed seventy years later, the *Weeks* Court "expressly recognized that the commands of the Fourth Amendment were addressed to both the courts and the Executive Branch".[59]

> The effect of the Fourth Amendment is to put *the courts* of the United States and Federal officials, in the exercise of their power

---

the Exclusionary Rule Rest on a "Principled Basis" Rather than an Empirical Proposition?, 16 Creighton L.Rev. 561, 590 & note 162 (1983).

[57] Allen, *supra* note 3, at 536 note 90. Even Chief Justice Burger, one of the exclusionary rule's most severe critics, recognized, before ascending to the Supreme Court, that *Weeks* "rest[s] on the Court's unwillingness to give even tacit approval to official defiance of constitutional provisions by admitting evidence secured in violation of the Constitution. The idea of deterrence may be lurking between the lines of the opinion but is not expressed." Warren E. Burger, *Who Will Watch the Watchman?*, 14 Am. U. L. Rev. 1, 5 (1964).

[58] 232 U.S. at 393–94.

[59] Justice Brennan, joined by Marshall, J., dissenting in United States v. Leon, 468 U.S. 897, 936 (1984).

and authority, under limitations and restraints as to the exercise of such power and authority.... [The Fourth Amendment's] protection reaches all alike, whether accused of crime or not, and *the duty of giving to it force and effect is obligatory upon all entrusted under our federal system with the enforcement of the laws.* The tendency of those who execute the criminal laws of the country ... to obtain conviction by means of unlawful seizures ... *should find no sanction in the judgment of the courts which are charged at all times with the support of the Constitution* and to which [all] people have a right to appeal for the maintenance of such fundamental rights.[60]

In the thirty-five years following *Weeks*, the Court had very little to say about the rationale for the exclusionary rule.[61] However, the stirring Holmes–Brandeis dissents in the famous wiretapping case, *Olmstead v. United States*,[62] do shed light on the original basis and purpose of the exclusionary rule. In the course of urging the Court to extend the *Weeks* doctrine to situations where the federal government had not violated the Constitution, or even federal law, but only a state wiretapping statute, Justices Holmes and Brandeis embellished the *Weeks* Court's reasoning:

[N]o distinction can be taken between the Government as prosecutor and the Government as judge. If the existing code does not permit district attorneys to have a hand in such dirty business [obtaining evidence by an unlawful act], it does not permit the judge to allow such inequities to succeed.[63]

The Court's aid is denied only when he who seeks it has violated the law in connection with the very transaction as to which he seeks legal redress. Then aid is denied despite the defendant's wrong. It is denied in order to maintain respect for the law; in order to promote confidence in the administration of justice; in order to preserve the judicial process from contamination.[64]

To declare that in the administration of the criminal law the end justifies the means—to declare that the Government may commit crimes in order to secure the conviction of a private criminal—would bring terrible retribution. Against that pernicious doctrine this Court should resolutely set its face.[65]

The Holmes–Brandeis dissents underscore that the exclusionary rule, at least in the pre-*Wolf* era, was based on principle—one might also say

---

[60] *Weeks*, 232 U.S. at 391–92 (emphasis added).

[61] *See* Kamisar, *supra* note 56, at 601–06.

[62] *See* Olmstead v. United States, 277 U.S. 438, 469, 471 (1928).

[63] *Id*. at 470. (Holmes, J., dissenting.)

[64] *Id*. at 484. (Brandeis, J., dissenting.)

[65] *Id*. at 485. (Brandeis, J., dissenting.)

that it had an important symbolic quality—not on estimates of how significantly the exclusion of evidence affects police conduct.

The famous dissents of Holmes and Brandeis, and the *Weeks* case itself, were based on what has been called the " 'one-government' conception" or the "unitary model of a government and a prosecution."[66] According to this view, by excluding illegally seized evidence "the court stops the entire government, of which it is a part, from consummating a wrongful course of conduct begun but by not means ended when the police invade the defendant's privacy."[67] But the *Wolf* Court took a very different view of the exclusionary rule.

2. *Wolf v. Colorado*

In *Wolf*, a 5–4 majority, per Frankfurter, J., resolved "the tension produced by the recognition of the objective of fair procedure, on the one hand, and the demands of federalism, on the other"[68] in favor of federalism. The Court had no hesitation in saying that "[t]he security of one's privacy against arbitrary invasion by the police—which is at the core of the Fourth Amendment—is basic to a free society" and thus "enforceable against the states through the Due Process Clause."[69] But "the ways of enforcing such a basic right" was another matter.[70]

According to the *Wolf* Court, excluding the illegally seized evidence was only one among a range of options. A state court could reject the

---

[66] Thomas Schrock & Robert Welsh, *Up From Calandra: The Exclusionary Rule as a Constitutional Requirement*, 59 Minn. L. Rev. 251, 255 (1974). But *see* Larry Yackle, *The Burger Court and the Fourth Amendment*, 26 Kan. L. Rev. 335, 417 (1978) maintaining that although the approach to the exclusionary rule in the Holmes–Brandeis *Olmstead* dissents is related to the approach taken in *Weeks*, it is also somewhat different.

[67] *See id.* Consider, too, Justice Brennan, joined by Marshall, J., dissenting in United States v. Leon, 468 U.S. 933, 938 (1984):

[B]y admitting unlawfully seized evidence, the judiciary becomes a part of what is in fact a single government action prohibited by the terms of the [Fourth] Amendment.

* * *

[The *Weeks* Court] recognized that, if the Amendment is to have any meaning, police and the courts cannot be regarded as constitutional strangers to each other; because the evidence-gathering role of the police is directly linked to the evidence-admitting function of the courts, an individual's Fourth Amendment rights may be undermined as completely by one as by the other.

In *Leon*, the majority adopted a so-called good faith (actually a "reasonable mistake") exception to the search and seizure exclusionary rule.

[68] Francis A. Allen, *The Supreme Court, Federalism, and State Systems of Criminal Justice*, 8 DePaul L. Rev. 213, 240 (1959).

[69] 338 U.S. at 27–28.

[70] *See id.* at 28:

exclusionary rule so long as it relied on some other remedy (such as a private tort action against the offending officer(s) or the internal discipline of the police) "which, if consistently enforced, would be equally effective."[71] (The Court gave no indication whether or how it would go about determining if an alternative to the exclusionary rule *was being* "consistently enforced.")

As one critic expressed it, the author of the *Wolf* opinion performed "the unusual, if not unprecedented, feat of simultaneously creating a constitutional right and denying the most effective remedy for violation of that right."[72] As another critic put it, "the *Wolf* case leaves the federal 'right' of privacy ... more largely in the realm of wish than reality."[73]

Moreover, by "driving a wedge between [the protection against unreasonable search and seizure] and the exclusionary rules,"[74] "inject[ing] the instrumental rationale of deterrence of police misconduct into [the Court's] discussion of the exclusionary rule,"[75] and "using the empirically-based, consequentialist rationale of deterrence as support for [the Court's] refusal to apply the exclusionary rule to the states,"[76] the *Wolf* opinion not only made the result reached in that case seem more palatable, but it planted the seeds of destruction for the exclusionary rule—in federal as well as state cases.[77]

* * *

But the ways of enforcing such a basic right raise questions of a different order....
[W]hat remedies against [such arbitrary conduct] should be afforded, the means by which the right should be made effective, are all questions that are not to be so dogmatically answered as to preclude the varying solutions which spring from an allowable range of judgment on issues not susceptible of quantitative solution.

[71] *Id.* at 31. "We cannot ... regard it as a departure from basic standards," maintained Frankfurter, "to remand [the victims of illegal searches], together with those who emerge scatheless from a search, [to remedies other than the exclusionary rule]." *Id.*

[72] T. S. L. Perlman, *Due Process and the Admissibility of Evidence*, 64 Harv.L.Rev. 1304 (1951).

[73] Francis A. Allen, *The Wolf Case: Search and Seizure, Federalism, and the Civil Liberties*, 45 Ill.L.Rev. 1, 30 (1950). *See also* Allen, *supra* note 15, at 5: "The basic difficulty was that in [*Wolf*] the Court's reach had exceeded its grasp ... The federal 'right of privacy' was relegated to the tender mercies of the state for its enforcement."

[74] William J. Mertens & Silas J. Wasserstrom, *Foreword: The Good Faith Exception to the Exclusionary Rule: Deregulating the Police and Derailing the Law*, 70 Geo. L.J. 365, 380 (1981).

[75] *Id.* at 379.

[76] *Id.*

[77] Consider Justice Brennan, joined by Marshall, J., dissenting in *Leon, supra* note 67, at 931, 938–40:

Justice Frankfurter appears to have been heavily influenced by Judge (later Justice) Cardozo's famous 1926 opinion in *People v. Defore*, the New York case that had rejected the exclusionary rule when the states still had an option.[78] Cardozo had noted that there was no shortage of alternatives to the exclusionary rule: "The officer might have been resisted, or sued for damages, or even prosecuted for oppression."[79] Although Justice Frankfurter's list of other remedies was not as extensive as Cardozo's (Frankfurter did not include resisting the officer!), the *Wolf* opinion, too, "smells of the lamp."

Thus, the temptation to attack, and to defeat, Justice Frankfurter *on his own battleground* must have been strong. Justice Murphy, who wrote the principal dissent in *Wolf*, yielded to that temptation. He examined the other available remedies[80] and reached what he called the

---

At bottom, the Court's decision turns on the proposition that the exclusionary rule is merely a " 'judicially created remedy designed to safeguard Fourth Amendment rights generally through its deterrent effect, rather than a personal constitutional right.' " The germ of that idea is found in *Wolf v. Colorado*, and although I had thought that such a narrow conception of that rule had been forever put to rest by our decision in *Mapp v. Ohio*, it has been revived by the present Court and reaches full flower with today's decision.

* * *

[T]he question whether the exclusion of evidence would deter future police misconduct was never considered a relevant concern in the early cases from *Weeks* to *Olmstead....* A new phase in the history of the rule, however, opened with the Court's discussion in *Wolf....* Notwithstanding the force of the *Weeks* doctrine that the Fourth Amendment required exclusion, a state court was free to admit illegally seized evidence, according to the Court in *Wolf*, so long as the State had devised some other "effective" means of vindicating a defendant's Fourth Amendment rights.

Twelve years later, in *Mapp* ... however, the Court restored the original understanding of the *Weeks* rule, by overturning the holding in *Wolf* and repudiating its rationale.... In the [*Mapp*] Court's view, the exclusionary rule was not one among a range of options to be selected at the discretion of judges; it was "an essential part of both the Fourth and Fourteenth Amendments"....

Despite [the statements in *Mapp*], however, the Court since *Calandra* [v. United States, 414 U.S. 338 (1974), which took into account only the deterrence rationale in holding that a grand jury witness may not decline to answer questions on the ground they were based on illegally seized evidence] has gradually pressed the deterrence rationale for the [exclusionary] rule back to center stage.

[78] 150 N.E. 585 (N.Y. 1926).

[79] *Id.* at 587.

[80] 338 U.S. at 41. (Murphy, J., joined by Rutledge, J., dissenting.) It is important to compare the exclusionary rule with "currently available" alternatives. There is no shortage of *theoretically possible* ways, aside from the exclusion of evidence, to make the Fourth Amendment viable. As I have said elsewhere, Yale Kamisar, *Remembering the "Old World" of Criminal Procedure: A Reply to Professor Grano*, 23 U. Mich. J.L. Ref. 537, 564 (1990),

"inescapable" conclusion that "but one remedy exists to deter violations of the search and seizure clause"—the exclusionary rule.[81]

Justice Murphy's belittling of the available alternatives to the exclusionary rule might have been a mistake in strategy. The better course might have been to avoid attacking Frankfurter on the grounds he chose, but to underscore the "one-government" approach that pervades both *Weeks* and the *Olmstead* dissents, an approach that gives no weight to the availability of possible alternatives to the exclusionary rule. But surely Justice Murphy's disparagement of the available alternatives to the exclusionary rule was well-founded.[82]

Justice Stewart may have summed up the situation as well as anyone when, shortly after stepping down from the court, he observed:

> Taken together, the currently available alternatives to the exclusionary rule satisfactorily achieve some, but not all, of the necessary functions of a remedial measure. They punish and perhaps deter *the grossest* of violations, as well as government policies that legitimate those violations. They compensate some of the victims of *the most*

"the problem is not a lack of *imagination or intellectual capacity*. Rather, it is a lack of *political will*."

As one commentator has recently reminded us, Tracey Maclin, *When the Cure for the Fourth Amendment is Worse than the Disease*, 68 S. Cal. L. Rev. 1, 60 note 289 (1994), ever since the 1930s, commentators have been underscoring the inadequacy of existing tort remedies against offending police officers and proposing what are now called "fortified" tort remedies. But nothing has come of any of these proposals. Do we have any reason to expect similar proposals made in our day to fare any better?

[81] 338 U.S. at 44.

[82] By the time of *Wolf* a number of commentators had already called attention to the ineffectiveness of alternatives to the exclusionary rule. *See, e.g.,* LESTER ORFIELD, CRIMINAL PROCEDURE FROM ARREST TO APPEAL 28–31 (1947); Jerome Hall, *The Law of Arrest in Relation to Contemporary Social Problems*, 3 U. Chi. L. Rev. 345, 346 (1936); William T. Plumb, Jr., *Illegal Enforcement of the Law*, 24 Cornell L.Q. 337, 386–88 (1939); Comment, *Judicial Control of Illegal Search and Seizure*, 58 Yale L.J. 144, 146–56 (1948). Since then, the number of commentators deprecating the available alternatives to the exclusionary rule has grown to the point where it is fair to say that there is an overwhelming consensus that all the available alternatives are woefully inadequate. The classic article is Caleb Foote, *Tort Remedies for Police Violations of Individual Rights*, 39 Minn. L. Rev. 493 (1955). *See also, e.g.,* Anthony G. Amsterdam, *Perspectives on the Fourth Amendment*, 58 Minn. L. Rev. 349, 378–79, 429–30 (1974); Donald Dripps, *Akhil Amar on Criminal Procedure and Constitutional Law: "Here I go Down that Wrong Road Again,"* 74 N.C.L. Rev. 1559, 1606 (1996); Daniel J. Meltzer, *Deterring Constitutional Violations by Law Enforcement Officials: Plaintiffs and Defendants as Private Attorneys General*, 88 Colum.L.Rev. 247, 284–86 (1988); Pierre J. Schlag, *Assaults on the Exclusionary Rule: Good Faith Limitations and Damage Remedies*, 73 J. Crim. L. & Criminology 875, 907–13 (1982); and William A. Schroeder, *Deterring Fourth Amendment Violations: Alternatives to the Exclusionary Rule*, 69 Geo. L.J. 1361, 1386–1410 (1981). *But see* Guido Calabresi, *The Exclusionary Rule,* 26 Harv. J.L. & Pub. Pol'y 111, 112 (2002); Christopher Slobogin, *Why Liberals Should Chuck the Exclusionary Rule,* 1999 U. Ill. L. Rev. 364.

egregious violations. But they do little, if anything, to reduce the vast majority of fourth amendment violations—the frequent infringements motivated by commendable zeal, not condemnable malice. For these violations, a remedy is required that inspires the police officer to channel his enthusiasm to apprehend a criminal toward the need to comply with the dictates of the fourth amendment. There is only one such remedy—the exclusion of illegally obtained evidence.[83]

* * *

Justice Frankfurter often remarked that "[o]n the question you ask depends the answer you get."[84] He illustrated his point in the *Wolf* case by formulating one of the longest and most convoluted "questions presented for consideration" ever to appear in a Supreme Court opinion:

> The precise question for consideration is this: Does a conviction by a State court for a State offense deny the "due process of law" required by the Fourteenth Amendment, solely because evidence that was admitted at the trial was obtained under circumstances which would have rendered it inadmissible in a prosecution for violation of a federal law in a court of the United States because there deemed to be an infraction of the Fourth Amendment as applied in *Weeks* . . .?[85]

The question presented in *Wolf* could easily have been phrased differently. For example:

> The question for consideration is whether a state conviction resting on evidence secured in violation of a right so important as to be deemed "basic to a free society" may be allowed to stand without making the courts themselves accomplices in disobedience of the constitutional command.[86] Or—

> The question presented is whether we can admit evidence produced by police conduct which violates the security of one's privacy against arbitrary invasion by government officials—a right basic to a free society—without affording police lawlessness the cloak of law.[87] Or—

> The question for consideration is whether a failure to put a curb on the use of evidence obtained by illegal state searches and seizures in state prosecutions would only invite the very police methods deemed

---

[83] Stewart, *supra* note 16, at 1388–89 (emphasis added).

[84] HENRY FRIENDLY, *Mr. Justice Frankfurter*, in BENCHMARKS 318, 319 (1967).

[85] 338 U.S. at 25–26.

[86] *Cf.* McNabb v. United States, 318 U.S. 332, 345 (1943) (Frankfurter, J.).

[87] *Cf.* Rochin v. California, 342 U.S. 165, 173 (1952) (Frankfurter, J.).

inconsistent with the concept of human rights enshrined in the history and legal documents of our people.[88] Or—

In three other cases decided today,[89] we have reversed state convictions based on "involuntary" confessions without disputing the assertion that "[c]hecked with external evidence, [the] confessions in each case are inherently believable [and] not shaken by anything that occurred at the trial."[90] The question presented is whether the problem of coerced confessions and the problem of unreasonable searches or seizures can be treated separately for purposes of Fourteenth Amendment due process without establishing an indefensible double standard in defining the requirements of due process as they relate to state criminal proceedings.[91]

It might be objected that these formulations of the question are so appealing from the defendant's viewpoint that they suggest an answer in his favor. But if the alternative formulations of the question lead the reader to answer them as the writer wishes, the same may be said for the question Justice Frankfurter actually posed in *Wolf*. Moreover, the alternative formulations of the question presented I have offered are based almost entirely on how the author of the *Wolf* opinion elsewhere viewed the question of admitting unconstitutionally or illegally obtained evidence in other Supreme Court cases.[92]

In suggesting alternative ways of stating the question presented in the *Wolf* case I have assumed that the case stands for the proposition

---

[88] *Cf* Nardone v. United States, 308 U.S. 338 (1939) (Frankfurter, J.).

[89] *See* Harris v. South Carolina, 338 U.S. 68 (1949); Turner v. Pennsylvania, 338 U.S. 62 (1949); Watts v. Indiana, 338 U.S. 49 (1949). All three opinions of the Court were written by Justice Frankfurter.

[90] Justice Jackson, concurring in the result in *Watts* and dissenting in the companion cases, 338 U.S. at 58. *See also* Justice Frankfurter, observing in *Rochin, supra* note 12, at 173: "[Coerced confessions] are inadmissible under the Due Process Clause even though statements contained in them may be independently established as true. Coerced confessions offend the community's sense of fair play and decency."

[91] *Cf.* Allen, *supra* note 73, at 29:

"In both situations [coercive police interrogation and illegal searches] the perils arise primarily out of the procedures employed to acquire the evidence rather than from dangers of the incompetency of the evidence so acquired. Furthermore, if the demands of federalism are not such as to deny to the Court power to supervise the interrogating practices of state police officers in the interest of procedures most likely to preserve the integrity of basic individual immunities, such supervision of police practices in the interest of preserving basic rights of privacy seems likewise justifiable. Yet the consequence of the decision [in *Wolf*] ... is rigidly to separate the two problems [searches and confessions] and to create a dubious double standard in the definition of the requirements of due process as they relate to state criminal proceedings."

[92] *See* notes 86–90 *supra*.

that what would be a violation of the Fourth Amendment if carried out by a federal official constitutes a violation of the Fourteenth Amendment if committed by a state officer. This is not entirely clear. *Wolf* could conceivably have stood, or have come to stand, for the proposition that only certain "gross" or "aggravated" unreasonable searches or seizures—only those violations of the Fourth Amendment that strike at its very "core"[93]—offend Fourteenth Amendment Due Process.

However, if this were the meaning of *Wolf*, then whether a given search by state officers was not only unlawful but sufficiently "outrageous" to offend Fourteenth Amendment Due Process would turn on its particular facts. But no facts whatever are given about the search that occurred in *Wolf*. Not by Justice Frankfurter, writing for the majority, nor by any of the concurring or dissenting Justices.

Even if one were to read every word written by the five members of the Court who filed opinions in the case, one would have no idea who Wolf was (a practicing physician) or what crime he was convicted of (conspiracy to commit abortion) or what evidence was seized (appointment books from his office). As Justice Jackson pointed out five years later in his *Irvine* plurality opinion, "the opinions in *Wolf* were written entirely in the abstract."[94]

So far as one can tell, the *Wolf* case involved not a "shocking" or "aggravated" illegal search, but a "routine" one. If "the basic right to protection against arbitrary intrusion by the police"[95] were only violated when state police committed certain kinds of violations of the Fourth Amendment, the *Wolf* Court would have had *no need and no reason to reach the difficult question* whether a violation of "the basic right . . . demands the exclusion of logically relevant evidence."[96] The first order of business would have been to decide whether the illegal search by the Colorado police constituted the *kind* of illegal search that violated "the basic right."

Although he did not address the question explicitly, Justice Frankfurter seemed to equate the *substantive* protection against unreasonable searches and seizures provided by the Fourteenth Amendment with the specific guarantee of the Fourth. He seemed to say that even though the Fourteenth Amendment does *not require the exclusion* of the resulting

---

[93] *Cf. Wolf*, 338 U.S. at 27 (Frankfurter, J.): "The security of one's privacy against arbitrary intrusion by the police—which is at the core of the Fourth Amendment—is basic to a free society."

[94] Irvine v. California, 347 U.S. 128, 133 (1954). Justice Jackson then proceeded to discuss the facts in *Wolf*. *See id.*

[95] *Wolf*, 338 U.S. at 28 (Frankfurter, J.).

[96] *Id.*

evidence, the Amendment is violated when state police conduct *any* unreasonable search and seizure.[97]

Moreover, while concurring and dissenting opinions do not necessarily constitute the most accurate interpretations of majority opinions, it is at least noteworthy that concurring Justice Black "agree[d] with the conclusion of the Court that the Fourth Amendment's prohibition of 'unreasonable searches and seizures' is enforceable against the states,"[98] and Justice Murphy, author of the principal dissent, "agree[d] with the Court that the Fourteenth Amendment prohibits activities which are prescribed by the search and seizure clause of the Fourth Amendment."[99]

In any event, a decade later, in *Elkins v. United States*,[100] any disagreement over whether, as a result of *Wolf*, the Fourteenth Amendment had "incorporated" the *substantive* provisions of the Fourth Amendment was resolved in favor of "incorporation." Ironically, *Elkins* interpreted the *Wolf* opinion in a way that evoked strong protests from its author, Justice Frankfurter.[101]

---

[97] *See* 338 U.S. at 28, 33. For the view that the best reading of *Wolf* is that it viewed the Fourteenth Amendment as "incorporating" the substantive provisions of the Fourth Amendment but not the exclusionary rule, *see* Donald A. Dripps, *At the Borders of the Fourth Amendment: Why a Real Due Process Test Should Replace the Outrageous Government Conduct Defense*, 1993 U. Ill. L. Rev. 261, 267 note 43; Kamisar, *supra* note 43, at 1101–08. *See also* Allen, *supra* note 15, at 9, pointing out that although there is no indication that the search of Dr. Wolf's office was aggravated or egregious "the Court had apparently treated the police behavior in *Wolf* as violating the defendant's Fourteenth Amendment rights."

[98] *Id*. at 39.

[99] *Id*. at 41.

[100] 364 U.S. 206 (1960).

[101] Dissenting in *Elkins*, 364 U.S. at 206–07, Justice Frankfurter, joined by Clark, Harlan and Whittaker, JJ., maintained that the *Wolf* opinion had stated that "only what was characterized as the 'core of the Fourth Amendment,' not the Amendment itself, is enforceable against the States." But in his opinion of the Court in *Wolf* Justice Frankfurter never said that "only ... the 'core of the Fourth Amendment,' not the Amendment itself" applies to the states. What he did say was: "The security of one's privacy against arbitrary intrusion by the police—which is at the core of the Fourth Amendment—is basic to a free society" and therefore "enforceable against the States through the Due Process Clause." 338 U.S. at 25–26. Moreover, as noted earlier, Justice Frankfurter never discussed whether the illegal search that took place in *Wolf* did violate the "core of the Fourth Amendment"; in fact, he did not discuss the search at all.

It may strike many as anomalous for a majority of the Court to interpret an earlier opinion differently than the author of that opinion. But *Elkins* was not the only time Justice Frankfurter wrote a dissent maintaining that the majority had misread one of his earlier opinions for the Court. The same thing had happened six years earlier in Irvine v. California, 347 U.S. 128 (1954). Then, too, Frankfurter had written an angry dissent insisting that the Court had misread one of his earlier opinions (*Rochin, supra* note 12).

Elkins overturned the "silver platter" doctrine, the rule that a federal prosecutor may use evidence illegally seized by a *state* officer in a federal case so long as the evidence "secured by state authorities is turned over to the federal authorities on a silver platter."[102]

Although Justice Stewart, writing for the majority in *Elkins*, noted that "we are not here directly concerned" with "the ultimate determination in *Wolf*"[103] (the holding that the Fourteenth Amendment does not require the state courts to exclude illegally seized evidence), "*Wolf*'s underlying constitutional doctrine"[104] was another matter:

> [N]othing could be of greater relevance to the present inquiry than the underlying constitutional doctrine which *Wolf* established. For there it was unequivocally determined by a unanimous Court [on this point] that the Federal Constitution, by virtue of the Fourteenth Amendment, prohibits unreasonable searches and seizures by state officers....
>
> The foundation upon which the admissibility of state-seized evidence in a federal trial originally rested—that unreasonable state searches did not violate the Federal Constitution—thus disappeared in 1949.[105]

Not surprisingly, *Mapp* relied heavily on what might be called *Wolf*'s initial or underlying holding—that Fourteenth Amendment Due Process had "incorporated" the substantive provisions of the Fourth Amendment. *Mapp* took "incorporation" of the Fourth Amendment one step further:

> Since the Fourth Amendment's right of privacy has been declared enforceable against the States through the Due Process Clause of the Fourteenth, it is enforceable against them by the same sanction of exclusion as is used against the Federal Government.... [I]n extending the substantive protections of due process to all constitutionally unreasonable searches—state or federal—it was logically and constitutionally necessary that the exclusion doctrine—an es-

---

Moreover, Frankfurter was not the only Justice to have this experience. In Kirby v. Illinois, 406 U.S. 682 (1972), the Court interpreted Justice Brennan's majority opinion in United States v. Wade, 388 U.S. 218 (1967) (a landmark case dealing with the right to counsel at lineups), differently than he did. Brennan dissented. The same thing happened to Brennan again in United States v. Ash, 413 U.S. 300 (1973).

[102] Lustig v. United States, 338 U.S. 74, 78–79 (1949). *See generally* Kamisar, *supra* note 97.

[103] 364 U.S. at 214.

[104] *Id.*

[105] *Id.* at 213.

sential part of the right to privacy—be also insisted upon as an
essential ingredient of the right newly recognized by the *Wolf* case.[106]

3. *Rochin v. California*

Rochin, the noisome "stomach pumping" case,[107] demonstrates that
even in pre-*Mapp* days, even when the evidence seized was indisputably
trustworthy (it is hard to think of any evidence more trustworthy than
morphine capsules taken from a defendant's stomach), the sky was not
the limit for state law enforcement officials. *Rochin* arose as follows:[108]

Three Los Angeles County deputy sheriffs broke into defendant's
room. When they spotted two capsules on a night stand near defendant's
bed, they asked what they were. Rochin responded by grabbing the
capsules and putting them in his mouth. A struggle ensued, in the course
of which the deputies tried forcibly to extract the items from Rochin's
mouth. But he managed to swallow them. (The California courts found
that the deputies had unlawfully assaulted and battered defendant while
they were in his room.)

Rochin was then handcuffed and taken to a hospital. There, at the
deputies' direction and against defendant's will, a doctor forced an
emetic solution through a tube in Rochin's stomach. This "stomach
pumping" caused Rochin to vomit up the two capsules, which turned out
to contain morphine.

Even though *Wolf* was on the books, the police misconduct in
Rochin was more than the Supreme Court could bear. It reversed
Rochin's conviction without a dissent.[109] Justice Frankfurter delivered
the opinion of the Court. Applying the "general considerations" of due
process "to the circumstances of the present case,"[110] he declared:

---

[106] *Mapp*, 367 U.S. at 655–56.

[107] *Rochin* is discussed briefly in note 12 *supra*.

[108] This summary of the facts is based on the account set forth in the *Rochin* opinion,
342 U.S. at 166–67.

[109] However, both Justice Black and Justice Douglas wrote concurring opinions,
expressing strong disagreement with the approach taken by Justice Frankfurter, author of
the majority opinion. Black rejected the majority's view that "the Due Process Clause
empowers this Court to nullify any state law if its application 'shocks the conscience,'
offends 'a sense of justice' or runs counter to the 'decencies of civilized conduct.' " *Id.* at
175. Although he realized that a majority of the Court had refused to apply the Fifth
Amendment to the states, Black maintained that the "stomach pumping" had violated
Rochin's privilege against self-incrimination. *See id.* Douglas also expressed the view that
capsules taken from a person's stomach, over his objection were "inadmissible because of
the command of the Fifth Amendment." *Id.* at 179. According to him the majority's
approach (which asked whether the police had violated "the decencies of civilized conduct")
made the admissibility of evidence "turn not on the Constitution but on the idiosyncrasies
of the judges who sit here." *Id.*

[110] *Id.* at 172.

This is conduct that shocks the conscience.... [T]his course of proceeding by agents of government to obtain evidence is bound to offend even hardened sensibilities. They are methods too close to the rack and the screw to permit of constitutional differentiation.[111]

Perhaps because he wanted to put as much distance between *Wolf* and *Rochin* as he could, Justice Frankfurter's nine-page *Rochin* opinion "studiously avoided [the search-and-seizure question] and never once mentioned the *Wolf* case."[112] If *Mapp* started out as an obscenity case but became a search and seizure case along the way, it might be said that *Rochin* started out as an "aggravated" search and seizure case but wound up looking very much like a coerced confessions case:

[The coerced confession cases] are not sports in our constitutional law but applications of a general principle. They are only instances of the general requirement that States in their prosecutions respect certain decencies of civilized conduct. Due process of law [means] ... that convictions cannot be brought about by methods that offend "a sense of justice." *It would be a stultification of the responsibility which the course of constitutional history has cast upon this Court to hold that in order to convict a man the police cannot extract by force what is in his mind but can extract what is in his stomach.*

To attempt in this case to distinguish what lawyers call "real evidence" from verbal evidence is to ignore the reasons for excluding coerced confessions.... [Coerced confessions] are inadmissible under the Due Process Clause even though statements contained in them may be independently established as true. *Coerced confessions offend the community's sense of fair play and decency. So here,* to sanction the brutal conduct which naturally enough was condemned by the court whose judgment is before us, would be to afford brutality the cloak of law.[113]

Although everybody I have ever talked to about the "stomach pumping" case has agreed that the Court should have overturned the defendant's conviction, it is not easy to reconcile Justice Frankfurter's majority opinion in *Rochin* with his majority opinion in *Wolf* (which may be why Frankfurter's *Rochin* opinion never mentions *Wolf*).

---

[111] *Id.*

[112] Irvine v. California, 347 U.S. 128, 133 (1954) (principal opinion by Jackson, J.). Justice Jackson pointed this out in the course of rejecting dissenting Justice Frankfurter's argument that *Rochin* applied to the facts of *Irvine*. Jackson succeeded in arguing that *Rochin* did not apply to blatant or egregious illegal searches, but only to cases "involv[ing] coercion, violence or brutality to the person." *Id. See* text at notes 133–35 *infra.*

[113] 342 U.S. at 173 (emphasis added).

The *Wolf* Court was impressed by the fact that most of the state courts that had passed on the admissibility of evidence obtained by unlawful search and seizure had rejected the federal exclusionary rule.[114] But the *Rochin* Court did not consider it worth mentioning (although concurring Justice Douglas did) that "[t]he evidence obtained from the accused's stomach would be admissible in the majority of states where the question has been raised."[115]

The *Wolf* Court gave great weight to the fact that the many states that had rejected the federal exclusionary rule had "not left the right to privacy without other means of protection" (such as internal police discipline and tort actions and criminal prosecutions against offending police officers).[116] But the *Rochin* Court thought it irrelevant that the "stomach pumping" and the earlier physical struggle to retrieve the capsules from Rochin before he could swallow them constituted more than one tort and more than one crime.

Indeed, as the *Rochin* court itself informed us, "the [California] District Court of Appeal affirmed [Rochin's] conviction, despite the finding that the officers 'were guilty ... of unlawfully assaulting and battering defendant while in [his] room' and 'were guilty of unlawfully assaulting, battering, torturing, and falsely imprisoning the defendant at the alleged hospital.' "[117] Moreover, not only did the California courts make plain that the police officers had committed more than one tort and more than one crime, but, as the *Rochin* Court told us, "[a]ll the California judges who have expressed themselves in this case have condemned the conduct in the strongest language."[118]

Why, then, would upholding Rochin's conviction have amounted to "sanctioning" the police misconduct and "affording" it "the cloak of law"?[119] And if it would have had this effect, why didn't the Supreme Court's affirmance of Wolf's conviction have *the same effect*?

In overturning Rochin's conviction, the Court told us that it had been "brought about by methods that offend 'a sense of justice.' "[120] But how does this distinguish the *Wolf* case? The best reading of *Wolf* (and the reading that a majority of the Court was soon to give it),[121] is that,

---

[114] *See Wolf*, 338 U.S. at 29.

[115] *Id*. at 177 (Douglas, J., concurring).

[116] *Id*. at 30.

[117] *Rochin*, 342 U.S. at 166–67.

[118] *Id*. at 174.

[119] *See* text at note 113 *supra*.

[120] *Id*.

[121] *See* text at notes 105–06 *supra*.

although *Wolf* declined to make the exclusionary rule a limitation on the states, the police conduct at issue violated Fourteenth Amendment Due Process. Doesn't *every* police action that violates due process offend a sense of justice? (If not, why is it a violation of due process?)

One way to reconcile *Rochin* with *Wolf* is to say that although searches that would have violated the Fourth Amendment if conducted by federal officers do violate Fourteenth Amendment Due Process when made by state officers, *the use of evidence* so acquired in a state prosecution does not offend due process unless the police methods involved amount to an egregious or shocking violation of due process. But this is a curious proposition.

To say that state police conduct is unconstitutional—that it violates the minimal standards of due process—would seem to be as bad a label as one can put on police behavior. Why should any more have to be required? Why must the police be found to have violated *sub-minimal* standards before the evidence they obtained has to be excluded?[122]

Was the unlawful search in *Wolf*, unlike the police misconduct in *Rochin*, only a "bare" or "mild" violation of due process? How does one "barely" or "mildly" violate what is "basic to a free society" and "implicit 'in the concept of ordered liberty' "?[123]

One might say that the rights the police violated in *Wolf* were merely rights "basic to a free society" whereas the rights flouted in *Rochin* were rights "*very* basic to a free society."[124] However, to say the least, "[t]here is a certain inelegance" in speaking of constitutional rights that way.[125]

4. *Irvine v. California*

Although *Rochin* carved out an exception to *Wolf*'s rule of admissibility for evidence obtained by lawless state police, *Irvine v. California*[126] left no doubt that the exception was quite small. Because the police misconduct was so egregious—even the Justices who voted to uphold the defendant's convictions conceded that what the police had done "would be almost incredible if it were not admitted"[127]—*Irvine* was an excellent

---

[122] *See* the discussion in Kamisar, *supra* note 43, at 1121–29.

[123] *See Wolf*, 338 U.S. at 27–28: "The security of one's privacy against arbitrary intrusions by the police—which is at the core of the Fourth Amendment—is basic to a free society. It is therefore implicit in 'the concept of ordered liberty' and as such enforceable against the States through the Due Process Clause."

[124] *See* Allen, *supra* note 15, at 9.

[125] *See id.*

[126] 347 U.S. 128 (1954).

[127] *Id.* at 132.

case to test the limits of *Wolf*'s rule of admissibility. The Court's answer was clear: The latitude *Wolf* had given state courts to admit illegally seized evidence was far-reaching. (To put it another way, there might be a "shock the conscience" exception to *Wolf*, but what shocked the Court's conscience? According to *Irvine*, "not very much.")[128]

In *Irvine*, in order to overhear conversations between defendant (a suspected bookmaker) and his wife, the police made repeated illegal entries into his home, first to install a secret microphone in the hall, then to move it to the bedroom, and finally to move it to a closet. The electronic surveillance lasted for over a month. Officers were posted in a nearby garage to listen.[129]

Justice Jackson, who wrote the principal opinion,[130] did not spare the police:

> That officers of the law would break and enter a home, secrete a [microphone], even in a bedroom, and listen to the conversation for over a month would be almost incredible if it were not admitted. Few police measures have come to our attention that more flagrantly, deliberately, and persistently violated the fundamental principle declared by the Fourth Amendment as a restriction on the Federal Government. . . .[131]

Nevertheless, the Court, per Justice Jackson, rejected the efforts to bring *Irvine* "under the sway" of *Rochin*:[132] The key to *Rochin*, maintained Jackson, was "coercion . . . applied by a physical assault upon [defendant's] person to compel submission to the use of a stomach pump."[133] That factor was "totally lacking here."[134] However egregious

---

[128] Dale W. Broeder, *The Decline and Fall of Wolf v. Colorado*, 41 Neb. L. Rev. 185, 191 (1961).

[129] *See* 347 U.S. at 132.

[130] Justice Jackson was joined by Chief Justice Warren and Justices Reed and Minton. The fifth vote was provided by Justice Clark, who concurred in the judgment.

Clark had no love for *Wolf* (he stated at the outset of his concurrence that he would have applied the exclusionary rule to the states if he had been in the Court when *Wolf* was decided), but he had no love for *Rochin* either (*id*. at 138):

> Of course, we could sterilize the rule announced in *Wolf* by adopting a case-by-case approach to due process, in which inchoate notions of propriety concerning local police conduct guide our decisions. But . . . the practical result of this *ad hoc* approach is simply that when five Justices are sufficiently revolted by local police action, a conviction is overturned and a guilty man may go free. *Rochin* bears witness to this.

[131] *Id*. at 132.

[132] *Id*. at 133.

[133] *Id*.

[134] *Id*.

the facts in *Irvine*, "they do not involve coercion, violence or brutality to the person."[135]

Dissenting Justice Frankfurter insisted that *Rochin* called for the exclusion of the evidence at issue in *Irvine*. According to Frankfurter, the decisive factor in *Irvine* was the "aggravating" police conduct "which the Court finds repulsive."[136] Frankfurter continued:

> There was lacking here physical violence, even to the restricted extent employed in *Rochin*. We have here, however, a more powerful and offensive control over the Irvines' life than a single, limited physical trespass. Certainly the conduct here went far beyond a bare search and seizure.... Surely the Court does not propose to announce a new absolute, namely that even the most reprehensible means for securing a conviction will not taint a verdict so long as the body of the accused was not touched by State officials.[137]

For what it is worth, I agree with Justice Frankfurter. Indeed— because the police misconduct in *Irvine* lasted for over a month—I, for one, find it more "outrageous" and more "shocking" than the police misconduct in *Rochin*. (Perhaps this just illustrates the unmanageable, unprincipled nature of the *Rochin* "shock the conscience" test.)

Although I think Justice Frankfurter's reading of *Rochin* was better than Jackson's, the latter's reading was at least plausible. Although Frankfurter gave no indication he was aware of this, his opinion in *Wolf* had come back to haunt him in *Irvine*. At times it was hard to believe that the same Justice who dissented in *Irvine* had written the opinion of the Court in *Wolf*.

Although Justice Frankfurter had emphasized in *Wolf* that the exclusion of the illegally seized evidence was *not the only way* to enforce the security of one's privacy against lawless intrusions by the police, he protested in *Irvine*:

> Nor can we dispose of this case by satisfying ourselves that the defendant's guilt was proven by trustworthy evidence and *then finding, or devising, other means* whereby the police may be discouraged from using illegal methods to acquire such evidence.[138]

But isn't this the way the Court disposed of the *Wolf* case?

In *Irvine*, dissenting Justice Frankfurter maintained that not even suspending or dismissing or prosecuting the law enforcement officials

---

[135] *Id.*

[136] *Id.* at 146.

[137] *Id.* at 145–46.

[138] Id. at 148 (emphasis added).

responsible for the invasion of the Irvines' privacy could justify the use
of the resulting evidence in a state prosecution:

> If, as in *Rochin*, "[o]n the facts of this case the conviction of the
> petitioner has been obtained by methods that offend the Due Pro-
> cess Clause," *it is no answer to say* that the offending policemen and
> prosecutors who utilize outrageous methods should be punished for
> their misconduct.[139]

But why *was it* an answer to say that in *Wolf*? Wasn't *Wolf's*
conviction, no less than Irvine's, brought about by police methods that
offended due process? Why was the availability (or at least possibility) of
alternative ways of enforcing the protection against unreasonable search
and seizure so important in *Wolf* but so insignificant (indeed, according
to Frankfurter, irrelevant) in *Irvine*?[140]

Unlike his dissenting colleague, Justice Jackson thought *it was* a
good answer to say that the offending police officers whose "almost
incredible" conduct brought about Irvine's conviction should be punished. It appeared that the California police had committed a federal
crime, *i.e.*, "under color" of law, they had deprived the Irvines of "rights,
privileges or immunities secured or protected by the Constitution of the
United States."[141] Therefore, announced Justice Jackson, he was directing "the Clerk of this Court ... to forward a copy of the record in this
case, together with a copy of this opinion, for attention of the Attorney
General of the United States."[142]

Only the newest member of the Court, Chief Justice Warren, shared
Justice Jackson's view that the case should be sent to the Attorney
General for possible prosecution.[143] Would Jackson have picked up War-

---

[139] *Id.* (emphasis added).

[140] One who supported Frankfurter's position might say courts are content to rely on
alternatives to the exclusionary rule when the police violations of due process are
"ordinary" or "routine," but *not* when they are flagrant and deliberate. In these latter
cases, and *Rochin* and *Irvine* are good examples, the courts must exclude the evidence to
show their strong disapproval; alternative remedies simply will not suffice.

It strikes me, however, that the egregiousness of the police misconduct cuts the other
way. The *need to exclude the evidence* is *greater* in ordinary or routine cases of police
misconduct because the alternatives to excluding the evidence are much less likely to be
effective. "Routine" or "ordinary" cases of police lawlessness are *less likely* to attract the
attention of the press, *less likely* to lead to discipline of or prosecutions against the
offending officers and *less likely* to excite the sympathy of jurors when those mistreated by
the police seek damages. In short, if the courts cannot rely on alternatives to the
exclusionary rule in outrageous cases such as *Rochin* and *Irvine*, then they certainly cannot
and should not rely on such alternatives in less flagrant cases.

[141] *See id.* at 137–38.

[142] *Id.* at 138.

[143] *See id.* at 137.

ren's vote if he had not taken this step? We shall probably never know. But we do know that Jackson's move backfired.

It turned out that the police officers who had concealed the microphone in the Irvines' home had been acting under the order of the local chief of police and with the full knowledge of the local prosecutor. Therefore, concluded the Justice Department, "it would be both useless and inadvisable to present [the] matter to the Federal grand jury."[144]

All the Justices who sat on the *Mapp* Court probably knew that the pursuit of alternatives to the exclusionary rule in *Irvine*, one of the most outrageous cases of police behavior ever to reach the Supreme Court, had ended with a whimper. Chief Justice Warren certainly knew about it. The Justice Department official who had concluded that there was no point prosecuting the police involved in *Irvine* had been one of Warren's former deputies and remained one of his closest friends.[145]

According to one of his biographers, later in his career Warren repeatedly told the story of the *Irvine* case.[146] One of the lessons he drew from that case *and its aftermath* was that the Court could not rely on alternative remedies to the exclusionary rule.[147]

Two years before *Mapp* was handed down, I wrote:

[F]or better or worse, [the *Wolf*] doctrine seems more firmly imbedded in the law today than when first promulgated. For on its facts, *Irvine* goes much further. Yet, while *Irvine* well illustrates "the tendency of a principle to expand itself to the limits of its logic," there is also precedent for the view that a principle is never so vulnerable as when it is so expanded.[148]

In retrospect, "the demonstrated incapacity of the *Wolf* doctrine to meet the problem of the egregious wrong must be regarded as an important milestone on the road to *Mapp*."[149]

---

[144] *See* Comment, *State Police, Unconstitutionally Obtained Evidence and Section 242 of the Civil Rights Statute*, 7 Stan. L. Rev. 76, 94 note 75 (1954).

[145] *See* Cray, *supra* note 27, at 181, 270–71; JOHN D. WEAVER, WARREN: THE MAN, THE COURT, THE ERA 196, 198 (1967). The Justice official was Warren Olney, III, the assistant attorney general in charge of the criminal division.

[146] *See* G. EDWARD WHITE, EARL WARREN: A PUBLIC LIFE 266 (1982).

[147] *See id. See also* Cray, *supra* note 27, at 374.

[148] Kamisar, *supra* note 43, at 1198. The quotation about the tendency of a principle to expand is from BENJAMIN CARDOZO, THE NATURE OF THE JUDICIAL PROCESS 51 (1925).

[149] Allen, *supra* note 15, at 10.

5. *People v. Cahan*

Although it was only a state supreme case, *People v. Cahan*[150] (which saw California adopt the exclusionary rule on its own initiative) may be viewed as another milestone on the road to *Mapp*. In *Defore*, Cardozo had warned that the exclusionary rule could free a dangerous criminal simply because the constable had blundered.[151] But *Cahan* illustrated (as had *Irvine* only a year earlier) that the rule of admissibility could permit the use of evidence obtained by the most flagrant and deliberate police misconduct.

As one contemporary observer said of the police conduct involved in *Cahan*: The police illegality in this case "is illegality elaborately planned with the connivance of the Los Angeles Chief of Police. It is not the case of the over-eager rookie misjudging the fine lines of the law of arrest. It is constitutional violation as a matter of policy."[152]

"Cardozo's statements [in *Defore*] and his prestige have often been relied upon by opponents of the [exclusionary] rule."[153]

This is hardly surprising. After all, Cardozo was undoubtedly the most respected state judge of his generation. But Roger Traynor, author of the *Cahan* opinion, was widely regarded as the most respected state judge of *his* generation.[154] Moreover, when it came to the exclusionary rule, Traynor had a special credibility. In 1942, when he was a new judge, he had written the opinion of the California Supreme Court *reaffirming the admissibility* of illegally-seized evidence.[155] By 1955, however, it had become apparent to Traynor, as he later explained, that illegally seized evidence "was being offered and admitted as a routine procedure" and it had become "impossible to ignore the corollary that

---

[150] 44 Cal. 2d 434, 282 P.2d 905 (1955).

[151] *See* note 54 *supra*.

[152] Monrad G. Paulsen, *Safeguards in the Law of Search and Seizure*, 52 Nw. U. L. Rev. 65, 75–76 (1957). In *Cahan*, Los Angeles police officers, with the approval of their chief of police, had surreptitiously installed microphones in two houses occupied by some of the defendants. Then, after making forcible entries into the houses, the police had made various warrantless arrests, searches and seizures. The California Supreme Court called the police action a "flagrant violation" of both the federal and state constitutions. *See* 44 Cal. 2d at 436, 282 P.2d at 906.

[153] Weinstein, supra note 43 at 155–56.

[154] *See* Powe, *supra* note 11, at 199; Walter V. Schaefer, *Chief Justice Traynor and the Judicial Process*, 53 Calif. L. Rev. 11, 24 (1965).

[155] People v. Gonzales, 20 Cal. 2d 165, 124 P.2d 44 (1942). Ironically, Earl Warren was the California Attorney General who had successfully urged Traynor and his colleagues to take this position.

illegal searches and seizures were also a routine procedure, subject to no effective deterrent."[156]

Justice Traynor wrote a balanced, scholarly opinion. Indeed, the arguments of scholars and judges *in favor* of admitting illegally seized evidence "have seldom been stated more forcefully" than in the *Cahan* opinion.[157] But his opinion was also quite powerful:

> [W]ithout fear of criminal punishment or other discipline, law enforcement officers, sworn to support the Constitution of the United States and the Constitution of California, frankly admit their deliberate, flagrant acts in violation of both Constitutions and the laws enacted therein. It is clearly apparent from their testimony that they casually regard such acts as nothing more than the performance of their ordinary duties for which the City employs and pays them.
>
> * * *
>
> We have been compelled to [overrule our precedents permitting the use of illegally seized evidence] because other remedies have completely failed to secure compliance with the constitutional provisions on the part of police officers with the attendant result that the courts under the old rule have been constantly required to participate in, and in effect condone, the lawless activities of law-enforcement officers.[158]

In *Elkins*,[159] decided only a year before *Mapp*, the Court noted that "[t]he experience in California has been most illuminating,"[160] and proceeded to quote thirteen lines from Justice Traynor's *Cahan* opinion. (It also quoted, not approvingly, one sentence from Cardozo's opinion in *Defore*, the only other state case quoted in *Elkins*.)[161]

---

[156] Roger J. Traynor, *Mapp v. Ohio at Large in the Fifty States*, 1962 Duke L.J. 319, 321–22.

[157] Monrad G. Paulsen, *Criminal Law Administration: The Zero Hour Was Coming*, 53 Calif.L.Rev. 103, 107 (1965). Paulsen considered the *Cahan* opinion "a great achievement" because "[a]ll voices are heard and we are told why Reason chooses to follow one set of arguments rather than another." *Id.*

[158] 282 P.2d at 907, 911–12. As the quotation from the opinion in the text indicates, Justice Traynor was a proponent of the "one-government" approach to the admission of illegally seized evidence. *See also id.* at 912–13.

[159] *See* text at notes 100–05 *supra* and accompanying footnotes.

[160] 364 U.S. at 220.

[161] The *Mapp* Court thought it "significant" that California is "now following [the] exclusionary rule," 367 U.S. at 651, and noted that its highest court had declared in *Cahan* that it had been "compelled to reach that conclusion because other remedies have completely failed ..." *Id.* At another point, the *Mapp* Court observed that "[t]he experi-

The *Elkins* Court quoted something else, something that may have influenced some members of the Supreme Court as much, or even more than, the *Cahan* opinion itself—a statement by the California Attorney General that since *Cahan* was decided things were working out well:

> The over-all effects of the *Cahan* decision, particularly in view of the [search and seizure] rules now worked out by the [California] Supreme Court, have been excellent. A much greater education is called for on the part of all peace officers of California. As a result, they will be much better police officers. I think there is more cooperation with the District Attorneys and this will make for better administration of criminal justice.[162]

The Police–Prosecution Criticism of *Mapp*

The reaction of law enforcement officials when the Court finally imposed the exclusionary rule on all the states may well be the best evidence of the need for the rule. Many in law enforcement reacted as if the Fourth Amendment or its state constitutional counterpart had just been adopted.

New York City Police Commissioner Michael Murphy likened the *Mapp* case to a "tidal wave" and an "earthquake."[163] As the commissioner recalled some years later:

> I can think of no decision in recent times in the field of law enforcement which had such a dramatic and traumatic effect as [*Mapp*].... As the then commissioner of the largest police force in this country, I was immediately caught up in the entire problem of reevaluating our procedures, which had followed the *Defore* rule, and ... creating new polices and new restrictions for the implementation of *Mapp*.... [Decisions such as *Mapp*] create tidal waves and earthquakes which require rebuilding of our institutions sometimes from their very foundations upward. Retraining sessions had to be

---

ence of California that ... other remedies [than the exclusionary rule] have been worthless and futile is buttressed by the experience of other States." *Id.* at 652. (Once again, *Defore* was the only other state case bearing on the exclusionary rule quoted by the Court.)

[162] *Id.* at 220–21. The Court was quoting a letter from then Attorney General Edmund G. Brown to the *Stanford Law Review*, quoted in part in Note, Stan. L. Rev. 515, 538 (1957). For other extracts from this letter *see* Kamisar, *supra* note 43, at 1198.

Chief Justice Warren must have been impressed by both Justice Traynor's opinion in *Cahan* and the state attorney general's assessment of how the police were adjusting to it. Warren knew Traynor personally and, on the basis of his own dealings with him, respected him. *See* Weaver, *supra* note 144, at 74. As for the state attorney general's optimistic evaluation of how the police were adjusting to *Cahan*, this probably corroborated the Chief Justice's view that rulings criticized for "handcuffing the police" actually encouraged the police to work harder and to prepare their cases more carefully and thoroughly. *See* White, *supra* note 145, at 272, 277–78.

[163] *See* the quotation from Commissioner Michael Murphy set forth immediately below.

held from the very top administrators down to each of the thousands of foot patrolmen and detectives engaged in the daily basic enforcement function.[164]

Why did *Mapp* have "such a dramatic and traumatic effect"? Why did it necessitate "retraining" from top to bottom? What was the *old* search and seizure training like? *Was there any?* How does one "implement" *Mapp*, a case that simply imposed *a remedy* for a violation of a body of law the police were supposed to be obeying all along?

What did the commissioner mean when he tried to defend his department's disinterest in the law of search and seizure prior to *Mapp* by noting that his department "had followed the *Defore* rule"? To be sure, *Defore* permitted New York prosecutors to *use* illegally seized evidence, but it did not—as the commissioner evidently believed—allow the police to *commit illegal searches*.

As Donald Dripps has observed, "[i]f effective civil remedies carried the political appeal that would commend them to legislators, those remedies would have forced the police to comply with the Amendment in the [years before] *Mapp* [and] *Mapp* would have discomfited the police but little."[165]

It appears that, prior to *Mapp*, the police were not the only New York law enforcement officials unfamiliar with and unconcerned about the law of search and seizure. Professor Richard Uviller, a New York prosecuting attorney when *Mapp* was handed down, recalled that he quickly "cranked out a crude summary" of federal search and seizure law just before the next state convention of district attorneys took place and that he "had an instant runaway best seller. It was as though we had made a belated discovery that the fourth amendment applied in the State of New York."[166] Uviller's last comment, I believe, sums up the situation in New York before and after *Mapp* quite well.

---

[164] Michael Murphy, *Judicial Review of Police Methods in Law Enforcement: The Problem of Compliance by Police Departments*, 44 Tex. L. Rev. 939, 941 (1966).

Those who believed or assumed that various alternatives to the search and seizure exclusionary rule were adequate may have suffered an even greater blow when, unaware that there was a reporter in the audience, New York City Deputy Police Commissioner Leonard Reisman explained to a large group of detectives at a post-*Mapp* training session why they had to learn the law of search and seizure at this late date in their careers: "[In the past] nobody bothered to take out search warrants. . . . [T]he Supreme Court had ruled that evidence obtained without a warrant—illegally if you will—was admissible in state courts. So the feeling was, why bother?" Sidney Zion, *Detectives Get a Course in Law*, N.Y. Times, Apr. 28, 1965, at 50, col. 1 (nat'l ed.).

[165] Donald Dripps, *Akhil Amar on Criminal Procedure and Constitutional Law: "Here I Go Down that Wrong Road Again,"* 74 N.C. L. Rev. 1559, 1606 (1996).

[166] H. Richard Uviller, *The Acquisition of Evidence for Criminal Prosecution: Some Constitutional Premises and Practices in Transition*, 35 Vand. L. Rev. 501, 502 (1982).

The response of New York law enforcement officials to the imposition of the search and seizure exclusionary rule was hardly unique. When, six years earlier, in the *Cahan* case, the California Supreme Court adopted the exclusionary rule on its own initiative, the reaction of the Los Angeles Chief of Police, William Parker, was quite similar to the reaction his New York City counterpart would have when *Mapp* came down.

Chief Parker warned that as a result of *Cahan* his officers' "ability to prevent the commission of crimes has been greatly reduced."[167] But he promised that "[a]s long as the Exclusionary Rule is the law of California, your police will respect it and operate to the best of their ability within the framework of limitations imposed by that rule."[168]

However, the Exclusionary Rule does not impose any limitations on the police; the law of search and seizure does. And Chief Parker seemed to be saying that his officers would work within the "framework of limitations" imposed by the law of search and seizure *only so long as* "the Exclusionary Rule is the law of California."

In Pennsylvania, a young Philadelphia assistant district attorney (and a future U.S. Senator), Arlen Specter, made it clear that in his state, too, tort remedies, criminal prosecutions and internal police discipline had had little or no effect. He announced that *Mapp* had *"revolutionized"* police practice and prosecution procedures in the many states that had been admitting illegally seized evidence.[169] Indeed, he went so far as to call *Mapp* "the most significant event in criminal law since the adoption of the fourteenth amendment."[170]

Mr. Specter, too, seemed to confuse the *content* of the law of search and seizure (which proponents of the exclusionary rule need not, and have not always, defended) with the *exclusionary* rule—a *remedy*, a rule that "merely states the consequences of a breach of whatever principles might be adopted to control law enforcement officers."[171]

---

[167] WILLIAM H. PARKER, PARKER ON POLICE 117 (O.W. Wilson ed. 1957).

[168] *Id*. at 131.

[169] Arlen Specter, *Mapp v. Ohio: Pandora's Problems for the Prosecutor*, 111 U. Pa. L. Rev. 4 (1962) (emphasis added). As the New York City Police Commissioner had done, one Pennsylvania judge likened *Mapp* to a natural disaster—a "hurricane" which "swept over our fair land last June." *Id*. at 4. Another Pennsylvania judge "was so surprised by the *Mapp* holding that he said it applied only to Ohio so far as he was concerned until the Pennsylvania appellate courts told him otherwise." *Id*. at 4–5.

[170] *Id*. at 4.

[171] Monrad G. Paulsen, *The Exclusionary Rule and Misconduct by the Police*, 52 J. Crim. L. & Criminology & Police Sci. 255 (1961) (written on the eve of *Mapp*).

In Minnesota, however, the pattern of law enforcement responses to imposition of the exclusionary rule was broken. Another future U.S. Senator, and a future Vice President as well, Minnesota's young Attorney General, Walter Mondale, reminded an assemblage of distressed Minnesota officers that "the language of the Fourth Amendment is identical to the [search and seizure provision] of the Minnesota State Constitution" and that "*Mapp* did not alter one word of either the state or national constitutions."[172] Continued Mondale:

> [*Mapp*] does not reduce police powers one iota. It only reduces potential *abuses* of power. The adoption of the so-called "exclusionary rule" does not affect authorized police practices in any way. What was a legal arrest before, still is. What was a reasonable search before still is. . . .[173]

What Mondale said, in effect, was that if the police feared that the evidence they were acquiring in their customary manner would now be excluded by the courts, they must have been unmindful of the so-called alternative remedies to the exclusionary rule all these years and they must have been violating the guarantee against unreasonable search and seizure all along. That, I think, is the hard truth.

The "Original Understanding" of *Mapp*

A number of commentators have had great difficulty figuring out exactly what Justice Clark's rationale(s) for *Mapp* were. Thus, Thomas Schrock and Robert Welsh call Clark's statement that the exclusionary rule is "a clear, specific, and constitutionally required—even if judicially implied—deterrent safeguard without insistence upon which the Fourth Amendment would have been reduced to a form of words"[174] an "incorrigibly ambiguous" passage, "mixing in about equal portions vague constitutional references, deterrence rationale, and empirical generalization."[175] Larry Yackle similarly observes that *Mapp* "ultimately fastened the exclusionary rule on the states in reliance upon *all* the rationales thus far imposed."[176]

---

[172] Walter Mondale, *The Problem of Search and Seizure*, 19 Bench & B. Minn. 15, 16 (Feb. 1962).

[173] *Id.*

[174] 367 U.S. at 648.

[175] Schrock & Welsh, *supra* note 66, at 319, quoting 367 U.S. at 648.

[176] Yackle, *supra* note 66, at 418. Professor Yackle continues, *id.* at 418–19: "Thus the Court said that the exclusionary rule is 'an essential part' of the individual's personal rights under the Fourth and Fourteenth Amendments [367 U.S. at 657], that it gives to the courts 'that judicial integrity so necessary in the true administration of justice' [*id.* at 660], and also that its purpose 'is to deter—to compel respect for the constitutional guaranty in the only effectively available way by removing the incentive to disregard it' [*id.* at 656]."

William Mertens and Silas Wasserstrom are also unhappy with
Justice Clark's treatment of the exclusionary rule in *Mapp*. They do not
think *Mapp* did what it should have—mark a return to the days when
the Court "perceived a kind of natural, immutable affinity between the
fourth amendment and the exclusionary rule":[177]

> [A]lthough the Court in *Mapp* invoked a concatenation of normative
> principles to support the extension of the exclusionary rule to the
> states, the bulk of its opinion was devoted to a defense of the rule on
> the empirical basis that it has proved to be the only effective means
> of enforcing the fourth amendment.[178]

I have to disagree. The only discussion of the inadequacy of "other
means" of enforcing the right to privacy appears in Part II of Clark's
opinion where he yielded, as have others, to the temptation to meet the
author of the *Wolf* opinion on the latter's own battleground. However, all
that Clark had to say in his opinion about "other remedies" is contained
in sixteen lines.[179] So few lines in an eighteen page opinion does not seem
to warrant the conclusion that "the bulk" of Clark's opinion was devoted
to a defense of the exclusionary rule on an empirical basis.

Of course, it is not simply a matter of counting lines. Rather, it is a
matter of reading those lines in light of the totality of the opinion. A
quick look at the opinion follows:

• Part I of the *Mapp* opinion makes plain that it views the exclusionary rule as neither "a mere rule of evidence" or a product of the Court's
"supervisory powers," but as *a "constitutionally required" doctrine*.[180]

• Part II tells us that the *Wolf* Court's reasons for not considering
the exclusionary rule "essential to the right of privacy" "were bottomed
on factual considerations."[181] *"[W]hile not basically relevant to the constitutional consideration"*[182]—these factual matters "could not, in any analysis, now be deemed controlling."[183]

• Part III concludes: "We hold that all evidence obtained by
searches and seizure in violation of the Constitution is, *by that same
authority*, inadmissible in a state court."[184]

---

[177] Mertens & Wasserstrom, *supra* note 74, at 381.

[178] *Id.* at 382.

[179] *See* 367 U.S. at 651–53.

[180] *See id.* at 646–50 (emphasis added).

[181] *Id.* at 655 (emphasis added).

[182] *Id.* at 650–51.

[183] *Id.* at 653 (emphasis added).

[184] *Id.*

• The main thrust of Part IV is that "[s]ince the Fourth Amendment's right of privacy has been declared enforceable against the States," "it is enforceable against them by the same sanction of exclusion as is used against the Federal Government."[185] "[I]n extending the substantive protections of due process to all constitutionally unreasonable searches—state or federal—*it was logically and constitutionally necessary that the exclusion doctrine—an essential part of the right to privacy*— be also insisted upon as an essential element of the right newly recognized by the *Wolf* case."[186]

The *Wolf* case had downgraded the protection against unreasonable search and seizure by "conditioning" its "enforcement" in a way that no other basic constitutional right's enforcement had been restricted.[187] But from this point on, those days are over. The Fourth Amendment is going to be enforced as "strictly against the States" as are other fundamental rights—such as "the right not to be convicted by use of a coerced confession, however logically relevant it be, and without regard to its reliability."[188] This part of the opinion ends with the assurance that "*no man is to be convicted on unconstitutional evidence.*"[189]

• The fifth and last part of the Clark opinion begins by referring to "our holding that *the exclusionary rule is an essential part* of both the Fourth and Fourteenth Amendments."[190] It ends with the observation that "[b]ecause [the Fourth Amendment] *is enforceable in the same manner and to like effect as other basic rights secured by the Due Process Clause*, we can no longer permit it to be revocable at the whim of any police officer who ... chooses to suspend its enjoyment. Our decision ... gives to the individual no more than that which the Constitution guarantees him...."[191]

I do not deny that Justice Clark scrambled the analysis somewhat and caused some confusion by, for example, calling the exclusionary rule "a constitutionally required ... deterrent safeguard."[192] The trouble, I believe, was that Justice Clark was trying to get maximum approval for the overruling of *Wolf*. Evidently he thought he could do so by advancing as many reasons (or arguments) for the exclusionary rule he could find.

---

[185] *Id*. at 655.

[186] *Id*. at 656 (emphasis added).

[187] *Id*. at 656.

[188] *Id*.

[189] *Id*. at 657 (emphasis added).

[190] *Id*. (emphasis added).

[191] *Id*. (emphasis added).

[192] *See* text at note 174 *supra*.

Evidently Clark also thought he could do so by refuting all the arguments the rule's critics had ever made. (One of those, of course, was the claim that the exclusionary rule was not an effective deterrent or that it was not any better than "other methods" of enforcing the protection against unreasonable search and seizure.)

I agree with Steven Schlesinger and Bradford Wilson:

> It is true that Justice Clark discussed deterrence and concluded that "other remedies ... have been worthless and futile." ... Yet it is clear that he was only trying to counter *Wolf*'s claim that the exclusionary rule was bad law *from a* policy *standpoint*. The *only* reason Justice Clark engaged in that factual discussion was that he read *Wolf* to be "bottomed on factual considerations" [367 U.S. at 651] as opposed to constitutional analysis or deduction, and out of respect for the precedent he was overturning, he felt obliged to meet and defeat it on its own grounds first, before moving to the basis of his own position.[193]

It may well be that the Justices who voted to overrule *Wolf* were heavily influenced by the belief that all the alternatives to the exclusionary rule had turned out to be woefully inadequate. *But that is not the way Clark's opinion is written*. The way it is written, the exclusionary rule does not rest on an empirical proposition.[194] Rather, it is a command of the Constitution.

As I noted earlier, a number of commentators have read *Mapp* differently than I do. But they did so many years after *Mapp* was handed down. I cannot help wondering whether they were operating under what in this instance might be called the *handicap* of hindsight. They were looking back on the landmark search and seizure case through the filter of subsequent cases that have downgraded the exclusionary rule and misread or distorted Clark's opinion in *Mapp*.[195]

Professor Francis Allen, who wrote a major article on the *Mapp* case *the year it was decided*, seemed to have little trouble understanding the basic reasoning of the Clark opinion. Although the opinion "does not confine itself to the statement of a 'syllogism,' " Justice Clark's "essen-

---

[193] Steven R. Schlesinger & Bradford Wilson, *Property, Privacy and Deterrence: The Exclusionary Rule in Search of a Rationale*, 18 Duquesne L. Rev. 225, 235–36 (1980). Immediately after observing that *Wolf*'s rejection of the *Weeks* doctrine was "bottomed on factual considerations," 367 U.S. at 651, Clark said his opinion was going to consider "the factual grounds upon which *Wolf* was based" even though these factual considerations "are not basically relevant to a decision that the exclusionary rule is an essential ingredient of the Fourth Amendment." *Id*. A short time later, *see id*. at 653, Clark made this point again.

[194] *Cf*. Allen, *supra* note 3, at 537.

[195] *See* text at notes 200–233 *infra*.

tial position," reported Professor Allen, "is that the exclusionary rule is part of the Fourth Amendment; the Fourth Amendment is part of the Fourteenth; therefore, the exclusionary rule is part of the Fourteenth."[196]

Post-*Warren* Court Developments

Concurring in *Mapp*, Justice Douglas commented that the overruled *Wolf* case had evoked "a storm of constitutional controversy which only today finds its end."[197] He could not have been more wrong. The controversy was not only to intensify but to engulf the *Weeks* or *federal* exclusionary rule itself.[198]

Since *Mapp* relied to a significant extent on the premise that the exclusionary rule was an essential part of the Fourth Amendment and took the position that "in extending the substantive protections of due process to all constitutionally unreasonable searches—state or federal—it was logically and constitutionally necessary" to extend the exclusionary rule as well,[199] critics of *Mapp* soon began directing their fire at the efficacy, validity and constitutional basis of the *Weeks* or federal exclusionary rule itself. And they did so with great force and much success.

1. *The "Deterrence" Rationale and "Cost–Benefit" Analysis Gain Ascendancy—and the Thrust of the Exclusionary Rule Narrows*

In the post-Warren Court era, the "deterrence" rationale and "cost-benefit" analysis came to the fore.[200] This approach bloomed in *United*

---

[196] Allen, *supra* note 15, at 26. *See also id.* at 23–24. *Cf.* Weinstein, *supra* note 153, at 150. Francis Allen was not only a leading commentator on *Mapp*, but the earliest critic, and the most redoubtable critic, of *Wolf*. *See* Allen, *supra* note 73.

[197] 367 U.S. at 670.

[198] As Telford Taylor has noted, the Court's division in the *Mapp* case "did not concern the merits of the [federal or Fourth Amendment] exclusionary rule," but only the application of the rule to the states. "That is the issue on which the justices divided, and there is not a word in [Justice Harlan's dissenting opinion] suggesting that the rule is intrinsically bad," TELFORD TAYLOR, TWO STUDIES IN CONSTITUTIONAL INTERPRETATION 20–21 (1969).

[199] 367 U.S. at 655–56.

[200] One might say that the deterrence rationale came to the fore even before the Warren Court disbanded. Although the case could have been limited to its special facts, the deterrence rationale for the exclusionary rule is the dominant theme in Linkletter v. Walker, 381 U.S. 618 (1965), which declined to give *Mapp* full retroactive effect. The Court was under tremendous pressure to reach this result because applying the exclusionary rule announced in *Mapp* to cases which had become "final" (beyond direct review) before *Mapp* was decided "would tax the administration of justice to the utmost." *Id.* at 637. It is highly unlikely that in a case prosecuted in a pre-*Mapp* "admissibility" jurisdiction the defendant would have dwelt on the illegality of a search or seizure or that the court would even have allowed him to develop this point. But the understandably strong pressure to limit the

States v. Calandra,[201] the most important exclusionary rule case of the 1970s. In the course of ruling that grand jury witnesses may not refuse to answer questions on the ground that the questions were based on the fruits of an unlawful search, the *Calandra* Court did not treat the exclusionary rule with the constitutional respect *Mapp* had.

The *Calandra* majority, per Justice Powell, characterized the rule—one might say disparaged it—as a "judicially created remedy designed to safeguard Fourth Amendment rights generally through its deterrent effect rather than a personal constitutional right of the party aggrieved."[202] Thus, whether the exclusionary rule should be applied "presents a question not of rights but of remedies"—a question to be answered by weighing the "likely 'costs' " of the rules against the "likely 'benefits.' "[203]

---

impact of *Mapp* led the *Linkletter* Court (per Clark, J.) to rest the exclusionary rule almost entirely on an empirical basis.

As I have observed elsewhere, Kamisar, *supra* note 56, at 630, 631–32, "[o]ne might say that *Linkletter* applied *Wolf*'s way of thinking about the exclusionary rule 'retroactively' to *Mapp*.... [T]he *Linkletter* Court strongly implied ... that the exclusionary rule is 'an essential ingredient' of the fourth amendment only *because*, and only *so long as*, it is 'the only effective deterrent to lawless police action' " (quoting 381 U.S. at 636–37). *See generally* Kamisar, *supra*, at 627–33 and the authorities quoted and cited therein.

Despite their popularity in judicial opinions and the legal literature, the terms "deterrence" or "deterrent effects" in the search and seizure context are quite misleading. "Deterrence" suggests that the exclusionary rule is supposed to influence the police the way the criminal law is supposed to affect the general public. But the rule does not, and cannot be expected to, "deter" the police the way the criminal law is supposed to work. The rule does not inflict a "punishment" on police who violate the Fourth Amendment; exclusion does not leave the police in a worse position than if they had never violated the Constitution in the first place.

However, because the police are members of a structural governmental entity, the rule influences them, or is supposed to influence them, by "systemic deterrence," *i.e.,* through a department's institutional compliance with Fourth Amendment standards. *See* Wayne R. LaFave, *The Fourth Amendment in an Imperfect World: On Drawing "Bright Lines" and "Good Faith,"* 43 U. Pitt. L. Rev. 307, 319–20, 350–51 (1982); Mertens & Wasserstrom, *supra* note 74, at 394, 399; Pierre Schlag, *Assaults on the Exclusionary Rule: Good Faith Limitations and Damage Remedies,* 73 J. Crim. L. Criminology & P.S. 875, 882–83; Yackle, *supra* note 66, at 426.

Despite the widespread use of the "deterrence" terminology, it seems more accurate to view the exclusionary rule as a "disincentive" or "counterweight"—a means of eliminating significant incentives for making illegal searches, at least where the police contemplate prosecution and conviction. *See* Anthony G. Amsterdam, *Perspectives on the Fourth Amendment,* 58 Minn. L. Rev. 349, 431 (1974).

[201] 414 U.S. 338 (1974).

[202] *Id*. at 348.

[203] *Id*. at 348, 354, 349.

The post-*Mapp* way of thinking about the exclusionary rule enabled critics of the rule to gain some important victories. This is hardly surprising. The "costs" of the exclusionary rule are immediately apparent—the "freeing," for example, of a drug dealer—but the "benefits" of the rule are hard to grasp.

One *could* say that the benefits "involve safeguarding a zone of dignity and privacy for every citizen, controlling abuses of power [and] preserving checks and balances."[204] And one *could* regard these goals as "pretty weighty benefits, perhaps even invaluable ones."[205] But the Burger and Rehnquist Courts have not done so. Instead, they have characterized the benefits of the rule "as abstract [and] speculative."[206]

On the other hand, the Court has underscored what it thinks are the severe *costs* of the rule.[207] Thus, it has called the rule a "drastic

---

[204] Stephen J. Schulhofer, *The Constitution and the Police: Individual Rights and Law Enforcement*, 66 Wash. U. L.Q. 11, 19 (1988).

[205] *Id.*

[206] *Id.*

[207] However, a five-year empirical study of California data by Thomas Davies, called "[t]he most careful and balanced assessment conducted to date of all available empirical data," 1 WAYNE R. LaFAVE, SEARCH AND SEIZURE: A TREATISE ON THE FOURTH AMENDMENT 58 (3d ed. 1996), reveals that the exclusion of evidence in murder, rape, and other violent cases is extremely rare. *See* Thomas Y. Davies, *A Hard Look at What We Know (and Still Need to Learn) About the Costs of the Exclusionary Rule*, 1983 Am. B. Found. Res. J. 611, 640, 645. "The most striking feature of the data," reports Professor Davies, "is the concentration of illegal searches in drug arrests (and possibly weapons possession arrests) and the extremely small effects in arrests for other offenses, including violent crimes." *Id.* at 680.

The California data reveals that less than 0.3% (fewer than three in 1,000) of arrests for all non-drug offenses are rejected by prosecutors because of illegal searches. *Id.* at 619. Davies estimates that "the cumulative loss of drug arrests at all stages of felony processing in California is around 7.1%." *Id.* at 681. In United States v. Leon, 468 U.S. 897, 907 note 6 (1984), the Court, per Justice White, estimated that "the cumulative loss due to nonprosecution or nonconviction of individuals arrested on felony drug charges is probably in the range of 2.8% to 7.1%."

One may argue, as the Court did in *Leon*, that the small percentage of cases lost "mask a large absolute number." *Id.* As Davies points out, however, "raw numbers are not as useful for policy evaluation as percentages. In a system as large as the American criminal justice system . . . almost any nationwide measurement or estimate will look larger if expressed in raw numbers" Davies, *supra* at 670.

A proponent of the exclusionary rule could hardly resist the temptation to ask: What is all this talk about the "costs" of *the exclusionary rule*? Are the costs any different than those that would be exacted by *any* equally effective remedy? Doesn't a society whose police *comply with the Fourth Amendment in the first place* (because of an effective tort remedy or internal discipline or some other reason) "pay the same price" as the society whose law enforcement officials cannot use the evidence they obtained because they violated the Fourth Amendment? Don't both societies convict fewer criminals?

measure,"[208] an "extreme sanction,"[209] a rule that "exacts a costly toll
upon the ability of courts to ascertain the truth in a criminal case,"[210]
and one whose application is "contrary to the idea of proportionality that
is essential to the concept of justice."[211]

Given the Court's characterization of the "costs" and "benefits" to
be balanced, the outcome is quite predictable. Indeed, although cost-
benefit analysis sounds objective, even scientific, it is hard to avoid the
conclusion that in search-and-seizure cases, at least, it simply gives back
the values and assumptions the Court feeds into it.

During the cost-benefit analysis era, the Court failed to apply the
exclusionary rule to various settings. In the aforementioned *Calandra*
case, it declined to apply the rule in grand jury proceedings. In *Stone v.
Powell*,[212] it greatly limited the circumstances under which search-and-
seizure claims could be raised on federal habeas corpus proceedings. In
United States v. Janis,[213] it found the rule inapplicable in federal civil tax
proceedings. And in *I.N.S. v. Lopez–Mendoza*,[214] the Court deemed the
rule inappropriate in civil deportation proceedings.

The cost-benefit approach to the exclusionary rule culminated in
United States v. Leon,[215] the case that adopted a so-called good-faith
exception (actually a "reasonable mistake" exception) to the exclusionary rule. As the *Leon* majority saw it, the "marginal or nonexistent
benefits" produced by the exclusionary rule when the police reasonably
but mistakenly rely on a search warrant that turns out to be invalid
"cannot justify the costs of exclusion."[216]

Although *Leon* may appear to be little more than a routine application of the "cost-benefit" approach utilized in earlier cases, such as
Calandra, it is not. The earlier cases were based on the assumption that
the exclusionary rule—fully applicable in a criminal prosecution against
the direct victim of an illegal search or seizure—*need not also be applied*

---

[208] United States v. Janis, 428 U.S. 433, 459 (1976).

[209] United States v. Leon, 468 U.S. 897, 926 (1984).

[210] United States v. Payner, 447 U.S. 727, 734 (1980).

[211] Stone v. Powell, 428 U.S. 465, 489 (1976).

[212] *See* note 211 *supra*.

[213] *See* note 208 *supra*.

[214] 468 U.S. 1032 (1984).

[215] 468 U.S. 897 (1984).

[216] *Id.* at 922.

in certain "collateral" or "peripheral" contexts "where no significant *additional* increment of deterrence [was] deemed likely."[217]

Until *Leon* was handed down, one could still say that the post-Warren Court's "deconstitutionalization" of the exclusionary rule—its view that the rule is only a "judicially created" remedial device whose application turns on a "pragmatic analysis of [its] usefulness in a particular context"[218]—had not affected the rule in its central application: the prosecutor's case-in-chief against the direct victim of an unreasonable search and seizure. But *Leon* made clear that here, too, the rule would be subjected to "interest-balancing" or "cost-benefit" analysis. In this setting, too, the Court would ask whether the rule could "pay its way."

The fact that the Court carved out an exception to the exclusionary rule in its central application and the cost-benefit balancing it used to reach that result renders the exclusionary rule almost defenseless against "legislative repeal," for example, legislation that offers in its place what its proponents will undoubtedly assure us is an "effective" tort remedy. As Justice Brennan, who dissented in *Leon*, observed:

> By remaining within the redoubt of empiricism and by basing the rule solely on the deterrence rationale, the Court has robbed the rule of legitimacy. A doctrine that is explained as if it were an empirical proposition but for which there is only limited empirical support is both inherently unstable and an easy mark for critics.... Rather than seeking to give effect to the liberties secured by the Fourth Amendment through guesswork about deterrence, the Court should restore to its proper place the principle framed ... in *Weeks* that an individual whose privacy has been invaded in violation of the Fourth Amendment has a right grounded in that Amendment to prevent the government from subsequently making use of any evidence so obtained.[219]

So far the Court has not applied the "good faith" exception to all searches; it has confined *Leon* to those occasions where the police have acted pursuant to a warrant.[220] However, by applying "*Leon*-type reason-

---

[217] 1 LaFave, *supra* note 207, at 56.

[218] Stone v. Powell, 428 U.S. at 488.

[219] 468 U.S. at 943 (Brennan, J., joined by Marshall, J., dissenting in *Leon* and the companion case of Massachusetts v. Sheppard, 468 U.S. 981 (1984)).

[220] Nevertheless, warns Professor LaFave, "the possibility" that *Leon* and its companion case "will serve as stepping stones to a more comprehensive good faith exception to the Fourth Amendment exclusionary rule cannot be discounted.... Particularly noteworthy is the *Leon* majority's broad assertion that whenever the police officer's conduct was objectively reasonable the deterrence function of the exclusionary rule is not served and

ing" to instances where the police have relied on legislative and clerical action or inaction, the Court "has held admissible on 'good faith' grounds evidence obtained in warrantless police activity."[221]

Thus, *Illinois v. Krull* applied *Leon*'s rationale to a case where the police had acted in reliance on a state law authorizing the search in question even though the statute turned out to be in violation of the Fourth Amendment.[222] However, as the four dissenters protested, "[s]tatutes authorizing unreasonable searches were the core concern of the Framers of the Fourth Amendment."[223] Moreover, whereas a judicial officer's authorization of a search only "authorizes a single search under particular circumstances,"[224] "a legislature's unreasonable authorization of searches may affect thousands or millions" and therefore surely "poses a greater threat to liberty."[225]

The Court also applied the reasoning of *Leon* (and *Krull*) to the facts in *Arizona v. Evans*.[226] Defendant had been taken into custody because a patrol car's computer indicated he had an outstanding arrest warrant. In fact, the arrest warrant had been quashed several weeks earlier because of defendant's voluntary appearance in court. Evidently the court clerk had not notified the sheriff's department so that the warrant could be removed from the computer records.

The Court ruled the evidence admissible: "[T]here is no basis for believing that application of the exclusionary rule in these circumstances will have a significant effect on court employees responsible for informing the police that a warrant has been quashed."[227] But dissenting Justice Ginsburg argued that "[w]hether particular records are maintained by the police or the courts should not be dispositive where a single computer database can answer all calls."[228] Moreover, not only is the

---

that 'when law enforcement officers have acted in objective good faith or their transgressions have been minor, the magnitude of the benefit conferred on such guilty defendants offends basic concepts of the criminal justice system.'" 1 LaFave, *supra* note 207, at 93, quoting 468 U.S. at 908 (opinion of the Court by White, J.).

[221] 1 LaFave, *supra* note 207, at 93.

[222] 480 U.S. 340 (1987). The invalid statute had authorized warrantless inspections of the records of licensed motor vehicles and vehicular parts sellers.

[223] *Id.* at 362 (O'Connor, J., joined by Brennan, Marshall and Stevens, J. dissenting).

[224] *Id.* at 365.

[225] *Id.*

[226] 514 U.S. 1 (1995).

[227] *Id.* at 15.

[228] *Id.* at 29 (Ginsburg, J., joined by Stevens, J., dissenting).

distinction between court clerk and police clerk "artificial," in practice it is difficult to tell which official "caused the error to exist or to persist."[229]

As *Pennsylvania Board of Probation v. Scott*[230] illustrates, the Rehnquist Court has also continued to decline to apply the exclusionary rule to proceedings other than criminal prosecutions. But the reasoning of the Court leaves a good deal to be desired.

The officers who conducted the warrantless and apparently suspicionless search of Scott's home did so because they thought he might be keeping firearms there, a violation of one of the conditions of his parole as well as a crime. The officers *knew* that Scottt was a parolee. They themselves were parole officers. If Scott did turn out to possess firearms (and he did), the officers probably contemplated a revocation proceeding rather than a criminal prosecution. For, as the Supreme Court observed some thirty years ago, a parole revocation "is often preferred to a new prosecution because of the procedural ease of recommitting the individual on the basis of a lesser showing by the State."[231]

The *Scott* majority declined to apply the exclusionary rule, reminding us that the rule need not apply "in every instance in which it might provide marginal deterrence."[232] As Justice Souter pointed out for the dissenters, however, when the searching officers know, as these officers did, that the subject of their search is a parolee (or probationer), there is *nothing* "marginal" or "incremental" about application of the exclusionary rule. For the officers most likely assumed (and correctly so) that the revocation hearing would be *the only proceeding* in which the evidence would ever be offered.[233]

2. *The Fourth Amendment Is Subjected to a Prolonged Campaign of "Guerilla Warfare"*[234]

Narrowing the thrust of the exclusionary rule, that is, restricting the circumstances in which evidence obtained in violation of the Fourth Amendment must be excluded, is only one way to reduce the impact of *Weeks* and of *Mapp*. Another way is to shrink the scope of the Amendment itself, *e.g.*, to dilute what amounts to "probable cause" to arrest or to search; to take a grudging view of what constitutes a "search" or "seizure"; and to make it easy to establish "consent" to what otherwise would be an illegal search. These developments, too, give the police more

---

[229] *Id.*

[230] 524 U.S. 357 (1998).

[231] Morrissey v. Brewer, 408 U.S. 471, 479 (1972).

[232] *Id.* at 368.

[233] *Id.* at 374 (Souter, J., joined by Ginsburg and Breyer, J J., dissenting). Justice Stevens also wrote a separate dissenting opinion.

[234] *See* text at note 236 *infra* and accompanying footnote.

leeway to investigate crime and the defendant fewer opportunities to invoke the exclusionary rule.

On a few occasions the post-Warren Court did decide some search-and-seizure cases in favor of the defense,[235] but in the main it substantially reduced the impact of the exclusionary rule *both* by cutting back on the application of the rule itself *and by* downsizing the scope of the protection against unreasonable search and seizure.

What Albert Alschuler said of the Burger Court when it came to an end applies to the Rehnquist Court as well. And Professor Alschuler's observation applies with special force to the law of search and seizure:

> In place of the expected counterrevolution, the Burger Court waged a prolonged and rather bloody campaign of guerilla warfare. It typically left the facade of Warren Court decisions standing while it attacked those decisions from the sides and underneath.[236]

A few examples follow:

The heart of the Fourth Amendment is "probable cause." *Illinois v. Gates*[237] dismantled the existing probable cause structure[238] in favor of a

---

[235] *See* Kyllo v. United States, 533 U.S. 27, 34 (2001) (holding that the use of a thermal imager or, more generally, any "sense-enhancing" technology to obtain "any information regarding the interior of the home that could not otherwise have been obtained without physical 'intrusion into a constitutionally protected area' constitutes a search—at least where (as here) the technology in question is not in general public use"); Tennessee v. Garner, 471 U.S. 1 (1985) (police slaying of an unarmed, nondangerous felon in order to prevent his escape constitutes an "unreasonable seizure" within meaning of the Fourth Amendment); Payton v. New York, 445 U.S. 573 (1980) (police must be armed with a warrant before entering a suspect's home to make a routine arrest); Gerstein v. Pugh, 420 U.S. 103 (1975) (with some exceptions, the Fourth Amendment requires a prompt judicial determination of probable cause as a condition for any significant pretrial restraint on a suspect's liberty).

[236] Albert Alschuler, *Failed Pragmatism: Reflections on the Burger Court*, 100 Harv. L.Rev. 1436, 1442 (1987). *Cf.* Carol S. Steiker, *Counter-Revolution in Constitutional Criminal Procedure? Two Audiences, Two Answers*, 94 Mich. L. Rev. 2466, 2527–28 (1996) (not only have the Burger and Rehnquist Courts "promulgat[ed] 'inclusionary rules' that made possible the admission of evidence that has been obtained through unconstitutional conduct of law enforcement agents," but by changing rules governing the standard of review on appeal and on federal habeas corpus it has made it harder for the erroneous admission of unconstitutionally obtained evidence at trial to lead to the overturning of convictions).

[237] 462 U.S. 213 (1983), criticized in Yale Kamisar, *Gates, "Probable Cause," "Good Faith," and Beyond*, 69 Iowa L. Rev. 557 (1984); Wayne R. LaFave, *Fourth Amendment Vagaries (of Improbable Cause, Imperceptible Plain View, Notorious Privacy, and Balancing Askew)*, 74 J. Crim. L. & Criminology 1171, 1188–89 (1983); and Silas Wasserstrom, *The Incredible Shrinking Fourth Amendment*, 21 Am. Crim. L. Rev. 257, 329–40 (1984).

[238] The existing structure was known as the "two-pronged test," which consisted of the "veracity" prong and the "basis of knowledge" prong. Concurring in the judgment in

mushy "totality of the circumstances" test. The Court emphasized that it viewed "probable cause" as "a fluid concept—turning on the assessment of probabilities in particular factual contexts—not readily, or even usefully, reduced to a neat set of legal rules."[239] The *Gates* Court made it fairly clear that "probable cause" is *something less* than "more probable than not" (although how much less is anything but clear). At one point the Court told us that "probable cause requires only a probability or *substantial chance* of criminal activity."[240]

Moreover, because the rulings of magistrates are entitled to considerable deference, the issuing magistrate does not have to be right. It is enough that the magistrate had a "substantial basis" for believing probable cause existed.[241] When one combines *Gates* with *Leon*, decided a year later, the result is that "[u]nlawfully seized evidence [becomes] admissible when a police officer could have reasonably believed that a magistrate could have reasonably believed that a person could have reasonably believed that a search would uncover evidence of a crime."[242]

Police activity is not subject to any constitutional restraints if the activity does not amount to a "search" or "seizure." Both the Burger and Rehnquist Courts have taken a narrow, stingy view of these key terms.

Consider *California v. Greenwood*.[243] A garbage bag is a common repository for personal effects and a search of such bags can reveal intimate details about one's business dealings, political activities, sexual practices and personal hygiene. Yet *Greenwood* held that the police may tear open the sealed opaque trash bags people place at the curb for garbage pick-up and examine their contents for evidence of crime without engaging in a "search."[244]

Gates, Justice White summed up the two-pronged test as follows: "First, an affidavit based on an informant's tip, standing alone, cannot provide probable cause for issuance of a warrant unless the tip includes information that apprises the magistrate of the informant's basis for concluding that the contraband is where he claims it is (the 'basis of knowledge' prong) *and* the affiant informs the magistrate that the informant is credible (the 'veracity' prong)." *Id.* at 267.

[239] *Id.* at 232.

[240] *Id.* at 244 note 13 (emphasis added).

[241] *See id.* at 238–39.

[242] Alschuler, *supra* note 236, at 1445. *See also* Kamisar, *supra* note 237, at 589.

[243] 486 U.S. 35 (1988).

[244] It is unclear to what extent *Greenwood* is grounded on the notion that one has no legitimate expectation of privacy in materials one voluntarily turns over to a third person or to what extent the decision turns on the fact that Mr. Greenwood left his garbage bags for collection on the curb—outside the curtilage of his home.

To say that the use of a police investigating technique, *e.g.*, police examination of a person's garbage or police aerial surveillance of a fenced-in backyard[245] or police use of a pen register[246] is not a "search" is a drastic move. For it means the police activity is completely uncontrolled by the Fourth Amendment. On the other hand, to conclude that a particular investigatory technique *is* a "search" is not a drastic move. For such a conclusion does not ban the investigative technique at issue altogether.[247]

The Court has not only taken a cramped view of what constitutes a "search." It has also given the crucial term "seizure" a narrow reading. According to *Florida v. Bostick*,[248] if armed police board an interstate bus at a scheduled intermediate stop, announce their mission is to detect drug traffickers, randomly approach a passenger, ask to see his bus ticket and driver's license, and then ask permission to search his luggage, no "seizure" has taken place. Under these circumstances, with two armed officers filling the aisle and towering over him, we are supposed to believe that a reasonable person would feel free to terminate the encounter or to ignore the police presence and to return to what he was doing—for example, go back to reading his newspaper or working on his crossword puzzle.

Although the post-Warren Court has taken a grudging view of what amounts to a "search" or "seizure," it has taken a very relaxed view of what constitutes a consent to an otherwise illegal search or seizure. "Consent" is law enforcement's trump card. It is the easiest and most propitious way for the police to avoid the problems presented by the Fourth Amendment. Thus, the protection afforded by the Amendment will vary greatly depending on how difficult or easy it is for the police to establish consent. *Schneckloth v. Bustamonte*[249] made it all too easy.

If an officer lacks authority to conduct a search, he may request permission to search, but he cannot *demand* it. To many people who confront the police, however, the distinction is very thin—or nonexis-

---

[245] *See* California v. Ciraolo, 476 U.S. 207 (1986).

[246] Smith v. Maryland, 442 U.S. 735 (1979). The ruling that the government's use of a pen register, a device that records all numbers dialed from a given phone and the time they were dialed, is not a "search" or "seizure" was based on the ground that one who uses a phone "assumes the risk" the phone company will tell the government the numbers a person dialed.

[247] For example, one might conclude that the examination of the contents of sealed trash bags is a "search," but that it is not bounded by the same limitations applicable to a search of one's dwelling. Thus, although classified as a "search," police examination of sealed trash might not require traditional probable cause.

[248] 501 U.S. 429 (1991).

[249] 412 U.S. 218 (1973).

tent. "[W]hat on their face are merely words of request take on color from the officer's uniform, badge, gun and demeanor."[250]

All the police need do to make the distinction between "request" and "demand" meaningful is to advise a person that she has the right to refuse an officer's "request" and that such a refusal will be respected. But the *Schneckloth* Court dismissed such a requirement as "thoroughly impractical."[251] That such a warning would undermine what the Court called "the legitimate need for [consent] searches"[252] is quite clear; that such a warning would be "impractical" (as that word is normally defined) is not at all clear.

Now that *Schneckloth* is on the books, a person may effectively consent to a search even though she was never informed—and the government has failed to demonstrate that she was ever aware—that she had the right to refuse the officer's "request" to search her person, automobile, or home. After *Schneckloth*, the criminal justice system, in one important respect at least, does (to borrow a phrase from the *Escobedo* case) "depend for its continued effectiveness on the citizens' abdication through unawareness of their constitutional rights."[253]

The *Schneckloth* approach to consent searches reappeared in *Ohio v. Robinette*.[254] After stopping the defendant for speeding, issuing a verbal warning, and returning his license, Deputy Sheriff Newsome—who has enjoyed remarkable success in getting motorists to consent to searches of their cars[255]—added "One question before you get gone. Are you carrying any illegal contraband in your car? Any weapon of any kind, drugs, anything like that?"[256]

When the defendant replied in the negative, the deputy asked whether he could search the car. The defendant said he could. The search turned up a small amount of drugs. The Ohio Supreme Court held that the evidence should have been excluded because the defen-

---

[250] Caleb Foote, *The Fourth Amendment: Obstacle or Necessity in the Law of Arrest* 51 J. Crim. L. and Criminology and Police Sci., 402, 403 (1960).

[251] 412 U.S. at 231.

[252] *Id.* at 227.

[253] *Cf.* Escobedo v. Illinois, 378 U.S. 478, 490 (1964).

[254] 519 U.S. 33 (1996).

[255] Newsome testified that it was his routine practice to ask permission to search a motorist's car during a traffic stop. When asked in another case why he did so, he replied: "I need the practice." State v. Retherford, 639 N.E.2d 498, 502 (Ohio Ct. App. 1994). He has had a lot of practice. In one year alone he requested, and obtained consent to, a search incident to a traffic stop more than 750 times. *See id.* at 503 note 3.

[256] *Robinette*, 519 U.S. at 35–36.

dant's consent was obtained during an illegal detention (*after* every
aspect of the traffic stop had been brought to a conclusion) and the drugs
found were a product of that unlawful detention.[257] In order to prevent
the police from turning a routine stop "into a fishing expedition for
unrelated criminal activity," and to assure that the encounter immediately following the completion of the business relating to the traffic stop
would be truly consensual, the Ohio court required the following: *When
the police have completed the business of the traffic stop*, any attempt to
search a vehicle about an unrelated crime must be preceded by a police
warning: "At this time you are legally free to go" (or words to this
effect).[258]

It strikes me that the Ohio Supreme Court made a valiant effort to
deal with a practice that is hard to square with the Fourth Amendment.
However, to almost no one's surprise, the U.S. Supreme Court reversed.
Chief Justice Rehnquist, who wrote the majority opinion, thought it
would be "unrealistic" to require police officers to tell motorists detained
for traffic violations that they were "free to go" before asking them
whether they would consent to a search of their cars.[259]

Why would it be unrealistic? Keep in mind that Deputy Newsome,
and many other officers as well, routinely ask motorists who have been
stopped for a traffic violation and are about to leave, a series of questions
before asking whether they will consent to a search of their cars. It is
hard to see why advising a once-detained motorist that he is free to leave
is any more time-consuming or burdensome than the technique Newsome and his colleagues use in *working their way up* to asking a motorist
to consent to a search.

There is also the matter of third-party consent searches. *Illinois v.
Rodriguez*[260] tells us that a warrantless entry of one's home is valid when
the police reasonably, but mistakenly, believe that a third party (in this
case, a girlfriend of defendant who had in fact moved out of his
apartment) possesses common authority over the premises. Thus, even
though (a) no magistrate authorizes the search, (b) no probable cause
supports the search, and (c) no exigency requires quick action, the police
may enter a person's home on the basis of the "seeming consent" of a
third party.

---

[257] State v. Robinette, 653 N.E.2d 695, 698–99 (Ohio 1995).

[258] *Id.* at 696, quoted in *Robinette*, 519 U.S. at 36.

[259] *See Robinette*, 519 U.S. at 40.

[260] 497 U.S. 177 (1990). For extensive criticism of this case, *see* Thomas Y. Davies,
*Denying a Right by Disregarding Doctrine: How Illinois v. Rodriguez Demeans Consent,
Trivializes Fourth Amendment Reasonableness, and Exaggerates the Excusability of Police
Error*, 59 Tenn. L. Rev. 1 (1991). *See also* Tracey Maclin, *Justice Thurgood Marshall:
Taking the Fourth Amendment Seriously*, 77 Cornell L. Rev. 723, 796–99 (1992).

The *Rodriguez* dissenters forcefully argued that when confronted with the choice of either relying on the consent of a third party or obtaining a warrant, the police "should secure a warrant and must therefore accept the risk of error should they instead choose to rely on consent."[261] But the majority was not impressed. "What [a person] is assured by the Fourth Amendment," observed Justice Scalia, "is not that no government search of his house will occur unless he consents; but that no such search will occur that is 'unreasonable' "[262]—and a search is not unreasonable when the police "reasonably (though erroneously) believe that the person who has consented to their entry is a resident of the premises."[263]

New York Times columnist William Safire once said that "a strong reason must exist for commuters to go into hock to buy a car, to sweat out traffic jams [and] to groan over repair bills" and the reason is "the blessed orneriness called privacy."[264] Evidently, the post-Warren Court does not agree. For in the thirty-five years since Chief Justice Warren stepped down from the Court, the privacy the Fourth Amendment affords motorists has greatly diminished.

A goodly number of Supreme Court cases can be cited in support of this statement.[265] Ironically, the best case may be one where the police

---

[261] 497 U.S. at 193 (Marshall, J., joined by Brennan and Stevens, JJ., dissenting).

[262] *Id*. at 183.

[263] *Id*. at 187.

[264] Quoted in Lewis Katz, *Automobile Searches and Diminished Expectations in the Warrant Clause*, 19 Am. Crim. L. Rev. 557, 571 note 79 (1982). *See also* the discussion of how private automobile transportation has shaped American society in David A. Harris, *Car Wars: The Fourth Amendment's Death on the Highway*, 66 Geo. Wash. L. Rev. 556, 576–78 (1998).

[265] *See, e.g.*, California v. Acevedo, 500 U.S. 565 (1991) (whether the police have probable cause to believe that drugs are somewhere in a car and come upon a closed container that just happens to be there, or whether the probable cause has focused on a container that just happens to be in the vehicle, the police may make a warrantless search of the container, even if found in the locked car trunk); New York v. Belton, 453 U.S. 454 (1981) (even though police lack any reason to believe that a car contains evidence of crime, if they have adequate grounds to make a custodial arrest of driver they may make a warrantless search of the entire interior or passenger compartment of the car, including closed containers, whether or not the driver has been removed from the car and handcuffed); Thornton v. United States, 541 U.S. 615 (2004) (*Belton* rule, *supra*, applies even when an officer does not make contact with the arrestee until he has already left the vehicle); Maryland v. Pringle, 540 U.S. 366 (2003) (finding of drugs in backseat armrest of car validly stopped for traffic offense gives police probable cause to believe that front-seat passenger (and apparently all passengers in car) is guilty of possessing a controlled substance); Maryland v. Wilson, 519 U.S. 408 (1997) (police may order all passengers, as well as the driver, out of a lawfully stopped car absent any particularized suspicion that any occupant of the car is armed or dangerous).

undeniably had lawful grounds to stop the car. (*e.g.*, there is no question the police had probable cause to believe that various provisions of the traffic code, such as speeding and turning without signaling, had been violated.)[266]

The *Whren* defendants conceded they had violated certain provisions of the local traffic code. But they maintained that, given the enormous multitude of traffic and vehicular equipment regulations and the ease with which the police may find *anybody* violating one or more of them, allowing mere observation of a minor traffic offense automatically to justify a stop or arrest gives the police a great temptation to use traffic enforcement as a means of investigating other more serious violations as to which *no individual suspicion exists*. Probable cause as to a minor traffic violation can be so easily come by, argued the defendants, that its existence provides no effective protection against arbitrary police action.[267]

Therefore, contended the defendants, the Court should adopt a *"would have"* test, under which a traffic stop or arrest satisfies the Fourth Amendment *only if* a reasonable police officer *would have* been motivated to stop the car or arrest the motorist by a desire to enforce the traffic laws or—to put it another way—police action violates the Fourth Amendment if a reasonable officer would not have taken the action she did but for an underlying purpose or motivation that, *standing alone*, could not provide a lawful basis for the police action.

Applying this test to the facts of the *Whren* case would have been easy. The arresting officers were *plainclothes vice squad officers* in unmarked cars, patrolling what they call a "high drug area" of Washington, D.C.[268] District of Columbia police regulations permit plainclothes officers in unmarked cars to enforce traffic law *only when* the violation is "so grave as to pose an *immediate threat* to the safety of others"[269]—and that is a far cry from the violations that occurred in *Whren*.

---

[266] Whren v. United States, 517 U.S. 806 (1996).

[267] Moreover, there is reason to think that the police use *the pretext* of traffic enforcement to harass motorists because of the length of their hair, the style of their clothing, or the color of their skin. *See* Angela J. Davis, *Race, Cops and Traffic Stops*, 51 U. Miami L. Rev. 425 (1997); David A Harris, *"Driving While Black" and All Other Traffic Offenses: The Supreme Court and Pretextual Traffic Stops*, 87 J. Crim. L. & Criminology 544 (1997); Tracey Maclin, *"Black and Blue Encounters"—Some Preliminary Thoughts about Fourth Amendment Seizures: Should Race Matter?*, 26 Va. U. L. Rev. 243 (1991); David A. Sklansky, *Traffic Stops, Minority Motorists, and the Future of the Fourth Amendment*, 1997 Sup.Ct.Rev. 271.

[268] *Whren*, 517 U.S. at 808.

[269] *Id.* at 815 (quoting the Metropolitan Police Department, Washington, D.C., General Order).

But the Court, per Justice Scalia, rejected this approach (and, surprisingly, without a dissent). It held that a traffic stop or arrest is permissible so long as an officer in the same circumstances *could have* made the stop or arrest (because the officer had observed a traffic violation) *regardless* of whether a reasonable officer *would have* made the stop or arrest *had there not been* some reason or motivation beyond the traffic offense (such as a hunch that the driver or a passenger had drugs or guns in his possession).

After *Whren*, a traffic stop supported by adequate grounds to believe that a violation occurred satisfies the Fourth Amendment *whatever* the motives of the police, *whatever* internal police regulations may have to say about enforcing the traffic laws and *whatever* the usual or routine practice of the police department. In short, after *Whren* there is *no such thing* as a pretextual traffic stop.

As William Stuntz has observed:

In a world where trivial crimes stay on the books, or one where routine traffic offenses count as crimes, the requirement of probable cause to arrest may mean almost nothing. Officers can arrest for a minor offense—everyone violates the traffic rules—in order to search or question a suspect on a major one. This allows arrests and searches of suspected drug dealers without any ex ante support for the suspicion, the very thing the probable cause standard is supposed to forbid.[270]

3. *Revising Cardozo's Famous Epigram*

More than three-quarters of a century ago, when Cardozo delivered his memorable one liner about the criminal "go[ing] free because the constable has blundered,"[271] and even in 1961, when the Court imposed the exclusionary rule on the states as a matter of Fourteenth Amendment Due Process, the law of search and seizure probably did unduly restrict the police—*on paper*. But this is no longer true.

Mapp has had a large impact. Whether or not the Warren Court intended this result or foresaw it, *Mapp* and its progeny have greatly clarified and simplified the law of search and seizure—especially in favor of the police. Because the thrust of the exclusionary rule and the scope of the protection provided by the Fourth Amendment have been so narrowed, and the room the police have to maneuver safely so enlarged, Cardozo's famous epigram is outdated. Nowadays, the criminal rarely, if ever, "goes free" because the constable has made an honest blunder or a

---

[270] William J. Stuntz, *The Uneasy Relationship Between Criminal Procedure and Criminal Justice*, 107 Yale L.J. 1, 7 (1997). *See also* Harris, *supra* note 264, at 559–60.

[271] *See* note 54 *supra*.

technical one. If the criminal does go free it is most likely because the constable has *flouted* the Fourth Amendment—has blundered *badly*.

A Final Comment

A critic of *Mapp* might take all the search-and-seizure cases I have discussed in the previous section (as well as others I have not) and throw them back at proponents of the exclusionary rule. These cases demonstrate, she might say, that the rule puts tremendous pressure on the courts to avoid "freeing a guilty defendant." If *Mapp* had never imposed the rule on the states, she might argue, the Fourth Amendment would never have been construed as narrowly as it has been.

Thus, Judge Guido Calabresi recently observed:

[L]iberals ought to hate the exclusionary rule because the exclusionary rule, in my experience, is most responsible for the deep decline in privacy rights in the United States. Indeed, the existence of the exclusionary rule has been the reason for more diminutions in privacy protection than anything else going on today.

* * *

Judges—politicians' claim to the contrary notwithstanding—are not in the business of letting people out on technicalities. If anything, judges are in the business of keeping people who are guilty *in* on technicalities. . . .

This means that in any close case, a judge will decide that the search, the seizure, or the invasion of privacy was reasonable. That case then becomes the precedent for the next case. The next close case comes up and the precedent is applied: same thing, same thumb on the scale, same decision. The hydraulic effect, . . . or the slippery slope means that courts keep expanding what is deemed a *reasonable* search or seizure.[272]

But critics of the exclusionary rule overlook that *any effective alternative* to the exclusionary rule, such as a meaningful tort remedy or administrative sanction, would also exert strong pressure to make the rules governing search and seizure more "police-friendly."[273]

---

[272] *See* Calabresi, *supra* note 82; Slobogin, *supra* note 82.

[273] If civil law suits against offending police officers were the primary means of enforcing the Fourth Amendment, there would be great pressure to find the challenged search "reasonable." The same would be true if the primary means of enforcement were departmental discipline. The reason is that if damages were awarded with some regularity against officers who violated the Fourth Amendment or if they were suspended without pay or required to pay substantial fines, the police "would be afraid to conduct the searches they should make." Myron W. Orfield, Jr., Comment, *The Exclusionary Rule and Deterrence: An Empirical Study of Chicago Narcotics Officers*, 54 U. Chi. L. Rev. 1016, 1053

As Monrad Paulsen noted on the eve of the *Mapp* case:

Whenever the rules are enforced by meaningful sanctions, our attention is drawn to their content. The comfort of Freedom's words spoken in the abstract is always disturbed by their applications to a contested instance. Any rule of police regulation enforced in fact will generate pressure to weaken the rule.[274]

There is no denying that one of the effects of the exclusionary rule has been to diminish the protection the Fourth Amendment once provided—*on paper*. But a down-sized Fourth Amendment that is taken seriously is still a good deal better than an expansive, majestic Fourth Amendment that exists only in a theoretical world. Moreover, diminution of the Fourth Amendment's scope is undoubtedly the price we would have to pay for *any* means of enforcing the Amendment that had a bite—for *any* remedy that actually worked.

As the previous section of this paper spells out at some length, that price *has been* paid. However unrealistic search and seizure requirements may once have been, to a greater degree than ever before, they are no longer "obstacle[s] in a game but only a protection against arbitrary and capricious police action."[275] That is why the case for retaining the exclusionary rule today is even stronger than the case for adopting it was in 1914 or 1961.

(1987). *See also* William J. Stuntz, *The Virtues and Vices of the Exclusionary Rule*, 20 Harv. J.L. & Pub. Pol'y 443, 445 (1997): "[T]he usual legal tools [for enforcing the Fourth Amendment]—damages, fines, criminal punishment—are likely to cause more harm than good. If an officer faces serious loss whenever he makes a bad arrest, he will make fewer bad arrests, but also many fewer good ones."

[274] Paulsen, *supra* note 171, at 256.

[275] Paulsen, *supra* note 152, at 66.

*

3

Gideon v. Wainwright and *Strickland v. Washington*: Broken Promises

by David Cole*

With the possible exception of *Miranda v. Arizona*, no case in constitutional criminal procedure is as well known as *Gideon v. Wainwright*, the Supreme Court's 1963 decision declaring that indigent defendants in serious criminal cases have a right to a lawyer paid for by the state. Gideon's case was the subject of a popular book by former New York Times columnist Anthony Lewis, *Gideon's Trumpet*. Lewis's book was in turn made into a Hollywood movie, with Henry Fonda starring as Clarence Earl Gideon, the drifter whose case made it to the Supreme Court. Indeed, Gideon's story is so classic that if one didn't know it was true, one would assume that a Hollywood script writer conjured it up.

Gideon, an unemployed Floridian, was convicted in 1961 of breaking and entering a poolroom and attempting to steal money from a vending machine. He could not afford a lawyer at trial, and neither Florida nor federal law at the time guaranteed him a lawyer at the state's expense. He defended himself, and was found guilty. From his cell, Gideon scribbled a note and mailed it to the Supreme Court objecting to the fact that he was denied a lawyer in his trial. The Supreme Court receives over one thousand appeal requests each year, and virtually all of them are rejected, even when filed by well-heeled law firm lawyers. But the Court treated Gideon's handwritten note as a "petition for certiorari," and granted the petition, thereby agreeing to decide Gideon's case. It then appointed Abe Fortas, one of the most respected lawyers in the nation—and later a Supreme Court Justice himself—to represent Gideon in his appeal before the Supreme Court. Fortas, a name partner with the eminent Washington law firm of Arnold, Fortas and Porter, asked a law student working as a summer associate to help him on the case. The

* Some of the material in this chapter is adapted from material in David Cole, *No Equal Justice: Race and Class in the American Criminal Justice System* (New Press, 1999). I am indebted to my research assistant, Brian Baak, for excellent research in connection with this chapter.

student, John Hart Ely, was unknown at the time, but would go on to become one of the nation's leading constitutional scholars, teaching at Yale Law School, serving as dean of Stanford Law School, and writing one of the most influential books ever written on American constitutional law.[1] The Court then ruled that the Sixth Amendment guarantees all indigent criminal defendants the assistance of a lawyer paid for by the state. On retrial, represented by a lawyer, Gideon was acquitted.

Gideon's story reaffirms all that is best in the American justice system. Like Horatio Alger, Gideon prevailed over poverty—not by making himself lots of money, but by establishing the most important right in the criminal justice system. His story illustrates that the justice system can work for the most vulnerable among us, and his efforts led to the recognition of a formal constitutional right that makes that possible. And as he was acquitted on retrial, his is the story of an innocent man, wrongly accused, and ultimately vindicated with the help of the most powerful institution in American law.

In addition, the right recognized in *Gideon* is critical to perhaps the central premise of the American criminal justice system—the promise of equal treatment. As long as the rich could hire lawyers and the poor had to do without, the promise that all are "equal before the law" was patently illusory. Thus, while the right to counsel acknowledged in *Gideon* was explicitly founded on the Sixth Amendment, it was at least as much grounded in the guarantee of equality.

But the real story of the right to counsel is not Gideon's, but that of David Leroy Washington, a far less sympathetic protagonist with a far less satisfying story. No movies were made out of Washington's case, and to date no one has sought to write a book about it. But in a very real sense, it is Washington's case, *Strickland v. Washington*, decided in 1984, that determined the actual content of the right to counsel for the poor. Because he was tried after *Gideon* was decided, Washington had a lawyer paid for by the state; his claim was not that he lacked any representation, but that he lacked *effective* representation. In *Strickland v. Washington*, the Supreme Court affirmed that the right to counsel means the right to *effective assistance* of counsel. But it established a standard of "effectiveness" that virtually assures that the poor are *not* in fact guaranteed competent representation. If *Gideon* offers the promise of justice winning out over poverty, *Strickland* breaks that promise, allowing the forces of inequality to triumph as only the empty symbol of equality survives.

Gideon has certainly made a difference. Whenever the state seeks to take a criminal defendant's liberty, it must appoint him a lawyer. But despite the promise of "effective assistance" set forth in *Strickland*, in

---

[1] John Hart Ely, *Democracy and Distrust: A Theory of Judicial Review* (1980).

actuality as long as the state provides a warm body with a law degree and a bar admission, little else matters. Real estate lawyers with no criminal experience have been deemed competent to defend serious criminal cases, as have lawyers who have fallen asleep or been drunk during trial. Nothing in the Supreme Court's doctrine impels states to provide sufficient resources to defend the indigent competently, and all other incentives are to spend as little money as possible on lawyers for the poor. As a result, indigent defense counsel are generally underpaid, overworked, and given insufficient resources to conduct an adequate investigation and defense. And indigent defendants ultimately pay the price—with their freedom, and sometimes, their lives.

The numbers begin to tell the story. Nationwide, we spend more than $146.5 billion annually on criminal justice.[2] More than half of that goes to the police and prosecution, who together investigate, develop, and prosecute criminal cases. Indigent defense, by contrast, receives only 1.3 percent of annual federal criminal justice expenditures, and only two percent of total state and federal criminal justice expenditures.[3] We spend about twice as much on criminal prosecutors as we do on criminal defense counsel.[4] England and Wales spend about $34 per capita on indigent criminal defense; Americans spend only about $10 per capita.[5] Many states impose highly unrealistic caps on reimbursement for criminal defense—Illinois, for example, pays at most $150 for a misdemeanor case, and $1250 to defend a felony, rates so low that virtually no attorney will sign up for the work.[6] In 1990, Kentucky spent an average of only $162 on each indigent criminal case.[7] That came to a total of $11.4 million, approximately 1/1000 of the state budget, and four million dollars *less* than the University of Kentucky's athletic budget.[8] Meanwhile, public defenders are forced to carry impossible caseloads—in some parts of New York, public defenders handle as many as 1600 cases a

---

[2] Bureau of Justice Statistics, Sourcebook of Criminal Justice Statistics—2002, at 2 (Table 1.1) (reporting on figures from fiscal year 1999).

[3] Bureau of Justice Statistics, Sourcebook of Criminal Justice Statistics—1993, at 2 (Table 1.2) (reporting on total state and federal expenditure figures from fiscal year 1990); Bureau of Justice Statistics, Sourcebook of Criminal Justice Statistics—1996, at 14 (Table 1.12) (reporting on federal spending from fiscal year 1996).

[4] American Bar Assn, *Gideon's* Broken Promise: America's Continuing Quest for Equal Justice 14 (2004).

[5] *Id.* at 8.

[6] *Id.* at 9–10.

[7] Edward C. Monahan, Who Is Trying to Kill the Sixth Amendment?, Crim. Justice 24, 27 (Summer 1991).

[8] *Id.*

year; in Pennsylvania, eighteen public defenders were responsible for 8,000 cases in 2000.[9]

These shortcomings have been dutifully noted by various blue-ribbon commissions almost from the time *Gideon* was decided.[10] Yet we have made very little progress in making the promise of effective counsel a reality for the poor. The story of *Strickland* is the story of how and why the Supreme Court has failed to make good on the promise so dramatically made in *Gideon*. The Court is by no means the only culpable actor here; the political process must also bear substantial responsibility. But given the obvious lack of political clout of poor criminal defendants, and the very strong incentives to deny indigent defendants competent lawyers, the Court had a special obligation to ensure that the promise of equality it made in *Gideon* would be realized. By accepting a patently unacceptable status quo as the constitutional baseline for "effective" lawyering, the Court in *Strickland* practically guaranteed that indigent defendants would obtain effective assistance only through luck, not through a state-guaranteed right. Moreover, the failure to make good on *Gideon*'s promise is no mere mistake. Rather, it is perhaps the single most significant mechanism by which the courts and society ensure that the burden of ensuring rights is not fully borne by all in the United States.

Gideon: The Birth of a Right

The right declared in *Gideon v. Wainwright* was not born full-bloom in 1963. Like most rights, it developed over time, through a series of smaller steps, culminating in the right we now associate with *Gideon*. The starting point was not the Sixth Amendment to the Constitution, which guarantees that "In all criminal prosecutions, the accused shall enjoy the right ... to have the Assistance of Counsel for his defence,"

---

[9] ABA, *Gideon's* Broken Promise, *supra* note 4, at 17–18.

[10] *See* id.; Richard Klein & Robert Spangenberg, The Indigent Defense Crisis 10 (Aug. 1993) (prepared for ABA Section on Criminal Justice Ad Hoc Committee on the Indigent Defense Crisis) (discussing current crisis in indigent defense, and noting that the ABA issued similar reports in 1979, 1982, and 1986); President's Commission on Law Enforcement in Administration of Justice, The Challenge of Crime in a Free Society (128) (1967) (decrying gap between the ideal of a right to counsel for all and the reality of "assembly line justice"); National Legal Aid and Defendar Association, The Other Face of Justice (1973) (reporting that indigent defense systems are overburdened and underfunded); S. Krantz, D. Rossmann, P. Froyd & J. Hoffman, Right to Counsel in Criminal Cases (1976) (study undertaken for the Law Enforcement Assistance Administration criticizing underfunding of indigent criminal defense); Norman Lefstein, Criminal Defense Services for the Poor 2 (1982) (national study undertaken for the American Bar Association finding that "millions of persons in the United States who have a constitutional right to counsel are denied effective legal representation"); The American Bar Association, the National Legal Aid and Defender Association, Gideon Undone! The Crisis in Indigent Defense Funding 1–3 (1982) (finding that inadequate funding often leads to inadequate indigent representation).

but the Fourteenth Amendment, which merely provides in much more general terms that no person shall be deprived of life, liberty, or property without "due process of law."

The reason assistance of counsel began as a due process right was that the original understanding of the Sixth Amendment was much more limited. It was designed to bar federal courts from adopting the English common law practice, in which defendants facing felony charges were affirmatively *precluded* from having a lawyer, even if they were willing and able to pay for one. Twelve of the thirteen colonies had rejected that common law rule as a matter of state law.[11] The Sixth Amendment merely required the federal courts to do the same.

But the constitutional right to an attorney in federal criminal trials did not initially include the right to have the government pay for one's attorney. The Constitution generally does not obligate the government to provide affirmative assistance to those seeking to exercise constitutional rights. It says what the government *cannot* do, but does not generally tell the government what it *must* do. For example, while parents have a constitutional right to send their children to private schools,[12] indigent parents have no right to compel the government to pay private school tuition.

There are good arguments for treating the right to counsel in a criminal trial differently. The vast majority of criminal defendants are too poor to hire an attorney. About 80 percent of criminal defendants are indigent.[13] About three-quarters of all inmates in state prisons were represented by public defenders or some other publicly-provided attorney.[14] Without assistance, the vast majority of criminal defendants would simply go unrepresented. And that, in turn, would make a mockery of the adversarial process, which is predicated on arriving at the truth through a fair struggle. A persuasive argument can be made that a criminal proceeding is simply not fair unless both sides are represented by counsel. Moreover, the criminal justice system is predicated on the proposition that all are equal before the law, and that claim is difficult to sustain where only wealthy defendants have the help of a lawyer.

Over the years, attorneys arguing for the right to appointed counsel made all of these arguments. They contended that the Sixth Amendment guaranteed a right to appointed counsel paid for by the government. They objected that a trial without defense counsel was fundamentally

---

[11] Powell v. Alabama, 287 U.S. 45, 64–65 (1932).

[12] Pierce v. Society of Sisters, 268 U.S. 510 (1925).

[13] Caroline Wolf Harlow, Bureau of Justice Statistics, *Defense Counsel in Criminal Cases* 1 (Nov. 2000); Bureau of Justice Statistics, *Indigent Defense* 1 (Dec. 1995).

[14] *Id.*

unfair, in violation of the Fourteenth Amendment's Due Process Clause. And they claimed that allowing a criminal defendant's rights to turn on whether he had enough money to hire a lawyer contravened the Fourteenth Amendment's Equal Protection Clause. The right to counsel that the courts recognize today has its roots in all three arguments.

The Supreme Court's initial approach to this issue adopted a due process approach. In 1932, the Court reversed the convictions of nine young black men tried and convicted in Scottsboro, Alabama, on charges that they had raped two young white women on a freight train traveling from Chattanooga to Memphis.[15] The defendants, taken off the train at Scottsboro, narrowly escaped a lynch mob, but were then promptly sentenced to death within a matter of days, as thousands stood outside the courthouse door and cheered. The defendants could not afford counsel, so the judge appointed the whole bar of Scottsboro (six men) to represent them. Only one attorney agreed to do so, and he did so only on the morning of trial. Needless to say, he had no time to prepare or investigate the case. A group of concerned citizens from Chattanooga hired a Tennessee lawyer to assist the defendants, but he was unschooled in Alabama law, and met the defendants only moments before the trials began. After all eight defendants were sentenced to death by an all-white jury, the Communist Party took up the defendants' appeals, and transformed the Scottsboro case into a national and international cause celebre.

When the Scottsboro case reached the United States Supreme Court, the Court reversed the convictions on the ground that the defendants had been denied due process. It ruled that due process requires that a criminal trial be fundamentally fair, and that at least in the extreme circumstances presented, fundamental fairness required appointment of counsel. While the Scottsboro defendants were formally appointed lawyers, the Court found that the manner in which the counsel had been appointed was a charade.

The Scottsboro case was unique, however, and the Court made clear that its decision was limited to the especially strong facts presented: "All that it is necessary now to decide, as we do decide, is that in a capital case, where the defendant is unable to employ counsel, and is incapable adequately of making his own defense because of ignorance, feeble mindedness, illiteracy, or the like, it is the duty of the court, whether requested or not, to assign counsel for him as a necessary requisite of due process of law."[16] Thus, the Scottsboro case left unresolved whether

---

[15] The Scottsboro trial is the subject of a separate chapter in this volume. See Michael J. Klarman, *Powell v. Alabama: The Supreme Court Confronts "Legal Lynchings"*.

[16] Powell v. Alabama, 287 U.S. at 71.

appointed counsel would be required in non-capital cases, or in cases where the defendants were not "feeble minded."

Six years later, in *Johnson v. Zerbst*,[17] the Court held that in all *federal* criminal trials, the Sixth Amendment required the government to pay for a lawyer where the defendant could not afford one. The Court reasoned that the Sixth Amendment right to counsel "embodies a realistic recognition of the obvious truth that the average defendant does not have the professional legal skill to protect himself when brought before a tribunal with power to take his life and liberty."[18] However, since about 90% of criminal prosecutions are tried in state court, the *Johnson* decision, which applied only to federal trials, had limited effect. Just four years later, in 1942, the Court refused to extend the right to state criminal trials. The Sixth Amendment, like the rest of the original Bill of Rights, by its terms applies only to the federal government. Over time, the Court has interpreted the Fourteenth Amendment's Due Process Clause to "incorporate" and apply against the states those protections in the Bill of Rights that are "fundamental to ordered liberty." But in *Betts v. Brady*,[19] the Court held that the right to appointed counsel for the poor was not a "fundamental right." As a result, states remained free to prosecute and convict indigent defendants in one-sided proceedings in which the state was represented by a lawyer and the defendant was left to fend for himself.

Criminal defendants also challenged the denial of legal assistance on equal protection grounds. In 1956, the Supreme Court ruled for Judson Griffin, an indigent man convicted of armed robbery, who had been precluded from appealing his conviction because he could not afford to pay for the transcript from his trial. Stating that "there can be no equal justice where the kind of trial a man gets depends on the amount of money he has," the Supreme Court held that the state denied equal protection when it barred the defendant from appealing simply because he could not afford to pay the trial transcript fee.[20]

By the time Clarence Gideon's case reached the Supreme Court, the Court had already used the Sixth Amendment, the due process clause, and the Equal Protection Clause to address the problem of legal assistance for the poor in criminal cases. With this experience in mind, the Court in *Gideon* reversed *Betts v. Brady*, and held that the right to counsel for the poor was indeed a "fundamental right" applying to all criminal trials, state as well as federal. As Justice Harlan pointed out in

---

[17] 304 U.S. 458 (1938).

[18] 304 U.S. at 462–63.

[19] 316 U.S. 455 (1942).

[20] Griffin v. Illinois, 351 U.S. 12 (1956).

his concurring opinion, the ruling in *Gideon* was in some respect the organic outgrowth of the Court's initial step in the Scottsboro case. Since that case, the Court had found that an increasingly wide range of criminal trials without appointed counsel resulted in "fundamentally unfair" trials that violated due process. But the Scottsboro approach required time-consuming and inefficient case-by-case review, and failed to establish clear guidelines for lower courts or state legislatures regarding when appointment of counsel was required. The lesson of the Scottsboro approach, moreover, was that most serious cases required an attorney for the defendant if they were to be fair. At the same time, states had increasingly recognized a right to counsel in state criminal cases, so that Florida was a real outlier by the time *Gideon* was decided. In *Gideon*, the Court abandoned its case-by-case approach for a more easily administered across-the-board rule, reiterating the "obvious truth" it had previously recognized only for federal criminal trials: "that in our adversary system of criminal justice, any person haled into court, who is too poor to hire a lawyer, cannot be assured a fair trial unless counsel is provided for him."

Strickland: The Demise of a Right

If Clarence Earl Gideon's case was the ideal case to seek to establish the right to counsel, David Leroy Washington's was probably the worst possible case to set forth the parameters for effective assistance of counsel. On a two-week crime spree in September 1976, David Leroy Washington robbed and killed a minister because he was a homosexual; robbed and killed a woman in her home while her three elderly sisters-in-law watched while bound and gagged, and then shot all three of the sisters-in-law in the head; and kidnaped a man, stabbed him repeatedly, and eventually killed him.

When arrested and charged with capital murder and multiple related counts of robbery, breaking and entering, and kidnaping, Washington was appointed a public defender, Bill Tunkey. For a court-appointed lawyer, Tunkey was relatively experienced. He'd been a prosecutor for three years and a defense attorney for three and a half more. During that period, he estimated that he had handled over 1,000 cases as trial attorney. The judge who presided over Washington's post-conviction proceeding called Tunkey "one of the leading criminal defense attorneys in Dade County."[21] Other defendants facing death row have been appointed lawyers who have never tried a case in their lives, so at least in this regard, Washington was reasonably fortunate.

Washington was, to put it mildly, a difficult client. He repeatedly disregarded Tunkey's advice. Tunkey told him not to talk to the police,

---

[21] *Strickland v. Washington*, Appendix to Petition for Certiorari at A216.

but Washington disregarded that advice and confessed to all three murders. Tunkey recommended that Washington choose a jury trial, but Washington waived his jury trial right and pleaded guilty. And when Tunkey recommended that Washington invoke his right under Florida law to an advisory jury for capital sentencing, Washington again rejected the advice and waived that right as well.

At least initially, Washington had no complaints about Tunkey's performance. When he pleaded guilty, the trial judge asked Washington if he was satisfied with his attorney, and Washington responded, "I want to say this. I think this is about one of the best lawyers you could ever get." He went on to say that "if it was left up to him, he would fight this to the Supreme Court. But, I told him I would rather go ahead and plead because it don't make sense to try to hide it when I know I'm guilty."[22]

But that was before Washington was sentenced to death. Capital punishment trials are divided into two stages. The first decides guilt or innocence; Washington's plea made that stage unnecessary. The second, and generally more important stage, focuses solely on sentencing. At this stage, the jury (or judge in this case) is required to identify statutorily-specified "aggravating factors," which are supposed to identify the most heinous murders. Then the judge or jury must weigh the aggravating factors against any "mitigating factors" that the defendant chooses to put forward—a troubled childhood, drug, alcohol, or mental problems, evidence of good works, service to the country, behavior in prison, family connections, etc.—in short, anything that might make a judge or jury choose to spare the defendant's life, by issuing a sentence of life imprisonment instead of death.

Because guilt is often not a contested issue in death penalty cases, the lawyers' real work often focuses on preparation for the sentencing proceeding. That, after all, is where life and death are literally on the line. Life imprisonment is always a possibility, even with the most clearly guilty of defendants. Because the defendant can introduce literally any evidence he thinks might be helpful to him, preparation for sentencing requires a thorough investigation of the defendant's life history in order to find out what mitigating information might actually exist. Tunkey didn't do much. In his investigation for sentencing, he met with Washington in jail, and talked by phone to Washington's wife and mother, but never followed up with a face-to-face meeting. He pursued no other character witnesses. He did not request a psychiatric examination, a life history, or even a presentence investigation report. He subsequently explained that he chose not to present such evidence because that would "open the door" for the prosecution to present new evidence about Washington's criminal history or psychiatric state at

---

[22] *Strickland v. Washington*, Brief of Petitioner, 11–12.

sentencing, but he also complained that Washington's conduct left him feeling "hopeless," and that it was difficult to get in touch with Washington's family, seemingly inconsistent explanations for his actions.

In post-conviction proceedings, Washington's new lawyer argued that Tunkey had provided ineffective assistance of counsel. None of the lower courts found Tunkey's performance to be ineffective, but they disagreed markedly about what standard should govern whether counsel was indeed "ineffective." The Florida state courts and the federal district court adopted one standard, a panel of the U.S. Court of Appeals for the Fifth Circuit set forth a different standard, and the Fifth Circuit en banc imposed still a third test.[23] This confusion was emblematic of the disarray throughout the lower courts, and was attributable to the fact that while the Supreme Court had long suggested that defendants were entitled to "effective assistance" of counsel, it had never set forth any guidance for how to judge whether counsel was "effective."

The Supreme Court first intimated that the right to counsel implied "effective" assistance of counsel in its very first decision addressing the need for counsel—the Scottsboro case.[24] In that case, the defendants had been appointed lawyers, but in such a way as to preclude any meaningful representation. As noted above, the Court found that under the circumstances, the failure to provide effective assistance of counsel led to a fundamentally unfair proceeding in violation of due process. As long as the denial of counsel was conceived as a due process claim, it violated the defendant's rights only where it rendered the entire trial fundamentally unfair. Accordingly, under this due process approach, the analysis inevitably required a case-by-case evaluation of the whole trial, and of the role counsel played in the trial. Under this approach, most courts held that only when a lawyer's performance rendered the trial a "farce and mockery of justice" was due process infringed.[25]

In 1970, however, the Supreme Court ruled that the Sixth Amendment itself required a lawyer "within the range of competence demanded of attorneys in criminal cases."[26] If the right to effective assistance of counsel rested on the Sixth Amendment right to counsel rather than the Fifth Amendment right to a fair trial, a different standard for reviewing ineffectiveness claims seemed to be called for. Because the Fifth Amendment's concern is ultimately with a fair trial, analysis of a Fifth Amendment claim necessarily required review of the whole trial. But the Sixth

---

[23] *See* Strickland v. Washington, 466 U.S. 668 (1984), Brief for Petitioner, 76–82, and decisions cited therein.

[24] Powell v. Alabama, 287 U.S. 45 (1932).

[25] *See, e.g.,* Diggs v. Welch, 148 F.2d 667, 669 (D.C. Cir. 1945).

[26] McMann v. Richardson, 397 U.S. 759, 771 note 14 (1970).

Amendment right is much more specific—it guarantees the assistance of counsel in all criminal trials in which a sentence of incarceration is sought. Thus, assessing whether the Sixth Amendment was violated would not seem to require an assessment of the fairness of the whole trial, but simply of the attorney's performance therein.

In response to these arguments, courts began to develop a range of different tests for assessing Sixth Amendment claims of ineffective assistance of counsel. Some courts hewed to the "farce and mockery of justice" standard, not seeming even to acknowledge the shift to the Sixth Amendment analysis.[27] But the vast majority rejected that approach, and instead adopted a test that looked at two considerations: the attorney's performance; and the effect of the attorney's performance, often referred to as "prejudice." On the performance prong, most courts applied a kind of "malpractice" standard, requiring the defendant to show that his attorney's performance fell below the general range of competent lawyering.[28] But this was an extremely subjective inquiry, and simply accepted the status quo as "effective," whether it was or was not in fact of sufficient quality to provide an effective defense. Some courts adopted instead a "guidelines" approach, in which they tested the lawyer's conduct against a set of minimal duties or guidelines.[29] The standards most often looked to were those of the American Bar Association. For example, the Fourth Circuit required that a criminal defense attorney must at a minimum confer with his client promptly and as often as necessary to advise him of his rights and to elicit information regarding his defense, conduct appropriate investigations, both factual and legal, and allow himself sufficient time to prepare for trial.[30] Similarly, the California Supreme Court cited the ABA's Standards Relating to the Defense Function, and set forth a number of basic duties of all criminal defense counsel, including: a duty to investigate all defenses of fact and law that may be available; consulting with the client and advising him of his rights; seeking his release pending trial; and when appropriate, moving to suppress illegally obtained evidence and to obtain a pre-trial psychiatric examination.[31] Commentators virtually universally preferred the guidelines approach, because it was more susceptible to objective application and gave clear notice to attorneys and courts as to what was demanded. Critics argued that such an approach might lead to an over-

---

[27] United States v. Yanishefsky, 500 F.2d 1327, 1333 (2d Cir. 1974).

[28] J. Eric Smithburn & Theresa L. Springmann, *Effective Assistance of Counsel: In Quest of a Uniform Standard of Review*, 17 Wake Forest L. Rev. 497, 506–07 (1981).

[29] *Id.* at 507–08.

[30] Coles v. Peyton, 389 F.2d 224, 226 (4th Cir. 1968).

[31] People v. Pope, 23 Cal. 3d 412, 590 P.2d 859, 152 Cal. Rptr. 732 (1979).

bureaucratized approach to lawyering, in which attorneys were more concerned with checking off the tasks on the list than with doing the best job possible for their clients. But the guidelines were hardly the kind of straitjacket that would constrain a lawyer, and sought to do no more than identify what any lawyer would minimally have to do in order to prepare a competent defense.

There was also disagreement in the lower courts on the issue of "prejudice." Here, the disagreement centered around two issues: what sort of prejudice had to be shown, and who bore the burden on the prejudice issue. The vast majority of the courts, noting that the Supreme Court had identified the right to effective assistance as stemming from the Sixth Amendment right to counsel, required a showing that the counsel's deficient performance impaired the defense in a material way. A minority of courts required a much more difficult showing of prejudice—namely, a showing that the outcome of the trial would have been different had counsel been competent. By effectively requiring assessment of the whole trial, the latter test seemed to re-introduce through the back door the "farce and mockery of justice" standard that courts had largely rejected.

The lower courts also differed as to whether the defendant or the government should bear the burden to show prejudice or the absence thereof. Most courts, noting that information about a defense lawyer's performance was more likely to be accessible to the defendant than to the government, placed the burden on the defendant to show not only that the lawyer had been incompetent, but also that the incompetent performance had likely affected his defense in a material way.[32] But some courts put the burden on the government, maintaining that once a defendant showed that his attorney's performance was deficient, the government bore the burden of showing that the deficiency did not affect the result, much as the government must show "harmless error" when defendants identify other constitutional defects in their prosecution.[33]

Thus, when the Supreme Court finally took up the issue in *Strickland*, the lower courts' experience with this issue offered a variety of standards from which the Court might choose. In the end, it adopted a two-prong test, but notably chose the most pro-government of the existing standards on each prong. As to performance, the Court held that a defendant must show that his attorney's performance was "outside the wide range of professionally competent assistance."[34] It stressed that reviewing courts "must indulge a strong presumption that counsel's

---

[32] Smithburn & Springmann, *supra* note 28, at 510.

[33] *See, e.g.*, Coles v. Peyton, 389 F.2d at 227.

[34] *Strickland*, 466 U.S. at 690.

conduct falls within the wide range of reasonable professional assistance," and mandated a "highly deferential" standard of review.[35] Insisting that the Sixth Amendment was not designed to "improve the quality
of legal representation," the Court essentially limited claims of "ineffectiveness" to lawyering that fell substantially below the status quo norms
of criminal representation.[36] It rejected a guidelines approach as too
constraining.[37] And it warned that courts should avoid second-guessing
lawyers, and should generally defer to "tactical" judgments of defense
counsel, even if they were not the judgments the court might have made
in defense counsel's shoes.[38] With the possible exception of the "farce
and mockery" test that virtually every court had long rejected, this
standard was at least as onerous as any other court had defined the test
prior to *Strickland*.

The Court also imposed the most onerous existing standard on
defendants with regard to showing "prejudice." It not only squarely laid
the burden on defendants, but also required defendants to show not just
that the lawyer's deficient performance impaired the defense in a material way—the showing required by the majority of the lower courts at the
time—but a "reasonable probability that the result would have been
different" had counsel been competent.[39] This test essentially reverses
the usual "harmless error" analysis. For most constitutional violations,
courts indulge a presumption that the error infected the trial unless the
government can show that the error was harmless because the result
would have been the same without the error. For ineffectiveness claims,
by contrast, the presumption is that even abysmal lawyering has no
effect on the trial, unless the defendant can establish a reasonable
probability that the result would have been different with better lawyering. On issues like this, which by definition require speculation and
conjecture about counter-factuals ("what would have happened if . . .?"),
where the burden lies will often be determinative.

The bottom line is that short of embracing the "farce and mockery
of justice" standard, the Supreme Court in *Strickland* adopted the most
difficult existing test for defendants to meet with respect to ineffective
assistance claims. The Court was evidently driven by concerns about an
avalanche of such claims if the standard were too easy to meet. But the
Court seems to have wholly overlooked the danger on the other side of
the scale; namely, that atrocious lawyering would be excused as "effec-

[35] *Id.* at 689.

[36] *Id.*

[37] *Id.* at 688.

[38] *Id.* at 689–90, 699.

[39] *Id.* at 694.

tive" because the Court set the bar for "effective" so low. In fact, the Court's approach may have created the worst of all possible outcomes. Because the standard is fairly open-ended, and does not have the clarity of a "guidelines" approach, it does little to forestall the filing of ineffectiveness claims. And because the Court's standard uncritically accepts the status quo as "effective," it creates no incentive for states to improve on existing standards of legal representation for the poor. As the aftermath of *Strickland* demonstrates, that status quo is an embarrassment, and the Court's approach has only entrenched it.

The *Strickland* standard has proved virtually impossible to meet. Courts have declined to find ineffective assistance where defense counsel slept during portions of the trial,[40] where counsel used heroin and cocaine throughout the trial,[41] where counsel allowed his client to wear the same sweatshirt and shoes in court that the perpetrator was alleged to have worn on the day of the crime,[42] where counsel stated prior to trial that he was not prepared on the law or facts of the case,[43] and where counsel appointed in a capital case could not name a single Supreme Court decision on the death penalty.[44] In one case, a capital murder defendant's attorney was found effective even though he "consumed large amounts of alcohol each day of the trial ... drank in the morning, during court recess, and throughout the evening ... [and] was arrested [during jury selection] for driving to the courthouse with a .27 blood-alcohol content."[45]

Consider Gregory Wilson, on death row in Kentucky, Kentucky paid so little to lawyers defending indigents in capital punishment cases that the judge responsible for appointing a lawyer for Wilson hung a notice on the courthouse door that read, in capital letters, "PLEASE HELP—DESPERATE."[46] Local lawyer William Hagedorn responded. Wilson probably would have been better off without him. Hagedorn had never tried a death penalty case before. He had no office, and only a few out-of-date law books. He worked out of a room in his house that prominently featured a lighted "Budweiser" sign. A prosecution witness described Hagedorn as "a well-known drunk." Hagedorn filed only one pretrial

---

[40] People v. Tippins, 173 A.D.2d 512, 570 N.Y.S.2d 581 (N.Y. App. 1991).

[41] People v. Badia, 159 A.D.2d 577, 552 N.Y.S.2d 439 (N.Y. App. 1990).

[42] People v. Murphy, 96 A.D.2d 625, 464 N.Y.S.2d 882 (N.Y. App. 1983).

[43] People v. Dalton, 140 A.D.2d 993, 529 N.Y.S.2d 927 (N.Y. App. 1988).

[44] Stephen B. Bright, *Counsel for the Poor: The Death Sentence Not for the Worst Crime but for the Worst Lawyer*, 103 Yale L.J. 1835, 1839 (1994) (describing Birt v. Montgomery, 725 F.2d 587, 601 (11th Cir. 1984), *cert. denied*, 469 U.S. 874 (1984)).

[45] People v. Garrison, 765 P.2d 419, 47 Cal.3d 746 (Cal. 1989).

[46] Klein & Spangenberg, *Indigent Defense Crisis, supra* note 10, at 5–6.

motion, made no closing argument, didn't interview any of the other side's witnesses, and hired no experts. During the most crucial testimony in the case—that of the pathologist—Hagedorn wasn't even in the courtroom. Yet to date the courts have found Hagedorn's representation "effective."

Courts frequently excuse atrocious lawyering as a "tactical" decision, subject to deference under the Court's directive in *Strickland*. But as *Strickland* itself illustrated, almost any deficiency in performance can in hindsight be described as "strategic." Deborah Pilchak's lawyer, for example, made no opening statement to the jury, and did not object when the prosecutor introduced evidence of Pilchak's prior criminal convictions, which are generally inadmissible. Although the attorney was suffering from Alzheimer's disease during the trial, the court held that these lapses were not ineffective assistance, but "tactical decisions."[47] As one court has explained, "Even if many reasonable lawyers would not have done as defense counsel did at trial, no relief can be granted on ineffectiveness grounds unless it is shown that *no* reasonable lawyer, in the circumstances, would have done so."[48]

Courts also routinely deny ineffectiveness claims by finding that the defendant failed to demonstrate "prejudice." Assessing the damage that an incompetent attorney has done is extremely difficult, because the damage often will not show up on a cold record. The consequences of an attorney's failure to pursue a line of investigation, argument, or cross-examination are by definition speculative. And as capital defense attorney Stephen Bright has argued, the difference a good lawyer makes will often show up in such things as rapport with a defendant's family and witnesses, negotiating skills that may bring a favorable plea agreement, skilled questioning of prospective jurors, and pursuit of investigative leads—none of which will be apparent from the trial record.[49] It is particularly difficult to demonstrate prejudice where juries apply open-ended standards, as they do when they determine whether to impose a death sentence. How is a court to determine whether the jury might have struck a different balance between "mitigating" and "aggravating" factors had the attorney introduced a particular piece of mitigating evidence? As Justice Alan Handler of the New Jersey Supreme Court has noted, "as a judgment becomes more subjective, the task of assessing the extent to which that judgment might have been influenced by more competent representation becomes more difficult."[50] Yet courts routinely

---

[47] Pilchak v. Camper, 741 F. Supp. 782 (W.D. Mo. 1990), *aff'd*, 935 F.2d 145 (8th Cir. 1991).

[48] Rogers v. Zant, 13 F.3d 384, 386 (11th Cir. 1994).

[49] Stephen B. Bright, *Counsel for the Poor, supra* note 44, at 1864.

[50] State v. Davis, 561 A.2d 1082, 1116 (N.J. 1989) (Handler, J., dissenting).

reject ineffectiveness claims by finding no prejudice where a capital defendant's attorney failed to investigate or present mitigating evidence at sentencing.[51]

The same day that the Supreme Court decided *Strickland*, it also decided another "ineffective assistance" case, *United States v. Cronic*, which underscored both the low standard the Court had set for "effectiveness," and the Court's reluctance to entertain systemic challenges to indigent defense based on objective criteria such as the amount of resources or time that an appointed counsel is given to prepare her defense. Harrison Cronic did not face the death penalty, but his case was nonetheless quite complex. He was charged with fraudulent check kiting involving over nine million dollars. The government had spent four and one-half years investigating and preparing its case against Cronic. When Cronic's retained counsel withdrew from the case at the last minute, the judge appointed counsel for him: a real estate lawyer who had never tried a case to a jury before. The judge gave the newly appointed lawyer only 25 days to prepare a defense. Cronic was convicted, and sentenced to 25 years in prison.

The court of appeals in *Cronic* deemed it unnecessary to examine the trial record for specific errors committed by Cronic's lawyer because objective circumstances hade so hampered his preparation; as the court reasoned, "the prejudice from lack of preparation and experience cannot be nicely weighed."[52] The court accordngly looked to such objective factors as the time afforded Cronic's lawyer, the complexity of the case, and the lawyer's minimal experience, and determined that these factors made out a showing of ineffective assistance of counsel without regard to what transpired at trial.

The Supreme Court reversed, and in doing so rejected the court of appeals' approach.[53] The Court stated that absent extraordinary circumstances, such as the wholesale denial of counsel, or counsel's failure to subject the government's case to any adversarial testing at all, or the kind of sham appointment of counsel present in the Scottsboro case, the services of a defense lawyer must be presumed competent, and the defendant bears the burden of pointing to specific errors in the record to make out a claim of ineffective assistance. This result made any systemic challenges to the adequacy of counsel under the Sixth Amendment based on the inadequacy of funding and resources virtually impossible, and effectively required case-by-case adjudication of Sixth Amendment claims.[54]

---

[51] *See, e.g.*, Wilkerson v. Collins, 950 F.2d 1054, 1065 (5th Cir. 1992).

[52] United States v. Cronic, 675 F.2d 1126, 1128 (10th Cir. 1982).

[53] United States v. Cronic, 466 U.S. 648 (1984).

[54] As one commentator recently noted, "the *Strickland* standard is, by its nature, an ex post analysis; therefore, it cannot be used preemptively to challenge the effectiveness of an

As a result of the high bar set in *Strickland* and *Cronic*, ineffective assistance claims rarely succeed. Of 103 cases raising ineffective assistance claims in the California Supreme Court from January 1, 1989 through April 21, 1996, 94 were denied, 3 were remanded for further factual development, and only 6 were granted. Of 158 cases raising such claims in the United States Court of Appeals for the Fifth Circuit during the same period, 142 were denied, 10 remanded, and 6 granted. The message is clear: the vast majority of defense representation is adequate, and only a few extraordinary cases require reversal for ineffectiveness. In the end, the ineffectiveness standard does less to protect defendants from bad lawyers than it does to legitimate the poor quality of representation generally provided to criminal defendants. The fact that so few lawyers are deemed ineffective sends a message that the bulk of criminal defense representation is effective. And that in turn legitimates the skewed results of the criminal justice system, in which those who cannot afford to buy good representation are not likely to get it, and are therefore unlikely to have their constitutional claims effectively litigated.

Having an incompetent but not constitutionally "ineffective" attorney will often mean not only that a defendant's rights are less vigorously defended, but that the rights are forfeited altogether. This is because of a related doctrine, labeled "procedural default," which visits the sins and omissions of attorneys on their clients. Under this doctrine, if a lawyer fails to raise an objection or argument in a timely fashion, the client is barred from having *any* court rule on it, absent extraordinary circumstances. For example, Roger Keith Coleman was executed without obtaining appellate review of several legal arguments, because his attorney misinterpreted the local court rules, and filed his notice of appeal three days late.[55] Given the inadequate system of indigent defense that we maintain and tolerate, mistakes are entirely foreseeable. We are unwilling to pay for, and the Supreme Court has been unwilling to require, appointment of counsel who would make fewer mistakes. The ultimate

---

attorney, regardless of the limitations on time or resources that may hamper the attorney's ability to provide an adequate defense." Note, *Effectively Ineffective: The Failure of Courts to Address Underfunded Indigent Defense Systems*, 118 Harv. L. Rev. 1731, 1732 (2005). This statement overstates the problem somewhat, as the Scottsboro case illustrate; in extraordinary situations, limits on resources and time may be sufficient to establish ineffectiveness. However, the author of the Note goes on to illustrate that even in those rare instances where courts have undertaken systemic challenges to indigent defense systems, the cases have been "unable to facilitate long-term, sustainable reform." *Id.* at 1733, 1735–41.

[55] Coleman v. Thompson, 501 U.S. 722 (1991); Wainwright v. Sykes, 433 U.S. 72, 84–87 (1977).

cause of most mistakes, then, has absolutely nothing to do with the defendants themselves, and everything to do with our failure as a community—and the Court's failure as guardian of the process—to ensure that the indigent are adequately represented. The "procedural default" rules place the burden of those mistakes not on society, but on the indigent defendant.

Results: Indigent Defense Today

The Court's doctrine exerts no pressure on the political branches to fund indigent defense adequately. Since "ineffectiveness" will be found only where lawyering falls far below the status quo, there is literally no incentive to improve the status quo. And because good lawyering is costly, both because good lawyers can demand higher fees and because good lawyers file more motions and raise more legal issues in their clients' defense, states and the federal government have every incentive to cut corners on the funding of indigent defense. Finally, because the affected class consists of poor criminal defendants, overwhelmingly from minority communities, there is little or no political pressure to improve the situation.

How bad is the system of indigent defense today? The figures set forth in the opening of this essay show that whether you compare indigent defense funding to funding for prosecutors, to indigent defense funding in other countries, or to the amounts that lawyers can earn in other lines of legal work, the funding is abysmal. In 2004, more than 41 years after *Gideon v. Wainwright*, the American Bar Association issued a report on the right to counsel in criminal proceedings. It found that funding for indigent defense is "shamefully inadequate," and that indigent defense in the United States is in "a state of crisis, resulting in a system that lacks fundamental fairness and places poor persons at constant risk of wrongful conviction."[56]

In all, more than one-half of the states impose a per-case maximum fee for criminal cases.[57] In Kentucky, for example, the statutory maximum fee for defending a capital case is $12,500.[58] Studies have found that attorneys spend between 100 and 1500 hours in preparing for and

---

[56] ABA, *Gideon's Broken Promise, supra* note 4, at v.

[57] See The Spangenberg Group, Rates of Compensation for Court–Appointed Counsel in Non–Capital Felonies at Trial, July 2002 (American Bar Association), available at http://www.abanet.org/legalservices/downloads/sclaid/indigentdefense/compensationrates capital2002–table.pdf.

[58] The Spangenberg Group, 2002 Update on Rates of Compensation for Court–Appointed Counsel in Capital Cases at Trial: A State-by-State Overview 5 (April 2003).

trying a capital case, with the median ranging from 300–600 hours.[59] If an attorney were to spend 500 hours, a median amount, defending a capital case in Kentucky, her hourly rate would work out to $25./ Every extra hour that she works, moreover, would result in an effective decrease in her hourly rate. Rates in noncapital cases are substantially lower, even where very serious penalties are on the line. Tennessee and Maryland, for example, impose a $1000 maximum for all non-capital felony cases.[60] Illinois's statutory maximum is $1250.[61] In Virginia, the current maximum fee for misdemeanors is $112, for most felonies, $395; and for felonies carrying a sentence of more than 20 years, $1,096.[62] A study prepared for the Virginia General Assembly and State Bar in 1993 concluded that after taking into account overhead costs, the effective rate for appointed defense attorneys in capital cases was $13 an hour.[63] While some states'statutory caps may be waived by the judge, waivers are rarely granted.[64]

In one Mississippi death penalty case, two experienced attorneys spent 449.5 and 482.5 hours, respectively, on preparation and trial. They filed more than 100 motions, and took two interlocutory appeals. The prosecution sought to use witnesses who had been hypnotized, requiring the defense to retain expert assistance on the effects of hypnosis. There were nine days of pretrial hearings, and the trial itself lasted four weeks. Each attorney logged nearly 200 hours of in-court time alone. Yet the Mississippi statute limited compensation to $1000 per case, under which the attorneys would have earned just over two dollars an hour.[65] Accord-

---

[59] The Spangenberg Group, A Study of Representation in Capital Cases in Texas 61 (March 1993); *see also* Norman Lefstein, *Reform of Defense Representation in Capital Cases: The Indiana Experience and its Implications for the Nation*, 29 Ind. L. Rev. 495, 516–17 (1996) (discussing numerous studies). These studies, moreover, are themselves skewed by the limited compensation paid. Experts estimate that the minimum time required to prepare a capital trial adequately is 1,000 hours—500 hours for the guilt/innocence phase, and 500 hours for the sentencing phase. *Panel Discussion: The Death of Fairness? Counsel Competence and Due Process in Death Penalty Cases*, 31 Hous. L. Rev. 1105, 1108 (1994).

[60] Spangenberg Group, Rules of Compensation for Court-Appointed Counsel in Non-Capital Felonies at Trial, *supra* note 57.

[61] S.C. Code Ann. § 17–3–50 (Law. Co-op. 1990).

[62] The Spangenberg Group, A Comprehensive Review of Indigent Defense in Virginia 46–47 (2004).

[63] Klein and Spangenberg, *Indigent Defense Crisis, supra* note 10, at 7, The Spangenberg Group, A Study of Representation in Capital Cases in Virginia (1993).

[64] Albert C. Vreeland, III, *The Breath of the Unfee'd Lawyer: Statutory Fee Limitations and Ineffective Assistance of Counsel in Capital Litigation*, 90 Mich. L. Rev. 626, 628 note 23 (1991).

[65] Pruett v. State, 574 So.2d 1342 (Miss. 1990).

ing to Judge Reuben V. Anderson, "the court reporter was paid far more than defense counsel."[66]

The Mississippi Supreme Court upheld the cap. Rejecting the claim that such low compensation threatens a defendant's right to effective assistance of counsel, the court stated that "those rare cases where counsel has been ineffective may be handled and determined individually by the appellate courts."[67] Ironically, the court showed more sympathy for the lawyers' claim that appointment at such wages effectively constituted a taking of their property without just compensation. It addressed that concern by creatively construing the statute to permit attorneys to recover their overhead and out-of-pocket expenses, in addition to the $1000 in the statute, which the court characterized as "pure profit."[68] Thus, while attorneys in Mississippi assigned to indigent defense will now at least break even, they will never receive more than $1000 above their overhead expenses, no matter how long the trial and no matter how many hours they log.[69]

Contrary to the assurances of the Mississippi Supreme Court, it is unlikely that the "ineffective assistance" requirement will act as a safety net to guard against the abuses that such a system is certain to create. Since the ineffectiveness standard takes as a baseline the quality of defense representation generally provided in criminal cases, about 80% of which involve indigent defendants, and only identifies as "ineffective" radical departures from that baseline, it cannot possibly serve as a check on the general quality of representation obtained through unrealistically low compensation schemes. In Alabama, for example, the courts found "ineffective assistance of counsel" in capital cases only three times in fourteen years when the statutory cap on compensation for handling a capital trial was $1,000.[70]

Low hourly rates and statutory caps also induce attorneys who take

---

[66] *Id.* at 1350 (Anderson, J., dissenting).

[67] Wilson v. State, 574 So.2d 1338, 1341 (quoting State ex rel. Stephen v. Smith, 747 P.2d 816, 831 (Kan. 1987)) (companion case to *Pruett*).

[68] *Id.* at 1341.

[69] The Louisiana Supreme Court reached a similar result in a case involving appointment of private counsel to a capital case. The Court held that while counsel must be reimbursed for out-of-pocket expenses and overhead costs, there was no need to pay a fee for the lawyer's services, because it was part of the lawyers' "pro bono publico" obligations. The Court rejected the claim that the rights of the indigent defendants had anything to do with the appointed attorney's compensation, and treated the issue as solely a matter of the attorneys' rights. State v. Wigley, 624 So.2d 425 (La. 1993).

[70] Marcia Coyle, Counsel's Guiding Hand is Often Handicapped by the System It Serves, Nat'l L.J., June 11, 1990, at 35.

such cases to accept more cases than they can reasonably handle.[71] As a result, indigent cases are routinely underinvestigated and under-researched. A 1986 study found that in New York, three-quarters of all appointed counsel in homicide cases and 82 percent of appointed counsel in non-homicide cases did not even interview their clients, much less conduct any independent investigation.[72] Appointed counsel filed no discovery motions in 92 percent of homicide cases, and filed no pre-trial motions at all in 75 percent of such cases.[73] They consulted with experts in only 17 percent of homicide cases, even though the prosecution uses a medical expert in virtually every homicide case.[74] The study concluded that assigned counsel "were court functionaries, rather than adversarial representatives of the poor.... The system sustains only those lawyers who comply with its goals by providing cost-efficient, expeditious dispositions, and alienates those who view the defense function in adversarial terms."[75]

Although inadequate compensation is no doubt the most significant barrier to effective indigent defense, it is not the only barrier. Most jurisdictions have no experiential qualifications for who may be assigned to represent an indigent defendant. As a result, counsel are routinely appointed with virtually no relevant experience. Charles Bell, facing the death penalty in Mississippi, was represented by a recent law graduate who had never tried a criminal case to final judgment.[76] Donald Paradis's attorney had passed the bar six months before he was appointed to defend a capital murder case, had never taken criminal law, criminal procedure, or trial advocacy in law school, and had never before represented a criminal defendant.[77] Billy Sunday Birt, on trial for murder in Georgia, was represented by court-appointed counsel who, when asked to identify any criminal law decision from any court with which he was familiar, could name only *Miranda v. Arizona* and *Dred Scott v. Sanford*. (*Miranda*, which established that police must give a set of warnings before engaging in custodial interrogation, is known by virtually anyone who has ever watched a police show on television; *Dred Scott* is not even

---

[71] Paul Calvin Drecksel, *The Crisis in Indigent Criminal Defense*, 44 Ark. L. Rev. 363, 380 (1991).

[72] Michael McConville & Chester L. Mirsky, *Criminal Defense of the Poor in New York City*, 15 N.Y.U. Rev. L. & Soc. Change 581, 758 (1986–87).

[73] *Id.* at 761, 767.

[74] *Id.* at 764.

[75] *Id.* at 901–02.

[76] Bell v. Watkins, 692 F.2d 999, 1008 (5th Cir. 1982).

[77] Paradis v. Arave, 954 F.2d 1483, 1490–91 (9th Cir. 1992).

a criminal case.)[78]

A final impediment to effective representation, ironically, are judges themselves, who most often are responsible for appointing counsel in indigent cases. While many judges no doubt strive to appoint competent counsel, judges may also be tempted to appoint attorneys who they know will not make too much trouble. Ron Slick, for example, often gets appointed to defend indigent clients in Long Beach, California. He has had more clients sentenced to death than any other lawyer in California. A local public defender explained that judges like to appoint Slick because he was always ready to go to trial, even when it seemed he had inadequate time to prepare.[79] According to the Los Angeles Times, while it can often "take weeks or months to try complex capital cases . . . Slick sometimes spent just a few days."[80]

Similarly, Joe Frank Cannon, who boasts that he hurries through criminal trials "like greased lightning," has received repeated appointments in capital trials in Houston, Texas. The past president of the Harris County Criminal Lawyers Association stated in an affidavit that it is "generally reputed in the Harris County legal community" that Cannon gets appointments "because he delivers on his promises to move the courts' dockets." He has been accused of falling asleep repeatedly in court.[81] Ten of his clients have received the death penalty.[82]

By contrast, when an attorney demonstrates competence and dedication to his clients, he can find it difficult to get appointed for precisely that reason. George Kendall, an experienced capital defense attorney with the NAACP Legal Defense and Educational Fund, volunteered to take on Victor Roberts' case in 1984 when Roberts was on death row. He prevailed in federal court in 1992, demonstrating that several constitutional errors at trial required a re-trial. Yet when Roberts' case was sent back to be retried, the local judge in Fayette County, Georgia refused to appoint Kendall to the case.[83] Experienced capital defense attorneys Stephen Bright and William Warner faced a similar Georgia welcome after reversing a death sentence in Tony Amadeo's case before the

---

[78] Birt v. Montgomery, 725 F.2d 587, 598 note 25 (11th Cir.), *cert. denied*, 469 U.S. 874 (1984); *see* Bright, *Counsel for the Poor*, *supra* note 44, at 1839.

[79] Ted Rohrlich, The Case of the Speedy Attorney, L.A. Times, Sept. 26, 1991, at A1.

[80] *Id.*

[81] *See* Burdine v. Johnson, 262 F.3d 336 (5th Cir. 2001) (en banc) (finding that Cannon provided ineffective assistance of counsel when he slept through substantial parts of a death penalty trial).

[82] Paul M. Barrett, Lawyer's Fast Work on Death Cases Raises Doubts About System, Wall Street J., Sept. 7, 1994, at A1.

[83] Roberts v. State, 438 S.E.2d 905, 906 (Ga. 1994).

Supreme Court. The trial court refused to appoint them for Amadeo's resentencing, and instead appointed two lawyers with no experience in capital punishment litigation. Bright and Warner had to appeal to the Georgia Supreme Court merely to get appointed to continue to represent the man whose case they'd won in the United States Supreme Court.[84]

Why might trial judges appoint less than qualified counsel, and oppose the appointment of demonstrably effective lawyers? As the O.J. Simpson case demonstrated, capable defense attorneys can make both the prosecutor's and the trial judge's lives more difficult. Lawyers from Stephen Bright's Southern Center for Human Rights, specialists in death penalty litigation, often file 50–100 pre-trial motions, and expend considerable time and resources developing and presenting mitigating evidence at the sentencing phase of the trial, where the life or death decision is made. By contrast, a 1990 National Law Journal study of 20 randomly chosen Alabama death penalty trials found the average length of trial to be 4.2 days, with the penalty phase lasting on average only 3.6 hours.[85] A 1996 study of Alabama capital cases found that the average penalty phase—including jury deliberations—was less than three hours.[86] Competent attorneys are also more likely to ferret out and challenge constitutional error, and judges who rule in favor of a criminal defendant's claims of constitutional error may find re-election more difficult than if they efficiently process convictions.[87] In short, good lawyers make the task of convicting defendants more difficult.

More is at stake here even than reluctance to spend money on poor criminal defendants. Consider the fate of death penalty resource centers, a short-lived experiment in federally-funded legal aid offices for death row inmates. Congress created the centers in 1987, to save money and reduce delay in the death penalty appeal process. Indigent death row prisoners are entitled by statute to a federally-funded attorney in habeas corpus proceedings. Without resource centers, the government had to hire private attorneys to do this work, and paid those private lawyers between $75 and $125 an hour. Resource centers, by contrast, paid lawyers a relatively low salary, low even for public interest work. Bryan

---

[84] Amadeo v. State, 384 S.E.2d 181, 181 (Ga. 1989).

[85] Marcia Coyle, Counsel's Guiding Hand is Often Handicapped by the System it Serves, Nat'l L.J., June 11, 1990, at 35.

[86] The Equal Justice Initiative, *A Report on Alabama's Indigent Defense System: Capital Cases* (March 1997).

[87] *See generally*, Stephen B. Bright & Patrick J. Keenan, *Judges and the Politics of Death: Deciding Between the Bill of Rights and the Next Election in Capital Cases*, 75 B.U.L. Rev. 759 (1995); Thomas M. Ross, *Rights at the Ballot Box: The Effect of Judicial Elections on Judges' Ability to Protect Criminal Defendants' Rights*, 7 J. L. & Inequality 107 (1988).

Stevenson, for example, one of the best capital defense attorneys in the country, headed Alabama's death penalty resource center and drew an annual salary of only $27,000 in 1994. In addition, because resource center lawyers were "repeat players," they were more efficient. Because death penalty cases are so draining, emotionally and financially, private attorneys rarely take on more than one capital defense case in their careers, so the private appointment system requires the government to waste resources funding lots of attorneys to start from square one. A 1995 General Accounting Office study reported that hiring private attorneys to represent death row inmates costs the government more than twice as much as using resource centers to do the same work.

Yet in 1995, Congress cut off all federal funding for the resource centers. Representative Bob Inglis, who introduced the bill, called the centers "think tanks for legal theories that would frustrate the implementation of all death sentences." What bothered the center's critics was not that the centers were too costly, but that they were too *effective*. Congress was in effect willing to pay *more* money to ensure that death row inmates got *worse* lawyers, because good lawyers, as Representative Inglis put it, "frustrate the implementation of all death sentences." But a death sentence will be frustrated at the post-conviction stage only if a judge finds constitutional error that cannot be dismissed as "harmless." In those cases, the death penalty should be frustrated.

Congress's decision to pay more money for worse capital defense lawyers only makes economic sense because identifying and vindicating constitutional error is itself extremely costly. It may require resentencing or retrial. In rare cases, it may mean that a guilty man will go free. Better lawyers will raise more issues, investigate and litigate more aggressively, and identify more constitutional errors. All of that makes trying criminal cases more costly. Congress was willing to pay more for worse lawyers in order to avoid those social costs.

Broadly speaking, the Supreme Court's "right to counsel" jurisprudence has had much the same effect as Congress's decision to defund the resource centers. If the Court required better lawyers for the indigent, it would cost society not only in terms of the resources necessary to pay those lawyers, but also in terms of the costs of fully enforcing criminal defendants' constitutional rights. Better lawyers would mean more hard-fought trials, more evidence suppressed for constitutional error, fewer convictions, more acquittals, and more hung juries. As then-President of Harvard University Derek Bok candidly acknowledged,

> if Congress provided enough funds for legal aid, or if it agreed to offer the same support to legal defenders as it gives the prosecution, it could easily touch off a burst of litigation that would cost huge

sums of money and add heavily to the burdens and delays of the legal system.[88]

An adversary system in which both sides are evenly matched costs more than a system in which the prosecution's resources overwhelm the defense's, and despite our surface commitment to equality before the law, apparently neither society nor the Court is willing to require anything like an even playing field.

The present system of assigning indigent defendants poorly funded, overburdened, and often underqualified defense attorneys thus "saves" money in two ways: first, by reducing the direct costs of providing a decent defense; and second, and more significantly, by systematically underenforcing the constitutional rights of the indigent accused. Indeed, this is probably the single most significant cause of injustice and inequality in our criminal justice system. If one were looking for a mechanism to reduce the costs of constitutional rights without weakening rights protections for the privileged, one could do no better than ensuring that the poor systematically receive less qualified and competent legal representation than the rich. By denying the poor adequate lawyers, and then holding their lawyers' mistakes against them, we guarantee that we will never have to pay full cost for the constitutional rights we protect, and we achieve that saving without diluting the protections available to those who can afford competent counsel. The appointed counsel system creates an across-the-board double standard: those with the resources to hire a qualified attorney can take full advantage of their constitutional rights, while those without will often forfeit constitutional protections through incompetent lawyering. As the O.J. Simpson trial illustrated, the inequality created by the ability to hire competent counsel is predicated on class, not race. But because most minority defendants are poor, and because blacks and Hispanics disproportionately find themselves as criminal defendants, this class-based disparity also falls especially heavily on the minority community.

Signs of Hope for the Future?

The history of the implementation of the right to counsel over the forty-plus years that it has been a constitutional right offers little basis for hope of marked improvement in the future. However, there are a few rays of hope. A handful of states, sufficiently embarrassed by negative publicity about their indigent defense systems, have adopted improvements in recent years. In 2003, the Georgia legislature enacted a law setting up the state's first statewide public defender service, after sustained pressure from advocacy groups, the state bar, the Congression-

---

[88] Derek Bok, *A Flawed System of Law Practice and Teaching*, 33 J. of Legal Education 570, 575 (1983).

al Black Caucus, and some judges.[89] In 2001, Texas passed the Texas Fair Defense Act, which established statewide standards for indigent defense and an oversight commission, and provided partial state funding for indigent defense, which had previously been funded exclusively at the county level.[90] In 2003, in response to a lawsuit, New York increased compensation rates for court-appointed defense lawyers, from $25 per hour to $60 per hour for out-of-court work, and from $40 per hour to $75 per hour for in court work.[91] In 2004, Virginia created the Virginia Indigent Defense Commission, charged with overseeing all indigent defense, and setting performance standards and caseload limits.[92] And in 2005, the Massachusetts legislature finally raised its rates for indigent defense counsel. It raised rates for non-homicide criminal defense from $30–40 an hour to $50–60 an hour, and from $54 an hour to $100 an hour for homicide cases.[93] The success of these measures remains to be seen—in Virginia, for example, the legislature provided no additional funds for indigent defense, despite having some of the lowest fees in the nation. And New York and Massachusett's revised rates still pale in comparison to what lawyers in other fields can earn, or even to what criminal defense attorneys representing paying clients charge. Still, these reforms illustrate that despite the overwhelming political odds against it, there is some possibility of achieving political reform on the issue of indigent defense. These examples are, however, exceptions to the norm, and even these "success stories" may prove to be failures if the legislatures are not willing to provide sufficient funds to make the reforms possible.

Another ray of hope may be found in several recent decisions of the Supreme Court. For more than fifteen years after issuing its decision in *Strickland*, the Court found not a single case of ineffective assistance of counsel. Since 2000, however, it has found ineffective assistance in three death penalty cases—and more significantly, in each case it has relied heavily on the ABA's guidelines for criminal defense counsel. In *Williams v. Taylor*[94] and *Wiggins v. Smith*,[95] the Court reversed lower

---

[89] ABA, *Gideon's* Broken Promise, *supra* note 4, at 30.

[90] *Id.* at 30–31.

[91] *Id.* at 32–33.

[92] *Id.* at 31–32.

[93] Act of July 29, 2005, ch. 54, 2005 Mass. Acts (providing counsel to indigent persons); The Spangenberg Group, *Indigent Defense in Massachusetts: A Case History of Reform* 5 (August 2005), available at http://www.abanet.org/legalservices/downloads/sclaid/indigentde fense/MAindigdefreform2005.pdf.

[94] 529 U.S. 362 (2000).

[95] 539 U.S. 510 (2003).

courts and found ineffective assistance based on the lawyers' failure to investigate and present mitigating evidence at the sentencing phase of the defendant's capital trials. And in *Rompilla v. Beard*,[96] the Court similarly reversed a lower court, finding counsel ineffective because he failed to examine the court files on Rompilla's prior conviction, when he knew the prosecution would rely on the prior conviction as an aggravating factor at sentencing. In all three decisions, the Court noted that ABA standards require counsel to investigate potential mitigating evidence and all information in the possession of the prosecution.[97]

These decisions suggest that after two decades of experience with the *Strickland* approach, the Court may be gravitating toward a more guidelines-based approach. The Court has been careful to stress that the ABA standards are only guides, and not rigid requirements. But at least when it comes to questions of investigation, the standards do appear to provide a relatively clear and objective measure of adequate performance. The failure to investigate, after all, is rarely a tactical decision; indeed, reasonable investigation is often a prerequisite to an informed strategic decision.

It is dangerous to read too much into three Supreme Court decisions. But the tenor of these decisions does seem markedly different from *Strickland* itself, and the very fact that the Court is taking such cases and reversing lower courts at all is a departure from past practice. Three factors may be at play here. First, as the Court discovered with the right to counsel itself in the lead-up to *Gideon*, it may be learning through experience that the wholly open-ended standard set forth in *Strickland* is increasingly unsatisfactory. A more specific guidelines-based approach would provide for more clarity, and as long as the guidelines are limited to such basic tasks as investigating leads and consulting with one's client, they are unlikely to restrict counsel's discretion or to inundate the courts with claims. By its nature, ineffective assistance will never be susceptible to the kind of bright-line solution that *Gideon* provided, but more clarity would undoubtedly be helpful in making clear to the government and defense lawyers what is required, and in making litigation of ineffectiveness claims more efficient.

Second, the development of DNA analysis in recent years has demonstrated that a shocking number of wholly innocent defendants have not only been convicted of serious crimes, but sentenced to death.[98]

---

[96] 125 S.Ct. 2456 (2005).

[97] *Rompilla*, 125 S.Ct. at 2465–66; *Wiggins*, 539 U.S. at 524; *Williams*, 529 U.S. at 396.

[98] *See, e.g.*, Website of The Innocence Project, http://innocenceproject.org; ABA, *Gideon's* Broken Promise, *supra* note 4, Appendix C (listing sample of individuals exonerated in

This evidence has led to the pardons of many men on death row, and has spawned an "innocence" movement.[99] Prior to DNA, whether a defendant was guilty or innocent in a controversial case was always open to argument; DNA provides incontrovertible proof of innocence (and guilt) in many cases. The undeniable reality that the system the Court condoned with its status-quo-embracing *Strickland* test has led to a significant number of innocent people being erroneously convicted and even sentenced to death may make the Justices more inclined to take ineffective assistance claims more seriously than in the past.

Third, it is possible that the sheer weight of evidence of systemic problems in indigent representation has taken its toll on the Court. Ever since *Gideon* was decided, the ABA and other bodies have issued periodic reports detailing the shamefully inadequate level of funding for indigent defense. Horror stories of sleeping, drunk, and drug-addicted lawyers regularly appear in a variety of media, from mainstream newspapers to law reviews and specialized journals. In the face of this evidence, and in light of the fact that the situation shows little sign of improvement through the political process, the Court may finally be showing signs that it feels responsible to put some pressure on the system for positive change.

Whatever the reason, the three recent decisions do offer some hope that the Court is moving in the direction of taking more responsibility for improving the quality of representation for the indigent. Such a change in course is absolutely necessary if there is any hope of improving the quality of defense counsel for the poor. Episodic and isolated reforms in a handful of states cannot solve the problem, and even those reforms took extraordinary efforts. The problem of inadequate lawyers for the poor is one that the Court is well suited to take on; it does not require intruding on the inner workings of the other branches, but only candid acknowledgment of the infirmities in the judicial system itself. As long as the Supreme Court is content to embrace the status quo and provide remedies only for those who fall far below the status quo, there will be "no equal justice" in the American criminal courts.

U.S. in 2003–2004); Samuel R. Gross et al., *Exonerations in the United States, 1989–2003*, 95 Journal of Crim. L. & Criminology 523 (2005).

[99] *See, e.g.*, Jodi Wilgoren, After Sweeping Clemency Order, Ex–Gov Ryan Is a Celebrity, but a Solitary One, N.Y. Times, Feb. 7, 2003, at A16; Scott Turow, *Ultimate Punishment: A Lawyer's Reflection on Dealing with the Death Penalty* (2003).

4

Brady v. Maryland: From Adversarial Gamesmanship Toward the Search for Innocence?

Stephanos Bibas*

Brady v. Maryland[1] is unusual among the great landmark criminal procedure decisions of the Warren Court. *Brady* requires prosecutors to give criminal defendants evidence that tends to negate their guilt or reduce their punishment. In other words, *Brady* mandates limited discovery instead of trial by ambush. *Brady*'s test turns not on whether the prosecutor misled a jury or acted in good faith, but on whether the evidence is favorable and material to guilt or punishment. Thus, *Brady* marked a potentially revolutionary shift from traditionally unfettered adversarial combat toward a more inquisitorial, innocence-focused system. Yet, unlike *Mapp v. Ohio*[2] and *Miranda v. Arizona*,[3] *Brady* has sparked little public controversy or commentary. This may be because innocence is an appealing touchstone for criminal procedure, one with enormous potential to transform the adversarial criminal trial into a collaborative search for the truth.

Brady, however, has meant much less in practice than it could have. Few potential *Brady* claims come to light, and fewer defendants walk free, because our system remains an adversarial contest rather than a neutral inquiry into innocence. First, *Brady* requires prosecutors to look

* I am grateful to David Baldus, Todd Pettys, and Tung Yin for their comments on earlier drafts and to Jordan Esbrook, Brian Raimondo, and Robert Zink for their research assistance.

[1] 373 U.S. 83 (1963).

[2] 367 U.S. 643 (1961) (requiring exclusion from criminal proceedings of evidence obtained in violation of the Fourth Amendment).

[3] 384 U.S. 436 (1966) (requiring police to warn suspects in custody of their rights to remain silent and to consult with an attorney before questioning them).

out for defendants' interests, and adversarial-minded prosecutors are poorly suited to do that job. Second, *Brady* is hard to implement and enforce. Favorable evidence is often spread across many agencies' files; defendants cannot learn of evidence hidden in these files; and judges are loath to reverse convictions long after trial. Empirical evidence shows that few *Brady* claims succeed and that most *Brady* material is ambiguous enough that prosecutors can easily overlook it. Third, *Brady* requires relatively little discovery, though statutes and rules have broadened discovery beyond the constitutional minimum. Much broader discovery would alleviate many of the adversary system's problems, at the cost of more witness intimidation, fabricated alibis, and revelation of undercover and confidential informants. Fourth, *Brady* applies only at the trial stage, but hardly any defendants go to trial any more. About 95% plead guilty, and *Brady* may not even apply to the plea bargaining process, when defendants need this information most. Finally, though *Brady* ignores the prosecutor's good faith (mens rea), its test continues to require some prosecutorial misdeed (actus reus). It does not focus exclusively on the defendant's guilt or innocence of the crime or punishment.

Brady's ringing rhetoric of innocence, then, is in some ways a hollow promise. Far from transforming the adversarial system into a quest for truth, it has merely tinkered at its margins.

The Tradition of Adversarial Criminal Procedure

In much of continental Europe, magistrates and judges actively seek out evidence and question witnesses, even the defendant himself. This approach is known as the inquisitorial system, because judges themselves inquire directly into the truth of the case. Judges find both the facts and the law, and they can hop back and forth between digging up evidence and witnesses and hearing the testimony of those witnesses. Thus there is no separation between discovery and trial, and the parties cannot question or coach witnesses before judges take their testimony. While they may begin by hearing the evidence and witnesses proposed by either side, they may also pursue other leads, including names mentioned by witnesses. Thus judges, rather than prosecutors, run the show. Their job is to develop a full picture of the evidence that bears on guilt or punishment, not simply the case presented by either side. The English, however, rejected the inquisitorial system, as it reminded them of the Spanish Inquisition and the Star Chamber, which had used torture to extract confessions. Instead, England entrusted fact-finding to lay juries who heard the arguments of each party. Crime victims dug up their own evidence and witnesses and argued their own cases in court, and criminal defendants brought in their own evidence and defended themselves in court. Laymen, not lawyers, ran the system, which sharply divided pre-trial discovery from trial testimony.[4]

By the late eighteenth century, lawyers had taken over the criminal process. Public prosecutors (appointed or paid for by the state) took the place of victims, and criminal defense lawyers took the place of defendants who could afford them. The lawyers investigated the evidence before trial and then questioned witnesses at trial in front of juries. Prosecutors came to see police officers almost as their clients and worked closely with them to dig up evidence and witnesses and prepare witnesses' testimony for trial. Now that lawyers ran the show, judges could develop rules of procedure and evidence to regulate trials. Judges guarded the procedural fairness of trials but left substantive questions of guilt or innocence to juries. The adversarial system trusted that, if each side fought hard to present its own arguments, the truth would emerge from the collision of truth and error. The American colonies inherited this adversarial criminal process from England.

Each lawyer, then, was supposed to be a zealous partisan rather than a neutral arbiter of truth. The main limit on zealous advocacy was that lawyers were in some sense officers of the court. As such, they could not lie to or mislead the tribunal. Short of falsehood, however, lawyers were free to advance their own clients' interests and to leave issues of ultimate truth to the jury. If a fact hurt one's client or weakened an argument, that lawyer was under no obligation to find or disclose it; it was the opposing lawyer's job to do that. Thus, the parties did not have to reveal information to each other in discovery.

In theory, prosecutors hold themselves to even higher ethical standards. Prosecutors do not have human clients, but rather represent the State in its quest for justice. As the Supreme Court stated in 1935, the prosecutor "is the representative ... of a sovereignty whose interest ... in a criminal prosecution is not that it shall win a case, but that justice shall be done.... He may prosecute with earnestness and vigor—indeed, he should do so. But, while he may strike hard blows, he is not at liberty to strike foul ones."[5] If the adversarial trial remains a boxing match, at least the prosecutor must fight by the Marquis of Queensbury rules and avoid striking below the belt. Thus, beginning in 1935 with *Mooney v. Holohan*, the Supreme Court adopted narrow due process limits on prosecutorial misconduct. Prosecutors must not elicit testimony that

---

[4] I draw the account in this and the next paragraphs from the work of John Langbein. *See generally* John H. Langbein, *The Origins of Adversary Criminal Trial* (2003).

[5] Berger v. United States, 295 U.S. 78, 88–89 (1935) (reversing criminal conviction in part because the prosecutor had misstated facts, assumed facts not in evidence, badgered witnesses, and proclaimed personal opinion in closing argument).

they know is perjurious or misleading, because doing so would "deliberate[ly] dece[ive] court and jury."[6]

Fundamentally, though, the prosecutor remains an adversary, a boxer rather than a referee. If prosecution is a mere game or a sporting event, prosecutors may feel entitled to fight to win at all costs. Prosecutors are the heirs to the partisan role of victims, whom they supplanted. Their incentives also push them toward maximizing convictions: if they rack up many wins and few losses, they receive promotions or lucrative jobs in private practice.[7] Though conscientious prosecutors also want to free the innocent and show mercy on sympathetic guilty defendants, at root, they see their job as convicting and punishing the guilty. This adversarial mindset may endanger the quest for truth. Partisan prosecutors may conclude early on that defendants are guilty and so fail to see or discount the importance of later evidence that undercuts their case. And because partisan lawyers find and prepare witnesses, they may consciously or unconsciously coach them to slant their stories and omit unfavorable details. In particular, they may leave out crucial details that might contradict or impeach a witness's testimony. Or, lawyers may simply avoid calling witnesses who undercut their theory of the case. Unless the adversary system works perfectly and the other side finds all of the damaging information on its own, the jury will not hear the crucial damaging evidence. Defense counsel, however, often are underfunded and lack the broad subpoena powers and investigative agencies to which prosecutors have access. In addition, each side may not know the evidence and witnesses that the other will use, so each is in a poor position to investigate and poke holes in the other's evidence. Moreover, witnesses sympathetic to the defendant or victim may refuse to talk to opposing counsel, which impedes investigating the weaknesses in witnesses' stories. As a result, each side often will not find on its own the helpful evidence possessed by the other side.

John Brady's Crime

John Brady was a twenty-five-year old man who had bounced around from job to job. He had fallen in love with another man's wife, Nancy Boblit Magowan, and now she was expecting their child. Brady was broke but felt he had to come up with money to take care of Nancy and their child. On June 22, 1958, Brady had written her a post-dated

---

[6] Mooney v. Holohan, 294 U.S. 103, 112 (1935) (per curiam); *see also* Napue v. Illinois, 360 U.S. 264, 265, 267, 269–70 (1959); Alcorta v. Texas, 355 U.S. 28, 31 (1957) (per curiam) (reversing conviction because prosecutor knowingly elicited and failed to correct testimony that "gave the jury [a] false impression" even though it may have been technically truthful); Pyle v. Kansas, 317 U.S. 213, 216 (1942).

[7] *See* Stephanos Bibas, *Plea Bargaining Outside the Shadow of Trial*, 117 Harv. L. Rev. 2463, 2471–72 (2004).

check for $35,000 and promised her that he would come up with that money in the next two weeks.[8]

Together with Nancy's brother, Donald Boblit, Brady hatched a scheme to rob a bank. But to pull off the robbery, they needed a fast, reliable car. Brady suggested that they steal the new Ford Fairlane that his friend William Brooks had just bought. So, late on June 27, 1958, Brady and Boblit placed a log across the road near Brooks' home and waited for him to return home from work. When Brooks pulled up and got out of his car to move the log, one of the men hit him over the head with a shotgun, knocking him unconscious. Brady and Boblit put him into the back seat and stole his wallet, and Brady drove them to a secluded field ten miles away. The two men walked Brooks to a clearing at the edge of the woods, and one of the men strangled Brooks to death with a shirt. They both carried his corpse farther into the woods and left it there. The key issue in the case turned out to be the identity of the actual killer. Who had strangled Brooks–Brady or Boblit?

The Confessions

Brady later gave a series of statements to the police. In his first two statements, Brady said that he, not Boblit, had stolen the car, hit Brooks over the head with a pipe, loaded him into the back seat, and dumped him elsewhere. He made no mention of any murder or death.[9] In Brady's third statement, he asserted that after the two of them had stolen the car, Boblit had hit Brooks over the head. Boblit, he claimed, had suggested killing Brooks over Brady's opposition and had strangled Brooks as Brady stood by silently. He claimed that he had agreed to take the blame for Boblit.[10] In his fourth statement, Brady said that he and Boblit had agreed that Boblit would have to kill Brooks. Although Boblit had wanted to shoot him, Brady had suggested strangling him. Once again, Brady admitted that he had stood by silently.[11] At trial, Brady "admitted virtually everything set forth in his confessions"[12] but denied having personally killed Brooks.[13]

Boblit also gave a series of statements to the police, and in all but one of them he accused Brady of doing the actual killing. In the first and

---

[8] I draw the facts in this and the next paragraph from Richard Hammer, *Between Life and Death* 15–52 (1969).

[9] *Id.* at 85, 87.

[10] *Id.* at 103–07.

[11] *Id.* at 111–12.

[12] Brady v. State, 154 A.2d 434, 435 (Md. 1959).

[13] Brady v. State, 160 A.2d 912, 913 (Md. 1960), *rev'd and remanded*, 174 A.2d 167 (Md. 1961), *aff'd*, 373 U.S. 83 (1963).

second statements, Boblit said that he had helped Brady to rob Brooks but had not known that Brady would kill him. In both statements, he claimed that Brady had committed the actual killing. In the second statement, Boblit added that Brady had hit Brooks with a gun and that Boblit had told Brady not to kill him.[14] Boblit's third and fourth statements repeated the second one, except that Boblit admitted that he and Brady had both thought that "Brooks had to be killed."[15]

The key confession at the heart of *Brady v. Maryland* was Boblit's fifth statement, made on July 9, 1958. In that statement, Boblit admitted that he, not Brady, had hit Brooks on the head with the shotgun. He also said that after they got back into the car, he had planned to shoot Brooks, but Brady had persuaded him to strangle him instead. Boblit had strangled him, he admitted, and both men had carried his corpse into the woods.[16]

In short, both men repeatedly admitted to taking part in the robbery and murder, but each at times blamed the other for the actual killing. This disagreement was irrelevant to guilt but possibly relevant to whether one or the other deserved the death penalty.

Lower Court Proceedings

Before trial, Brady's lawyer asked the prosecutor for any confessions that Brady or Boblit had made. The prosecutor turned over Boblit's other statements but did not turn over Boblit's July 9 statement, in which he had admitted doing the actual killing.[17]

Brady and later Boblit were convicted at jury trials and sentenced to death. Afterwards, Brady's new lawyer read the transcript of Boblit's trial and learned of the July 9 statement, which Brady's trial lawyer had never received. He filed a collateral attack, requesting a new trial based on newly discovered evidence. The trial court denied the motion, but the Court of Appeals of Maryland reversed. It held that "the suppression or withholding by the State of material evidence exculpatory to an accused is a violation of due process."[18] Even though Brady did not claim that the prosecutor had acted out of "guile," the prosecutor's guile is irrelevant

---

[14] Hammer, *supra* note 8, at 97–98.

[15] *Id.* at 100.

[16] *Id.* at 114–15.

[17] Brady v. Maryland, 373 U.S. 83, 84 (1963). The State's Attorney claimed that he had never turned over any of Boblit's statements, but the courts appear to have credited Brady's lawyer's claim that he had received Boblit's other statements. *See id.*; Hammer, *supra* note 8, at 259–60.

[18] Brady v. State, 174 A.2d 167, 169 (Md. 1961).

to the due process violation.[19] Though it seriously doubted whether Boblit's confession would have done Brady any good, the court gave Brady the benefit of the doubt. It refused to order a new trial on the issue of guilt, as the withheld evidence cast no doubt on that issue. Instead, the court remanded for a new trial solely to determine punishment.[20]

In the Supreme Court

Brady petitioned for *certiorari*, seeking a new trial on both guilt and punishment. The Fourteenth Amendment's Due Process Clause, he contended, entitled him to use Boblit's statement throughout the trial to sway the jury, which might even have persuaded it to acquit.[21]

The Supreme Court of the United States affirmed. Writing for the majority, Justice Douglas "h[e]ld that the suppression by the prosecution of evidence favorable to an accused upon request violates due process where the evidence is material either to guilt or to punishment, irrespective of the good faith or bad faith of the prosecution."[22]

Brady did not further define materiality. But later cases held that evidence is material if there is "a reasonable probability" that disclosing it would have changed the outcome of the proceeding. "A 'reasonable probability' [is] 'a probability sufficient to undermine confidence in the outcome.'"[23] *Brady* also defined the reach of exculpatory evidence narrowly, as evidence that would tend to negate guilt or reduce punishment. *Giglio v. United States* expanded *Brady*'s rule to include evidence that would tend to impeach government witnesses,[24] such as payments to witnesses or promises of leniency.

---

[19] *Id.*

[20] *Id.* at 171–72. Today, courts bifurcate death-penalty trials into one phase on guilt and another one (or two) on punishment, but at the time the idea of a punishment minitrial was novel.

[21] Brady also invoked the Equal Protection Clause of the Fourteenth Amendment. 373 U.S. at 90–91. Future similarly situated defendants, Brady argued, would be able to use exculpatory evidence throughout their trials, and so he should have been able to do the same. Though Brady made this his lead argument, it was opaque. Neither the majority nor Justice White's concurrence devoted any space to it, presumably because the evidence would have been inadmissible as to guilt in any event.

[22] 373 U.S. 83, 87.

[23] United States v. Bagley, 473 U.S. 667, 682 (1985) (quoting Strickland v. Washington, 466 U.S. 668, 694 (1984)); *see also id.* at 685 (White, J., concurring in part and concurring in the judgment) (agreeing with the test set forth in the first of the two sentences quoted in the text).

[24] 405 U.S. 150, 153–54 (1972). Napue v. Illinois, 360 U.S. 264 (1959), had foreshadowed this rule by extending Mooney v. Holohan, 294 U.S. 103 (1935) to impeachment

The point of due process, the *Brady* Court stated, is not to punish prosecutorial misdeeds but to give defendants fair trials.[25] Even though Brady's prosecutor had not acted out of "guile," his actions had denied Brady's right to a fair trial.[26] In other words, prosecutors can violate due process even if they lack any mens rea and act in good faith. As the Court later put it, "[i]f the suppression of evidence results in constitutional error, it is because of the character of the evidence, not the character of the prosecutor."[27] The *Brady* Court accepted the Court of Appeals' holding that under state law, the suppressed evidence would not have been admissible on the issue of guilt. Thus, the Court affirmed.[28] Justice White concurred in the judgment. He pointed out that it was not clear whether the Maryland Court of Appeals had relied on the Maryland or Federal Constitution.[29] Moreover, the State had not cross-petitioned to challenge the due process holding below. Accordingly, the only issue properly before the Court was whether the Federal Constitution guaranteed Brady a new trial on guilt as well as punishment. Having decided that Brady had no such right, the majority should not have reached the broader due process issue, and its whole due process "hold[ing]" amounted to dictum.[30] Finally, the majority's sweeping opinion created a broad new rule of criminal discovery. The majority, he argued, should have left the scope of the right to legislation and rule-making in the first instance.[31]

Life After Death Row

After the Supreme Court affirmed, Brady was in limbo. He had a right to a new trial limited to the question of punishment. But he did not

---

evidence, though *Napue*'s holding was limited to "knowing[] use [of] false evidence" or allowing that evidence to go uncorrected. *See* 360 U.S. at 265, 267, 269–70.

[25] *Brady*, 373 U.S. at 87 (discussing *Mooney*, the seminal due process case in this area).

[26] *Id.*

[27] United States v. Agurs, 427 U.S. 97, 110 (1976).

[28] *Brady*, 373 U.S. at 90–91.

[29] *Id.* at 91 (White, J., concurring in the judgment).

[30] *Id.* at 92 ("[T]he due process discussion by the Court is wholly advisory"); *accord id.* at 92 note 1 (Harlan, J., dissenting) (agreeing with Justice White that the majority's due process discussion was unnecessary); *see id.* at 87 (majority opinion) ("We now hold that. . . .").

[31] *Id.* at 92 (White, J., concurring in the judgment).

Justice Harlan, joined by Justice Black, dissented. They were uncertain about whether Boblit's statement would have been admissible as to Brady's guilt under Maryland law, and so whether there was an equal protection violation. Thus, they preferred to vacate and remand for further proceedings in light of the governing constitutional principle set forth by the majority. *Id.* at 92–95 (Harlan, J., dissenting).

want to exercise this right, lest the jury again sentence him to death. The State had a right to retry Brady, but it had never conducted a punishment-only trial and was not sure how to do it. So for years neither side made a move. Brady was transferred off death row and housed in a series of prisons and jails and took part in a work-release program during the daytime. After fifteen years, his lawyers figured that the State's evidence had decayed too much to retry Brady, so they finally moved for a speedy trial. Rather than retry Brady, the Governor commuted his sentence to life imprisonment. After eighteen years, Brady was paroled.[32]

While on death row, Brady had married a Baltimore nurse. After his release, the two had several children before divorcing. Brady then moved south, married again, and started another family. He remains steadily employed as a truck driver and has not been in serious trouble with the law before or since the Brooks murder. He remains sorry that the murder occurred but maintains that he never intended to kill Brooks, who had been his friend.

Brady's Overbreadth

While Brady himself retired into obscurity, the Supreme Court case bearing his name eventually became famous for what seemed to be its sweeping holding. Justice Douglas's majority opinion went much further than was necessary to resolve Brady's case. First, Justice White is correct that the majority's famous "hold[ing]" was no more than dictum. Second, Brady's prosecutor never denied that he had possessed Boblit's July 9 statement and had known about it all along. Indeed, he had repeatedly tried to use that same statement at Boblit's trial.[33] Moreover, when Brady's lawyer had asked for Boblit's statements, the prosecutor had turned over the other four statements but not the fifth one.[34] This selective discovery created the misleading impression that there were no others. Given this evidence of mens rea, it is odd that the Supreme Court made its rule "irrespective of the good faith or bad faith of the prosecution."[35] Third, because the due process "hold[ing]" was on a point not briefed nor contested by either party, the Court lacked the benefit of a developed adversarial record. As Justice White notes, perhaps the Court should not have defined this sweeping new right on its own in the first instance. If its holding had been more modest, legislatures, the bar, and

---

[32] The information in this paragraph and the next one comes from Telephone Interview with Clinton Bamberger, counsel in the Supreme Court for John Brady (Mar. 3, 2005).

[33] Hammer, *supra* note 8, at 237.

[34] *Brady*, 373 U.S. at 84.

[35] 373 U.S. at 87.

lower courts could have experimented and developed the precise contours of this new right. In short, Justice White's suggestion of judicial activism is largely correct. Justice Douglas's majority opinion reached far beyond the questions presented and actual facts to create a broad new due process right.

The Emphasis on Innocence

To say that a decision is activist, however, is not to say that it is wrong. *Brady* came in the 1960s, a decade in which the Court created many broad new criminal-procedure protections. Many of these other decisions sparked great controversy and resistance. *Mapp v. Ohio*,[36] for example, led to decades of case law expanding and then narrowing the Fourth Amendment exclusionary rule, often over bitter dissents. *Miranda v. Arizona*[37] became famous and infamous, and Congress passed legislation in an unsuccessful effort to overturn the *Miranda* warning requirement.[38]

In contrast, *Brady* elicited hardly a peep of protest. This difference, I suspect, has to do with innocence. *Mapp* and *Miranda* let guilty criminal defendants walk free, in order to protect broader constitutional principles and values and punish or regulate police misconduct. Suddenly, guilty criminal defendants were the good guys and police were the bad guys, a flip-flop that many people resented. As crime rose in the turbulent 1960s, courts that freed guilty criminal defendants on technicalities seemed to be part of the problem. Richard Nixon successfully campaigned for president against the Warren Court and appointed Warren Burger Chief Justice, partly because Burger was hostile to criminal procedure technicalities.[39]

Innocence, however, is not a technicality tangential to the criminal process. It is the main touchstone of the criminal process. The justice system must not only strive to convict the guilty but also to acquit the innocent. If it mistakenly convicts the wrong person, it inflicts a grave injustice while leaving the guilty party free to commit more crimes. Due process is not simply about punishing prosecutors who lie or mislead. Instead of focusing on the prosecutor's mens rea, bad faith, or guile,

---

[36] 367 U.S. 643 (1961).

[37] 384 U.S. 436 (1966).

[38] *See* Title II, Omnibus Crime Control and Safe Streets Act of 1968, Pub. L. No. 90–351, 90th Cong., 2d Sess., 82 Stat. 210 (codified as amended at 18 U.S.C. § 3501). The Supreme Court declared this statute ineffective to abrogate *Miranda* in Dickerson v. United States, 530 U.S. 428 (2000).

[39] *See* Bob Woodward & Scott Armstrong, *The Brethren: Inside the Supreme Court* 4, 6–7 (1979).

Brady shifts the focus to the defendant's innocence. Prosecutors must now take affirmative steps so that the jury can discern the truth.

Moreover, *Brady* does not let defendants walk free. At most, it requires a new trial, at which the state will have a second opportunity to prove guilt beyond a reasonable doubt. And in *Brady* itself there was no danger that the punishment retrial would let Brady or Boblit walk free. The most that either could hope for was to avoid the death penalty and instead receive a life sentence. Brady was not innocent of murder, but he could plausibly claim to be innocent of a murder bad enough to deserve the death penalty. In the 1960s, the tide of judicial and popular opinion was turning against the death penalty. Some states abolished the death penalty, and polls showed that at the time only a minority of Americans favored it.[40] Courts scrutinized death sentences far more carefully than other sentences and halted many executions. As a result of these forces, the flow of executions slowed to a single-digit trickle by 1965, less than two years after the Supreme Court decided *Brady*.[41]

Even today, innocence has the potential to transform criminal procedure. DNA testing has documented many wrongful convictions of the innocent.[42] As a result, the governor of Illinois halted and later commuted all death sentences in that state.[43] In addition, scholars have highlighted flaws in interrogation and identification procedures and legislatures have considered increasing funding for defense counsel. As habeas corpus review grows ever narrower, compelling new evidence of actual innocence can still unlock the door to the courthouse or win executive clemency.

If one had taken *Brady* seriously, it would have portended a major shift away from the traditional adversarial system towards a focus on innocence. This major shift never occurred, however, because crucial features of *Brady* and our adversarial system have limited *Brady*'s impact upon trials. The remainder of this chapter will explain five basic features of our system that hobble *Brady*. First, despite *Brady*'s exhortation to do justice, prosecutors and police remain fundamentally *adversarial*. Second, *Brady* has a *weak enforcement mechanism*. Because it depends upon these partisans to dig through their own files to find information for the other side, *Brady* violations rarely come to light.

---

[40] *See* Hammer, *supra* note 8, at 287.

[41] *See id.* at 285–86.

[42] *See generally* Barry Scheck et al., *Actual Innocence: Five Days to Execution and Other Dispatches from the Wrongly Convicted* (2000).

[43] *See* Jodi Wilgoren, *Citing Issue of Fairness, Governor Clears Out Death Row in Illinois*, N.Y. Times, Jan. 12, 2003, § 1, at 1; Dirk Johnson, *Illinois, Citing Faulty Verdicts, Bars Executions*, N.Y. Times, Feb. 1, 2000, at A1.

When violations do surface, long after trial, judges are loath to reverse convictions and order retrials. Third, *Brady* is limited to *exculpatory* and impeachment evidence, rather than the incriminating evidence that is much more common. *Brady* is a very narrow discovery rule, and statutes and rules have expanded upon *Brady*'s discovery, but nonetheless neither side knows all of the other side's evidence. Fourth, though *plea bargaining* resolves most cases, *Brady* is designed for trials and poorly suited to plea bargaining. And finally, though prosecutorial "guile" is irrelevant, *Brady* still requires some *prosecutorial misconduct* and not simply innocence. In other words, while *Brady* requires no prosecutorial mens rea, it still requires some actus reus, some act of withholding favorable evidence.

Adversarial Barriers to Focusing on Innocence

The documented wrongful convictions reveal important flaws in our adversary system. While funding better defense counsel might prevent some of these errors, others are beyond defense counsel's control or capacity to investigate. Police and prosecutors are human, and humans tend to jump to conclusions and then discount later information that undercuts their earlier beliefs. Their adversarial mindset conditions them all the more to hypothesize guilt and then focus on finding corroborating evidence. Thus, police and prosecutors who become too convinced early on of a suspect's guilt may simply fail to appreciate or investigate contrary leads. Even if they come across exculpatory evidence, they may minimize or not see its significance.[44] (In other words, even if they see that the evidence is exculpatory, they may not see how it is material.) They may thus conclude that because a piece of evidence does not change their own minds about guilt, it would not change jurors' minds either and so is not *Brady* material. This over-stringent perspective could lead prosecutors to decide that nothing is *Brady* material unless it persuades them to dismiss a case, so the rate of *Brady* disclosures could approach zero. Prosecutors may also be too willing to believe paid informants who tell them what they want or expect to hear. In addition, their interrogations and line-ups may subtly communicate what they expect or hope to find, eliciting false or skewed evidence.

---

[44] *See* United States v. Agurs, 427 U.S. 97, 117 (1976) (Marshall, J., dissenting) (arguing that prosecutors naturally tend "to overlook evidence favorable to the defense, and [have] an incentive ... to resolve close questions of disclosure in favor of concealment."). Psychological studies confirm that people tend to interpret new evidence so as to confirm their initial judgments. *See, e.g.*, Charles G. Lord et al., *Biased Assimilation and Attitude Polarization: The Effects of Prior Theories on Subsequently Considered Evidence*, 37 J. Personality & Soc. Psychol. 2098, 2102 (1979); S. Plous, *Biases in the Assimilation of Technological Breakdowns: Do Accidents Make Us Safer?*, 21 J. Applied Soc. Psychol. 1058, 1059 (1991).

If the adversarial system is the problem, then maybe the inquisitorial system is the solution. Prosecutors could view their job not as a partisan struggle to convict, but as a neutral, detached investigation into the truth. *Brady v. Maryland* appeared to be a step in that direction. The Court took seriously prosecutorial rhetoric about seeing that justice is done. By obligating prosecutors to cooperate with defense counsel, the Court cast defense counsel not as enemies of prosecutors but as partners in the quest for justice. Rather than leaving adversarial combat unregulated, courts were to actively supervise the search for truth. At least one commentator, writing shortly after *Brady*, thought that prosecutors might have to turn over their entire files to trial judges. These judges would then review all the evidence in camera to find possible *Brady* material.[45] This move could have been the first step toward a more inquisitorial system, with active judicial oversight. As it turned out, judges did not take up this supervisory role. *In camera* review of all possible evidence would be extremely time-consuming, and judges are too busy to take on additional duties voluntarily. Moreover, judges traditionally have not been deeply involved in criminal cases until right before trial. They do not know the issues and the evidence, so usually they cannot see what evidence might fit with various possible defense theories of the case. Thus, they leave the *Brady* determination of favorable evidence up to the prosecutor, whose mindset is fundamentally partisan.

Simple exhortations to be neutral or pursue justice cannot transform our adversarial system into an inquisitorial one. The traditions, culture, and incentives of our adversarial system are deeply rooted and hard to change. As mentioned, prosecutors receive promotions and better jobs if they have favorable win-loss records and rack up many convictions. And as discussed below, most cases are strong and result in convictions, which makes finding or appreciating evidence of innocence like looking for a needle in a haystack. The press of business does not encourage this slow, detached rumination over the evidence.

Moreover, prosecutors face off against defense counsel who are paid to be zealous advocates. The ethical rules require zealous advocacy and rarely penalize overly aggressive behavior. The defense lawyer's flesh-and-blood client, of course, asks the lawyer to do whatever he can to win acquittal or a low sentence. Defense lawyers are not about to turn over inculpatory evidence to prosecutors, particularly because the privilege against self-incrimination and the attorney-client privilege forbid many disclosures. If defense lawyers are fighting hard and concealing their cards, a prosecutor might think, why should I show any more than the

---

[45] *See* James M. Carter, *Suppression of Evidence Favorable to an Accused*, 34 F.R.D. 87, 90–91 (1964). For a modern proposal to give judges a similar inquisitorial role, *see* Darryl Brown, *The Decline of Defense Counsel and the Rise of Accuracy in Criminal Adjudication*, 93 Calif. L. Rev. 1585 (2005).

bare minimum of mine? Because the system depends on prosecutorial self-policing, defense counsel are unlikely ever to learn of *Brady* violations. And if they do come to light at trial, judges may treat any error as harmless, as defense counsel winds up with the evidence in time for trial. Thus, prosecutors do not fear being penalized for violating *Brady* or interpreting it very narrowly.

The adversarial norms and roles of each side keep reinforcing each other. In America, unlike England, lawyers serve exclusively on one side or the other of this divide, at least for a period of years. Thus, pro-prosecution lawyers become full-time prosecutors and pro-defendant lawyers become full-time defense counsel. Each group of lawyers then works and socializes in offices filled with like-minded people, which reinforces and polarizes their original leanings. Each also practices against adversaries who are similarly polarized, which may antagonize and exacerbate the gulf between them.

Brady's Weak Enforcement Mechanism

Brady's enforcement difficulties and weak, retrospective enforcement mechanism exacerbate these problems. Many different federal, state, and local agencies share overlapping responsibilities for investigation and prosecution. For any moderately complex conspiracy spanning several states, half a dozen police and prosecutorial offices may have information relevant to the case. Defense counsel cannot search these files, and a single prosecutor may not know about, let alone be able to search, all of them. How far does the *Brady* obligation go? Courts have charged prosecutors with the knowledge that is in their offices and their investigative agencies,[46] but not other jurisdictions' files. As a practical matter, however, prosecutors will never learn of much of this material, and it will never come to light.

This problem highlights another one: *Brady* relies on ineffective prosecutorial self-policing in the first instance. Because *Brady* material is hidden in prosecutors' and police files, defense lawyers probably will never learn of its existence. Most defendants lack the investigative resources to dig up *Brady* material. (The next Section discusses how modern discovery has alleviated this problem somewhat.)

---

[46] *See, e.g.*, Kyles v. Whitley, 514 U.S. 419, 437 (1995) (charging the individual prosecutor with "a duty to learn of any favorable evidence known to the others acting on the government's behalf in the case, including the police"); Pennsylvania v. Ritchie, 480 U.S. 39, 43, 51, 67 (1987) (requiring *Brady* disclosure of information in the files of a government agency that investigates child abuse and neglect); Giglio v. United States, 405 U.S. 150, 154 (1972) (charging each prosecutor with knowledge of all promises made by other lawyers in the same office, whether or not the prosecutor had actual knowledge or was negligent).

Furthermore, *Brady*'s test is a retrospective one. In other words, reviewing courts ask ex post whether the withheld evidence was material in light of all the evidence presented at trial. But prosecutors must determine whether evidence is material ex ante, before trial. Because of the adversary system, prosecutors have a poor sense of the defense's evidence and theory of the case until trial. And before trial, prosecutors expect to plea-bargain away most cases, so often they do not finish investigation and familiarize themselves with the evidence until trial is imminent. Prosecutors, unfamiliar with their own and the other side's evidence, have difficulty forecasting before trial what evidence will in retrospect seem to have been material.

In addition, the only enforcement mechanism is retrospective. If *Brady* material somehow does come to light, it most likely surfaces after the time has expired for a motion for new trial or appeal. Defendants must instead file collateral attacks such as habeas corpus petitions, seeking to reopen convictions that have already become final. By this time, however, defendants no longer have a right to court-appointed counsel, so most proceed pro se. Courts are flooded with other pro se habeas petitions, many of which are frivolous and few of which succeed. The volume of meritless claims may easily lead courts to view the entire exercise as a waste of time. In other words, jaded judges find it hard to spot the occasional innocence needle in the haystack.[47]

The psychology of hindsight exacerbates this problem. Psychologists have noted that people suffer from an inevitability bias. In other words, once people learn what actually happened, that outcome seems to have been inevitable all along. Thus, when reviewing convictions, people discount evidence that might have led to a different outcome, such as an acquittal.[48] A related problem is that of jumping to conclusions: people latch onto the evidence that they learn first and discount or explain away evidence that conflicts with their initial impressions. On habeas, a judge reviews a conviction by a trial court that an appellate court has also upheld. Judges see trial records that convinced juries of guilt beyond a reasonable doubt, and they are wary of second-guessing those verdicts. Psychologically, it is easier to discount the new piece of evidence than to upset the entire factual premise and solemn verdict of the trial.

---

[47] *See* Brown v. Allen, 344 U.S. 443, 537 (1953) (Jackson, J., concurring in result) ("It must prejudice the occasional meritorious application to be buried in a flood of worthless ones. He who must search a haystack for a needle is likely to end up with the attitude that the needle is not worth the search.").

[48] For a discussion of how this same problem infects retrospective review of ineffective-assistance-of-counsel claims, together with citations of the psychological literature, see Stephanos Bibas, *The Psychology of Hindsight and After-the-Fact Review of Ineffective Assistance of Counsel Claims*, 2004 Utah L. Rev. 1.

The intrusiveness of the remedy also makes judges reluctant to upset convictions based on *Brady* violations. Retrials before juries are cumbersome and time-consuming. In inquisitorial justice systems, judges (not juries) find the facts at trial, often based on paper records or dossiers. The emphasis is not on live, dramatic, in-court testimony before a jury. Thus, if an appellate court finds an evidentiary error at trial, it can simply fix the error and decide for itself whether the conviction stands or not. In our adversarial system, however, we claim that juries are the sole arbiters of facts. If a *Brady* violation prevented the jury from hearing exculpatory evidence, the appellate court cannot overtly fix the error, as that would intrude upon the jury's province. Instead, it must order an entire new trial, even if years have passed and witnesses have long since died.

The judge's temptation is to claim that the evidence was not material to the outcome—that there is no reasonable probability that the evidence would have produced a different result. Of course, if the withheld evidence is a DNA test that positively proves innocence, no judge will block that claim. But then again, a prosecutor would have to be both evil and stupid to bring such a case in the first place, or not to dismiss it as soon as that evidence came to light. The much more common *Brady* situations are ambiguous ones, where a piece of evidence might have bolstered a claim of reasonable doubt, but there is still much evidence of guilt. The prosecutor may think the evidence creates only a fleeting doubt as to guilt (and so probably is not material). Defense counsel, in contrast, might view the doubt as substantial (which probably is material). Because the two sides read the same evidence through different partisan lenses, each side is overly confident in its own arguments. If this evidence surfaces on habeas corpus, what is a judge to do? The judge may not be comfortable ordering a new trial for a defendant who is 85% or maybe 99% likely to be guilty, particularly if that judge has to run for re-election. The evidence arguably creates a reasonable doubt as to guilt, but arguably it does not. The judge's inclination may be to minimize the evidence's materiality and so find no *Brady* violation.

Empirical Evidence of How Rarely *Brady* Works in Practice

Empirical evidence confirms that, perhaps for these reasons, *Brady* claims infrequently succeed. I examined 210 *Brady* and *Giglio* cases decided in 2004. Of the sixty-three *Giglio* claims, thirteen (20.6%) succeeded (typically meaning a retrial), three others (4.8%) were remanded for evidentiary hearings, and forty-seven (74.6%) were unsuccessful. Non-*Giglio Brady* claims are even less successful. Of the 148 cases in this category, twelve (8.1%) succeeded, eight (5.4%) were remanded, and 128 (86.5%) were unsuccessful.[49] If one combines the two categories, one finds that twenty-five of 210 claims (11.9%) succeeded, eleven (5.2%) were remanded, and 174 (82.9%) were unsuccessful.

My sense as a former prosecutor is that not many cases involve significant *Brady* material and that smoking guns are almost unheard of, for otherwise the prosecutor would never have brought the case. The exception is that government informants and cooperating witnesses can frequently be impeached with their criminal records and cooperation agreements. But prosecutors routinely air this information during witnesses' direct examinations, to comply with *Giglio*, and juries very often convict anyway.

Empirical evidence confirms that most *Brady* and *Giglio* claims involve not smoking guns but ambiguous evidence, which prosecutors can easily overlook. My research assistants and I reviewed 448 *Brady* and *Giglio* claims that succeeded or were remanded between 1959 and August 2004.[50] This sample of cases is weighted toward and most comprehensive over the last decade. Success typically means that the court sent the case back for a new trial. Of these cases, 315 (70.3%) involved exculpatory information while 262 (58.5%) involved impeachment information. (Some cases involved both.) The most common claims involved undisclosed plea agreements or promises of leniency or immunity to witnesses, which occurred in sixty-four cases (14.3% of the overall total). Other commonly concealed *Giglio* information included witnesses' criminal records (32 cases, 7.1%), financial or other tangible incentives to testify (six cases, 1.3%), witnesses' prior inconsistent statements unrelated to identification (fifty-four cases, 12.1%), witnesses' having been hypnotized (nine cases, 2.0%), and other evidence of witness bias (thirteen cases, 2.9%). In thirty-six cases (8.0%) the *Brady* material consisted of the prosecution's failure to identify or make available witnesses who might have had helpful information. In twenty-one cases (4.7%) other evidence tended to support an affirmative defense. Twenty-six cases (5.8%) involved witness statements that related to misdescriptions, misidentifications, or failures to identify defendants. Seventy-one cases (15.8%) involved forensic, physical, or documentary evidence, and most

---

[49] On April 3, 2005, my research assistant ran the search SY,DI(Giglio (Brady /3 Maryland) (Brady /s (material claim exculpatory))) & DA(AFT 12/31/2003) & DA(BEF 1/1/2005). The search returned 214 hits, of which 210 were relevant. One of the cases contained *Giglio* and non-*Giglio Brady* evidence, so it falls into both categories.

[50] I drew these cases from the Capital Defense Network's lists of successful and remanded *Brady* claims in the United States Supreme Court, United States District Court, and state courts, updated through August 2004 (*available at* http://www.capdefnet.org/ in the Habeas Assistance and Training directory, WebSite Contents, Constitutional Issues, Exculpatory Evidence, Successful Brady Cases and Cases Remanded (last visited Apr. 26, 2005)). The lists attempt to be and appear to be comprehensive.

of the forensic involved weaknesses in forensic methodology, failures to test evidence, or evidence that the defendant or victim was intoxicated during the crime. In about seven of these cases (1.6%) the withheld forensic evidence strongly supported innocence. In other words, only about one-fourteenth of the successful or remanded cases fall into the most compelling categories: identification evidence or strong forensic evidence. Of all the cases in the sample, only twenty-seven (6.0%) persuaded me that the defendant was likely innocent. (Perhaps that just goes to show how partisan and jaundiced an ex-prosecutor's perspective is.)

What is striking to an ex-prosecutor is that, even in the small universe of successful cases, most of the *Brady* and *Giglio* evidence is quite consistent with guilt. Juries often convict in the face of impeachment evidence, for example. Indeed, in *Brady* itself the Maryland Court of Appeals doubted that the identity of the strangler was significant but gave Brady the benefit of the doubt. From the defense's perspective this evidence might create a reasonable doubt as to punishment, but in the heat of battle prosecutors may not see it that way. Thus, prosecutors can easily overlook this evidence.

Brady's Failure to Reach Incriminating Evidence, and Discovery

Another complaint about *Brady* is that it is limited to exculpatory and impeachment material. Defendants would prefer discovery that went far beyond *Brady* in two ways. First, most defendants have little money and few investigative resources of their own. Appointed defense counsel are often chronically underfunded, overworked, and of uneven competence.[51] Some are hardly able to function as the vigorous, effective adversaries idealized by the adversary system. The government, in contrast, has superior resources, more investigative powers, and sometimes better knowledge of the case. Thus, defendants would like the government not only to turn over exculpatory material that it already has, but also to investigate and develop other possible exculpatory leads. In other words, they would prefer a quasi-inquisitorial system, with a neutral magistrate who is charged with digging up the truth. Due process, however, does not require the police "to use a particular investigatory tool."[52] It does not even forbid the good-faith destruction of evidence that might be exculpatory.[53]

Second, defendants would prefer that prosecutors turn over inculpatory as well as exculpatory evidence. While few cases involve significant

---

[51] *See* Bibas, *supra* note 7, at 2476, 2479, 2481–82.

[52] Arizona v. Youngblood, 488 U.S. 51, 59 (1988).

[53] *Id.* at 58; California v. Trombetta, 467 U.S. 479, 488–89 (1984).

exculpatory evidence, all involve much inculpatory evidence. One chronic complaint about the adversary system is that it encourages trial by surprise or ambush, in which each side must guess about the other side's strength and theory of the case. It is difficult to plan a defense in the dark. Each side would prefer to know the other's key contentions and evidence and to research and prepare for them ahead of time.

Once again, the Supreme Court has refused to require this drastic departure from the traditional adversarial model. "Whether or not procedural rules authorizing [routine disclosure of prosecutors' entire files] might be desirable, the Constitution surely does not demand that much."[54] As a matter of constitutional law, the Court is right: there is no text, history, or tradition that requires open-file discovery. But, as a matter of policy, the traditional trial by ambush is troubling, exalting an extreme sporting theory of justice over the quest for truth. Oddly, since the 1930s criminal discovery has been far more restrictive than civil discovery. In civil cases, the parties can depose each other's witnesses, submit interrogatories, request admissions, and request extremely broad document discovery.[55] In criminal cases, however, most civil discovery devices do not exist. For example, very few states allow pre-trial depositions, in which each side can question the other side's witnesses on the record. This discovery imbalance seems backwards. Because more is at stake in criminal cases, one might think that criminal cases would allow even broader discovery. But traditionally, the opposite has been true.

Brady was part of a larger trend toward requiring more cooperation between the traditional adversaries. Even though the Constitution did not require it, the federal government and all states guaranteed defendants more discovery than *Brady*'s constitutional minimum. Three years after *Brady*, for example, Federal Rule of Criminal Procedure 16 authorized pre-trial disclosure of defendants' statements, examination or test results, documents, and tangible objects. In its current form, Rule 16 is even broader, requiring disclosure of all of these items if the government intends to use them at trial. It also requires disclosure of the defendant's

---

[54] United States v. Agurs, 427 U.S. 97, 109 (1976); *accord* United States v. Bagley, 473 U.S. 667, 675 (1985) (*Brady*'s "purpose is not to displace the adversary system as the primary means by which truth is uncovered, but to ensure that a miscarriage of justice does not occur. Thus, the prosecutor is not required to deliver his entire file to defense counsel...." (footnotes omitted)); Weatherford v. Bursey, 429 U.S. 545, 559 (1977) ("There is no general constitutional right to discovery in a criminal case"); *see also Agurs*, 427 U.S. at 112 note 20 (rejecting a defendant's right to all evidence that would help trial preparation, because "that standard would necessarily encompass incriminating evidence as well as exculpatory evidence, since knowledge of the prosecutor's entire case would always be useful in planning the defense.").

[55] *See* Fed. R. Civ. P. 30, 33, 34, 36.

criminal record and reports of expert witnesses whom the government intends to use at trial.[56] Once the case reaches trial, the government must disclose written or recorded statements by witnesses that relate to the subject of their testimony.[57] A majority of states provide similar discovery. A solid minority of states go even further than the federal rules. They require disclosure of the names, addresses, and (in some states) even prior statements of witnesses whom the government intends to call at trial.[58]

To prosecutors, this unilateral discovery seemed to be lopsided and unfair. After all, if defendants needed evidence to prepare their defenses, so too did prosecutors. If defendants needed a preview of the government's theory of the case, prosecutors needed a preview of the defense. The common refrain of these critics was that discovery ought to be a two-way street.[59]

Thus, the pendulum swung again, and procedural rules began to require discovery from the defense. In 1974, for example, the Federal Rules of Criminal Procedure were amended to require reciprocal discovery.[60] Today, in the federal and many state systems, defendants must notify prosecutors before trial that they intend to raise certain defenses, such as alibi, insanity, or self-defense. They must also disclose the names of the witnesses who will support these defenses.[61] In addition, if defendants seek documents, books, tangible objects, and expert reports from the government, they must reciprocate with the same kinds of evidence.[62]

---

[56] Fed. R. Crim. P. 16(a)(1); Fed. R. Crim. P. 16 advisory committee's note (1966).

[57] 18 U.S.C. § 3500(a), (B); Fed. R. Crim. P. 26.2(a).

[58] E.g., Alaska R. Crim. P. 16(b); Ariz. R. Crim. P. 11.4, 15.1; Ark. R. Crim. P. 17(1); Fla. R. Crim. P. 3.220(b)(1); N.J. Ct. R. 3:13–3(c)(6), (7) (also requiring disclosure of witnesses' past statements and criminal records).

[59] One might have thought that the privilege against self-incrimination forbade discovery from defendants. But Williams v. Florida, 399 U.S. 78, 81–86 (1970), upheld discovery of a defendant's alibi defense against a Fifth Amendment challenge, opening the way for other discovery obligations.

[60] As the Advisory Committee on the Federal Rules of Criminal Procedure explained, in the course of proposing the 1974 amendments: "[P]rosecution and defense discovery ... are related and ... the giving of a broader right of discovery to the defense is dependent upon giving also a broader right of discovery to the prosecution." Fed. R. Crim. P. 16 advisory committee's note (1974).

[61] E.g., Fed. R. Crim. P. 12.1, 12.2; Alaska R. Crim. P. 16(c)(5); Ariz. R. Crim. P. 15.2(b); Ark. R. Crim. P. 18.3.

[62] E.g., Fed. R. Crim. P. 16(b); Ala. R. Crim. P. 16.2, 25.5; Alaska R. Crim. P. 16(c)(4), (6) (expert reports and physical evidence only); Ariz. R. Crim. P. 11.4, 15.2(c); Ark. R. Crim. P. 18.2 (reports of medical and scientific tests only).

Brady Is Designed for Trials, Not Plea Bargaining

All of these expansions of discovery have reduced the ambush factor. But in most states, pre-trial discovery does not reach the evidence defendants want most: the names and statements of lay fact witnesses, such as eyewitnesses to a crime. Simply opening all prosecutorial and police files to defense inspection would eliminate trial by ambush, but at a high cost. Prosecutors are reluctant to disclose this information because they fear a variety of repercussions: Defendants may kill, intimidate, or bribe government witnesses into staying silent or changing their stories, particularly in violent, gang, and drug cases. Defendants may tailor their stories and alibis to fit the evidence. And many government witnesses are undercover agents or confidential informants. Revealing their names prematurely could not only jeopardize their safety but also undermine their usefulness in ongoing or future investigations.

In the federal and many state systems, defendants receive witnesses' names and statements at or on the eve of trial.[63] This trial timing is consistent with *Brady*'s focus on "avoidance of an unfair trial to the accused."[64] *Brady* is designed to give juries the information they need in time to reach accurate verdicts. So long as the defense has these statements shortly in advance of cross-examination, it can use them to impeach witnesses and prepare the defense case. (Some pieces of evidence, however, might require investigative follow-up, which would take longer.) Defendants are therefore less susceptible to trial by ambush. The prosecution may still be surprised, as the defense usually does not have to reveal its witnesses' names or statements until the close of the government's case.

Trials, however, are the exception rather than the rule. Today, only about 5% of adjudicated cases go to trial. 95% plead guilty, and most of these pleas result from plea negotiations and bargains between the prosecution and defense. *Brady* and discovery rules are designed to "avoid[] an unfair trial" by informing the jury, on the assumption that there will be a trial and a jury. Their timing is geared towards trial preparation and cross-examination, not plea negotiations. Most discovery rules require some prosecutorial disclosures shortly after indictment, but typically not witnesses' names and statements until trial.

The parties sometimes choose to supplement this discovery with informal discovery, giving each other a preview of their proof to facilitate plea bargaining. If, for example, the prosecution reveals to the defendant that five eyewitnesses saw him commit the crime, he may see that a trial conviction is inevitable and plead guilty. But informal discovery is

---

[63] *E.g.*, 18 U.S.C. § 3500; Fed. R. Crim. P. 26.2.

[64] 373 U.S. at 87.

sporadic and incomplete, and prosecutors are least likely to reveal their cards when they are bluffing with weak hands.

Because defendants do not have this information in time for plea bargaining, they must bargain in the dark. Typically, guilty defendants know that they are guilty and have a rough idea of what witnesses and other proof might link them to the crime. But defendants who are innocent or were intoxicated or mentally ill at the time of the crime have little knowledge of the evidence against them. Defendants who may be the most sympathetic may thus be at the greatest disadvantage in plea bargaining. They may be most susceptible to prosecutorial bluffing.

Some courts tried to extend *Brady* to plea bargaining, accelerating its timing to require disclosure in time for bargaining. They reasoned that disclosure was essential to the integrity of the plea-bargaining process. They contended that defendants needed exculpatory and impeachment information to make voluntary, knowing, intelligent pleas. And they saw *Brady* and *Giglio* information as necessary to ensure that guilty pleas are accurate and reliable.[65]

The Supreme Court, however, appears to have rejected these arguments. In *United States v. Ruiz*, the Court held that plea bargains may require defendants to waive their rights to impeachment material.[66] In a unanimous opinion, the Court reasoned that defendants have no right to impeachment information before trial. *Brady* is designed to prevent juries from being deceived at trial, the Court reasoned, not to facilitate plea negotiations and tactical decisions. Thus, this trial right does not apply before trial. Though the Court's holding is limited to *Giglio* impeachment material, much of its reasoning could apply with equal force to classic *Brady* exculpatory material.[67] True, most states require prosecutors to disclose *Brady* material at some point before trial.[68] But in the rest of the states, as well as the federal system, plea bargaining can continue to go on in the dark.

Whether this secrecy is a good or a bad thing depends on why prosecutors want to keep their cards hidden. If prosecutors bluff despite doubts about factual guilt, then actually innocent defendants might be convicted instead of persevering to possible acquittal at trial. The trade-

---

[65] *See, e.g.*, Sanchez v. United States, 50 F.3d 1448, 1453 (9th Cir. 1995); Banks v. United States, 920 F. Supp. 688, 691 (E.D. Va. 1996); Fambo v. Smith, 433 F. Supp. 590, 598–99 (W.D.N.Y.), *aff'd*, 565 F.2d 233 (2d Cir. 1977).

[66] 536 U.S. 622, 628–33 (2002).

[67] *See id.* at 629–33 (citing both *Brady* and *Giglio*).

[68] *See* Stanley Z. Fisher, *The Prosecutor's Ethical Duty to Seek Exculpatory Evidence in Police Hands: Lessons from England*, 68 Fordham L. Rev. 1379, 1417 note 206 (2000) (cataloguing forty-three states that require *Brady* disclosures at some point before trial).

off is more complex when witnesses die: revealing their deaths may let factually guilty defendants walk free, but concealing them induces guilty pleas from those who could never have been convicted at trial.

Often, prosecutors have good reasons to hide their cards besides covering up holes in the evidence. First, as noted, they fear witness intimidation and tampering and alibi fabrication and offer plea discounts to avoid these risks. Second, they offer plea discounts to keep undercover agents and confidential informants from having to testify, so they can develop future cases. Third, prosecutors want to spare traumatized witnesses, such as child-molestation and rape victims, from having to relive their victimization. If they can avoid releasing victims' names, sexual histories, or accounts of victimization, they plea-bargain cases away to do so. Fourth, prosecutors may be so overwhelmed with cases that they offer especially generous deals in exchange for not having to search for discovery. For example, to dispose of the flood of immigration cases swiftly, federal prosecutors in much of the Southwest offer huge discounts in exchange for waivers of all rights and immediate pleas.[69]

In short, prosecutors sometimes have legitimate reasons to buy off discovery rights with favorable plea bargains, and defendants have good reason to take these deals. Without more information, we cannot know how often non-disclosure jeopardizes innocent defendants and how often it simply protects witnesses, saves time and effort, and speeds up cases. *Brady* simply does not speak to the issue. Its focus on jury trials leaves plea-bargaining discovery unregulated by the Constitution.

The odd thing about the plea-bargaining system is that it looks vaguely like an inquisitorial model, with prosecutors trying unsuccessfully to fill judges' shoes.[70] Prosecutors sift evidence and make quasi-adjudicatory decisions about whether to charge and what punishments defendants actually deserve. Prosecutors and defense counsel cooperate and negotiate seemingly just compromises instead of fighting to complete victory or utter defeat. Yet, at root, prosecutors and defense counsel still come out of the traditional adversarial culture. They may cooperate much more than they used to, but at bottom prosecutors still see themselves not as neutral examiners but as partisan advocates.

Why Require Prosecutorial Misdeeds, Not Just Innocence?

A fifth limit on *Brady* is that, while it purported to disregard prosecutorial "guile," it nonetheless required a prosecutor's wrong rather than just a defendant's innocence. The Court's pendulum has swung back and forth on whether to emphasize the lawyers' and police's

---

[69] *Id.* at 625.

[70] *See generally* Gerard E. Lynch, *Our Administrative System of Criminal Justice*, 6 Fordham L. Rev. 2117, 2124–51 (1998).

blameworthiness, the defendant's innocence, or some of both. In *Mooney* it required knowing prosecutorial use of perjury, but in *Brady* it treated the prosecutor's good faith as irrelevant. In cases involving preservation of possibly exculpatory evidence, however, the Court swung back again. *Arizona v. Youngblood* held that destruction of evidence does not violate due process unless the defendant can prove that the police acted in bad faith.[71] The same pendulum has swung back and forth on the importance of defense counsel's diligence. In *United States v. Agurs* the Court's materiality test hinged on defense counsel's actions. A piece of evidence was more likely to qualify as material when defense counsel specifically requested it than when defense counsel made no request or only a general request.[72] But in *United States v. Bagley*, the Court rejected the *Agurs* framework. *Bagley* applies the same standard of materiality regardless of whether defense counsel specifically requests a piece of evidence.[73] (If, however, the prosecutor has rebuffed a specific request, a court will be more likely to find that the defense lawyer relied on the prosecutor's answer, so good defense lawyers still make specific requests.) In short, the Court is torn between emphasizing the badness of the lawyers and police and the innocence of the defendant. It wants both to punish misconduct and to free the innocent, but each goal may compete with the other. The bottom line today is that prosecutorial mens rea and defense counsel requests are largely irrelevant (except in destruction-of-evidence cases). But, as we shall see, prosecutorial misconduct (actus reus) still matters greatly.

If *Brady* is fundamentally about innocence and not prosecutorial misconduct, why should it depend on whether the prosecutor happened to have a material fact and withheld it? In other words, should courts reverse convictions wherever there is significant new evidence of actual innocence, regardless of whether the police and prosecutor ever found it?

The law focuses on procedural violations rather than substantive innocence in order to preserve the jury's privileged place in the adversary system. Recall that judges supervise procedural issues and juries

---

[71] 488 U.S. 51, 58 (1988); *see also* California v. Trombetta, 467 U.S. 479, 488–89 (1984).

[72] *Compare* United States v. Agurs, 427 U.S. 97, 104–06 (1976) ("When the prosecutor receives a specific and relevant request, the failure to make any response is seldom, if ever, excusable."), *with id.* at 112 (in general-request or no-request cases, evidence is material "if the omitted evidence creates a reasonable doubt that did not otherwise exist").

[73] 473 U.S. at 682 (opinion of Blackmun, J.) (holding that the same standard covers specific requests, general requests, and no requests: "The evidence is material only if there is a reasonable probability that, had the evidence been disclosed to the defense, the result of the proceeding would have been different. A 'reasonable probability' is a probability sufficient to undermine confidence in the outcome."); *id.* at 685 (White, J., concurring in part and concurring in the judgment) (agreeing with the test set forth in the first quoted sentence of the previous parenthetical).

determine substantive ones. A trial or appellate judge cannot simply find a defendant innocent or guilty, as that would intrude on the jury's sacred province. Rather, the judge usually has to find a procedural error. For example, the judge may rule that the prosecutor made an improper kind of argument or introduced a prejudicial piece of evidence. The ordinary remedy is to send the case back for another jury trial. (A judge may, however, occasionally find that the evidence was insufficient to sustain a conviction or that the interests of justice require a new trial.) In other words, defendants argue their innocence to juries, but legal points to judges. A defendant who wants to challenge a conviction after trial or on appeal must argue that there was a procedural defect in the trial. If the trial or appellate court agrees, the remedy is a whole new trial, unless the procedural error was not properly preserved or was harmless.

Judges are human and are most willing to reverse convictions when they think that defendants may be factually innocent. But claims of factual innocence, by themselves, do not show any procedural errors in jury verdicts. To persuade, defendants must take claims of factual innocence and dress them up as procedural errors. For example, they may argue that their lawyers were ineffective and that there is a reasonable probability that the jurors would have acquitted if counsel had made a certain argument. In other words, while doubt about guilt may sway a judge's heart, a defendant also needs the hook of a procedural claim to open the courthouse door.[74]

In inquisitorial systems, in contrast, judges find both facts and law, without juries and the elaborate procedures surrounding them. Judges focus on the substantive questions of guilt and punishment instead of evidentiary and procedural rules. On appeal, defendants can again argue their innocence. If the trial court neglected to consider a piece of evidence, the appellate court need not send the case back for trial. It can decide for itself on the paper record whether, in light of the additional evidence, the defendant is guilty.

Brady claims exemplify the adversary system's blend of procedural error and substantive doubts about guilt. The *Brady* test requires that evidence be both exculpatory and material—there must be a reasonable probability that it would have led to acquittal or lesser punishment. But it also requires that the prosecution withheld or suppressed this evidence. Perhaps prosecutorial withholding is a proxy for very damaging

---

[74] The Supreme Court has left open the possibility that "a truly persuasive demonstration of 'actual innocence'" might itself trigger a due process right to federal habeas relief, even without any other procedural error. But even if the Constitution guarantees such a due process right, the standard is an extremely high one that defendants will rarely satisfy. *See* Herrera v. Collins, 506 U.S. 390, 417 (1993).

evidence,[75] but it is at best an imperfect proxy. Even though *Brady* purports to ignore prosecutorial fault, it still requires some prosecutorial withholding or suppression, whether intentional or not. Under this standard, some guilty defendants receive windfalls simply because their adversaries goofed, while some innocent defendants receive no relief because their prosecutors played by the rules. In this way, the sporting theory of justice lives on.

CONCLUSION

Brady was a significant step toward making adversarial combat fairer, and it was part of a trend towards liberalizing discovery on both sides. It indirectly promotes reliability by modestly leveling the adversarial playing field, compensating a bit for prosecutors' superior resources and access to evidence. *Brady* could have meant much more, though. It could have portended a shift away from adversarial combat at trial towards a joint search for guilt or innocence. Ultimately, though, our proceduralized adversarial model has rendered *Brady*, if not a dead letter, not a very vigorous one either. Judges are too weak, prosecutors are too partisan, enforcement is too difficult, discovery is too limited, and plea bargains are too widespread for *Brady* to influence many cases. *Brady* remains an important symbol but in some ways a hollow one.

One can only speculate about whether *Brady*'s activism contributed to its failings. When the Court creates a sweeping new rule, without the benefit of common-law experimentation, it cannot know how the rule will fare in practice. The Court could instead have let courts, legislatures, and the bar experiment with more workable rules and enforcement mechanisms. Perhaps, if it had, *Brady* would have had more impact on our adversary system. Justice White's concurrence may have been prescient after all.

---

[75] *See* Arizona v. Youngblood, 488 U.S. 51, 58 (1988) (confining the police duty to preserve evidence to "those cases in which the police themselves by their conduct indicate that the evidence could form a basis for exonerating the defendant.").

5

Miranda v. Arizona: A Modest But Important Legacy

Stephen Schulhofer

The story of *Miranda*[1] is in large part a doctrinal story centered on the evolution and content of Fourteenth Amendment "due process" and the Fifth Amendment's self-incrimination clause. *Miranda* is also, of course, the story of interrogation as an important tool of criminal investigation. More generally, the *Miranda* story is in microcosm the story of the twentieth-century development of policing as a profession.

But even these large topics are among the narrower facets of the complete *Miranda* story. *Miranda* epitomizes the importance and difficulty of outside efforts to regulate law-enforcement behavior. *Miranda* is the poster child for the Supreme Court's fluctuating commitment to safeguarding the fairness of the criminal justice system as a whole. More broadly yet, it is no exaggeration to say that, more than any other word or phrase in our lexicon, *"Miranda"* stands for judicial activism, for the volatile dynamics of crime-control politics, and for the problematic legitimacy and effectiveness of Supreme Court attempts to assure justice in American social arrangements at any or all levels.

The approach of *Miranda*'s fortieth birthday signals more than an interesting anniversary. Today only our most senior judges, lawyers and detectives know at first hand the world before *Miranda*. Soon none of that generation will remain professionally active. Their world, legally and operationally, was very different from the criminal justice world we inhabit today.

Interrogation and Constitutional Law Before 1960

The Fourteenth Amendment, ratified in 1867, imposed on states, for the first time, an obligation to respect "due process of law." But, as interpreted prior to the 1960s, the Fourteenth Amendment did not require states to follow any particular rules of criminal procedure. "Due process" meant only that criminal investigations and trials must comport with fundamental fairness, a loose and highly permissive concept

---

[1] Miranda v. Arizona, 384 U.S. 436 (1966).

applied on a rough case-by-case basis.[2] States were free, if they wished, to permit searches and seizures without warrants or probable cause, or to prohibit such searches but allow their courts to use evidence illegally obtained.[3] States were free to try felony defendants without a jury.[4] Absent "shocking" circumstances, they were not required to provide indigent defendants any assistance of counsel whatever.[5] And states could formally compel a prospective criminal defendant to give testimony under oath, even when the testimony was potentially incriminating.[6]

Police interrogation was governed by the same flexible standard. Over time, certain particularly brutal tactics were ruled impermissible per se. But even in the 1950s, milder physical force—a few slaps and kicks, for example—did not necessarily render a subsequent confession inadmissible.[7] Police legally could—and often did—use almost any methods short of direct physical violence. The resulting confessions were admissible unless they were considered "involuntary" in the sense that police tactics had "overborne" the particular suspect's will in light of the totality of the circumstances.[8] From the 1930s through the early 1960s, the Supreme Court became progressively less willing to condone intense pressure and psychological abuse. But the Court continued to uphold the admissibility of confessions obtained after long hours of nonstop interrogation and after repeated police refusals to honor a suspect's pleas to be left alone or to be allowed to contact family or counsel.[9]

The tactics deployed in a New York City police investigation of the late 1950s were by no means atypical. *Spano v. New York*[10] involved a young, emotionally unstable foreign-born suspect who had already been indicted. The method of interrogation included continuous custodial questioning for eight hours, from late evening till early morning; the use

---

[2] *E.g.* Palko v. Connecticut, 302 U.S. 319 (1937); *see* Sanford H Kadish, Methodology and Criteria in Due Process Adjudication—A Survey and Criticism, 66 Yale L.J. 319 (1957).

[3] *E.g.* Wolf v. Colorado, 338 U.S. 25 (1949). In *Wolf* the Court suggested that it would violate due process for a state to affirmatively authorize unreasonable searches, but the Court refused to require states to provide any remedy for such searches.

[4] Compare Duncan v. Louisiana, 391 U.S. 145 (1968).

[5] Betts v. Brady, 316 U.S. 455 (1942).

[6] Adamson v. California, 332 U.S. 46 (1947).

[7] Stroble v. California, 343 U.S. 181 (1952).

[8] *E.g.*, Watts v. Indiana, 338 U.S. 49 (1949). *See* Yale Kamisar, What is an Involuntary Confession?, 17 Rutgers L. Rev. 728 (1963).

[9] *E.g.* Crooker v. California, 357 U.S. 433 (1958). *See* Catherine Hancock, Due Process Before Miranda, 70 Tul. L. Rev. 2195 (1996).

[10] 360 U.S. 315 (1959).

of teams of detectives in relays; repeated denials of Spano's requests to contact the lawyer he had already retained; and deceptive use of a childhood friend, who repeatedly implored Spano to talk, falsely telling him that his refusal to cooperate had placed the friend's job in jeopardy. The Court drew a line of sorts, holding Spano's confession involuntary. But in reversing the conviction, the Court made clear that none of the police tactics was inherently improper in itself. Eight hours of nonstop interrogation of an unwilling, foreign-born suspect, for example, or the deceptive use of a childhood friend, was perfectly permissible, except (perhaps) in combination with some—or all—of the other factors that had made the *Spano* interrogation especially unfair. And that opinion was written—in 1959—by Chief Justice Earl Warren himself.

The Criminal Procedure Revolution

All this changed dramatically, in a breathtakingly short period of time. In 1961, the Court ruled in *Mapp v. Ohio*[11] that states could no longer admit evidence obtained by unreasonable search and seizure. In 1963 *Gideon v. Wainwright*[12] held that indigent felony defendants could no longer be tried without being offered the assistance of counsel. In 1964 the Court in *Malloy v. Hogan*[13] required states to respect the privilege against self-incrimination; the compulsion of a formal subpoena could no longer be used to force a criminal defendant to testify against himself in court. In 1966, *Miranda* held that the self-incrimination privilege also applied in police interrogation. Two years later, *Duncan v. Louisiana*[14] required states to provide jury trials in serious criminal cases.

This was a genuine, full-fledged revolution. Scholars still debate the nature and scope of changes on the ground, but there is no doubt that the Court's doctrinal moves amounted to a sea change in the capacity and obligation of federal judges to supervise state police practices and state criminal trials. The Fourth, Fifth and Sixth Amendments, previously irrelevant to criminal justice in the states, became—almost overnight—a comprehensive "code of criminal procedure." And the adoption, elaboration and ultimate responsibility for enforcement of this code was placed entirely in the hands of the U.S. Supreme Court.

---

[11] Mapp v. Ohio, 367 U.S. 643 (1961). *Mapp* is the subject of a separate chapter in this volume.

[12] 72 U.S. 335 (1963). *Gideon* is the subject of a separate chapter in this volume, along with Strickland v. Washington, 466 U.S. 668 (1984).

[13] 378 U.S. 1 (1964).

[14] 391 U.S. 145 (1968). *Duncan* is the subject of a separate chapter in this volume.

Why did this happen? To anyone with a rosy view of American democracy in the Eisenhower and Kennedy years, the development must seem a mixture of the incomprehensible, the illegitimate, the benighted and the outrageous. Yet the Justices who accomplished (or perpetrated) this coup were no ivory-tower academic theorists pushing an abstract ideological agenda. Nor for that matter were they, like most of today's Justices, people who had spent long stretches of their careers in the rarefied atmosphere of the federal appellate courts. Clark (author of *Mapp*), Black (author of *Gideon*), Warren (author of *Miranda*), and White (author of *Duncan*) were sophisticated politicians and intensely practical men, all of them had moved from high political office directly to the Supreme Court, and none had hints of what we would today consider civil-libertarian credentials.[15] Yet they knew at first hand the realities of police behavior, prosecutorial practice, state criminal trials and—above all—the daunting politics of state and federal legislative reform. They knew these matters intimately, in ways that contemporary academic critics of Warren Court activism can at best only imagine.

What concerns preoccupied these Justices? There was, most obviously, the appalling police behavior repeatedly made evident in the Court's cases of the 1940s, 1950s and early 1960s. The problems were acute in the Southern states, especially in cases with racial overtones. But the difficulties were national in scope; several of the Court's most troubling cases of this period involved the police of New York City, Los Angeles,

---

[15] None of them, moreover, had had significant judicial experience prior to their Supreme Court appointments; their credentials lay in the world of politics. Tom Clark was an Assistant Attorney General, Criminal Division (1943–45), and Attorney General (1945–49) immediately before he was appointed to the Supreme Court. *See* R. Kirkendall, Tom C. Clark, in The Justices of the United States Supreme Court 1789–1969, at 2665–67 (L. Friedman & F. Israel, eds., 1969).

Hugo Black, after a brief stint as a police court judge in Birmingham, Alabama (1911–12), had served as a county solicitor (1914–17) and U.S. Senator (1927–37) before being appointed to the Court in 1937. *See* Roger Newman, Hugo Black 29–32, 36–47, 125–36, 237–38 (1997). Black had been a member of the Ku Klux Klan from 1923–26. *Id.*, at 91–92, 103.

Earl Warren had been a District Attorney (1925–38), Attorney General of California (1939–43), Governor of California (1943–53), and Republican candidate for vice-president on the Dewey ticket (1948), prior to his appointment to the Court in 1953. *See* G. Edward White, Earl Warren 27–34, 47–49, 100–07, 137–40 (1982). As Attorney General of California, Warren had played a major role in supporting and implementing the internment of Japanese–Americans during World War II. *See id.*, at 67–78.

Byron White served as Colorado state chairman of the Kennedy presidential campaign (1960) and Deputy Attorney General (1961–62) prior to joining the Court. *See* Dennis Hutchinson, The Man Who Once Was Whizzer White 232–33, 241–63 (1998). At the Justice Department White had played a leading role in law enforcement efforts of the period, including Attorney General Robert Kennedy's initiatives against crime and labor racketeering. *See id.*, at 272–87.

and Cleveland.[16] And the existence of a serious problem was not in itself in dispute. Virtually all the Justices agreed that the practices coming to light were egregious and intolerable; the main disagreements within the Court were over the propriety of judicial action to stamp them out.

Beyond these problems of police misconduct in general, the interrogation cases posed a distinctive set of problems. The effort to separate legitimate police questioning from illegal abuse was framed by the "voluntariness" test. But in nearly three decades of experience using this test, its practical problems had become impossible to ignore. The voluntariness standard left police without essential guidance in what they were permitted to do. Its vagueness left judges without guidance as well and impaired the forward-looking value of appellate review. Decisions were fatally dependent on resolution of a "swearing contest" between police and the suspect, with no reliable way to assess the subtleties of pressure in the interrogation room or even the more straightforward facts about what had occurred. The test endorsed application of a "suction process"[17] to unwilling suspects and allowed considerable interrogation pressure that many considered inherently incompatible with "voluntary" choice. Minority suspects, the unsophisticated and the psychologically vulnerable were especially susceptible to manipulation and abuse. That factor in turn was not only troubling in itself, but it also posed a major risk of eliciting false confessions. Meanwhile, hardened criminals were left at a relative advantage. And extreme physical brutality, while clearly illegal, was not adequately checked by the test and in some ways was indirectly encouraged by the "suction process" it legitimated.

As with the broader problems of police misconduct, the interrogation cases often left strong judicial majorities in agreement that unacceptable methods had been used. Again, the important disagreements within the Court were only over the best way to remedy the consequences and prevent their recurrence.

Here other factors enter the picture, shaping the disagreements as they evolved during the 1950s: the absence, over several decades, of any serious state legislative efforts to rein in such practices; the virtual paralysis of the federal legislative process in matters touching the autonomy of the Southern states in the areas of civil liberties and civil

---

16 *See, e.g.*, Spano v. New York, 360 U.S. 315 (1959) (New York City); Mapp v. Ohio, 367 U.S. 643 (1961) (Cleveland); Rochin v. California, 342 U.S. 165 (1952) (Los Angeles). An extensive discussion of many such examples appears in Miranda, 384 U.S., at 445–48 & notes 6–7.

17 Watts v. Indiana, 338 U.S. 49, 53 (1949) (opinion of Frankfurter, J.). For more detailed discussion of these problems posed by the voluntariness test, *see* Stephen J. Schuhofer, Confessions and the Court, 79 Mich. L. Rev. 865, 869–72 (1981) (hereinafter cited as Schulhofer, Confessions).

rights; the continuing willingness of state judges to condone or ignore egregious police misconduct; and the persistence of such police behavior even in the face of Supreme Court pronouncements repeatedly and forcefully condemning it.

Political solutions to these problems, through community mobilization on the ground, had begun but were being blocked by distinctly non-democratic processes. Black citizens whose only offense was their effort to register to vote were met with violent intimidation on a wide scale and outright murder, perpetrated with impunity thanks to the connivance of local law-enforcement officials and juries.[18] More distant factors probably played a role as well: the then-recent horrors of Nazi Germany; the resulting sensitivity to police-state tactics, racial injustice, and judicial passivity in the face of them; and the perceived urgency of the Cold War struggle to win third-world hearts and minds that were questioning the justice and fairness of American democracy.[19]

All these concerns drove "incorporation"—the application to the States of pertinent provisions of the federal Bill of Rights—and especially the three pieces of incorporation that preceded *Miranda*: the exclusionary rule (*Mapp*, 1961), the right to counsel (*Gideon*, 1963), and the privilege against self-incrimination (*Malloy*, 1964). These prior decisions of course are important in their own right and worthy of separate discussion. But *Miranda* cannot be understood without reference to them; they are crucial pieces of the *Miranda* story itself. More than mere background or illustrations of the Warren Court mind-set, *Mapp, Gideon* and *Malloy* made it impossible for the Warren Court to avoid direct confrontation with new challenges to police interrogation as then practiced.

First, consider *Malloy*. It held that the states were subject not only to the Fourteenth Amendment ban on involuntary statements but also to the Fifth Amendment ban on "compel[ed]" incriminating statements.

Despite the verbal affinity between the operative terms (compelled and involuntary), it was clear to all concerned that the Fifth Amendment prohibition had much wider reach. Involuntary statements, though variously defined, are in essence those obtained by something akin to breaking a witness's will, and such statements can never be used for any purpose. But statements obtained by threat of some less grievous penalty (obtained by subpoena, for example) normally are not problematic at all. Indeed the process of *compelling* witnesses to testify is routine—the bread and butter of litigation.[20] It is worth repeating this contrast

---

[18] *See* Todd Gitlin, The Sixties: Years of Hope, Days of Rage 151 (1987).

[19] *See* Margaret Raymond, Rejecting Totalitarianism: Translating the Guarantees of Constitutional Criminal Procedure, 76 N.C. L. Rev. 1193 (1998).

[20] *See* United States v. Nixon, 418 U.S. 683, 709 (1974). *See generally* Stephen J. Schulhofer, Miranda, Dickerson, and the Puzzling Persistence of Fifth Amendment Excep-

between the two concepts, because—although the contrast is clear and indispensable—it is so easily and so often overlooked. Long before *Malloy,* states had been barred from ever using "involuntary" incriminating statements, but *Malloy* also barred use of "compelled" incriminating statements. The dissenters in *Malloy* were well aware that this holding brought more than redundancy or a mere change in terminology. They understood clearly that the Fifth Amendment prohibition swept much more broadly than that of the Fourteenth, and they forcefully protested the imposition of the more stringent restriction on the states.[21]

The compulsion at issue in *Malloy* itself was that of judicial subpoena. But the Court could not long avoid deciding whether informal pressures should be considered equivalent to those of a formal subpoena. And if informal pressures could ever qualify, it would be difficult to deny that the informal pressures brought to bear in police interrogation—pressures intentionally designed to elicit incriminating information from unwilling suspects—easily qualified as "compelling" in the Fifth Amendment sense, even when they did not rise to the level of coercion that breaks the suspect's will.[22]

Gideon added further, wholly independent concerns. The case involved a defendant who had requested counsel at trial. But in light of Sixth Amendment doctrines previously settled, *Gideon* by itself took the Court 90% of the way to *Miranda.* The case law had already made clear that the right to counsel applied not only at the trial but early enough to permit "effective aid in the preparation and trial of the case."[23] And just a year after *Gideon,* the Court in *Escobedo* held that post-arrest interrogation designed to elicit a confession, after suspicion had already "focus[ed]" on the arrestee, was a "critical ... stage when legal aid and advice are surely needed."[24] Therefore, the Court held, the Sixth Amendment (with the exclusionary-rule concept inspired by *Mapp*) required suppression of the resulting confession.

Escobedo (arguably a natural application of the "critical stage" concept) cast a dark shadow over customary police interrogation practices, as once again the decision's proponents and critics both understood. The only wiggle room left for police interrogators, short of asking the Court to overrrule *Escobedo* (or *Gideon!*) was the fact that the

---

tionalism, 99 Mich. L. Rev. 941, 944–48 (2001) (hereinafter cited as Schulhofer, Exceptionalism).

[21] Malloy, 378 U.S., at 14–20 (Harlan, J., dissenting).

[22] *See* Stephen J. Schulhofer, Reconsidering Miranda, 54 U. Chi. L. Rev. 435, 440–46 (1987).

[23] Powell v. Alabama, 287 U.S. 45, 71 (1932).

[24] Escobedo v. Illinois, 378 U.S. 478, 488 (1964) (internal quotation marks omitted).

defendants in those cases knew their rights and had requested counsel specifically. If the Sixth Amendment right could be limited to those circumstances, *Gideon* and *Escobedo* would not require police to warn suspects of their rights.

But Sixth Amendment doctrine had already settled this point too, and in a clear fashion that left little room for compromise. Even absent an affirmative request, the Sixth Amendment required access to counsel except when the defendant had made "an intentional relinquishment or abandonment of a known right."[25] Unless the Court was prepared to reverse itself and announce (counterfactually) that police interrogation was *not* a critical stage, or unless it was willing to except police interrogation from the normal principle that the right to counsel cannot be lost by ignorance or failure to make an affirmative request, the essential parameters of *Miranda* had been fixed, and police interrogation as theretofore practiced had been doomed, from the moment that *Gideon*—one of the Warren Court's most universally celebrated decisions—had been decided. Indeed, *Gideon* and related Sixth Amendment principles cast an even wider shadow, because the earlier cases had already recognized that the right to assistance at critical stages applied even when the defendant was not in custody.[26]

Thus, *Gideon* and *Malloy*—decisions that are never considered controversial today—made something very much like *Miranda*, or an even more restrictive decision, very difficult for a principled Court to avoid.

Finally, the voluntariness test then used to assess interrogation added momentum from an independent direction. Even as the test grew more sensitive and restrictive, the Court had become increasingly dissatisfied with its effectiveness. The 1959 *Spano* case had prompted four concurring Justices (not yet with Warren's support) to conclude that a new framework completely severed from voluntariness "balancing" was necessary.[27] In 1961, Justice Frankfurter made a monumentally elaborate effort to provide workable parameters for a rehabilitated voluntari-

---

[25] Johnson v. Zerbst, 304 U.S. 458, 464 (1938).

[26] *E.g.* Powell v. Alabama, 287 U.S. 45 (1932). *Powell*, or "the Scottsboro Boys" case, is the subject of a separate chapter in this volume. The *Powell* defendants were in custody, but the Court's decision was based on the need for counsel *before trial*, to assure adequate opportunity for preparation. The *Powell* principle clearly applies to defendants not in custody. *See, e.g.*, Massiah v. United States, 377 U.S. 201 (1964). For the classic discussion of the tension between the right to counsel at trial and the pre-*Escodebo* refusal to recognize a right to the assistance of counsel during pre-trial interrogation, *see* Yale Kamisar, Equal Justice in the Gatehouses and Mansions of American Criminal Procedure, in Criminal Justice in Our Time 19–36 (Y. Kamisar, F. Inbau & T. Arnold, eds. 1965).

[27] Spano, 360 U.S. at 324 (Douglas, J., concurring) (joined by Justices Black and Brennan); *id.*, at 326 (Stewart, J., concurring) (joined by Justices Douglas and Brennan).

ness test.[28] Yet the effort was patently unsuccessful; only one other Justice was willing to join his opinion. The Court's decisions were replete with expressions of frustration with the voluntariness test and recognition, by its opponents and its erstwhile supporters alike, that over decades of experience, it had proved completely unworkable in practice.[29] Matters could not long continue in that vein, in any Court committed to controlling police-interrogation abuses.

In sum, against a background of unusually powerful political and social developments, three strands of specific doctrinal evolution (voluntariness, self-incrimination and the right to counsel) converged in the run-up to *Miranda*, a perfect storm poised to engulf investigation routines that had been commonplace for generations.

The *Miranda* Decision

As every law student and nearly all television viewers know, *Miranda* held that before questioning a suspect in custody, police must deliver a now-familiar four-part warning—that the suspect has the right to remain silent, that anything he says can be used against him, that he has the right to the assistance of counsel, and that if he cannot afford one, counsel will, on request, be appointed for him at state expense. This understanding of *Miranda*, while not wrong as far as it goes, misses nearly all the important features of the opinion, both analytically and operationally.

Analytically, the key to *Miranda* is the Court's decision to rely on Fifth Amendment principles, applying the ban on "compulsion" to stationhouse questioning but *rejecting* the broader restrictions that a Sixth Amendment right to counsel would have triggered. Operationally, the crucial portions of the holding are those that require police to follow specific procedures *after* the warnings are given. Questioning cannot proceed until the police obtain the suspect's "knowing and intelligent" waiver of his rights, they must not use inducements or trickery to obtain that waiver, and if the suspect indicates at any time that he no longer wishes to talk, then all questioning must cease.

This last step, the cut-off rule, is the real heart of *Miranda*. Neither the famous warnings nor the waiver requirement imposed radically new limits on police practices, but the automatic cut-off rule was a dramatic change in permissible interrogation tactics.

Political and Jurisprudential Fallout

Miranda drew bitter opposition, literally from day one. Prosecutors protested loudly that the Court had handcuffed the police, usurping

---

[28] Culombe v. Connecticut, 367 U.S. 568 (1961) (plurality opinion)(joined by Justice Stewart).

[29] *See* Schulhofer, Confessions, *supra* note 16, at 869.

legislative prerogatives by imposing detailed rules that allegedly guaranteed the release of thousands of violent criminals. Two years later, after contentious hearings and biting criticism of the Court, Congress, in a provision of the "Omnibus Crime Control and Safe Streets Act of 1968," purported to overrule *Miranda* and reinstate "voluntariness" as the sole criterion for determining the admissibility of a confession.[30]

Even then, the political firestorm did not abate. Richard Nixon had observed Barry Goldwater's attempt to raise "law and order" as a major theme in the 1964 presidential campaign.[31] For two years prior to *Miranda*, Nixon had been exploring ways to make the argument work more successfully against liberal opponents and the Democratic Party. For Nixon, *Miranda* came at the perfect time and provided just the highly visible opening he needed. Sharply escalating crime rates in the mid–1960s and urban rioting throughout the country in 1968 gave the issue powerful political traction. Judges and politicians who were "soft on crime" became Nixon's specific target in the 1968 presidential campaign, which gave prominent place to his pledge to appoint "strict constructionists" and remake the Warren Court.

Once elected, Nixon did just that, appointing Warren Burger as Chief Justice and adding William Rehnquist soon thereafter. And the Burger Court moved quickly in the direction that Nixon and much of the country desired. Although the Court (and the Nixon Justice Department) both ignored the 1968 statute's purported repeal of *Miranda*, the Court adopted a long list of qualifications and exceptions to the *Miranda* requirements and repeatedly found ways to avoid reversing convictions in cases involving *Miranda* violations.[32] By the mid–1970s the Burger Court had decided numerous cases presenting *Miranda* issues and had not reversed a single conviction on *Miranda* grounds.[33]

Making matters worse, the Burger Court seemed determined to pull the ground out from under *Miranda's* conceptual foundation and to cast doubt on the decision's legitimacy. The Court repeatedly referred to *Miranda* in grudging terms, even to the point of stating that the *Miranda* rules were not constitutionally required, that *Miranda* "sweeps more broadly than the Fifth Amendment itself,"[34] and that confessions

---

[30] U.S.C. § 3501.

[31] *See* Lia Baker, Miranda: Crime, Law and Politics 40–42 (1983).

[32] *E.g.*, Oregon v. Elstad, 470 U.S. 298 (1985); New York v. Quarles, 467 U.S. 649 (1984); Michigan v. Tucker, 417 U.S. 433 (1974).

[33] *See* Geoffey R. Stone, The Miranda Doctrine in the Burger Court, 1977 Sup. Ct. Rev. 99.

[34] Elstad, 470 U.S., at 306.

taken in violation of *Miranda* were not necessarily compelled.[35] *Miranda*, the leading symbol of Warren Court activism, seemed headed for oblivion.

Yet the Court hesitated to deliver the *coup de grace*. And as time passed, the Court's impetus to do so seemed to slacken, perhaps because subsequent decisions seemed to have softened *Miranda*'s impact or because the catastrophic law-enforcement consequences so confidently predicted in 1966 never materialized.[36]

When Edwin Meese became President Reagan's Attorney General, he pressed the Department of Justice to complete this piece of unfinished business by attacking *Miranda* head on.[37] But he ran into surprising resistance—from his own Solicitor General,[38] from professional prosecutors and even from police chiefs nationwide.[39] Though antipathy to *Miranda* remained, especially among those like Meese whose law-enforcement careers had begun in the 1950s, there was now a widespread impression that *Miranda* was not so bad after all.

By the 1980s a common view among police chiefs was that *Miranda* did not substantially impede the flow of confessions and even had some advantages for police.[40] *Miranda* made clear the steps necessary to insure a confession's admissibility and in some cases even helped interrogators get confessions in the first place, probably by inducing suspects to let down their guard and encouraging them to believe that they could safely attempt to talk their way out of trouble. More broadly, *Miranda*, once seen as a symbol of illegitimate judicial activism, had become for the police a legitimating symbol of their own professionalism, a highly public affirmation of their respect for the rights of suspects and for the rule of law.[41]

---

[35] *Id.*, at 312, suggesting that a genuine violation of the Fifth Amendment requires proof of "physical violence or other deliberate means calculated to break the suspect's will."

[36] Mich L. Rev 2475, 79–85.

[37] *See* Phillip Shenon, "Meese Seen as Ready to Challenge Rule on Telling Suspects of Rights," N.Y. Times, Jan. 22, 1987, p. 1.

[38] Charles Fried, Order and Law 46 (1990).

[39] *See, e.g.*, Eduardo Paz–Martinez, "Police Chiefs Defend Miranda Against Meese Threats," Boston Globe, Feb.5, 1987, pp. 25, 29.

[40] *See* Stephen J. Schulhofer, Miranda's Practical Effect: Substantial Benefits and Vanishingly Small Social Costs, 90 Nw. U.L.Rev. 500, 503–04 & notes 9 & 13 (1996) (hereafter cited as Schulhofer, Practical Effect).

[41] *See* Richard A. Leo. The Impact of Miranda Revisited, 86 J. Crim. L. & Criminology 621, 680 (1996).

Miranda's most committed opponents nonetheless persisted in their efforts to overturn it. And in 2000 they finally managed to get the attention of the Supreme Court when a federal appellate court held (rejecting the Justice Department's position in support of *Miranda*) that the 1968 statute had validly superceded *Miranda* and replaced its strictures with the old due-process voluntariness test.[42]

By this point there were decades of Supreme Court precedent insisting that *Miranda*'s rules were not constitutionally required. But in decisions rendered at the same time and thereafter, there were also numerous Supreme Court judgments that reversed state criminal convictions on *Miranda* grounds,[43] an action that would be untenable, indeed inconceivable, if *Miranda*'s rules were not constitutionally required. Observers on both sides of the issue hoped that the Court would resolve this paradox, either by firmly endorsing *Miranda*'s constitutional credentials or by disavowing them and wiping the *Miranda* rules off the books once and for all.

In the end neither side got all it had hoped for. In *Dickerson v. United States*[44] the Supreme Court reaffirmed *Miranda* and held that both state and federal courts must comply with its requirements. That ruling, moreover, came on a surprisingly strong 7–2 vote, with an opinion authored by none other than *Miranda*'s most prominent Supreme Court critic, Chief Justice William Rehnquist. Yet the opinion also reaffirmed prior decisions casting doubt on *Miranda*'s constitutional foundations. While insisting that compliance with *Miranda* was obligatory, the *Dickerson* majority to some extent perpetuated the *Miranda* paradox by refusing to characterize the *Miranda* rules as constitutional requirements, and by using only weaker formulations that treated *Miranda* as "constitutionally based," with "constitutional underpinnings."[45] *Dickerson* also endorsed the previously created exceptions to *Miranda*. And the Court's most recent decisions make clear that it intends to give those exceptions a broad reading, leaving police free to use most indirect fruit of interrogations that disregard *Miranda*,[46] at least absent proof of deliberate efforts to circumvent the requirements.[47]

---

[42] United States v. Dickerson, 166 F.3d 667 (4th Cir. 1999).

[43] *E.g.*, Minnick v. Mississippi, 498 U.S. 146 (1990); Arizona v. Roberson, 486 U.S. 675 (1988); Edwards v. Arizona, 451 U.S. 477 (1981).

[44] 530 U.S. 428 (2000).

[45] *Id.*, at 440 & note 5.

[46] United States v. Patane, 542 U.S. 630 (2004).

[47] Missouri v. Seibert, 542 U.S. 600 (2004).

Did we wind up in the right place? To what extent has *Miranda* really changed police behavior for the better, and at what cost in terms of lost confessions and lost convictions? Should a Court fully cognizant of its doctrinal obligations and the limits of the judicial role have been more cautious from the outset? Or should such a Court have been even more interventionist? And would greater caution or greater activism have produced better results in the long run? The remainder of this Chapter considers these practical and jurisprudential dimensions of the *Miranda* story.

Assessing *Miranda*

The *Miranda* rules, as we have seen, consist principally of three requirements. The first and best known is that prior to custodial questioning, police must give the suspect a specific, four-part warning. Less well known are two requirements that *Miranda* imposes on police actions thereafter. Before initiating interrogation, the police must obtain a "knowing and intelligent" waiver, and if the suspect indicates that he no longer wishes to talk, all questioning must cease.

Viewed in this way, the *Miranda* holding has the troubling feel of detailed legislation, inappropriate for a court.[48] In this conventional picture, moreover, the decision compounds that failing by seeming to obliterate years of precedent under the voluntariness test and to trump any alternative approach; hence the charge, common then and now, that *Miranda* precluded more flexible case-by-case approaches and creative legislative solutions.[49] And as conventionally understood, *Miranda* had the added and particularly disturbing feature that it seemed to "handcuff" the police, making it likely that the guilty would demand lawyers immediately and force the prosecution to turn them loose for lack of sufficient evidence. This last effect, we now know, did not materialize, but only, it is widely believed, because subsequent decisions "tamed" the holding in ways that the original *Miranda* Court supposedly never intended.

Yet if we put aside the *Miranda* we know from popular fiction and from off-hand portrayals that academics themselves often perpetuate, these common criticisms of *Miranda* collapse. If we trace carefully the doctrinal and operational dimensions of the actual decision, a very different picture emerges.

---

[48] *E.g.*, Edwin Meese III, Square Miranda Rights With Reason, Wall St. J.22 (June 13, 1986).

[49] *E.g.*, William J. Stuntz, Miranda's Mistake, 99 Mich. L. Rev. 975, 977–78 (2001); Paul G. Cassell, Miranda's Social Costs: An Empirical Reassessment, 90 Nw. U. L. Rev. 387, 498 (1996).

Miranda did not involve an illegitimate form of adjudication, it did not impose "code-like" rules, it did not supplant the voluntariness test, and it did not preclude legislative solutions. *Miranda* took a conventional judicial approach to constitutional interpretation, and the Court's doctrinal conclusions were—on their merits—solidly grounded. If the Court's conclusions are analytically vulnerable, it is only because they represent a retrenchment, pulling back from broader Fifth and Sixth Amendment restrictions that previous cases had foreshadowed.

Nor, from a practical perspective, did *Miranda* "handcuff" the police, even in its original Warren Court formulation. Operationally, *Miranda* gave police free rein to continue using a wide range of interrogation practices, the opinion deliberately avoided language that would have imposed more restrictive requirements, and it chose not to address many of the most serious defects in the voluntariness test. Seen in light of what the *Miranda* opinion actually says, and the details of what it actually does, the portrait conventionally drawn by *Miranda's* critics turns out to be almost a mirror image of the reality.

This section first considers the constitutional principles on which *Miranda* rests and then takes a close look at *Miranda's* operational requirements, both as the *Miranda* opinion originally formulated them, and as they have worked in practice.

Constitutional Foundations

(1) *The Sixth Amendment right to counsel.* On the eve of *Miranda*, the Court seemed poised to hold (and many said *Escobedo* had already held) that the Sixth Amendment barred *all* police questioning, in or out of the stationhouse, after suspicion had focused on the accused, unless counsel was actually present or unless counsel had been waived under scrupulously guarded conditions. Many said as well that whatever one thought of *Escobedo,* the universally acclaimed *Gideon* decision required the same restrictions in any event.

Miranda's first analytic step was to reinterpret *Escobedo* as a Fifth Amendment—*not* a Sixth Amendment—case.[50] While focusing attention on interrogation's potential for compulsion, the Court in effect *eliminated* broader and more restrictive right-to-counsel concerns from the equation in typical interrogation situations, even inside the stationhouse. And the Court left police with almost unrestricted freedom to question suspects outside the stationhouse, at least prior to the time when formal judicial proceedings began.[51] On the right-to-counsel issues at least, *Miranda* was an unequivocal victory for law enforcement, a victory

---

[50] Miranda, 384 U.S. at 444 note 4.

[51] *See, e.g.*, Beckwith v. United States, 425 U.S. 341 (1976); Berkemer v. McCarty, 468 U.S. 420 (1984).

based, moreover, on an unusual (and previously unprecedented) formalism in interpreting the Sixth Amendment's crucial critical-stage concept.[52] On this score, if there is any objection to *Miranda*'s legitimacy, it is that the Court eliminated Sixth Amendment concerns by fiat, in a terse footnote that suggests no principled basis, indeed no explanation whatever, for the Court's departure from the functional approach that had guided critical-stage assessments for more than three decades.

An explanation can be imagined, of course—the explanation that practical law enforcement needs require this exception from the usual Sixth Amendment standards. That explanation, however, simply underscores again the fact that the Court gave law-enforcement concerns great weight, and did so *in spite of* the more traditional criteria of judicial decision-making and constitutional interpretation.

(2) *Fifth Amendment compulsion.* Three elements of *Miranda*'s holding focused on the Fifth Amendment. The Court held first that Fifth Amendment compulsion can be either formal or informal and, second, that absent warnings and a waiver, all interrogation in a custodial setting is inherently compelling. Third, the Court held that police can "dispel" this inherent compulsion in either of two ways—by delivering the prescribed warnings and obtaining the suspect's statement of his willingness to talk, or by taking any other steps equally effective in informing the suspect of his rights and assuring his ability to exercise them. And as a corollary of this third point, once the warned suspect voluntarily waives his rights, compulsion has been dispelled, and thereafter, police can proceed to question the suspect in the isolated custodial setting after all. Indeed, *Miranda* holds, such questioning can continue indefinitely, unless and until the suspect indicates that he no longer wishes to talk. Any statement made prior to that point will be admissible, provided only that it is voluntary.

Seen through this lens—that is, through the lens of the opinion itself—*Miranda* involved conventional, not illegitimate modes of constitutional interpretation, and it left ample room for legislatures to prescribe alternative approaches. *Miranda*'s Fifth Amendment foundation is not only "legitimate," but substantively solid, as we can see by taking each of its three elements in turn.

(a) Informal pressure. In holding that the word "compel" includes *informal* pressure, the Court was, of course, engaged in an entirely conventional act of judicial interpretation. And on the merits, *Miranda*'s holding on this point, though a departure from Supreme Court precedent of the early to mid-Twentieth Century, was clearly correct, in accord with common sense and with the early historical understanding (so far as it is known) of the self-incrimination privilege. That piece of the

---

[52] Compare Powell v. Alabama, 287 U.S. 45 (1932).

holding is also in accord with a strong line of uncontroversial precedent in post-*Miranda* cases outside the interrogation setting. Today, virtually none of *Miranda*'s many critics suggests that Fifth Amendment compulsion should be limited to formal penalties only.[53]

(b) The per se rule. *Miranda*'s second step—the holding that absent warnings, *any* custodial interrogation involves "compelling" pressure— poses, again, a conventional question of interpreting constitutional text. Yet critics often suggest that because of the emphatically per se character of the Court's holding, the Court adopted a "prophylactic rule," that the Court cannot properly do such a thing in constitutional adjudication, and therefore that this feature renders the *Miranda* holding illegitimate.[54]

This criticism is commonplace, and a source of discomfort even for some of *Miranda's* defenders. Nonetheless, it is untenable. There is nothing illegitimate—or even unusual—about per se rules in constitutional adjudication. They are commonplace in First Amendment settings, for example.[55] And such per se rules are especially commonplace—even predominant—in cases, both before and after *Miranda*, that are concerned with defining "compulsion" in Fifth Amendment settings outside the stationhouse.[56]

To take only one of many possible examples, a threat to discharge a public employee for refusing to testify—or even for refusing to explain his misconduct informally—is impermissibly compelling per se.[57] Numerous circumstantial factors affect the actual force of such a threat for any given employee, but the Court has expressly held that such circumstances are irrelevant. The threat is automatically deemed compelling, regardless of a particular employee's specific economic situation. And none of the Justices has ever condemned precedents of this sort as improper "prophylactic rules" or illegitimate usurpations of legislative prerogatives.

Even in the Court's police-interrogation voluntariness case law, the area that most quintessentially requires case-by-case judgments under

---

[53] *See, e.g.*, Stephen J. Markman, The Fifth Amendment and Custodial Questioning: A Response, 54 U. Chi. L. Rev. 938, 939 (1987) (criticizing *Miranda* but conceding that *Miranda*'s first holding—that "compulsion" can include informal pressure—was "obviously correct.")

[54] *See, e.g.*, Joseph D. Grano, Prophylactic Rules in Criminal Procedure: A Question of Article III Legitimacy, 80 N. W. U. L. Rev.100 (1985).

[55] *See* David A. Stauss, The Ubiquity of Prophylactic Rules, 55 U. Chi. L. Rev.190 (1988).

[56] For cases illustrating these points, *see* Schulhofer, Exceptionalism, *supra* note 20, at 946–48.

[57] Lefkowitz v. Cunningham, 431 U.S. 801 (1977).

the totality of the circumstances, the Court had, long before *Miranda*, adopted many per se rules. For example, the Court had made explicit since the 1940s that confessions obtained by dozens of hours of continuous interrogation are automatically deemed involuntary, regardless of any surrounding circumstances.[58] The same rule no doubt applies today to confessions obtained by punching or kicking the accused.[59] And these points again are uncontroversial. None of those who attempt to suggest that *Miranda's* per se rule is somehow illegitimate cast any doubt whatever on the legitimacy or substantive soundness of the rule that confessions obtained by a punch or a kick are involuntary per se.

A more nuanced criticism concedes that per se rules can be *legitimate* but argues that *Miranda's* particular per se rule is not sound *on its merits*. The argument here is that a conclusive presumption of compulsion is inappropriate because unwarned custodial interrogation often is not sufficiently coercive to *overbear* a defendant's will.[60] But coercion of this sort is normally not considered necessary to establish a Fifth Amendment violation. At least in contexts outside that of custodial police interrogation, Fifth Amendment compulsion is satisfied by any significant pressure or penalty that the state deploys against a suspect for the specific purpose of getting him to reveal incriminating testimonial information.[61] The effort to paint the *Miranda* per se rule as extreme can be considered plausible only from two perspectives. That effort can be considered plausible if we ignore the restrictions beyond Fourteenth Amendment voluntariness that *Malloy* and the Fifth Amendment bring into play. Or it can be considered plausible if we accept a kind of Fifth Amendment *exceptionalism*, under which the standards used to assess compulsion in the context of police interrogation are different from—and more demanding than—the standards uncontroversially accepted for determining Fifth Amendment compulsion in every other setting.[62]

Against the background of generally accepted Fifth Amendment conceptions of compulsion, is a per se rule appropriate in making judgments about custodial police interrogation? Given the relative infrequency of cases in which compelling pressures will truly be absent and the difficulties of case-by-case decision-making in this area, a conclusive presumption of compulsion is in fact a responsible tool of adjudication.

---

[58] *E.g.*, Ashcraft v. Tennessee, 322 U.S.143 (1944).

[59] *See, e.g.*, Stein v. New York, 346 U.S. 156, 182 (1953).

[60] *See, e.g.*, Dickerson v. United States, 530 U.S. at 444 (Scalia, J., dissenting).

[61] For detailed discussions of this point, *see* Schulhofer, Reconsidering Miranda, *supra* note 22, at 445.

[62] For development of this argument, *see* Schulhofer, Exceptionalism, *supra* note 20, at 944–51.

Indeed, the problem of determining compulsion in the context of police interrogation could fairly be placed right at the top of any list of constitutional issues that properly demand some form of pre se rule.[63]

(c) The warnings. *Miranda's* next step required that the suspect receive a complex, four-part warning of his rights. More precisely, *Miranda* required either that police give the four-part warning or put in place some other, equally effective system to inform a suspect of his right to remain silent and assure that he will have the opportunity to exercise that right.

Here, the complaints about illegitimate judicial legislation seem at first glance to have some substance. The Court had apparently mandated a detailed, "code-like" warnings system. And the Court seemed to reinforce the legislative character of that holding by stating that the warnings procedure was *not* in itself constitutionally required. The Court seemed, in the name of the Constitution, to be requiring state and local police to take steps that even the *Miranda* Court did not view as a constitutional mandate.

What the Court meant, of course, was that *some* system of protection from the custodial pressures was constitutionally required. And absent effective alternatives, the *Miranda* warnings therefore *would be* every bit as obligatory as any other constitutional requirement. Rather than leave state and local police guessing about what kind of a system would suffice, the Court chose an approach that in effect gave police officers the best of both worlds. The Court offered them a model system of safeguards that they could use with confidence, guaranteeing that it would pass constitutional muster, all the while leaving state legislatures and the police the option—indeed expressly encouraging them—to develop any other approach that would be equally effective.

The approach that the *Miranda* Court chose was—odd as it may seem to say so—*diffident*. It showed respect for legislative prerogatives and allowed the maximum flexibility that was consistent with the suspect's right to protection from unconstitutionally compelling pressures. Yet, paradoxically, the Court's approach was seized upon by critics and distorted to support claims that the Court had overreached and imposed mandatory rules that the Constitution itself did not require. *Miranda's* diffidence allowed unsympathetic Courts in later years to state with apparent accuracy that the rights announced in *Miranda* are "not themselves rights protected by the Constitution,"[64] and that a failure to follow the *Miranda* rules "is not in itself a violation of the

---

[63] *See* Schulhofer, Reconsidering Miranda, *supra* note 22, at 451–53.

[64] Michigan v. Tucker, 417 U.S. 433, 444 (1974).

Fifth Amendment.''[65] But where alternative safeguards were not deployed, as was invariably the case, then the police had carried out an interrogation while impermissibly compelling pressures were still in place. If *Miranda*'s underlying constitutional principles are correct, police interrogation without following *Miranda's* subsidiary rules (or some comparable substitute) *is* "in itself a violation of the Fifth Amendment."

Miranda's supposedly offensive code of rules, in short, not only do not constrain legislatures inappropriately; they also do not "handcuff" the police. Indeed the code doesn't restrict the police at all. What it does is precisely the opposite. If the Court was correct in holding that any interrogation in the custodial setting is inherently compelling, then far from handcuffing the police, the warnings act to liberate the police. The warnings grant police officers a green light to continue questioning the isolated suspect who is held against his will in the confines of the stationhouse, a process that otherwise would violate the Constitution itself—not merely some derivative system of prophylactic rules.

The notion that police-initiated warnings really can "dispel" that inherent compulsion seems dubious at best. But however that may be, the warnings unquestionably serve—and from the outset were designed to serve—the function of permitting custodial interrogation to continue. Whether and to what extent those requirements, even as originally written—imposed real operational constraints remains to be considered.

Miranda's Operational Rules

(1) Access to counsel. *Miranda*, as we have seen, reinterpreted *Escobedo* as a Fifth Amendment case and as a result eliminated Sixth Amendment constraints from most interrogation situations inside the stationhouse. And because the *Miranda* rules that replace *Escobedo* apply *only* in custodial situations, the Court left police with largely unrestricted freedom to question suspects *outside* the stationhouse, at least prior to the time when formal judicial proceedings began.[66]

Miranda does, to be sure, use quite a lot of right-to-counsel language, and it even states that suspects facing custodial interrogation have such a right. But the *Miranda* right to counsel is not the suspect's affirmative Sixth Amendment right to comprehensive legal assistance in the suspect's defense. Rather it is (at most) only a Fifth Amendment tool for helping to dissipate the custodial pressures. And in practice this right is even more limited than that, because it comes into play only when a suspect in the grip of those very pressures chooses to invoke it. Having

---

[65] Oregon v. Elstad, 470 U.S. 298, 307 & note 1 (1985).

[66] *See, e.g.,* Beckwith v. United States, 425 U.S. 341 (1976).

detailed in powerful language the ways that a suspect in the isolated police station environment, "surrounded by antagonistic forces,"[67] faces intimidating pressures that can "operate very quickly to overbear the will of one merely made aware of his privilege by his interrogators,"[68] the *Miranda* Court granted a right to have counsel present only "if the defendant so desires."[69] And the Court assumed that the suspect's decision to express this desire could be "unfettered"[70] even when it must be made while he remains in the isolation of the interrogation room, and when it must be communicated to the same antagonistic forces whose hostility created the need for counsel's protection in the first place. The choice of that approach cannot have been a product of inadvertence or naive optimism. The *Miranda* Court knew what it was doing.

(2) The warnings. Having dispensed with an effective, affirmative right to counsel grounded in the Sixth Amendment, the *Miranda* Court proceeded to require that the suspect be told *by the police* that he can choose to remain silent. No doubt such a warning can help assure a suspect that the police acknowledge his rights and are prepared to respect them. No doubt the inherent pressures of the custodial situation are thereby mitigated to some degree, and no doubt some officers anticipated that this requirement would pose an obstacle or at best a troublesome nuisance. For the Warren Court to have taken this step and imposed the warning requirement was not nothing.

Nor, however, was it a lot. The Court was well aware of the difficulty of determining after the fact, without recorded evidence or written documents, exactly what had transpired in the interrogation room. The *Miranda* opinion discusses that problem at length[71] but then does nothing whatever about it. The Court required no written or recorded corroboration of how—or indeed whether—the warnings were in fact delivered.

Likewise, the Court was well aware that warnings entrusted to the police are easily blunted. Here too the Court itself makes the point explicitly: "A once-stated warning, delivered by those who will conduct the interrogation, cannot itself suffice to [assure that the individual's right to choose between silence and speech remains unfettered] among those who most require knowledge of their rights...."[72] Yet once again

---

[67] Miranda, 384 U.S. at 461.

[68] *Id.*, at 469–70.

[69] *Id.*, at 470.

[70] *Id.*, at 469.

[71] Miranda, 384 U.S. at 445, 448.

[72] *Id.*, at 469–70.

the Court does nothing whatever to address the problem. In the conventional picture of an activist Warren Court determined to subject the police to tight restrictions and perhaps even to stamp out the use of confessions altogether, the oversight has to seem inexplicable. But again, the Court surely knew what it was doing.

(3) Waiver. Once the warnings are given, the police cannot initiate questioning until the suspect freely agrees to talk. But what are the standards by which the validity of such a waiver is to be judged? The waiver cannot be prompted by any persuasion, cajolery or deception, and the opinion stresses that the police have a "heavy burden" to prove waiver.[73]

These are not meaningless restrictions, but again, they are far from airtight. In essence the test for a valid waiver remains what it was before *Miranda*—voluntariness under the totality of the circumstances. (To be sure, there is an important difference: police cannot apply the previously permissible "suction process" to obtain such a waiver.)

And once again, the swearing-contest problem remains as well. In imposing a "heavy burden," the *Miranda* Court must have meant, at a minimum, that a police officer's testimony about waiver would have to appear sincere and convincing. But at the same time that it stressed the dangers of interrogation-room secrecy, the Court chose not to require that the waiver be made in writing, recorded, or witnessed by any neutral observer. It is no doubt too cynical to assume that the *Miranda* Court deliberately contemplated and invited police perjury on this point; perhaps the Court hoped to tackle the swearing contest soon after. But it is fair to wonder whether a Court seeking a truly effective package of prophylactic rules should have started where *Miranda* starts and postponed what *Miranda* postponed.

(4) After Waiver. We now know that most suspects facing interrogation waive their *Miranda* rights and agree to talk.[74] In light of the porous character of the first three *Miranda* safeguards (counsel, the warnings and waiver), this result should not have been surprising. It should have been apparent, and indeed from the outset it *was* apparent to perceptive observers, that the guts of *Miranda* was the set of rules it established for interrogations conducted after waiver.

But what are those rules? Even the most attentive television viewer might understandably conclude that *Miranda* has nothing to say on this subject.[75] Indeed, one important potential requirement was strikingly

---

[73] *Id.*, at 475.

[74] *See* Schulhofer, Practical Effect, *supra* note 40, at 560.

[75] *See, e.g.*, Akhil Reed Amar, "OK, All Together Now: 'You Have the Right to…'" L.A. Times, Dec. 12, 1999, at M1 (equating the *Miranda* rights with the *Miranda* warnings

omitted. *Miranda* forbids the use of cajolery or deception to *obtain* a waiver. But the opinion is silent, no doubt deliberately so, on the propriety of using cajolery and deception *after waiver*. And just three years after *Miranda*, the Court, in an opinion by Justice Thurgood Marshall, held that the use of deceptive tactics did not render a confession "involuntary."[76] "Because the admissibility of statements given after a valid waiver ... must be determined on the basis of the voluntariness test,"[77] a suspect who attempts to explain himself to his captors waives his right to be protected from cajolery, deception and psychological ploys designed to test his story. In that respect, interrogation after a *Miranda* waiver remains very much the same process that it was during the 1950s.

There is one extremely important difference. *Miranda*, unlike the voluntariness test, provides that when a suspect indicates at any point during interrogation that he no longer wishes to talk, then "the interrogation must cease."[78] Under the voluntariness test, police had been permitted to continue questioning, challenging, cajoling and deceiving the unwilling, resisting suspect, as they did (though ultimately to an excessive extent) in the *Spano* case. *Miranda*'s cut-off rule is, operationally, the heart of the *Miranda* system and arguably its only real teeth. But for the suspect who fails to state unequivocally that he wants to remain silent or consult an attorney, the only limits that apply to interrogation tactics are identical to those in effect before *Gideon*, *Malloy*, *Escobedo* and *Miranda*—the amorphous balancing concepts of the due process voluntariness test.

Unlike the due-process voluntariness test, *Miranda* doctrine does not overtly balance each suspect's dignity interests against the law-enforcement interests of the state in his case. Rather, under *Miranda*, the suspect's Fifth Amendment rights are ostensibly absolute. But under the system *Miranda* puts in place, the police retain ample room to pursue their law-enforcement interests, even by methods that bring considerable pressure to bear on the suspect. *Miranda* does not, any more than the due-process test, come directly to grips with the dilemma arising from our simultaneous commitments to the privilege against self-incrimination and to a law-enforcement system in which police interrogation is perceived as a necessity.

---

and asserting that the public knows the *Miranda* rights because it knows the *Miranda* warnings).

[76] Frazier v. Cupp, 394 U.S. 731 (1969).

[77] Welsh S. White, What is an Involuntary Confession Now?, 50 Rutgers L. Rev. 2001, 2004 (1998).

[78] Miranda, 384 U.S. at 474.

The Consequences in Practice

Almost as soon as it was announced, *Miranda* prompted district attorneys and police chiefs throughout the country to monitor its effects, and many of their early studies claimed that the decision had had catastrophic effects on law enforcement.[79] Precipitous declines in confession rates and conviction rates were reported. Yet most of these early studies were crudely designed, and often, on closer examination, their results proved to be fatally flawed. Subsequent studies presented quite a different picture. The weight of the evidence suggested that any negative impact on confession and conviction rates was small and rapidly diminishing over time. The informal impressions of law enforcement personnel and other criminal justice practitioners were in accord with these conclusions.[80]

The currently prevailing view, even among police and prosecutors, that *Miranda's* impact on conviction rates is negligible and that it does not present serious problems for law enforcement.[81] Typically, only 20% to 25% of suspects invoke their right to silence at any point prior to or during interrogation.[82] Carefully conducted studies indicate that in roughly 55–65% of all interrogations, the police ultimately succeed in obtaining an incriminating statement—rates comparable to those that commonly prevailed prior to *Miranda*.[83]

---

[79] *See, e.g.*, Baker, *supra* note 31, at 180–81, 403–05; Yale Kamisar, Police Interrogation and Confessions 47–49 & note 11 (1980).

[80] *See, e.g.*, Stephen L. Wasby, Small Town Police and the Supreme Court (1976); ABA Special Comm'n on Criminal Justice in a Free Society, Criminal Justice in Crisis 28 (1988).

[81] *See* Roger Parloff, "Miranda on the Hot Seat," New York Times Magazine, Sept. 26, 1999, pp. 84, 87; Schulhofer, Practical Effect, *supra* note 40, at 504. There has been one dissenting voice, a law professor who revisited the early empirical studies, made several adjustments, and concluded that *Miranda* was responsible for the loss of a conviction in 3.8% of all serious criminal cases. Cassell, *supra* note 49. The 3.8% attrition figure could in itself be taken as a refutation of the apocalyptic claims of *Miranda's* detractors. But on close examination, even the claim of a 3.8% impact proved to be artificially inflated and unsupportable. When the available before/after studies are reanalyzed with all appropriate qualifications in mind, *Miranda's* empirically detectable harm to law enforcement shrinks in effect to zero. *See* Schulhofer, Practical Effect, *supra* note 40, at 544–45. For other studies concluding that Miranda has caused no empirically detectable harm to law enforcement, *see, e.g.*, George C. Thomas III, Plain Talk About the Miranda Empirical Debate: A "Steady State" Theory of Confessions, 43 UCLA L.Rev. 933, 935–36, 952–55 (1996); Richard A. Leo, Inside the Interrogation Room, 86 J. Crim. L. & Criminology 266, 280 (1996); Peter Carlson, You Have the Right to Remain Silent, Washington Post, Sept., 13, 1998, at 9; John J. Donohue III, Did Miranda Diminish Police Effectiveness?, 50 Stan. L. Rev. 1147 (1998).

[82] *See, e.g.*, Cassell, *supra* note 49, at 496.

[83] *See, e.g.*, Leo, *supra* note 81, at 280; Thomas, *supra* note 81, at 935–36, 946–53.

Indeed, experienced law-enforcement officials typically believe that the *Miranda* rules are appropriate and that they offer substantial benefits for the police. *Miranda* procedures are less difficult for police officers to follow than the vagaries of the voluntariness standard. By assuring the public that police must operate within defined rules, *Miranda* provides legitimacy to the process of interrogation behind closed doors. Law-enforcement institutions "have not only successfully adapted ... to Miranda, but have publicly embraced Miranda as a legitimating symbol of their professionalism and commitment to fairness in the criminal process."[84]

If *Miranda* has had no impact on the flow of confessions, some might conclude that the decision was a failure—not simply because confessions have survived (eliminating them was never a goal that could plausibly be attributed to *Miranda*), but because a continuing flow of confessions seems to imply continuation of the pressures police deploy to obtain confessions. But recent observational studies of police interrogation tactics demonstrate that today's suspects typically confess not because of fear of mistreatment but primarily because of misplaced confidence in their own ability to talk their way out of trouble. Modern police questioning has become an elaborate "confidence game," in which detectives subtly establish rapport with their "mark" and dupe the suspect into believing that he can help himself by letting out a portion of the facts or by inventing a plausible alibi.[85]

CONCLUSION

For those who consider only the "bottom line" of confessions rates and convictions, *Miranda* may appear an irrelevancy. But our best available evidence suggests that today's confessions are primarily the result of persuasion, deception and the suspect's overconfidence, rather than the product of pressure and fear. That is no merely technical difference. The Fifth Amendment protects and any decent society should protect suspects from state-orchestrated compulsion to convict themselves. But our Constitution does not protect and a decent society ought not to protect suspects from misplaced confidence in their ability to outsmart the police. *Miranda* seems to have moved us closer to a system that relies more on the latter method and less on the former.

That said, *Miranda* left many of the most serious problems in police interrogation untouched. *Miranda* did not substantially reduce the possibilities for physically abusive questioning, and it stopped far short of protecting suspects from all pressure to waive their Fifth Amendment

---

[84] Leo, *supra* note 41, at 680.

[85] *See* David Simon, Homicide 197–202 (1991); Richard A. Leo, Miranda's Revenge: Police Interrogation as a Confidence Game, 30 L. & Soc'y Rev. 259 (1996).

rights. *Miranda* did nothing at all about police dominance of the swearing contest over what had actually occurred behind the closed doors of the interrogation room. It did almost nothing about the problem of false confessions. In all these respects, a Court determined to implement the Fifth Amendment privilege could have done much more.

Miranda, in short, was a compromise. It was carefully structured to preserve police interrogation as an investigative tool and to preserve the shrouds of secrecy that protect the practice from the prying eyes of judges and the public. Nothing in *Miranda* prevents a state from requiring its police to videotape their interrogations whenever possible. Indeed no conceivable law-enforcement interest—at least no *legitimate* law-enforcement interest—stands in the way of such a requirement. Yet to this day only a handful of jurisdictions require videotaping, and only a handful of police departments preserve videotapes showing anything more than the end result—the confession itself, but not the dynamic that produced it. The resistance prompted by *Miranda*'s prophylactic safeguards against compulsion would likely seem tame in comparison to the massive opposition that prophylactic safeguards against police perjury would have provoked.

Seen from that perspective, *Miranda* is a grand but largely symbolic gesture. The symbolic importance of criminal procedure guarantees, however, should not be underestimated. Symbols like *Miranda* underscore our societal commitment to a government of limited powers. Such symbols serve, however imperfectly, to encourage restraint in an area where emotion easily runs uncontrolled. They can help educate and persuade the thousands of front-line officials upon whose voluntary compliance the constitutional order ultimately depends. As the Court has said in a related context, "[O]ver the long term, [the] demonstration that our society attaches serious consequences to violation of constitutional rights is thought to encourage those who formulate law enforcement policies, and the officers who implement them, to incorporate [constitutional] ideals into their value system."[86] Over the course of a generation, *Miranda* appears to have had just such an effect, a subtle but by no means modest accomplishment.

---

[86] Stone v. Powell, 428 U.S. 465, 492 (1976).

*

6

Hoffa v. United States: Secret Agents in Private Spaces

Tracey Maclin*

Introduction

Sometimes there is an untold story behind a Supreme Court ruling. The Court's opinion in *Hoffa v. United States*[1] fails to reveal the story of the decade-long battle between two of the most famous and controversial men in America. On one side was Bobby Kennedy, brother of the President and hard-charging Attorney General of the United States. On the other side was Jimmy Hoffa, head of the Teamsters Union and considered one of the most powerful (and corrupt, according Kennedy) labor bosses in the country. Kennedy and Hoffa hated each other, or so the public believed.

Kennedy's pursuit of Hoffa began in the 1950's, when he served as counsel on Senator Joseph R. McCarthy's Permanent Investigations Subcommittee. His investigation of Hoffa continued when, at the age of 29, he was appointed Chief Counsel of Senator John McClellan's "Rackets Committee." Kennedy believed that Hoffa led a corrupt union, and that Hoffa and the Teamsters were bedfellows with organized crime figures. Hoffa, on the other hand, believed that Kennedy was a spoiled rich kid, who pursued a vendetta against him and the Teamsters.

The battles between Kennedy and Hoffa, which often were relayed to the public in front page news stories, were both real and mythical. For example, in March 1957, Hoffa was prosecuted in a federal bribery case for attempting to get John Cheasty a job on the McClellan Committee. Cheasty was to furnish Hoffa with secret information from the committee's files.[2] At a press conference after Hoffa's arrest, Kennedy confidently asserted, " 'If Hoffa isn't convicted, I'll jump off the Capitol dome.' "[3] After Hoffa was acquitted, Edward Bennett Williams, Hoffa's trial law-

---

* I want to thank Alison Passer for her excellent work as my research assistant.

[1] 385 U.S. 293 (1966).

[2] ARTHUR A. SLOANE, HOFFA 72–76 (The MIT Press 1991).

[3] *Id.* at 74.

yer, jokingly offered to give Kennedy a parachute.[4] Kennedy and Hoffa did not keep their animosity towards each other private. On the eve of the Cheasty trial, Kennedy and Hoffa publicly "argued about who could do more push-ups and those American people who cared about this sort of thing couldn't wait to find out."[5]

Another Washington legend spins the tale that one night Kennedy, while "driving home at midnight after his usual eighteen-hour day, spied the light on in Hoffa's Teamsters office and turned his own car around and went back to work."[6] Hoffa, according to one of his attorneys, believed the legend and would "leave the office lights on intentionally after he did leave his third-floor suite for the night, in an effort to trick Kennedy into repeating the performance."[7] The animosity between the two even surfaced in the *beau monde* pages of the *Washington Post*. In one of her gossip columns, *The Post's* Maxine Cheshire told the story of Ethel Kennedy and her children riding near the capitol. At a red light, Ethel points to a building.

"What's up there?"

"The Teamsters Union," responded four or more little Kennedy voices.

"And what do they do?"

"Work overtime to keep Jimmy Hoffa out of jail!"

"And?" Ethel prompted.

"Which is where he belongs!" was the happy response.[8]

But *Hoffa* involved more than the larger-than-life personalities of Bobby Kennedy and Jimmy Hoffa. The case also raised serious and important constitutional questions with which the Supreme Court had struggled since 1921. Specifically, the case posed the question of whether law enforcement officials have the unfettered authority to send a secret spy into the private quarters of an individual, not to gather evidence of known criminal conduct, but to keep an eye on the activities of the target and to look for evidence of possible future crimes. Prior to *Hoffa*, the Court had issued only a few decisions on the constitutionality of government officials planting or utilizing informants to rummage around for information or monitor conversations in private places. Moreover, in the few rulings that did exist, the rule of law was unsettled and seemed

---

[4] Victor S. Navasky, Kennedy Justice 452 (iUniverse.com, Inc. 2000) (1971).

[5] *Id.* at 454.

[6] *Id.* at 453.

[7] Sloane, *supra* note 2, at 157.

[8] Navasky, *supra* note 4, at 454.

to be moving in the direction toward tighter controls on the government's authority to use informants, at least where electronic equipment was employed to record private communications. Finally, the Justices were divided on what constitutional restraints, if any, should control the power of the government to employ secret agents. Thus, to understand the significance of *Hoffa*, it is important to know who the individuals were and the historical background of the legal issues. The misdemeanor that started in a Nashville courtroom would be transformed into a Supreme Court ruling giving government free license to spy on its citizens.

The Personalities: Jimmy Hoffa v. Bobby Kennedy

1. *Jimmy Hoffa*

Jimmy Hoffa was born February 14, 1913, in Brazil, Indiana. His father, a coal prospector, died when Hoffa was seven. When he was ten, his mother moved him and his three siblings to Detroit, where they all took jobs to support the family. Hoffa quit school after seventh grade and began to work at a department store, followed by a job unloading trucks and railroad boxcars at the produce warehouse dock of Kroger's. Aggravated by long hours and little pay, Hoffa and the other men employed at the dock decided they needed a union. When they refused to unload a strawberry truck, Kroger's gave in. The men formed a union, which became part of Teamsters Local 337 in 1932. Shortly after, Hoffa was appointed business agent of Local 299, and later became its president.[9]

Hoffa's work for the unions during the Depression demonstrated his relentless commitment to improve the plight of laborers. He was constantly recruiting members, putting up picket lines, and organizing strikes. Although strikers' efforts were met with resistance (they fought against police, tear gas, and bullets) and arrests (Hoffa unashamedly recalled being arrested eighteen times in one day), Hoffa never seemed to lose his drive to organize workers. Eventually, Hoffa was elected president of the Teamsters Union, and he converted the Teamsters from a disjointed confederation of local unions into a powerful, national union.[10]

After attaining a leadership position in the Teamsters, Hoffa became the focus of federal investigators, particularly Bobby Kennedy. But despite his never-ending legal problems, Hoffa succeeded in maintaining the support of union workers, due to his ability to relate to the rank-and-file and his constant efforts to get them better contracts. The sentiments

---

[9] John Bartlow Martin, *The Struggle to Get Hoffa, Part Two: The Making of a Labor Boss*, The Sat. Evening Post, July 4, 1959, at 54.

[10] *Id.*

expressed by a Teamster truck driver is representative of many of Hoffa's loyal supporters: "Hoffa did steal from us, but he also gave us a hell of a lot. For what he did for the driver, I'd take a chance on him again. If he robbed a little, what the hell."[11]

Hoffa first met Kennedy at the home of Eddie Cheyfitz on February 19, 1957. Cheyfitz, a Washington lawyer and former Teamster public relations official who was friends with both Kennedy and Hoffa, convinced them to meet at his home for dinner. Cheyfitz believed the two men might like each other because

> the patrician Kennedy and the rough-edged Hoffa actually had a lot in common. Both were ambitious, combative, feisty bantamweights. Each was a confirmed workaholic but also a devoted family man. Both prided themselves on candor. Both were nonsmoking physical fitness addicts. Each demanded, and received, total loyalty from his staff. Each was frequently described as "charismatic" by admirers, and as "ruthless" by detractors.[12]

By the end of the evening, however, it was clear that Hoffa and Kennedy did not like each other.[13] Kennedy thought that Hoffa "was a 'bully' hiding behind a façade of toughness, compelled to brag and boast about his strength and power because of self-doubts that he really had such an ability to excel."[14] Hoffa's views of Kennedy were similarly negative. After the dinner, Hoffa recalled: "I can tell by how he shakes hands what kind of fellow I got. I said to myself, 'Here's a fella thinks he's doing me a favor by talking to me,'" and asserted that [Kennedy] was "'a damn spoiled jerk.'"[15]

2. *Bobby Kennedy*

When Bobby Kennedy became the Chief Counsel for Senator John McClellan's Permanent Subcommittee on Investigations, neither the subcommittee nor Kennedy intended their investigations to focus on the activities of corrupt unions in general or Jimmy Hoffa in particular. Kennedy's investigations originally focused on trade with Red China and conflict-of-interest cases involving federal officials. Kennedy began focusing on the activities of corrupt unions, however, once he became convinced that earlier investigations of union officials had been "fixed

---

[11] A.H. Raskin, *What the "Little Fellow" Says to the Teamsters is What Counts*, N.Y. TIMES, May 30, 1971, § 6 (Magazine), at 12.

[12] SLOANE, *supra* note 2, at 77.

[13] *Id*. at 77–78; John Bartlow Martin, *The Struggle to Get Hoffa, Part One: Kennedy Sets a Snare*, The Sat. Evening Post, June 27, 1959, at 21, 92.

[14] SLOANE, *supra* note 2, at 77.

[15] *Id*. at 78.

because of political pressure, something that presumably would not be a factor" with Kennedy.[16]

The information uncovered in the McClellan Committee's two and a half years in existence confirmed Kennedy's belief that under Hoffa, the Teamsters Union was "a conspiracy of evil."[17] As chief counsel, Kennedy was responsible for deciding what was investigated, how it was handled, and what witnesses would be called to testify.[18] Kennedy's early work on the committee had been instrumental in removing David Beck as president of the Teamster union. After Beck left, Hoffa became president of the Teamsters. Thus, ironically, Kennedy's success in ousting Beck paved the way for Hoffa's election as Teamsters president.[19]

The testimony Kennedy heard during the committee hearings led him to believe that Hoffa was guilty of misusing union funds for his own profit, and that Hoffa had close associations with members of the Mafia. Kennedy also worried that Hoffa, as president of the Teamsters, had the power to damage the country's economy by instigating a nationwide labor strike. Kennedy explained his views on the Jack Paar Show. He stated Hoffa and the Teamsters believe that, "nobody can touch them, that they can fix juries, that they can fix judges, that they can fix members of the legislature. . . . They have enough money. They have— Mr. Hoffa has said in the past, every man has his price! So they don't worry."[20] Based on evidence uncovered by Kennedy's work on the McClellan Committee, the federal government brought Hoffa to court three times—once on charges of bribery and twice on charges of wiretapping. The government lost each time.

Kennedy became Attorney General in 1961, but he did not forget Hoffa. Kennedy appointed Walter Sheridan to head a group of attorneys in the Organized Crime Section of the Criminal Division of the Justice Department. Sheridan, a non-lawyer and former FBI agent, worked for Kennedy on the McClellan Committee. Sheridan's group became known better as the "Get Hoffa Squad," and was responsible for completing the McClellan Committee's investigations of Hoffa and the Teamsters. The Hoffa Squad's *raison d'etre* seemed to be not a subject area but a target: Jimmy Hoffa."[21] Sheridan's mission was to send Hoffa to the federal penitentiary.

---

[16] *Id.* at 49.

[17] Robert F. Kennedy, The Enemy Within 162 (Harper & Brothers 1960).

[18] Martin, *supra* note 13, at 92.

[19] Navasky, *supra* note 4, at 455.

[20] *Id.* at 451.

[21] *Id.* at 457.

Kennedy and Sheridan's combined enthusiasm and effort to get Hoffa were assisted by a large and impressive team. One scholar estimates that the "Get Hoffa Squad" employed sixteen lawyers and thirty FBI agents full time.[22] In addition to going after Hoffa directly, the "Get Hoffa Squad" also prosecuted lower-ranking Teamsters and their associates, believing that the key to bringing down Hoffa was to tear down his support system. Soon after Kennedy took power, there were fifteen grand juries investigating Hoffa and the Teamsters.[23]

During Kennedy's tenure as Attorney General, the Justice Department prosecuted Hoffa three times, and obtained two convictions. Also, federal indictments brought were against one hundred Teamster officials and ninety of their associates. In total, the Department convinced grand juries to issue one hundred and ninety indictments, and it obtained one hundred and fifteen convictions in Teamster-related prosecutions. "By any standard Kennedy's anti-Hoffa campaign, if that's what it was, represented an extraordinary administrative accomplishment."[24]

At the time, many considered Kennedy's work in prosecuting and sending Hoffa to prison a successful undertaking. But Kennedy's actions against Hoffa as Attorney General also raised serious constitutional issues and "the profoundest of questions of prosecutor[ial] discretion."[25] As soon as he became Attorney General, Kennedy targeted Hoffa for imprisonment. "Under the Kennedys," Victor Navasky wrote, "the U.S. government considered itself at war with Jimmy Hoffa and the Teamsters."[26] Kennedy and his subordinates seem to have no qualms about utilizing constitutionally questionable law enforcement methods in their pursuit of Hoffa.

While Attorney General, Kennedy urged Congress to enact legislation authorizing federal law enforcement officers to wiretap telephone conversations. Kennedy, "was, on balance, pro-wiretapping."[27] Although Kennedy and Sheridan denied that the Justice Department ever bugged

---

[22] LUCAS A. POWE, JR., THE WARREN COURT AND AMERICAN POLITICS 402 (The Belknap Press of Harvard Univ. Press 2000).

[23] NAVASKY, *supra* note 4, at 462.

[24] *Id.* at 447. Professor Monroe Freedman notes that, by comparison, Kennedy's Justice Department brought "more prosecutions against Jimmy Hoffa than there were civil rights cases in the entire state of Mississippi, and more prosecutions against officers of the Teamsters than there were civil rights cases in the entire country." Monroe H. Freedman, *The Professional Responsibility of the Prosecuting Attorney*, 55 GEO. L.J. 1030, 1035, note 25 (1967).

[25] NAVASKY, *supra* note 4, at 447.

[26] *Id.* at 446.

[27] *Id.* at 80.

or wiretapped Hoffa,[28] Sheridan had Hoffa under constant surveillance. Sheridan admitted: " 'I knew where he was twenty-four hours a day.' "[29] Other Justice Department officials insisted that extraordinary means were required to deal with an extraordinary target. Nathan Lewin, a lawyer on the "Get Hoffa Squad," described how many members of the group rationalized their work and methods:

> "On the other side, you had a group of criminal defendants prepared to do total and unreserved battle.... That included jury-tampering, bribery, you name it. They had limitless funds and used them, and they didn't play by the rules. Hoffa didn't care about lower courts because he could go to a higher court. They were not ordinary criminal defendants. During the Nashville case Hoffa had six high-priced lawyers sitting in a hotel room to consult with the four other lawyers they had in the courtroom. That's more than the government had working on the trial. He probably spent as much money defending himself as the government spent bringing him to justice. You had to meet that with similar resources and flexibility from the government side."[30]

The "Test Fleet" Case

The Test Fleet case, which began as a misdemeanor charge, was the first step in a long legal process that eventually ended with the Supreme Court's ruling in *Hoffa v. United States*. Hoffa and a business partner, Bert Brennan, established Test Fleet, Inc. in 1949 in their wives' names. Test Fleet specialized in leasing trucking equipment to Commercial Carriers, a Detroit trucking company. Although Hoffa insisted that there was no conflict of interest regarding his ownership of Test Fleet and his Teamsters position, Kennedy's Justice Department charged him with a federal misdemeanor for violating the Taft–Hartley law.[31]

The Test Fleet case was prosecuted in Nashville, Tennessee between October 22 and December 23, 1962. Hoffa was the only defendant. Before the trial began, however, Edward Grady Partin, contacted the Justice Department. Partin was a Teamster official from Louisiana who, at the time, was awaiting prosecution in a Louisiana jail. Partin had a long criminal history, which included "breaking and entering, a bad conduct discharge from the Marines, indictments for rape, embezzlement and falsifying records, forgery and first-degree manslaughter."[32] He was

---

[28] *Id.* at 464–65.

[29] *Id.* at 463.

[30] *Id.* at 465.

[31] NAVASKY, *supra* note 4, at 470.

[32] *Id.* at 474; SLOANE, *supra* note 2, at 297.

under federal indictment for misuse of union funds when he contacted federal officials about Hoffa. Partin initially told Justice Department officials that Hoffa had asked for his help in assassinating Bobby Kennedy in a plan "remarkably similar to the one actually used in the John F. Kennedy killing."[33]

Partin was soon released from jail and was on his way to Nashville to see Hoffa, who was staying at the Andrew Jackson Hotel during the Test Fleet trial. Partin was given Sheridan's telephone number (who was in Nashville himself) and became Hoffa's confidante and doorman at Hoffa's hotel suite.

Only Kennedy, Sheridan "and one or two others knew of [Partin's] double-agent role."[34] According to Sheridan, Partin was " 'a perfect informant.' "[35] Sheridan noted that the " 'FBI wouldn't work with [Partin]—they didn't trust him—but I worked with him, and every time he told me something I had the FBI check it out, and it always checked out just like he said.' "[36] Partin told Sheridan about several attempts by Hoffa and members of his entourage to bribe jurors in the Test Fleet case. The Test Fleet trial ended in a mistrial when the jury was unable to reach a verdict after an initial seven-to-five jury vote for acquittal.

Hoffa was not retried for the misdemeanor charge that was the subject of the Test Fleet case. However, the information about jury tampering obtained by Partin while acting as a government informant in the Hoffa camp was used to prosecute and convict Hoffa and his co-defendants in a later federal trial in Chattanooga. Immediately after the announcement of Hoffa's conviction in the jury tampering trial, Sheridan ran out of the courtroom in Chattanooga and placed the call that, in one form or another, Robert Kennedy had been awaiting for seven years. Sheridan's first words to his superior were, "We made it!" A jubilant Kennedy responded to the man whose input had been so vital to the conviction, "Nice work."[37]

Without the information obtained by Partin and his later testimony, Kennedy and Sheridan would never have been able to celebrate Hoffa's conviction. The jury tampering convictions of Hoffa and his co-defendants were ultimately appealed to the Supreme Court. Hoffa's strongest argument, and the claim that received the most attention from the Justices during oral argument, was that Partin's conduct violated the

---

[33] SLOANE, *supra* note 2, at 283.

[34] NAVASKY, *supra* note 4, 476.

[35] *Id*. at 474.

[36] *Id*.

[37] SLOANE, *supra* note 2, at 301 (footnote omitted).

Fourth Amendment's prohibition against unreasonable searches and seizures. The Court rejected this claim and Hoffa's other constitutional claims.[38] The next section of this chapter describes the three legal developments that influenced the Court's thinking about *Hoffa*. The two preceeding sections explain the results in *Hoffa* and a companion case, *Lewis v. United States*,[39] and provides a critique of *Hoffa*. The final section discusses the state of the law in a post-*Hoffa* world where there are no constitutional checks on the type of informant spying that was responsible for sending Jimmy Hoffa to prison.

The Legal Background on the Fourth Amendment and Informants

Prior to *Hoffa*, the Court had issued only a handful of decisions on the constitutionality of the government's authority to send covert agents into the private lives of Americans. And the few opinions announced by the Court were not all of a piece. Perhaps because there were only a few rulings on the topic, the Court had not definitively resolved several basic questions on whether the use of an informant was consistent with Fourth Amendment principles. For example, if the target of a police investigation unwittingly admits a secret police agent into his home or hotel suite and the agent observes incriminating information that is later used against the target, should the agent's behavior trigger Fourth Amendment scrutiny?

After all, the Fourth Amendment was placed in the Bill of Rights to guard against *forcible* intrusions into privacy. It was the violent breaking down of doors and rummaging through private spaces by British customs officers under the authority of general warrants and writs of assistance that enraged the colonists. When an informant gains entry into a home or office through deceit, he or she is not effectuating a forcible search or seizure. Would the answer to this threshold question change if the target admits a disguised agent into his home or office to discuss a crime or to buy narcotics? Should it matter whether it is the target or the agent who initiates the discussion to purchase narcotics?

---

[38] Hoffa also argued that Partin's conduct violated his rights under the Self Incrimination Clause of the Fifth Amendment and the Sixth Amendment's Right to Counsel Clause. These claims were rejected. *See* 385 U.S. at 303–312. In a third, independent prosecution, Hoffa and other co-defendants were convicted of mail and wire fraud involving activities related to the Central States, Southeast and Southwest Areas Pension Fund of the International Brotherhood of Teamsters. Hoffa and his co-defendants appealed their convictions to the Court. The Court did not address the merits of their claims, but did remand their cases to the District Court to determine whether a FBI wiretap of one of the defendants tainted the convictions of any of the defendants. *See* Hoffa v. United States, 387 U.S. 231 (1967) (*per curiam*).

[39] 385 U.S. 206 (1966).

Moreover, after gaining entry into a private place, if a police spy hears only what the target intends for him to hear, or sees only what is in plain view, why has an unreasonable search or seizure occurred? Even assuming that words can be searched or seized, did the spy's actions violate the Fourth Amendment? If the target has invited or acquiesced in the spy's entry, hasn't the target also consented to whatever search or seizure the spy accomplishes while remaining in the target's presence? Under traditional Fourth Amendment norms, neither a warrant nor probable cause is needed if a person consents to police search or seizure. Although the Court's early secret spy cases, discussed below, had raised these and other issues, the Court's opinions sent mixed signals about the proper way to answer these questions.

In addition to its prior rulings on informants, the Justices in *Hoffa* were influenced by two other developments. The rulings in the early informant cases were emerging at the same time that the Court was reconsidering the constitutionality of telephone wiretapping and electronic bugging by police officials. If unfettered wiretapping and bugging were inconsistent with search and seizure norms, then a reasonable argument could be made that covert agent spying also implicated constitutional concerns.

The final and most important factor that influenced the result in *Hoffa* came from an unlikely source. *Hoffa* rested on a legal framework first conceived by Justice Brennan, who "was widely regarded as the leading voice of liberalism on the Court and (a view held by many of his critics as well as his admirers) as one of the most influential and effective Justices in the Court's history."[40] Rather than relying on the same theories that supported its rulings in the wiretapping and bugging contexts, the *Hoffa* Court turned to Brennan's "assumption of risk" theory to explain why informant spying did not invoke Fourth Amendment protection. Each of these developments is discussed in greater detail below.

1. *The Early Cases: More Questions Than Answers*

The Court's initial covert agent case, *Gouled v. United States*,[41] raised more questions than it answered. In *Gouled*, a government agent, who was a friend of Gouled, went to Gouled's office to gather information about an alleged conspiracy to defraud the United States Army. Acting under direction of Army Intelligence Department officers, the friend, "pretending to make a friendly call," obtained admission to Gouled's office and "in [Gouled's] absence, without warrant of any

---

[40] Yale Kamisar, *Remembering the "Old World" of Criminal Procedure: A Reply to Professor Grano*, 23 U. MICH. J.L. REF. 537, 541 (1990).

[41] 155 U.S. 298 (1921).

character, seized and carried away several documents," one of which was later introduced at Gouled's prosecution for fraud.[42]

Gouled asserted that the agent's actions violated his Fourth Amendment rights, but the government had two responses to this claim. First, the government insisted that a forcible intrusion was the essence of an unreasonable search or seizure. Although the agent had taken advantage of his friendship with Gouled to obtain entry into the office, the government argued that this ploy did not implicate constitutional interests. The government contended that the Fourth Amendment did not bar such conduct, provided no force or legal compulsion was exerted against Gouled.[43] Alternatively, even assuming that the agent's conduct constituted a search or seizure, the government argued that Gouled consented to the agent's entry. Once the agent had gained access to the office, the Fourth Amendment did not "require him to shut his eyes to any evidence of crime that may be open to his observation."[44]

A unanimous Court summarily rejected the government's arguments and ruled that Gouled's Fourth Amendment rights had been violated. First, the Court expressly dismissed the claim that force or coercion was a necessary element of a Fourth Amendment intrusion. The Court explained that an intrusion by stealth implicates the same constitutional concerns as a forcible intrusion. Although *Gouled* left no doubt that a stealthy intrusion triggers Fourth Amendment scrutiny, the Court's reply to the government's consent argument was cryptic. The Court stated: "[W]hether entrance to the home or office of a person suspected of crime be obtained by a [government agent] by stealth, or through social acquaintance, or in the guise of a business call, and whether the owner be present or not when he enters, any search and seizure subsequently and secretly made in his absence, falls within the scope of the prohibition of the Fourth Amendment."[45]

Interestingly, the *Gouled* Court did not address the government's argument that Gouled consented to the *entry*. Instead, the Court focuses on the "search and seizure subsequently and secretly made in [Gouled's] absence."[46] If, however, the seizure of the paper in Gouled's absence was the crux of the constitutional violation, then the *manner* of the agent's entry is unimportant. What matters is Gouled's ignorance of the seizure. If Gouled witnessed the seizure without objection, then he would have no constitutional complaint. But because he was momentarily absent

---

[42] *Id.* at 304.

[43] *Id.* at 299–301.

[44] *Id.* at 301.

[45] *Id.* at 306.

[46] *Id.*

during the agent's seizure of the incriminating documents and did not
learn of the government's possession of them until later, Gouled was
unable to protect or assert his Fourth Amendment rights when it
mattered most.

Decades later, *Gouled* would be interpreted by the Court and most
commentators as establishing the narrow proposition that a clandestine
search or seizure in the absence of the target violates the Fourth
Amendment. At the same time, *Gouled* was also read to establish that if
a person unwittingly grants access to private premises or communications and knowingly reveals private information to a covert spy, no
Fourth Amendment intrusion has occurred. But the conclusion that
Gouled permits the use of secret informants is problematic for two
reasons. First, the traditional view of *Gouled*—that the use of a secret
spy raises no Fourth Amendment issues, provided no information is
seized in the absence of the target—races far ahead of the facts and
holding in *Gouled*. Second, and most importantly, the traditional view
that no Fourth Amendment violation occurs when the target unwittingly
grants access to a covert spy *assumes* that the target has consented to
the entry, but the *Gouled* Court did not endorse the government's
consent argument.

On the first point, consider two slightly altered variations of the
Gouled facts. In one hypothetical case, after gaining entry to Gouled's
office by "pretending to make a friendly call,"[47] the informant spies an
incriminating document while Gouled is still in the room, but does not
snatch the document while Gouled's back is turned. The informant
reports his observation to his superiors, and later the government
obtains a search warrant to seize the document. In the second hypothetical, the informant is unable to locate the incriminating document he was
sent to find, but while chatting with Gouled observes a gallon-sized
bottle of contraband liquor in plain view on a shelf above Gouled's desk.
After reporting his failure to locate the incriminating document to his
superiors, the informant mentions noticing the contraband liquor. A
warrant to search for the illegal alcohol is then obtained. While execut-
ing that warrant, agents seize both the liquor and the incriminating
document which is discovered in plain view on the same shelf holding
the whiskey bottle.

In both hypotheticals, Gouled is in the room. Yet, the logic of *Gouled*
would seem to proscribe both intrusions. Both hypotheticals involve
covert and deliberate government conduct that invaded Gouled's security
and privacy and constituted a "search and seizure ... as much against
his will"[48] as the actual intrusion in *Gouled*. When the hypothetical

---

[47] *Id*. at 304.

[48] *Id*. at 305–06.

agent came to Gouled's office to determine whether incriminating material was present, he certainly "searched" the office. In the second hypothetical, although the agent failed to find the incriminating document, he did observe contraband liquor, which was also a "search" of the office. If a search is still a search even though nothing of great personal value is exposed, deliberate governmental action that discloses the existence of private information or communications is certainly no less a search. As the Court noted seven years prior to *Gouled*, "a search ordinarily implies a quest by an officer of the law."[49] Both hypotheticals depict a government agent on a quest for information.

To be sure, *Gouled* did not confront facts raised by either of these hypotheticals. On the other hand, there is no indication in the terse *Gouled* opinion to suggest that the Court would allow either of these intrusions. In fact, a small number of lower courts and a few commentators had interpreted *Gouled* to proscribe secret governmental intrusions even when the target of the search was present and the informant only saw or heard information knowingly revealed by the target.[50]

The second problem with the traditional interpretation of *Gouled*— that it permits entries by disguised agents in order to search and seize, provided the agent does not see, hear or take anything not contemplated by the target—is that the traditional view ignores the fact that the *Gouled* Court did not address, let alone, adopt the government's consent argument. The most that can be said about the government's consent claim is that *Gouled* remained neutral on the point.

But did Gouled consent to the search? It is too easy to say that Gouled consented. When *Gouled* was decided in 1921, the Court had not yet addressed whether "consent" under the Fourth Amendment turned on the individual acting voluntarily, or whether consent required an intentional waiver of a known right, although a case decided on the same day as *Gouled*, *Amos v. United States*[51] suggested that the Court was inclined to view consent as requiring an intentional waiver of one's right. Granted, the Constitution generally, and the Fourth Amendment specifically, does not protect against stupidity, or even against a private friend

---

[49] Weeks v. United States, 232 U.S. 383, 397 (1914).

[50] *See, e.g.*, Hajdu v. State, 189 So. 2d 230, 231–32 (Fla. Dist. Ct. App. 1966), *cert. denied*, 196 So. 2d 923 (Fla. 1967); Osmond K. Fraenkel, *Recent Developments in the Law of Search and Seizure*, 13 MINN. L. REV. 1, 11 note 87 (1928) (asserting that *Gouled* "condemned a taking by stealth whether in the presence or absence of the owner").

[51] 255 U.S. 313, 317 (1921) (rejecting the claim that "the constitutional rights of defendant were waived when his wife admitted to his home," without a warrant, officers demanding entry under government authority, and refusing to consider "whether it is possible for a wife, in the absence of her husband, thus to waive his constitutional rights, for it is perfectly clear that under the implied coercion here presented, no such waiver was intended or effected").

who later reveals incriminating information to the authorities. The Fourth Amendment, however, does protect against unfettered, deliberate efforts by *government* officials to obtain information from one's home or office. Indeed, prior to *Hoffa*, a number of lower courts read *Gouled* to establish the rule that incriminating evidence obtained by deceit violates the Fourth Amendment.[52] When Gouled opened his office to his friend, he had no knowledge of, and did not consent to, the planned *governmental* intrusion that occurred. As one modern commentator has described:

> Undercover agents often violate [the] sanctity [of a home or office] when they gain access to a person's home or workplace without a warrant. They may be invited in, but only because of deception—under the guise of friendship, a business partnership, or through the access granted a phony housing inspector or meter reader. It is sophistry to argue that such searches are voluntary. A person may give consent to a meter reader, but only to have the meter read, not to have the house searched. Consent is highly circumscribed; if the target was not duped, access would be denied. When the public-private boundary can be transgressed at will, whether through deception or coercion and force, liberty is impossible. Liberty exists partly because there are private and personal spaces that are beyond official reach.[53]

Put simply, fictive notions of consent cannot undercut the basic tenet that planned, covert intrusions of a protected area or activity implicate Fourth Amendment values, just as open and forcible invasions do.

The Court's next informant case, *On Lee v. United States*,[54] paid little attention to what the Court had decided and left undecided in *Gouled*. Whereas *Gouled* made clear that an intrusion by stealth or deceit implicates the same constitutional values implicated by a forcible intrusion, *On Lee* dismissed the defendant's attempt to invoke Fourth Amendment protection against a covert intrusion because the informant had not committed a trespass on his property. In a similar vein, although

---

[52] *See, e.g.,* United States v. Sclafani, 265 F. 2d 408, 415 (2d Cir., 1959) (stating that the rule of *Gouled* condemns fraudulently obtained consent to search); United States v. Reckis, 119 F.Supp. 687, 690 & note 1 (D. Mass. 1954) (interpreting *Gouled* to stand for the proposition that incriminating statements and evidence obtained by means of fraud violate the Fourth Amendment); People v. Dent, 19 N.E. 2d 1020, 1021–22 (Ill. 1939) (relying upon *Gouled* to hold that permission to enter a home, given in ignorance of the identity and purpose of those seeking admission, renders a subsequent entry and search invalid); Commonwealth v. Wright, 190 A.2d 709, 711 (Pa. 1963) (relying upon *Gouled* to hold that "consent [to search] may not be gained through stealth, deceit or misrepresentation").

[53] GARY T. MARX, UNDERCOVER: POLICE SURVEILLANCE IN AMERICA, 1960–1972 99–100 (Univ. of Cal. Press 1989).

[54] 343 U.S. 747 (1952).

the *Gouled Court* did not endorse the government's position that Gouled had consented to a search when he unwittingly allowed an informant access to his office, *On Lee* proceeded as if the use of a covert spy raised no legitimate issue concerning the target's consent.

In *On Lee*, Chin Poy, a friend and former employee of defendant On Lee, went to On Lee's laundry shop. Unknown to On Lee, Chin Poy was a government informant "wired for sound, with a small microphone in his inside overcoat pocket and a small antenna running along his arm."[55] A federal Narcotics Bureau agent, Lawrence Lee, was stationed outside the laundry shop and equipped to listen to the conversation between On Lee and Chin Poy. Several days later, a conversation between On Lee and Chin Poy, which took place on the street, was monitored by agent Lee. During both conversations, On Lee made incriminating statements regarding illegal narcotics. At trial, agent Lee was permitted to testify about On Lee's incriminating statements.

Speaking for a majority of the *On Lee* Court, Justice Jackson concluded that "the conduct of Chin Poy and agent Lee did not amount to an unlawful search and seizure such as is proscribed by the Fourth Amendment."[56] Jackson explained that "no trespass was committed" by Chin Poy; on the contrary, "Chin Poy entered a place of business with the consent, if not by the implied invitation, of the [defendant]."[57] Jackson opined that the additional argument that agent Lee had committed a trespass because the electronic equipment concealed on Chin Poy allowed Lee to secretly overhear what transpired in On Lee's laundry bordered on the "frivolous." Only a "physical entry," such as one associated with force, submission to legal coercion, or without any sign of consent, would trigger constitutional protection against this type of covert surveillance.[58] Finally, Jackson saw no reason to view informant spying as the equivalent of police wiretapping. The use of a radio wire suggested only "the most attenuated analogy to wiretapping." According to Jackson: "It would be a dubious service to the genuine liberties protected by the Fourth Amendment to make them bedfellows with spurious liberties improvised by farfetched analogies which would liken eavesdropping on a conversation, with the connivance of one of the parties, to an unreasonable search or seizure."[59]

Justice Burton's dissent challenged Jackson's conclusion that there was no illegal entry because On Lee had consented to Chin Poy's search

---

[55] *Id*. at 749.

[56] *Id*. at 751.

[57] *Id*. at 751–52.

[58] *Id*. at 752–53.

[59] *Id*. at 753–54.

and seizure. This claim "overlooks the fact that Chin Poy, without warrant and without [On Lee's] consent, took with him the concealed radio transmitter to which agent Lee's receiving set was tuned." In effect, Chin Poy was "surreptitiously bringing Lee with him" when he entered the laundry.[60] Without elaborating, Justice Burton observed that Chin Poy, "who was lawfully in [On Lee's] room, could have testified as to what he, himself, saw or heard there."[61] But Burton believed that agent Lee's monitoring of the conversation was accomplished without On Lee's consent.

The tension between *On Lee* and *Gouled* is apparent. First, consider Justice Jackson's conclusion that because no trespass or "physical entry" had occurred, On Lee's constitutional argument, to use his phrase, "verges on the frivolous." But why was On Lee's submission frivolous? Didn't the Court, thirty years earlier in *Gouled*, settle the argument over whether a police intrusion must be accompanied by force or violence to trigger Fourth Amendment scrutiny? Didn't a unanimous Court in *Gouled* resolve this issue *against* the government? Jackson fails to reconcile this aspect of *Gouled*.

Nor does he acknowledge that *Gouled* left the consent issue open. Jackson concluded On Lee consented to Chin Poy's entry into his office. But if On Lee's unwitting acquiescence to Chin Poy's entry was a valid consent, then Gouled also consented when he unwittingly allowed similar access to a friend-turned-government-spy. Didn't this discrepancy merit some discussion? It is not a "frivolous" argument to urge that the crux of the constitutional harm in *On Lee* occurred when Chin Poy, "pretending to make a friendly call,"[62] and "without warrant of any character,"[63] was sent into On Lee's laundry to capture private conversations. On Lee no more consented to this secret and deliberate seizure of his words than did Gouled when he invited his friend into his office.

While Justice Jackson did not reconcile his conclusions in *On Lee* with *Gouled*, nine years later in the next informant case, four members of the Court were ready to overrule *On Lee*. In that case, *Lopez v. United States*,[64] only three Justices remained from the Court that had decided *On Lee*, and two of the three, Black and Douglas, thought at the time that the evidence obtained by Chin Poy's covert surveillance should have

---

[60] *Id.* at 766 (Burton, J., dissenting).

[61] *Id.*

[62] *Gouled*, 255 U.S. at 304.

[63] *Id.*

[64] 373 U.S. 427 (1963).

been excluded from trial.[65] In *Lopez*, the defendant appealed his conviction for the attempted bribery of an Internal Revenue agent. The agent had visited Lopez's business to inquire about the payment of excise taxes. During the visit, Lopez offered the agent a bribe. Pretending to go along with the bribery scheme, the agent returned to Lopez's office several days later, equipped with a pocket recorder. During this second visit, Lopez made additional incriminating statements. At Lopez's trial, the agent testified about the conversation that Lopez had initiated, and a tape recording of the conversation was played to corroborate the agent's testimony. In the Supreme Court, Lopez argued that the agent's testimony, as well as the tape recording, were inadmissible because the agent's conduct violated the Fourth Amendment.

The *Lopez* Court disagreed. Writing for the majority, Justice Harlan found that there was no illegal invasion of Lopez's office because the agent obtained Lopez's "consent, and while there [the agent] did not violate the privacy of the office by seizing something surreptitiously without Lopez's knowledge."[66] Although Justice Harlan believed Lopez's consent and knowledge of the agent's mission was enough to distinguish the facts in *Lopez* from *Gouled*, interestingly, Harlan did not reaffirm *On Lee*'s rationale or its holding. Perhaps Harlan thought that explicit reliance on *On Lee* would lose votes of one or more members of the majority. (Justice Black, for example, a member of the *Lopez* majority, voted to exclude the evidence obtained in *On Lee* based on the Court's supervisory authority over the federal judiciary.) Or perhaps, Harlan himself had doubts about the validity of *On Lee*'s "trespass" or "consent" theories. Whatever the reason, Harlan did not purport to follow *On Lee* or state that *On Lee* controlled the result in *Lopez*.

Finally, Justice Harlan was careful to point out that the facts in *Lopez* did not raise an issue concerning the constitutionality of electronic wiretapping or eavesdropping, an issue which had bitterly divided the Court since 1928. For Harlan, the permissibility of eavesdropping, electronic or otherwise, was not addressed in *Lopez* because "[t]he government did not use an electronic device to listen in on conversations it could not otherwise have heard."[67] On the contrary, according to Harlan, the electronic recording equipment "was used only to obtain the most reliable evidence possible of a conversation in which the Government's

---

[65] In *On Lee*, Justice Black wrote that agent Lee's testimony should have been excluded under the Court's supervisory authority over the federal courts, *see* 343 U.S at 758, while Justice Douglas thought agent Lee's testimony was the product of an illegal electronic listening device. Justice Clark, the third Justice that sat on both *On Lee* and *Lopez*, joined the majority opinion in *On Lee*.

[66] 373 U.S. at 438.

[67] *Id*. at 439.

own agent was a participant and which that agent was fully entitled to disclose."[68] When viewed from this angle, a ruling in favor of Lopez would be the equivalent to holding that Lopez has "a constitutional right to rely on possible flaws in the agent's memory, or to challenge the agent's credibility without being beset by corroborating evidence that is not susceptible of impeachment."[69]

In sum, when the Court granted Jimmy Hoffa's petition to review his case, the government's authority to insert secret agents into the private lives of citizens was hardly settled. To be sure, there was a consensus among the Justices to read *Gouled* narrowly. *Gouled* was understood as establishing the limited rule that a covert agent's clandestine search or seizure in the absence of the target violates the Fourth Amendment. But students of the Court could also discern that, after *Lopez*, much of *On Lee*'s reasoning rested on a shaky analytical foundation, and a majority of the Court was unwilling to endorse its holding. Given these circumstances, and the fact that four Justices in *Lopez* expressly called for overruling *On Lee*, the continued permissibility of using covert spies as informants to gather information in constitutionally protected areas was an open question. Under this view, *Lopez* merely announced that the Fourth Amendment imposed no restraint on a government officer testifying about incriminating statements made to him, and no rule against the use of electronic equipment to corroborate the officer's testimony. But *Lopez* had not settled the issue, first raised in *Gouled*, whether entry procured by deceit amounted to consent under the Fourth Amendment. Three years later, the Court would grant certiorari in *Hoffa* and *Lewis v. United States* to finally resolve this question.[70]

2. *The Uneasy Mix of Technology, Wiretapping and Bugging on the Development of the Informant Cases*

Technological advances had a significant impact on the Court's view of the constitutionality of using informants to discover private information. As electronic surveillance equipment became more sophisticated, law enforcement officials took advantage of technological innovations in their fight against crime. But as technology became more advanced and better able to capture communications between persons in private places, a growing number of the Justices took the position that electronically-wired informants threatened the privacy interest that was at the core of the Fourth Amendment's protective scope.

---

[68] *Id*. at 439.

[69] *Id*.

[70] 382 U.S. 1024 (1966).

Moreover, the informant cases were being decided at the same time that the Court's thinking on wiretapping and bugging was evolving. During the time that the Court was reconsidering and preparing to overrule *Olmstead v. United States*,[71] which had held that telephone wiretapping was not covered by the Fourth Amendment, the Court was deciding *On Lee*, *Lopez*, *Lewis* and *Hoffa*. Addressing the constitutionality of planting informants into constitutionally sensitive areas while at the same time reconsidering the constitutionality of wiretapping posed an interesting juxtaposition for the Justices.

On the one hand, if the Justices thought unfettered government wiretapping and bugging was inconsistent with the Fourth Amendment, it is understandable why they would also take a jaundiced view of informants, particularly electronically wired spies who deliberately sought and obtained private communications. After all, a secret informant acts as a "human bug" for the government. On the other hand, if the Court were prepared to permit limited forms of wiretapping and electronic bugging, especially if such surveillance were supervised by a neutral judge, there was no apparent reason why informant surveillance ought to be *per se* unconstitutional. Put another way, if the Court were willing to tolerate wiretapping and bugging, albeit under judicial oversight, it would be illogical to conclude that the Fourth Amendment barred the use of informants even in constitutionally sensitive areas.

Although no electronic equipment was used in *Gouled*, the rationale of *Gouled* was ironically initially questioned in a wiretap case, *Olmstead v. United States*. *Olmstead* held that police wiretapping of telephone conversations fell outside the protection of the Fourth Amendment. Employing a narrow and literal reading of the amendment, *Olmstead* held that words spoken into a telephone were not tangible things and thus could not be subject to search or seizure. The Court also reasoned that because wiretapping could be accomplished without a trespass, there was no physical invasion of property to justify invoking Fourth Amendment protection. Finally, the Court *assumed* that a person who uses the telephone "intends to project his voice to those quite outside."[72]

The defendants in *Olmstead* argued that because *Gouled* held that the amendment covers stealthy as well as forcible intrusions on privacy, wiretapping was also covered by the amendment even though no trespass was involved. The *Olmstead* Court was not impressed with this theory. *Olmstead* observed that *Gouled* "carried the inhibition against unreasonable searches and seizures to the extreme limit." The *Olmstead* Court then distinguished wiretapping from the facts in *Gouled* by noting that in *Gouled* "[t]here was actual entrance into the private quarters of

---

[71] 277 U.S. 438 (1928).

[72] *Id.* at 466.

defendant and the taking away of something tangible. Here we have testimony only of voluntary conversations secretly overheard."[73]

Although *Olmstead*'s conclusion that telephone wiretapping did not trigger Fourth Amendment scrutiny was subjected to stinging criticism both on and off the Court, *Olmstead*'s holding remained the constitutional rule for almost forty years. In the meantime, law enforcement officials took advantage of technological innovations to spy on individuals in ways unimaginable to the Framers. Various studies chronicled the development of technological devices that could secretly intrude on private activities and communications.[74] In the first case addressing the constitutionality of electronic bugging, *Goldman v. United States*,[75] the Court ruled that the placement of a detectaphone against the wall of a private office, which enabled officers to monitor conversations on the other side of the wall, did not amount to a search or seizure. The defendants in *Goldman* had sought to distinguish electronic eavesdropping from telephone wiretapping by noting that *Olmstead* had relied on the assumption that one who uses the telephone intends to project his words outside of his home, and thus assumes the risk that his words may be intercepted. In contrast, persons who speak inside an office intend for their words to remain within the confines of the office, and thus, do not assume the risk that their communications will be overheard by a detectaphone. The *Goldman* Court thought this distinction "too nice for practical application of the Constitutional guarantee," and accordingly saw no "reasonable or logical" distinction between the use of a detectaphone and telephone wiretapping.[76]

While a slim majority of the Court in *Olmstead* and *Goldman* established that wiretapping and electronic bugging were beyond the reach of the Fourth Amendment, it was obvious that the strength of those majority opinions would soon be tested. In *Goldman* itself, Chief Justice Stone and Justice Frankfurter pointedly noted that had a majority of their colleagues been willing to overrule *Olmstead*, they would have been "happy to join them."[77] In *Silverman v. United States*, a "spike mike" was inserted into the party wall of an adjoining row house and made contact with a heating duct, which converted the heating duct into a "conductor of sound," enabling officers to hear conversations in the adjoining home. A unanimous Court ruled that this was a search.[78]

---

[73] *Id.* at 464.

[74] *See, e.g.*, ALAN F. WESTIN, PRIVACY AND FREEDOM (Atheneum 1967).

[75] 316 U.S. 114 (1942).

[76] *Id.* at 135.

[77] *Id.* at 136 (separate opinion of Stone, C.J., & Frankfurter, J.).

[78] 365 U.S. 505 (1961).

Silverman recognized that the only difference between the use of a "spike mike" and a "detectaphone," which was allowed in *Goldman*, was the trivial fact that the "spike mike" required a physical intrusion extending only a few inches into a party wall. Nevertheless, the *Silverman* Court was unwilling to re-examine *Goldman's* reasoning. But the Court was also unwilling "to go beyond [*Goldman's* logic], by even a fraction of an inch."[79]

The debate on overruling *Olmstead* had not been resolved between the time when *Goldman* and *Silverman* were decided. In 1952, ten years after *Goldman*, but nine years prior to *Silverman*, the Court decided *On Lee*. It was evident in the various opinions written in *On Lee* that the "wiretapping" debate and its reverberations were affecting the Justices' thinking about informant spying. For example, although the *On Lee* majority refused to reconsider *Olmstead's* holding, the Court noted overruling *Olmstead* would not aid On Lee's constitutional claim because the "presence of a radio set [attached to an informant] is not sufficient to suggest more than the most attenuated analogy to wiretapping."[80] The Court also insisted that the police use of a radio transmitter to capture private communications was no different than the use of bifocals, field glasses or a telescope to capture otherwise private activity. By contrast, dissenting Justices Frankfurter and Douglas called for overruling *Olmstead*. In his separate dissent, Justice Douglas admitted that he was wrong to join the *Goldman* majority. Douglas was now taking the position that there was no principled distinction between the telephone wiretap used in *Olmstead*, the detectaphone used in *Goldman*, and the " 'walky-talky' " radio device used in *On Lee*.[81]

The debate over wiretapping and electronic bugging was even more vigorous in *Lopez*. The *Lopez* Court was badly divided over whether the use of a transmitter to record the conversation between Lopez and the Internal Revenue agent triggered Fourth Amendment protection. Four Justices in *Lopez* declared that both *Olmstead* and *On Lee* were wrongly decided.[82] As noted earlier, Justice Harlan's majority opinion in *Lopez* did

---

[79] *Id.* at 512.

[80] *On Lee*, 343 U.S. at 753.

[81] *Id.* at 765 (Douglas, J., dissenting).

[82] Chief Justice Warren and Justices Brennan, Douglas and Goldberg thought *On Lee* should be overruled. Chief Justice Warren argued that *Lopez* and *On Lee* were different cases. In *On Lee*, "[t]he use and purpose of the transmitter . . . was not to corroborate the testimony of [the informant], but rather, to obviate the need to put him on the stand." 373 U.S. at 443 (Warren, C.J., concurring in result). For the Chief Justice, electronic surveillance, when used in the manner at issue in *On Lee*, raised substantial questions of due process. Justice Brennan, speaking for the other two Justices, contended that *On Lee* and *Lopez* were indistinguishable.

not reaffirm *On Lee*. But he did conclude that the *Lopez* facts raised no constitutional concerns because the transmitter had been "used only to obtain the most reliable evidence possible of a conversation in which the Government's own agent was a participant and which that agent was fully entitled to disclose."[83] The dissenters, on the other hand, argued that the presence of a recording device was constitutionally significant because it allowed third parties to monitor private conversations. As Justice Brennan put it for the dissenters, both *On Lee* and *Lopez* impose the unreasonable risk "that third parties, whether mechanical auditors like the Minifon or human transcribers of mechanical transmissions as in *On Lee*—third parties who cannot be shut out of a conversation as conventional eavesdroppers can be, merely by a lowering of voices, or withdrawing to a private place—may give independent evidence of any conversation."[84]

The debate among the Justices over the constitutionality of wiretapping and electronic bugging would soon be resolved, but not before the Court announced its opinion in *Hoffa*. By the end of 1967, a year after *Hoffa* had been decided, the Court concluded in two cases that electronic bugging and telephone wiretapping did trigger Fourth Amendment scrutiny.

The first case, *Berger v. New York*, involved electronic bugging.[85] *Berger* addressed a constitutional challenge to a New York statute allowing court-authorized electronic surveillance. The defendants were convicted of conspiracy to corrupt the New York State Liquor Authority. The incriminating evidence against some of the defendants was obtained pursuant to several court-ordered bugs authorized by the statute. A majority of the *Berger* Court ruled that the state law was facially unconstitutional under the Fourth Amendment for essentially two reasons: the statute did not require that a judge find probable cause before issuing an electronic surveillance warrant, and the statute failed to limit the nature, scope or duration of the electronic surveillance. The second ruling, *Katz v. United States*,[86] was a replay of the facts in *Olmstead*. In *Katz*, the defendant argued that FBI agents violated the Fourth Amendment by attaching an electronic listening and recording device to the outside of a public telephone to monitor his conversations. The Court agreed and reversed Katz's conviction, and in the process overruled *Olmstead* and *Goldman*.

---

[83] 373 U.S. at 439.

[84] *Id.* at 450 (Brennan, J., dissenting).

[85] 388 U.S. 41 (1967).

[86] 389 U.S. 347 (1967). *See* the chapter on *Katz* in this volume.

Judges and legal scholars universally agree that Justice Stewart's opinion in *Katz* signaled that the old ways of analyzing search and seizure issues were no longer acceptable.[87] The Justices who decided Jimmy Hoffa's case, however, would not have the benefit of *Katz*'s reformulation of Fourth Amendment law. Although *Katz*'s redefinition of search and seizure doctrine had yet to be announced, the Justices who decided *Hoffa* did not return to the "trespass" or "consent" theories that had badly divided the Court during *Olmstead* and *On Lee*'s reign. Instead, the Justices turned to a different theory to resolve the search and seizure question at stake in *Hoffa*. Ironically, that theory had been suggested in Justice Brennan's dissent in *Lopez* on an issue that was not germane to the *Lopez* facts. Justice Brennan's assumption of risk theory is the third development that explains *Hoffa* and clarifies how the Court reconciles informant spying and Fourth Amendment principles.

3. *Justice Brennan's Contribution to* Hoffa

As noted in the previous section, the *Lopez* Court was badly split over whether the use of an electronic transmitter to capture Lopez's conversations with an Internal Revenue agent was covered by the Fourth Amendment. Although closely divided on this issue, all of the Justices in *Lopez* agreed that the agent's oral testimony was admissible at trial and not the product of an unreasonable search or seizure. The logic supporting this agreement was articulated in a little-noticed section of Justice Brennan's dissent. In that section, Justice Brennan introduced his assumption of risk theory regarding informant spying.

Justice Brennan's reasoning was similar to a theme that first surfaced in *Olmstead*. The *Olmstead* Court justified its conclusion that wiretapping was not a search or seizure by speculating about the subjective views of the "reasonable" person. "The reasonable view is that one who installs in his house a telephone instrument with connecting wires *intends* to project his voice to those quite outside, and that the wires beyond his house and messages while passing over them are not within the protection of the Fourth Amendment."[88]

In *Lopez*, Justice Brennan proffered a comparable model in explaining why ordinary conversations between an individual and a disguised government informant fall outside the scope of the Fourth Amendment. According to Brennan, such conversations "do not seriously intrude upon the right of privacy. The risk of being overheard by an eavesdropper or betrayed by an informer or deceived as to the identity of one with

---

[87] *See, e.g.,* 1 WAYNE R. LaFAVE, SEARCH AND SEIZURE § 2.1(b), at 385 (3d ed. 1996) (describing *Katz* as a "landmark" ruling).

[88] 277 U.S. at 466 (emphasis added).

whom one deals is probably inherent in the conditions of human society. It is the kind of risk we necessarily assume whenever we speak.''[89]

Justice Brennan's comments were gratuitous and unfortunate. First, his remarks on the risks we assume were an unnecessary detour from the facts in *Lopez*. *Lopez* could have been decided on straightforward consent grounds, since unlike Gouled and On Lee, Lopez knew he was conversing with a federal law enforcement officer. Further, Lopez had initiated the conversation and encouraged the agent to return to his office. Thus, Brennan's discussion on the risk of being betrayed by secret police informants and eavesdroppers was unnecessary because such activity was not even remotely at issue in *Lopez*.

Second, Brennan's comments were unfortunate because his conclusion on the risks we assume by speaking to third parties was no more based on facts than was the conclusion assumed in *Olmstead* that a person who uses a telephone inside his home or office intends to project his voice to those outside. Nor were Brennan's views tied to a principle embraced by the Fourth Amendment. It was simply his conclusion about how most folks live their lives. Three years later, however, an overwhelming majority of the Court would adopt Justice Brennan's assumption of risk model in *Hoffa*.

In summary, three developments affected the Court's thinking on the eve of *Hoffa*. First, the Court's prior rulings on informants had left unsettled the government's authority to send covert spies into the private lives of citizens. In the most recent case on the topic, *Lopez*, the majority had refused to reaffirm *On Lee*'s holding, and four Justices had expressly wanted to overrule *On Lee*. Second, the Court was on the brink of declaring telephone wiretapping and electronic bugging unconstitutional. If police officials were no longer free to decide for themselves whether to wiretap or bug a target's home or office in order to gather information or evidence, reasonable persons could ask why officials should be free to send a covert agent into a person's home or office to do the same. Finally, when the Court again attempted to reconcile informant surveillance with Fourth Amendment values, it would turn to a theory that had not been subjected to careful scrutiny among the Justices. Rather than rely on the trespass or consent models that had divided the Court in previous cases, the Court justified informant spying under Justice Brennan's assumption of risk theory.

Hoffa and *Lewis*: Informant Spying Without Constitutional Restraint

Hoffa and *Lewis* were decided on the same day, and the cases have sometimes been treated as a matched pair, but there are significant

---

[89] 373 U.S. at 465 (Brennan, J., dissenting).

factual and legal differences between the cases. *Lewis* will be discussed first. The facts in *Lewis* were undisputed. An undercover officer misrepresented his identity during a telephone conversation and obtained Lewis's invitation to visit his home to purchase narcotics. It was conceded that that conversation provided probable cause to believe a narcotics offense would be committed at Lewis's home, and thus would have justified the issuance of a warrant to search the home. The officer came to the home and purchased the narcotics. A second visit, encouraged by Lewis, resulted in a similar purchase. The narcotics and the officer's testimony concerning his conversations with Lewis were admitted at trial.

In rejecting Lewis's constitutional claim, the Court was careful to frame the issue narrowly. Chief Justice Warren emphasized that there was no question about whether a "search" of the home had occurred or whether "anything other than the purchased narcotics [had been] taken away." The only issues were whether "in the absence of a warrant, any official intrusion upon the privacy of a home constitutes a Fourth Amendment violation" and whether Lewis's invitation can "be held a waiver when the invitation was induced by fraud and deception."[90]

Lewis argued that *Gouled* controlled, but the Chief Justice disagreed. *Gouled*, according to Warren, involved a "secret and general ransacking" while the target was absent. In contrast to *Gouled*, the officer in *Lewis* did not "see, hear, or take anything that was not contemplated, and in fact intended, by [Lewis] as a necessary part of his illegal business." The Chief Justice opined that a different result would impose a *"per se"* constitutional bar on the use of undercover officers.[91]

Sensitive to the fact that the officer had entered Lewis's home, the Chief Justice explained that the traditional protections afforded a home are unavailable where a house is transformed into a commercial center to do illegal business. "A government agent, in the same manner as a private person, may accept an invitation to do business and may enter upon the premises for the very purposes contemplated by the occupant."[92] Without saying so expressly, the Chief Justice inferred that Lewis had "waived" his Fourth Amendment rights. Interestingly, however, Chief Justice Warren never used the term "consent" in explaining why the entry into Lewis's home was constitutionally reasonable. What the Chief Justice implied, concurring Justice Brennan made explicit: Lewis's home "was not an area protected by the Fourth Amendment as related to the transactions in the present case." Brennan insisted that a

---

[90] 385 U.S. at 208.

[91] *Id.* at 210.

[92] *Id.* at 211.

homeowner can "waive his right to privacy" and does so "to the extent that he opens his home to the transaction of business and invites anyone willing to enter to come in to trade with him."[93]

In *Hoffa*, as already discussed, Edward Grady Partin reported to Walter Sheridan incriminating conversations he overheard while a member of Jimmy Hoffa's entourage, including conversations that were spoken inside Hoffa's hotel suite. Finding it unimportant to the Fourth Amendment issue, the Court chose to assume that Partin was a government informer. But instead of announcing a narrow ruling, as it did in *Lewis*, the *Hoffa* Court spoke broadly.

Relying expressly on Justice Brennan's dissent in *Lopez*, Justice Stewart's opinion began by explaining that it was "evident that no interest legitimately protected by the Fourth Amendment [was] involved" in *Hoffa*.[94] There was no entry by force or stealth, nor was there any surreptitious eavesdropping. The most that could be said about Hoffa's constitutional interest was that "he was relying upon his misplaced confidence that Partin would not reveal his wrongdoing."[95] That interest, however, was not protected by the Fourth Amendment. Recalling the unanimity of the *Lopez* Court regarding the revenue agent's oral testimony, Stewart resurrected and recast Justice Brennan's assumption of risk theory into a constitutional norm: The Fourth Amendment does not protect "a wrongdoer's misplaced belief that a person to whom he voluntarily confides his wrongdoing will not reveal it."[96]

Before carefully examining *Hoffa*'s legal analysis, one should note the differences, between *Hoffa* and *Lewis*. First, Lewis invited a stranger to his home to purchase narcotics. In contrast, Partin was a friend of Jimmy Hoffa who was working for the government. Some have argued that these factual distinctions make Lewis's constitutional claim less compelling than Hoffa's. After all, if Lewis thought so little about the privacy of his home to invite a stranger inside to purchase illegal drugs, the argument continues, why afford overriding constitutional protection to his home when Lewis himself was so cavalier about who he admitted inside? As Professor LaFave has noted, a fact of central importance in *Lewis* is that the undercover officer "indicated in advance that it was *his* purpose to participate in the criminal activity."[97]

---

[93] *Id.* at 213 (Brennan, J., concurring).

[94] 385 U.S. at 302.

[95] *Id.*

[96] *Id.*

[97] 3 Wayne R. LaFave, Search and Seizure, § 8.2(m) at 703 (3d. ed. 1996).

Hoffa, on the other hand, involved a situation where the government took advantage of Partin's friendship with Jimmy Hoffa to gain access to Hoffa's privacy that was otherwise unavailable to the government. Jimmy Hoffa would never have given a stranger the same access as Partin. Furthermore, unlike Lewis, Hoffa had not invited Partin into his hotel suite to commit a crime. "Hoffa had not opened his hotel suite for the conduct of any business, and no specificity of purpose or duration limited Partin's presence there. Rather, once having been admitted, Partin spent an extensive period of time both conversing with Hoffa and his companions and listening to conversations not directed to him, all with the broad, indefinite purpose of gathering evidence of illegal activity."[98] Thus, the intrusion in *Hoffa* is more troublesome.

The other notable difference is the Court's framing of the issue and articulated holding in each case. Even though the facts in *Lewis* favored the government, Chief Justice Warren narrowly framed the issue. The Court could have easily and quickly dismissed Lewis's constitutional claim with a citation to *Lopez*, but did not. Even though no electronic recording equipment was involved, the *Lewis* Court proceeded on the premise that the undercover officer's entry into Lewis's home "raised a serious Fourth Amendment problem."[99] Most importantly, the Chief Justice is careful to confine the Court's holding to the specific facts involved.

By contrast, Justice Stewart makes no effort to carefully frame the issue in *Hoffa* or to restrain its holding. "It seems curious that the Court, while so carefully limiting its holding in *Lewis*, at the same time approved the extensive intrusion in *Hoffa* without even acknowledging the substantial differences in the breadth of the searches involved in the two cases."[100] Interestingly, Justice Stewart does not rely on *Lewis* to support his holding. He does, however, cite *Lewis* in "an enigmatic" footnote suggesting that if Partin had been a stranger to Hoffa the Court would be faced with a different, and more difficult, issue.[101]

---

[98] *The Supreme Court, 1966 Term*, 81 HARV. L. REV. 69, 193 (1967) [hereinafter, *1966 Term*].

[99] Edmund W. Kitch, Katz v. United States: *The Limits of the Fourth Amendment*, 1968 SUP. CT. REV. 133, 144.

[100] *1966 Term*, *supra* note 98, at 193 (footnote omitted).

[101] Kitch, *supra* note 99, at 150. The constitutional distinction referenced in the footnote—the difference between a stranger and a friend or acquaintance—is hardly self-evident. "[N]othing in the logic of [*Lewis* and *Hoffa*] or the policy considerations surrounding the fourth amendment supports such a distinction. Indeed, if there is any distinction between stranger and friend, it would seem to point the other way, since where the informant is an acquaintance, defendant is likely to be more readily deceived and to allow greater incursions into his private life." *1966 Term*, *supra* note 98, at 193, note 13.

Critiquing *Hoffa*

The result in *Hoffa* was a turning point for the Court. After years of debating the constitutionality of covert agents being used to spy on citizens, the Court had finally reached a consensus justifying secret and deliberate government surveillance. No Fourth Amendment interest was jeopardized by Partin's spying. Under *Hoffa*'s logic, whenever one invites another person into his home or office, or engages in private conversations, he assumes the risk that the other may be a government spy. Although Justice Stewart never uses the terms "waiver" or "consent," *Hoffa*'s reasoning posits that the individual either waives the security the Constitution ordinarily provides against deliberate and stealthy invasions of privacy, or consents to a secret police search of their home or seizure of their private communications.

At first glance, *Hoffa* appears to be a sensible, if not correct decision. After all, Jimmy Hoffa knew that he was a "marked man," and if he truly valued his privacy, he should have been more careful with his associations. Although reasonable minds may differ over the wisdom of Hoffa's judgment in associating with Partin, Hoffa's caution regarding the friends he chose was irrelevant to the constitutional issues before the Court. Indeed, the holding in *Hoffa* is more serious, and dangerous to the right of privacy, than the Court's opinion would lead one to believe.[102]

There are at least three troublesome aspects to the Court's opinion. First, it is difficult to reconcile the result in *Hoffa* with a central feature of the history and purpose of the Fourth Amendment: controlling police discretion to invade the privacy of the citizenry. Second, the Court's assumption of risk theory is a flawed model for deciding whether government officials should have unrestrained authority to send secret agents into the private lives of citizens to gather information or to monitor communications. The third problem with *Hoffa* concerns not what the Court said, but what the Court did not say, or at least did not consider. A companion case to *Hoffa*, *Osborn v. United States*,[103] upheld a judicially-approved use of a wired-informant to record the private communications of a lawyer who the government had probable cause to believe was engaged in jury tampering. However, the *Hoffa* Court apparently never bothered to ask whether informant spying should also be conditioned on the approval of a neutral and detached magistrate.

1. Informant Spying and Controlling Police Discretion

If one accepts the fundamental historic tenet that the Fourth Amendment reflected the Framers' distrust of police power and was

---

[102] *Cf. Hoffa*, 385 U.S. at 320 (Warren, C.J., dissenting) (observing that the government's conduct in *Hoffa* raises "serious" Fourth Amendment questions).

[103] 385 U.S. 323 (1966).

designed to limit the discretionary authority of the police to invade one's home,[104] the *Hoffa* Court paradoxically gave the government license to plant spies into one's home and other private places. Like the customs officers who forced open the doors of colonial homes, the secret informant is on a similar mission for the state. "The modern police undercover agent operation is in purpose, if not in detail, the same as any traditional police investigative technique: to gather information from and about private citizens on possible violations of the law."[105] This description accurately captures Partin's goals. After all, Partin did not arrive at Hoffa's hotel suite by accident. Rather, "Partin made an effort to spend as much time as possible in the suite, and the government not only encouraged him to do so but made it possible for him to be in Nashville to do so.... The penetration [into Hoffa's hotel suite] was active and deliberate; Hoffa's willingness to talk freely there was not merely a consequence of his 'misplaced confidence' in Partin, but also of his assumption that the government would not attempt to spy on him in the privacy of his hotel room."[106]

Put simply, it is hard to reconcile the result in *Hoffa*, which grants the government uncontrolled authority to send undercover officers and secret spies into our homes and other private places to search for and obtain private information, with the purpose of the amendment, which was designed to control the government's discretionary power to invade private places in order to search and seize.

2. *Assumption of Risk as a Fourth Amendment Principle*

Justice Stewart dismissed Hoffa's attempt to liken Partin's spying to a warrantless search of the hotel suite. According to Stewart, Hoffa was not relying on the security of the hotel suite. Rather, "he was relying upon his misplaced confidence that Partin would not reveal his wrongdoing." The Fourth Amendment, however, does not protect "a wrongdoer's misplaced belief that a person to whom he voluntarily confides his wrongdoing will not reveal it."[107] Relying on Justice Brennan's assump-

---

[104] *See* Thomas Y. Davies, *Recovering the Original Fourth Amendment*, 98 MICH. L. REV. 547, 556 (1999) (explaining that the "larger purpose" for which the Framers adopted the amendment was "to curb the exercise of discretionary authority by officers"). *But cf.* Carol S. Steiker, *Second Thoughts About First Principles*, 107 HARV. L. REV. 820, 824 (1994) (cautioning against undue reliance on the original purpose of the Fourth Amendment because the provision "more than many other parts of the Constitution, appears to require a fairly high level of abstraction of purpose; its use of the term 'reasonable' (actually, 'unreasonable') positively invites constructions that change with changing circumstances").

[105] Joseph R. Lundy, Note, *Police Undercover Agents: New Threat to First Amendment Freedoms*, 37 Geo. Wash. L. Rev. 634, 664 (1969).

[106] William D. Iverson, Note, *Judicial Control of Secret Agents*, 76 YALE L.J. 994, 1012 (1967).

[107] 385 U.S. at 302.

tion of risk model, Stewart adopts Brennan's theory to conclude that Hoffa assumed the risk that Partin would be a government informer.

This analysis is seriously flawed. First, factually speaking, Partin was not, as Justice Stewart implied, a friend who subsequently decided to betray Jimmy Hoffa, but a government spy right from the start:

> [T]he reality to which Hoffa was exposed was not that Partin would decide to tell but that he was in fact working for the government at the very time Hoffa spoke. Partin did not turn out to be a friend who later "revealed wrongdoing." He was exactly what he did not appear to be—a government agent—and Hoffa was induced to speak to him because of this very deception. It is one thing to say that people must take the risk that their friends will report wrongdoing. It is another thing to say that people must take the risk that their friends have already promised to report whatever they do and say to the government.[108]

Second, *Hoffa*'s assumption of risk theory is a legal conclusion masquerading as legal analysis. There is no principled distinction between Justice Stewart's conclusion that Hoffa assumed the risk that Partin would be a government informer and the Court's prior conclusion in *Olmstead* that an individual who uses a telephone intends to project his voice to those outside. Why is the former conclusion constitutionally reasonable but not the latter? There was no more empirical support for *Hoffa*'s conclusion that citizens assume certain risks whenever they speak to or associate with a third party than there was for the now-discredited assumption in *Olmstead*. Moreover, if someone in Jimmy Hoffa's shoes assumes the risk that his companions are police agents, "then why does one using the phone not 'assume the risk' that the police will be tapping the wire? And why does one using the mails not assume the risk that the police will be reading his letters? Are these other risks small only because the Court has made them so?"[109]

People do not assume the risk that the police are listening to telephone conversations or opening mail, because the Court has inter-

---

[108] KITCH, *supra* note 99, at 151–52.

[109] YALE KAMISAR ET AL., MODERN CRIMINAL PROCEDURE: CASES, COMMENTS AND QUESTIONS 380 (West 10th ed. 2002). *Cf.* DONALD A. DRIPPS, ABOUT GUILT AND INNOCENCE: THE ORIGINS, DEVELOPMENT, AND FUTURE OF CONSTITUTIONAL CRIMINAL PROCEDURE 53 (2003) (Praeger Press) ("*Katz* holds that when one talks to another over the telephone one has a reasonable expectation of privacy in the communications. [The informant cases] all hold that this expectation is not reasonable when one's interlocutor is a government spy. But if the theory is that speakers assume the risk that their words will be repeated, why does the fact that the interlocutor is a spy make any difference? If the *risk* that one's audience includes a spy suffices to make conversations unprivate, the government should have the right to tap telephones at will, for there is always the chance that one party may betray the other.").

preted the Fourth Amendment to require that the police satisfy the procedural safeguards of probable cause, particularity, and reasonableness before such intrusions may occur. The Court's conclusion that telephone conversations and mail are constitutionally protected was not based on the amendment's text or empirical data about the risks people assume. Instead, it came from a distrust of unchecked police power that threatens the interests embodied in the Fourth Amendment. Since the amendment restrains the discretion of the police to wiretap or "bug" private conversations, it should also restrain the discretion of the police to decide whether to plant a secret informer in constitutionally sensitive areas in order to gather information or monitor private communications. After all, as Chief Justice Warren acknowledged, "Partin became the equivalent of a bugging device which moved with Hoffa wherever he went."[110]

Finally, *Hoffa*'s conclusions about the risks assumed by criminals are a faulty gauge to measure the scope of the Fourth Amendment's protection. Indeed, in other search and seizure contexts, the Court has recognized that the risk theory utilized in *Hoffa*, which focuses on the risks and assumptions of criminals, rather than innocent persons, distorts the meaning of the Fourth Amendment. For example, when deciding whether a police-citizen encounter triggers constitutional scrutiny, the Court has instructed that the intrusiveness of police conduct must be judged from the perspective of the innocent person.[111] If a similar analysis is employed where informants are used to infiltrate homes and other constitutionally sensitive contexts, the flaw in *Hoffa*'s assumption of risk theory is evident. There is simply no basis, empirical or otherwise, for the conclusion that ordinary citizens assume that government informers and spies will filter in and out of their lives. The "risks" discussed in *Hoffa* are not assumed by the ordinary innocent person. On the contrary, "these risks come to him" because the Court has granted the government "a license to unilaterally decide whether to monitor his private activities" by sending an informer into his home or office.[112]

The Court has also recognized, in another post-*Hoffa* ruling, that a person can raise a legitimate Fourth Amendment claim against government conduct even when similar conduct by a private party does not

---

[110] 385 U.S. at 319 (Warren, C.J., dissenting). *See also*, H. Richard Uviller, *Evidence from the Mind of the Criminal Suspect: A Reconsideration of the Current Rules of Access and Restraint*, 97 Col. L. Rev. 1137, 1195 (1987) ("The Court in *Hoffa* should have regarded Partin as the human bug he was and treated his intrusions as a search and seizure.").

[111] Florida v. Bostick, 501 U.S. 429, 438 (1991).

[112] Eric F. Saunders, Case Comment, *Electronic Eavesdropping and the Right to Privacy*, 52 B.U. L. Rev. 831, 843 (1972).

trigger constitutional protection. In *Marshall v. Barlow's, Inc.*,[113] the Court explained that there is a critical difference between governmental intrusion and a similar intrusion by a private individual. Defending a scheme of warrantless administrative searches of factories for health and safety violations, the government unsuccessfully argued that an employer has a diminished privacy interest in those areas of a factory where employees and other third parties have access. The disclosure of limited information to a private party, *Barlow's Inc.* explained, does not justify federal officers entering a place from which the general public is barred to conduct searches. *Barlow's Inc.* recognizes that when determining whether a search occurs, the relevant inquiry is the target's privacy interest vis-à-vis the government, not what has been disclosed to a private party. Stated simply, *Barlow's Inc.* recognizes what the *Hoffa* Court should have understood: "Because the [F]ourth [A]mendment protects citizens from government, logic and reason would seem to dictate that the relevant inquiry focus on the expectations that citizens have about governmental intrusion into their privacy," and not what is exposed to private persons.[114]

In the final analysis, the assumption of risk theory utilized in *Hoffa* cannot be confined to the Jimmy Hoffas or other "wrongdoer[s]" of the world. After *Hoffa*, the risks assumed by someone in Jimmy Hoffa's shoes are the same risks assumed by "Everyman."[115] Once government is given a license to send informers into our homes or offices, everyone, the innocent and guilty alike, assumes the risk that the person we invite into our homes or to whom we speak is a government spy.

3. *Why Not Treat Informants Like Wiretaps and Bugs?*

Six months after *Hoffa* was decided, the Court decided *Berger v. New York*. Six months later, *Katz* was decided. As discussed earlier, *Berger* and *Katz* ruled that electronic bugging and wiretapping were subject to Fourth Amendment protection. But these rulings, particularly *Katz*, did not impose insurmountable bars against electronic surveillance. When *Katz* was announced, more than a few Court-watchers thought the Justices were signaling their willingness to accept some types of judge-supervised electronic surveillance. This view was partially supported by the result in *Osborn v. United States*, which upheld a judicially authorized use of a wired-spy to secretly tape-record the conversations of an attorney alleged to have attempted to bribe jurors in the Test Fleet case. When *Osborn* was combined with *Katz*, many saw a potential blueprint

---

[113] 436 U.S. 307 (1978).

[114] Joseph D. Grano, *Perplexing Questions About Three Basic Fourth Amendment Issues: Fourth Amendment Activity, Probable Cause, and the Warrant Requirement*, 69 J. CRIM. L. & CRIMINOLOGY 425, 432 (1978).

[115] Brinegar v. United States, 338 U.S. 160, 181 (1949) (Jackson, J., dissenting).

to support wiretap legislation. In 1968, Congress accepted the challenge and enacted a comprehensive law that authorized wiretapping and electronic bugging, provided enumerated constitutional and statutory safeguards were observed.[116] As one observer of the Court noted at the time, Congressional wiretap legislation "did not come in spite of the Supreme Court; it was encouraged by it."[117]

The enactment of federal and state laws regulating electronic surveillance has, practically speaking, ended the debate over the constitutionality of wiretapping and bugging. While these types of police intrusions are now subject to judicial oversight, informant spying, whether wired or not, remains free of constitutional restraints. *Hoffa*, of course, never addressed whether informant spying should be subjected to the safeguards of the Warrant Clause because the Court concluded Partin's conduct was not a search. But that conclusion ignores the reality of Partin's mission and the intrusiveness of his activities. Indeed, a fundamental question arises in a post-*Katz* world: If wiretapping and bugging are subject to constitutional restraint, and a comprehensive wiretapping law can be structured in a manner consistent with the demands of probable cause and the other requirements of the Warrant Clause, why not subject informant spying to constitutional restraint?

Some argue that it is impractical to apply Fourth Amendment safeguards to informant spying. For example, it has been said that because informants "must be developed or placed over a long period of time and the objectives of their 'search' will almost always be broad and impossible to delineate with any precision in advance,"[118] the particularity requirement of the amendment cannot be satisfied. Others contend that Fourth Amendment restrictions on informant spying would be too burdensome on law enforcement in light of the fact that certain "types of crime are particularly difficult to investigate because their perpetrators are able to restrict sharply the traces of criminal activity they leave behind."[119] For example, in victimless crimes such as drug trafficking and bribery, where in light of the fact that it is unlikely anyone would come forward, planting spies is an effective way to catch criminals. Similar claims were raised when Congress and the Court were debating whether to impose constitutional restrictions on police wiretapping and electronic bugging.

---

[116] *See* Title III of the Omnibus Crime Control and Safe Streets Act of 1968. Pub. L. No. 90–351, § 802, 82 Stat. 197, 211–21 (codified as amended at 18 U.S.C. §§ 2510–2522 (1994)).

[117] FRED P. GRAHAM, THE SELF-INFLICTED WOUND 261 (The Macmillan Company 1970).

[118] Kitch, *supra* note 99, at 142.

[119] Philip B. Heymann, *Understanding Criminal Investigations*, 22 HARV. J. ON LEGIS. 315, 333 (1985).

It would not have taken too much prescience for the *Hoffa* Court to imagine how search and seizure norms might apply to informant spying. *Osborn* was decided on the same day that *Hoffa* was announced. Writing for the majority in *Osborn*, Justice Stewart praised the process wherein two federal judges, after reviewing a detailed factual affidavit alleging the commission of a serious crime by Osborn, authorized the use of electronic recording equipment to seize private communications between a secret government informer and Osborn. This process, according to Stewart, was an excellent example of "the procedure of antecedent justification before a magistrate that is central to the Fourth Amendment as a precondition of lawful electronic surveillance."[120] The reasoning and results in *Berger* and *Katz* would be established a year later.

Osborn, *Berger* and *Katz* provided a framework for applying Fourth Amendment norms to wiretapping and bugging. That same framework could have been applied to informant spying so that it too would comply with the Fourth Amendment. For example, the probable cause rule, which partially helps to deter the promiscuous and rampant intrusions inherent in wiretapping, would also check the intrusions associated with informant spying. As in wiretapping and bugging, the probable cause requirement defines and limits the person, location, communications, and time period targeted for informant surveillance. Many of the same constitutional evils that *Berger* and *Katz* found in discretionary wiretapping are extant where the police decide for themselves when to infiltrate a home or record a private conversation with an informant. The constitutional requirements of probable cause, particularity, minimization and necessity—all vital elements of a valid wiretap or electronic bug—can and should be applied to informant spying.

Informant Spying After *Hoffa* and *Katz*

A year after the rulings in *Lewis* and *Hoffa*, the Court decided *Katz*. When *Katz* was announced, many legal commentators believed that the Court had adopted a fundamental change in Fourth Amendment law. Not only did *Katz* overrule the "trespass" theory that supported *Olmstead* and *Goldman*, but it also contained several statements indicating that the Court would take a new and expansive view of the Fourth Amendment's scope. Comments like "the Fourth Amendment protects people, not places,"[121] and "[n]o less than an individual in a business office, in a friend's apartment, or in a taxicab, a person in a telephone booth may rely upon the protection of the Fourth Amendment,"[122] strongly suggested that "the effect of *Katz* [was] to expand rather than generally to reconstruct the boundaries of fourth amendment protec-

---

[120] *Osborn*, 385 U.S. at 330 (internal quotation marks omitted).

[121] 389 U.S. at 351

[122] *Id*. at 352 (footnotes omitted).

tion."[123] Indeed, when these comments were read in conjunction with the Court's conclusion that listening to and recording Katz's words infringed "the privacy upon which he justifiably relied"[124] it seemed *Katz* was establishing a new and more realistic vision of Fourth Amendment protection against government surveillance in the modern world.

While *Katz* appeared to signal a new approach toward defining the scope of the amendment generally, it did not take long to discover that the reasoning of *Katz* would have no impact on the law governing the use of informers and secret agents. *United States v. White*,[125] a case that mirrored the facts of *On Lee*, came before the Court four years after *Katz*, and a plurality ruled that *Katz*'s holding did not affect the assumption of risk theory that supported the results in *Lopez* and *Hoffa*. At issue in *White* was whether the testimony of federal officers about conversations between the defendant and a government informant, which were overheard by the officers monitoring the frequency of a radio transmitter carried by the informant, implicated the Fourth Amendment. As did *On Lee*, the *White* Court found that this conduct was not a search.

Acknowledging the Court's prior holdings, the *White* plurality conceded that the "trespass" theory of *On Lee* had not survived *Katz*. However, *White* noted that *On Lee* was supported by a second and independent rationale—namely, On Lee, like Hoffa, assumed the risk that the person who he confidentially and indiscreetly trusted was a government informant. The *White* plurality then explained that if an individual assumes the risk that a secret informant, acting without electronic equipment, might later reveal the contents of a conversation, the risk is the same when the informant simultaneously records and transmits the conversation to a third party. "If the law gives no protection to the wrongdoer whose trusted accomplice is or becomes a police agent, neither should it protect him when that same agent has recorded or transmitted the conversations which are later offered in evidence to prove the State's case."[126] In either situation, "the risk is his," and the Fourth Amendment offers no protection against police efforts to obtain information in this manner.[127]

Ironically, Justice Harlan, the author of *Lopez*, dissented in *White*. Although he had been unwilling to overrule *On Lee* when *Lopez* was

---

[123] Anthony G. Amsterdam, *Perspectives On The Fourth Amendment*, 58 MINN. L. REV. 349, 385 (1974) (footnote omitted).

[124] 389 U.S. at 353.

[125] 401 U.S. 745 (1971).

[126] *Id*. at 752 (plurality opinion).

[127] *Id*. In United States v. Caceres, 440 U.S. 741, 744 & note 2 (1979), a majority of the Court indicated its acceptance of the reasoning of the *White* plurality.

decided, Harlan concluded that *On Lee*'s holding could no longer stand. Harlan rested his change of view partially on the fact that since *Osborn* the Court's rulings "have shown no tolerance for the old dividing lines resting, as they did, on fiction and common-law distinctions without sound policy justification in the realm of values protected by the Fourth Amendment."[128]

Harlan had also reconsidered the assumption of risk theory, which he indirectly endorsed in *Lopez*.[129] Harlan was now taking the position that risk theory was a flawed principle for assessing the scope of the Fourth Amendment's protection. "Our expectations and the risks we assume, are in large part reflections of laws that translate into rules the customs and values of the past and present." He then cautioned that judges should not "merely recite the expectations and risks without examining the desirability of saddling them upon society."[130] For Harlan, there was a critical difference between *Lewis* and *Hoffa* on the one hand, and *On Lee, Lopez* and *White*, on the other hand. The difference turned on the judgment that cases like *On Lee* and *White* fail to protect the interest of the ordinary citizen, "who has never engaged in illegal conduct in his life, that he may carry on his private discourse freely, openly, and spontaneously without measuring his every word against the connotations it might carry when instantaneously heard by others unknown to him and unfamiliar with his situation or analyzed in a cold, formal record played days, months, or years after the conversation."[131]

Since *White*, the Court has decided no other case involving informants and the Fourth Amendment. Moreover, the lower courts have not read *Lewis* or *Hoffa* narrowly.[132] The rulings of the lower courts are not

---

[128] 401 U.S. at 778 (Harlan, J., dissenting).

[129] *See Lopez*, 373 U.S. at 439 ("We think the risk that [Lopez] took in offering a bribe to [the government agent] fairly included the risk that the offer would be accurately reproduced in court, whether by faultless memory or mechanical recording.").

[130] *White*, 401 U.S. at 786 (Harlan, J., dissenting).

[131] *Id.* at 790 (Harlan, J., dissenting). While Harlan reasoned that the Fourth Amendment should control the type of third-party monitoring involved in *On Lee* and *White*, he was prepared to live with the results in *Lewis* and *Hoffa* because in those cases "[n]o surreptitious third ear was present." *Id.* at 784 (Harlan, J., dissenting). Justice Harlan's distinction between wired and unwired informants is not convincing. Certainly from "the perspective of informational privacy," there is no principled distinction between wired and unwired informants. Grano, *supra* note 114, at 435. Indeed, "[t]he only difference [between an informant wired for sound and an informant without a wire] is that under electronic surveillance you are afraid to talk to anybody in your office or over the phone, while under a spy system you are afraid to talk to anybody at all." Amsterdam, *supra* note 123, at 407.

[132] *See* 3 LAFAVE, *supra* note 97, at 702–05 (explaining that although *Lewis* can be read to apply only in a context where the target permits entry into his home for an *illegal* transaction, the lower courts have not read *Lewis* narrowly).

surprising given the *White* Court's embrace of *Hoffa*'s assumption of risk theory, and its refusal to distinguish between wired and unwired informants. Indeed, in light of *Hoffa*'s broad ruling, there have been very few controversies in the lower courts over its meaning. Thus, the Court has had few occasions to revisit or reconsider *Hoffa*. Nevertheless, there is an interesting postscript to *Hoffa*'s legacy.

Sometime in 1974, the Memphis, Tennessee police department began investigating one Arthur Wayne Baldwin. An undercover officer, Joseph Honig, applied for and obtained employment as Baldwin's chauffeur and general handyman. In that capacity Honig worked for Baldwin for approximately six months. During this time, Honig also worked at Baldwin's Playgirl Clubs as a bartender and club manager. In the first few months of Honig's employment, he and Baldwin shared a two-bedroom apartment. Later, Honig moved with Baldwin into a house, and occupied a downstairs bedroom. Throughout this six month period, Honig had access to all parts of Baldwin's residences, including his bedrooms. Honig saw Baldwin use and distribute cocaine. Eventually, Honig seized samples of cocaine that he discovered on a tabletop in Baldwin's bedroom and on the floorboard of Baldwin's car. Some of these samples were introduced at trial when Baldwin was prosecuted for possession and distribution of cocaine. After Baldwin was convicted of these charges and the Court of Appeals affirmed his conviction, Baldwin filed a certiorari petition which argued that Honig's conduct violated the Fourth Amendment.

On April 6, 1981, the Court declined to review Baldwin's case.[133] Justice Marshall, however, wrote a dissent from the Court's denial of certiorari. Justice Marshall asserted that the Court of Appeals had erred in its interpretation of *Lewis* and *Hoffa*. In Marshall's view, both *Lewis* and *Hoffa* were narrow rulings and did not give police *carte blanche* to send informants into the homes and offices of individuals to gather evidence.

First, Marshall contended that the facts in *Baldwin* were distinguishable from *Lewis* because Baldwin "neither invited the undercover agent into his home for any illegal purpose nor gave up his expectation of privacy in the home by converting it into a center of unlawful business."[134] Marshall also argued that Baldwin's case was not controlled by *Hoffa*. He wrote that *Hoffa* focused on the narrow question "whether the Fourth Amendment precluded the Government from benefiting from a 'wrongdoer's misplaced belief that a person to whom he voluntarily confides his wrongdoing will not reveal it.' "[135] According to Marshall,

---

[133] Baldwin v. United States, 450 U.S. 1045 (1981).

[134] *Id.* at 1048.

[135] *Id.*, *quoting Hoffa*, 385 U.S. at 302.

the *Hoffa* Court made clear that Hoffa's constitutional claim, unlike Baldwin's petition, "was not based on any asserted violation of his right to privacy."[136] Justice Marshall closed his dissent by opining that if the police conduct in *Baldwin* did not trigger Fourth Amendment protection, "it is hard to imagine what sort of undercover activity would." Accordingly, he believed that the Court of Appeals had mistakenly extended *Lewis* and *Hoffa*, its ruling on Baldwin's Fourth Amendment claim was "probably wrong," and that, "at the very least," the ruling below merited full review by the Court.[137]

Students of the modern Court will not be surprised by Justice Marshall's dissent in *Baldwin*. Marshall was not on the Court when *Lewis* and *Hoffa* were decided, and he dissented in *White*, expressing the view that *Katz* had robbed *On Lee* of its viability. Moreover, throughout his time on the Court, Marshall consistently gave the Fourth Amendment a broad reading and pointedly refused to embrace the Court's assumption of risk theory when it was extended in subsequent rulings.[138] Indeed, it is fair to surmise that had Marshall been on the Court when *Hoffa* was decided, he would have dissented from the majority's ruling, or would have been unwilling to endorse the assumption of risk theory adopted by the majority.

Nor would students of the Court be surprised to learn that only Justice Brennan joined Marshall's dissent. Between the rulings in *White* and *Baldwin*, Justices Rehnquist, Powell and Stevens joined the Court. The background of these Justices provides no indication that they shared Marshall's narrow view of *Hoffa*'s holding. Finally, Chief Justice Burger and Justices White, Stewart and Blackmun, the four Justices who comprised the *White* plurality, were still on the Court when Baldwin's petition was denied. Indeed, what would be startling is that any of these Justices agreed with Marshall's interpretation of *Hoffa*.

Marshall's attempt to distinguish *Baldwin* from *Hoffa* seems strained. The premise of his argument is that the result in *Hoffa* would have been different had Hoffa's Fourth Amendment claim been based on a "right of privacy." But Marshall never explains why this is so.

To be sure, the *Hoffa* Court did not frame the issue as a "right of privacy." But that fact is unimportant. The crux of *Hoffa* concerned whether Partin's conduct was a search; the Court concluded that it was not. The Court's holding employs the phraseology of a "wrongdoer's" assumed risks, but there is nothing in the *Hoffa* opinion itself, nor does

---

[136] *Id*. at 1049.

[137] *Id*. at 1049–50.

[138] *See* Tracey Maclin, *Justice Thurgood Marshall: Taking the Fourth Amendment Seriously*, 77 CORNELL L. REV. 723, 731–45 (1992).

Justice Marshall provide any other proof or substantive argument in
Baldwin, to indicate that the result in *Hoffa* would have been different if
the Court had addressed whether Partin's conduct violated Hoffa's right
of privacy. Put differently, once the Court concluded that Hoffa had
assumed the risk that Partin was a secret informant who would reveal
Hoffa's private conversations, the Court had simultaneously found that
Hoffa's conversations with Partin were not protected by the right of
privacy. Labeling Hoffa's claim under the rubric of a "right of privacy"
would not have made a difference. Rather than straining to distinguish
Hoffa, Justice Marshall might have been more convincing had he asserted that the reasoning of *Katz* overruled *Hoffa*.[139]

But neither Justice Marshall's dissent, nor the fact that no other
Justice (beside Brennan) joined that dissent, makes *Baldwin* an interesting postscript to *Hoffa*. What is intriguing about *Baldwin* is that Justice
Brennan—the originator of the assumption of risk theory, whose dissent
in *Lopez* provided "the doctrinal basis [for the Court's] subsequent
Fourth Amendment decisions"[140] in this area—joins Marshall's dissent.
At this point, one can only speculate why. Perhaps Brennan was having
second thoughts about how the assumption of risk theory had been
applied in *Hoffa*. That possibility, however, seems unlikely in light of the
fact that Brennan joined Justice Stewart's opinion in *Hoffa* without
comment, and did not criticize *Hoffa*'s logic five years later in his
separate opinion in *White*, while he reiterated his criticism of *On Lee* and
Lopez.

Another possibility is that Brennan felt that *Hoffa* had not survived
Katz, but that explanation is undermined by the fact that Brennan did
not proffer this concern in his *White* concurrence, which was written
four years after *Katz*. Finally, it is possible that by 1981 Brennan still
believed that *Hoffa* was correctly decided, but that the lower courts were
improperly extending *Hoffa*'s holding, as Marshall had argued in *Baldwin*. The problem with this account is the one discussed above. Justices
Brennan and Marshall were too savvy to believe that two more of their
colleagues were prepared to say that the result in *Hoffa* would have been
different had Hoffa's constitutional claim rested on the right of privacy.
Indeed, it was Brennan himself—in his *Lopez* dissent—who said that this
type of informant spying "do[es] not seriously intrude upon the *right of
privacy*."[141]

---

[139] *Cf.* YALE KAMISAR *et al., supra* note 109, at 386–87 (asking whether *Katz* should be
read as overruling *Hoffa*, and inquiring whether it may be "said of the *Hoffa* case—using
the language in *Katz*—that the government's use of defendant's trusted friend to obtain
evidence against him 'violated the privacy upon which [defendant] justifiably relied' and
thus constituted a 'search' or 'seizure'?").

[140] *White*, 401 U.S. at 778, note 12 (Harlan, J., dissenting).

[141] 373 U.S. at 465 (Brennan, J., dissenting) (emphasis added).

For whatever reason, Justice Brennan joined Marshall's dissent in *Baldwin*.

Although Marshall's characterization of *Hoffa*'s holding may not have been persuasive, he did accurately describe the impact of *Hoffa* on Fourth Amendment law. After *Hoffa*, police officials appear to have unfettered discretion to disguise its officers and informers "as repairmen, babysitters, neighbors, maids, and the like, [in order] to gain entry into an individual's home by ruse rather than force in order to conduct a search."[142]

CONCLUSION

Whether intentional or not, the tone of Justice Stewart's opinion in *Hoffa* does not convey the magnitude of the personalities and legal issues at stake in the case. His opinion never mentions Bobby Kennedy's name or Kennedy's perpetual targeting of Hoffa for prosecution. Nor does it acknowledge the existence of the "Get Hoffa Squad" or even acknowledge what many knew at the time to be true: "that had the defendant not been Hoffa and had the Attorney General not been Kennedy, the [Test Fleet] case would not have been brought."[143]

Furthermore, Justice Stewart's opinion addresses the Fourth Amendment issue at stake in a matter-of-fact tone. No mention is made of the decades-long struggle on the Court to reconcile informant spying with the Fourth Amendment. There is no analysis of whether Hoffa "consented" to the spying of Partin. And Stewart has no reply to the Chief Justice's reasonable conclusion that "Partin became the equivalent of a bugging device which moved with Hoffa wherever he went."[144] Instead, the reader is left with the impression that *Hoffa* posed an easy constitutional question, deserving of a simple resolution, which is what Justice Stewart's opinion provides.

Edward Bennett Williams, Hoffa's "ranking lawyer" ever since he helped to secure Hoffa's acquittal in the Cheasty trial,[145] is said to have quipped that "only Jimmy Hoffa could escalate a misdemeanor into a felony."[146] To be sure, Hoffa's jury tampering in the Test Fleet case did transform a misdemeanor case into a Supreme Court ruling granting the government free license to spy on its citizenry. And it is also true that a "government that can 'get' Jimmy Hoffa can get anyone."[147] But Jimmy

---

[142] *Baldwin*, 450 U.S. at 1049 (Marshall, J., dissenting).

[143] NAVASKY, *supra* note 4, at 472.

[144] *Hoffa*, 385 U.S. at 319 (Warren, C.J., dissenting).

[145] SLOANE, *supra* note 2, at 163.

[146] NAVASKY, *supra* note 4, at 472.

[147] POWE, *supra* note 22, at 402.

Hoffa does not deserve sole blame (or credit) for the result in *Hoffa*. When Americans mull over the fact that the Fourth Amendment appears to impose no restraint on the government's power to infiltrate homes or other private places with covert agents, they can blame (or credit) Bobby Kennedy, Walter Sheridan, a majority of the Supreme Court Justices, and most particularly, Justice William Brennan.

*

7

Katz v. United States: The Limits of Aphorism

David A. Sklansky

Some landmark cases stay controversial because there is lingering disagreement about whether they were correctly decided. Other times there is doubt whether a famous decision proved as momentous as it initially seemed. And sometimes there are arguments that a relatively obscure ruling should, in retrospect, be seen as pivotal.

Charlie Katz's interstate wagering case is different. When the Supreme Court reversed Katz's conviction in 1967, holding that the federal government had violated his Fourth Amendment rights against "unreasonable searches and seizures" by bugging a pair of phone booths he used, everyone understood it was a watershed decision. The Justices thought so; the lawyers on both sides thought so; the public thought so. Decades later, *Katz v. United States*[1] is still viewed, almost universally, as one of the most important Fourth Amendment cases ever decided. There is broad consensus, moreover, that the Court was right to rule as it did. Nonetheless the decision remains the subject of great debate. The uncertainty surrounding *Katz* has to do with *why* the case matters as much as everyone seems to agree that it does.

In the standard, celebratory history of American constitutional law, the significance of *Katz* is straightforward and dramatic: it changed the Fourth Amendment from a protection against trespass to a protection of "reasonable expectations of privacy." There is plenty of truth to that account. The most famous sentence in *Katz*, after all, memorably declares that the Fourth Amendment "protects people, not places."[2] But it has never been clear what makes an expectation of privacy "reasonable," or how substantially the practical consequences of the new approach differ from those of the old. And what seemed important about *Katz* at the time of the decision was *not* the shift from trespass to expectations of privacy—a shift that earlier decisions had unmistakably foreshadowed—but the surprising announcement that electronic eavesdropping was

---

[1] 389 U.S. 347 (1967).

[2] *Id.* at 351.

constitutionally permissible, so long as it proceeded pursuant to a judicial warrant.

The confusion surrounding *Katz* arises in part because the case forms a key chapter of three separate, grand narratives of criminal procedure law over the past century: the shifting understanding of what the Fourth Amendment protects; the evolving legal treatment of electronic eavesdropping; and the struggle to apply the language of the Fourth Amendment, framed in response to very particular abuses of the eighteenth century, to the novel challenges of the modern world. Revisiting the story of *Katz* can help us to untangle these three larger narratives, as well as to see how they are connected.

The Catching of Charlie Katz

Charlie Katz was a Damon Runyon character plopped into 1960s Los Angeles. Katz was a professional bettor: "gambler" does not quite capture how he made his living. Katz wagered on sports events, sometimes for himself and sometimes on commission for others. He specialized in basketball games, and he had his own, elaborate system for ranking teams and predicting outcomes. In February 1965, he was living in a poolside hotel room on the Sunset Strip.

For reasons that are not entirely clear, Katz preferred to place bets with out-of-state bookmakers. He may have wanted to spread his business around, or he may have been operating as a bookmaker himself and hedging his exposure. Katz's own explanation, following his arrest, was that Los Angeles bookmakers had a reputation for not paying off.[3] Whatever the reason, Katz conducted much of his business via interstate telephone calls. That brought the Federal Bureau of Investigation into the picture.

The FBI in 1965 was less stretched for personnel than it is today. After an informant tipped the Bureau off about Katz, a team of agents, ultimately numbering five, began to watch him.[4] They saw him leave his hotel most mornings and walk a few blocks east on Sunset Boulevard to a bank of three telephone booths, place some brief calls, and then return to the hotel. Eager to learn—and to document—what Katz was saying, the agents eventually took the step that would take the case to the Supreme Court and into the annals of history. They attached a tape recorder on top of the roof of the middle telephone booth.

It was a stereophonic tape recorder, with two microphones. The agents taped the microphones to the backs of two of the telephone

---

[3] *See* Record at 45, 148, Katz v. United States, 389 U.S. 347 (1967) (No. 35).

[4] *See id.* at 112.

booths, and they put a sign on the third saying "Out of Order."[5] At this point the surveillance kicked into high gear. Every morning, when Katz left his hotel, an agent stationed outside would radio the news to an agent stationed near the telephone booths. The second agent would turn on the tape recorder and then watch Katz make his calls. After Katz finished his calls and walked away, the tape recorder was turned off, and the tape was retrieved. This went on for a week.

The tape recorder picked up only Katz's side of the conversations, but that was enough to make clear what they were about. When the tapes were transcribed, a typical passage read, "Give me Temple minus ten and a half for a dime. Pass. Pass. Pass. Pass. Pass. Pass. Give me Duquesne minus 7 for a nickel."[6] (A "dime" was bookmaking parlance for $1000; a "nickel" meant $500.[7]) The telephone company, meanwhile, confirmed that the calls went out of state, a necessary predicate for federal jurisdiction over the offense. Katz was arrested and charged with interstate wagering.[8]

The tapes from the telephone booths were not the only evidence against Katz. For two days, toward the end of the surveillance, an FBI agent had occupied the hotel room next to Katz's and, whenever he saw Katz come in from the pool, had placed his ear next to an electrical outlet on the wall between the two rooms. The agent overheard snippets of conversation similar to what the tape recorder over the telephone booths had captured: "Oregon minus 4 ... Northwestern plus 5 ... Sammy is the most honorable person in the world. Don't worry about the money. Also don't worry about the line. I called Boston three times today."[9] The agents made surreptitious copies of the notes Katz took while in the telephone booths, by hiding sheets of carbon paper in the armrests that served as writing surfaces.[10] The day Katz was arrested,

---

[5] The trial court record indicates that the agents "placed one phone booth out of order." *Id.* One of the agents told the author several years ago that this was accomplished simply by attaching a sign to the door of the booth.

[6] *Id.* at 117.

[7] *See id.* at 165.

[8] The applicable statute, 18 U.S.C. § 1084, made it a felony for anyone "engaged in the business of betting or wagering" knowingly to use a "wire communication facility for the transmission in interstate commerce of bets or wagers ... on any sporting event or contest."

[9] Record at 136.

[10] There is no indication of this tactic in the record, apparently because the Office of the United States Attorney decided not to use the evidence. But two law enforcement officials involved with the case—an FBI agent and a Los Angeles Police Department officer who served as an expert witness—independently mentioned the carbon paper in the armrests to the author.

the agents executed a search warrant in his hotel room, and the search turned up a variety of wagering records, including 148 pages of coded, handwritten notes about college basketball teams. And Katz made a number of incriminating statements following his arrest. He complained, in particular, about the seizure of his records: he said they had taken years to compile, that he could not bet without them, and that betting was the only trade he knew. He also promised, albeit in a manner the agents took to be facetious, that if he continued to bet he would lead them to "the big fellows."[11]

The tapes, though, were the principal basis for the arrest of Katz and the search of his hotel room, and they became the heart of the prosecution's case at trial. They also were the focus of most of the arguments during pretrial litigation, and later, following Katz's conviction, on appeal. To understand the context for those arguments, we first need to turn the clock back an additional half century.

Lt. Olmstead's Legacy

In 1965, when Charlie Katz was arrested, the seminal Supreme Court decision on the constitutionality of electronic surveillance—and, more broadly, on the scope of the Fourth Amendment—was *Olmstead v. United States*.[12] That Prohibition-era case concerned the dramatic downfall of Roy Olmstead, the "bootleg king of Puget Sound."

Olmstead was an up-and-coming lieutenant in the Seattle Police Department until 1920, when he was caught smuggling Canadian whiskey into the country. Thrown off the force, he turned full-time to rum running. Olmstead soon had fifty employees: "salesmen, telephone operators, watchmen, warehousemen, deliverymen, truck drivers, bookkeepers, a lawyer, and even an official fixer, though Olmstead himself remained on intimate terms with some of his old police colleagues."[13] Liquor was brought from England on freighters chartered by Olmstead, ferried ashore by motorboats he owned, trucked to a ranch outside of Seattle and to distribution centers throughout town, and delivered to customers by a fleet of four cars. The operation moved as many as 200 cases a day, had gross revenues of up to $200,000 a month, and turned an annual profit, after expenses and bribes, of close to $50,000. Olmstead

---

[11] Record at 37–42, 148, 154, 158–59. Some of these statements were made on the day of the arrest, and some were made the following day, when Katz was already out on bail. Two FBI agents returned to his hotel that day, purportedly to return a nail clipper and a key chain seized by mistake during the search. *See id.* at 153–55.

[12] 277 U.S. 438 (1928).

[13] Walter F. Murphy, Wiretapping On Trial 16–17 (1965).

bought a mansion in the best part of Seattle. He was a dapper man-about-town. His employees called him the "Big Boy."[14]

Like any up-to-date businessman in the early 1920s, Olmstead ran much of his operation over the telephone. This proved to be his undoing. Wiretapping was frowned upon at the time: many states, including Washington, criminalized the practice, and at the federal level it was against the official policy of both the Justice Department and the Treasury Department.[15] But Prohibition agents in Seattle, eager to bring down the Big Boy, employed the tactic anyway. Beginning in summer 1924 and continuing well into the fall, they eavesdropped on seven telephone lines, including the one to Olmstead's house. What they overheard was enough to convict Olmstead and twenty of his associates of conspiracy.[16]

The Supreme Court granted review in the case to consider the defendants' argument that admitting the wiretap evidence violated their rights under the Fourth and Fifth Amendments. On a vote of 5 to 4, the Court affirmed the convictions. Writing for the majority, Chief Justice Taft explained that there had been no violation of the Fifth Amendment bar against compulsory self-incrimination, because no one forced Olmstead and his codefendants to talk—the same, simple line of reasoning the Court was to use, decades later, in affirming the jury-tampering conviction of Jimmy Hoffa.[17] The Fourth Amendment analysis in *Olmstead* was almost as simple, but it merits a bit more discussion. It was this analysis that, decades later, the Court was to revisit in *Katz*.

The Fourth Amendment has two clauses. The first protects the "right of the people to be secure in their persons, houses, papers, and effects, against unreasonable searches and seizures." The second prohibits the issuance of warrants, except "upon probable causes, supported by Oath or affirmation, and particularly describing the place to be searched, and the persons or things to be seized." Historically, both clauses have been understood to be reactions against a particular set of eighteenth-century abuses: the "general warrants" that English judges had struck down in a celebrated series of decisions in the 1760s, and the "writs of assistance" about which the American colonists had repeatedly protested in the years leading up to the Revolutionary War. Both of these legal

---

[14] *Id.*; see also, e.g., Norman H. Clark, *Roy Olmstead, A Rumrunning King on Puget Sound*, 54 Pacific Northwest Q. 89 (1963); Emmett Watson, *Seattle's Colorful Past*, Seattle Post–Intelligencer, Oct. 20, 1974, at A1, A2.

[15] *See id.* at 13, 128; Orin S. Kerr, *The Fourth Amendment and New Technologies: Constitutional Myths and the Case for Caution*, 102 Mich. L. Rev. 801, 840–43 (2004).

[16] *See* 277 U.S. at 471 (Brandeis, J., dissenting); Murphy, *supra* note 13, at 18–30.

[17] *See* 277 U.S. at 462; Hoffa v. United States, 385 U.S. 293 (1966). See the chapter on *Hoffa* in this volume.

instruments had authorized ransacking of personal property without significant judicial oversight.[18]

The *Olmstead* majority reasoned that this history, along with the literal language of the Fourth Amendment, limited the scope of the Amendment to searches and seizures of "material things—the person, the house, his papers, or his effects."[19] The wiretapping in Seattle, the Court concluded, had therefore involved no "search" or "seizure" within the meaning of the Constitution. The agents simply listened: there had been no "entry of the houses or offices of the defendants."[20] And this struck the Court as an altogether sensible result. The "reasonable view" was "that one who installs in his house a telephone instrument with connecting wires intends to project his voice to those quite outside, and that the wires beyond his house, and messages while passing over them, are not within the protection of the Fourth Amendment."[21]

Four justices filed dissents in *Olmstead*. One of those dissents, by Justice Brandeis, was soon more famous than the majority opinion, and it saw some vindication fifty years later in *Katz*. Brandeis argued that the Fourth Amendment should be interpreted liberally, in order to protect against new threats to what he took to be its underlying concern: government invasions of privacy. On this score, he thought, "writs of assistance and general warrants are but puny instruments of tyranny and oppression when compared with wire tapping."[22]

Roy Olmstead served his four-year prison sentence and returned to Seattle. He became a Christian Science practitioner and Bible teacher, regularly visiting jails and prisons. He died quietly in 1966, while the *Katz* case was on appeal.[23]

The *Olmstead* doctrine outlived its namesake, although not for long. It, too, had a strange career.

Federal Surveillance Law at Mid-century

Olmstead was controversial from the start. The press denounced the decision as condoning "universal snooping." When Nicholas Murray

---

[18] *See, e.g.,* Nelson B. Lasson, The History and Development of the Fourth Amendment to the United States Constitution 42–78 (1937); Telford Taylor, *Search, Seizure, and Surveillance, in* Two Studies in Constitutional Interpretation 19, 24–38 (1969).

[19] 277 U.S. at 464.

[20] *Id.*

[21] *Id.* at 466.

[22] *Id.* at 476 (Brandeis, J., dissenting).

[23] *See* Clark, *supra* note 14, at 103; *Roy Olmstead, Prohibition–Era Figure*, Seattle Times, May 4, 1966, at 24; Don Duncan, *"Bootleg King" Now Religious Worker*, Seattle Times, Apr. 11, 1965, at 14.

Butler, the President of Columbia University, tried to defend the ruling at the 1928 Republican Convention, he was shouted down from the floor. But defenders of the decision were also combative. Taft wrote to his brother that if Brandeis and "[h]is claques in the law school contingent" thought the Court would be "frightened in our effort to stand by the law and give the public a chance to punish criminals," they were "mistaken." And while the Justice Department and its newly formed Bureau of Investigation continued to bar wiretapping, the Prohibition Bureau responded to *Olmstead* by openly embracing the practice. So did state police agencies across the country.[24]

Within a decade, the Court began to backtrack, but in a limited and roundabout way. Unwilling to overrule *Olmstead* directly, it curtailed the significance of the decision through a creative exercise in statutory interpretation. In 1934, in the course of revising and recodifying federal regulations over radio broadcasting, Congress prohibited the unauthorized interception or divulgence of radio or wire communications. The prohibition, codified at 47 U.S.C. § 605, said nothing about the admissibility of intercepted communications, and nothing in the legislative history suggested that Congress intended to modify the *Olmstead* rule.[25] When Frank Nardone, a New York bootlegger convicted with wiretap evidence, argued that his conviction should be overturned because section 605 made the intercepted conversations inadmissible, the Second Circuit rejected the argument out of hand.[26] But the Supreme Court reversed. Over the objections of the only two members of the *Olmstead* majority still serving, the Court reasoned that testifying about telephone conversations counted as "divulging" them and therefore fell within the legislative prohibition.[27] Nardone was convicted in a retrial, but the Supreme Court again reversed the conviction, this time on the ground that section 605 prohibited the introduction not only of the intercepted conversations themselves, but also of any evidence derived through the investigative use of those conversations.[28]

The majority opinions in the two *Nardone* cases made perfectly clear what drove the statutory analysis: a changed set of intuitions about the constitutional questions lying in the background. Perhaps, the Court speculated in the first case, Congress had "thought it less important that some offenders should go unwhipped of justice than that officers should resort to methods deemed inconsistent with ethical standards and de-

---

[24] Murphy, *supra* note 13, at 125–29, 133.

[25] *See id.* at 133.

[26] United States v. Nardone, 90 F.2d 630, 632 (2d Cir. 1937).

[27] Nardone v. United States, 302 U.S. 379, 382 (1937).

[28] Nardone v. United States, 308 U.S. 338, 340–43 (1939).

structive of personal liberty." Indeed, the Court suggested, section 605 might well have been motivated by "[t]he same considerations . . . as evoked the guaranty against practices and procedures violative of privacy, embodied in the Fourth and Fifth Amendments of the Constitution."[29] The Court was even more emphatic when reversing Nardone's second conviction, explaining that its earlier decision had been based not on "a merely meticulous reading of technical language" but instead on "broad considerations of morality and public well-being."[30]

For several reasons, though, the *Nardone* decisions fell far short of undoing *Olmstead*. First, the Department of Justice interpreted the opinions to prohibit, under section 605, the introduction of wiretap evidence, or the introduction of evidence obtained from leads provided by wiretaps—but not the wiretapping itself.[31] Second, the Supreme Court later ruled that section 605 did not bar state prosecutors from using wiretap evidence obtained by state officers—despite the absence of anything in the statutory language or legislative history supporting a distinction between state and federal wiretaps or between state and federal testimony.[32] Finally, the *Nardone* rules applied only to wiretaps, and the Court interpreted *Olmstead* to sweep more broadly.

Olmstead itself could have been read to exempt from the Fourth Amendment only the interception of messages intentionally "project[ed] . . . to those quite outside." It could have been limited, that is to say, to wiretapping. That was the interpretation urged on the Court in *Goldman v. United States*[33] by the lawyers for three defendants convicted of bankruptcy fraud, in part based on evidence obtained through use of a "detectaphone"—a device that amplified sound waves passing through a wall. Federal agents used the detectaphone to eavesdrop on conversations taking place in the office of one of the defendants, and on what that defendant said when talking on the telephone from his office. The defendants argued that, even after *Olmstead*, eavesdropping on conversations taking place entirely within a private office constituted a search.

---

[29] 302 U.S. at 383.

[30] 308 U.S. at 340.

[31] Murphy, *supra* note 13, at 136–37.

[32] Schwartz v. State of Texas, 344 U.S. 199 (1952). The Court's opinion in *Schwartz* analogized to Wolf v. Colorado, 338 U.S. 25 (1949), which refused to extend the Fourth Amendment exclusionary rule to state prosecutions. The analogy made even clearer that the Court understand the *Nardone* decisions as only nominally about statutory interpretation. In Benanti v. United States, 355 U.S. 96 (1957), the Supreme Court applied the *Nardone* rules to state wiretap evidence introduced in a federal prosecution. *Wolf* was later overruled by Mapp v. Ohio, 367 U.S. 643 (1961), which is the subject of separate chapter in this volume.

[33] 316 U.S. 129 (1942).

But the Court saw no distinction between the eavesdropping in *Goldman* and the wiretapping in *Olmstead*: the critical fact, in both cases, was the absence of any physical trespass. The *Nardone* protections, on the other hand, were deemed inapplicable in *Goldman*, on the ground that section 605 barred interception of communications only in the course of wire or radio transmission.[34]

The combined effect of all of these rulings was that *Olmstead* remained largely intact throughout the 1940s and 1950s. Evidence obtained by wiretaps was inadmissible in federal criminal cases, ostensibly on statutory grounds. The wiretapping itself was not viewed as illegal, though, and the evidence it produced was admissible in state prosecutions. Moreover, electronic surveillance that involved neither a physical trespass nor the interception of an electronic transmission was left largely unregulated. Section 605 did not apply, and neither, under *Olmstead* and *Goldman*, did the Fourth Amendment.

The edifice began to crack in 1961, when the Court unanimously overturned the convictions in *Silverman v. United States*.[35] The case involved evidence obtained with a foot-long "spike mike" inserted into a party wall that the defendants' rowhouse shared with an adjacent, abandoned house. The Court distinguished *Goldman* on the ground that the microphone in *Silverman* made contact with a heating duct serving the defendants' house, and the heating duct served as a sounding board.[36] Writing for the majority, Justice Stewart described this as "usurping" part of the defendants' property: the heating duct became, in effect, "a giant microphone, running through the entire house." It made no difference whether or not there had been "a technical trespass;" there had been a "physical encroachment within a constitutionally protected area," and the Court had "never held that a federal officer may without warrant and without consent physically entrench into a man's office or home, there secretly observe or listen, and relate at the man's subsequent criminal trial what was seen or heard." If the result in *Silverman* seemed inconsistent with the spirit of *Goldman*, so be it. The majority found "no occasion to re-examine *Goldman*," but it refused to extend the earlier decision, "even by a fraction of an inch."[37]

Silverman thus made clear not just that eavesdropping could constitute a "search" or "seizure" within the meaning of the Fourth Amendment—a matter *Olmstead* had left in great doubt—but also that the Court was no longer comfortable tying Fourth Amendment rights to

---

[34] *Id.* at 133–35.

[35] 365 U.S. 505 (1961).

[36] *See id.* at 506–07.

[37] *Id.* at 509–12.

"ancient niceties of tort or real property law."[38] Justice Douglas, who had joined the majority opinion in *Goldman*, called in *Silverman* for reversing it outright, along with *Olmstead*.[39] Two years later Justice Brennan took the same position, in a dissent joined by Justice Douglas and by Justice Goldberg.[40] A year after that, the Court took the distinction drawn in *Silverman* to its logical extreme, finding a Fourth Amendment violation because a listening device had been attached to the outside of an apartment wall by a thumb tack:[41] "had it merely been taped to the wall, the conversations would have been admissible."[42] By this point it was apparent that the trespass test was falling rapidly out of favor; it seemed destined to be replaced with a focus on infringements of privacy in "protected areas."[43]

And then the FBI tape recorded Charlie Katz placing bets from a telephone booth.

Katz in the Lower Courts

Katz was represented in court by Burton Marks, an experienced Los Angeles defense attorney. Two weeks after Katz was arrested, Marks moved to suppress all of the prosecution's evidence, based in part on a claim that the surreptitious tape recording of Katz had violated the Fourth Amendment and had tainted the entire investigation. Marks argued in a short memorandum supporting the motion that *Silverman* had rendered *Olmstead* a "dead letter": electronic eavesdropping was now unconstitutional. Nor did the location matter: "Surely a man has as much right to be let alone in a private telephone booth as in his own home"[44]

Unsurprisingly, the government saw things differently. *Silverman* was distinguishable on two grounds: there had been no "physical intru-

---

[38] *Id.* at 511.

[39] *Id.* at 512–13 (Douglas, J., concurring). Justice Douglas first announced his view that *Olmstead* and *Goldberg* had been wrongly decided in On Lee v. United States, 343 U.S. 747, 762–65 (1952).

[40] Lopez v. United States, 373 U.S. 427, 446 (1963).

[41] Clinton v. Virginia, 377 U.S. 158 (1964) (mem.), *rev'g* 130 S.E.2d 437 (Va. 1963).

[42] Samuel Dash, Katz—*Variations on a Theme by* Berger, 17 Cath. U. Am. L. Rev. 296, 304–05 (1968).

[43] *See, e.g., id.* at 304; Telford Taylor, *Search, Seizure, and Surveillance, in* Two Studies in Constitutional Interpretation 17, 74 (1969).

[44] Notice of Motion to Suppress Evidence and for Return of Evidence (Exhibits and Points and Authorities in Support Thereof), United States v. Katz, Misc. No. 1209, at 4 (C.D. Cal.) (filed Mar. 11, 1965). A pleasing typographical error in the original motion changed the "right to be let alone" to the "right to bet alone." *Id.*

sion" here, and a telephone booth, unlike a home, was "not a constitutionally protected area."[45] And *Olmstead* and *Goldman* were still on the books—whatever "the law might or might not be at some time in the future."[46]

District Judge Jesse Curtis Jr. agreed. The suppression motion raised "a very interesting and exciting constitutional question," and the applicable law was "rapidly changing." *Silverman* threw the continued validity of *Goldman* into "great doubt"; it seemed likely the Supreme Court would decide *Goldman* differently today. Still, "for lack of a new and different pronouncement," *Goldman* remained the law. And under *Goldman* there had been no violation of the Fourth Amendment. Judge Curtis denied the motion.[47]

The trial lasted two days. The chief evidence against Katz consisted of his tape recorded statements over the telephone, the records seized from his hotel room, and expert testimony from a vice officer in the Los Angeles Police Department, who decoded the bookmaking lingo and opined on the significance of Katz's records. Katz waived a jury. Judge Curtis found Katz guilty and fined him $300.[48]

On appeal before the Ninth Circuit, Marks renewed his contention that tape recording Katz's telephone calls had violated the Fourth Amendment as interpreted in *Silverman*. The appellate panel had even less trouble than Judge Curtis rejecting this claim. District Judge Charles Powell, sitting by designation, wrote for a unanimous court. He suggested in passing that a telephone booth, unlike a home, was not a protected area under the Fourth Amendment: by way of comparison, he noted that the Ninth Circuit had found no Fourth Amendment violation when police spied on "events" in a public toilet stall.[49] But the key point for Judge Powell was that there had been "no physical entrance" of the telephone booths.[50] The case was therefore governed by *Goldman*, and by the Ninth Circuit's recent application of *Goldman* in *Corngold v. United States*[51]—a case to which we will have occasion to return later in this chapter. Melvin Corngold had been convicted of trafficking in stolen

---

[45] Opposition to Defendant's Motion for Suppression of Evidence and for Return of Evidence; and Memorandum of Points and Authorities, *Katz*, Misc. No. 1209, at 3–7 (C.D. Cal.) (filed Mar. 29, 1965).

[46] Record at 63, Katz v. United States, 389 U.S. 347 (1967) (No. 35).

[47] *Id.* at 72–73.

[48] *See id.* at 93–206; Katz v. United States, 369 F.2d 130, 131–33 (9th Cir. 1966).

[49] 369 F.2d at 133 (citing Smayda v. United States, 352 F.2d 251 (9th Cir. 1965)).

[50] 369 F.2d at 134.

[51] 367 F.2d 1 (9th Cir. 1966).

watches. Some of the evidence against him had been obtained by using a "scintillator" to detect radiation emitted from the watches, which had radium-treated dials. The Court of Appeals reasoned that under *Goldman* the use of the scintillator did not violate the Fourth Amendment, even when the watches were in Corngold's apartment, because the agents stood outside in a public hallway.[52] The surveillance of Katz, Judge Powell reasoned, was just like the surveillance upheld in *Corngold*, and steered clear of the Fourth Amendment in the same manner.[53] Katz's conviction was affirmed.

In retrospect there are two striking things about the Fourth Amendment arguments advanced for Katz in the lower courts.

First, Marks never challenged the notion that, in order to prevail, he needed to establish both that no physical trespass was required for a search, and that a telephone booth, like a home, was a "protected area" under the Fourth Amendment. The suppression motion argued that when in a "private" telephone booth, as when at home, a person had the right "to be let alone." Before the Ninth Circuit, Marks urged that when Katz closed the door to the telephone booth for the purpose of placing a call, he was "in effect in his own residence."[54] In this respect Marks was following conventional legal wisdom. As we have seen, it was widely believed at the time that trespass test was destined soon to be replaced with a focus on protected areas of privacy.

Second, Marks never suggested that the secret monitoring of his client's telephone calls would have been constitutional if only the agents had first obtained a warrant. The thrust of the argument seemed to be that the monitoring was flatly unconstitutional, not that it was unconstitutional only because the government had failed to follow proper procedures. In this respect, too, the arguments advanced for Katz in the lower courts reflected the era in which the case arose. There was widespread uncertainty at the time regarding whether warrants could validate electronic eavesdropping. The reasons for that uncertainty merit a brief detour.

The Dubious Status of Surveillance Warrants

When the Supreme Court reversed the convictions in *Silverman*, on the nominal ground that the government had commandeered the defendants' heating duct, the Justices suggested in passing that a warrant might have cured the problem. Never, the Court explained, had it "held that a federal officer may *without warrant* and without consent physical-

---

[52] *Id.* at 3.

[53] 369 F.2d at 133–34.

[54] *Id.* at 133.

ly entrench into a man's office or home, there secretly observe or listen, and relate at the man's subsequent criminal trial what was seen or heard."[55] The notion that a warrant could validate electronic surveillance also found its way into state surveillance laws. By the mid–1960s, most states had laws against wiretapping, although usually not against "bugging"—i.e., electronic eavesdropping not involving the interception of radio or wire communications. Most of state wiretap statutes made some sort of exception for law enforcement, sometimes requiring officers to get a warrant before commencing surveillance. Those few states that regulated bugging generally required warrants for that practice as well. New York, in particular, had imposed a warrant requirement on wiretaps since 1942 and on bugging since 1958.[56]

Nonetheless there was considerable doubt regarding the validity of surveillance warrants. The problems were threefold.

First, the Supreme Court had held in 1921 that the Fourth Amendment did not permit search warrants for "mere evidence," as opposed to contraband, criminal proceeds, or instrumentalities of crime.[57] The idea was that there was something objectionable about confiscating and using property to convict the owner of crime—something analogous to compelling self-incriminating testimony—unless the government or a third party had a superior right to possess the property. A warrant could not be used "solely for the purpose of making search to secure evidence to be used . . . in a criminal or penal proceeding."[58] By the 1960s the "mere evidence" rule was widely criticized, and courts had grown adept at working around it.[59] But it was still the law, and it was difficult to reconcile with the idea of surveillance warrants. It was hard to see how the government could claim a paramount right to possess the words "seized" through electronic eavesdropping. Wiretapping or bugging "usually could serve no other purpose than the collection of evidence," and therefore seemed flatly contrary to the "mere evidence" rule.[60]

Second, it was hard to see how surveillance warrants could comply with the "particularity" requirement: the explicit command in the Fourth Amendment that every warrant must "particularly describe[e] the place to be searched, and the persons or things to be seized." It

---

[55] 365 U.S. at 683 (emphasis added).

[56] See Dash, supra note 42, at 303; Kerr, supra note 15, at 846; Taylor, supra note 18, at 78.

[57] See Gouled v. United States, 255 U.S. 298 (1921).

[58] Id. at 309.

[59] See Taylor, supra note 18, at 51.

[60] Dash, supra note 42, at 308–09; see also Taylor, supra note 18, at 78.

might be "possible to describe the 'place' to be put under surveillance"—although even here some there was some awkwardness in applying this concept to a wiretap—but it seemed "quite impossible to describe at all—let alone 'particularly'—the 'persons or things' to be seized."[61] By its very nature, electronic eavesdropping involved the collection of evidence that did not exist until the moment of its interception. It seemed uncomfortably similar to the indiscriminate searches infamously authorized by general warrants and writs of assistance, the paradigmatic abuses against which the Fourth Amendment had taken aim.

Precisely for this reason, and also because "words ... are ordinarily mere evidence and not the fruits or instrumentalities of crime," Justice Brennan speculated in 1963 that the Fourth Amendment might forbid wiretapping and bugging altogether, although he left open the possibility that an acceptable warrant for electronic surveillance might be devised.[62] Justice Douglas and Justice Goldberg joined Brennan's opinion, and three years later, while *Katz* was on appeal, Douglas announced his conclusion that the Constitution in fact barred all electronic searches. Wiretaps and bugs, he reasoned, "invariably involve a search for mere evidence," and a "warrant authorizing such devices is no different from the general warrants the Fourth Amendment was intended to prohibit."[63]

Justice Brennan's 1963 opinion also touched on the third reason for doubt about the constitutionality of surveillance warrants. Search warrants, although issued *ex parte*, generally are disclosed, and thereby made subject to challenge, as soon as they are executed. Surveillance orders, though, must be kept secret even when they are executed; disclosure would defeat the purpose of the surveillance. Brennan worried that "without some form of notice" electronic searches would be "intolerable intrusions into ... privacy," and he was not alone in this concern. Because electronic surveillance had to remain clandestine throughout its duration, there was considerable uncertainty whether surveillance warrants could ever survive constitutional scrutiny, even aside from the "mere evidence" problem and the requirement of "particularity."[64]

---

[61] Taylor, *supra* note 18, at 80–81.

[62] Lopez v. United States, 373 U.S. 427, 463–65 (1963) (Brennan, J., dissenting).

[63] Osborn v. United States, 385 U.S. 323, 352–53 (1966) (Douglas, J., dissenting).

[64] *See* Taylor, *supra* note 18, at 81–85. Professor Taylor believed the Court was right to conclude in *Olmstead* that communications sent out over telephone lines were unprotected by the Fourth Amendment. *See id.* at 75–77. But he thought it clear that warrants authorizing the bugging of a home "would have been regarded as highly 'unreasonable' under the original understanding of the first clause of the fourth amendment," because "a period of clandestine surveillance of one's private doings and sayings in the home is a far

Katz Reaches the Supreme Court

When Marks petitioned the Supreme Court for certiorari in *Katz*, his argument was in all pertinent respects the same one he had made in the lower courts. Once again, there was no suggestion that the tape recording of Katz's telephone calls required a warrant or could have been validated by a warrant. The suggestion was instead that the taping was flatly prohibited by the Fourth Amendment. Once again, Marks implicitly conceded that, in order to prevail, he needed to establish both that a public telephone booth was a protected area under the Fourth Amendment, and that a violation of the Amendment could occur without any physical intrusion into the phone booth. Indeed, Marks told the Court that resolving the legality of the electronic eavesdropping on Katz required answering two separate questions: first, whether "a public telephone booth is a constitutionally protected area," and second, whether "physical penetration of a constitutionally protected area is necessary" for a violation of the Fourth Amendment.[65] As below, Marks relied heavily on *Silverman*. And he elaborated slightly on his analogy between a telephone booth and a home. "Doors," he suggested, "are placed on telephone booths for no other purpose than to guarantee its occupant privacy."[66]

As had Judge Powell's opinion for the Ninth Circuit, the Solicitor General's memorandum opposing the petition for certiorari challenged both legs of Marks's argument. The government's chief point was that, even after *Silverman*, a violation of the Fourth Amendment required a physical "intrusion into a constitutionally protected area."[67] Here, there was no intrusion, because the tape recorder and microphones were outside of the telephone booths. In a footnote, moreover, the government pointed out that one district court had held that a public telephone booth was not a "constitutionally protected area" to begin with. "Whatever the validity of this ruling," the Solicitor General suggested, it was "at least clear that a public telephone booth is not generally considered as a private sanctuary, as is one's home or office."[68]

In March 1967, the Supreme Court granted certiorari in *Katz*. The Court asked for briefing and argument not only on the electronic

---

greater invasion of privacy than a single search, conducted in one's presence, for specified physical objects." *Id.* at 83–84.

[65] Petition for Writ of Certiorari to the United States Court of Appeals for the Ninth Circuit at 3, Katz v. United States, 389 U.S. 347 (1967) (No. 895).

[66] *Id.* at 6–7.

[67] Memorandum for the United States in Opposition at 6, *Katz* (No. 895).

[68] *Id.* at 5 note 4.

surveillance issue, but also on an immunity question[69] and on the issue
of the validity of the search warrant executed at Katz's hotel room.[70]
When it finally decided the case, the Court dismissed the immunity
question and the challenges to the warrant in a footnote.[71] The case is
remembered for what the Court said about the surveillance.

Briefing

Between March 1967, when the Supreme Court agreed to review the
Ninth Circuit's decision in *Katz*, and September 1967, when the opening
brief on the merits was filed, the Court handed down three major
decisions interpreting the Fourth Amendment. Together, these cases
significantly altered the terrain on which *Katz* would be fought.

Warden v. Hayden, decided in late May 1967, finally abandoned the
"mere evidence" rule, calling it an obsolete remnant of the "discredited"
notion that "property interests control the right of the Government to
search and seize." The modern view, the Court explained, was that the
Fourth Amendment served chiefly to protect "privacy rather than property"; among the authority cited for this proposition was *Silverman*.[72]

---

[69] The immunity issue was raised in the Solicitor General's memorandum opposing the
petition for certiorari. Shortly after the Ninth Circuit affirmed his conviction, Katz had
testified under a statutory grant of transactional immunity before a federal grand jury in
Florida, as part of an investigation into illegal interstate wagering, and he had been asked
about some of the calls that formed the basis of his prosecution in Los Angeles. The
applicable statute barred a witness from being "subjected to any penalty ... for or on
account of any transaction, matter, or thing concerning which he is compelled, after having
claimed his privilege against self-incrimination, to testify." 47 U.S.C. § 409(*l*) (repealed
1970). (Later, in 1970, Congress would replace all federal transactional immunity statutes
with a new statute, providing protection only against the actual use of immunized
testimony, or evidence located through use of immunized testimony. *See* 18 U.S.C. §§ 6002
& 6003; Kastigar v. United States, 406 U.S. 441 (1972)). The difficulty raised by Katz's
immunized testimony was that the District of Columbia Circuit had recently ruled that a
grant of immunity to a defendant appealing a conviction voided the conviction, if the
subject matter of the immunized testimony "relat[ed] to the matters involved in the
conviction." Frank v. United States, 347 F.2d 486, 491 (D.C. Cir. 1965), *vacated on other
grounds sub nom.* Leon v. United States, 384 U.S. 882 (1966). After flagging the issue, the
Solicitor General suggested that the ruling by the District of Columbia Circuit was
erroneous and should not be followed. Memorandum for the United States in Opposition at
2–3, *Katz* (No. 895).

[70] 386 U.S. 954 (1967). Marks had argued in the lower courts, and reiterated in his
petition for certiorari, that the warrant was invalid on three separate grounds: it lacked
probable cause, it authorized a search for "mere evidence," and it was insufficiently
particular in describing the items to be seized.

[71] Katz v. United States, 389 U.S. 347, 349 note 3 (1967) (holding that the immunity
statute did not reach prosecutions carried out before compelling the defendant's testimony,
and that the challenges to the warrant were moot in light of the Court's ruling on the
surveillance issue).

[72] 387 U.S. 294, 304 (1967).

One week later, in *Camara v. Municipal Court*, the Court held that nonconsensual administrative inspections, no less than nonconsensual searches for criminal evidence, could not proceed without warrants—a ruling that considerably bolstered the position of the warrant requirement as the "one unifying principle" of search and seizure law.[73]

The really big news, though, was *Berger v. New York*,[74] handed down the week after *Camara*. *Berger* involved the New York statute authorizing state judges to issue warrants for wiretapping or electronic bugging by law enforcement. In a long and fractured set of opinions, the Court struck down the statute on a 5–4 vote. The opinion for the Court, written by Justice Clark, faulted the New York surveillance warrants for lacking probable cause and particularization regarding the conversations to be "seized," for failing to impose a termination date, and for failing to require notice.[75] Justice Clark took no explicit position regarding whether those faults could feasibly be remedied, but Justice Douglas, who provided the fifth vote for the majority, argued in a separate, concurring opinion that they could not.[76] Both Justice Clark and Justice Douglas had strong words about the threats that electronic eavesdropping posed to a free society, and both were plainly skeptical of claims that outlawing the technique would cripple law enforcement.[77] On the other hand, Justice Stewart, who concurred narrowly in the result, and Justice Black, Justice Harlan, and Justice White, who dissented, all took the view that the surveillance warrants authorized by the New York statute were fully consistent with the Fourth Amendment.[78]

---

[73] 387 U.S. 523, 528–29 (1967).

[74] 388 U.S. 41 (1967).

[75] *Id.* at 55–63. The separate objection that electronic eavesdropping constituted a search for "mere evidence" was rejected in a brief footnote citing *Warden v. Hayden. See id.* at 44 note 2.

[76] *Id.* at 64–68 (Douglas, J., concurring). Thus Professor Taylor's assessment of *Berger*: "Mr. Justice Clark ... wrote an opinion for the Court in which three other members concurred. A fifth member, Mr. Justice Douglas, said that he concurred in the opinion, but in fact he didn't." Taylor, *supra* note 18, at 100.

[77] *See* 388 U.S. at 62–63 (opinion of the Court); *id.* at 64–68 (Douglas, J., concurring).

[78] *See id.* at 68 (Stewart, J., concurring); *id.* at 70 (Black, J., dissenting); *id.* at 89 (Harlan, J., dissenting); *id.* at 107 (White, J., dissenting). Justice Stewart concurred in the result only because he concluded that the warrant applications in the particular case before the Court did not make an adequate showing of probable cause. *Id.* at 69 (Stewart, J., concurring).

The combined effect of *Hayden*, *Camara*, and *Berger* was the following. The "mere evidence" rule, which might have made electronic
surveillance *per se* unconstitutional, was now discarded. The centrality of
the warrant requirement to the Fourth Amendment was underscored.
And it was uncertain whether warrants for electronic surveillance could
be drawn in such a fashion to satisfy the Fourth Amendment. Four
members of the Supreme Court thought they could—and in fact had
been in New York. One member of the Court thought they could not.
And the position of the remaining Justices was not entirely clear. In
retrospect, it seems plain enough that Justice Clark's opinion gave
legislatures a reasonably simple road map for drafting an electronic
surveillance statute that the Court would uphold.[79] To many observers at
the time, though, that was not apparent.[80] Justice Black would later
note, in his dissenting opinion in *Katz*, that *Berger* had "set up what
appeared to be insuperable obstacles to the valid passage of . . . wiretapping laws."[81]

The doctrinal shifts in *Hayden*, *Camara*, and *Berger* significantly
altered the arguments put forward in *Katz*, but the full effects were not
seen immediately. Once the Supreme Court granted certiorari in the
case, Marks brought on another attorney, a recent law school graduate
named Harvey Schneider. All the talk about "reasonableness" reminded
Schneider of his first-year torts class; he thought the "reasonable man"
test for negligence provided a good model for thinking about electronic

---

[79] *See, e.g.,* Charles H. Kennedy & Peter P. Swire, *State Wiretaps and Electronic
Surveillance After September 11*, 54 Hastings L.J. 971, 975 (2003). The clearest indication,
perhaps, was Justice Clark's treatment of the Court's recent decision in Osborn v. United
States, 385 U.S. 323 (1966). In *Osborn* the Court approved the use of a tape recorder
secreted on the person of a confidential informant, and noted approvingly that the tactic
had been authorized in advance by a "precise and discriminate" court order. *Id.* at 329.
The business about the court order seemed "quite unnecessary to the disposition," Taylor,
supra note 18, at 92, because the Court had earlier held, and reaffirmed in *Osborn*, that the
Fourth Amendment did not protect the confidentiality of a conversation with an undercover agent of the government, or prohibit the agent from secretly tape recording the
conversation, *see* 385 U.S. at 327; Lopez v. United States, 373 U.S. 427, 438 (1963). In
Berger, though, Justice Clark read *Osborn* to approve "an invasion of the privacy protected
by the Fourth Amendment," on the ground that the surveillance in question had been
authorized by a narrowly drawn court order, which he contrasted favorably with the
surveillance warrants permitted by the New York statute. 388 U.S. at 56–58.

[80] *See, e.g.,* Taylor, *supra* note 18, at 106, 110 (arguing that surveillance statutes and
surveillance warrants could "readily be drawn so as to meet the Court's requirements,"
but noting that *Berger* had been "attacked as making surveillance practically impossible").

[81] Katz v. United States, 389 U.S. 347, 364 (1967) (Black, J., dissenting); *see also, e.g.,*
Fred P. Graham, *High Court Eases Curbs on Bugging*, N.Y. Times, Dec. 19, 1967, at 1
(noting that the Court's decision in *Katz* "erased an impression" created by *Berger* "that
the Supreme Court would insist on such elaborate procedures in connection with [surveil-
lance] warrants that bugging would become virtually useless as a police tool").

surveillance.[82] That notion found expression in the opening brief, which suggested that the test for determining whether a conversation was covered by the Fourth Amendment should be, "Would the average reasonable man believe that the person whose conversation had been intercepted intended and desired his conversation to be private?"[83] Katz's lawyers argued that *Hayden* and *Berger* made clear that "the primary concern of the Fourth Amendment" was "the individual's right to privacy."[84]

For the most part, though, the opening brief for Katz tracked the approach of the petition for certiorari. The central argument was rooted in two claims: that no physical trespass was required for violation of the Fourth Amendment, and that the telephone booth was a "constitutionally protected area."[85] The question about the "reasonable man," in fact, was presented as simply another way to ask, "Does the area in question have the 'attributes of privacy?' "[86] Marks and Schneider argued that a telephone booth being used by a paying customer did have such "attributes," and they supported their claim by pointing to cases where the Court had held the Fourth Amendment applicable to physical searches in offices, hotel rooms, automobiles, and even taxicabs. "Surely," they argued, someone using a public telephone booth "has the same right to exclusive control and use as does the taxicab occupant."[87]

What is most striking in retrospect about the opening brief in *Katz* is the absence of any hint that what made the surveillance illegal was the lack of a warrant. Marks and Schneider did argue that the secret taping of Katz shared the imprecision and excessive duration of the monitoring struck down in *Berger*; they claimed those flaws would make the telephone booth surveillance "unreasonable" under the Fourth Amendment even if the booths were not "constitutionally protected area[s]."[88] But they never suggested that the constitutional violation could have been cured with a warrant.

That suggestion, ironically, first entered the case in the government's brief on the merits. As when opposing certiorari, the government argued first and foremost that, even after *Silverman*, a search required a

---

[82] Interview of Harvey Schneider, Los Angeles, Cal., July 26, 2004.

[83] Brief for Petitioner at 13, *Katz* (No. 35).

[84] *Id.* at 11.

[85] *Id.* at 8–14.

[86] *Id.* at 13.

[87] *Id.* at 13–14 (citing, *inter alia*, Gouled v. United States, 255 U.S. 298 (1921) (office); United States v. Jeffers, 342 U.S. 48 (1951) (hotel room); Henry v. United States, 361 U.S. 98 (1959) (automobile); Rios v. United States, 364 U.S. 253 (1960) (taxicab)).

[88] Brief for Petitioner at 16–17, *Katz* (No. 35).

"physical invasion," if not a "technical trespass." Sensing, however, that the Court's decision to review *Katz* might signal a desire to revisit the physical invasion requirement, the government placed new weight on the contention that a telephone booth was not a "constitutionally protected area." A public booth was not like a home or an office or an automobile; it was more like a public street or undeveloped acreage—areas that the Court had long treated as "open fields" that could be searched without triggering the Fourth Amendment.[89]

In the alternative, the government argued that, even if a telephone booth was a "protected area" under the Fourth Amendment, it should receive less protection than the home—just as automobile searches had long been evaluated under looser standards than residential searches.[90] In particular, the government urged, the "occupant's interest in a public telephone booth" was too "limited" to justify imposition of a warrant requirement.[91]

This was enough of a hint for Marks and Schneider. The reply brief argued that the lack of a search warrant made the monitoring of Katz's telephone calls "patently unconstitutional."[92] And by this point Schneider had evidently convinced Marks to jettison reliance on the notion that a telephone booth was a "protected place" under the Fourth Amendment. Instead, the reply brief reiterated, this time without equivocation, that the proper question was whether "the average reasonable man" would have thought the conversations in question were intended to be private. No places were beyond Fourth Amendment protection. If this required parting with the "open fields" doctrine, it was good riddance: "if two persons believed that an uninhabited open field was the safest and most private place to conduct a conversation," then their conversation *should* be protected by the Fourth Amendment.[93] By now Katz's lawyers were going for broke.

Oral Argument

The Supreme Court heard oral argument in *Katz v. United States* on October 17, 1967. It was clear from the start that Katz's lawyers would

---

[89] Brief for the Respondent at 13–15, *Katz* (No. 35). The "open fields" doctrine dated back to Hester v. United States, 265 U.S. 57, 59 (1924). There Justice Holmes, writing for the Court, declared that "the special protection accorded by the Fourth Amendment to the people in their 'persons, houses, papers and effects,' is not extended to the open fields," because "[t]he distinction between the latter and the house is as old as the common law." *Id.* at 59.

[90] Brief for the Respondent at 18, *Katz* (No. 35).

[91] *Id.* at 19 & note 8.

[92] Reply Brief for the Petitioner at 2, *Katz* (No. 35).

[93] *Id.* at 4–5.

not play it safe. Ordinarily the first rule of litigating before the Supreme Court, or any appellate court, is to minimize the novelty of your claim. "We ask only for a straightforward application of existing law," the advocate typically argues, "but deciding against us would require over-ruling settled precedent." But the late 1960s were not an ordinary time, at the Supreme Court or elsewhere, and Katz's lawyers couched their argument frankly—maybe even with a degree of exaggeration—as a call for innovation.

Marks and Schneider split the argument for Katz. Schneider, giving the opening argument, set the tone early. The facts of the case, he told the Court, were "quite simple," but the applicable law was "really something else again."[94] He framed the Fourth Amendment issues in a way that all but eliminated the traditional concern with "protected places." "Whether or not a telephone booth or any other area is constitutionally protected," he argued, was "the wrong initial inquiry."[95] Instead, he urged, the test should be simply whether "a reasonable person, objectively looking at the communications setting, the situation and location of the communicator and communicatee, would ... reasonably believe that the communication was intended to be confidential."[96] The "physical location" of the communication was a "factor" to be considered in making that assessment, but only one factor—and not a terribly important factor at that. The point of the Fourth Amendment was to protect "the right to privacy," and that right "follow[ed] the individual": in assessing whether a communication should be deemed confidential, it was "not determinative" whether it took place "in a space enclosed by four walls and a ceiling and a roof, or in an automobile, or in any other physical location." Equally if not more important was "the activity engaged in by the enforcement officer"—the lengths to which the officer had to go in order to overhear the conversation.[97]

Schneider made no effort to root any of this in case law. He mentioned *Berger* favorably in passing,[98] but for the most part he referred to precedents only to identify the rulings he was asking the Court to overrule. *Goldman* certainly could "no longer stand" if the Court were to adopt "this new test, or anything similar to it."[99] *Hester v. United States*, which declared the protection of the Fourth Amendment unavailable in "open fields," had "to go, as well"; the "open fields"

---

[94] Oral argument at 1, *Katz v. United States* (No. 35).

[95] *Id.* at 5.

[96] *Id.*

[97] *Id.* at 6–8; *see also id.* at 11–12.

[98] *See id.* at 4.

[99] *Id.* at 8; *see also id.* at 10.

doctrine was inconsistent "with any test similar to that which we propose."[100] "We think," Schneider explained, "that if a confidential communication was intended, and all the other aspects of confidentiality are present, ... it makes no different whether in you're in an open field or in the privacy of your own home."[101]

If Schneider couched his argument as doctrinally innovative, though, he was careful to soften its practical implications. He was not asking the Court to outlaw electronic surveillance of confidential communications; he was simply asking the Court to apply the warrant requirement. The monitoring of what Katz said in the telephone booth was unconstitutional not because it was a "search" within the meaning of the Fourth Amendment, but because it was a search carried out "without a warrant."[102] And although Schneider "[a]s a private citizen ... would not be in favor of any kind of bugging device," he believed "[a]s a constitutional lawyer" that the practice was permissible if "sufficient protections" were present. That was what *Berger* had "indicated": the warrant procedure could be used to make electronic surveillance constitutional.[103]

Not surprisingly, the Court pressed him on this point: "So here, it's a constitutionally protected area. You would say, with the right procedures you might be able to invade this area, but here there were no such procedures?" Schneider resisted "the emphasis on whether or not you have a constitutionally protected area." But he reiterated his position that "very specific measures," interposing "a detached magistrate" between law enforcement officers and their targets, could make bugging constitutional.[104]

Marks, in his rebuttal argument, was even more emphatic. *Berger* made clear that telephonic eavesdropping was constitutional, as long as a proper warrant was obtained beforehand. It would have been "very simple" for the officers investigating Charlie Katz to get such a warrant, but they did not.[105] The Justices pressed Marks, as they had pressed Schneider: "[Y]ou think that would have been valid, under *Berger*?" Yes, there was "no question" in Marks's mind.[106] The whole case boiled down

---

[100] *Id.* at 11.

[101] *Id.* at 5.

[102] *Id.* at 4.

[103] *Id.* at 7.

[104] *Id.*

[105] *Id.* at 34–35

[106] *Id.* at 36.

to the failure to get a warrant. "We're forced to the conclusion, from *Berger*, that this is a search warrant case."[107]

The government's argument was presented by John Martin, an attorney in the Solicitor General's office. Martin seized on the expansiveness of Schneider's argument. This was indeed a call for "a radical change in the concept of the Fourth Amendment."[108] The "open fields" doctrine of *Hester v. United States* was a critical part of that concept. Surely, Martin argued, government agents were permitted to *watch* a telephone booth to see who placed a call from it—something they might do, for example, if they were trying to catch a kidnapper who had used the booth for an earlier call. There would be no invasion of privacy there, because the telephone booth was out in public. "An occupant in a public telephone booth is just as subject to visual surveillance as a man standing in an open field." And the same was true for audio surveillance. "These phone booths are neither designed, nor are they considered to be, totally soundproof."[109]

The Court pressed Martin on the difference between watching a telephone booth and eavesdropping on it. No one could go into a glass telephone booth and reasonably expect to remain unseen, but surely someone could enter the same booth reasonably expecting to carry out a private conversation? Martin held firm; he did not "see drawing a distinction between 'overhearing' and 'viewing.' "[110] The Fourth Amendment "was designed to protect the public from trespass by law enforcement officers"; it therefore applied at all only in those areas where a person "had the right to withdraw" and "to exclude others."[111]

At times the Court's questioning of Martin digressed into a discussion of telephone booth architecture. What was the point of the glass walls, if not to protect the privacy of the occupant's conversation? Martin suggested the walls served chiefly "to exclude some of the extraneous noise." Moreover, he noted that the walls were not as common as they used to be: "you ... now have a movement toward the open-type of booth." And surely the telephone company, in deciding which kind of pay telephone to install, did not think it was "conferring greater or lesser privacy rights."[112]

---

[107] *Id.* at 38.

[108] *Id.* at 15.

[109] *Id.* at 15–16; *see also id.* at 22.

[110] *Id.* at 15–16.

[111] *Id.* at 28.

[112] *Id.* at 30.

Moreover, even if the Fourth Amendment *did* apply in a telephone booth, Martin argued in the alternative that the surveillance here was reasonable—with or without a warrant. The tape recorder was installed only after the FBI had watched Katz long enough to have good reason to think he was using these particular telephone booths to place illegal interstate bets. They were careful to turn the tape recorder on only when Katz was approaching, and to turn it off promptly when he left. Only once was an innocent third party accidentally recorded, and the agents never listened to that conversation.[113] That should satisfy the Fourth Amendment: the protections in a telephone booth should not be "coextensive with the protection we provide for a home."[114] Justice Black told Martin, "You seem to be taking the position that a man's telephone booth is not his castle"; Martin was happy to agree.[115]

Decision

The Supreme Court handed down its decision in *Katz v. United States* on December 18, 1967, just two months after hearing argument in the case. The result was virtually everything that Marks and Schneider had hoped for. The Court voted 7–1 to reverse. (Justice Marshall, who as Solicitor General had opposed certiorari in *Katz*, did not participate in the Court's consideration of the case.) More striking even than the lopsided vote was the sweeping rhetoric of Justice Stewart's opinion for the Court, rhetoric that, on the question of electronic eavesdropping, seemed to embrace every position Schneider and Marks had taken in oral argument.

The " 'trespass' doctrine" of *Olmstead* and *Goldman* had been "so eroded" that it could "no longer be regarded as controlling." The absence of any "physical penetration" of the telephone booth thus had "no constitutional significance."[116] More fundamentally, the Court followed Schneider's lead in de-emphasizing physical locations altogether in Fourth Amendment analysis. There was no point in trying to decide "in the abstract" whether a telephone booth was a "constitutionally protected area." The whole notion of a "constitutionally protected area" diverted attention from the real issues in the case. The heart of the matter, Stewart declared for the Court, was that "the Fourth Amendment protects people, not places." Therefore "[w]hat a person knowingly exposes to the public, even in his own home or office, is not a subject of Fourth Amendment protection," whereas "what he seeks to preserve as

---

[113] *See id.* at 18, 22, 24.

[114] *Id.* at 29.

[115] *Id.* at 30.

[116] Katz v. United States, 389 U.S. 347, 352–53 (1967).

private, even in an area accessible to the public, may be constitutionally protected."[117] In particular, a person placing a call from a public telephone booth was "surely entitled to assume that the words he utters into the mouthpiece will not be broadcast to the world." A contrary ruling, Stewart explained, would "ignore the vital role that the public telephone has come to play in private communication." Nor did it matter that the walls of the booth were transparent, for what Katz "sought to exclude ... was not the intruding eye" but "the uninvited ear."[118]

Since eavesdropping on Katz's telephone conversations was a "search" within the meaning of the Fourth Amendment, the only remaining question was whether the search was "unreasonable" and therefore unconstitutional. Here, again, the Court adopted precisely the position urged by Schneider and Marks. The "search" was unreasonable because it had taken place without a warrant. It was "clear" that a constitutionally acceptable warrant *could* have been issued for "narrowly circumscribed" monitoring of the telephone booths: that, Justice Stewart explained, was the import of *Osborn* and *Berger*.[119] By foregoing a warrant, the FBI had circumvented " 'the procedure of antecedent justification' " that was " 'central to the Fourth Amendment.' "[120]

Justice Black, the lone dissenter in *Katz*, objected that calling eavesdropping a "search" distorted the language of the Fourth Amendment and departed without justification from its traditional interpretation—the interpretation applied, for example, in *Olmstead* and *Goldman*.[121] What was striking here was not just that Justice Black wrote only for himself, but that he was arguing in terms wholly alien to the analysis found in the majority opinion. Justice Stewart's opinion for the Court gave little attention to history, and none whatsoever to constitutional language.

Perhaps the most striking thing about the Court's reasoning in *Katz*, though, was how vague and ambiguous it was. Justice Black complained that the majority had neglected language and history in favor of "broad policy discussions and philosophical discourses on such nebulous subjects as privacy."[122] But in fact there was little discussion of policy or philosophy in the Court's opinion. In particular, Stewart explicitly disavowed any reliance on "a general constitutional 'right to

---

[117] *Id.* at 350–51.

[118] *Id.* at 352.

[119] *Id.* at 355–56.

[120] *Id.* at 359 (quoting *Osborn*, 385 U.S. at 330).

[121] *Id.* at 364–74 (Black, J., dissenting).

[122] *Id.* at 364.

privacy' ": the protections of the Fourth Amendment went beyond that, and often had "nothing to do with privacy."[123] Stewart's opinion did contain a hint of a policy argument: the suggestion that finding the Fourth Amendment inapplicable in this case would "ignore the vital role that the public telephone has come to play in private communication."[124] That aside, though, the affirmative case for deeming the monitoring of the telephone booths a "search" was left largely unstated; the Court simply asserted that a telephone booth customer was "surely entitled" to Fourth Amendment protection of his conversation.[125] More broadly, the Court gave little indication what kinds of considerations it thought should substitute for the traditional focus on property rights in interpreting the Fourth Amendment. The most famous sentence in *Katz*—the ringing declaration that "the Fourth Amendment protects people, not places"—sounded modern, forward-looking, and pragmatic. But it begged the critical question: *How* did the Fourth Amendment protect people? What rights did it provide? No wonder one prominent scholar, commenting on this aphorism, complained that its "only merit" was "its brevity."[126]

In a short concurring opinion, Justice Harlan tried to clarify the import of the Court's decision. He explained that the Fourth Amendment protected "reasonable expectation[s] of privacy," which required "first that a person have exhibited an actual (subjective) expectation of privacy and, second, that the expectation be one that society is prepared to recognize as 'reasonable.'" And, notwithstanding the rhetoric of the majority opinion, Harlan suggested that Fourth Amendment protection typically *did* attach to particular locations. *Of course*, he agreed, the Fourth Amendment protected "people, not places." But the question was what protection it gave those people, and answering that question would ordinarily require "reference to a 'place.'" In *Katz* itself, Harlan reasoned, the Fourth Amendment applied only because "an enclosed telephone booth is an area where, like a home . . . occupants' expectations of freedom from intrusion are recognized as reasonable."[127] At least for some purposes, a man's telephone booth *was* his castle.

---

[123] *Id.* at 350–51 (opinion of the Court).

[124] *Id.* at 352.

[125] *Id.*

[126] Taylor, *supra* note 18, at 112. Professor Taylor's reaction was not idiosyncratic. *See, e.g.,* Edmund W. Kitch, Katz v. United States: *The Limits of the Fourth Amendment*, 1968 Sup. Ct. Rev. 133, 135 (noting that, in overturning "the property principle of *Olmstead* . . . [t]he Court has been eager to abandon the limiting principle of the past, but inattentive to the more difficult task of articulating and applying a limiting principle for the future").

[127] 389 U.S. at 360–61 (Harlan, J., concurring).

There was one final ambiguity in *Katz*, this one narrower and entirely explicit. In a footnote, the Court expressly declined to reach the question "[w]hether safeguards other than prior authorization by a magistrate would satisfy the Fourth Amendment in a situation involving the national security."[128] Justice White made clear in his concurring opinion that he thought national security wiretaps were different: "successive Presidents" had authorized them without warrants, and appropriately so.[129] Justice Douglas, on the other hand, saw utterly no reason to exempt national security wiretaps from the warrant requirement, and his concurring opinion, setting forth this view, was joined by Justice Brennan.[130] As we will see, this was an issue to which the Court soon returned.

Electronic Surveillance After *Katz*

The Supreme Court's decision in *Katz* had a three-part legacy. First, it established an enduring legal framework for electronic surveillance. Second, and more broadly, it set the terms for future discussions of the reach of the Fourth Amendment. Third, and even more broadly, it signaled the arrival of a new, more forward-looking approach to the Fourth Amendment, an approach less focused on text and history and more focused on current realities of law enforcement. The broader aspects of this legacy—the lessons *Katz* taught about the overall scope of the Fourth Amendment and about the role of text and history in search-and-seizure jurisprudence—are the ones that receive the most attention today. At the time that *Katz* was decided, though, what seemed most important about it was the compromise it struck regarding electronic surveillance.

Before *Katz*, as we have seen, there was a good deal of uncertainty both about whether electronic surveillance was permissible at all, with or without a warrant. Indeed there was uncertainty about whether court orders authorizing wiretapping or bugging could comply the traditional restrictions on warrants, including the particularity requirement explicitly imposed by the Fourth Amendment. Many lawyers read the Supreme Court's opinion in *Berger v. New York* to answer that question in the negative. When the Supreme Court decided *Katz*, what seemed most newsworthy about the decision was the green light it gave for electronic surveillance warrants. The *New York Times*, for example, reported that the Court's abandonment of the trespass test "had been expected by most lawyers."[131] The surprise in the decision was the statement, by a

---

[128] *Id.* at 358 note 23 (opinion of the Court).

[129] *Id.* at 362–63 (White, J., concurring).

[130] *Id.* at 359 (Douglas, J., concurring).

[131] Fred P. Graham, *New Tack in Bugging*, N.Y. Times, Dec. 20, 1967, at 37.

solid majority of the Court, that the bugging of the telephone booth would have been lawful if only the agents had sought prior judicial approval.[132]

The *Katz* compromise—electronic surveillance is lawful, as long as conducted pursuant to warrant—had immediate and lasting effect. The Johnson Administration had backed a bill, then pending before Congress, that would have outlawed bugging and wiretapping except in national security cases. The bill faced strong opposition even before *Katz*, but whatever chances it had for passage were eliminated by the Supreme Court's unambiguous embrace of electronic surveillance warrants.[133] At the same time, *Katz* gave a shot in the arm to legislative efforts at both the federal and state levels to establish clear procedures for court-ordered electronic eavesdropping.[134] At the federal level, those efforts soon culminated in Title III of the Omnibus Crime Control and Safe Streets Act of 1968, which to this day provides the principal regulatory framework for electronic surveillance orders issued by federal courts, and minimum requirements for similar warrants issued by state courts.[135] Title III was consciously crafted to comply with requirements of *Berger* and *Katz*: it requires not only a showing of probable cause, but also strict time limits on authorized monitoring, procedures to minimize interception of unrelated conversations, and prompt notification to the subjects of the investigation following termination of the surveillance.[136]

Title III in turn has served as the model for a range of other surveillance statutes, at both the federal and the state levels. A key move in this regard was the extension of the *Katz* compromise to national security wiretaps. As we have seen, the Court in *Katz* sidestepped the question whether warrants were required for electronic eavesdropping for purposes of national security. Congress, too, dodged the question when enacting Title III, which by its terms did not apply to actions taken by the President to protect against a "clear and present danger to the structure and existence of the Government."[137] The Supreme Court finally addressed the question head-on in 1972, in a case with facts far more dramatic than those in *Katz*.

---

[132] *See id.*; Graham, *supra* note 81, at 1; Fred J. Ostrow, *Supreme Court Rules Bugging is Subject to Legal Standards*, L.A. Times, Dec. 19, 1967, at 1.

[133] *See* Ostrow, *supra* note 132, at 1.

[134] *See, e.g.,* Graham, *supra* note 131, at 37.

[135] 18 U.S.C. §§ 2510–2522.

[136] *See, e.g.,* Kerr, *supra* note 15, at 850–52.

[137] 18 U.S.C. § 2511(3) (subsequently repealed).

The case began in September 1968, three short months after the passage of Title III, when a bomb went off at the CIA recruiting office in Ann Arbor Michigan.[138] Three members of a local radical group, the "White Panthers," were eventually arrested and charged with the bombing. During pretrial proceedings the government disclosed that conversations involving one of the defendants had been intercepted in 1969, when he spoke over the telephone with members of the Black Panther Party in Berkeley and San Francisco whose lines the government was tapping. Those wiretaps had been conducted without a warrant, but the government took the position that they were constitutional because President Nixon's Attorney General, John Mitchell, had authorized them in the interest of national security. The district judge in Michigan, Damon Keith, disagreed. He ordered the government to turn over the contents of the conversations to the defense, for purposes of determining the extent to which the illegal wiretapping had tainted the prosecution's evidence. The government asked the Sixth Circuit to set aside Judge Keith's order. (The case is sometimes referred to as *Keith*, instead of its more cumbersome, formal title: *United States v. United States District Court*.) When the Sixth Circuit refused, the government sought and received certiorari from the Supreme Court.

Once the Supreme Court reached the merits of the controversy, however, it too agreed with Judge Keith.[139] Writing for the Court, Justice Powell explained that the requirement of judicial preauthorization was so central to the logic of the Fourth Amendment that it applied even in cases of national security. Justice Douglas concurred separately, reiterating his view that conforming an electronic eavesdropping warrant with the particularity requirement of the Fourth Amendment "would be extremely difficult if not impossible," and that therefore wiretapping and bugging should be deemed flatly unconstitutional.[140] But by 1972 his was a voice in the wilderness. The *Katz* compromise had triumphed.

Congress, in fact, extended the model of court orders for electronic surveillance even further than the Supreme Court required. The ruling in *Keith*, for example, applied only to "the domestic aspects of national security"; the Court expressly declined to reach "the issues which may be involved with respect to activities of foreign powers or their agents."[141] Rather than wait for a ruling on those issues, though, Congress went ahead and created a separate apparatus, parallel to Title

---

[138] *See* William B. Treml, *City CIA Office Bombed*, Ann Arbor News, Sept. 30, 1968, at 1.

[139] United States v. United States District Court, 407 U.S. 297 (1972).

[140] *Id.* at 324–34 (Douglas, J., concurring).

[141] *Id.* at 321–22 (opinion of the Court).

III, for issuing surveillance orders in foreign intelligence cases, an apparatus that includes a special district court and a special court of appeals, each of which meets in secret.[142] Congress later did something similar for the monitoring of digital communications and for cordless telephones, statutorily requiring court orders without waiting to see if the Supreme Court would demand them.[143]

Congress has even extended the Title III model to certain forms of electronic surveillance that the Supreme Court has declared unregulated by the Fourth Amendment. For reasons we will explore later, the Supreme Court has held that neither pen registers, which record the numbers dialed by a telephone, nor trap and trace devices, which record similar information for incoming calls, constitute "searches" or "seizures" within the meaning of the Fourth Amendment, so neither requires a warrant. Nonetheless, Congress has required federal investigators seeking to install either of these devices to first seek a court order.[144] These are not warrants: no showing of probable cause is necessary. But it is noteworthy that, even in this setting, Congress has chosen to follow the general pattern of Title III, authorizing the surveillance but requiring a court order. The same pattern was later followed for monitoring the destination of outgoing email messages, and the source of incoming messages.[145]

The Title III model for electronic monitoring is by now so firmly rooted that courts have applied it, without hesitation, to covert *video* surveillance—without any statutory authorization. In the immediate aftermath of the Supreme Court's decision in *Katz*, some commentators thought it "unlikely" that the decision would be applied outside the context of "overheard conversations."[146] And Title III applies by its terms only to monitoring of "conversations."[147] In the 1980s, though, law enforcement agents began to apply for warrants to install and operate hidden cameras in offices, safe houses, and private yards where they suspected drugs were being sold, money was being laundered, currency

---

[142] Foreign Intelligence Surveillance Act of 1978, Pub. L. No. 95–511, 92 Stat. 1783 (codified in pertinent part, as amended, at 50 18 U.S.C. §§ 1801–1811).

[143] Electronic Communications Privacy Act of 1986, Pub. L. No. 99–508, 100 Stat. 1848, (codified as amended at 18 U.S.C. §§ 2510–21) (digital communications); Communications Assistance for Law Enforcement Act, Pub. L. No. 103–414, § 202(a), 108 Stat. 4279 (1994) (codified at 18 U.S.C. § 2510(1), (12)) (cordless telephones).

[144] *See* 18 U.S.C. § 3121(a).

[145] *See* Pub. L. 107–56, Title II, § 216(c)(1)-(4), 115 Stat. 290 (amending 18 U.S.C. § 3127).

[146] Dash, *supra* note 42, at 304 note 44.

[147] *E.g.*, 18 U.S.C. § 2511(1).

was being counterfeited, bombing were being planned, or other serious crimes were being carried out. Uniformly, courts analogized to audio surveillance and reasoned that the requirements set forth in Title III should govern the constitutionality of video monitoring, as well.[148] By the end of the century it was well established that the statutory requirements for wiretapping defined the constitutional bounds on video surveillance—a result one commentator aptly characterized as "extraordinary."[149] There could be no clearer testament to the triumph of the *Katz* compromise. By now it seems obvious to most lawyers and judges that the Fourth Amendment permits electronic surveillance, but only pursuant to judicial warrant. The compromise seems so obvious, in fact, that it is easy to forget how controversial it was, before it received the Supreme Court's blessing in *Katz*.

The Scope of the Fourth Amendment After *Katz*

If Title III has extended outside the context of intercepted conversations, the *Katz* decision, which provided the blueprint to Title III, has been applied even more broadly. *Katz* quickly came to be understood as providing a new test for determining the scope of the Fourth Amendment, replacing the old "trespass" test of *Olmstead* and *Goldman*. The new test, drawn from Justice Harlan's concurring opinion in *Katz*, asked whether a particular investigative step infringed on a "reasonable expectation of privacy"—defined as "an actual (subjective) expectation of privacy ... that society is prepared to recognize as 'reasonable.' "[150] Justice Stewart's opinion for the Court in *Katz* seemed to promise that the new test would differ dramatically in its application from the old, now discredited requirement of a physical trespass into a "protected place." That was the import, presumably, of the Court's grand declaration that "the Fourth Amendment protects people, not places," and of the Court's elaboration of that remark: "What a person knowingly exposes to the public, even in his own home or office is not a subject of Fourth Amendment protection," but "what he seeks to preserve as private, even in an area accessible to the public, may be constitutionally protected." Regardless where a person went, the Court explained, "he is entitled to know that he will remain free from unreasonable searches and seizures."[151]

---

[148] The cases are discussed in Ric Simmons, *Can* Winston *Save Us From Big Brother? The Need for Judicial Consistency in Regulating Hyper–Intrusive Searches*, 55 Rutgers L. Rev. 547, 557–60 (2003).

[149] *Id.* at 559.

[150] *Katz*, 389 U.S. at 360–61 (Harlan, J., concurring).

[151] *Id.* at 351, 359 (opinion of the Court).

The Court lost little time adopting Justice Harlan's suggestion, in his concurring opinion in *Katz*, that the Fourth Amendment protected a person's "reasonable expectations of privacy"—expectations that the person actually held, and that were objectively reasonable. The Court embraced this gloss on *Katz* in *Terry v. Ohio*,[152] decided just six months after *Katz*, and it has adhered to it ever since. But both the subjective and the objective prongs of the "reasonable expectation of privacy" test soon raised difficulties. Conditioning Fourth Amendment protection on a suspect's "actual (subjective) expectation of privacy" had the odd implication that people who suspected the government were spying on them (of whom there were quite a few by the end of the 1960s), might for that very reason lose much of their protection against what they feared.[153] That in turn suggested the government could defeat expectations of privacy simply by declaring its intention to violate them: for example, by "announcing half-hourly on television ... that we were all being placed under comprehensive electronic surveillance."[154] To avoid these results, the Court placed greater emphasis on the objective prong of Justice Harlan's test, the requirement "that the expectation be one that society is prepared to recognize as 'reasonable' "[155] But how were judges to tell which expectations society was in fact "prepared to recognize" as "reasonable"? The inquiry proved distressingly indeterminate, and many observers, on and off the Court, came to think it circular: an expectation of privacy was reasonable if the Court was willing to protect it.[156]

Perhaps for that reason, the results reached under the new, "expectation of privacy" test looked surprisingly like the results that would have reached under the old, "trespass" test. The "open fields" doctrine, for example, which both sides in *Katz* had argued was inconsistent with a more flexible focus on reasonable expectations, turned out to survive under the new test. The Court reasoned that owners of undeveloped land could not reasonably expect privacy on their property, even if they put up fences and "No Trespassing" signs, in part because measures of that kind generally were not effective in barring the public from viewing

---

[152] 392 U.S. 1, 9 (1968).

[153] *See, e.g.,* John M. Burkoff, *When Is a Search Not a "Search"? Fourth Amendment Doublethink*, 15 Toledo L. Rev. 515, 527 (1984); John M. Junker, *The Structure of the Fourth Amendment: The Scope of the Protection*, 79 J. Crim. L. & Criminology 1105, 1166 (1989).

[154] Anthony G. Amsterdam, *Perspectives on the Fourth Amendment*, 58 Minn. L. Rev. 349, 384 (1974).

[155] *See, e.g.,* Hudson v. Palmer, 468 U.S. 517, 525 & N.7 (1984); Smith v. Maryland, 442 U.S. 735, 740 note 5 (1979); Burkoff, *supra* note 153, at 528–29.

[156] Justice Scalia, for example, made precisely this charge in 1999, in an opinion joined by Justice Thomas. *See* Minnesota v. Carter, 525 U.S. 83, 97 (1998) (Scalia, J., concurring).

vacant land.[157] Peering into a backyard from an airplane flying overhead turned out to violate no reasonable expectation of privacy, because the observation took place from "public navigable airspace" and was "physically nonintrusive."[158] The use of electronic tracking devices did not constitute searches or seizures when used on public highways, but implicated the Fourth Amendment the minute they sent signals from inside a home.[159] Pen registers did not trigger the Fourth Amendment, because a caller had no reasonable expectation of privacy in numbers that he or she "voluntarily conveyed . . . to the telephone company."[160] Garbage left for collection "in an area accessible to the public" was likewise unprotected by the Fourth Amendment.[161] The use of an undercover agent or confidential informant did not constitute a search, even when the agent or informant secretly transmitted or recorded his conversations with the suspect, as long as the suspect was speaking voluntarily: there was no reasonable expectation of privacy in misplaced confidences.[162] The pattern soon became clear. To a remarkable extent, police tactics turned out to violate reasonable expectations of privacy only when they involved physical intrusions into constitutionally protected places.[163]

But not always. Three and a half decades after *Katz*, just when many people had stopped taking the "reasonable expectation of privacy" test seriously, it proved to have surprising vitality. The context was the use of a "thermal imager"—essentially, an infrared camera—to detect the use of high-intensity lamps in a home. By the late 1990s, narcotics investigators around the country were using this tactic to help identify indoor cultivation of marijuana. Every federal appeals court to consider the issue ultimately concluded that pointing a thermal imager at a home infringed on no reasonable expectation of privacy. The reasoning, typically, was that the device simply measured "waste heat" from a public place and involved no physical intrusion—essentially the same considerations that had led the Ninth Circuit, in the pre-*Katz* era, to rule that the Fourth Amendment did not reach the use of a scintillator to detect radiation emitted from within an apartment. Aside from substituting

---

[157] See Oliver v. United States, 466 U.S. 170 (1984).

[158] California v. Ciraolo, 476 U.S. 207, 213–14 (1986); see also Florida v. Riley, 488 U.S. 445 (1989).

[159] See United States v. Karo, 468 U.S. 705 (1984); United States v. Knotts, 460 U.S. 276 (1983).

[160] Smith v. Maryland, 442 U.S. at 745.

[161] California v. Greenwood, 486 U.S. 35, 41 (1988).

[162] See United States v. White, 401 U.S. 745 (1971).

[163] See Kerr, *supra* note 15, at 805–15.

language about "reasonable expectations of privacy" for language about "trespasses," the reasoning in the thermal imaging cases was identical to what it would have under *Olmstead*. None of the lower courts seemed troubled by that, and the Supreme Court was not widely predicted to be, either.[164]

Those predictions proved wrong. When, in *Kyllo v. United States*, the Court finally addressed the constitutionality of thermal imaging, it brushed aside the government's arguments about the absence of physical intrusion. *Katz*, the majority explained, had "rejected such a mechanical interpretation of the Fourth Amendment," and had "decoupled" search-and-seizure law from property rights.[165] Writing for the Court, Justice Scalia—who previously had complained that the "reasonable expectation of privacy" test was entirely circular[166]—now reasoned that the test made a certain amount of sense, at least when it came to protecting the privacy of the home, "the prototypical area ... of protected privacy." Accordingly, Scalia concluded for the majority, the Fourth Amendment generally came into play, and required a warrant, whenever the government wished to use "sense-enhancing technology" to learn anything about the interior of a home that could otherwise have been learned only by a physical intrusion.[167]

There was a good bit of irony, of course, in *Katz* finding vindication in an opinion that placed so much emphasis on the special sanctity of the home. That emphasis is hard to reconcile with the notion that "the Fourth Amendment protects people, not places"—so much so that some commentators thought *Kyllo* a "return to the pre-*Katz* world."[168] But the business about "people, not places" was always something of an empty promise, even before *Kyllo*. The Court sometimes succeeded in decoupling Fourth Amendment law from property rights, but it never proved able to decouple it from geography. The Court never tired of reiterating that "the Fourth Amendment protects people, not places."[169] In case after case, though, the Court made clear that the Fourth Amendment

---

[164] The cases are discussed in David A. Sklansky, *Back to the Future:* Kyllo, Katz, *and Common Law*, 72 Miss. L.J. 143, 169–77 (2002).

[165] 533 U.S. 27, 31, 35 (2001).

[166] *See supra* note 156.

[167] 533 U.S. at 34. The Court left for another day whether the result would be different if the technology was "in general public use." *Id.*

[168] David Cole, *Scalia's Kind of Privacy*, Nation, July 23, 2001, at 6.

[169] *See* Minnesota v. Carter, 525 U.S. 83, 88 (1998); Minnesota v. Olson, 495 U.S. 91, 95. note 5 (1990); Segura v. United States, 468 U.S. 796, 810 (1984); United States v. Mendenhall, 446 U.S. 544, 550 (1980); Smith v. Maryland, 442 U.S. 735, 739 (1979); United States v. Chadwick, 433 U.S. 1, 7, 9 (1977); United States v. Dionisio, 410 U.S. 1, 8 (1973); Desist v. United States, 394 U.S. 244, 246 (1969); Terry v. Ohio, 392 U.S. 1, 9 (1968).

offered heightened protection inside the home.[170] In other places—automobiles, highways, fields, offices, even backyards—Fourth Amendment protection, as a practical matter, either vanished entirely or dropped off dramatically.[171]

The sharp curtailment of Fourth Amendment protection outside the home has had large costs, particularly for people not rich enough to live in large and comfortable homes.[172] Still, there is a good deal to be said for the notion, first put forward in Justice Harlan's concurring opinion in *Katz*, that the reasonableness of a person's expectation of privacy typically will depend heavily on where the person is—and even for the further proposition that searches of homes, in particular, should face special restrictions.[173] To say that the Fourth Amendment provides the same protection on the street as in the home would be to say that it provides no greater protection in the home than on the street.[174] Even Justice Stewart's opinion for the Court in *Silverman v. United States*, which laid the groundwork for the overruling of *Olmstead* in *Katz*, stressed that any "sane, decent, civilized society must provide some . . . insulated enclosure, some enclave, some inviolate place."[175]

The difficulty, though, has been reconciling this kind of sensitivity to place with the specific result in *Katz*, which continues to strike most people as correct and important. Justice Harlan's tactic was to analogize a telephone booth to a house. An "enclosed telephone booth," he reasoned, was "an area where, like a home," a person could reasonably expect privacy; it was "a temporarily private place."[176] Justice Scalia read *Katz* the same way in *Kyllo*: an occupant was entitled to rely on "the privacy of the telephone booth."[177] But that reading of *Katz* seems

---

[170] *See, e.g.*, Wilson v. Layne, 526 U.S. 603 (1999); United States v. Karo, 468 U.S. 705, 714 (1984); *Segura*, 468 U.S. at 810; Payton v. New York, 445 U.S. 573 (1980).

[171] *See, e.g.*, Christopher Slobogin, *Technologically-Assisted Physical Surveillance: The American Bar Association's Tentative Draft Standards*, 10 Harv. J.L. & Tech. 383, 390–91 (1997). For the particularly low level of protection provided inside automobiles, see, e.g., California v. Acevedo, 500 U.S. 565 (1991); *Chadwick*, 433 U.S. at 12.

[172] *See* Amsterdam, *supra* note 154, at 404; William J. Stuntz, *The Distribution of Fourth Amendment Privacy*, 67 Geo. Wash. L. Rev. 1265, 1270 (1999).

[173] *See* Sklansky, *supra* note 164, at 190–94.

[174] *Cf.* Taylor, *supra* note 18, at 114 ("No doubt it is comforting to be told that one's privacy is as fully protected in a public telephone booth as it is at home. But it is less reassuring to realize that one's privacy is no better protected at home than in a public telephone booth.").

[175] 365 U.S. 505, 511 note 4 (quoting United States v. On Lee, 193 F.2d 306, 315–16 (2d Cir. 1951) (Frank, J., dissenting)).

[176] *Katz*, 389 U.S. at 360–61 (Harlan, J., concurring).

[177] *Kyllo*, 533 U.S. at 32–33.

to trivialize the opinion, and to make it close to irrelevant in a world where cellular telephones are rapidly proliferating and where pay telephones, when they still exist, rarely are enclosed. Even when Katz was decided, this part of Harlan's argument seemed implausible. "Would the case have been different," asked one commentator incredulously, "if the pay phone had not been surrounded by a booth?"[178]

Of course, even if Fourth Amendment protection *generally* is triggered by a place, it might not *always* be. Sometimes, perhaps, Fourth Amendment privacy is triggered by a *communication*. The Court itself once described *Katz* as recognizing that "that the Fourth Amendment protects a person's private communications as well as his private premises."[179] Some commentators, as we have seen, read *Katz* that way when the decision came out.[180] There is a good deal to be said for that reading.[181] It accommodates the intuition that the ruling did not rely on the architecture of the telephone booth, without threatening the notion that Fourth Amendment protection is *usually* place-dependent. It makes full sense of Justice Stewart's declaration in *Katz* that "[t]o read the Constitution more narrowly is to ignore the vital role that the public telephone has come to play in private communication." It accords with the special protection that search-and-seizure law has long provided to letters, and with the explicit reference in the text of the Fourth Amendment to the security of "papers," along with "persons, houses, . . . and effects."[182] And, looking to the future, it provides a promising point of entry for applying the Fourth Amendment in cyberspace—which, after all, has been memorably described as "that place you are in when you are talking on the telephone."[183]

Nevertheless, by the end of the 1960s *Katz* was almost universally understood as a decision about the overall scope of the Fourth Amendment, not a decision about the application of the Fourth Amendment to conversations. The Fourth Amendment protected "people, not places"— and not, by implication, activities. It might have been different had the Court declared in *Katz* that the Fourth amendment protected "communications, not just places." But that would not have had the same ring.

---

[178] Kitch, *supra* note 126, at 140.

[179] Alderman v. United States, 394 U.S. 165, 178 (1969).

[180] *See supra* note 146 and accompanying text.

[181] For a more extended argument, see Sklansky, *supra* note 164, at 194–200.

[182] *See* United States v. Van Leeuwen, 397 U.S. 249 (1970); *Ex parte* Jackson, 96 U.S. 727, 733 (1878); Eric Schnapper, *Unreasonable Searches and Seizures of Papers*, 71 Va. L. Rev. 869 (1985).

[183] Philip Elmer–DeWitt, *Welcome to Cyberspace: What Is It? Where Is It? And How Do We Get There?*, Time, Mar. 22, 1995, at 4, 8 (quoting John Perry Barlow).

Nor, as we will see, would it have signaled so strongly the Court's commitment to reorient Fourth Amendment law away from the past and toward the future.

Katz and the Future

We have examined two parts of *Katz*'s legacy: the now-pervasive model it created for the legal treatment of electronic surveillance, and the surprisingly uncertain impact it had on the general scope of Fourth Amendment protection. There remains a third and final aspect of *Katz*'s legacy: the prominent role it played in the Supreme Court's efforts, in the 1960s, to modernize search-and-seizure law, by turning its focus away from the past, toward the present and the future.

Through the first half of the twentieth century, Fourth Amendment law was strikingly rooted in the past. The constitutional treatment of searches and seizures was heavily guided by the eighteenth-century text of the Fourth Amendment and by general warrants and writs of assistance, the chief abuses against which the amendment originally took aim. *Olmstead*, as we have seen, exemplified this approach. "Searches" and "seizures" within the meaning of the Fourth Amendment required a physical trespass on a "person", "paper," "house," or "effect"—because these were the only items given explicit protection in the constitutional text, and general warrants and writs of assistance both had authorized physical trespasses on them. Dissenting in *Olmstead*, Justice Brandeis famously argued for a more forward-looking interpretation of the Fourth Amendment, an approach that offered protection against the new threats to privacy made possible by advancing technology.

Although the Court's opinion in *Katz* disavowed reliance on Brandeis's notion that the Fourth Amendment helped to create a general right to privacy, it vindicated, in several different ways, his call to modernize search-and-seizure law. First, the "reasonable expectation of privacy" test—especially when read in light of the Court's emphasis on "the vital role that the public telephone has come to play in private communication"—focused attention on the lived realities of modern life, rather on the form that abusive searches and seizures took in the eighteenth century. Second, the Court's opinion, like the argument by *Katz*'s counsel that it largely followed, paid little attention to constitutional history and virtually none to constitutional text. The Court's methodology in *Katz* signaled the arrival of a new consensus, shared by the Court and its academic critics, that when interpreting the Fourth Amendment, "[i]ts language is no help and neither is its history."[184] Third, the premium that *Katz* placed on *mobility*—on Fourth Amend-

---

[184] Amsterdam, *supra* note 154, at 395.

ment protection following a person wherever he or she may be[185]—responded to the modern, urban values of speed, fluidity, and spontaneity.[186] That may have been why the business about the Fourth Amendment protecting "people, not places" resonated so strongly, despite the maddening difficulty of giving the notion some content.

The modernizing aspects of *Katz* were mirrored in certain other criminal procedure decisions of the 1960s, particularly *Terry v. Ohio*,[187] decided the year after *Katz*. *Terry* shared with *Katz* the spirit of doctrinal iconoclasm, the turn away from text and history as interpretative guides, and the focus on modern urban realities.

Katz may well have represented the high point of the Court's enthusiasm for refocusing Fourth Amendment law on the present and future rather than the past. Even *Terry*, by sanctioning the "stop and frisk" tactic, may have signaled the limits of the Court's enthusiasm for the unrestrained freedom of modern urban life. As we have seen, the "reasonable expectation of privacy" test turned out, in application, to have a surprising similarity to the old, "trespass" test that the Court had jettisoned. And by the 1990s the Court was rediscovering in search-and-seizure law, as elsewhere, the attractions of originalism—a development spurred in part by the frustrations some Justices experienced attempting to apply functional, ahistoric doctrines like the "reasonable expectation of privacy" test.[188]

Still, the modernizing aspirations of *Katz* never really lost their allure. Even Justice Scalia, who led the Court's swing toward originalism in search-and-seizure law as elsewhere, stressed in *Kyllo* the need to "take the long view, from the original meaning of the Fourth Amendment forward," in order to limit the "power of technology to shrink the realm of guaranteed privacy."[189] In proclaiming that Fourth Amendment law protected "people, not places," the Court seemed to promise search-and-seizure law that was not only less tied to specific locations, but also less hidebound, more open to the opportunities and needs of a modern, mobile society. The Justices have never quite made good on that promise, but they keep repeating it, because it retains much of its appeal.

---

[185] *See* Katz, 389 U.S. at 359.

[186] On these values, see, e.g., James Miller, Democracy Is in the Streets: From Port Huron to the Siege of Chicago 147 (paperback ed. 1994).

[187] 392 U.S. 1 (1968). *Terry* is the subject of a separate chapter in this volume.

[188] *See* David A. Sklansky, *The Fourth Amendment and Common Law*, 100 Colum. L. Rev. 1739, 1745–70 (2000).

[189] 533 U.S. at 34, 40.

8

Duncan v. Louisiana: How Bigotry in the Bayou Led to the Federal Regulation of State Juries

Nancy J. King*

The criminal jury remains one of the nation's most vital democratic institutions, enabling ordinary citizens to block tyrannical action by government. It is fitting then that the case in which the Court extended the right to a jury trial to state defendants began in one of the most undemocratic and hierarchical communities in the United States in the 1960s—Plaquemines Parish, Louisiana, 50 miles south of New Orleans.

In 1965, the parish remained in the iron grip of segregationist Judge Leander H. Perez, Sr., a cigar-chomping, thickset, fist-clenching, explosive political leader,[1] with a deep voice[2] and a grey pompadour.[3] Perez had amassed a fortune after welcoming the oil industry to the parish and helping himself to some of the resulting revenues.[4] Serving as District Judge in the parish for five years, then as District Attorney and Parish Council President for nearly fifty years after that, he exercised unquestioned control over all political offices and government services in the parish. He was enormously influential in state politics, saving Huey

* Special thanks to Janet Hirt, Vanderbilt University Law School Librarian and Lecturer in Law, for her miraculous research, and to Richard Sobol, George Strickler, and Dorothy Worblette, who kindly spoke with me by telephone.

[1] Reese Cleghorn, *The Perils of Plaquemines: Leander H. Perez*, New Republic, Sept. 21, 1963, at 8.

[2] Lester Velie, *Kingfish of the Dixiecrats*, Collier's, Dec. 17, 1949, at 10.

[3] Richard Austin Smith, *Oil, Brimstone, and "Judge" Perez*, Fortune, March 1958, at 145.

[4] *Segregation Planner: Leander Henry Perez Sr.*, N.Y. Times, Nov. 28, 1960, at 34 (noting also that Perez had a house in New Orleans, on fashionable Newcomb Boulevard just down the street from Federal Judge J. Skelly Wright, who ordered the integration of New Orleans schools and who bore the brunt of Perez's most violent vocal attacks).

Long from impeachment, and masterminding Earl Long into the governor's mansion.[5] The state's "most ardent segregationist,"[6] Perez was convinced that Jews were Communists who wanted to conquer America for the Soviet Union by undermining Caucasian stock with miscegenation.[7]

To motivate segregationists, Perez would ask "How would you like it if your little girl came back home ravished from a forced racially integrated school?"[8] "Don't wait for your daughter to be raped by these Congolese," he would exhort his followers. "Don't wait until the burrheads are forced into your schools. Do something about it now."[9]

Violence followed his speeches.[10] A Catholic school that dared to admit African–American children had its windows shot out and was then bombed.[11] Perez's resistance to integration of Catholic schools led the

---

[5] Velie, *supra* note 2; Lester Velie, *'Democracy' in the Deep Delta*, Collier's, Dec. 24, 1949, at 21.

[6] John G. Warner, *Sheriff's Aide Among 17 Seized in New Orleans School Fracas*, Wash. Post, Nov. 16, 1960, at A3; James F. Clayton, *New Orleans Now Realistic in Desegregation Attitude*, Wash. Post, Sept. 11, 1961, at A6 ("the most militant of all"); Claude Sitton, *Citizens' Council Fuels Louisiana Resistance*, N.Y. Times, Nov. 27, 1960, at E6 ("chief of [the] segregationist triumvirate").

[7] Glen Jeansonne, *Leander Perez: Remembering the Bonaparte of the Bayou on His 100th Birthday*, Baton Rouge Sunday Advoc., Jul. 14, 1991, at 17 (quoted as saying Negroes are "animals right out the jungle," and that there are two kinds of Negroes: "Bad ones are niggers and good ones are darkies"; attributed the movement to desegregate Southern schools "back to all those Jews who were supposed to have been cremated at Buchenwald and Dachau but weren't, and Roosevelt allowed 2 million of them illegal entry into our country"); Claude Sitton, *Citizens' Council Fuels Louisiana Resistance*, N.Y. Times, Nov. 27, 1960, at E6 (Perez regarded desegregation as part of a communist conspiracy to overthrow the United States).

[8] Claude Sitton, *Atlanta Sit–In Tension Imperils Peaceful Integration of Schools*, N.Y. Times, Feb. 19, 1961, at 71.

[9] *Segregation Planner: Leander Henry Perez Sr.*, N.Y. Times, Nov. 28, 1960, at 34; *Racist Leader*, Time, Dec. 12, 1960, at 21 (reports this as said at a meeting of the New Orleans Citizens Council, responding to the four Negro girls in the city's first integrated schools).

[10] Claude Sitton, *2,000 Youths Riot in New Orleans*, N.Y. Times, Nov. 17, 1960, at 30 (reporting that mobs of anti-integration demonstrators pelted ice at bus passengers, knocked a woman unconscious, tossed lighted paper wads into cars, smashed windshields with bats in cars and trucks driven by Blacks).

[11] John Corporon, Church Triumphant in New Orleans Desegregation Fight, Wash. Post, Mar. 24, 1963, at E3; Cleghorn, *supra* note 1 (reporting that Our Lady of Good Harbor school was bombed when a gasoline ignited explosion after a woman called that afternoon saying if the school opened with any Negroes "we're going to blow up the school and you in it"; the priest of Our Lady complained gunfire had wrecked windows) Glen Jeansonne, Leander Perez: Boss of the Delta 267–70 (1977).

archbishop of New Orleans to excommunicate him.[12] When court-ordered desegregation came to the state, Perez pushed through the Louisiana legislature a concurrent resolution warning banks and businesses that compliance with the federal court order was illegal and that violators would lose their funds.[13]

Voting rights and other civil liberties in the parish suffered as well. The "Bonaparte of the Bayou"[14] selected the occupant of each post. Elections were a sham. Perez once said of democracy, "I hate that word."[15] One of his candidates was found to have received 1800 more votes than there were voters registered, causing the unsurprised residents of New Orleans to conclude, "The muskrats must be voting down there."[16] Voters voted in alphabetical order in one election; in another, Babe Ruth, Charlie Chaplin, Herbert Hoover were registered to vote.[17] By August 1965, the United States Attorney General declared Plaquemines Parish one of the nine most discriminatory counties in the nation, with less than 100 of more than 2000 eligible African–American voters registered to vote.[18] After the voting registrar of the parish failed her own voting test, being unable to calculate age based on birth date,[19] and federal investigators arrived, the parish police jury took out an advertisement urging readers not to cooperate with the federal agents.[20] Eventually federal registrars were deployed to the parish, but Perez used them to boost registration of new white voters, outstripping the number of newly registered African–American voters.[21] Perez forbade the local librarian to

---

[12] JACK BASS, UNLIKELY HEROES 287 (1981).

[13] Sitton, *supra* note 10.

[14] Jeansonne, *supra* note 7; Richard Austin Smith, *Oil, Brimstone, and "Judge" Perez,* FORTUNE, March 1958, at 145 (dubbing Perez "the swampland Caesar").

[15] JAMES CONAWAY, JUDGE: THE LIFE AND TIMES OF LEANDER PEREZ 63 (1973).

[16] Jack Langguth, *Louisiana Parish Fights Pentagon: Leander Perez Keeps Area Bastion of Segregation,* N.Y. TIMES, Sept. 5, 1963, at 20.

[17] Jeansonne, *supra* note 7.

[18] John Herbers, *9 Counties to Get Vote Aides Today,* N.Y. TIMES, Aug. 10, 1965, at 1; *La. County Resists FBI Vote Probe,* WASH. POST, Aug. 19, 1961, at A2 (reporting only 44 of 4135 non-white voters registered). *See also* Homer Bigart, *Parish of Leander Perez Shaken As 50 Negroes Register to Vote,* N.Y. TIMES, Aug. 11, 1965, at 20 (reporting until today only 96 of more than 2000 eligible black voters have registered).

[19] Claude Sitton, *Atlanta Sit–In Tension Imperils Peaceful Integration of Schools,* N.Y. TIMES, Feb. 19, 1961, at 71; *Louisiana Registrar Fails Test She Gives to Poll Applicants,* N.Y. TIMES, May 6, 1961, at p. 23.

[20] *Panel Exhorts Voters: Louisianans Urged to Oppose Rights Commission Inquiry,* N.Y. TIMES, Aug. 19, 1961, at 10 ("Tell them they are not welcome.").

[21] Robert E. Baker, *Katzenbach Gives Defense of Use of Federal Registrars,* WASH. POST, Oct. 1, 1965, at A1.

order books discussing the United Nations, Franklin Delano Roosevelt, or any book "showing a liberal viewpoint," and barred African Americans from checking out books.[22]

He enforced his control over the political, economic, and social life of the parish using first his power as District Attorney, an office he held from 1924 until 1960, when he turned it over to his son, Leander Perez, Jr., then his position as parish Commission Council president from 1961 to 1967 when the presidency passed to his other son, Chalin.[23] Said the elder Perez, "Always take the offensive. The defensive ain't worth a damn."[24] To deter civil rights activists from coming to Plaquemines, Perez converted an abandoned fort in the middle of a swamp into a concentration camp for "racial demonstrators." Accessible only by boat, crawling with snakes, and mosquitoes so thick that cattle couldn't breathe,[25] the fort was given an electrified fence and guard towers by Perez. He gave tours to television crews in which he explained just how he would confine agitators.[26]

In August of 1966, the United States Department of Justice, federal District Judge Christenberry and the Perez establishment were engaged in the opening battles of a vicious desegregation fight. After the school board was notified of the Justice Department's complaint in July,[27] Perez's council order transferred all public school property to the Parish Council.[28] He announced the establishment of a private school for whites.[29] White public school teachers signed contracts with the new private schools after the school board notified them that new contracts

---

[22] Langguth, *supra* note 16; *see also Louisiana Librarian Resigns Charging Political Interference*, Libr. J., May 1, 1962, at 1754.

[23] Bigart, *supra* note 18; *Perezes lose ruling on telling wealth*, Baton Rouge Morning Advoc., June 29, 1985, at 23D.

[24] *Racist Leader*, *supra* note 9.

[25] Jeansonne, *supra* note 7; *Our Man on the Mississippi* (NBC television broadcast, Feb. 2, 1964) ("The place is useless for any ordinary purpose. For example, cattle cannot be kept here because the mosquitoes are so thick the cattle will breathe in mosquitoes until they choke to death").

[26] *Id.; Prison–Perez Style: Ready for Race Demonstrators*, U.S. News & World Rep., Nov. 4, 1963, at 16 (Parish has leased the 200–year-old Fort St. Phillip, and fitted the powder magazines out as a prison. It is surrounded by water. On hand are two boats equipped with cattle pens; into these, Mr. Perez told a newsman, "We can pack a hundred demonstrators . . . if necessary."); Jeansonne, *supra* note 11, at 280–83.

[27] *Perez's Parish Sued by U.S. over Schools*, N.Y. Times, Jul. 22, 1966, at 9 (U.S. files suit to desegregate Plaquemines Parish schools).

[28] Jeansonne, *supra* note 11, at 288–89.

[29] *Id.* at 298–302; *Former Perez Home to Take White Pupils*, Wash. Post, Sept. 3, 1966, at A2.

with public schools would not be forthcoming.[30] Pianos, audio equipment, maps, aquariums, athletic equipment, textbooks, and new school buses left with the white teachers and students for the new private schools.[31]

By the start of the school year, the five public high schools in the parish had only about half of the students they'd had the year before. At some public schools gyms and auditoriums were reserved for the use of white students from private schools. Public school students had to forego assemblies, organized athletics, and field trips. Damage to the public schools from devastating hurricane Betsy the previous year was ignored,[32] the prices of school lunches tripled, and bookmobiles (the only library service) were rerouted to the new private schools.

Bert Grant and Bernard St. Ann, two African–American boys about 12 years old began to attend the formerly all-white Boothville Venice High School that September.[33] They were immediately physically assaulted, threatened, and harassed.[34] On October 18, after being threatened with violence at school again, Bert and Bernard were walking home. Four white boys about the same age as Bert and Bernard crossed the road to confront them. Bert and Bernard's cousin, Gary Duncan, age 19, happened to drive by. Duncan, a husband and father, earned about $65 a week[35] as a boat captain.[36] Duncan stopped his car, got out, and asked his cousins what was going on. Bert replied that the white boys wanted to fight, and Duncan told his cousins to get into his car.[37] As they did,

---

[30] United States v. Plaquemines Parish School Board, 11 Race Rel. L. Rptr. 1764 (E.D. La. August 26, 1966).

[31] Just before the start of the school year, Judge Christenberry, of the E.D. La in N.O., entered a preliminary injunction against Plaquemines Parish officials ordering them to desegregate its public school system. United States v. Plaquemines Parish School Board, 11 Race Rel. L. Rep. 1764 (E.D. La. Aug. 26, 1966); *Judge Orders School Mix for Plaquemines*, NEW ORLEANS TIMES-PICAYUNE, Aug. 27, 1966 (Judge Christenberry ordered desegregation in Plaquemines Parish barred council from selling school property to set up private school); *Compromise Hinted in Plaquemines Parish*, WASH. POST, Sept. 17, 1966, at A4 (faculty quit to join Perez school).

[32] *See* Roy Reed, *"Hard–Headed" Residents of Perez's Parish Tell How They Clung to Life in the Hurricane*, N.Y. TIMES, Sept. 15, 1965, at 32 (Hurricane Betsy crushes Plaquemine Parish, hundreds of houses destroyed, only a handful dead).

[33] Sobol v. Perez, 289 F. Supp. 392, 396 (E.D. La. 1968).

[34] Duncan v. Louisiana, Petition in the Louisiana Supreme Court, at p. 6; *Two Attorneys Give Testimony*, NEW ORLEANS TIMES-PICAYUNE, Jan. 25, 1968, sec. 2, at 4 (reporting Negro students were beaten by white students).

[35] *Sobol v. Perez*, 289 F. Supp. at 396–97.

[36] Duncan v. Louisiana, Statement of Jurisdiction, at p. 65 (trial transcript).

[37] Duncan v. Louisiana, Statement of Jurisdiction, at p. 5; *Sobol v. Perez*, 289 F. Supp. at 396.

Herman Landry, Jr., one of the white boys present, muttered, "You must think you're tough."[38] Duncan then touched Landry on the arm— just how forcefully later became a matter of dispute—urged him to head home, and drove off with Bert and Bernard.

From about 250 feet away, Bert Latham, president of the new private school association established to avoid integration, saw the incident and immediately called the sheriff's office to report that Duncan had slapped Landry's arm. A deputy stopped Duncan's car and took him back to the scene. There the deputy questioned the white boys.[39] Landry was not hurt and displayed no bruise.[40] The deputy released Duncan, telling him that he did not believe that he'd struck the boy.[41] Landry's father had other ideas. He sought out a justice of the peace and swore out an affidavit supporting Duncan's arrest.[42] On October 21, Gary Duncan was jailed on the charge of cruelty to a juvenile.[43] He was released after his employer posted the $1000 bond.[44]

Gary Duncan and his family doubted that any local attorney would defend him.[45] His concerns were well founded: Leander Perez, Jr., the District Attorney, had stated publicly, "[i]f any known agitator were to appear in Plaquemines Parish, his mere presence would amount to a disturbance of the peace, since he was an outsider."[46] The parish had no

---

[38] Duncan v. Louisiana, Statement of Jurisdiction, at p. 47 (trial transcript).

[39] *Sobol v. Perez*, 289 F. Supp. at 396.

[40] Duncan v. Perez, 321 F. Supp. 181, 184 (E.D. La. 1970), *aff'd*, 445 F.2d 557 (5th Cir. 1971).

[41] *Sobol v. Perez*, 289 F. Supp. at 396.

[42] Duncan v. Perez, 445 F.2d 557 (5th Cir. 1971).

[43] LSA–RS. § 14:93; Sobol v. Perez, 289 F. Supp. at 396; Duncan v. Perez, 321 F. Supp. at 181.

[44] Duncan v. Louisiana, Statement of Jurisdiction, at p. 63 (trial transcript).

[45] Duncan v. Perez, 321 F. Supp. at 182.

[46] Sobol v. Perez, 289 F. Supp. 392, 401 (E.D. La. 1968). Fearing intimidation, harassment, violence, and the KKK, African–American attorneys as well as the six or seven white lawyers in the parish wouldn't touch a case like Duncan's. *Negroes Can't Get Legal Help, Say Rights Leaders,* NEW ORLEANS TIMES-PICAYUNE, Jan 30, 1968, p. 17, c.1 (reporting testimony in Sobol's case); *Two Attorneys Give Testimony,* NEW ORLEANS TIMES-PICAYUNE, Jan. 25, 1968, sec. 2, at 4 (attorney received "crank telephone calls to himself and his family and hate letters"); *No Protest Given on Role with Case Earlier–Sobol,* NEW ORLEANS TIMES-PICAYUNE, Jan. 31, 1968, sec. 2, at 4 (reporting that the witness the state called testified on cross examination that he was accosted by five deputies with blackjacks in the dark parking lot after arguing an election dispute before the Parish Democratic Executive Committee, seeking to qualify for an election, and that another witness testified that his organization's headquarters were raided by the District Attorney); *Amadee Tells of Being Afraid: Threatened by Perez, Says Negro Attorney,* NEW ORLEANS TIMES-PICAYUNE, Feb. 1,

African–American attorneys, and African–American lawyers in surrounding areas were reluctant to venture there, after being threatened and
compelled to leave in earlier incidents. Some feared that Perez would
plant narcotics on them if they went to Plaquemines.[47] One white
attorney explaining why he couldn't take a civil rights case said, "These
people in town will kill me."[48] Any parish attorney was worthless,
Duncan had concluded. As he said later, "all he would have done is get
me to plead guilty."[49]

Duncan's parents turned to the Lawyers Constitutional Defense
Committee (LCDC), an organization dedicated to litigating civil rights
issues in Mississippi, Alabama, and Louisiana. Under the leadership of
civil rights attorney Alvin Bronstein and the African–American firm of
Niles R. Douglas, Lolis E. Elie, and Robert F. Collins,[50] LCDC had just
opened an office in New Orleans. The office and its growing caseload was
soon staffed by Richard Sobol, a young white attorney who had moved to
New Orleans in August with his wife and two children, taking a leave of
absence from Arnold and Porter in Washington, D.C.[51] A meeting was
scheduled between Duncan, his witnesses, Sobol, and members of the
Douglas, Elie and Collins firm. After the meeting, Sobol and Collins, who
later became the Deep South's first African–American United States
District Court Judge,[52] took the case. They were already hard-pressed to
cover dozens of other pending cases needing attention,[53] and knew that

---

1968, sec. 1, at 6 (attorney testified that "Perez made a reference to violence which had
taken place in Alabama in connection with a bus load of 'Freedom Riders' and told him
that the same thing would happen to him").

[47] *State Lawyers Said Bypassed: Lack of Confidence in Rights Cases Cited*, NEW
ORLEANS TIMES-PICAYUNE, Jan. 23, 1968, sec. 1, at 10 (testimony in Sobol's later civil suit
describing of intimidation of lawyers).

[48] *Id.*

[49] *Negroes Can't Get Legal Help, Say Rights Leaders*, NEW ORLEANS TIMES-PICAYUNE, Jan.
20, 1968, p. 17, c.1 (reporting Duncan's testimony in *Sobol v. Perez*)

[50] JACK BASS, UNLIKELY HEROES 292 (1981).

[51] *Id.*

[52] Collins, the African–American attorney who represented both Duncan and Perez
along with Bronstein in their civil suits, (during Duncan's trial, Judge Leon repeatedly
called Sobol "Mr. Collins") went on to be appointed in 1978 as the Deep South's first
African–American federal judge. He resigned in 1993, the first federal judge to be convicted
of taking a bribe in the 200 years of the judiciary. Targeted in a 1989 sting operation, he
had been convicted of taking money from a man seeking a lenient sentence in a drug case.
Elie and Douglas were inducted into the National Bar Association Hall of Fame.

[53] Author's telephone interview with Richard Sobol, November 1, 2004 ("We were very
busy. When I got [to the LCDC office], the attorney filling in handed me a stack of cards
about 6 inches thick each one representing a pending case.").

the case would involve substantial costs that they would never recover, but they pursued it because "the arrest and prosecution was nothing more than a form of harassment undertaken in retaliation for the fact that Gary Duncan's relatives chose to go to the school previously reserved exclusively for whites."[54]

Duncan's arraignment was held in late November, in the chambers of Judge Eugene E. Leon in the parish courthouse in Pointe à la Hache.[55] Collins and Sobol, the first attorneys ever to venture into Perez's domain on a civil rights matter,[56] appeared and filed a motion to quash the information on the ground that one of the elements of the charged crime was a parental relationship between the defendant and the juvenile. This was a line of argument the District Attorney's office obviously was not prepared to counter. Judge Leon set the motion for hearing, the conference broke up, and Assistant District Attorney Daryll Bubrig immediately advised Landry's parents that because the juvenile charge was probably invalid, an affidavit charging simple battery[57] should be filed. Mrs. Landry promptly signed an affidavit charging Duncan with simple battery and as a result he was arrested for a second time. A new bond was set at $1500, double the $750 figure for simple battery in the suggested bond schedule.[58]

Duncan's trial took place on January 25, 1967. At the state's table sat Bubrig, accompanied by his boss, Leander Perez, Jr. Sobol appeared for Duncan. He began by filing a jury demand based on the Sixth and Fourteenth Amendments of the United States Constitution. Judge Leon denied the request. In Louisiana, the crime of simple battery was a misdemeanor, punishable at that time by a term of two years' imprisonment and a fine of $300.[59] Crimes not punishable by "imprisonment *at hard labor*" were defined under Louisiana law as misdemeanors,[60] and defendants charged with misdemeanors had no right to trial by jury under Louisiana law.[61]

---

[54] Sobol v. Perez, 289 F. Supp. 392, 397 (E.D. La. 1968); Duncan v. Perez, 321 F. Supp. at 182.

[55] Sobol v. Perez, 289 F. Supp. at 397.

[56] *Louisiana to Out-of-State Lawyers: Get Out*, NEW REPUBLIC, Feb. 24, 1968, at 17–18.

[57] LSA–RS. § 14:35.

[58] Duncan v. Perez, 321 F. Supp. 181, 182 (E.D. La. 1970), *aff'd*, 445 F.2d 557 (5th Cir. 1971).

[59] LSA–RS. § 14:35.

[60] LSA–RS. § 14:2.

[61] Art. 779 of La. Code of Crim. Proc.

Duncan and his cousins all testified that Duncan had merely touched Landry's elbow, as a manner of expression, while telling him that it would be best if he went home.[62] Latham testified that he saw Duncan slap the white boy in a hostile manner.[63] Although Bubrig conducted the prosecution for the state, during Sobol's attempt to establish acts of violence at school against the two boys, Perez cut in arguing, "[T]hese two colored boys who are witnesses of the defendant had been proven to be the ones who were the aggressors, and I can't understand any further questions along these lines, which to me seemed to tend to prove the guilt of the defendant."[64] Judge Leon too seemed impatient with this line of testimony, and urged Sobol to stick with "what went on on the side of the road."[65] Ultimately, Judge Leon found the testimony of Latham and Landry more credible than that of the African–American witnesses and convicted Duncan.

At sentencing, Sobol asked for a suspended sentence, but Judge Leon sentenced Duncan to $150, costs, and sixty days in prison, with an additional twenty days if the fine and costs were not paid. This was an extraordinarily stiff sentence for the crime of simple battery. Later facing Sobol in a deposition, Judge Leon explained that the following considerations had affected his sentencing decision:

> Your representation as a member of the Lawyer's Constitutional Defense Committee, you all found the proper forum, which was Plaquemines Parish, you all found the proper name, which was L.H. Perez, and also you found the proper time, the integration of the parish school system.... You at no time ... attempted to defend this man of the charges, your sole attempt was to have the Constitution of the State of Louisiana where it dealt with jury trials and misdemeanors, you wanted that declared unconstitutional, and that's the only thing you did, sir.[66]

Sobol then filed notice that he was seeking review in the Louisiana Supreme Court, and after another few hours in jail, Duncan posted an additional $1500 bond imposed by Judge Leon, this time for release pending appeal.[67]

---

[62] *See also Judge to Bar Duncan Trial*, New Orleans Times-Picayune, Oct. 22, 1970, sec. 1, at 5.

[63] Duncan v. Perez, 321 F. Supp. at 182.

[64] Duncan v. Louisiana, Statement of Jurisdiction at p. 37 (trial transcript).

[65] Duncan v. Louisiana, Statement of Jurisdiction at p. 37 (trial transcript).

[66] Duncan v. Perez, 321 F. Supp. at 182.

[67] Sobol v. Perez, 289 F. Supp. 392, 398 (E.D. La. 1968).

Duncan in his petition for review in the Louisiana Supreme Court argued that the state law permitting trial without jury for a two-year offense violated Duncan's right to a jury trial under the Sixth and Fourteenth Amendments of the United States Constitution. Jury trial, Duncan's attorneys argued, was a fundamental right for those accused of crime, part of the due process guaranteed prior to the deprivation of liberty. The United States Supreme Court had decades earlier rejected this argument; Duncan's attorneys were hoping the Warren Court might see it otherwise.[68] At the time, only two states other than Louisiana denied the right to trial by jury in cases where the defendant faced a sentence of more than six months. The defense argued that "racial overtones were expressed at the trial," and that "in this atmosphere, only a jury composed of a fair representation of the community could impartially assess the evidence and render a just verdict." The petition was summarily denied, due to "no error of law."[69]

The next day, calling Judge Leon's chambers for an appointment so that Duncan's bond could be continued pending an appeal to the United States Supreme Court, Sobol was advised by the judge's secretary to come by after noon. In the meantime, Judge Leon passed along Sobol's intent to Assistant District Attorney Bubrig, who phoned his boss, Perez, Jr. The District Attorney immediately signed an information charging Sobol with practicing law without a license on the theory that he was not a member of the state bar and had at times been appearing without local counsel. That afternoon, receiving Sobol, Judge Leon said nothing of the allegations against Sobol, refused Sobol's request to continue Duncan's appellate bond and insisted that Duncan must be rearrested and incarcerated until he posted yet another $1500 bond, pending an appeal to the United States Supreme Court.[70]

After leaving Judge Leon's chambers, while still in the courthouse, Sobol was arrested by a sheriff's deputy.[71] Up until that moment, not a word had been said to him by the District Attorney or the judge to indicate to him he was practicing law improperly. "It was a complete surprise to me," he recalled.[72] Sobol was taken downstairs to the sheriff's office, fingerprinted, photographed, relieved of his briefcase with all of

---

[68] The Court had rejected trial by jury as part of the due process guaranteed state defendants in Maxwell v. Dow, 176 U.S. 581 (1900). *See also* Snyder v. Massachusetts, 291 U.S. 97 (1934).

[69] State v. Duncan, 250 La. 253, 195 So.2d 142 (1967).

[70] Duncan v. Perez, 321 F. Supp. at 183.

[71] Sobol v. Perez, 289 F. Supp. at 392.

[72] Interview with Sobol, *supra* note 53.

Duncan's case papers over his objection, and held for four hours before being released on bond.[73]

Soon after Sobol was released on bond, Alvin Bronstein was in New Orleans, asking the federal court to enjoin Perez's prosecution of Sobol.[74] The United States Supreme Court had recently backed Judge Minor Wisdom's effort to restrain Louisiana officials from harassing civil rights workers with criminal prosecution.[75] Civil rights attorneys all over the Fifth Circuit were seeking injunctive relief in federal court, attempting to fend off arrests by local officials who hoped to slow civil rights activity by using criminal prosecution.[76]

At about the same time, with no notice to Duncan's counsel, Judge Leon granted a hearing to District Attorney Perez and issued a warrant for Duncan's arrest. Late at night on February 23, Duncan was arrested, for the fourth time, and taken from his home to the parish prison. Both the timing of the arrest and the transportation to prison were "highly unusual."[77] For about 24 hours, Duncan and persons acting on his behalf tried repeatedly to post the new bond with the sheriff's office, including pledging property worth $1500, but the sheriff's office maintained the position that the bond could be met only if property with an assessed value of *double* that amount was pledged. This was contrary to state law and past practice.[78] Eventually both Duncan and Sobol were released, and they began preparing Duncan's appeal to the United States Supreme Court.

Sobol's brief in which he was joined by civil rights attorneys Alvin Bronstein,[79] Anthony Amsterdam, and Donald Juneau, argued that Duncan had a right to a jury trial on the battery charge, a right guaranteed by the Fourteenth Amendment's Due Process Clause. Louisiana law denying him a jury trial on the charge carrying up to two years' imprisonment was unconstitutional. Specifically, they asked the Court to

---

[73] *Id.*

[74] Sobol v. Perez, 289 F.Supp. 392 (E.D.La. 1968).

[75] Dombrowski v. Pfister, 380 U.S. 479 (1965).

[76] *See* Jack Bass, Unlikely Heroes 291 (1981); City of Greenwood v. Peacock, 384 U.S. 808 (1966); Georgia v. Rachel, 384 U.S. 780 (1966). *See also* Owen Fiss, *Dombrowski*, 86 Yale L.J. 1103 (1977); Douglas Laycock, *Federal Interference with State Prosecutions: The Cases Dombrowski Forgot*, 46 U. Chi. L. Rev. 636 (1979); Frank L. Maraist, *Federal Intervention in State Criminal Proceedings: Dombrowski, Younger, and Beyond*, 50 Tex. L. Rev. 1324 (1972).

[77] Duncan v. Perez, 321 F.Supp. 181, 183 (E.D.La. 1970).

[78] *Id.*

[79] Alvin J. Bronstein, went on to lead the ACLU's National Prison Project for nearly a quarter century.

overrule its earlier decisions in which it had found that in state court trial by jury, rather than judge, was not required by the Fourteenth Amendment,[80] and that the right to a jury trial in all but petty criminal cases, a right protected by the Sixth Amendment, applied in state prosecutions as well as federal.

The time was right for Duncan's claim. The Warren Court was well underway in what came to be known as the "criminal procedure revolution," in which it expanded the federal judiciary's oversight of state criminal justice by extending to state defendants, one case and constitutional clause at a time, the protections of the Fourth, Fifth, Sixth, and Eighth Amendments previously reserved for federal prosecutions. Over the preceding five terms, the Court had found that due process guaranteed to state as well as federal defendants several other Sixth Amendment guarantees, including the right to a speedy[81] and public[82] trial, a jury that is impartial,[83] compulsory process,[84] and the right to counsel.[85] Once a right was held to apply to the states, all of the decisions interpreting that right in the federal context were equally applicable to state prosecutions.[86] Through this process of "selective incorporation," the Warren Court had already made it clear that the Constitution regulated the jury process whenever states made it available by barring race discrimination in jury selection, and guaranteeing a jury that was impartial.[87] Duncan's lawyers argued, "It would be ironic indeed if a state were permitted to nullify this Court's carefully developed protections of the jury system by substituting for trial by jury trial by a single judge, who cannot represent a fair cross section of the community and who is frequently exposed to official and unofficial influences prejudicial to the defendant."[88]

---

[80] Maxwell v. Dow, 176 U.S. 581 (1899). *See also* Snyder v. Massachusetts, 291 U.S. 97 (1934); Palko v. Connecticut, 302 U.S. 319, 325 (1937) ("The right to trial by jury and the immunity from prosecution except as the result of an indictment may have value and importance. Even so, they are not of the very essence of a scheme of ordered liberty.... Few would be so narrow or provincial as to maintain that a fair and enlightened system of justice would be impossible without them.")

[81] Klopfer v. North Carolina, 386 U.S. 213 (1967).

[82] In re Oliver, 333 U.S. 257 (1948).

[83] Turner v. Louisiana, 379 U.S. 466 (1965).

[84] Washington v. Texas, 388 U.S. 14 (1967).

[85] Gideon v. Wainwright, 372 U.S. 335 (1963).

[86] *See generally* WAYNE R. LAFAVE, JEROLD H. ISRAEL & NANCY J. KING, 1 CRIMINAL PROCEDURE § 2.5 (2d ed. 1999).

[87] Turner v. Louisiana, 379 U.S. 466 (1965) (decided just two years earlier establishing that the sixth amendment right to a jury that is impartial applies to the states).

[88] Duncan v. Louisiana, Brief of Appellant, at 18.

Duncan's attorneys argued that the prosecution of their client was just the sort of case where the protection of a jury against the power of judge and prosecutor was most vital, as the prosecution was "part of the general official effort to discourage the exercise of rights under the federal court order" desegregating the local schools. Their argument concluded with a quote from Blackstone, "In times of difficulty and danger, more is to be apprehended from the violence and partiality of judges appointed by the Crown, in suits between the King and the subject, than in suits between one individual and another. . . ."

But Sobol and his colleagues were fighting a two-front war in Plaquemines during that summer of 1967. After filing their briefs with the Supreme Court in Duncan's case, they continued their effort to block the prosecution of Sobol himself. Sobol deposed Perez and Judge Leon in Plaquemines,[89] while hundreds of miles away on October 2 in Washington, D.C., Court of Appeals Judge Thurgood Marshall was confirmed as the first African–American U.S. Supreme Court Justice in the nation's history.[90]

On October 9, exactly one week after Judge Marshall was sworn in as Associate Justice of the United States Supreme Court, the Court noted probable jurisdiction in Duncan's case, and set a date for oral argument.[91] The same day, down in New Orleans, Judge Cassibry granted a motion to allow Arnold and Porter to participate as amici in Sobol's lawsuit. Ultimately Sobol's cause was joined by the United States Department of Justice,[92] the NAACP, and thirty of the nation's leading law firms.[93]

None of this seemed to faze the Perez establishment in the least. Attorneys in the Perez camp, while simultaneously resisting Duncan's appeal, fighting off Sobol's suit, and sabotaging the federal efforts to end segregation and African–American disenfranchisement in the parish, continued to deal with political enemies by locking them up. That December, one foe who was alleged to have threatened Judge Perez was forced to post over $31,000 in bonds in order to gain his freedom.[94] And

---

[89] Docket sheet, *Sobol v. Perez,* on file with author.

[90] Lisa Paddock, Facts About the Supreme Court of the United States 334 (1996) (oath taken October 2, 1967).

[91] The same day the Court refused to reexamine the contempt convictions of Dr. Martin Luther King, Jr. and other ministers who led desegregation demonstrations in Birmingham in 1963 in violation of Alabama law. *Dr. King is Denied a Rehearing; Faces 5–Day Term for Contempt,* N. Y. Times, Oct. 10, 1967, at p. 40.

[92] Attorney General Ramsey Clark was granted permission to intervene on Sobol's behalf for the United States.

[93] *Louisiana to Out-of-State Lawyers: Get Out,* New Republic, Feb. 24, 1968, at 18.

[94] *Trial of Perez Foe Continues,* New Orleans Times–Picayune, Dec. 21, 1967 at p. 17 (reporting that Rousselle, a political foe of Perez, was prosecuted for conspiracy to inflict

in a ironic twist, while Duncan's case was winding its way through its appellate stages, parish officials defending against the Justice Department's school desegregation suit protested that they were "entitled to the right of trial by jury," in the case "because the government's suit against it was in the nature of a suit to try the title to land," a claim summarily rejected by the federal court.[95]

In the United States Supreme Court

Duncan's attorneys argued to the Court that extending the right of criminal jury trial to the states was imperative in order to end racial injustice in the Deep South. Factual findings by judges, in particular credibility determinations like the ones Judge Leon had made in Duncan's case, were virtually unreviewable.

> [I]n cases such as this—where the personal and political leanings of the trial judge will often be antagonistic to the defendant—the potential for a factual determination that is influenced by considerations other than the evidence of record is very great. This situation, particularly in civil rights related prosecutions in the Deep South, is not uncommon. Because of the accepted limitation on federal review and state appellate review of factual determinations in state trial courts, the only effective remedy is to guarantee the accused the right to have the crucial factual determination of guilt or innocence made by a jury, rather than by a judge. . . .[96]

To this instrumentalist justification, they added historical practice, as well as the weight of authority in other states, arguing that the right to a jury trial in non-petty offenses was fundamental, so fundamental that it was part of the due process guaranteed by the Fourteenth Amendment.[97]

Louisiana Attorney General Jack Gremillion selected attorney Dorothy Wolbrette to brief and argue Duncan's case for the state. One of only three women in her graduating class, Wolbrette had been editor-in-chief of the *Tulane Law Review* in 1944–45, and had practiced law with her father prior to landing a job with the state.[98] Wolbrette remembered, "All these liberal groups had sent us this big, thick brief that they

---

great bodily harm on Perez, had to post over $31,000 in bonds, after five men testified they heard him make threats against Perez).

[95] Plaquemines Parish School Bd. v. United Status,, 415 F.2d 817, 824 (5th Cir. 1969).

[96] Duncan v. Louisiana, Brief of Appellant, at 23.

[97] *Id.* at 6–12.

[98] Nick Marinello, *Where the girls were: Alumnae remember the challenges and rewards of serving as gender pioneers in the study and practice of law*, TULANE LAWYER, Fall/Winter 2002, at 25.

researched for ages and had been waiting to use."[99] The *Duncan* case, she later said, was about the political and social sensibilities of the 1960s.[100] Gremillion would later recall, "I was at the helm of the state's legal team during all the cases when Louisiana lost its sovereignty to the federal government."[101]

Louisiana argued to the Court that history did not support treating the right to a jury trial as a fundamental right, that a fair trial did not depend upon the presence of a jury, and even if the Sixth Amendment did guarantee a right to trial by jury, surely it wouldn't extend to a case in which the defendant was charged with an offense classified as a misdemeanor under state law and treated as a petty offense in almost every jurisdiction, for which the defendant received only 60 days' imprisonment.[102] Any jury required by due process, the state argued, need not mirror exactly the Sixth Amendment jury that federal defendants enjoyed—a twelve-person, unanimous jury for any offense carrying a penalty of over six months' imprisonment.

This plea for less than wholesale application of all aspects of an individual right to the states had a basis in some prior opinions of the justices. But adherents for complete application were dwindling. Repeatedly in earlier cases, the Court had required states to comply with all features of what formerly had been strictly federal rights. Only a minority of the justices had expressed opposition to applying all specific aspects of each right against the states. These justices preferred instead to require only those processes that were required by "fundamental fairness."[103]

Justice Byron White drafted the majority opinion reversing the Louisiana Supreme Court's rejection of the right to jury. In his proposed opinion, he admitted that there was no settled "test for determining whether a right extended by the Fifth and Sixth Amendments with respect to federal criminal proceedings is also protected against state action by the Fourteenth Amendment."[104] Phrasings had included "whether the right is among those 'fundamental principles of liberty and justice which lie at the base of all our civil and political institutions,' . . . whether it is 'basic in our system of jurisprudence,' . . . and whether it is

---

[99] *Id.* In 1976 she was appointed administrative law judge for the Social Security Administration, a post she held until her retirement in 1988.

[100] *Id.*

[101] Bill Grady, *Politico Recalls Colorful Career*, New Orleans Times-Picayune, June 8, 1992 at B1.

[102] Duncan v. Louisiana, Brief of Appellee.

[103] See generally LaFave, Israel & King, *supra* note 86, at § 2.2–2.5.

[104] Duncan v. Louisiana, 391 U.S. 145, 148 (1968).

'a fundamental right, essential to a fair trial' "[105] White concluded that the right to trial by jury met all of these tests, but he tucked into a footnote his own approach to the problem:

> Earlier the Court can be seen as having asked, when inquiring into whether some particular procedural safeguard was required of a State, if a civilized system could be imagined that would not accord the particular protection. ... In recent cases, on the other hand, we have proceeded upon the valid assumption that state criminal processes are not imaginary and theoretical schemes but actual systems bearing virtually every characteristic of the common-law system that has been developing contemporaneously in England and in this country. The question thus is whether given this kind of system a particular procedure is fundamental—whether, that is, a procedure is necessary to an Anglo–American regime of ordered liberty. ... A criminal process which was fair and equitable but used no juries is easy to imagine. It would make use of alternative guarantees and protections which would serve the purposes that the jury serves in the English and American systems. Yet no American State has undertaken to construct such a system. Instead, every American State, including Louisiana, uses the jury extensively, and imposes very serious punishments only after a trial at which the defendant has a right to a jury's verdict.[106]

Reviewing the history of jury trial up to and after the Founding, he concluded, "Even such skeletal history is impressive support for considering the right to trial by jury in criminal cases to be fundamental to our system of justice...."[107] Expanding upon the function of the jury trial, he added what has become the most frequently referenced explanation of the purposes of Sixth Amendment's right to trial by jury:

> A right to trial by jury is granted to criminal defendants in order to prevent oppression by the Government. Those who wrote our constitutions knew from history and experience that it was necessary to protect against unfounded criminal charges brought to eliminate enemies and against judges too responsive to the voice of higher authority. The framers of the constitutions strove to create an independent judiciary but insisted upon further protection against arbitrary action. Providing an accused with the right to be tried by a jury of his peers gave him an inestimable safeguard against the corrupt or overzealous prosecutor and against the complaint, biased, or eccentric judge. If the defendant preferred the common-sense

---

[105] *Id.* at 148–49.

[106] *Id.* at 150.

[107] *Id.* at 153.

judgment of a jury to the more tutored but perhaps less sympathetic reaction of the single judge, he was to have it. Beyond this, the jury trial provisions in the Federal and State Constitutions reflect a fundamental decision about the exercise of official power—a reluctance to entrust plenary powers over the life and liberty of the citizen to one judge or to a group of judges. Fear of unchecked power, so typical of our State and Federal Governments in other respects, found expression in the criminal law in this insistence upon community participation in the determination of guilt or innocence. The deep commitment of the Nation to the right of jury trial in serious criminal cases as a defense against arbitrary law enforcement qualifies for protection under the Due Process Clause of the Fourteenth Amendment, and must therefore be respected by the States.[108]

Turning to the question of which cases require jury trials, Justice White rejected the expansive view that "all crimes" must be tried by jury stating instead that crimes "carrying possible penalties up to six months do not require a jury trial if they otherwise qualify as petty offenses."[109] But he refused to "settle in this case the exact location of the line between petty offenses" which do not require a jury, "and serious crimes" which do. Louisiana had contended that the right to trial by jury guaranteed by due process ought to turn on the seriousness of the penalty actually imposed, but White explained that the *authorized* penalty is a " 'gauge of [the legislature's] social and ethical judgments' of the crime. . . ."[110] The crime in this case, carrying up to two years' imprisonment and a fine is not an offense that may be tried without a jury, White concluded. He relied upon "objective criteria, chiefly the existing laws and practices in the Nation."[111] In all but one state, "crimes subject to trial without a jury . . . are punishable by no more than one year in jail."[112] In the late eighteenth century, he continued, "crimes triable without a jury were for the most part punishable by no more than a six-month prison term."[113] Declining to go further than a pronouncement that two years is too long, he did note in another pregnant footnote, that "there appear to be only two instances, aside from the Louisiana scheme,

---

[108] *Id*. at 155–56.

[109] *Id*. at 159.

[110] *Id*. at 160.

[111] *Id*. at 161.

[112] *Id*.

[113] *Id*.

in which a State denies jury trial for a crime punishable by imprisonment for longer than six months."[114]

Justice White's opinion also did not resolve whether the incorporation of the right to trial by jury would require states to abandon de novo trial procedures, non-unanimous jury decisions, or juries of less than twelve members.[115] Justice White stated blithely in a footnote, "It seems very unlikely to us that our decision today will require widespread changes in state criminal processes.... [M]ost of the States have provisions for jury trial equal in breadth to the Sixth Amendment.... Only in Oregon and Louisiana can a less-than-unanimous jury convict for an offense with a maximum penalty greater than one year."[116] Justices Brennan and Marshall promptly joined White's opinion.[117]

Justice Harlan circulated a dissenting opinion, a forceful argument for federal restraint.[118] He wrote, "The Due Process Clause of the Fourteenth Amendment requires that [a state's] procedures be fundamentally fair in all respects. It does not, in my view, impose or encourage nationwide uniformity for its own sake; it does not command adherence to forms that happen to be old; and it does not impose on the States the rules that may be in force in the federal courts except where such rules are also found to be essential to basic fairness."[119] Justice Harlan assailed the entire "incorporation" enterprise, with particular venom directed at Justice Black's argument in earlier cases that the Fourteenth Amendment required total incorporation of the first eight amendments. "The overwhelming historical evidence ... demonstrates, to me conclusively, that the Congressmen and state legislators who wrote, debated, and ratified the Fourteenth Amendment did not think they were incorporating the Bill of Rights...."[120] "[N]either history, nor sense, supports using the Fourteenth Amendment to put the States in a constitutional straitjacket with respect to their own development in the administration

---

[114] *Id.* at note 33.

[115] "The Fourteenth Amendment guarantees a right of jury trial in all criminal cases which—were they to be tried in a federal court—would come within the Sixth Amendment Guarantee." *Id.* at 149.

[116] *Id.* at 158 note 30.

[117] Memorandum from Justice Brennan to Justice White (March 13, 1968) (on file with the Library of Congress, Papers of William J. Brennan, Box I: 172, folder 10); Memorandum from Justice Marshall to Justice White (March 13, 1968) (on file with the Library of Congress, Papers of Thurgood Marshall, Box 46, folder 3).

[118] Memorandum from Justice Harlan to the Conference (March 13, 1968) (on file with the Library of Congress, Papers of William J. Brennan, Box I: 172, folder 10).

[119] *Duncan*, 391 U.S. at 172 (Harlan, J., dissenting).

[120] *Id.* at 174.

of criminal or civil law."[121] Opting for the "much more discriminating process" of attempting to define the words liberty and "due process of law" in a way that "accords with American traditions and our system of government," Harlan considered the Bill of Rights as "evidence ... of the content Americans find in the term 'liberty' and American standards of fundamental fairness."[122] The Court, he accused, was not true to this approach in this case. Instead, "[i]t has simply assumed that the question before us is whether the Jury Trial Clause of the Sixth Amendment should be incorporated into the Fourteenth, jot-for-jot and case-for-case, or ignored." Harlan found it obvious that a guarantee of exactly twelve jurors, for example, "is not fundamental to anything: there is no significance except to mystics...."[123] and that unanimity had already been abandoned in Britain.[124]

Harlan concluded that there is no "significant new evidence" that suggested the Court was wrong when it had already concluded in earlier decisions that the right to grand jury review and trial by jury were "not fundamental in their nature but concern merely a method of procedure."[125] The "principal original virtue of the jury trial—the limitations a jury imposes on a tyrannous judiciary," he wrote, "has largely disappeared.... Judges enforce laws enacted by democratic decision, not by regal fiat. They are elected by the people or appointed by the people's elected officials, and are responsible not to a distant monarch alone but to reviewing courts, including this one."

[126] One imagines that for minority citizens in Plaquemines Parish in 1967, Justice Harlan's praise of the limiting power of democracy would ring hollow indeed.

Justice Fortas issued an opinion joining the result reached by White, but concurring with Harlan's objections to the "implication" that a twelve-person, unanimous jury is constitutionally required. "I do believe ... that the right of jury trial is fundamental, [but] it does not follow that the particulars of according that right must be uniform. We should be ready to welcome state variations which do not impair—indeed, which may advance—the theory and purpose of trial by jury."[127]

---

[121] *Id.* at 175–76.

[122] *Id.* at 176–77.

[123] *Id.* at 182.

[124] *Id.*

[125] *Id.* at 185–86.

[126] *Id.* at 188.

[127] Draft opinion by Justice Fortas at 4, Duncan v. Louisiana, 391 U.S. 145 (1968) (No. 410—October Term, 1967) (on file with the Library of Congress).

The opinions of Harlan and Fortas prompted Black to revise what had been a one-sentence concurrence into a heated ten-page defense of the "incorporation" process.[128] The exchange remains one of the classic debates in constitutional law, read by law students ever since. After summarizing the basis for his disagreement about what the historical record had to say about the meaning of the Fourteenth Amendment, Black turned to his key objection to Harlan's approach. "[D]ue process, according to my Brother Harlan, is to be a word with no permanent meaning, but one which is found to shift from time to time in accordance with judge's predilections and understandings of what is best for the country. If due process means this, the Fourteenth Amendment, in my opinion, might as well have been written that 'no person shall be deprived of life, liberty or property except by laws that the judges of the United States Supreme Court shall find to be consistent with the immutable principles of free government.' "[129] Due process does not mean "a guarantee of a trial free from laws and conduct which the courts deem at the time to be 'arbitrary,' 'unreasonable,' 'unfair,' or 'contrary to civilized standards.' The due process of law standard for a trial is one tried in accordance with the Bill of Rights and laws passed pursuant to constitutional power, guaranteeing to all alike a trial under the general law of the land."[130]

Rejecting the suggestion that his approach undermines state sovereignty, Justice Black argued, "[T]he due process approach of my Brothers Harlan and Fortas restricts the States to practices which a majority of this Court is willing to approve on a case-by-case basis. No one is more concerned than I that the States be allowed to use the full scope of their powers as their citizens see fit. And that is why I have continually fought against the expansion of this Court's authority over the States through the use of a broad, general interpretation of due process that permits judges to strike down state laws they do not like."[131]

This battle in *Duncan* eventually proved decisive in the incorporation conflict in the Supreme Court. Harlan's opinion would be joined only by Justice Stewart, and Justice Black's opinion only by Justice Douglas. The Chief Justice joined White's opinion, making the final vote seven to two in Duncan's favor. That same term, the Court had agreed to hear, and decided against the government, no less than four additional

---

[128] Papers of Thurgood Marshall, Draft opinion of Mr. Justice Black, circulated March 20, 1968 (on file with the Library of Congress).

[129] *Duncan*, 391 U.S. at 168.

[130] *Id.* at 170.

[131] *Id.* at 171.

cases related to the right to trial by jury. In *Bloom v. Illinois*,[132] the Court extended the right to trial by jury to state criminal contempt cases, overruling a 1958 decision. In *United States v. Jackson*,[133] the Court struck down a federal statute permitting the death penalty to be imposed only by a jury, because the law in imperiling the lives of only those who demanded a trial, had an undue chilling effect on the exercise of the right to trial by jury. *Bruton v. United States*[134] barred the introduction of a non-testifying codefendant's confession, based upon the jury's inability to follow instructions to ignore such powerful evidence when evaluating the guilt of one defendant but not the other. Finally, in *Witherspoon v. Illinois*,[135] the Court prohibited judges in capital cases from excusing for cause potential jurors who have doubts about the death penalty, but who are not automatically opposed to it in every case.

When the Supreme Court announced its decision in *Duncan* on May 20, 1968, the *New York Times*[136] and the *New Orleans Times–Picayune*[137] gave it front page coverage. Within twenty-four hours, attorneys were predicting disaster in both New York and Louisiana, two of the three states that denied juries to defendants facing more than six months' incarceration. Louisiana Attorney General Gremillion warned that the decision would bring the state's courts to a standstill.[138] The state legislatures in Louisiana and New Jersey quickly reduced the sentences for some crimes to six months to avoid the anticipated burden of providing juries for the thousands of minor prosecutions previously tried to the court.[139] It must have been an enormous relief to state officials when, within weeks, the Court held that *Duncan* did not apply retroac-

---

[132] 391 U.S. 194 (1968).

[133] 390 U.S. 570 (1968).

[134] 391 U.S. 123 (1968).

[135] 391 U.S. 510 (1968).

[136] Fred P. Graham, *Justices Extend Five Legal Rights in Criminal Cases*, N.Y. Times, May 21, 1968, at A1.

[137] *Court Decision on Jury Trials Get Criticism*, New Orleans Times Picayune, May 21, 1968, § 1, at 1; New Orleans Times–Picayune, June 8, 1968, p. 2 c. 1.

[138] *Court Decision on Jury Trials Get Criticism*, New Orleans Times Picayune, May 21, 1968, § 1, at 1; New Orleans Times–Picayune June 2, 1968 p. 27 c.1

[139] The Louisiana legislature reduced the maximum sentence for nineteen offenses, including battery, from two years to six months. *See* La. Acts 1968, No. 647, cited in Judith M. Arnette, *Jury Trial in Louisiana—Implications of Duncan*, 39 La. L. Rev. 126–127 (1968). *See also* State v. Orr, 253 Or. 752, 755–56, 219 So.2d 775, 776 (1969) (describing emergency legislation); Robert E. Tomasson, *Hogan Seeks Curb on Trial by Jury,* N.Y. Times, Sept. 13, 1968, at p. 36; State v. Owens, 102 N.J. Super. 187, 207 note 2, 245 A.2d 736, 746 note 2 (App. Div. 1968).

tively.[140]

Duncan's Legacy

The *Duncan* decision did not resolve many of the issues that so occupied the justices at oral argument: If the states must provide jury trials in some cases, which cases, and what kinds of juries? If cases defining the Sixth Amendment right governed state as well as federal prosecutions, the decision threatened bench trials for crimes carrying more than six months' incarceration in three states, de novo trial procedures in ten states, non-unanimous verdicts in six states, and juries of less than twelve in twenty states. Was a jury required to determine punitive damages, sentences, or juvenile delinquency? Today, thirty-six years later, the Court continues to decide, case-by-case, just when the Constitution requires a jury trial, and what attributes of a proceeding are essential to that right.

When is a Jury Required?

The Court's first opportunity to address the petty/serious distinction arose when New York State refused after *Duncan* to amend its statute denying a jury trial for crimes in New York City carrying up to a year's incarceration. A wave of *Duncan* claims followed, including those of nearly 900 anti-war demonstrators arrested at Columbia University.[141] By 1970, the case of a pickpocket convicted of "jostling" presented the issue squarely. With Justice White again writing for the majority, as he was to do in several of the post-*Duncan* jury cases, the Court announced a bright line rule in *Baldwin v. New York*: "no offense can be deemed petty for purposes of the right to trial by jury where imprisonment for more than six months is authorized."[142] Drawing on history once again, the Court also noted, "In the entire Nation, New York City alone denies an accused the right to interpose between himself and a possible prison term of over six months, the commonsense judgment of a jury of his peers. . . . This near-uniform judgment of the Nation furnishes us with the only objective criterion by which a line could ever be drawn—on the basis of the possible penalty alone—between offenses that are and that are not regarded as 'serious' for purposes of trial by jury."[143]

---

[140] DeStefano v. Woods, 392 U.S. 631 (1968) (per curiam); *Court Says Jury Trial Rule Will Not Apply Retroactively*, N.Y. TIMES, June 18, 1968, at 33.

[141] Martin Tolchin, *900 Columbia Rebels Granted Writ on Jury Trials*, N.Y. TIMES, Aug. 30, 1968 at p. 26.

[142] 399 U.S. 66 (1970).

[143] *See also* Blanton v. City of North Las Vegas, 489 U.S. 538 (1989) (holding no jury right for DUI offense carrying potential prison sentence of six months, plus $1000 fine, community service, and license suspension).

In a companion case to *Duncan*, *Bloom v. Illinois*,[144] the Court tackled the issue of the right to jury in contempt cases, and held that Bloom, a lawyer, was entitled to a jury before being convicted of contempt and sentenced to two years' imprisonment for filing a will he had forged. In this and a series of cases that followed,[145] the Court, with Justice White penning the majority opinion, was to adapt the petty/serious distinction to the unique crime of contempt, which lacked the "objective criterion" of a statutory maximum sentence, used to trigger the jury right under *Baldwin*. The actual sentence *imposed* would furnish the proxy in contempt cases.

But *Duncan*, *Bloom*, and *Baldwin* did not sweep as broadly as some had hoped and others had feared. The Court soon rejected the right to trial by jury for juveniles,[146] and also held that a capital defendant is not entitled to have a jury select a sentence.[147] Nor did the right to trial by jury expand to include assessments of punitive damages, the imposition of civil penalties, or the civil commitment decision, as some had predicted.[148] The Court also confirmed in a later case that the right to trial by jury was to be assessed per charge, not per case. The Sixth Amendment metric was the legislature's assessment of seriousness, and this measure did not require a jury when prosecutors chose to join several non-serious offenses for trial, even though consecutive sentencing exposed a defendant to a total sentence longer than six months.[149] By capping the sentence for any give offense at six months or less, states could avoid jury trials altogether.

Yet drawing the line between elements of crime (which must go to a jury) and sentencing facts used to determine sentence (which need not go to a jury) has proved to be particularly controversial for the Rehnquist Court. Several sentencing statutes of the 1970s and 1980s attempted to control disparity in sentencing by limiting a judge's discretion. New presumptive sentences and sentence ranges could be exceeded only if the judge found at sentencing specific aggravating facts about the offense or offender. In a line of cases—*Apprendi v. New Jersey*,[150] *Ring v. Arizona*,[151]

---

[144] 391 U.S. 194 (1968).

[145] Codispoti v. Pennsylvania, 418 U.S. 506 (1974); Muniz v. Hoffman, 422 U.S. 454 (1975).

[146] McKeiver v. Pennsylvania, 403 U.S. 528 (1971).

[147] Spaziano v. Florida, 468 U.S. 447 (1984).

[148] Note, Trial By Jury in Criminal Cases, 69 Colum. L. Rev. 419, 429 (1969).

[149] Lewis v. United States, 518 U.S. 322 (1996).

[150] 530 U.S. 466 (2000).

[151] 536 U.S. 584 (2002).

Blakely v. Washington,[152] and *Booker v. United States*[153]— the Court has held that the government must establish to a jury, not a judge, any fact other than the fact that the defendant has been convicted before, which operates to raise the maximum penalty beyond that authorized for conviction alone. It is remarkable how the reaction to these later decisions of the Rehnquist Court have resembled the reaction to the *Duncan* and *Baldwin* decisions handed down by the Warren Court thirty-six years earlier. The decisions in *Duncan* and *Baldwin* limited a state's ability to choose judge over jury, and were resented by those who saw the Court's interpretation of the Fourteenth Amendment as an unwarranted expansion of federal power over state autonomy. Many predicted that the Warren Court's interpretation of the right to trial by jury would mean "chaos and doom" for states that must retry thousands of prisoners convicted by judge alone, and provide jury trials where none were provided before.[154] Over three decades later, when the Court insisted in *Blakely* that the Sixth Amendment guaranteed the right to a jury determination of maximum-enhancing facts, even more states and the federal government were left scrambling to minimize the impact of this new jury mandate on past and future prosecutions.[155]

The immediate catastrophic impact of *Duncan* and *Baldwin* never materialized for four reasons: First, the Court refused to apply the rule retroactively to cases preceding the decision.[156] Second, legislatures quickly amended state law to avoid further constitutional challenges.[157] Third, plea bargaining absorbed much of the shock until uncertainty subsided. To be sure, in a tiny proportion of cases, the value of the right to a jury trial is the actual jury itself along with the possibility that it would acquit when a judge would not. But for most defendants, the value of the right to trial by jury is the burden its exercise creates for prosecutors and courts. Because prosecutors will pay to avoid this burden with charge and sentencing discounts in settlements that judges willingly endorse, after any expansion of the jury right some deals get a little better for a little while. In the six months following *Baldwin*, the

---

[152] 542 U.S. 296 (2004).

[153] 125 S.Ct. 738 (2005) (the U.S. cite for *Booker* is 543 U.S. 220 (2005). As of publication of this book, the case is not yet paginated in the US Reports.)

[154] *Jury Trials of Misdemeanants in New York City: The Effects of Baldwin,* 7 COLUMBIA J. OF L AND SOCIAL PROBLEMS, 173, 173, 182–191 (1971) (characterizing predictions as "anguished cries of impending chaos and doom").

[155] *See* sources collected at www.sentencing.typepad.com (collecting commentary, court decisions, and legislative action following the Court's decision in Blakely v. Washington and Booker v. United States). *Booker* is discussed at length in a separate chapter in the volume on *United States v. Mistretta,* 488 U.S. 361 (1989).

[156] DeStefano v. Woods, 392 U.S. 631 (1968).

[157] *See* note 139 *supra.*

length of sentences in New York shifted markedly downward. Concluded one researcher, "The prosecution is now willing to give the defendant a better bargain ... in order to avoid a jury trial."[158] The predicted catastrophic impact of *Blakely,* decades after *Duncan,* is being softened by the same adaptive forces.[159]

What Kind of Jury?

The fourth reason that state systems rebounded quickly from the shock of the new federal constitutional guarantee announced in *Duncan* was the limited reading the Court subsequently gave to the jury right itself. Justice Harlan in his *Duncan* dissent warned that "a major danger of the 'incorporation' approach' " is "that provisions of the Bill of Rights may be watered down in the needless pursuit of uniformity."[160] The robust federal right—requiring a jury of twelve, voting unanimously— might be reduced to a lower common denominator so as not to disrupt the varied state systems, he predicted. Those fears were soon realized.

In *Williams v. Florida,*[161] decided during same term as *Baldwin,* the Court, with Justice White again writing for the majority, held that a jury of six was constitutional, a decision that spared at least eight states the trouble of redrafting their law. The "essential feature of a jury obviously lies in the interposition between the accused and his accuser of the commonsense judgment of a group of laymen, and in the community participation and shared responsibility that results from that group's

---

[158] *See e.g., Jury Trials for Misdemeanants in New York City: The Effects of Baldwin,* 7 Colum. J. L. & Soc. Probs. 173, 198 (1971) (reporting that in the six months before *Baldwin* was decided about half of those sentenced received less than three months, in the same period after *Baldwin,* 72% did; the percentage of less severe sentences rising by about 18% and the percentage of more severe sentences decreasing by the same percentage).

[159] In addition, the Court has held that the failure to submit an element to the jury can be harmless error, making relief for defendants seeking relief even less likely. *See* Neder v. United States, 527 U.S. 1 (1999). *See also* United States v. Cotton, 535 U.S. 625 (2002) (failure to include element in indictment does not require automatic reversal but must instead be reviewed under plain error standards).

[160] *Duncan,* 391 U.S. at note 21 (Harlan, J., dissenting). *See also* Chimel v. California, 395 U.S. 752, 769 (1969) (Harlan, J., concurring); Ker v. California, 374 U.S. 23, 45–46 (1963) (Harlan, J., concurring); Williams v. Florida, 399 U.S. 78, 129 (1970) (Harlan, J., dissenting) (complaining that the majority's acceptance of a six-person jury in a state case was a "backlash" that "dilutes a federal guarantee in order to reconcile the logic of 'incorporation ... with the reality of federalism' "). Even Justice Brennan stated in 1986 that "For several years now, there has been an unmistakable trend in the Court to read the guarantees of individual liberty restrictively, which means that the content of the rights applied to the states is likewise diminished." He called the trend, "the Court's contraction of federal rights and remedies on grounds of federalism." William J. Brennan, Jr., *The Bill of Rights and the States: The Revival of State Constitutions as Guardians of Individual Rights,* 61 N.Y.U. L. Rev. 535, 546–48 (1986).

[161] 399 U.S. 78 (1970).

determination of guilt or innocence." The Court concluded that six was as good as twelve in achieving this: "large enough to promote group deliberation, free from outside attempts at intimidation, and to provide a fair possibility for obtaining a representative cross-section of the community."[162] Seven years later, bombarded with post-*Williams* jury studies demonstrating the significant loss of diversity, consistency, accuracy, and deliberation that can result from reduction in jury size, a new majority held the constitutional line at six jurors, striking down convictions for non-petty offenses by juries of five jurors,[163] and invalidating laws in several states, including Louisiana.[164]

Unanimity was next, and Louisiana Attorney General Gremillion and civil rights attorney Richard Sobol both returned to the Supreme Court to contest the constitutionality of state law authorizing non-unanimous jury verdicts.[165] In three successive decisions, two with plurality opinions authored by Justice White,[166] the Court abandoned the unanimity requirement as part of the jury required for state criminal defendants, upholding verdicts of 9–3 under Louisiana law in *Johnson v. Louisiana,* and 10–2 under Oregon law in *Apodaca v. Oregon.*[167] But there was a point at which a jury lacking unanimity failed to meet constitutional standards. Once again Louisiana had reached that point and gone beyond it. In the third unanimity case, *Burch v. Louisiana,* the Court found unconstitutional the Louisiana law authorizing verdicts of 5–1, finding that the "threat to preservation of the substance of the jury trial guarantee" is similar to that posed by a five-person jury. Pointing out that Louisiana was joined by only one other state in authorizing such a process, the Court once again relied on the "near-uniform judgment of the Nation" in "delimiting the line between those jury practices that are constitutionally permissible and those that are not."[168] Finally, despite an earlier holding barring de novo trials in federal court under the Sixth Amendment,[169] the Court refused to extend that ruling to the states, and upheld the two-tier system in place in several states that provided a jury

---

[162] *Id.* at 100.

[163] Ballew v. Georgia, 435 U.S. 223 (1978).

[164] *See* Arnette, *supra* note 139.

[165] Sobol represented the defendant in *Apodaca.*

[166] *See* Apodaca v. Oregon, 406 U.S. 404 (1972) (plurality opinion) (White, J.) and Johnson v. Louisiana, 406 U.S. 356 (1972) (White, J., for the Court).

[167] *Johnson,* at 361–362.

[168] Burch v. Louisiana, 441 U.S. 130 (1979).

[169] Callan v. Wilson, 127 U.S. 540 (1888).

trial only if the defendant was convicted first at a bench trial, then appealed.[170]

In these post-*Duncan* cases, the justices continued to argue over the appropriate interpretation of the Due Process Clause, the debate at the heart of the *Duncan* decision.[171] In *Williams*, Justice Harlan persisted in his argument that the Court's selective incorporation of federal rights was flawed because it must necessarily "be tempered to allow the States more elbow room in ordering their own criminal systems.... But to accomplish this by diluting constitutional protections within the federal system itself is something to which I cannot possibly subscribe."[172] Justice Powell, who provided the fifth vote to uphold non-unanimous verdicts in *Apodaca*, concurred specially to express agreement with Harlan's objection, and with Justice Fortas's earlier opinion in *Duncan*. Powell argued that the Sixth Amendment required unanimity in federal trials, but the Fourteenth Amendment did not incorporate, "jot-for-jot," each and every aspect of the Sixth Amendment Jury Clause against the states. "A uniform treatment," Justice Powell wrote, "derogates principles of federalism that are basic to our system ... deprives the States of freedom to experiment with adjudicatory processes different from the federal model ... [and] has culminated in the dilution of federal rights that were, until these decisions, never seriously questioned."[173] Powell's position was not shared by a majority of the justices, who favored uniform application to state and federal defendants alike, but it salvaged the unanimity requirement in federal courts, and it did pick up two more votes (Justice Rehnquist and Chief Justice Burger) in *Ballew*.[174] Since *Apodaca*, however, arguments to depart from the uniform application of criminal procedure rights in state and federal courts have essentially disappeared from the Court's decisions, urged only now and then by legal scholars.[175]

---

[170] Ludwig v. Massachusetts, 427 U.S. 618, 625–26 (1976).

[171] *See* Jerold Israel, *Selective Incorporation: Revisited*, 71 GEO. L.J. 253, 298–301 (1982). For a comprehensive and updated treatment of the incorporation saga in criminal procedure, *see* LAFAVE, ISRAEL, & KING, *supra* note 86, at pp. 467–628 (2d ed. 1999 & annual supp.).

[172] *Id. See also* George C. Thomas III, *When Constitutional Worlds Collide: Resurrecting the Framers' Bill of Rights and Criminal Procedure*, 100 MICH. L. REV. 145 (2001) (arguing that the "process of incorporation took a sledgehammer to the federal criminal procedure guarantees," rendering the "the federal Bill of Rights ... a fresh lump of clay for the Court to refashion into a new, less protective body of doctrine." ... [T]he Court "sacrificed the twelve-person federal jury on the altar of incorporation.").

[173] *Apodaca*, 406 U.S. 366, at 374 (Powell, J., concurring).

[174] Justice Powell was joined by Justice Rehnquist and Chief Justice Burger in *Ballew*, where he stated: "I do not agree, however, that every feature of jury trial practice must be the same in both federal and state courts." 435 U.S. 223, 244 (Powell, J., concurring).

Specifically, the Court in the years following *Duncan* refused to dilute one aspect of the jury right that was essential to eliminating racial bias in state criminal courts, and that was its regulation of the jury selection process. The *Duncan* decision extended to state defendants the right to a jury, but in many communities for many years, that jury was all male and all white. Proving intentional discrimination in jury selection under the Equal Protection Clause was difficult; progress in integrating juries was slow. *Duncan* laid the groundwork for a new means of combating discrimination in state courts—claims based on the Sixth Amendment requirement that jury panels be drawn from a "cross-section" of the community. In 1975, in yet another case out of Louisiana, *Taylor v. Louisiana*,[176] the Court held that distinctive groups in the community cannot be systematically excluded unless necessary to an important state interest. Establishing a violation of the cross-section requirement was easier than establishing an equal protection violation, which required a showing of *intentional* discrimination. *Duncan*, then *Taylor,* combined with advances in technology, eventually led to the widespread adoption of random selection procedures and the inclusion of more minorities and women in jury pools.

Aftermath

But what of Duncan and Sobol, both of whom in the summer of 1968 were still threatened with criminal charges in Plaquemines Parish after remand by the Supreme Court? On July 22, 1968, a panel made up of United States Court of Appeals Judge Robert Ainsworth, and District Judges Frederick J.R. Heebe and Fred J. Cassibry, enjoined Perez's criminal prosecution of Sobol. After ten days of hearings and numerous depositions[177] they had concluded, "[T]his was an unlawful prosecution which was undertaken for purposes of . . . deterring Sobol and other lawyers similarly situated from helping to provide legal representation in civil rights cases and to deter Negroes like Duncan from seeking their representation."[178] The stakes were summed up by one African–Ameri-

---

[175] *Compare* LaFave, Israel, & King, *supra* note 86, at § 2.6 (c) note 87 (concluding that the Rehnquist Court "has displayed not the slightest interest" in revisiting the selective incorporation doctrine, and quoting Justice Scalia's response upon being asked the question if he " 'would try to overturn the longstanding doctrine making states subject to the Bill of Rights': 'I'm a serious constitutional scholar, not a nut.' ") *with* Thomas, *supra* note 172; Donald Dripps, *On the Costs of Uniformity and the Prospects of Dualism in Criminal Procedure*, 45 St. Louis U. L.J. 433 (2001).

[176] 419 U.S. 522 (1975).

[177] *Louisiana to Out-of-State Lawyers: Get Out*, New Republic, Feb. 24, 1968, at 17–18.

[178] Duncan v. Perez, 445 F.2d 557 (5th Cir. 1971).

can attorney, Zelma Wyche, testifying early in the trial of *Sobol v. Perez*. Wyche said Sobol's arrest "shook me up.... [I]f ... Sobol was really found guilty and the LCDC lawyers were restricted from practicing law in Louisiana, I knew then that the Negroes of Louisiana who were trying to secure equal rights would be in a bad fix."[179] The decision was not appealed.

After Perez sought to retry Duncan—without a jury because the penalty for simple battery had been reduced[180]—Duncan's attorneys again sought relief from the federal courts. Alvin Bronstein's complaint in *Duncan v. Perez* charged that Perez meant only to harass Duncan and deter other African Americans from exercising their right to hire an attorney of their choice.[181] On October 20, 1970, almost exactly four years after Duncan's first arrest, United States District Judge Cassibry permanently enjoined Leander Perez, Jr., from further prosecuting Duncan on the battery charge, a decision affirmed upon appeal by the Fifth Circuit. "The multiple arrests, the unusually high bond [and] sentence, the unlawful demand that double bond be posted, the arrest of Sobol, and the comments of the defendant [Perez] and the state District Judge [Leon], all taken together established that these authorities are personally hostile to Duncan and have altered established principles of criminal procedure in an effort to punish Duncan for his exercise of federally secured rights."[182] Furthermore, "the charge against Duncan would not have been prosecuted, and certainly not reprosecuted, were it not for the civil rights context out of which the case arose, for Duncan's selection of civil rights attorneys to represent him, and for the vigor of his defense." Given Duncan's nominal violation of state law,[183] the state had no legitimate interest in pursuing the prosecution. Moreover, Judge Cassibry concluded, "If Duncan were required to face retrial, it would constitute an unmistakable message to Negroes in Plaquemines Parish that it is unprofitable to step outside familiar patterns and to seek to rely on federal rights to oppose the policies of certain parish officials. The destructive effect on the exercise of federal rights could not be corrected by Duncan's possible subsequent success in state or federal court."[184] "That was the end of it," Sobol later recalled.[185]

---

[179] JACK BASS, UNLIKELY HEROES 290 (1981).

[180] Duncan v. Perez, 445 F.2d 557 ("defendant faced retrial without a jury").

[181] *Provensal responded no basis for interference by feds*, NEW ORLEANS TIMES-PICAYUNE, Nov. 7, 1968 p. 6 c.2; NEW ORLEANS TIMES-PICAYUNE, Jan. 5, 1969, sec. 5, p. 27 c. 6.

[182] Duncan v. Perez, 321 F.Supp. 181, 184 (E.D.La. 1970).

[183] Duncan v. Perez, 445 F.2d 557 (5th Cir. 1971).

[184] *Id.*.

[185] Interview with Sobol, *supra* note 53.

Despite the important victories of Sobol and Duncan, it was business as usual in Plaquemines Parish for some time. One determined Perez opponent, Lawrence Rousselle, was arrested by Leander Perez, Jr., for plotting to assassinate Judge Perez. Rousselle had dared to encourage whites to attend integrated schools and support a candidate challenging Chalin Perez, Jr. for council president. Held for two weeks on a $75,000 bond, ordered reduced by the Supreme Court of Louisiana, he was finally released after Chalin Perez won the election, with no indictment or information ever filed.[186] Prosecuted again the next year, Rousselle filed false imprisonment claims and dashed off to federal court in New Orleans to seek removal of the state criminal charges to federal court.[187]

The day Judge Perez died in 1969, five young African–American men, entered a parish bar and "rashly announced their intention to celebrate." The five were quickly arrested, charged, and convicted of drunkenness and disturbing the peace (neither offense triggering the right to trial by jury under *Duncan*) and sentenced to jail with no option of paying a fine.[188] One wonders whether bar patrons celebrating something else would have paid as high a price.

Voting efforts had actually lost ground. As of 1970 only 184 African Americans were registered to vote in the parish, out of nearly 3000 eligible African–American residents.[189] Plaqueminians did not have their first free election until the early 1980s, when Judge Perez's two sons turned against each other, creating an opening for opposition forces.[190] Lea, Jr., started investigating the council in the late 1970s, and the grand jury indicted his brother Chalin in 1981.[191] But in 1982, the grand jury indicted Lea Perez, Jr., and Judge Leon with conspiracy and

---

[186] *See* note 94 *supra. See also* Complaint, Rousselle v. Perez, on file with author.

[187] *See* Complaint, *supra*; Rousselle v. Leon, *et al.*, Complaint for Damages for False Imprisonment (on file with author); State v. Rousselle, Petition for Removal, U.S. D.Ct. E.D. La, New Orleans Division (on file with author); *Rousselle Case Transferred*, New Orleans Times–Picayune, Feb. 21, 1968, at Section 1, page 21. One report states that Perez, Jr. and his aides tried to seize Rousselle and his attorney outside the federal courthouse for contempt. Reportedly, Smith, Rousselle's attorney, fought back, and pounded on door to the courtroom. An angry federal judge emerged and ordered Perez, Jr., and his men to leave Smith and his client alone while removal proceedings were pending. Bruce W. Eggler, *Plaquemines Without the Great White Father*, New Republic, May 24, 1969, at 11, 12.

[188] *Id.* at 11.

[189] Roy Reed, *Life of Blacks in South Affected by White Resistance as Well as Racial Gains*, N.Y. Times, Feb. 8, 1970, at 50.

[190] *The Ends of the Earth* (film documentary, on file with author).

[191] *Leander Perez, Jr. succumbs at 68*, Baton Rouge Morning Advocate, Oct. 6, 1988, at 1A.

malfeasance involving their role in the early discharge of a 1981 grand jury that was allegedly planning to indict Perez, Jr.[192] By 1983, Chalin Perez had been ousted from the council presidency. Lea Perez, Jr., chose not run for re-election as District Attorney. A suit against the Perez family by the Parish government seeking millions in oil royalties accumulated unlawfully between 1936 and 1983 was settled in 1987 for $12 million and future oil earnings.[193] Darryl Bubrig, the Assistant District Attorney who had tried the battery charge against Duncan to Judge Leon, took the reins from Leander Perez, Jr., in 1984 and is still today the Plaquemines District Attorney.[194]

Duncan later bought a shrimp boat, and when it was destroyed by a collision with a dangerous underwater oil jacket, he hired Sobol to represent him in a successful suit against the oil company. Still piloting boats in the parish today, Duncan was selected to receive the local 2003 Black History Month Award, and is pictured here next to his attorney, Richard Sobol, with that award.

CONCLUSION

The *Duncan* decision and the cases that followed were products of two of the most powerful forces modern criminal procedure—the quest for equal justice and federalism. Like the facts of so many other criminal cases reviewed by the Court during that period, the circumstances in *Duncan* vividly illustrated the civil rights struggle in the Deep South.[195] The conflict between parish officials and Gary Duncan grew out of the violent response of white citizens to school desegregation, and grew into a fight for the rights of minority citizens to secure legal counsel of their choice. The decision also became the focus of one of the most fundamental controversies in constitutional law, a decision in which the justices openly debated federal regulation of state government. The Court's selective incorporation approach in *Duncan,* hardly controversial now, was an explosive state's rights issue at the time. As Justice Brennan later wrote, it was in *Duncan* that the Court "attempted to explain the theoretical basis for its decisions requiring the states to adhere to certain provisions of the Bill while excluding others."[196]

---

[192] *Id.* Both Perez and Leon were acquitted of these charges in 1986. *Jury acquits Perez, Leon,* BATON ROUGE MORNING ADVOCATE, Feb. 14, 1988, at 4B.

[193] *Monument to Judge Perez now overgrown, repudiated,* BATON ROUGE MORNING ADVOCATE, Nov. 21, 1988, at 4B.

[194] *See* http://www.plaqueminesparish.com/Government.php.

[195] *See, e.g.,* Michael Klarman, *Racial Origins of Modern Criminal Procedure,* 99 MICH. L. REV. 48 (2000).

[196] Brennan, *supra* note 160.

That the right to trial by jury became the focus of this controversy is not surprising. Of all of the rights of those accused of crime, it is the only right of the accused that is enshrined in all of the original state constitutions, and in the body of the United States Constitution itself in addition to the Bill of Rights. Not even the right to counsel shares this distinction. The jury is more than a safeguard against inaccuracy or prosecutorial overreaching; it is a unique political force. Ordinary jurors can thwart the power of the judiciary in ways that procedures guaranteed by other individual rights cannot. Federal judicial oversight of state criminal prosecutions threatened state autonomy from without, but jury rights, like voting rights, threatened state power from within. *Duncan*'s holding that the Due Process Clause limits a state's power to deny jury trials was a key element of the Warren Court's expansive efforts to ensure that the criminal process would not be used as a weapon against those struggling to assert their civil rights.

*

9

Terry v. Ohio: The Fourth Amendment Reasonableness of Police Stops and Frisks Based on Less Than Probable Cause

By John Q. Barrett*

Terry v. Ohio, 392 U.S. 1 (1968), is a landmark Supreme Court decision concerning the Fourth Amendment prohibition on "unreasonable searches and seizures." In *Terry*, the Court decided that the Fourth Amendment applies to police activities known as "stops" and "frisks"—they are, respectively, "seizures" and "searches" within the meanings of those Fourth Amendment terms. But the *Terry* Court also decided that such stops and frisks can be constitutionally "reasonable" under the Fourth Amendment even when police lack "probable cause," the level of justification that the Fourth Amendment requires for government-issued warrants. *Terry* thus extended Fourth Amendment limits to street policing methods that occur without the judicial permission that is the essence of the warrant process. But the Supreme Court in *Terry* applied those constitutional limits in a more permissive fashion than it would have if it had interpreted the Fourth Amendment to require that *all* seizures and searches, including street stops and frisks, be based on probable cause.

Introduction: Detective McFadden and Street Policing

The protagonist of *Terry v. Ohio* was a Cleveland, Ohio, cop. Martin McFadden, born in 1901, was raised and spent his whole life in Cleveland. After attending high school, he went to work as a timekeeper for the Cleveland Railway Company. In 1925, McFadden joined the Cleveland Police Department. Five years later, he was promoted to its detective bureau, and in 1934 he joined the fraud unit. For the remainder of

*I am grateful to Carol Steiker for her excellent work on this project and to Eleni Zanias, Jessica Duffy and Nikia O'Neal for skillful research and editorial assistance.

his career, which lasted until he retired in 1970, Detective McFadden patrolled downtown Cleveland. He specialized in spotting pickpockets on the streets and protected city stores from fraud artists.[1]

For many years, Detective McFadden was semi-famous, at least in Cleveland, for his frequent arrests of a pickpocket named Louis ("Louie the Dip") Finkelstein.[2] A local newspaper, *The Cleveland Press*, reportedly once had files that were filled with clippings detailing McFadden–Finkelstein street encounters, including one at a Republican rally and another at a St. Patrick's Day parade. McFadden was so persistent in his pursuit of Finkelstein that "Louie the Dip" began to call McFadden "the persecutor." Later in life, Detective McFadden recalled these encounters with evident pride: "I remember four straight years I arrested Louie at the Ice Capades. In those days all we had to do was see Louis in a crowd and we arrested him."[3] To McFadden, his knowledge of Finkelstein's pocket-picking past apparently was reason enough to arrest him on sight, even when McFadden had no information about what Finkelstein was up to in a current moment.

The Fourth Amendment, however, has never been interpreted to permit arrest on sight for crimes that were prosecuted in the past, or that are so far in the past that they are beyond present prosecution. To the contrary, the Supreme Court has held repeatedly that the Fourth Amendment demands that all arrests be based on probable cause, which it defines as a substantial basis to believe that a prosecutable crime has been committed or is being committed by a particular person.[4] When McFadden referred to "arrest" in the context of his dealings with Louie

---

[1] *See* Jerry Kvet, *Nemesis of Downtown Desperadoes Retires*, CLEV. PRESS, Oct. 12, 1970; Bus Bergan, *Illegal Search Is Charged at Concealed Weapons Trial*, CLEV. PRESS, Sept. 22, 1964.

[2] *See* E.J. Kissell, *Court Ruling Is Gratifying to Detective in Frisk Case*, CLEV. PLAIN DEALER, June 11, 1968.

[3] Kvet, *supra* note 1; *accord* George Condon, *Louie the Dip Sticks in Memory*, CLEV. PLAIN DEALER, Nov. 15, 1981 ("The police book on Louie the Dip begins in 1909 and runs through 1959, with 121 arrests.").

By 1968, McFadden recognized that constitutional criminal procedure had developed generally to prohibit his practice of taking someone into custody based merely on his reputation. *See* E.J. Kissell, *supra* note 2 ("McFadden yesterday reminisced about his late adversary, Louie the Dip: 'It used to be when he saw me he'd walk over, because he knew I was going to throw him in the klink overnight, preventing somebody from being taken by him. But times have changed, as you know, and the police can't do that anymore.' "); *cf.* *Pickpockets' Nemesis Retiring From His Beat*, CLEV. PLAIN DEALER, Oct. 14, 1970 ("When Martin J. McFadden first patrolled Euclid Avenue downtown, a policeman could arrest a character if he looked strange or was loitering. 'It was fundamental preventive detention,' McFadden said yesterday as he cleared the papers from his desk in the Hotel and Checks Unit of the Cleveland Police Department.").

[4] *See, e.g.*, Brinegar v. United States, 338 U.S. 160 (1949).

the Dip, however, the detective apparently did not mean the kind of arrest that leads to arraignment, trial and thus the possibility of criminal conviction. What he meant, instead, was simply a detention of Louie's person. This kind of seizure would allow McFadden to investigate what Finkelstein was up to, or at least to begin a process of moving him away from some place where McFadden did not want him to be. McFadden apparently believed that he could do this to Louie whenever he pleased.

These police practices—seizing a person by stopping him on the street, and doing so in the absence of the probable cause that would legally justify his real, full-blown arrest for engaging in criminal activity, and then perhaps also searching him to the extent of patting down the outer surfaces of his clothing—are the issues that the Supreme Court addressed in *Terry v. Ohio*. As the case name suggests, it had nothing to do with Louis Finkelstein. It had everything to do with Detective McFadden and officers like him throughout the country who patrol public places, observe people behaving suspiciously, commence to investigate them and, as they come into proximity to these quarries, expose themselves to danger if such persons are armed with weapons.

Terry, the routine Cleveland case that went all the way to the Supreme Court, was decided in McFadden's—in street policing's—favor. It made him immortal, at least in the annals of constitutional criminal procedure, and it gave Fourth Amendment approval to police conduct that had not previously been subjected to constitutional evaluation.

II. The Case: McFadden, Chilton, Terry and Katz

A. Stop, Frisk, Arrest

Terry v. Ohio began on the afternoon of Halloween 1963 with two black men on a street in downtown Cleveland.[5] One, Richard D. Chilton, had moved to Cleveland from Chicago and worked as a printer. The other man was named John W. Terry.

Chilton and Terry's legal troubles together began on a corner in Cleveland's commercial district.[6] On the afternoon of Thursday, October

---

[5] For extensive material and varying perspectives on *Terry* and its impact, see Terry v. Ohio *30 Years Later: A Symposium on the Fourth Amendment, Law Enforcement & Police–Citizen Encounters*, 72 St. John's L. Rev. 721–1524 (Summer–Fall 1998).

[6] At the time, this downtown Cleveland area was known as Playhouse Square. For a street map that depicts the locations of the *Terry* stops, frisks and arrests, see Jill Dinneen's scale map, *id.* at 1384, and my key to these events, *id.* at 1385.

The above text reflects Chief Justice Warren's version of events in his opinion for the *Terry* Court. For text and detail from the arrest report that Detective McFadden filed, see Lewis R. Katz, Terry v. Ohio *at Thirty–Five: A Revisionist View*, 74 Miss. L.J. 423, 431, 434 (2004) (quoting McFadden's Oct. 31, 1963, report).

31, 1963, Detective Martin McFadden, who was white, observed two younger black men behaving suspiciously. From across the street, McFadden observed the men for about twelve minutes. He saw them take turns walking several hundred feet down the block from the corner, peering into the window of a store or an airline ticket office, and then returning to the corner. McFadden suspected that the men were "casing," or planning to stick-up, a business. He then saw a third man walk to the corner, speak briefly to the first two and then depart. McFadden then saw the first two men leave the corner and walk down the adjacent street. McFadden followed them around the corner and down the next block.[7] He saw them meet up there, in front of a haberdashery, with the third man. McFadden then approached the men, identified himself as a police officer and asked for their names. Receiving a mumbled response, McFadden turned one of the men (who turned out to be Terry) around and quickly patted down the outside of his clothing. McFadden felt a hard object that he recognized as a gun, but he could not pull it out of the man's coat, so the detective pulled the coat off and then took possession of the weapon. McFadden then ordered all three men into the nearby store. He patted down the second black man (Chilton), felt a gun in his coat pocket too, and seized it. McFadden then patted down the third man (Carl Katz), who was white, and found that he was unarmed. McFadden placed the men under arrest and had them transported to a police station. Chilton and Terry, but not Katz, later were charged with carrying concealed weapons.

B. Suppression Hearing, Trial, Judgment, Appeal

Chilton and Terry obtained fine legal representation. Their attorney Louis Stokes (also a black man) had been a lawyer for ten years and by 1963 he was one of Cleveland's leading criminal defense attorneys.[8] He handled these cases all the way to the Supreme Court. Cuyahoga County Assistant Prosecutor Reuben Payne, another black man, was assigned to prosecute Chilton and Terry.[9] Payne also handled the cases all the way up the line and ultimately won *Terry v. Ohio* in the Supreme Court.

---

[7] Although this fact was never noted in the subsequent litigation, this new location is just beyond an alley/underpass that leads back, as a secluded shortcut, to their original street location.

[8] In 1967, Louis Stokes helped his younger brother Carl B. Stokes win election as mayor of Cleveland. The next year, within months of the Supreme Court's *Terry* decision, Louis Stokes was elected to the United States House of Representatives. He was reelected fourteen times and served in the House from 1969 until his retirement in 1999. For more biographical information on Stokes, see 72 St. John's L. Rev. at 1393. For his memoir of the *Terry* case, see Hon. Louis Stokes, *Representing John W. Terry*, *id.* at 727.

[9] For more biographical information on Payne, see 72 St. John's L. Rev. at 1391. For his memoir of the *Terry* case, see Reuben M. Payne, *The Prosecutor's Perspective on* Terry: *Detective McFadden Had a Right to Protect Himself*, *id.* at 733.

In Cleveland, the *Chilton* and *Terry* cases were assigned to a newly-appointed Cuyahoga County Court of Common Pleas judge, Bernard Friedman.[10] On behalf of both clients, defense attorney Stokes filed motions to suppress the guns and the bullets on which the charges were based. He argued that Detective McFadden had stopped and frisked Chilton and Terry without probable cause, in violation of their Fourth Amendment rights.[11] Judge Friedman, who first received briefs from the parties and then held a suppression hearing that included testimony by McFadden, denied the motions.[12] Payne then won Chilton's and Terry's convictions at separate bench trials and each was sentenced to prison. The Ohio Court of Appeals affirmed the convictions[13] and the Ohio Supreme Court denied review. Stokes then petitioned the Supreme Court of the United States to review his clients' convictions, claiming violations of their Fourth Amendment rights.

III. The *Terry* Litigation in the Supreme Court

A. The Emergence of the Stop & Frisk Issues

The legal road that led to a Supreme Court decision addressing the constitutionality of police stops and frisks based on less than probable cause was surprisingly long. For decades prior to the 1960s, police officers had been stopping, questioning, and frisking people on the street without having arrests warrants or probable cause to make arrests,[14] but the legal system was slow to focus on the constitutionality of these practices. One explanation may be that police stops and frisks always have been low visibility practices—they often do not result in seizures of tangible evidence, arrests or, ultimately, prosecutions and criminal convictions. As a result, many innocent persons who experience police stops and frisks are probably glad when these encounters end and, understandably, they choose not to make legal issues of why and how they were stopped and frisked at all.

---

[10] For more biographical information on Friedman, see *id*. at 1393–95.

[11] Since Wolf v. Colorado, 338 U.S. 25 (1949), the Supreme Court had applied the Fourth Amendment to the states, and since Mapp v. Ohio, 367 U.S. 643 (1961), the Court had held that the remedy for state violations of the Fourth Amendment was exclusion from trial of evidence obtained through unconstitutional searches or seizures.

[12] Annotated transcripts of the *Chilton* and *Terry* suppression hearing and trials, including Judge Friedman's bench opinion, are published as *Appendix,* State of Ohio v. Richard D. Chilton *and* State of Ohio v. John W. Terry: *The Suppression Hearing and Trial Transcripts*, 72 St. John's L. Rev. at 1387–1524.

[13] *See* Ohio v. Terry, 214 N.E.2d 114 (Ohio Ct. App. 1966).

[14] One early judicial opinion, for example, describes a police officer in Brooklyn, New York, who was shot and killed while he was "engaged in searching Italians." People v. Marendi, 107 N.E. 1058, 1060 (N.Y. 1915).

By the 1960s, various legal forces and actors were not waiting for the Supreme Court to address the constitutionality of stops and frisks. In 1964, New York took the lead among the states by enacting a statute that affirmatively authorized such police activity.[15] In 1967, President Johnson's Commission on Law Enforcement and Administration of Justice recommended that all states define police officer authority to stop persons for brief questioning. Lower courts, as in the *Terry* case itself, also were deciding challenges to stops and frisks and offering increasingly substantive analyses of the Fourth Amendment issues they raised. Scholarly research and writing about law enforcement matters also were focusing attention on these issues. It was only a matter of time before the Court addressed the constitutional questions regarding police stops and frisks.

B. The Supreme Court Takes the Stop and Frisk Cases

The Court that decided *Terry* was the Warren Court late in, but fully in, its prime. Earl Warren had been the Chief Justice of the United States since 1953, and in 1967 he was beginning what he hoped would be his final Term on the Court before retirement. The Associate Justices who were serving with Warren were the two surviving and long-serving Roosevelt appointees, Hugo L. Black and William O. Douglas; three seasoned Eisenhower appointees, John Marshall Harlan, William J. Brennan, Jr., and Potter Stewart; one Kennedy appointee, Byron R. White; President Johnson's appointee Abe Fortas; and, in his first Term on the Court, a second Johnson appointee, Thurgood Marshall.

Chilton and Terry petitioned the Supreme Court for writs of *certiorari* on March 18, 1967. Their joint petition asked the Court to decide whether Detective McFadden had, by frisking them, arrested them without probable cause in violation of the Fourth and Fourteenth Amendments, requiring suppression of the guns and bullets.[16] On May 29, the Court granted the petition.[17] A few weeks later, Richard Chilton was killed during a shoot-out with police as he and three other armed men attempted to rob a drugstore.[18] Thus in the end, the only Ohio stop

---

[15] *See* Act of Mar. 2, 1964, ch. 86, § 2, 180–a, 1964 N.Y. Laws 111 (authorizing a police officer to "stop any person ... whom he reasonably suspects is committing, has committed or is about to commit" a crime and to search that person if the officer "reasonably suspects that he is in danger of life or limb") (codified at N.Y. Code Crim. Proc. 180–a) (1964) (current version at N.Y. Crim. Proc. Law 140.50 (McKinney 2005)).

[16] *See* Terry v. Ohio, 35 U.S.L.W. 3357 (U.S. Apr. 11, 1967) (No. 1161). The petition presented one question to the Court: "Did [the] police officer's mid-afternoon stopping and frisking of suspects constitute unlawful arrest without probable cause, rendering evidence so obtained inadmissible under [the] Fourth and Fourteenth Amendments?"

[17] *See* Terry v. Ohio, 387 U.S. 929 (1967).

[18] *See* James T. Cox, *Bullets Write Finish to Chilton Case*, CLEV. PLAIN DEALER, June 18, 1967; *Prints in Getaway Car Checked in Columbus Holdup*, CLEV. PRESS, June 20, 1967.

and frisk case that the Supreme Court decided—the legal landmark—
was the case of John W. Terry.

Terry actually was the fourth stop and frisk case that the Court
agreed in 1967 to review. The first, *Wainwright v. New Orleans*, arose
from police forcibly stopping and frisking a pedestrian in the French
Quarter.[19] The second, *Sibron v. New York*, raised Fourth Amendment
questions about a police officer who, after observing a man meet with
known drug dealers, reached into the man's pocket and seized glassine
envelopes that turned out to contain heroin.[20] The third case, *Peters v.
New York*, arose from a police officer chasing suspected burglars, catch-
ing one, questioning him, frisking him for a weapon and, feeling something hard in his pocket, removing what turned out to be burglar's
tools.[21] These cases, and in particular the questions they raised about
constitutional limits on "frisks," turned out to be secondary to the *Terry*
landmark.

C. Briefing & Oral Argument

When the Supreme Court decided in 1967 to hear the stop and frisk
cases, the interested legal community responded aggressively. The Court
received the parties' extensive briefs on the merits of each case and, in
addition, submissions by numerous *amici curiae*. The *amici* who urged
the Court to give its constitutional imprimatur to police stops and frisks
in the absence of probable cause to arrest included Americans for
Effective Law Enforcement, an Illinois non-profit corporation; the National District Attorneys Association; the Attorney General of the State
of New York; and, on behalf of the United States, Solicitor General
Erwin N. Griswold. The Court also received an *amicus* brief on the other
side of the Fourth Amendment issue from the national, New York and
Ohio offices of the American Civil Liberties Union and a separate *amicus*
brief from the NAACP's Legal Defense and Educational Fund, Inc.[22] The
NAACP brief argued that citizens needed more protection from aggressive street police investigative tactics and urged the Court to "hold that
neither stops nor frisks may be made without probable cause."[23]

---

[19] *See* Wainwright v. New Orleans, 385 U.S. 1001 (1967) (granting petition for writ of
certiorari).

[20] *See* Sibron v. New York, 386 U.S. 954 (1967) (granting petition for writ of *certiorari*).

[21] *See* Peters v. New York, 386 U.S. 980 (1967) (granting petition for writ of *certiorari*).

[22] Each of these briefs is reprinted in 66 LANDMARK BRIEFS AND ARGUMENTS OF THE SUPREME
COURT OF THE UNITED STATES: CONSTITUTIONAL LAW (Philip B. Kurland & Gerhard Casper eds.,
1975) ("LANDMARK BRIEFS").

[23] *Id*. at 645.

On December 11 and 12, 1967, the Supreme Court heard oral argument in the *Sibron*, *Peters* and *Terry* cases.[24] In each, and especially in the *Terry* argument,[25] the Justices asked many questions about the underlying facts, including the nature of the downtown Cleveland street where Detective McFadden had arrested Terry four years earlier, the specifics of McFadden's policing experience, and his stated reasons for suspecting, stopping, frisking and arresting Chilton, Terry and Katz. They also probed quite actively the issues and doctrinal complexities that would be involved in applying the Fourth Amendment, including its "probable cause" requirement, to such police practices.

One aspect of the case that became explicit during oral argument was race. Defense attorney Stokes, an African–American, described his client Terry and the late Mr. Chilton as "two Negro males." Stokes also stated to the Justices that McFadden had testified that he, on first spotting these men, "didn't like them." Prosecutor Payne, also African–American, later stated that McFadden's testimony had been that he "didn't like their looks."[26] Payne explained—during an exchange with Justice Marshall, who of course at that time was the Court's first ever and only black Justice—that McFadden had not "meant by that any reference to pigmentation or anything else." What McFadden had meant, according to Payne, was that on the "entire record"—"the fact that this was in a downtown area, that there people were not continuing in the regular flow of commerce as were other people on the street"— these men "beared watching." (Stokes, in his rebuttal argument, did not dispute Payne's explanation of McFadden's race-neutral suspicions about Chilton and Terry,[27] and the Court apparently was satisfied—no Justice

---

[24] *See* 36 U.S.L.W. 3245–49 (Dec. 19, 1967) (summarizing and quoting from the oral arguments in the three cases). *Wainwright* had been argued on October 9 and 10. Thereafter, the Justices were so troubled its factual ambiguities and legal complications that they voted in conference to dismiss the petition as improvidently granted, but they had not do so by the December oral arguments.

[25] An imperfect transcript of the *Terry* oral argument is published in Landmark Briefs, *supra* note 22, and the argument itself is available as an audio file at www.oyez.org/oyez/resource/case/378/audioresources.

[26] In fact, McFadden's suppression hearing testimony was that he "didn't like their actions on Huron Road, and I suspected them of casing a job, a stick-up. That's the reason," he testified, that he had approached the men, turned Terry around and frisked him. At Chilton's subsequent trial, McFadden testified on cross-examination, "Well, to be truthful with you, I didn't like them. I was just attracted to them, and I surmised that there was something going on when one of them left the other one and did the walking up, walk past the store and stopped and looked in and come back again. When he come back, then I observed the other man doing the same thing."

[27] *Cf.* Hon. Louis Stokes, *supra* note 8, at 729 (" 'Mac,' as we called him, was really a guy that we liked. He was straight. One thing about him—as a police officer, he came

in their private conference suggested that *Terry* might be a case of racist policing, and the ultimate *Terry* opinions do not mention the races of McFadden, Chilton, Terry and Katz.[28])

IV. Supreme Court Decision-making

A. The Conference

On Wednesday, December 13, 1967, the day after the oral arguments had concluded, the nine Justices met privately to discuss and vote on the four stop and frisk cases.[29] In *Wainwright*, the Justices voted again to dismiss the petition as improvidently granted. In *Sibron*, the Justices voted eight to one to reverse the conviction. In *Peters* and *Terry*, the Justices voted unanimously to affirm the respective convictions.

The Justices' handwritten conference notes support the following observations about their discussion:

- Of the four cases, only *Terry* sparked debate about central Fourth Amendment issues.

- The Justices did not discuss clearly how Detective McFadden approaching, detaining and questioning Chilton, Terry and Katz— what we today call the *"Terry* stop"—implicated, if it did at all, the Fourth Amendment. Had the men been "seized" within the meaning of the Fourth Amendment? Most Justices implied that the stops were Fourth Amendment seizures, for they discussed whether McFadden's reasons amounted to "probable cause," which is Fourth Amendment phraseology. But only two Justices, Black and White, spoke squarely to this issue, and they said that the questioning McFadden had done did not raise Fourth Amendment issues.

- By contrast, there was no serious debate about the constitutional status of McFadden's frisks of the men—those acts were, in the view of each Justice, Fourth Amendment "searches."

- Applying the Fourth Amendment to such stops (seizures) and frisks (searches), what level of justification must a police officer

---

straight down the line. You did not have to worry about him misrepresenting what the facts were.").

[28] Chief Justice Warren's opinion for the *Terry* Court did acknowledge, however, that "minority groups, particularly Negroes, frequently complain" about "wholesale harassment by certain elements of the police community...." *Terry*, 392 U.S. at 14.

[29] For an extensive recreation and analysis of this conference, see John Q. Barrett, *Deciding the Stop and Frisk Cases: A Look Inside the Supreme Court's Conference*, 72 St. John's L. Rev. 749, 778–793 (1998). The conference notes of Justices Douglas, Brennan and Fortas are transcribed and correlated to each other in an appendix to the article. *See id.* at 845–890.

have for such conduct? In conference, the Justices answered this question preliminarily in a manner that is, in the end, directly at odds with what we have come to understand, down through *Terry* itself and subsequent Supreme Court decisions, as its "reasonable suspicion" holding. The Justices' conference answer to the justification question was the language of the Fourth Amendment itself; the requirement was "probable cause."

- There is no record that any Justice mentioned that the Fourth Amendment prohibits only "unreasonable" searches and seizures, or that the concept of reasonableness played any role in their conference discussion of the constitutionality of McFadden's conduct.

As the conference discussion concluded, Chief Justice Warren, who would be writing for the Court, stated some of his own ideas about how he would write *Terry*. Warren said that he planned to explain, in a lengthy opinion, that the police power to stop and frisk stems from, and goes only as far as permitted by, the Fourth Amendment. He hoped that his opinion would "lay down hard rules for stop and frisk" practices.

B. The Drafting

Chief Justice Warren's strong personal preference was for the Court to decide the stop and frisk cases by drafting a model statute, much as the Court had done two Terms earlier in *Miranda v. Arizona* for police interrogation practices.[30] His colleagues did not want to take a *Miranda*-type approach, however, and the Chief Justice deferred to their preference for an opinion that applied Fourth Amendment textual concepts— "search"; "seizure"; "probable cause"—to police stops and frisks.

In February 1968, Chief Justice Warren circulated a proposed *Terry* opinion to the other Justices.[31] It explained that a police stop of a pedestrian is a "seizure," and that a frisk that carefully explores the outer surfaces of his clothing is a "search." To conduct such stops and frisks, Warren wrote, police must have probable cause, not a lesser basis called "reasonable suspicion." Warren's draft then focused specifically on the frisk, explaining that the probable cause required to justify this type of search is specific to its self-protective objective: it is probable cause to believe that someone is armed and dangerous. Applying these standards to McFadden's treatment of Chilton, Terry and Katz, Warren

---

[30] 384 U.S. 436 (1966). Chief Justice Warren's opinion for the *Miranda* Court decreed that a police officer must give specified warnings to a suspect in custody and obtain his waiver of those rights before the officer lawfully may commence to interrogate the suspect. *See id.* at 444–45.

[31] For a complete account of the Justices' draft opinion circulations and correspondence in *Terry* and its companion cases, see John Q. Barrett, *supra* note 29, at 793–835.

wrote that the detective's observations of their street activities warranted further investigation, that McFadden had probable cause to believe that they were armed and casing a store for robbery, and that he therefore quite properly seized the defendants and searched them for weapons. His conduct was reasonable in scope, Warren wrote, because he seized them based on probable cause, and because his search was limited to searching the men for weapons.

Chief Justice Warren's proposed approach generally did not satisfy his fellow Justices. Justice Harlan, for one, believed that it was a mistake to address police stops and frisks, which raised unique problems, using the constitutional rules that governed more intrusive and familiar police practices such as arrests—Harlan recognized, and he was the first Justice to explain at length in writing, that using known Fourth Amendment concepts in this new context, although well-intended, might generally dilute their established, and important, meanings. Harlan thus advocated more Court candor, and new constitutional approaches, to address the stop and frisk problem.

In the end, Justice Brennan first rethought his own commitment to the probable cause approach and then persuaded Chief Justice Warren also to abandon it. In Brennan's new view, the proper constitutional question in *Terry* was the "reasonableness" of stops and frisks under the Fourth Amendment's Reasonableness Clause (*i.e.*, its prohibition on "unreasonable searches and seizures"), not the presence or absence of the probable cause required by its Warrant Clause—probable cause is not relevant, Brennan explained as he rewrote Warren's draft opinion, in determining the constitutional reasonableness of police activity that is not of the warrant type. Instead, in Brennan's words, the case concerned "whether it is always unreasonable for a policeman to seize a person and subject him to a limited search for weapons unless there is probable cause to make an arrest." And the reasonableness of non-warrant-type police activity, Brennan urged, must be determined by, first, identifying the government interest that is involved and, second, by determining whether specific and articulable facts justify a particular intrusion. Explaining these concepts further in the context of *Terry*, Brennan said that the government interests that were involved in McFadden approaching the three men—the stops—were its broad, almost omnipresent, interests in crime investigation and/or prevention, and that the interests that were involved in McFadden searching the men—the frisks—were the much less common need of a police officer to protect himself. Regarding the latter interest, Brennan wrote that it would be constitutionally unreasonable to deny a police officer the power to frisk where he is justified in believing that a person is armed and presently dangerous.

Justice Brennan closed his rewrite of Chief Justice Warren's proposed *Terry* opinion by explaining the objective reasonableness of Detective McFadden's conduct. He had observed behavior that was a preface to a stick-up, which demonstrated that stopping the men for questioning was reasonable. His subsequent frisks also were reasonable because a prudent officer would believe, while investigating this suspicious behavior, that Terry and his colleagues were armed threats to the officer's safety. Furthermore, nothing occurred at any point during McFadden's encounter with the men that dispelled his objectively reasonable beliefs. Brennan also noted that, although the precise Fourth Amendment limits of a frisk would have to be developed in the concrete circumstances of future cases, the protective rationale for this kind of search defined a limit on its scope, and that McFadden had not exceeded this limit.

In May 1968, Chief Justice Warren, accepting the substantial redrafting assistance of Justice Brennan, prepared and circulated a new draft *Terry* opinion taking this "reasonablessness" tack. Unlike the Chief Justice's earlier effort, this draft impressed his colleagues. It quickly garnered a Court, losing only the vote of Justice Douglas, who decided to dissent.

C. The *Terry* Decision

On Monday, June 10, 1968, Chief Justice Warren announced his opinion for the Supreme Court in *Terry v. Ohio*. It stated the issue narrowly: Is it "always unreasonable for a policeman to seize a person and subject him to a limited search for weapons unless there is probable cause for an arrest"? The Court's answer was no, which the Chief Justice explained further in his final paragraph:

> Each case of this sort will, of course, have to be decided on its own facts. We merely hold today that where a police officer observes unusual conduct which leads him reasonably to conclude in light of his experience that criminal activity may be afoot and that the persons with whom he is dealing may be armed and presently dangerous, where in the course of investigating this behavior he identifies himself as a policeman and makes reasonable inquiries, and nothing in the initial stages of the encounter serves to dispel his reasonable fear for his own or others' safety, he is entitled for the protection of himself and others in the area to conduct a carefully limited search of the outer clothing of such persons in an attempt to discover weapons which might be used to assault him. Such a search is a reasonable search under the Fourth Amendment, and any weapons seized may properly be introduced in evidence against the person from whom they were taken.[32]

---

[32] *Terry*, 392 U.S. at 30–31.

Justice Harlan, one of the eight in the *Terry* majority, filed a concurring opinion "to fill in a few gaps" in the Court's opinion.[33] Noting that the Court was approving frisks that police officers make to protect themselves from people they have stopped, Harlan stressed that frisks are second-step events—before police can establish the constitutional reasonableness of self-protective frisk, he explained, they first must establish the reasonableness of the forcible stop that put the potentially dangerous person in proximity to them in the first place. In a case such as *Terry*, Harlan continued, where the basis for a lawful stop is "an articulable suspicion of a crime of violence," that same suspicion makes it reasonable to frisk "immediately and automatically." Putting these elements together, Harlan categorized and explained *Terry* itself as "a proper stop and an incident frisk."

The Supreme Court in *Terry* was not, however, unanimous. Justice Douglas, in a biting dissent, attacked the majority for approving Fourth Amendment seizures and searches in the conceded absence of Fourth Amendment probable cause.[34] The Court's holding gave police "greater authority to make a 'seizure' and conduct a 'search' than a judge has to authorize such action," Douglas wrote, and he called that development "a long step down the totalitarian path." Because Douglas was in the hospital recovering from surgery when *Terry* was announced in June 1968, Chief Justice Warren announced this dissent for his colleague.

Terry v. Ohio made headlines. In a time of great social unrest, the Supreme Court generally was applauded for its sensitivity to the safety interests of law enforcement officers.[35]

D. *Sibron, Peters* and *Wainwright*

On the same day on which he announced *Terry*, Chief Justice Warren also announced the Court's decisions in the New York cases, *Sibron* and *Peters*.[36] In a combined opinion that addressed both cases, the Court held that drug evidence that had been seized from Mr. Sibron should be suppressed because the officer who had searched him had no basis to believe that he was armed and dangerous, and because the search in the case exceeded the permitted scope of a frisk—reaching into a person's pocket is more than a self-protective frisk of the outer

---

[33] *See id.* at 31–34 (Harlan, J., concurring).

[34] *See id.* at 35–39 (Douglas, J., dissenting).

[35] THE NEW YORK TIMES, for example, editorialized "that the Supreme Court's 8–1 [Terry] decision ... will help persuade policemen that the Court does not lie awake nights dreaming up ways to increase the hazards of their jobs." *"Unreasonable" Still Stands*, N.Y. TIMES, June 12, 1968, at 46; *accord* Fred P. Graham, *High Court Backs Rights Of Police To Stop And Frisk*, N.Y. TIMES, June 11, 1968, at 1.

[36] *See* Sibron v. New York, 392 U.S. 40 (1968).

surfaces of his clothing.[37] In *Peters*, by contrast, evidence had been properly seized because the underlying Fourth Amendment events had been not merely a stop and a frisk based on suspicion, but instead an arrest based on probable cause and a proper search of the person incident to that arrest.[38] Justice Harlan again concurred, this time in the results.[39] He took the occasion to state flatly that *Terry* had decided that a street "stop may indeed be premised on reasonable suspicion,"[40] which was consistent with his earlier recommendation that the Court employ "reasonable suspicion" phraseology but went further than did the *Terry* opinion itself.

Wainwright v. New Orleans was still on hold when the Court decided the other stop and frisk cases. On Monday, June 17, 1968, it announced its decision to dismiss Wainwright's petition as improvidently granted and, in the case, the filing of separate concurring opinions by Justices Harlan and Fortas and separate dissenting opinions by Chief Justice Warren and Justice Douglas.[41] Douglas took the occasion to emphasize his dissenting view that the Court had improperly changed "traditional Fourth Amendment standards" in *Terry*.[42]

V. Understanding the 1968 Deciding of *Terry*

In the realm of modern constitutional criminal procedure, which has come to be a collection of doctrinal categories, *Terry v. Ohio*, almost forty years old, is a Supreme Court decision that we know well. We know that the *Terry* Court identified police conduct short of formal arrest as nonetheless constituting "searches" and "seizures" under the Fourth Amendment. We know that the Court, by balancing the relative intrusiveness and public purposes of this police conduct, approved the constitutional "reasonableness" of stops where the police have objective and articulable bases to believe that crime is afoot, and of frisks where the police have objective and articulable bases to believe that persons lawfully stopped are armed and pose dangers to the police or others. Many thus think of *Terry* and the law of "stop and frisk" as a well-settled matter, a

---

[37] *Id*. at 62–66.

[38] *Id*. at 66–67.

[39] *See id*. at 70–79 (Harlan, J., concurring in the result).

[40] *Id*. at 71.

[41] *See* Wainwright v. New Orleans, 392 U.S. 598 (1968) (*per curiam*).

[42] *Id*. at 610 (Douglas, J., dissenting). He also noted his "fear," for example, "that with *Terry* and with *Wainwright* we have forsaken the Western tradition and taken a long step toward the oppressive police practices not only of Communist regimes but of modern Iran, 'democratic' Formosa, and Franco Spain, with which we are now even more closely allied." *Id*. at 615.

sensible balancing of public interests in law enforcement against relatively lesser intrusions on personal freedom, and a measure of constitutional justification—"reasonable suspicion"—that police officers on the street, and also courts evaluating police conduct after the fact, can use effectively in deciding whether a particular intrusion is constitutionally permitted.

Before *Terry v. Ohio* was all of that, it and its companion cases asked the Justices of the Supreme Court in the October Term 1967 to consider and decide among competing analytical approaches to applying the Fourth Amendment to police stops and frisks. The Justices, concerned to control abusive police practices on the streets without unduly hampering law enforcement, carefully sorted through difficult legal and policy issues connected with each approach. Some thought that they should decide *Terry* as only a "frisk" case, and that they should do so by imposing real limits on the police power to frisk, leaving questions about on-the-street questioning and investigative detentions for later cases. Others thought that, as an analytical matter, the frisk issue could not be decided without first resolving "stop" questions. The latter view ultimately prevailed through a process of persuasion and compromise by the Justices.

Although we think of *Terry* and the constitutional law of stops and frisks as well-settled rules and categories, there was, from the time of the Court's conference through the drafting process that ended in the stop and frisk decisions of June 1968, an openness to multiple possibilities and doctrinal outcomes. One path that ultimately was not taken is the approach that Chief Justice Warren wanted in his heart of hearts: promulgating a *Miranda*-like frisk rule. It is of course impossible, without knowing the exact language of such a rule and the contingent course of subsequent events, to evaluate how this approach would have worked doctrinally, politically or practically. The *Terry* result itself eliminated the need, and thus political interest, to enact stop and frisk laws to empower the police. On the other hand, one way to view *Terry* itself is as something of a common law rule. *Terry* has, as developed in later decisions, become a known formula. Thus, while Chief Justice Warren never embarked consciously on the project of writing a stop and frisk "statute," his Court and the later Supreme Courts may well have done so in effect, with Fourth Amendment law ending up on the path that Warren wanted all along.

An alternative path, contemplated in the Justices' conference discussion and in Chief Justice Warren's first drafting effort, was to stick to the "probable cause" requirement of the Fourth Amendment's Warrant Clause. This approach took a unitary view of police actions that constitute Fourth Amendment "searches" or "seizures." According to Warren's early drafts, this approach would have required police officers to satisfy the requirements of the Warrant Clause whenever they searched or seized or, where obtaining a warrant was impossible, at least to justify their conduct with the "probable cause" that is a component of that Clause. When Warren tried to write an opinion that used this standard, however, the Court quickly fractured, coming together again only after Justice Brennan persuaded the Chief Justice to ground the opinion in a third approach: the Reasonableness Clause.

What if the Court had approved only stops and frisks that were based on Fourth Amendment probable cause? Justice Douglas, in his *Terry* dissent, implied that once some stops and frisks could be justified on less than probable cause, the protections of this Fourth Amendment component would erode in all contexts, including in the context of full-blown arrests where "probable cause" should retain its full constitutional meaning. The past decades may provide some support for this claim, but the converse proposition—that sticking with the "probable cause" rubric in all Fourth Amendment decision-making would have preserved its full meaning as a significant limit on the police—is not self-evident. As some Justices seemed to recognize in *Terry*, staying on the probable cause path for stops and frisks would have meant at least beginning the process of developing unique meaning for that level of justification in differing search and seizure contexts. Even if that development would not have led necessarily to later decisions pulling all "probable cause" requirements down to the level of its weakest form, the Court certainly would have been devising separate concepts that each claimed to be the same constitutional thing: "probable cause."

Did the Court then make a mistake in *Terry* by not going all the way and announcing with a new label—"reasonable suspicion"—that it was approving stops and frisks based on less justification than the Fourth Amendment requires for a lawful arrest? In 1968, most of the Justices were unwilling to take that step in the direction of semantic candor. Later Courts, following Justice Harlan's 1968 lead,[43] have not been so reserved, however, and "reasonable suspicion" is today, of course, a well-used measure of Fourth Amendment justification.[44]

The Justices' notes and the proposed stop and frisk opinions that the Court circulated in 1968 do not say explicitly why the Warren Court

---

[43] *See Terry*, 392 U.S. at 31 (Harlan, J., concurring); *Sibron*, 392 U.S. at 70 (Harlan, J., concurring).

[44] *See, e.g.*, Richards v. Wisconsin, 520 U.S. 385 (1997) (holding that if police have a "reasonable suspicion" that the announcement of their presence "would be dangerous or futile, or that it would inhibit the effective investigation of the crime," a "no-knock" entry is justified); Maryland v. Buie, 494 U.S. 325, 334–36 (1990) (concluding that the Fourth Amendment allows a "protective sweep" of premises that are an arrest scene if the searching officer has a "reasonable suspicion of danger"); Michigan v. Long, 463 U.S. 1032, 1049–50 & note 14 (1983) (authorizing area searches during investigative detentions by police who "have the level of suspicion identified in *Terry*").

was reluctant to embrace "reasonable suspicion" in 1968. These papers suggest that fidelity to the words of the Fourth Amendment played a role, and also that pragmatic considerations were present throughout the Court's stop and frisk deliberations. The Court was, and it knew that it was, deciding these cases in a particularly turbulent time. Events that occurred during the pendency of the stops and frisk cases included a crime explosion across the country; destructive urban riots; unrest in so-called ghettos, some of it arising from racial tensions between residents and the police; further unrest, among students and generally, regarding the Vietnam War; Richard Nixon campaigning for the presidency by highlighting the crime problem and attacking the Warren Court's crimi-nal law decisions; President Johnson's efforts to pass new anti-crime legislation; his decision not to seek reelection; and catastrophic acts of gun violence, including the assassinations of Dr. Martin Luther King, Jr. and, just days before the Court announced its *Terry* decision, U.S. Senator and Democratic presidential candidate Robert F. Kennedy.

The many compromises that *Terry* embodies and the genuine trepi-dation with which at least some Justices gave constitutional approval to police stops and frisks developed later into regrets. Justice Marshall, who as a newcomer to the Court was relatively uninvolved in the internal arguments over the stop and frisk cases, all but stated in later cases that he had voted wrong in *Terry*.[45] Justice Brennan, the shadow author of the Court's *Terry* opinion, never made so flat a statement, but some of his later opinions are very hard to square with the approach that he

---

[45] In Adams v. Texas, which came four years after *Terry*, the Supreme Court had what Justice Marshall described as its "first opportunity to give some flesh to the bones of" that 1968 decision. 407 U.S. 143, 153 (1972) (Marshall, J., joined by Douglas, J., dissenting). The *Adams* Court, including four Justices who had joined the Court after Terry, held 6–3 vote that a police officer did not violate the Fourth Amendment when he, responding to an informant's tip that a man sitting in parked car possessed narcotics and had a gun in his waistband, commanded this man to open the car, reached into his waistband, seized a gun, arrested him immediately for gun possession and, upon searching him incident to that arrest, found and seized narcotics. *See id.* at 144–45. Justice Marshall, dissenting, described the Court's analysis as inconsistent with *Terry*, which "never meant to approve this kind of knee-jerk police reaction." *Id.* at 159. In addition, in a separate, concluding section of his dissent, Marshall offered reflections that seemed almost to retract his vote in *Terry*:

> Mr. Justice Douglas was the sole dissenter in *Terry*. He warned of the "powerful hydraulic pressures throughout our history that bear heavily on the Court to water down constitutional guarantees...." 392 U.S., at 39. While I took the position then that we were not watering down rights, but were hesitantly and cautiously striking a necessary balance between the right of American citizens to be free from government intrusion into their privacy and their government's urgent need for a narrow exception to the warrant requirement of the Fourth Amendment, today's decision demonstrates just how prescient Mr. Justice Douglas was.

> It seems that the delicate balance that *Terry* struck was simply too delicate, too susceptible to the "hydraulic pressures" of the day. As a result of today's decision, the balance struck in Terry is now heavily weighted in favor of the government. And the

persuaded Chief Justice Warren and, through him, the Court to take in 1968.[46] But that is the ultimate point: it was 1968, and the Justices of the Warren Court did what they could then to apply the Constitution logically, sensibly to the stop and frisk problem.[47]

VI. Whatever Became of. . . .?

The known fate of John W. Terry was unfortunate. In August 1966, having already served penitentiary time for his gun possession conviction that was on its way to the Supreme Court and been paroled, Terry was arrested again, this time on a charge of heroin possession. While his Supreme Court case was pending, he was confined to the State Hospital at Lima, Ohio, as a narcotics user.[48] Thereafter, with the exception of a later arrest,[49] his activities are unreported.

Judge Bernard Friedman, whose original denials of Chilton's and Terry's motions to suppress evidence on Fourth Amendment grounds were in effect affirmed by the Supreme Court, was "very pleased" with *Terry v. Ohio*.[50] But in his post-decision comment, Judge Friedman

---

Fourth Amendment, which was included in the Bill of Rights to prevent the kind of arbitrary and oppressive police action involved herein, is dealt a serious blow. Today's decision invokes the specter of a society in which innocent citizens may be stopped, searched, and arrested at the whim of police officers who have only the slightest suspicion of improper conduct.

Id. at 161–62. In subsequent cases, Justice Marshall did write or join opinions that referred to *Terry* with approval, but only in contexts where *Terry* was invoked to describe Fourth Amendment *limits* on police practices. *See* Berkemer v. McCarty, 468 U.S. 420, 439–40 & note 32 (1984) (Marshall, J., for the Court); Florida v. Royer, 460 U.S. 491, 498–501 (1983) (White, J., joined by Marshall, Powell & Stevens, JJ.).

[46] *See, e.g.*, New Jersey v. T.L.O., 469 U.S. 325, 359–60 (1985) (Brennan, J., joined by Marshall, J., concurring in part and dissenting in part); Florida v. Royer, 460 U.S. 491, 509–10 (1983) (Brennan, J., concurring in the result); Dunaway v. New York, 442 U.S. 200, 213–14 (1979) (Brennan, J., joined by Stewart, White, Marshall, Blackmun and Stevens, JJ., for the Court).

[47] *See* Mark Tushnet, *The Warren Court as History: An Interpretation*, in THE WARREN COURT IN HISTORICAL AND POLITICAL PERSPECTIVE 23–24 (Mark Tushnet, ed., 1993) (characterizing *Terry* as a not atypical instance of the Warren Court's realism triumphing over its idealism); *but see* MORTON J. HOROWITZ, THE WARREN COURT AND THE PURSUIT OF JUSTICE 95–96 (1998) (explaining that *Terry* marked the end of the Warren Court's efforts to reform the criminal justice system).

[48] *See High Court Decision Awaited in Police "Stop and Frisk" Case*, CLEV. PRESS, Feb. 14, 1968.

[49] According to a wire service report, Terry was arrested on May 7, 1990, for breaking into a pharmacy in West Virginia. *See Noted Defendant Is Arrested Again*, BOSTON GLOBE, May 16, 1990, at 27, *available in* 1990 WL 5819851.

[50] *Police Won't Abuse Frisk Power Upheld by High Court, Says Blackwell*, CLEV. PRESS, June 11, 1968.

stressed that the stop and frisk practice he had approved was not unlimited:

> The court's decision gives police a vehicle through which to properly stop and search a suspicious person.
>
> In the [Chilton and Terry] trial, I limited this right to stopping and searching for weapons. This is necessary for the protection of the officer when he is acting on the basis of his experience and there is strong suspicion of wrong-doing.
>
> I don't believe there should be indiscriminate frisking for other contraband and I so indicated in this case.[51]

Detective Martin McFadden took rightful pleasure in the *Terry* decision. While the case was pending in the Supreme Court, he had worried that the Justices might rule that his treatment of Chilton and Terry had violated the Constitution.[52] After the decision validated his conduct, however, he crowed a bit: "I knew I was right, and I was, because the U.S. Supreme Court in Washington said I was."[53]

The later activities and fate of the intriguing "Louie the Dip" Finkelstein, McFadden's nemesis on the streets of Cleveland, deserve further research.

---

[51] *Id.*

[52] *See High Court to Eye Frisk Case*, CLEV. PLAIN DEALER, Dec. 11, 1967 ("McFadden, like many policemen who fear the effects of recent Supreme Court decisions on law enforcement, is afraid the court may take away his right to stop and frisk suspicious persons. 'If they do that, there's no use in being a policeman,' [McFadden] said yesterday. McFadden thinks his case is clear cut.").

[53] Kissell, *supra* note 2; *accord Right to Frisk Gets Supreme Court OK*, CLEV. PRESS, June 10, 1968, at A12 ("McFadden said: 'The court couldn't have made any other ruling. As far as I could see, it was a perfect case. I watched Perry [sic] and Chilton for about 15 minutes. They made 14 or 15 trips back and forth in front of the jewelry store window. I suspected they were looking it over in preparation for a robbery.' ").

*

10

United States v. Brignoni–Ponce and United States v. Martinez–Fuerte: The Road to Racial Profiling

Bernard E. Harcourt

March 8, 1989. Early morning at the Kansas City airport. Braniff Flight 650, the red-eye from Los Angeles, has just landed. DEA agent Carl Hicks and two local detectives are on the concourse, eyeing passengers as they deplane, looking for suspects. Hicks has intelligence information from the DEA that, in his words, "all-black street gangs from Los Angeles called the Crips and the Bloods are notorious for transporting cocaine into the Kansas City area from Los Angeles for sale. Most of them are young, roughly dressed male blacks."[1]

Arthur Weaver fits the description well: African–American, young, male, and roughly-dressed, he is deplaning the flight from Los Angeles. Plus, he's carrying two bags and walking so fast, according to Hicks, he's almost running down the concourse to the taxi stand—"common characteristics" of a drug courier at the airport. The officers lock on Weaver. They run after him, display a badge, and begin asking questions. They want to see the airline ticket. They want to see some ID. Weaver, apparently, gets nervous. His voice is unsteady, his speech is rapid, his hands shake, his body sways—or at least the officers claim later. After a few more exchanges, the agents conduct a pat down and search Weaver's two bags. They find six pounds of crack cocaine and over $2,500 in currency.[2]

At trial, Weaver challenges the search on the ground that the officers did not have a reasonable basis to suspect any wrongdoing. His motion to suppress is denied. Weaver enters a conditional guilty plea, reserving the right to appeal the denial of his suppression motion later. He is sentenced to twelve-and-a-half years in prison, five years super-

---

[1] United States v. Weaver, 966 F.2d 391, 394 note 2 (8th Cir. 1992).

[2] Id. at 392–93.

vised release, ten thousand dollars in fines, and a special assessment. And he takes his case to the Eighth Circuit Court of Appeals.

That court rejects Weaver's appeal, concluding that non-racial factors alone gave agent Hicks sufficient reason to conduct the search.[3] In a strong dissenting opinion, Chief Judge Arnold raises the issue of race: there was no good evidence to believe that race was a valid predictor of being a drug-courier. Using race, Judge Arnold writes, "simply reinforces the kind of stereotyping that lies behind drug-courier profiles. When public officials begin to regard large groups of citizens as presumptively criminal, this country is in a perilous situation indeed."[4] The majority relegates its response—and its entire discussion of race—to a footnote:

> We agree with the dissent that large groups of our citizens should not be regarded by law enforcement officers as presumptively criminal based upon their race. We would not hesitate to hold that a solely race-based suspicion of drug courier status would not pass constitutional muster. Accordingly, had [DEA agent] Hicks relied solely upon the fact of Weaver's race as a basis for his suspicions, we would have a different case before us. As it is, however, *facts are not to be ignored simply because they may be unpleasant*—and the unpleasant fact in this case is that Hicks had knowledge, based upon his own experience and upon the intelligence reports he had received from the Los Angeles authorities, that young male members of black Los Angeles gangs were flooding the Kansas City area with cocaine. To that extent, then, race, when coupled with the other factors Hicks relied upon, was a factor in the decision to approach and ultimately detain Weaver. *We wish it were otherwise, but we take the facts as they are presented to us, not as we would like them to be.*[5]

On December 14, 1992, the United States Supreme Court denies Weaver's petition for writ of certiorari.

How could the police use Arthur Weaver's race—the very fact that he is African–American—as a grounds to search him, consistent with the Fourth Amendment? How come the whole issue of race, in a criminal case involving a twelve-and-a-half year sentence, is relegated to an embarrassed footnote and an apology? Why doesn't the court conduct more rigorous analysis of the use of racial categories along the lines of strict scrutiny review? How come there is no discussion of the government's compelling interest? Why is race treated so differently in this law

---

[3] *See id.* at 396 (finding that Weaver's walking quickly toward a taxi, lacking a copy of his plane ticket and identification, and appearing nervous, constituted reasonable suspicion that Weaver carried drugs).

[4] *Id.* at 397 (Arnold, J., dissenting).

[5] *Id.* at 394 note 2 (emphasis added).

enforcement context than in other areas such as employment or education?

The answers to these questions lie on the long, winding, and often unpleasant road to racial profiling—a circuitous path characterized, more than anything, by an unwillingness to properly address the issue of race in policing.[6] On that road, two United States Supreme Court decisions—*United States v. Brignoni–Ponce*[7] and *United States v. Martinez-Fuerte*[8]—played a pivotal role. *Brignoni-Ponce* and *Martinez-Fuerte*, decided in 1975 and 1976, are the first and, to this date, the *only* United States Supreme Court decisions to expressly approve the use of race or ethnicity as a factor in the decision to stop and investigate an individual. As such, they remain today the leading Supreme Court cases addressing the use of race in policing.

Both cases involve the use of racial or ethnic profiling in identifying people illegally crossing the United States—Mexico border. By placing the first discussion of racial profiling at the Southern border with Mexico, the Supreme Court made race and ethnicity relevant to the policing enterprise in a uniquely powerful way. In the process, the Court paved a constitutional path to racial profiling in the United States, constructing a four-part legal structure that frames consideration of the use of race in policing. That constitutional structure consists of the following four legal distinctions:

(1) The first distinction, for purposes of Fourth Amendment analysis, draws a line between using race as the only factor versus using race as one among other factors in the decision to investi-

---

[6] In this chapter, "racial profiling" is defined as the knowing use by the police of race as a factor in the decision to investigate a suspect, based on the assumption that persons of the designated race or ethnicity are more likely to be offenders. The term "racial profiling" is of recent vintage. See generally Bernard E. Harcourt, *Rethinking Racial Profiling*, 71 U. Chi. L. Rev 1275, 1276 note 2 (2004); Jerome H. Skolnick and Abigail Caplovitz, *Guns, Drugs, and Profiling: Ways to Target Guns & Minimize Racial Profiling, in* Guns, Crime, and Punishment in America 249–79 (Bernard E. Harcourt, ed., NYU Press 2003) (discussing the history of the "racial profiling" expression). There is today some controversy over the definition of the term "racial profiling." Some commentators argue that the term "racial profiling" should be limited more narrowly to those cases where the police rely on race exclusively; others use the term when race is a significant factor among others in the decision to investigate. For discussions of the controversy, see, for example, Katheryn K. Russell, *Racial Profiling: A Status Report of the Legal, Legislative, and Empirical Literature*, 3 Rutgers Race & L. Rev. 61, 65–68 (2001); Albert W. Alschuler, *Racial Profiling and the Constitution*, 2002 U. Chi. Legal F. 163, 168–73 & n 24 (2002); Samuel R. Gross & Katherine Y. Barnes, *Road Work: Racial Profiling and Drug Interdiction on the Highway*, 101 Mich. L. Rev. 651, 738 & notes 278–82 (2002). The definition used in this chapter includes using race alone or as one factor among others in the decision to stop and search.

[7] 422 U.S. 873 (1975).

[8] 428 U.S. 543 (1976).

gate. Claims of racial profiling that fall in the latter category— which, not surprisingly, cover most, if not all cases since *Brigno-ni-Ponce*—tend to survive Fourth Amendment scrutiny.

(2) The second distinction separates Fourth Amendment protections against unreasonable searches from the Fourteenth Amendment guarantee of equal treatment. Implicitly in *Brignoni-Ponce* and *Martinez-Fuerte,* and more explicitly in the later decision in *Whren v. United States,*[9] the Supreme Court diverted issues of *intentional racial discrimination* to the Equal Protection Clause. Thus, claims that the police have acted in a racially biased manner are subject to equal protection analysis; however, if the use of race *is* relevant to the policing activity in question—as it is to stops on the Southern border with Mexico—then the police action does not trigger equal protection review.

(3) The third distinction is located narrowly in Equal Protection analysis, and holds that the use of race based on an eyewitness racial identification is different in kind from the use of race with no individualized suspicion (based only, for example, on the assumption that certain racial groups offend more than others). The former is generally excluded from Fourteenth Amendment scrutiny.

(4) The fourth and final distinction, also squarely in the Equal Protection context, demarcates claims of intentional discrimination established by evidence of specific discriminatory acts from those supported only by statistical evidence of disparate treatment. Challenges that do not establish *intent* to discriminate do not survive. As a result, proof that the police disproportionately stop and search African–American or Hispanic motorists—even disproportionate to their traffic offending rates—does not meet the intent requirement of the Fourteenth Amendment.

The practical result of these four pillars is that practically no federal constitutional challenges to racial profiling have prevailed since the *Brignoni-Ponce* case.[10] Federal challenges have either failed due to one or more of these legal distinctions[11] or have been settled out of court,

---

[9] 517 U.S. 806 (1996).

[10] For a critique of these four legal distinctions and the four-part structure of constitutional analysis in the racial profiling context, see Bernard E. Harcourt, *Rethinking Racial Profiling, supra* note 6, at 1335–54.

[11] *See, e.g.,* Gross and Barnes, *supra* note 6, at 727. There is one notorious state court exception, in which a New Jersey Superior Court permitted the requisite discriminatory intent to be inferred from statistical evidence. *See* State v. Soto, 734 A.2d 350, 360 (N.J. Super. Ct. 1996). For commentary on *Soto,* see Harcourt, *supra* note 6, at 1346–47; Gross and Barnes, *supra* note 6, at 723–30; David Harris, *Profiles in Injustice: Why Racial*

primarily for injunctive relief.[12] Given the reality of contemporary policing—especially the fact that a police officer usually has a number of
reasons why he or she may focus attention on one particular suspect—
the Supreme Court's early decisions in *Brignoni-Ponce* and *Martinez-
Fuerte,* allowing race or ethnicity to be considered as one among a
number of factors in the decision to search, essentially paved the
constitutional path to racial profiling.

Democratic politics—not the Supreme Court, nor the United States
Constitution—would later cast doubt on the policy of racially profiling
African–Americans and Hispanics, and ultimately led, toward the end of
the twentieth century, to a consensus in public opinion that profiling on
race is harmful to the social fabric of this country. The terrorist attacks
of September 11, 2001, however, fundamentally changed this emerging
consensus, generating renewed support for police profiling. As a constitutional matter, *Brignoni-Ponce* and *Martinez-Fuerte* remain the principal
Supreme Court cases on point. In this sense, these two Supreme Court
cases began a debate about the constitutionality of racial profiling that
continues to the present with extreme renewed interest after the events
of 9/11.

The trailhead on the road to racial profiling, though, begins back on
the dirt roads and interstates near the Mexican border—at the road
blocks, INS checkpoints, and roving border patrols policing illegal border
crossings. By starting the story at the border, the Supreme Court
effectively opened the door at the most sensitive location—a place where
ethnicity and appearance were at their most salient. Let's start the
story, then, on the Mexican border.

Profiling Cannot Work 53 (New Press 2002); David Rudovsky, *Law Enforcement by
Stereotypes and Serendipity: Racial Profiling and Stops and Searches without Cause,* 3 U.
Pa. J. Const. L. 296, 351 (2001).

[12] See Gross and Barnes, *supra* note 6, at 727–28; Brandon Garrett, *Remedying Racial
Profiling,* 33 Colum. Hum. Rts. L. Rev. 41, 75–81, 98–105 (2001). This is not to suggest,
though, that the litigation has not had significant effects in raising awareness of the issue
of racial profiling, in generating policy responses within police departments, and in
promoting agreements between police departments and anti-racial profiling organizations.
An example of one such agreement entered into as a result of voluntary mediation—
between the St. Paul Police Department and the St. Paul Chapter of the NAACP—is
reproduced as an appendix to Lorie Fridell, et al, Racially Biased Policing: A Principled
Response (Police Executive Research Forum 2001). That report also details six key policy
responses—including police department accountability and supervision, education and
training, and minority community outreach—that a number of police departments are
implementing. *Id.* at ch. 3–8. *See also* John J. Farmer, Jr. & Paul H. Zoubek, Final Report
of the State Police Review Team (New Jersey State Police Review Team 1999) (detailing a
list of recommendations for reforms of the New Jersey State Police on the subject of racial
profiling).

The Landscape of the Southern Border

Much of the United States was, in fact, part of Mexico until the close of the war with Mexico in 1848 and the signing of the treaty of Guadaloupe–Hidelgo. Under the terms of the treaty, "the United States annexed one million square miles of Mexican land, a territory equivalent in size to that of western Europe, and absorbed 100,000 Mexican citizens and 200,000 Native Americans living in the annexed territory. All or part of ten states resulted from the treaty: Texas, Arizona, New Mexico, Oklahoma, Wyoming, Colorado, Kansas, Utah, Nevada, and California."[13]

It would take many years from the signing of the treaty for the border to become a political issue. From 1848 through the early twentieth century, the United States paid little attention to the Mexican border. Control of the border was so lax, in fact, that no records were kept until near the turn of the twentieth century.[14] The United States government put little time or effort into patrolling the border. "As of 1919, there were only 151 immigrant inspectors; they were responsible for more than 2,000 miles of boundary, and most were obligated to remain at one of the twenty official ports of entry. At times, the Immigration Service had a total force of mobile guards that numbered no more than 60."[15] And the few immigration agents that patrolled had no enforcement power until the Immigration Act of 1925.

One explanation for the lack of concern is that many believed that immigrants had no interest in staying in the United States. It was generally assumed that most illegal immigrants would work for a while and then return home. The Dillingham Commission on Immigration—a federal government panel—expressed just this view in 1911, declaring that "The Mexican immigrants are providing a fairly adequate supply of labor. . . . While they are not easily assimilated, this is of no very great importance as long as most of them return to their native land."[16]

President Franklin Delano Roosevelt was one of the first to raise national security concerns about the border, and this only in connection with World War II. In 1940, Roosevelt doubled the size of the Border Patrol—an easy task given its size—with congressional spending of approximately two million dollars for 712 new Border Patrol officers.[17] But even as the Roosevelt administration was hiring more border patrol officers, "farmers along the U.S. side of the boundary actively encour-

---

[13] Joseph Nevins, Operation Gatekeeper: The Rise of the "Illegal Alien" and the Making of the U.S.-Mexico Boundary 19 (New York: Routledge, 2002).

[14] *Id.* at 25.

[15] *Id.* at 26–28.

[16] *Quoted in id.* at 104.

[17] *See id.* at 30.

aged Mexican workers to step across the line and work on their farms.''[18] Political economy—especially the needs of agricultural labor—led to what is known as a "revolving door policy": "the INS would effectively 'open' and 'shut' the boundary depending on the needs of domestic economic interests."[19] And while the illegal immigrants themselves were open to sanction and arrest, farmers on the United States side were not subject to any sanctions for employing Mexican workers.[20]

The 1970s marked the beginning of a restrictionist movement that now characterizes the United States' attitude towards Mexican immigration. It was a period of build-up in political initiatives and, correspondingly, in public opinion. As Joseph Nevins observes, "[the] preoccupation with 'illegal' immigrants and boundary enforcement—at least in a sustained manner with widespread popular support—is of relatively recent origin. The national Platform of the Republican Party, for example, did not mention immigration enforcement for the first time until 1980."[21] The Reagan administration expanded the INS to "unprecedented levels" as part of the war on drugs.[22] "Congressional funding appropriations increased 130.... The majority of these funds went to the INS Enforcement Division," and much of that went to increasing border patrols along the US–Mexico border.

Policing the Border

As politicians became increasingly concerned with illegal immigration, the INS Border Patrol refined its techniques for detecting illegal

---

[18] *Id*. at 31.

[19] *Id*. at 35.

[20] In this sense, it might be possible to trace the Fourth Amendment framework to the political economy of labor supply in this country along the lines drawn by Georg Rusche and Otto Kirchheimer in their 1939 monograph, Punishment and Social Structure (New York: Institute for Social Research, 1939). In their research, Rusche and Kirchheimer argued that the combination of population demographics and labor markets significantly influence the way that social institutions criminalize and punish. The definition of crimes and the modes of punishment and policing are heavily shaped by labor supply needs and methods of economic production. "Every system of production," Rusche and Kirchheimer wrote, "tends to discover punishments which correspond to its productive relationships. It is thus necessary to investigate the origin and fate of penal systems, the use or avoidance of specific punishments, and the intensity of penal practices as they are determined by social forces, above all by economic and then fiscal forces." Along such lines, the ebb and flow of labor supply needs, especially agricultural and service labor in the United States, may have played a critical role in the policing of illegal border crossings from the South. The economic dimensions are also reflected in the contrast between immigration regulation and NAFTA—which ensures that while people cannot cross the border, goods would be free to do so.

[21] *Nevins, supra* note 13, at 111.

[22] *Id*. at 67.

aliens traveling inland, narrowing its primary arsenal to three main devices—the fixed INS checkpoint, the temporary checkpoint, and roving patrols. These three inland devices supplemented the "line watch agents" stationed at the actual border checking papers and guarding the paved entrances to the United States.

Fixed INS checkpoints were placed on larger highways and interstates, about 25 to 100 miles from the actual border with Mexico. These checkpoints were essentially roadblocks that would bring northbound traffic to a snail's pace, allowing Border Patrol agents to look into every passing car and to detain motorists for short questioning and for the production of documents. The checkpoints were generally marked ahead with large black-on-yellow signs and flashing lights, and subsequent warnings as motorists got closer. Here is a good description of one of these fixed checkpoints in Southern California:

> Approximately one mile south of the checkpoint is a large black on yellow sign with flashing yellow lights over the highway stating "ALL VEHICLES, STOP AHEAD, 1 MILE." Three-quarters of a mile further north are two black on yellow signs suspended over the highway with flashing lights stating "WATCH FOR BRAKE LIGHTS." At the checkpoint, which is also the location of a State of California weighing station, are two large signs with flashing red lights suspended over the highway. These signs each state "STOP HERE—U.S. OFFICERS." Placed on the highway are a number of orange traffic cones funneling traffic into two lanes where a Border Patrol agent in full dress uniform, standing behind a white on red "STOP" sign checks traffic. Blocking traffic in the unused lanes are official U.S. Border Patrol vehicles with flashing red lights. In addition, there is a permanent building which houses the Border Patrol office and temporary detention facilities. There are also floodlights for nighttime operation.[23]

At some of the checkpoints, a "point agent" would visually screen all northbound traffic—which had come to a virtual, if not complete stop. Standing between the two lanes, the point agent would allow most motorists to proceed without any verbal inquiry or further inspection. But the point agent would select a number of motorists for further investigation, directing them to a secondary inspection site for questioning about the citizenship and immigration status of the motorists. Those further investigations would last on average three to five minutes— unless, of course, they led to arrest. At other checkpoints, Border Patrol officers might stop all northbound traffic for brief questioning. Local inhabitants who the officers recognized would be waived through, but all others would be stopped for interrogation.

---

[23] United States v. Baca, 368 F. Supp. 398, 410–11 (S.D. Cal. 1973).

According to the INS Border Patrol Handbook from 1972, the primary factors used to locate the permanent checkpoints included:

1. "A location on a highway just beyond the confluence of two or more roads from the border, in order to permit the checking of a large volume of traffic with a minimum number of officers."

2. "Terrain and topography that restrict passage of vehicles around the checkpoint, such as mountains, desert, [or a military installation]."

3. "Safety factors: an unobstructed view of oncoming traffic, to provide a safe distance for slowing and stopping; parking space off the highway; power source to illuminate control signs and inspection area, and bypass capability for vehicles *not* requiring examination," and

4. "Due to the travel restrictions of the I–186 nonresident border crosser to an area 25 miles from the border (unless issued additional documentation) the checkpoints, as a general rule, are located at a point beyond the 25 mile zone in order to control the unlawful movement inland of such visitors."[24]

"Temporary checkpoints" were set up in a similar way, but generally maintained on back roads where the traffic was less intense and in locations "where the terrain allows an element of surprise. Operations at these temporary checkpoints are set up at irregular intervals and intermittently so as to confuse the potential violator."[25] The third major technique, "roving patrols," consisted of mobile Border Patrol tactical units that roamed the back roads near larger interstates to stop and search automobiles at points removed from the actual border. These "roving patrols" would often work in combination with the fixed checkpoints to make sure that motorists were not trying to evade larger highways to avoid being stopped at a roadblock.

The Development of Criminal Profiling in the 1970s

By the early 1970s, it had become routine for Border Patrol officers to use the appearance of Mexican ancestry as one factor—and sometimes as the only factor—in the decision to stop and investigate motorists. This is evidenced in the *Brignoni-Ponce* case itself, where the Border Patrol agents conceded in court that "their only reason for [stopping Brignoni-Ponce's car] was that its three occupants appeared to be of Mexican descent."[26] In this sense, border policing in the 1970s reflected the larger turn to criminal profiling in law enforcement. The first criminal profiles

---

[24] *Baca*, 368 F. Supp. at 406.

[25] *See* INS Border Patrol Handbook at 9–3 (discussed in *Baca*, 368 F. Supp. at 406).

[26] 422 U.S. at 875.

were developed in the context of airline highjackers in the early 1970s, and expanded rapidly to drug-courier profiling at airports and bus terminals.

Most students of the drug-courier profile trace it back to two former DEA agents, John Marcello and Paul Markonni, who are considered the "Godfathers" of the profile.

In the early 1970s, Marcello and Markonni started identifying the common characteristics of illegal drug couriers disembarking from planes at U.S. airports.[27] "The majority of our cases, when we first started," Markonni explains, "involved cases we made based on information from law enforcement agencies or from airline personnel. And as these cases were made, certain characteristics were noted among the defendants."[28] The airplane highjacker profile was an important source of information, because stops based on that profile often netted persons in possession of drugs.[29] Those characteristics eventually became known as the drug-courier profile, first implemented in a surveillance and search program at the Detroit airport in the fall of 1974.

The profiles first used in the Detroit experiment were based on empirical observations collected over eighteen months of surveillance at the airport, observations that were focused on the conduct and appearance of travelers.[30] The experiment was deemed a success, and the program went nationwide by the mid 1970s.[31]

The Legal Landscape at the Border

Criminal profiling—and, especially, racial profiling—would come under challenge first at the Southern border with Mexico. The Supreme Court had addressed Border Patrol investigations on a number of occasions and set forth some contours of permissible police intervention. Stops, interrogations, and searches right at the border or its functional equivalent—say, an international flight landing at O'Hare in Chicago—were constitutionally permitted without warrant or probable cause, as a routine matter.[32] Fourth Amendment protections applied, however, in areas removed from the border—including areas *near* the Mexican–United States border.

---

[27] Harris, *supra* note 11, at 20; Charles L. Becton, *The Drug Courier Profile: "All Seems Infected That Th" Infected Spy, As All Looks Yellow to the Jaundic'd Eye*, 65 N.C. L. Rev. 417, 426, 433–34 (1987).

[28] Becton, *supra* note 27, at 426.

[29] *See id*. 426–27.

[30] *Id*. at 430 note 72.

[31] *See id*. at 417 note 2, 417–18.

[32] *See, e.g.,* Almeida-Sanchez v. United States, 413 U.S. 266, 272 (1973).

In *Almeida-Sanchez v. United States*,[33] the Court ruled that the Fourth Amendment precluded the Border Patrol from using "roving patrols" to stop and search automobiles without a warrant or probable cause at any point removed from the actual border. Under *Almeida-Sanchez,* in the absence of a judicial warrant allowing roving patrols in a designated area, probable cause was necessary before roving patrol agents could stop and search a vehicle in the general vicinity of the border. In *United States v. Ortiz*,[34] a companion case to *Brignoni-Ponce,* the Court extended the same requirements of probable cause or judicial warrant for any search conducted at a permanent INS checkpoint.

There were also legislative statutes purporting to regulate the conduct of Border Patrol agents. Under the Immigration and Nationality Act, at least two provisions were on point. Section 287(a)(1) authorized any officer or employee of the INS "to interrogate any alien or person believed to be an alien" without a warrant "as to his right to be or to remain in the United States."[35] And Section 287(a)(3) authorized any officer of the INS without a warrant "within a reasonable distance from any external boundary of the United States, to board and search for aliens any vessel with the territorial waters of the United State and any railway car, aircraft, conveyance, or vehicle."[36] Moreover, under federal regulations implemented by the INS after notice and public comment, the authority under Section 287(a)(3) could be exercised anywhere within 100 air miles of the border.[37]

Many questions, though, were left open. First, on the question of race and ethnicity, whether the appearance of Mexican ancestry was a constitutionally valid reason to stop, question, or search anyone. Second, whether questioning under Section 287(a)(1) should be treated differently than searches under Section 287(a)(3). And third, whether differences in police practices—roving patrols versus fixed checkpoints versus temporary checkpoints—would make any difference in these equations. These rules and these questions would first be put to the test in the case of *Brignoni-Ponce.*

The *Brignoni–Ponce* Case

March 11, 1973. It's early morning near the permanent INS checkpoint at San Clemente, 65 miles north of the Mexican border on

---

[33] 413 U.S. 266 (1973).

[34] 422 U.S. 891 (1975).

[35] 8 U.S.C. § 1357(a)(1).

[36] 8 U.S.C. § 1357(a)(3).

[37] C.F.R. § 287.1(a) (1975).

Interstate 5 between San Diego and Los Angeles. The United States Border Patrol usually maintains a roadblock there, but due to inclement weather, the checkpoint is closed. Two INS Border Patrol agents sit in their patrol car by the side of the road and observe the northbound traffic. It's dark, so the officers use their headlights to inspect the passing cars. A car drives by. The three occupants appear to be of Mexican descent, so the agents decide to investigate. In fact, the agents say later, that's the only reason they decide to investigate.[38] They pursue and interrogate. They discover that the two passengers were in the country illegally, arrest all three, and charge the driver, Felix Humberto Brignoni–Ponce, with transporting two illegal immigrants in violation of the Immigration and Nationality Act.[39]

Prior to trial, Brignoni–Ponce moves to suppress the evidence concerning the immigration status of the two passengers, arguing that the evidence was the product of an illegal seizure under the Fourth Amendment. The trial court denies the motion, and its ruling is affirmed by a panel of the Ninth Circuit. Sitting *en banc,* the Court of Appeals for the Ninth Circuit reverses, siding with Brignoni–Ponce.[40] The stop involved a "roving patrol" of the kind discussed in *Almeida-Sanchez,* the *en banc* court found, and as a result, under *Almeida-Sanchez,* an officer stopping a motorist on suspicion of illegal immigration status must have a "founded suspicion" that one or more of the motorists are in the country illegally. Mexican ancestry alone, the *en banc* court ruled, does not provide such a "founded suspicion."[41]

The Supreme Court granted certiorari, limiting its analysis to the narrow question whether a roving Border Patrol agent can stop a motorist *based on race alone.* The government, the court emphasized, conceded that the patrol officers were engaged in a roving patrol. It conceded that *Almeida-Sanchez* should apply retroactively to Brignoni–Ponce. And it conceded that the location of the stop was not at the border or its functional equivalent, but near the border. As such, the Court explained, "The only issue presented for decision is whether a roving patrol may stop a vehicle in an area near the border and question its occupants when the only ground for suspicion is that the occupants appear to be of Mexican ancestry."[42] In other words, whether being of Mexican ancestry satisfies the required "founded suspicion." By a unani-

---

[38] 422 U.S. at 875.

[39] 422 U.S. at 874–75.

[40] 499 F.2d 1109 (1974).

[41] *Id.*

[42] 422 U.S. at 878.

mous vote, though with different reasoning, the Court declared that it did not.

Justice Powell wrote an opinion joined by Justices Brennan, Stewart, Marshall, and Rehnquist. Powell first easily dismissed the government's arguments from statutory authority, repeating cursorily that "no Act of Congress can authorize a violation of the Constitution."[43] The stops and questioning involve seizures and therefore trigger the scrutiny of the Fourth Amendment.

On the constitutional analysis, Powell engaged a traditional balancing of interests analysis, weighing the governmental interest in having effective measures to police the border and prevent the illegal entry of Mexicans against the individual liberty interests of persons traveling in the border areas—the "balance between the public interest and the individual's right to personal security free from arbitrary interference by law officers."[44] Powell emphasized the limited nature of the stop. The intrusion, Powell said, is "modest." It lasts no more than a minute. There is no search (unless further evidence develops). All that is required, as the government explained and Powell reiterated, "is a response to a brief question or two and possibly the production of a document evidencing a right to be in the United States."[45] These conditions are similar, Powell suggested, to the limited intrusion of the pat-down search in *Terry v. Ohio* or the brief stop of a suspicious individual in *Adams v. Williams*. On the other side of the scale, the public's interest in preventing illegal immigration from Mexico, Powell asserted, was "valid."[46] "The INS now suggests there may be as many as 10 or 12 million aliens illegally in the country," Powell explained.[47] This has the potential of creating significant social and economic problems for citizens, as well as for the immigrants themselves.

Accordingly, building on *Terry* and *Adams*, Powell declared that Border Patrol agents may constitutionally conduct a limited stop to investigate without full blown probable cause. All that is needed is that "an officer's observations lead him reasonably to suspect that a particular vehicle may contain aliens who are illegally in the country."[48] As in *Terry*, the scope of the police intervention had to be tailored to the more limited scope of reasonable suspicion. The Border Patrol agent could stop

---

[43] *Id.* at 877 (quoting *Almeida-Sanchez*, 413 U.S. at 272).

[44] *Id.* at 878.

[45] *Id.* at 880.

[46] *Id.* at 879.

[47] *Id.* at 878.

[48] *Id.* at 881.

the vehicle briefly and investigate, but not engage in a full blown search unless other evidence developed: "The officer may question the driver and passenger about their citizenship and immigration status, and he may ask them to explain suspicious circumstances, but any further detention or search must be based on consent or probable cause."[49]

It is important to recognize, Powell maintained, that most of the traffic on these roads near the border is legitimate. A number of large towns now sit on the border, he emphasized, including San Diego in California, with a population at the time of 1.4 million residents, and El Paso and Brownsville in Texas, with combined populations of almost 700,000. "We are confident that substantially all of the traffic in these cities is lawful and that relatively few of their residents have any connection with the illegal entry and transportation of aliens," Powell asserted.[50] To allow roving patrols without any limitations whatsoever would be to interfere too greatly in the lives of ordinary citizens living near the border. This, Powell maintained, would give the Border Patrol too much discretion. "If we approved the Government's position in this case," Powell concluded, "Border Patrol officers could stop motorists at random for questioning, day or night, anywhere within 100 air miles of the 2,000–mile border, on a city street, a busy highway, or a desert road, without any reason to suspect that they have violated any law."[51]

On the key question of racial profiling, Powell declared the Court unwilling to let Mexican ancestry alone substitute for reasonable suspicion. Mexican appearance, Powell declared for the Court, may be one "relevant factor" but is not alone sufficient to support a police stop. "Large numbers of native-born and naturalized citizens have the physical characteristics identified with Mexican ancestry, and even in the border area a relatively small proportion of them are aliens."[52] There are many other factors that can and should be taken into account, Powell explained: erratic driving behavior, obvious evasion from the police, certain station wagons with large compartments, or cars that appear more heavily weighted down than they should. These are all factors that Border Patrol agents may consider. In addition, Powell said, they can and should be allowed to consider Mexican appearance. "The Government also points out that trained officers can recognize the characteristic appearance of persons who live in Mexico, relying on such factors as the mode of dress and haircut."[53] This, Powell declared, is acceptable. "In all

---

[49] *Id.* at 881–82.

[50] *Id.* at 882.

[51] *Id.* at 883.

[52] *Id.* at 886.

[53] *Id.* at 885.

situations the officer is entitled to assess the facts in light of his experience in detecting illegal entry and smuggling."[54]

But Mexican appearance *alone* would not suffice: "The likelihood that any given person of Mexican ancestry is an alien is high enough to make Mexican appearance a relevant factor, but standing alone it does not justify stopping all Mexican–Americans to ask if they are aliens."[55] The bottom line on race, then, is that it may be one factor, but not the only factor in a roving patrol decision to stop and question.

The result of the *Brignoni-Ponce* decision can be most clearly understood by a simple two-by-two table relating the type of police intervention (fixed checkpoint vs. roving patrol) to the specific police action (stop and search vs. stop and questioning):

	Roving Patrol	Fixed Checkpoint
Stop & Search	*Almedia-Sanchez* (1973): Judicial warrant or probable cause	*Ortiz* (1975): Judicial warrant or probable cause
Stop & Question	*Brignoni-Ponce* (1975): Reasonable suspicion; ethnic appearance is a relevant factor, but standing alone is not adequate.	Open question

Justice Powell's reasoning was endorsed by four of his colleagues—Justices Brennan, Stewart, Marshall, and Rehnquist—though the last, then Associate Justice, added a separate concurring paragraph to emphasize the limited nature of the holding. Rehnquist wrote separately to make clear that the decision did not render suspect other law enforcement practices, such as a highway roadblock intended to apprehend a known fugitive or agricultural inspections. "[A] strong case may be made," Rehnquist added, "for those charged with the enforcement of laws conditioning the right of vehicular use of a highway to likewise stop motorists using highways in order to determine whether they have met the qualifications prescribed by applicable law for such use."[56] Such stops, Rehnquist suggested, should be permissible without probable cause or founded suspicion, but as a matter of course.

The four other justices—Chief Justice Burger and Justices Blackmun, White, and Douglas—did not join Powell's opinion, but instead

---

[54] *Id.* at 885.

[55] *Id.* at 886–87.

[56] *Id.* at 887 (Rehnquist, J., concurring).

wrote or joined in separate concurring opinions. All agreed with the
result in this particular case. The first three, however, expressed reluctance at the holding and dismay at the direction of Fourth Amendment
analysis; Justice Douglas, in contrast, would have gone further.

Chief Justice Burger and Justice White concurred only in the result
and wrote separate opinions both joined by Justice Blackmun and both
sounding deep notes of anxiety and frustration regarding illegal immigration from Mexico and the flow of dangerous drugs into this country.
The result, Burger and White conceded, was foreordained by the Court's
1973 decision in *Almeida-Sanchez*, which required probable cause or a
warrant for searches conducted by roving patrols. But the consequences,
Burger and White emphasized, would be terrible for the country: the
flow of illegal immigrants from Mexico was already causing devastating
social, economic, and political problems. Burger emphasized that over 12
million illegal aliens were in the country and appended to his opinion a
lengthy, fourteen-page extract from a judicial opinion by United States
District Judge Turrentine of the Southern District of California in
United States v. Baca.[57] The excerpt, captioned "THE ILLEGAL ALIEN
PROBLEM," chronicled the problems associated with illegal immigrants
living in the United States—including the fact that they compete with
citizens for jobs, "perpetuate poor economic conditions by frustrating
unionization," and pose "a potential health hazard to the community
since many seek work as nursemaids, food handlers, cooks, housekeep-
ers, waiters, dishwashers, and grocery workers"[58]—as well as the challenges facing law enforcement and the lack of true enforcement.[59]

Any further hampering of law enforcement—including the result in
Brignoni-Ponce—will only aggravate the problem, wrote Burger and
White. "As the Fourth Amendment now has been interpreted by the
Court," Burger suggested, "it seems that the Immigration and Natural-
ization Service is powerless to stop the tide of illegal aliens—and dangerous drugs—that daily and freely crosses our 2,000–mile southern boundary."[60] White added: "the Court has thus dismantled major parts of the
apparatus by which the Nation has attempted to intercept millions of
aliens who enter and remain illegally in this country."[61]

Both Burger and White expressed hope that the Court would, in
future cases, give greater weight to the interests in law enforcement. "I

---

[57] 368 F. Supp. 398, 402–08 (S.D. Cal. 1973).

[58] United States v. Ortiz, 422 U.S. 891, 904 (Burger, C.J., concurring) (quoting United
States v. Baca, 368 F. Supp. 398).

[59] *Id.* 904–14 (Burger, C.J., concurring) (quoting United States v. Baca, 368 F. Supp.).

[60] *Id.* at 899 (Burger, C.J., concurring).

[61] *Id.* at 915 (White, J., concurring).

would hope," Burger wrote, "that when we next deal with this problem we give greater weight to the reality that the Fourth Amendment prohibits only '*unreasonable* searches and seizures' and to the frequent admonition that reasonableness must take into account all the circumstances and balance the rights of the individual with the needs of society."[62] But their tone sounded of despair. "Perhaps these decisions will be seen in perspective as but another example of a society seemingly impotent to deal with massive lawlessness," wrote Burger. "In that sense history may view us as prisoners of our own traditional and appropriate concern for individual rights, unable—or unwilling—to apply the concept of reasonableness explicit in the Fourth Amendment in order to develop a rational accommodation between those rights and the literal safety of the country."[63]

In sharp contrast, Justice Douglas would have gone further in *Brignoni-Ponce* and required probable cause rather than mere reasonable suspicion. Douglas agreed whole-heartedly that the stops were unreasonable and that the reliance on Mexican ancestry "was a patent violation of the Fourth Amendment."[64] In his concurrence, however, Douglas objected strenuously to the adoption of the less stringent reasonable suspicion standard. Douglas had dissented from the Court's opinion in *Terry* as an "unjustified weakening of the Fourth Amendment's protection of citizens from arbitrary interference by the police,"[65] and voiced those similar concerns here. In fact, Douglas argued, this and other recent cases demonstrated well the problems with the lower reasonable suspicion test. "The fears I voiced in Terry about the weakening of the Fourth Amendment have regrettably been borne out by subsequent events."[66] Douglas recounted border cases where motorists were stopped because their car was riding low or they had a spare tire in the back seat—stops that were upheld under the reasonable suspicion test. "The vacationer whose car is weighted down with luggage will find no comfort in these decisions; nor will the many law-abiding citizens who drive older vehicles that ride low because their suspension systems are old or in disrepair. The suspicion test has indeed brought a state of affairs where the police may stop citizens on the highway on the flimsiest of justifications."[67]

---

[62] *Id*. at 900 (Burger, C.J., concurring).

[63] *Id*. at 899 (Burger, C.J., concurring).

[64] *Id*. at 888 (Douglas, J., concurring).

[65] *Id*.

[66] *Id*.

[67] *Id*. at 889–90 (Douglas, J., concurring).

At the end of the day, though, *Brignoni-Ponce* stood for the proposition that ethnic appearance was a valid and reasonable factor to consider in deciding whether to stop and question an individual, but could not be the *only* factor. The *Brignoni-Ponce* case was the first constitutional step in the direction of allowing racial profiling.

Take Two: *United States v. Martinez–Fuerte*

The following term, the Supreme Court returned to the border, this time addressing the constitutionality of fixed immigration checkpoints. The case would resolve the question left open in *Brignoni-Ponce,* namely whether Border Patrol agents required any articulable suspicion to stop and question motorists at a roadblock within 100 miles of the Mexican border. Powell again would write the Court's opinion. And again, Powell would emphasize that ethnic appearance is relevant. But this time, he pulled the stops and allowed for even wider police discretion.

Martinez-Fuerte involved consolidated cases that arose from arrests made at two different permanent immigration checkpoints within 100 miles of the Mexican border, one in California, the other in Texas. The California checkpoint was located in familiar territory, on northbound Interstate Highway 5 near San Clemente, between San Diego and Los Angeles, 66 miles north of the Mexican border—very close to where Brignoni–Ponce had been stopped. The other checkpoint was located on U.S. Highway 77 near Sarita, Texas, north of Brownsville and about 65 to 90 miles north of the Mexican border.

Both checkpoints were marked in the traditional fashion with large black-on-yellow signs and flashing lights, and subsequent warning signs as motorists got closer. At the San Clemente checkpoint, the point agent visually screened all northbound traffic, but did not conduct questioning. Instead the agent would select a number of motorists for further investigation at a secondary inspection site, where other agents would stop and question the motorists about their citizenship and immigration status. At the time of the arrests at the San Clemente checkpoint, a magistrate had issued a "warrant of inspection" which authorized the Border Patrol to conduct roadblock operations at the site. At the Sarita checkpoint, Border Patrol officers would stop all northbound traffic for brief questioning, with the exception of local residents who the officers recognized. Also, in contrast to the San Clemente checkpoint, there was no judicial warrant regarding the operations at Sarita.

Several arrests were consolidated for purposes of review by the Supreme Court in *Martinez-Fuerte.* One group of defendants was arrested at the San Clemente checkpoint: Amando Martinez–Fuerte was directed to the secondary inspection area for questioning, where it was determined that his two female passengers were illegal Mexican aliens.

Martinez–Fuerte was charged under the same statute as Brignoni–Ponce, 18 U.S.C. 1324(a)(2), for illegally transporting aliens. In separate cases, Jose Jiminez–Garcia and Raymond Guillen were also arrested for similar violations. Before trial, Martinez–Fuerte moved to suppress the evidence from the stop at the checkpoint, but his motion was denied. In the other two cases, the same motion was granted. The Court of Appeals for the Ninth Circuit consolidated all these appeals, and ruled, over the dissent of one judge, that the Border Patrol agents needed to have articulable reasons to stop a motorist for inquiry.

Rodolfo Sifuentes was arrested at the Sarita checkpoint in Texas for illegally transporting aliens. The trial court denied his motion to suppress, and the Fifth Circuit affirmed, ruling that fixed checkpoint stops with no reason to believe a motorist is transporting illegal aliens present no Fourth Amendment problem.

The Supreme Court granted certiorari to resolve the circuit split. In a 7-to-2 opinion, written by Justice Powell, the Court sided with the Fifth Circuit and held that neither articulable suspicion nor a judicial warrant was necessary as a precondition for a search at an immigration roadblock. The composition of the Court had changed slightly since *Brignoni-Ponce*, with Justice Douglas no longer sitting and Justice John Paul Stevens now in his place. But the change had little effect on the outcome. Justices Brennan and Marshall were the only ones in dissent.

Justice Powell began, again, by considering the balance of interests. Permanent checkpoints, the government had maintained before the court, are "the most important of the traffic-checking operations."[68] And, Powell found, they are highly effective. The San Clemente checkpoint, for instance, resulted in the apprehension of 17,000 illegal aliens in 1973 from traffic of about 10 million cars. Their effectiveness, Powell intimated, would be greatly diminished if stops had to be based on reasonable suspicion: such a requirement "would be impractical because the flow of traffic tends to be too heavy to allow the particularized study of a given car that would enable it to be identified as a possible carrier of illegal aliens. In particular, such a requirement would largely eliminate any deterrent to the conduct of well-disguised smuggling operations, even though smugglers are known to use these highways regularly."[69] In contrast, the intrusion on liberty was relatively minor—in Powell's words, "quite limited."[70] All that was required was a "brief detention of travelers," "a response to a brief question or two," and "possibly the

---

[68] *Martinez-Fuerte*, 428 U.S. at 556.

[69] *Id.* at 557.

[70] *Id.* at 557.

production of a document evidencing a right to be in the United States."[71]

In many ways, the balance of interests seemed similar to that in *Brignoni-Ponce*. The police practice in question—immigration road-blocks—went hand-in-hand with roving patrols as two parts of the interdiction strategy. The intrusions were similar in both cases. In fact, Justice Powell relied on his opinion in *Brignoni-Ponce* to explain the general level of the intrusion. Nevertheless, Powell identified what he considered to be an important difference: the *subjective* intrusion is "appreciably less in the case of a checkpoint stop."[72] By subjective intrusion, Powell meant the feelings of fear or concern among the motorists. These, he argued, were less troubling than in the case of roving patrol stops. Checkpoint stops involve less discretion on the part of the agents, less interference with legitimate traffic, and less potential for abuse. Overall, there is less room for harassment than in the case of roving patrols.

Even the secondary stops at the San Clemente checkpoint, Powell argued, involve "minimal" intrusion. Those referrals are "made for the sole purpose of conducting a routine and limited inquiry into residence status" and involve an "objective intrusion" that remains "minimal," Powell suggested. "Selective referral may involve some annoyance, but it remains true that the stops should not be frightening or offensive because of their public and relatively routine nature."[73] As a result, and because of the more limited expectation of privacy in cars relative to homes, Justice Powell concluded that no individualized suspicion *at all* is needed "at reasonably located checkpoints."[74]

The implications for racial profiling were significant. At those secondary inspection areas, Powell was prepared to assume that the referrals were made almost, if not entirely on the basis of Mexican ancestry. Powell wrote: "even if it be assumed that such referrals are made largely on the basis of apparent Mexican ancestry, we perceive no constitutional violation."[75] Powell then dropped two footnotes. In the first, footnote 16, Powell suggested—relying on a dubious statistical analysis[76]—that Bor-

---

[71] *Id.* at 558 (also quoting *Brignoni-Ponce*, 422 U.S. at 880).

[72] *Id.* at 558.

[73] *Id.* at 560.

[74] *Id.* at 562.

[75] *Id.* at 563.

[76] *Id.* at 563 note 16. Powell reasons that less than one percent of motorists are stopped for questioning, but that between 13 to 18 percent are likely to appear to have Mexican ancestry. From this, Powell concludes that the Border Patrol does not rely exclusively on apparent Mexican ancestry. Another equally plausible interpretation of the

der Patrol agents do not rely on Mexican ancestry *alone* to refer motorists to the secondary area. In the second, footnote 17, Powell added that, "to the to the extent that the Border Patrol relies on apparent Mexican ancestry at this checkpoint, see note 16, *supra,* that reliance clearly is relevant to the law enforcement need to be served."[77] But even if they did rely on the appearance of Mexican ancestry *entirely,* there is no Fourth Amendment problem. "As the intrusion here is sufficiently minimal that no particularized reason need exist to justify it, we think it follows that the Border Patrol officers must have wide discretion in selecting the motorists to be diverted for the brief questioning involved."[78] This discussion—these footnotes—were sufficiently cryptic that they allowed the issue to continue to percolate, to fester, and to wind its way through the lower courts.

The *Martinez-Fuerte* case filled in the missing entry in our earlier table:

	Roving Patrol	Fixed Checkpoint
Stop & Search	*Almedia-Sanchez* (1973): Requirement of judicial warrant or probable cause	*Ortiz* (1975): Requirement of judicial warrant or probable cause
Stop & Question	*Brignoni-Ponce* (1975): Requirement of reasonable suspicion (and race alone is not adequate).	*Martinez-Fuertes* (1976): No requirement (and reliance on race alone or in part is fine).

Justice Brennan wrote a heated dissent, which Justice Marshall joined. Brennan described the result as the "defacement of Fourth Amendment protections,"[79] declaring that "Today's decision is the ninth this Term marking the continuing evisceration of Fourth Amendment protections against unreasonable searches and seizures."[80] What Brennan objected to most was the lack of any objective standard whatsoever to evaluate the reasonableness of the stop. Whereas in previous cases— *Almeida-Sanchez, Ortiz,* and *Brignoni-Ponce*—the Court had required some modicum of reasonableness, in *Martinez-Fuerte* the Court had

---

data is that the Border Patrol rely exclusively on apparent Mexican ancestry, but only have the resources to stop 1/16th of those persons.

[77] *Id.* at 564 note 17.

[78] *Id.* at 563–64.

[79] *Id.* at 569 (Brennan, J., dissenting).

[80] *Id.* at 567 (Brennan, J., dissenting).

abandoned the reasonableness standard completely: "We are told today ... that motorists without number may be individually stopped, questioned, visually inspected, and then further detained without even a showing of articulable suspicion, let alone the heretofore constitutional minimum of reasonable suspicion, a result that permits search and seizure to rest upon 'nothing more substantial than inarticulate hunches.' "[81]

Brennan could not fathom any difference in the weighing of interests as between roving patrols and secondary checkpoint referrals: "the governmental interests relied on as warranting intrusion here are the same as those" in the case of roving patrols. "Absent some difference in the nature of the intrusion, the same minimal requirement should be imposed for checkpoint stops."[82] Brennan rejected the idea that the subjective intrusion felt by the motorist was any less than in the case of a roving patrol stop. The motorist, he suggested, would feel just as much resentment at his detention and inspection—and just as much concern at being picked out of the crowd.

But even more troubling, the ruling would allow for unfettered racial profiling. By requiring no standard whatsoever, the Court was giving the Border Patrol free rein to profile all persons of Mexican ancestry for secondary questioning and inspection. The limitation from *Brignoni-Ponce* would have no effect whatsoever. Brennan exclaimed:

> In abandoning any requirement of a minimum of reasonable suspicion, or even articulable suspicion, the Court in every practical sense renders meaningless, as applied to checkpoint stops, the *Brignoni-Ponce* holding that "standing alone, [Mexican appearance] does not justify stopping all Mexican–Americans to ask if they are aliens." Since the objective is almost entirely the Mexican illegally in the country, checkpoint officials, uninhibited by any objective standards and therefore free to stop any or all motorists without explanation or excuse, wholly on whim, will perforce target motorists of Mexican appearance. The process will then inescapably discriminate against citizens of Mexican ancestry and Mexican aliens lawfully in this country for no other reason than that they unavoidably possess the same "suspicious" physical and grooming characteristics of illegal Mexican aliens.[83]

The *Marinez-Fuerte* decision, Brennan concluded, would allow reliance on race and ethnicity—and not just partial reliance, but entire reliance.

---

[81] *Id.* at 569–70 (Brennan, J., dissenting).

[82] *Id.* at 570 (Brennan, J., dissenting).

[83] *Id.* at 571–72 (Brennan, J., dissenting).

The Immediate Impact on Policing

Brignoni-Ponce and *Martinez-Fuerte* had an important impact not only on Fourth Amendment jurisprudence, but on border patrol and policing more generally. The decisions signaled a green light to criminal profiling—including racial profiling. The Court had given law enforcement a clear message that the use of a multiple factor profile, including as one factor race or ethnicity, were constitutional and legitimate police techniques. At the national level, the DEA began implementing criminal profiling, especially the drug-courier profile, with vigor. The original Detroit experiment was deemed a success, and the program went nationwide after *Brignoni-Ponce* and *Martinez-Fuentes*. Between 1976 and 1986 there were in excess of 140 reported court decisions involving DEA stops of passengers at airports across the country based on the drug-courier profile.[84] In the *Mendenhall* case from 1980, for example, the suspect was stopped in part on the basis of the following profile attributes:

> (1) the respondent was arriving on a flight from Los Angeles, a city believed by the agents to be the place of origin for much of the heroin brought to Detroit; (2) the respondent was the last person to leave the plane, "appeared to be very nervous," and "completely scanned the whole area where [the agents] were standing"; (3) after leaving the plane the respondent proceeded past the baggage area without claiming any luggage; and (4) the respondent changed airlines for her flight out of Detroit.[85]

Several scholars, David Cole in particular, have compiled lists of the drug-courier profile characteristics, which are often internally contradictory.[86] With time, the profiles have proliferated. As Charles Becton explains:

> Not only does each airport have a profile, but a single DEA agent may use multiple profiles of his or her own. Paul Markonni, the person most often credited with developing the drug courier profile, and clearly the agent most often listed in drug courier profile cases, has articulated several slightly varying profiles in reported cases. One court has used different profiles for incoming and outgoing flights. The United States Court of Appeals for the Ninth Circuit in *United States v. Patino* made reference to a "female" drug courier profile. The United States Court of Appeals for the Fifth Circuit referred to a regional profile in *United States v. Berry*, and a profile

---

[84] *See Becton, supra* note 27, at 417 note 2, 417–18.

[85] United States v. Mendenhall, 446 U.S. 544, 547 note 1 (1980).

[86] *See, e.g.,* David Cole, No Equal Justice: Race and Class in the American Criminal Justice System 48–49 (New York: Free Press, 1999); Becton, *supra* note 27, 421.

associated with particular agents in *United States v. Elmore*. And, contributing to the proliferation of the drug courier profile, state and local law enforcement agencies have instituted their own profile programs.[87]

According to former Justice Lewis Powell, concurring in *Mendenhall*, the drug-courier profile was a "highly specialized law enforcement operation."[88] Former chief Justice William Rehnquist referred to the profile as "the collective or distilled experience of narcotics officers concerning characteristics repeatedly seen in drug smugglers."[89] In 1982, the National Institute of Justice—the research arm of the Department of Justice—conducted a systematic study of the drug-courier profile.[90] The study required DEA agents to fill out a report for all encounters they instigated and a log of passengers observed during an eight month period in 1982. Of about 107,000 passengers observed, the agents approached 146. According to the report, most of the encounters (120 of the total 146) were triggered by a combination of behavioral and demographic peculiarities of the passengers—matches to a profile. The results of these encounters were as follows:[91]

	Number	Percentage
Total passengers stopped	146	100%
No search after questioning	42	29%
Consent searches	81	55%
Searches with warrant or incident to arrest	15	10%
Contraband found or other evidence of crime	49	34%

The study was considered by many as proof that the drug-courier profile worked.

Meanwhile, on the Mexican border, the political climate continued to heat up in the aftermath of *Brignoni-Ponce* and *Martinez-Fuerte*. The 1980s and 90s saw renewed public concern and political rhetoric surrounding illegal immigration. In 1993, Democratic President William Clinton, under attack by Republicans, pledged his support to increased surveillance: "In September 1993 the administration proclaimed Operation Hold-the-Line in El Paso, Texas, . . . an effort to curtail illegal

---

[87] *Becton, supra* note 27, 433–34.

[88] *Mendenhall*, 446 U.S. at 562 (1980) (Powell, J., concurring, joined by Burger, C.J., and Blackmun, J.).

[89] Florida v. Royer, 460 U.S. 491, 507 (1983).

[90] *See* Zedlewski, *The DEA Airport Surveillance Program: An Analysis of Agent Activities* (1984), reported in John Monahan and Laurens Walker, *Social Science in Law: Cases and Materials* (Westbury: Foundation Press 2006).

[91] *Id.*

entrants by deploying Border Agents at close intervals along the border itself, and in September 1994 Attorney General Janet Reno proclaimed the initiation of Operation Gatekeeper in San Diego."[92] These were not just empty policy promises: "The government increased the overall size of the Border Patrol by 51 percent from 1993 to 1995 bringing the number of agents to more than 4,500.... In mid–1995 Congress also approved a special $328 million enhancement for concentrated border enforcement."[93] Joseph Nevins suggests that this huge increase was due to political pressure generally and specifically as a response to California's ballot initiative, proposition 187, also entitled "SOS (Save our State)", which would deny medical and health services to illegal immigrants.

As for illegal passage from Mexico itself, "[an] INS report said that during much of the 1990s, around 700,000 illegal aliens entered the U.S. each year, a figure that increased to around 817,000 by 1998 and nearly one million by 1999."[94]

The Impact on Racial Profiling

The most significant constitutional implication of *Brignoni-Ponce* and *Martinez-Fuerte*, though, was that race or ethnicity, if relevant to the policing objective, could be used as one factor among others—and in some limited cases as the only factor—in determining whether there is sufficient reason to conduct police investigation, such as a stop and questioning.[95] In this sense, these decisions allowed the use of race as a factor in policing. And they set up a four-part distinction that still governs today the consideration of race in policing.

---

[92] Nevins, *supra* note 13, at 271.

[93] *Id.*

[94] Jon E. Dougherty, Illegals: The Imminent Threat Posed by Our Unsecured U.S.-Mexico Border 31 (Nashville: WND Books, 2004).

[95] The cases, especially *Martinez-Fuerte*, also undermine the requirement of individualized suspicion. Fourth Amendment law, as evidenced more recently in City of Indianapolis v. Edmond, 531 U.S. 32 (2000), requires individualized suspicion for Fourth Amendment searches intended to advance a general interest in crime control. *See id.* at 44 (declaring that "we are particularly reluctant to recognize exceptions to the general rule of individualized suspicion where governmental authorities primarily pursue their general crime control ends"). Justice Powell recognized this in *Martinez-Fuerte*: "The defendants note correctly that to accommodate public and private interests some quantum of individualized suspicion is usually a prerequisite to a constitutional search or seizure." 428 U.S. at 560. But not always, Powell continued: "the Fourth Amendment imposes no irreducible requirement of such suspicion." 428 U.S. at 561. As a result, Powell concluded, "we hold that the stops and questioning at issue may be made in the absence of any individualized suspicion at reasonably located checkpoints." 428 U.S. at 562. To be sure, *Martinez-Fuerte* limits its holding to cases of stop and questioning, not a full search. But more recent commentary seems to tow the line of individual suspicion more than in *Martinez-Fuerte*.

1. Legal Distinction #1: Race as a, but not the factor

Commentators most often cite *Brignoni-Ponce* for the proposition that race may be used as "one factor" in a police officer's decision to conduct investigation.[96] *Martinez-Fuerte* muddied the waters a bit, by allowing the use of race *alone* where there is no need for any articulable reason. The Supreme Court offered little or no guidance in the years following *Brignoni-Ponce* and *Martinez-Fuerte,* and the result has been some confusion among the lower federal courts. What has emerged, though, is a rough judicial norm that partial, but not exclusive use of race is constitutionally permissible.

Most federal courts either ignore the race question or allow the use of race *sub judice. United States v. Weaver*[97] is a prime example of the latter approach; but many other courts have simply sidestepped the race issue by relying on non-racial factors either to find or not find reasonable suspicion.[98] Still other lower federal courts have struck down the use of race under circumstances suggesting that race was one among other factors used to stop or search a suspect.[99] One panel of the Ninth Circuit, in fact, has held in the case of *United States v. Montero–Camargo* that the appearance of Mexican ancestry is of little, or no probative value at INS checkpoints because the majority of people who pass through checkpoints are Hispanic.[100] The Ninth Circuit declared there that His-

---

[96] *See, e.g.,* Kevin R. Johnson, *September 11 and Mexican Immigrants: Collateral Damage Comes Home,* 52 DePaul L. Rev. 849, 868 (2003); Deborah A. Ramirez, Jennifer Hoopes, & Tara Lai Quinlan, *Defining Racial Profiling in a Post–September 11 World,* 40 Am. Crim. L. Rev. 1195, 1204–06, note 40 (2003); Devon W. Carbado, *Eracing the Fourth Amendment,* 100 Mich. L. Rev. 946, 997–1000 (2002).

[97] 966 F.2d 391 (8th Cir. 1992).

[98] *See generally* Gross and Barnes, *supra* note 6, at 735, discussing Derricott v. State, 611 A.2d 592 (Md. 1992), and United States v. Davis, 11 Fed.Appx. 16 (2d Cir. 2001). Some courts have also used the same logic—reliance on non-racial traits justifies the stop and vitiates the constitutional claim—in the Equal Protection context. Alschuler, for example, has identified several cases from the Sixth Circuit that do just this: Where the police used other legitimate reasons to interview a suspect, the legitimacy of those other reasons cancels out the Equal Protection violation of improperly relying on race. *See* Alschuler, *supra* note 6, at 178. State courts are split on their approach to the use of race. *See generally* Gross and Barnes, *supra* note 6, at 734 & notes 253–54 (discussing state court holdings).

[99] *See* United States v. Laymon, 730 F. Supp. 332, 339 (D. Colo. 1990) (finding traffic stop based on defendant's weaving was a pretext for an impermissible stop based on the defendant's out-of-state license plates and race); United States v. Nicholas, 448 F.2d 622, 625 (8th Cir. 1971) (holding impermissible a search based on "a generalized suspicion that any black person driving an auto with out-of-state license plates might be engaged in criminal activity").

[100] United States v. Montero–Camargo, 208 F.3d 1122, 1131 (9th Cir. 2000) (the Court affirmed the conviction because other grounds were sufficient).

panic appearance is "of such little probative value that it may not be considered as a relevant factor where particularized or individualized suspicion is required" and that Hispanic appearance "is also not an appropriate factor."[101] The *Montero-Camargo* opinion takes issue with *Brignoni-Ponce*'s demographic analysis and finds that Hispanics make up too much of the population in the border area for there to be any probative value in using Hispanic appearance as a factor. Other courts do not widely cite this element of the holding, though it remains good law in the Ninth Circuit; and no other circuit has followed the "race can't be a factor" element of the *Montero-Camargo* holding.[102] At the end of the day, though, there has emerged a loose legal distinction between using race exclusively and using race as one among other factors. The first use of race is practically unanimously condemned. In fact, if the police in *Weaver* had argued that the legitimacy of the search rested entirely on the race of the suspect, there is no doubt that the court would have struck down the search. As the court said, "had [DEA agent] Hicks relied solely upon the fact of Weaver's race as a basis for his suspicions, we would have a different case before us."[103] The second use of race—as one among other factors—is only slightly more controversial, but is generally avoided by focusing on the other factors that raise suspicion.[104]

2. Legal Distinction #2: Fourth vs. Fourteenth Amendment

Brignoni-Ponce and *Martinez-Fuerte* also signaled that Fourth Amendment analysis differs in kind from Equal Protection analysis, and that claims of racial bias should be addressed to the latter, not the former. It would take, however, another twenty years before the Court would make this explicit in the case of *Whren v. United States*.[105] In *Whren*, the police used a minor traffic violation as a pretext to stop and investigate two motorists for drugs. The police suspected the two young

---

[101] *Montero-Camargo*, 208 F.3d at 1135.

[102] *See, e.g.*, United States v. Harold Bridges, 2000 WL 1170137 at 16 (S.D.N.Y.2000) (acknowledging the *Montero-Camargo* holding to mean " 'Hispanic appearance' is not a proper factor for the Border Patrol to consider in determining whether there is reasonable suspicion to stop suspects in light of the large number of Hispanics in the border area" but rejecting that holding's application to different facts).

[103] *Id.* at 394 note 2 (emphasis added).

[104] *See* R. Richard Banks, *Race-Based Suspect Selection and Colorblind Equal Protection Doctrine and Discourse*, 48 UCLA L. Rev. 1075, 1086–87 note 47 (2001) ("The consensus view seems to be that race may be considered as one of many factors, but may not be the only factor in an officer's decision to stop an individual."). *See also* Gross and Barnes, *supra* note 6, at 733 (suggesting that there is "a general view that race may not be the sole basis for deciding who to stop or search, but that it may constitutionally be considered as one factor among others").

[105] 517 U.S. 806 (1996).

African–American men, who were sitting in a Pathfinder with temporary license plates, because they were stopped for a longer than usual amount of time—more than 20 seconds—at a stop sign in a high-drug area and the driver was apparently looking down into the lap of his companion. The two men challenged the pretextual stop as unreasonable under the Fourth Amendment, and argued that allowing such practices would enable the police to stop motorists based on an impermissible factor: race.[106]

The Supreme Court rejected their argument. The Fourth Amendment, the Court declared, does not concern itself with the subjective intentions of police officers, including their possible reliance on race, so long as they had reasonable suspicion or probable cause to justify the seizure—in this case, the traffic violation. Race claims should be addressed to the Equal Protection clause, not the Fourth Amendment. "We of course agree with petitioners that the Constitution prohibits selective enforcement of the law based on considerations such as race," the Court declared. "But the constitutional basis for objecting to intentionally discriminatory application of laws is the Equal Protection Clause, not the Fourth Amendment."[107] Consideration of race is not a problem for Fourth Amendment analysis, so long as there is sufficient ground for the search.

This doctrinal framework of bifurcated Fourth and Fourteenth Amendment analysis has guided lawyers and lower courts. Most legal discussions of racial profiling today address each claim separately. Most constitutional scholars, including notably Carol Steiker, have criticized this practice and argued that notions of equal protection should inform our interpretation of the Fourth Amendment.[108] Despite criticism, the legal distinction has stuck and continues to hold today.

3.   Legal Distinction #3: Eye-witness Identification

The third constitutional pillar of racial profiling analysis is focused on Equal Protection analysis. It draws a distinction between using race absent any individualized suspicion about a particular suspect and using race where there is an eyewitness identification based on race. The first

---

[106] *Id.* at 808–09.

[107] *Id.* at 813.

[108] *See, e.g.*, Carol S. Steiker, *Second Thoughts about First Principles*, 107 Harv. L. Rev. 820, 844 (1994); Alschuler, *supra* note 6, at 193 & note 121 (characterizing the Court's "compartmentalization" as "artificial" and gathering commentary reaching same conclusion); Anthony C. Thompson, *Stopping the Usual Suspects: Race and the Fourth Amendment*, 74 NYU L. Rev. 956, 961 (1999) (asserting that the Supreme Court "took a wrong turn" in writing race out of the Fourth Amendment); Rudovsky, *supra* note 11, at 348 (arguing that "artificial doctrinal lines that the Supreme Court has drawn around the Fourth and Fourteenth Amendments" create "disquiet[ing]" results).

is generally associated with racial profiling—the idea of stopping a minority motorist because minority motorists are assumed to offend at higher rates. The second is what we generally associate with detective work—namely, getting an identification from a witness and tracking down suspects who match that description. Most courts hold that the latter is not "using race." Most often, the reason is that the reliance on an identification is a race-neutral policy; the content may be race-specific, but the policy itself is race neutral.[109]

The leading case for this proposition is *Brown v. City of Oneonta*.[110] In that case, a victim identified a burglar as a young African–American male; according to the reported decision, the description included a knife wound to the hand, allegedly inflicted during a struggle with the victim.[111] In response, police officers interrogated every African–American male student at the local college and conducted a sweep of the town "stopping and questioning non-white persons on the streets and inspecting their hands for cuts."[112] The African–American population in Oneonta was in the neighborhood of 300 people, with another 150 at the state university. Several residents sued the police for violating their civil rights. The court and the attorneys, naturally, addressed the Fourth Amendment and Equal Protection clause arguments separately.[113]

With regard to the Equal Protection claim, the Second Circuit ruled that the police had not purposely classified by race or engaged in intentional discrimination based on race when it questioned African–American residents and students. Instead, the police had relied on a race-neutral technique, focusing attention on persons who matched the eyewitness identification. The policy itself—namely "to investigate crimes by interviewing the victim, getting a description of the assailant, and seeking out persons who matched that description"[114]—was race-

---

[109] *See, e.g.*, Brown v. City of Oneonta, 221 F.3d 329, 337 (2d Cir. 2000) (deeming race-neutral the state policy of "investigat[ing] crimes by interviewing the victim, getting a description of the assailant, and seeking out persons who matched that description").

[110] 221 F.3d 329 (2d Cir. 2000).

[111] *Id.* at 334. Purportedly based on this information, the police accosted suspects to look at their hands. According to some media accounts, however, the victim never made any statement about the knife wound. *See, e.g.*, *60 Minutes II: The Black List* (CBS television broadcast Feb. 13, 2002) (reporting the contents of the original police investigative record).

[112] *Oneonta*, 221 F.3d at 334.

[113] With regard to the Fourth Amendment claim, the Second Circuit held that "a description of race and gender alone will rarely provide reasonable suspicion justifying a police search or seizure." *Id.* The court remanded the case to allow certain plaintiffs who had been seized to pursue their claim under a Fourth Amendment theory. *Id.* at 341–42. The court's treatment of the Fourth Amendment claim is in accordance with my argument.

[114] *Id.* at 337.

neutral on its face, the court declared. And even though the policy as applied here had a disparate racial impact, without an additional showing of intent to discriminate, "the disparate impact of an investigation such as the one in this case is insufficient to sustain an equal protection claim."[115]

Many constitutional commentators endorse this distinction. In fact, as Richard Banks correctly observes, "Even the harshest scholarly critics of racial profiling endorse police use of suspect descriptions."[116] Samuel Gross and Deborah Livingston write, for instance, that "[i]t is not racial profiling for an officer to question, stop, search, arrest, or otherwise investigate a person because his race or ethnicity matches information about a perpetrator of a specific crime that the officer is investigating. That use of race . . . does not entail a global judgment about a racial or ethnic group as a whole."[117] David Rudovsky similarly defines racial profiling so as to exclude witness identification cases—"except where police are acting on a racial description of the perpetrator of a crime."[118] And many commentators do not place the same type of limits on eyewitness racial identifications. So, for instance, Rudovsky observes: "Certainly police can consider race where a physical description is provided, but absent that factor, or other self-limiting factors, race cannot be considered in the decision to stop, detain, or search."[119] It is

---

[115] *Id.* at 338.

[116] Banks, *supra* note 104, at 1078. See also Alschuler, *supra* note 6, at 265–66 ("Almost no one seeks to prevent the police from using race as a partial description of physical appearance."). *Consider* U.S. Department of Justice, *Guidance Regarding the Use of Race by Federal Law Enforcement Agencies* (June 2003), *available at* at http://www.usdoj.gov/crt/split/documents/guidance_on_race.htm (visited Oct. 14, 2005) (prohibiting racial profiling in federal law enforcement activities "except that officers may rely on race and ethnicity in a specific suspect description").

[117] Samuel R. Gross and Debra Livingston, *Racial Profiling Under Attack*, 102 Colum. L. Rev. 1413, 1415 (2002). *See also* Gross and Barnes, *supra* note 6, at 655 note 10 ("[I]t is not racial profiling for an officer to stop, question, search, or arrest a person because his race matches the description of the perpetrator of a specific crime that has been reported."). Gross and Barnes note that "racial profiling is impossible once the police are looking for a particular person—the victim's partner, the woman in the surveillance video, Osama bin Laden." *Id.* at 655.

[118] Rudovsky, *supra* note 11, at 299 note 27.

[119] *Id.* at 328. *See also id.* at 308 note 79 ("Race is an appropriate factor in stops where the police have been provided with a description of a criminal suspect."). Sheri Lynn Johnson similarly writes: "The use of race to identify a particular perpetrator, for example, does not disadvantage any racial group and thus does not require strict scrutiny. Although the suspect's race is noted and weighed in the decision to detain, no *generalizations* about the characteristics, behavior, or appropriate treatment of the racial group are employed." Sheri Lynn Johnson, *Race and the Decision to Detain a Suspect*, 93 Yale L.J. 214, 242–43 (1983).

fair to say that the "consensus view of legal scholars casts . . . race-based suspect descriptions as innocuous and unquestionably legitimate."[120]

There is, however, a minority position advocated by a few commentators—Richard Banks and Albert Alschuler especially—and they seem to have the better of the argument.[121] When the police work from an eyewitness identification, they use probabilities in exactly the same way as when they rely on racial correlations with crime. Ironically, they may be working off *less reliable* information; eyewitness identification is notoriously untrustworthy.[122] Whether race may be considered should depend on whether race functions sufficiently to narrow down the suspect pool. In many cases, eyewitness racial identification will likely satisfy this standard. The fact that race-based suspect identification should be subject to equal protection review does not mean that it should be prohibited. Nevertheless, courts have uniformly taken the opposite position.

4. Legal Distinction #4: Intent to Discriminate

The final pillar of racial profiling law draws on the Supreme Court's decisions in *McCleskey v. Kemp*[123] and *United States v. Armstrong*[124]— which extend the *Washington v. Davis*[125] requirement of intent to the criminal justice sphere. This sets up the final major legal distinction, the requirement that a successful equal protection challenge rest on evidence of intentional discrimination rather than on inference from unexplained disparate treatment.[126]

Many commentators have criticized the intent requirement in the racial profiling context—as well as in other criminal justice contexts.[127]

---

[120] Banks, *supra* note 104, at 1083. *See generally id.* at 1083–85 (compiling list of authoritative legal scholars who endorse the use of race-based suspect descriptions).

[121] *See generally* Bernard E. Harcourt, *Rethinking Racial Profiling, supra* note 6, at 1345.

[122] *See generally* Elizabeth F. Loftus, Eyewitness Testimony (Harvard 1979).

[123] 481 U.S. 279 (1987). In *McClesky*, the Court rejected an Equal Protection claim for lack of a showing of actual discriminatory intent, where petitioner produced evidence that murderers of white victims are 4.3 times more likely to be sentenced to death than murderers of African–American victims. *Id.* at 287, 291–99.

[124] 517 U.S. 456 (1996). In *Armstrong*, the Court required evidence of discriminatory purpose in the context of a selective prosecution challenge. *Id.* at 465.

[125] 426 U.S. 229 (1976). In *Davis*, the Court articulated the principle that the Equal Protection Clause bars only intentional discrimination. *Id.* at 239–41.

[126] *See generally* Rudovsky, *supra* note 11, at 322–29.

[127] *See, e.g., id.* (providing critical commentary on both *McCleskey* and *Armstrong*); Alschuler, *supra* note 6, at 201–07 (critiquing *Armstrong*); Gross and Barnes, *supra* note 6, at 741 (lamenting the "near impossibility" of meeting the actual-intent requirement).

Al Alschuler, for instance, suggests that courts should substitute social meaning for intent: "Targeting only black street gangs or only black drug dealers, for example, clearly conveys the message that blacks are more to be feared than whites. The Equal Protection Clause should require the government to justify its delivery of this message."[128] Gross and Barnes, in their discussion of the notorious New Jersey case *State v. Soto*,[129] suggest another promising alternative. In the *Soto* case, the lower state court, relying in part on New Jersey precedent, carved an exception to the *McCleskey* requirement on the grounds that the decision to stop and search involves fewer variables—fewer factors that the police use— than the decision to sentence someone to death. The reduction in variables narrows and simplifies the claim of racial discrimination and therefore, the *Soto* court suggested, statistical evidence may be sufficient to prove intentional discrimination in the racial profiling context.[130] The decision to stop and search involves not only fewer variables than the decision to sentence to death, but also fewer decisionmakers. In the first case, the decisionmakers are all police officers, generally from the same patrol unit; in the second, they include prosecutors, grand jurors, petit jurors, judges, and defense attorneys. Although, as Gross and Barnes observe, the New Jersey court did not rely on this second distinction, it is important—perhaps even more important than the first. Courts, however, have not gone down this path, but abide, instead, on the fourth distinction's requirement of intent.

Epilogue

There was a thawing of border and immigration issues in the late 1990s—an effort to ease the difficulties facing the large population of illegal aliens from Mexico. President George W. Bush offered proposals to allow for temporary residence and a number of initiatives to cooperate with the administration of President Vincente Fox of Mexico. During the summer of 2001, in fact, the two country's leaders were talking about making immigration from Mexico "safe and legal."[131]

At the same time, there was also an emerging consensus in the context of racial profiling more generally that profiling on race was wrong. As Albert Alschuler writes, by the end of the 1990s, "almost everyone condemned racial profiling. President Bill Clinton called the practice 'morally indefensible' and 'deeply corrosive.' President George W. Bush pledged, 'We will end it.' A federal court observed, 'Racial

---

[128] Alschuler, *supra* note 6, at 212.

[129] 734 A.2d 350 (N.J. Super. Ct. 1996).

[130] *See id.* at 360. *See also* Gross and Barnes, *supra* note 6, at 723–26 (discussing the *Soto* decision).

[131] John Aloysius Farell, *Bush Courting Hispanics*, Denver Post, Jan. 8, 2004, at A1.

profiling of any kind is anathema to our criminal justice system.' 81 percent of the respondents to a 1999 Gallup poll declared their opposition."[132] Practically everyone seemed to agree. President Bush's first Attorney General, John Ashcroft, declared that "racial profiling is an unconstitutional deprivation of equal protection under our Constitution."[133] Robert Mueller, director of the F.B.I., added that "Racial profiling is abhorrent to the Constitution, it is abhorrent in any way, shape or form."[134] Senator Orrin Hatch of Utah agreed: "There has emerged a consensus concerning the fundamental point of the debate: racial profiling, also known as bias-based policing, is wrong, it is unconstitutional, and it must not be practiced or tolerated."[135]

This emerging consensus collapsed with the fall of the Twin Towers on September 11, 2001. The terrorist attacks changed the conversation on racial profiling. Many people shifted opinion. Shortly after 9/11, "58 percent of the respondents to a Gallup poll said that airlines should screen passengers who appeared to be Arabs more intensely than other passengers. Half the respondents who voiced an opinion favored requiring people of Arab ethnicity, including United States citizens, to carry special identification cards."[136] The Attorney General of New Jersey, John Farmer, Jr., argued in print:

> More than 6,000 people are dead, some would argue, because of insufficient attention to racial or ethnic profiles at our airports.... Let's be blunt: How can law enforcement not consider ethnicity in investigating these crimes when that identifier is an essential characteristic of the hijackers and their supposed confederates and sponsors, and when law enforcement's ignorance of the community heightens the importance of such broadly shared characteristics? Law enforcement tactics must be calibrated to address the magnitude of the threat society faces.[137]

Paul Sperry of the Hoover Institution defended profiling of young Muslim men in a *New York Times* op-ed titled "When the Profile Fits

---

[132] Alschuler, *supra* note 6, at 163.

[133] *Id.* (quoting *Black Caucus, Ashcroft Have Tense Meeting: Attorney General Cites "Candid Exchange" and Stresses Agreement on Profiling*, Washington Post, Mar. 1, 2001, at A6).

[134] *Id.* (quoting 147 Cong. Rec. S8683 (Aug 2, 2001)).

[135] *Id.* at 163 note 3 (quoting End Racial Profiling Act of 2001, Hearing on S. 989 Before the Senate Committee on the Judiciary Subcommittee on the Constitution, Federalism and Property Rights, 107th Congress, 1st Sess (2001)).

[136] Alschuler, *supra* note 6, at 163.

[137] *Id.* at 163 (quoting John Farmer, Jr., *Rethinking Racial Profiling*, Newark Star–Ledger § 10, Sept. 23, 2001, at 1).

the Crime." The facts suggest, he argued, that any likely offender is going to be young, male, and of Arab descent: "Young Muslim men bombed the London tube, and young Muslim men attacked New York with planes in 2001. From everything we know about the terrorists who may be taking aim at our transportation system, they are most likely to be young Muslim men."[138] Therefore, the police should profile: "Critics protest that profiling is prejudicial. In fact, it's based on statistics. Insurance companies profile policyholders based on probability of risk. That's just smart business. Likewise, profiling passengers based on proven security risk is just smart law enforcement."[139]

Those who supported increased control at the border have taken full advantage of the concerns about terrorism generated by 9/11. Steven Camarota, research director at the Center for Immigration Studies, for instance, argues that "If a Mexican day laborer can sneak across the border, so can an al Qaeda terrorist.... We can't protect ourselves from terrorism without dealing with illegal immigration."[140] The administration of George W. Bush responded to the heightened concern by promising tougher control at the border: "In January 2003, Homeland Security Director Tom Ridge pledged to merge four agencies responsible for border security into one, allegedly to plug gaps in a border-security system whose weaknesses were laid bare by the 9–11 attacks."[141]

Following the attacks, the new Department of Homeland Security implemented regulations regarding the deportation of illegal aliens intercepted within the 100–mile radius. Effective August 2004, the new rules allow border agents to deport, without judicial oversight, undocumented immigrants who: 1) are caught within 100 miles of the Mexican and Canadian borders and 2) have spent up to 14 days within the United States.[142] This power to deport without the oversight of immigration courts had already been granted to officials at airports and seaports.[143] The DHS "[says] that border agents [who will exercise these powers] would be trained in asylum law and that immigrants who showed

---

[138] Paul Sperry, *When the Profile Fits the Crime*, New York Times, July 28, 2005 (available at http://www.nytimes.com/2005/07/28/opinion/28sperry.html (last visited Oct. 14, 2005)).

[139] *Id.*

[140] Dougherty, *supra* note 94, at 32.

[141] Dougherty, *supra* note 94, at 132.

[142] See Rachel L. Swarns, *U.S. to Give Border Patrol Agents the Power to Deport Illegal Aliens*, New York Times, Aug. 11, 2004, at A1.

[143] *See id.* (noting that this was the second time since September 11th that the government expanded the "expedited removal" process).

credible fear of persecution would be provided hearings before immigration judges, not returned to hostile governments."[144]

In sum, the terrorist attacks of 9/11 revived the policy debates over racial profiling. They may also bring back to life the constitutional debate. In that debate, the United States Supreme Court decisions in *Brignoni-Ponce* and *Martinez-Fuerte* will once again play a central role. And with some luck, Justice Brennan's final words in *Martinez-Fuerte* will guide us in our deliberations:

> The cornerstone of this society, indeed of any free society, is orderly procedure. The Constitution, as originally adopted, was therefore, in great measure, a procedural document. For the same reasons the drafters of the Bill of Rights largely placed their faith in procedural limitations on government action. The Fourth Amendment's requirement that searches and seizures be reasonable enforces this fundamental understanding in erecting its buffer against the arbitrary treatment of citizens by government. . . . [A]s Mr. Justice Frankfurter reminded us, "[t]he history of American freedom is, in no small measure, the history of procedure."[145]

---

[144] *Id.*

[145] United States v. Martinez–Fuerte, 428 U.S. at 578 (Brennan, J., dissenting) (quoting Frankfurter, J., in Malinski v. New York, 324 U.S. 401, 414 (1945)).

*

11

Bordenkircher v. Hayes: Plea Bargaining and the Decline of the Rule of Law

William J. Stuntz

Important cases are usually important for obvious reasons. A particular set of facts produced a particular result, and the result mattered—either because the fact situation is so common, or because it is intrinsically important, or because millions of people watched on Court TV. That is the way law works in contemporary America.

Most of the time. But not in *Bordenkircher v. Hayes*.[1] *Bordenkircher* is the legal equivalent of a card trick; everything is misdirection. The defendant, Paul Hayes, took his case to trial—but the biggest effect of the case was on the millions of defendants who plead guilty each year. Hayes's legal claim challenged the criminal charge filed against him. But the case was really about sentencing, not charging. As for the sentence: Hayes got life in prison under Kentucky's "three strikes" statute—but the biggest effect of the case was on defendants who *aren't* sentenced under three-strikes laws. Misdirection.

But this is not a piece of casual entertainment like some magician's trick. *Bordenkircher* mattered a lot, more so than many cases whose names are much better known. More than two million men and women make their beds in prison and jail cells in America today.[2] Many thousands of them (no one knows *how* many) live where they live because of what happened to Paul Hayes, and what the Supreme Court had to say about it.

The Case

The case began with a small-time crime in Lexington, Kentucky. Sometime shortly before November 20, 1972, Paul Hayes stole a check

---

[1] 434 U.S. 357 (1978).

[2] According to the Bureau of Justice Statistics, there were 2,232,717 inmates in America's prisons and jails in 2003. U.S. Dep't of Justice, Bureau of Justice Statistics, *Corrections Statistics* (available on-line at http://www.ojp.usdoj.gov/bjs/correct.htm).

belonging to the Brown Machine Works, a local business.[3] Hayes made
out the check to the Pic Pac grocery for 88 dollars and 30 cents, and
forged the signature. In January 1973 he was charged with "uttering a
forged instrument," a crime that carried a sentence of two to ten years
in prison.[4]

That is not the sort of case one wants to take to trial, since there is
no good way to explain why Hayes was signing a check that wasn't his.
So Hayes was, predictably, looking for a deal. But he had a history.[5] In
1961, when he was seventeen, Hayes and an older man were charged in a
sexual assault case. The other man ended up serving a long prison
sentence. Hayes denied participating but nevertheless agreed to plead
guilty to "detaining a female," a low-grade felony under Kentucky law.
He was sentenced to seven years in the state reformatory.[6] With good
time credits, he got out five years and three months later. In April 1970,
three years after his release, he was charged with and convicted of
robbery. He got probation. Hayes was still on probation when he gave
the forged check to the Pic Pac grocery in November 1972.

Glen Bagby, the prosecutor in Hayes's case, was understandably
concerned about this record. Excepting his time in confinement, Hayes
had committed his three felonies (the only crimes the state knew about,
but likely not the only ones Hayes had committed) in a span of six years.
And while the 88–dollar check was a marginal felony at worst, that track
record suggested more than marginal prison time. Or so Bagby must
have thought. He offered Hayes a deal: Plead guilty on the forgery
charge and take a five-year prison sentence. The offer was backed up by
a threat: If Hayes refused, Bagby would charge him under Kentucky's
habitual criminal statute.[7] Today we would call that statute a "three
strikes" law; it mandated life in prison for anyone convicted of three
felonies. Hayes already had two felony convictions. The forgery charge
was his third strike.

---

[3] Bordenkircher v. Hayes, 434 U.S. 357 (1978), No. 76–1334, App. to Pet. for Certiorari
12 [hereinafter cited as "App."].

[4] App. 12, 47.

[5] Hayes's account of his criminal history appears at App. 38–41.

[6] Here is Hayes's description of the difference between the reformatory and the state
prison:

> The penitentiary has a wall, maximum security, and the State Reformatory has a
> fence, you know. See ... uh ... the penitentiary, you spend most of your time in cells,
> but at LaGrange it is just like a college, you do—just walk around the campus and
> things, you know. App. 38–39.

[7] App. 42–43.

Hayes balked. Five years seemed like a long time, and he may not have believed that Bagby would carry out his threat. So Hayes rejected the deal, whereupon Bagby did as he said. Under the terms of the habitual criminal law, Hayes would have a two-stage trial. At the first stage, the jury was to decide whether Hayes was guilty of forging the check. If Hayes was found guilty on that charge (as seemed likely) the case would proceed to stage two, where the jury would decide whether Hayes qualified for treatment as a habitual criminal. That question in turn depended on another: whether Hayes had indeed been convicted of two other felonies, not counting the forged check. If the answer to that question was "yes," the jury then had to sentence Hayes to life in prison under Kentucky law.[8] That sentence was fixed by law: once the jury convicted Hayes on the forged check charge and once it found that Hayes had two previous "strikes," a life sentence was mandatory. Neither the judge nor the jury was permitted to show Hayes any mercy on his sentence.

Twenty-first-century readers will find Kentucky's habitual criminal law familiar. Three-strikes statutes proliferated in the 1980s and 1990s; a few states lowered the threshold, declaring defendants "out" after only two strikes.[9] They were less familiar in 1973, though a scattering existed even then; Kentucky was hardly alone. Such laws first became common during the mid–1920s, when a New York legislator named Caleb Baumes sponsored a measure like Kentucky's in response to a rise in Prohibition-era criminal violence.[10] At least sixteen states passed these laws in the 1920s. A few other states, including Kentucky, had such laws in force even earlier.[11] When crime started to fall in the 1930s, the "Baumes laws" (as they were then known) became more controversial. Press coverage began to focus on the small-time defendants threatened with life sentences: a New York Times article in 1931 told of an 80–year-old woman charged with theft who had narrowly escaped liability under the original Baumes law.[12] As crime fell through the 1930s, 1940s, and much of the 1950s, such laws either were repealed or fell into disuse—only to arise again from the ashes after crime exploded in the 1960s and 1970s.

---

[8] App. 23–24.

[9] For a good general discussion, see Linda S. Beres & Thomas D. Griffith, *Do Three–Strikes Laws Make Sense? Habitual Offender Statutes and Criminal Incapacitation*, 87 GEO. L.J. 103 (1998).

[10] For a fascinating account of this development, see V.F. Nourse, *Rethinking Crime Legislation: History and Harshness*, 39 TULSA L. REV. 925, 930–35 (2004).

[11] *See id.* at 938–39 (listing state statutes).

[12] *Id. at* 931 & note 31 (citing *Woman, 85, Escapes Life Term as Thief: State Permits Mrs. LaTouche to Plead Guilty to Minor Charge Because of Her Age*, 80 N.Y. TIMES 17 (Sept. 1, 1931)).

A decade or two earlier, Hayes would probably have been charged with the stolen check, pled guilty, and gone to prison for two years, the low end of the statutory sentencing range. By 1973, local prosecutors like Bagby were beginning to take a tougher stance toward repeat criminals like Hayes. Hence the five-year offer. Bagby had not wanted to send Hayes away for life—the habitual criminal law was a means of getting Hayes to accept Bagby's offer, nothing more. But once Hayes declined the offer, Bagby had little choice but to go ahead and file the habitual criminal charge. If he caved, word would get around among local defense attorneys to hang tough in plea negotiations because Bagby was the kind of prosecutor who liked to bluff. Plea bargaining is what academics call a "repeat-play" game; the same lawyers negotiate pleas over and over again. A prosecutor who becomes known as a pushover will be taken advantage of, not once but many times.[13] So while Bagby's threat to use Kentucky's three-strikes law may have been unwise or unfair even in Bagby's eyes, once the threat was made, it had to be carried out.

As Hayes's trial date approached, the government's position looked unassailable. There was little doubt that Hayes was guilty on the forgery charge and no doubt at all about the existence of the two prior convictions. The case looked like a slam-dunk.

For Hayes, there were few hopeful scenarios. A favorable jury verdict seemed a near-impossibility. The government's case was strong on the forged check[14] and irrefutable on the two prior convictions. Hayes had to depend on the jury nullifying—ignoring the trial judge's instructions and voting to acquit notwithstanding the law and the evidence. But that was extremely unlikely, for three reasons. First, juries rarely nullify. Jury acquittals in the teeth of uncontested or overwhelming evidence of guilt, as in O.J. Simpson's criminal trial—still two decades in the future when Paul Hayes was tried—are more rare than one might think from an occasional glance at Court TV. Jurors are generally told what Hayes's jury was told: that, if they find that the evidence proves the defendant guilty of the charged crime beyond a reasonable doubt, they "shall" or "must" convict.[15] In fact, the law is otherwise. The jury may acquit for any reason or no reason at all, and if it does so, its decision is final; no judge can overturn it.[16] Because most jurors do not know how much power they have, the power is rarely exercised.

---

[13] For a detailed discussion of the parties' bargaining incentives, see Robert E. Scott & William J. Stuntz, *Plea Bargaining as Contract*, 101 YALE L.J. 1909 (1992).

[14] According to Bagby, Hayes was caught in the grocery store and his accomplice had made a statement implicating him. App. 49.

[15] "Shall" was the word used in the jury instructions in Hayes's case. App. 23.

[16] *See* Fong Foo v. United States, 369 U.S. 141 (1962).

Second, when juries *do* nullify, they tend to do so on behalf of sympathetic defendants. Hayes was a 29–year-old black man with three felony convictions—an acquittal on the check charge was nearly inconceivable; the nullification, if it happened, had to be at the second stage of the trial. And Kentucky in 1973—a border South state with a history of racial segregation, less than twenty years after *Brown v. Board of Education*[17] and less than a decade after the Civil Rights Act of 1964— was not a racially enlightened place. Black men with criminal records were not likely to tug at the heartstrings of white Kentuckians.

Which leads to the third reason why Hayes had little hope of a favorable jury verdict: Hayes's jury could easily have been all-white. (The record does not reveal the jury's racial composition.) When juries are selected for criminal trials, both the prosecutor and the defense attorney are allowed to "strike" a set number of potential jurors—to eliminate them from the jury—for any reason they may choose. Historically, prosecutors often used *their* peremptory challenges to eliminate all blacks from the jury pool, especially when a black defendant was on trial. Today that practice is illegal, due to the Supreme Court's decision in *Batson v. Kentucky*[18] (note the state), in which the Court held that the race-based use of peremptory challenges violates the Fourteenth Amendment's Equal Protection Clause.[19] But in 1973, *Batson* was still thirteen years in the future, and the race-based use of peremptory challenges was both permissible and routine.

Finally, juries tend to nullify when it's possible to articulate at least *some* doubt about the facts. O.J. Simpson looked guilty to most of us, but it was possible (barely) to imagine that someone else had murdered Nicole Brown Simpson and Ronald Goldman. In Hayes's case, there simply was no doubt about those two prior convictions. So it came as no surprise when the jury returned guilty verdicts on both the forgery and habitual criminal charges. Along with the latter verdict came a life sentence, as required by Kentucky law.

All of which was completely predictable once Hayes turned down Bagby's offer. From that moment on, Hayes's lawyer had only one shot at avoiding a life sentence for his client: he could argue that the decision to charge Hayes under the habitual criminal law was unconstitutional— and therefore that his conviction and the sentence attached to it should be set aside. The argument would not be easy. The habitual criminal law was plainly valid—in 1975 it would be repealed; in place of an automatic

---

[17] 347 U.S. 483 (1954).

[18] 476 U.S. 79 (1986).

[19] *Batson* is the subject of a chapter in this volume. *See* Pamela S. Karlan, *Batson v. Kentucky*: The Constitutional Challenges of Peremptory Challenges.

life sentence Kentucky's legislature would authorize a sentencing range of ten to twenty years.[20] But that was too late to help Hayes. And prosecutors traditionally have unlimited discretion to decide when to charge under valid criminal statutes, and when not to. In April of 1973, the same month as Hayes's trial, the Second Circuit Court of Appeals handed down its decision in *Inmates of Attica Correctional Facility v. Rockefeller*.[21] That case arose out of the Attica prison riot; 32 prisoners were killed as the guards regained control of the prison. The killings were retaliation for the prisoners' takeover, during which one guard had been killed and several others beaten. Federal and state officials refused to prosecute any of the guards, notwithstanding substantial evidence that they were guilty of multiple homicides and felony assaults. Prisoners and their relatives sued to force prosecution. The Court of Appeals dismissed the claim—regardless of the strength of the case against the guards, the decision to prosecute or not was solely in the hands of the prosecutors. Hayes would later testify that he knew of *six*-time felons who weren't charged under the habitual criminal law. Under *Inmates of Attica*, it didn't matter. If the statute was valid, and if Hayes's crimes fell within its terms, the case was over.

But there was an exception to the principle of *Inmates of Attica*. The Supreme Court had held that criminal defendants could not be punished for exercising their constitutional rights.[22] Such punishment was "vindictive," the Court said, and vindictive punishment was unconstitutional. The habitual-criminal charge against Hayes was filed after, and because, Hayes decided he wanted a jury trial. The right to a jury trial is protected by the Sixth Amendment. The habitual criminal charge thus appeared to be punishment for Hayes's decision to exercise that right.

Hayes's counsel made that argument to every court that would hear the case, for the next five years. The state offered the same response, every time: what Hayes called vindictiveness was nothing more than ordinary plea bargaining. All plea bargains have the same basic structure: the defendant agrees to plead guilty, and in return the government

---

[20] Ky. Rev. Stat. § 532.080 (Supp. 1977), cited in Bordenkircher v. Hayes, 434 U.S. at 359. The revised statute established several requirements for enhanced sentences: the defendant must have been eighteen or older at the time of each offense, the sentence for each prior offense must have been at least one year in prison, and the defendant must have served at least a portion of that prison time for each prior offense at the time of the current offense. Hayes fit none of these criteria: he was seventeen at the time of his sexual assault offense, had served time in a reformatory, not the state's prison, and had received probation after his robbery conviction. *See* Hayes v. Cowan, 547 F.2d 42, 42 note 1 (6th Cir. 1976).

[21] 477 F.2d 375 (2d Cir. 1973). The decision in *Inmates of Attica* was handed down on April 18. Judgment was entered against Hayes on April 23. App. 27.

[22] See North Carolina v. Pearce, 395 U.S. 711 (1969).

drops some of the charges or agrees to a more favorable sentence. That government offer can also be expressed as a threat: if the defendant insists on going to trial, the government will jack up the charges and push for a harsher sentence. If that threat amounts to impermissible punishment for exercising the right to trial, plea bargaining is either unconstitutional or nearly so. The implications of the vindictiveness argument were radical.

As the case wound its way through the Kentucky and federal court systems, one court after another reached the state's conclusion: Plea bargaining lies at the heart of the criminal justice system, Hayes's argument would cast a constitutional shadow over the practice, and that consequence is simply too radical to permit. The trial court, the Kentucky Court of Appeals, and the federal district judge who adjudicated Hayes's habeas corpus petition all dismissed the argument out of hand.

Then came the decision of the Court of Appeals for the Sixth Circuit, authored by Judge Wade McCree, later named Solicitor General by Jimmy Carter; he would be the second African American (Thurgood Marshall was the first) to hold that post. Judge McCree's opinion granted Hayes's claim,[23] but with a twist. Recall the sequence of events: Hayes was charged with "uttering a forged check;" Bagby offered Hayes a five-year sentence if he would plead guilty to that charge; Hayes rejected the offer; Hayes was then charged with violating Kentucky's habitual criminal statute. According to McCree, Bagby's "vindictiveness" had everything to do with timing. If Hayes had been charged under the habitual criminal law to begin with—if Bagby had offered to *drop* that charge in exchange for a guilty plea (instead of threatening to *add* it if a plea were not forthcoming)—the proceedings would have been, constitutionally speaking, above reproach. But adding the charge *after* Hayes refused the deal was "vindictive."[24] The timing made the life sentence a punishment for Hayes's decision to exercise his right to trial.

The Court of Appeals' decision took the sting out of Hayes's vindictiveness argument. In a sense, it also made the argument pointless: if the decision stood, every prosecutor would respond by charging the longest and most severe set of crimes possible, then offering to drop some of the charges in exchange for a guilty plea. Defendants would get no better deals than before. The deals might even be worse; sentences like Hayes's might be *more* common. In cases that draw attention in the local press, it is politically difficult to drop serious criminal charges;

---

[23] Hayes v. Cowan, 547 F.2d 42 (6th Cir. 1976).

[24] The key sentence follows: "Although a prosecutor may in the course of plea negotiations offer a defendant concessions relating to prosecution under an existing indictment, ... he may not threaten a defendant with the consequence that more severe charges may be brought if he insists on going to trial." *Id.* at 44.

voters may think the local district attorney's office is soft on crime.
Failing to add those charges in return for a plea is much less likely to
attract notice. (Who will tell the newspaper about the charge that wasn't
filed? Not defense counsel and not the prosecutor, since both have an
incentive to keep their mouths shut.) So, under the Court of Appeals'
rule, defendants would more frequently face trial on the most serious
possible charge—precisely what Paul Hayes had wanted to avoid. It
seems clear that defendants as a class would be no better off under the
Court of Appeals' rule. They would probably be worse off, at least
slightly and maybe substantially. Hayes had won, but for criminal
defendants, it was a Pyrrhic victory.

The Supreme Court's Decision

The state—nominally, the warden of the prison where Hayes was
housed; his name was Bordenkircher—appealed Judge McCree's decision, and the Supreme Court agreed to hear the case on June 6, 1977.[25]

The parties made what were by now the familiar arguments.
Hayes's counsel contended that the habitual criminal charge was "vindictive." The government answered with the claim that if the Court
adopted Hayes's position, plea bargaining would be unconstitutional; the
government criticized Judge McCree's timing rule as an inappropriate
interference with prosecutors' charging decisions. Each side could point
to clear, direct language from prior Supreme Court cases. For Hayes,
Blackledge v. Perry[26] seemed telling. The defendant in *Blackledge* was
charged with and convicted of misdemeanor assault. Under then-govern-
ing North Carolina law, the defendant could appeal his conviction and
thereby obtain a new trial in a different state court. The defendant
exercised that right, whereupon the prosecutor filed a new charge: felony
assault with intent to kill.[27] The Court saw that charging decision as
punishing the right to trial:

> A prosecutor clearly has a considerable stake in discouraging
> convicted misdemeanants from appealing and thus obtaining a [new
> trial] in the Superior Court, since such an appeal will clearly require
> increased expenditures of prosecutorial resources.... And, if the
> prosecutor has the means readily at hand to discourage such ap-
> peals—by "upping the ante" through a felony indictment whenever
> a convicted misdemeanant pursues his statutory appellate remedy—
> the State can insure that only the most hardy defendants will brave
> the hazards of a [new] trial.

---

[25] Bordenkircher v. Hayes, 431 U.S. 953 (1977).

[26] 417 U.S. 21 (1974).

[27] *Id.* at 22–23.

... A person convicted of an offense is entitled to pursue his statutory right to a trial ..., without apprehension that the State will retaliate by substituting a more serious charge for the original one, thus subjecting him to a significantly increased potential period of incarceration.[28]

Hayes's increased sentence was a lot more than "potential," and Bagby's behavior looked at least as retaliatory as the conduct the Court condemned in *Blackledge*.

The government pointed to cases affirming the constitutionality and desirability of plea bargaining. Consider this passage from *Santobello v. New York*,[29] a 1971 decision on remedies for broken plea bargains:

... The disposition of criminal charges by agreement between the prosecutor and the accused, sometimes loosely called "plea bargaining," is an essential component of the administration of justice. Properly administered, it is to be encouraged. If every criminal charge were subjected to a full-scale trial, the States and the Federal Government would need to multiply by many times the number of judges and court facilities.

Disposition of charges after plea discussions is not only an essential part of the process but a highly desirable part.... It leads to prompt and largely final disposition of most criminal cases; ... and, by shortening the time between charge and disposition, it enhances whatever may be the rehabilitative prospects of the guilty when they are ultimately imprisoned.[30]

Since plea bargaining was so clearly permissible, and since the threat of more severe charges was a necessary incident of plea bargaining, the government argued, the habitual criminal charge against Hayes must be permissible as well.

Given those arguments and the authorities that backed them up, there were three possible outcomes. First, the Court might hold that a prosecutor behaved "vindictively" anytime she threatened negative consequences from taking a case to trial (which is what the quoted language from *Blackledge v. Perry* suggested). Second, the Court could decide that Judge McCree was right—that Hayes's constitutional rights were violated because he was charged with being a "habitual criminal" *after* he chose to go to trial. Had the charge been filed ahead of time and had Bagby offered to drop it in exchange for a plea, Hayes would be out of luck. Third and finally, the Court could decide that the concept of

---

[28] *Id.* at 27–28.

[29] 404 U.S. 257 (1971).

[30] *Id.* at 260–61.

"vindictive prosecution" simply has no application to plea bargaining: Whatever the timing of the criminal charges, prosecutors may threaten to impose greater liability on defendants who exercise their right to trial than on defendants who don't as a means of inducing guilty pleas. And if prosecutors can make those threats, it follows that they can carry them out when bargaining fails and defendants insist on going to trial, as Hayes did.

The first outcome might mean the end of plea bargaining, or at least the above-the-table version that was and is common in the United States. Prosecutors might still extract guilty pleas with threats of greater punishment, but the threats would have to be communicated with winks and nods, not openly as in Hayes's case. The second outcome, ratifying Judge McCree's opinion, would mean very little. Prosecutors would file their charges in advance instead of waiting until the bargaining process had reached a dead end; the bottom line would either be the same or defendants would be worse off, as prosecutors might be loath to drop charges once filed. The third outcome would mean no change; the criminal process could continue as it had been. Each of the three outcomes was legally plausible. *Blackledge v. Perry* seemed to dictate a defense victory, but plea bargaining cases like *Santobello* suggested the opposite decision. McCree's decision split the difference. Whichever way the Court ruled, it would have caselaw on its side.

To non-lawyers, that sounds bizarre: how can the law point in opposite directions at once? But American constitutional law often works that way. The text of the Constitution is hardly crystal clear ("due process of law" can mean almost anything), and the Court's cases offer a wide array of intersecting doctrines and arguments. Frequently, the Justices have the flexibility to go either way—as they did in *Bordenkircher*. When that is so, political and social context matter as much as, often more than, legal arguments. In *Bordenkircher v. Hayes*, that context pointed strongly toward a government victory.

Begin with crime rates. From the 1930s through the mid–1950s, crime in America had declined by about half;[31] the 1950s saw the lowest crime rates in American history. Men and women who came of age during these decades—including the nine Justices, whose law school graduation dates ranged from 1931 to 1952[32]—grew accustomed to an

---

[31] For an excellent brief discussion of homicide rates in American history, including the substantial fall in such rates from the 1930s to the 1950s, see Eric Monkkonen, *Homicide Over the Centuries*, in THE CRIME CONUNDRUM 163, 166–69 (Lawrence M. Friedman & George Fisher eds., 1997). Before the 1960s, homicide rates are generally used as a proxy for overall crime rates, because data on homicides are so much better.

[32] Chief Justice Burger graduated from the St. Paul College of Law in 1931. Justices Brennan and Blackmun graduated from Harvard Law School in 1931 and 1932, respective-

America where crime was a modest problem. Especially urban crime: throughout these years, the nation's murder rate was higher than New York City's,[33] an unimaginable statistic to Americans of the last generation. Fear of street crime played no role in national politics. When crime surfaced as a political issue, it generally involved political corruption, often with some Mafia angle. That was true of the two biggest politics-of-crime stories of the 1950s: the Kefauver Committee's investigation of Mafia-run gambling networks and their ties to big-city Democratic machines, and the Senate Rackets Committee's investigation of Mafia-dominated labor unions like the Teamsters (an investigation that later led to a prison term for Jimmy Hoffa). Such investigations could dominate the front pages only in a country where day-to-day street crime was under control.

All that changed in the 1960s and 1970s. The FBI's crime index—a compilation of violent felonies and major thefts—nearly tripled between 1960 and 1975.[34] The number of murders more than doubled; rapes tripled; robberies quadrupled. Cities were particularly hard hit. New York's murder rate more than *quintupled* in the two decades beginning in 1957[35]—and a number of other cities were a good deal more violent than New York. America had seen crime waves before, but not of this magnitude. And this wave did not recede: crime rose steeply, then stayed high. Not until the 1990s, long after *Bordenkircher*, would the country see a significant drop in crime levels. Even today, crime rates are vastly higher than anything Americans knew in the 1950s.[36]

Higher crime rates meant different politics. Prior to the 1960s, crime had never been a significant issue in a presidential election. In 1968, Richard Nixon and George Wallace won fifty-seven percent of the

---

ly. Lewis Powell graduated from Washington & Lee Law School in 1931, and earned a graduate law degree from Harvard in 1933, the same year that Thurgood Marshall graduated from Howard University's law school. Potter Stewart attended Yale Law School, from which he graduated in 1941. Justice White also graduated from Yale, in 1946. Finally, Justice, later Chief Justice Rehnquist graduated from Stanford Law School in 1952.

[33] This was true throughout most of American history before the late 1950s. Since then, New York's murder rate has been a multiple of the nation's. *See generally* ERIC MONKKONEN, MURDER IN NEW YORK CITY (2001).

[34] In 1960, the FBI's figures show a rate of 1,887 index crimes per 100,000 population; in 1975, the figure was 5,299. The data are drawn from the annual volumes of the FBI, UNIFORM CRIME REPORTS: CRIME IN THE UNITED STATES, and are available on-line at http://members.aol.com/dpen98/ucrus.htm.

[35] The figures are taken from data used by Eric Monkkonen in his history of homicide in New York City. *See* Monkkonen, *supra* note 33.

[36] According to the FBI's figures, the rate of index crimes—violent felonies plus major thefts—per 100,000 population was 1,887 in 1960; forty years later, the number was 4,124. FBI, UNIFORM CRIME REPORTS—CRIME IN THE UNITED STATES 2000, tbl. 1.

vote, and both men made crime in the streets the centerpiece of their presidential campaigns. (Nixon won, and went on to appoint four of the Justices who decided *Bordenkircher*.) Of course, no Supreme Court Justices were on the ballot that year, or any other for that matter. Judging has a political component; still, Justices are not wet fingers testing political winds. But the change in the politics of crime during the 1960s and 1970s was more than a change in wind direction. It was a hurricane.

The Justices noticed, a full decade before *Bordenkircher* reached the Court. Throughout the 1950s and 1960s, Earl Warren's Court had steadily raised the level of constitutional regulation of policing. *Mapp v. Ohio*,[37] the 1961 case that imposed the Fourth Amendment's exclusionary rule on state courts—meaning that illegally obtained evidence could not be used against criminal defendants—ensured that these constitutional limits had teeth. But in the summer of 1968—*before* Richard Nixon's election—the Court upheld police officers' authority to stop and frisk suspects on the street based on reasonable suspicion, a much more generous standard than probable cause. The case in which the Court made this ruling, *Terry v. Ohio*,[38] was widely seen as a big win for law enforcement, and it came from a Supreme Court that had been notably unfriendly to law enforcement in the past. The change was not due to changes in the Court's composition; actually, the Court that decided *Terry* was politically farther to the left than the Court that had decided *Mapp*. Three Justices left the Court between *Mapp* and *Terry*: Charles Whittaker, Felix Frankfurter, and Tom Clark. Whittaker and Frankfurter regularly voted with the government in criminal cases, and Clark frequently did so. Their three replacements in *Terry* were Byron White, Abe Fortas, and Thurgood Marshall. White voted roughly the same as Frankfurter in criminal cases. Fortas and Marshall were much more prodefendant than Whittaker and Clark. By any reasonable definition, the *Terry* Court was the most liberal and pro-defendant Court in American history. The Court's decision did not rest on legal principle or political ideology. *Terry* was about political *necessity*.[39]

Warren wrote the majority opinion in *Terry*; his law clerk at the time has said that the Justices "were unwilling to be—or to be perceived

---

[37] 367 U.S. 643 (1961). For a detailed discussion of *Mapp*, see Yale Kamisar, *Mapp v. Ohio: The First Shot Fired in the Warren Court's Criminal Procedure "Revolution"*, in this volume.

[38] 392 U.S. 1 (1968). For a detailed discussion of *Terry*, see John Q. Barrett, *Terry v. Ohio: The Fourth Amendment Reasonableness of Police Stops and Frisks Based on Less than Probable Cause*, in this volume.

[39] The argument in this paragraph is developed in William J. Stuntz, *Local Policing After the Terror*, 111 YALE L.J. 2137, 2151–53 (2002).

as—the agents who tied the hands of the police" in a time of growing street violence.[40] *Terry* marked a clear change in direction for the Court. The change was a consequence of rising public fear of urban crime.

The years after *Terry* saw this change in direction confirmed time and again. State and federal governments usually lost criminal cases in the Supreme Court in the dozen years before 1968. They usually won afterward—and on a range of issues, not just police searches and seizures. One example was particularly important to the decision in *Bordenkircher*. For a long time, plea bargaining had occupied a strange, not-quite-legal status. It was practiced everywhere, but appellate courts behaved as though this universal practice did not exist. The Supreme Court had never acknowledged it, much less approved of it. Some language in Court opinions suggested that plea bargaining was unconstitutional because it rested on government threats to impose harsher sentences on defendants who went to trial.[41] This was, of course, Hayes's claim. In 1970 in *Brady v. United States*,[42] the Court rejected that position, and held that a guilty plea given in exchange for a government promise not to seek the death penalty was constitutionally valid—even if the death penalty statute was later invalidated.[43] If government threats of invalid death sentences were permissible, it was hard to argue that the threat of a legally valid life sentence wasn't.

Plea bargaining took on increased importance as crime rates rose. By 1978, criminal dockets were rising, and prison populations were rising with them. Given the massive increase in crime of the preceding generation, it was obvious that further increases were coming. (Both the number of felony prosecutions and the number of prison inmates more than doubled in the dozen years after *Bordenkircher*.[44]) Rising caseloads were not accompanied by rising prosecutorial budgets. In most states, district attorneys' offices are paid for by local tax dollars, and local governments were already strapped for cash. The only way the system

---

[40] Earl C. Dudley, Jr., *Terry v. Ohio*, the Warren Court, and the Fourth Amendment: A Law Clerk's Perspective, 72 St. John's L. Rev. 891, 893 (1998).

[41] Consider, for example, this statement from Justice Douglas's opinion for the Court in Boykin v. Alabama, 395 U.S. 238, 242–43 (1969): "[A] plea of guilty is more than an admission of conduct; it is a conviction. Ignorance, incomprehension, coercion, terror, inducements, subtle or blatant threats might be a perfect cover-up of unconstitutionality." All plea bargains involve government "inducements" to plead guilty, and those inducements can plausibly be characterized as "subtle or blatant threats."

[42] 397 U.S. 742 (1970).

[43] Brady had been charged with kidnapping under a federal statute that authorized the death penalty for that offense. The death penalty provision of that statute was invalidated in United States v. Jackson, 390 U.S. 570 (1968).

[44] *See infra* notes 71–72 and accompanying text.

could process many more defendants without hiring many more prosecutors was by getting more guilty pleas. That meant more aggressive use of plea bargaining. A constitutional shadow on plea bargaining, something a defense victory in *Bordenkircher* might produce, would make it harder for prosecutors to extract guilty pleas. More defendants would go to trial, and the plea rate would fall. At a time of high crime and steeply rising dockets, that result was unacceptable.

So a broad victory for Hayes—a holding that barred any threat to increase the charge or sentence if a defendant took his case to trial—was not in the cards. Nor was it likely that the Court would adopt the Sixth Circuit's timing rule, barring the filing of more serious charges *after* the defendant decided to go to trial. Again, such a rule might well harm defendants in Hayes's position, since prosecutors might find it politically problematic to drop serious charges once those charges were filed. It would seem strange to give Hayes a victory at the cost of giving thousands of defendants like him a serious defeat.

The only option left was the status quo: Leave plea bargaining alone. Hold that the vindictiveness analysis of *Blackledge v. Perry* had no application to plea negotiations—regardless of whether the defendant pled guilty or, as in Hayes's case, decided to go to trial.

That is precisely what the Court did. Five Justices rejected Hayes's argument completely. Four dissenters accepted the Sixth Circuit's timing rule—and acknowledged, explicitly, that prosecutors could evade that rule by filing the more severe charge up front. No one voted for the strong version of Hayes's claim: that all threats of harsher treatment for defendants who go to trial are impermissible.

Justice Stewart's majority opinion was chiefly devoted to defending plea bargaining. After a brief statement of facts, Stewart dismissed the Court of Appeals' timing rule as beside the point: "As a practical matter, in short, this case would be no different if the grand jury had indicted Hayes as a recidivist from the outset, and the prosecutor had offered to drop that charge as part of the plea bargain."[45] Stewart then proceeded to extol the existing system of plea negotiations: "[T]he guilty plea and the often concomitant plea bargain" were "important components of this country's criminal justice system. Properly administered, they can benefit all concerned."[46]

Then came the most important passage of the opinion, where Stewart distinguished the Court's vindictive punishment cases:

In those cases the Court was dealing with the State's unilateral imposition of a penalty upon a defendant who had chosen to exercise

---

[45] 434 U.S. at 360–61.

[46] *Id*. at 361–62.

a legal right to attack his original conviction—a situation "very different from the give-and-take negotiation common in plea bargaining between the prosecution and defense, which arguably possess relatively equal bargaining power."[47]

Notice the theme: in a case like *Blackledge v. Perry*, the prosecutor was exercising "unilateral" power over a helpless defendant. In a plea negotiation like the one in *Bordenkircher*, by contrast, the two sides "arguably possess[ed] equal bargaining power" in a "give-and-take" exchange. (Hayes could be excused for thinking that he had done all the giving and Bagby had done all the taking.) The emphasis was on "mutuality of advantage," with both sides gaining by agreements to have defendants plead to lesser charges. This mutuality still held, in the Court's view, even if the defendant's plea was "induced by promises of a recommendation of a lenient sentence or a reduction of charges, and thus by fear of the possibility of a greater penalty upon conviction after a trial."[48] It was entirely proper, Stewart maintained, that plea bargaining was deemed constitutionally permissible, even though "the prosecutor's interest at the bargaining table is to persuade the defendant to forgo his right to plead not guilty."[49]

For the Court, then, the only real question was whether Hayes "was properly chargeable under the recidivist statute."[50] Plainly, he was. Accordingly, it was proper for Bagby to threaten the charge him under that statute. And if the threat was proper, carrying it out was permissible. That was that. Even though Hayes had not pled guilty, the issue in the Supreme Court was the legal status of plea bargaining. Plea bargaining won, and Hayes lost.

Four Justices—Brennan, Marshall, Blackmun, and Powell—dissented from the second of those propositions, though not from the first. Justice Blackmun wrote the chief dissenting opinion. After noting that, as a matter of simple logic, vindictiveness was vindictiveness whether or not it happened during the course of a plea negotiation, Blackmun went on to discuss the merits of McCree's timing rule:

> It might be argued that it really makes little difference how this case, now that it is here, is decided. The Court's holding gives plea bargaining full sway despite vindictiveness. A contrary result, however, merely would prompt the aggressive prosecutor to bring the greater charge initially in every case, and only thereafter to bargain.

---

[47] *Id.* at 362 (quoting Parker v. North Carolina, 397 U.S. 790, 809 (1970) (opinion of Brennan, J.)).

[48] *Id.* at 363.

[49] *Id.* at 364.

[50] *Id.*

The consequences to the accused would still be adverse, for then he
would bargain against a greater charge, face the likelihood of increased bail, and run the risk that the court would be less inclined
to accept a bargained plea. Nonetheless, it is far preferable to hold
the prosecution to the charge it was originally content to bring and
to justify in the eyes of its public.[51]

For anyone accustomed to reading Supreme Court dissents, this is
remarkably candid language. Justices may on occasion advocate legal
positions that are likely to prove meaningless in practice, but they
generally do not own up to the meaninglessness. Blackmun did, squarely:
"The consequences to the accused would still be adverse"—indeed *more*
adverse, since he would have to "bargain against a greater charge" and
fare worse in subsequent proceedings once that charge was on the
record. Though Blackmun did say that it was "far preferable" to hold
prosecutors to their original charges, it plainly wasn't "preferable" for
defendants: he had just finished explaining why defendants should prefer
the majority's result. A more halfhearted dissent would be hard to find.

Except for Justice Powell's, the other *Bordenkircher* dissent. Powell
added frustration to Blackmun's halfheartedness. On the one hand,
Powell clearly believed that Hayes was the victim of an injustice. After
noting that five years in prison for an 88–dollar forged check—the deal
Hayes declined—"hardly could be characterized as a generous offer,"[52]
Powell recounted the story of Hayes's three felonies, the basis for his life
sentence under the habitual criminal law. Powell observed that Hayes
had served a little over five years in "a reformatory" for "detaining a
female," an offense committed while he was still a minor, and had served
no time at all for robbery.[53] "[Y]et the addition of a conviction on a
charge involving $88.30 subjected respondent to a mandatory sentence of
imprisonment for life. Persons convicted of rape and murder often are
not punished so severely."[54]

On the other hand, like Blackmun, Powell recognized that his
solution left prosecutors completely free to generate more such injustices:

The majority suggests ... that this case cannot be distinguished
from the case where the prosecutor initially obtains an indictment
under an enhancement statute and later agrees to drop the enhancement charge in exchange for a guilty plea. I would agree that these
two situations would be alike only if it were assumed that the

---

[51] *Id*. at 368 (Blackmun, J., dissenting).

[52] *Id*. at 369 (Powell, J., dissenting).

[53] *Id*. at 370 (Powell, J., dissenting).

[54] *Id*. (Powell, J., dissenting).

hypothetical prosecutor's decision to charge under the enhancement statute was occasioned not by consideration of the public interest but by a strategy to discourage the defendant from exercising his constitutional rights. In theory, I would condemn both practices. In practice, the hypothetical situation is largely unreviewable. The majority's view confuses the propriety of a particular exercise of prosecutorial discretion with its unreviewability.[55]

Like Blackmun, Powell conceded that his proposed rule was meaningless, but he faulted the majority for failing to adopt it anyway.

Bordenkircher is a strange case, and Powell's dissent highlights the key to the strangeness: the mismatch between Hayes's legal claim and the wrong that was done to him. The vindictiveness argument on which the defense relied had nothing to do with the severity of the sentence Hayes received—the charge would have been equally "vindictive" if the habitual criminal sentence had been six years rather than life. Yet, as Powell noted, the basic problem in the case was *precisely* the severity of the life sentence.

To put the point another way, the vindictiveness argument was all-or-nothing. If the argument was right, *no* threat of an increased sentence was permissible. If the argument was wrong, *any* threat was permissible. Differences of degree, the harshness of the sentence Hayes actually received, didn't matter. Given the choice between effectively banning plea bargaining and tolerating the status quo, every court that heard Hayes's argument—including the Court of Appeals—chose the status quo. Even Justices Blackmun and Powell chose the status quo, as they both admitted.

But that all-or-nothing argument bore little relation to Hayes's real complaint, which (as Justice Powell recognized) had everything to do with the harshness of the life sentence imposed on him. Here is what Hayes himself said about his dealings with Bagby, picking up from the point where the prosecutor had offered him a plea and a five-year sentence:

> I say, "No, man, I can't handle the five. . . ." I say that I want a jury trial, you know. He say, "if you don't take the five years, I am going to indict you on the habitual criminal." . . . I told him, "Look, man, you know, I have been in the State Reformatory one time and had one number on my back, you know," and, I said, "there's guys who have had six and seven numbers on their back and they never was tried on the habitual criminal. . . . "[56]

---

[55] *Id*. at 371 note 2. (Powell, J., dissenting).

[56] App. 42–43.

In truth, Hayes had two other "numbers" (felony convictions) on his back, not one. But his point remained: others have done worse than I did, and *they* didn't have this sentence imposed on *them*. The point was not that the prosecutor was trying to get Hayes to plead—as the *Bordenkircher* majority rightly noted, that is what prosecutors do. Rather, there were two potential problems with the proceedings against Paul Hayes. First, Hayes was treated worse than others with worse records than his. And second, Hayes was treated worse than he deserved.

One suspects that Paul Hayes understood those two problems intuitively. But the Supreme Court missed them, or at least ignored them, because that is what the lawyers and courts that had handled the case before had done. Which is why *Bordenkircher v. Hayes* reads as though the Court were deciding a different case—an ordinary plea bargain, a case in which the defendant responds to the threat of a modestly harsher post-trial sentence by pleading guilty. Faced with an up-or-down choice as to the legality of plea bargaining, the Court was bound to go with "up." In order to have a serious chance at victory in the Supreme Court, Hayes's counsel needed to find some way of posing a different choice, some argument that would lead to the conclusion that threatening to put Hayes away for life was wrong, without casting a shadow on the hundreds of thousands of ordinary plea bargains that happened each year.

There are a number of ways to make such an argument; Hayes's counsel had raised two of them earlier in the litigation. Counsel had argued that a life sentence was disproportionate to Hayes's crime, and hence violated the Eighth Amendment's ban on "cruel and unusual punishments." Justice Powell apparently thought the argument had merit. He saw even the five-year sentence Hayes turned down as "hardly ... a generous offer," so he must have seen life in prison as grossly excessive, notwithstanding Hayes's past crimes. Interestingly, a majority of the Court reached that conclusion just five years after *Bordenkircher*, with Powell writing the Court's opinion. The defendant in *Solem v. Helm*[57] was charged with passing a bad check for a hundred dollars—not very different from Hayes's stolen 88–dollar check to the Pic Pac grocery. The same defendant had six prior felony convictions: three for third-degree burglary, and one apiece for fraud, grand larceny, and driving while intoxicated.[58] This was a substantially longer rap sheet than Hayes's. Nevertheless, the *Solem* Court held that a life sentence in that case was too harsh to be consistent with the Eighth Amendment.[59]

---

[57] 463 U.S. 277 (1983).

[58] *Id.* at 279–83.

[59] *Id.* at 290–300.

Solem v. Helm was a large help to the Paul Hayeses of the world (albeit not to Paul Hayes himself), but the decision had a brief shelf life. In 1991, the Court overruled *Solem*;[60] in 2003, the Court upheld life sentences imposed pursuant to California's three-strikes statute.[61] The Eighth Amendment argument that the Court didn't hear in *Borden-kircher* is no more than a dream today.

Hayes's lawyer had also raised a discrimination claim: the problem with the life sentence is not that it was disproportionate, but that Hayes was arbitrarily selected to receive it. Hayes himself made this claim when he said that other defendants with six or seven "numbers" on their backs had escaped liability under the habitual criminal statute. But discrimination claims are notoriously hard to prove. Especially in a legal system structured as America's is. The huge majority of criminal prosecutions in the United States are brought by local prosecutors like Bagby.[62] They work for district attorneys who are elected by the voters of their city or county. Evidence of prosecutorial patterns from other counties won't suffice to prove intentional discrimination; claimants like Hayes have to establish the discriminatory pattern in their own jurisdictions in order to have a chance at success. That makes proof very difficult. In practice, it's more than difficult—it's impossible, because of a decision the Supreme Court handed down eighteen years after *Borden-kircher*. *United States v. Armstrong*[63] holds that anyone claiming discriminatory prosecution must point to similarly situated defendants (no one knows how many) who could have been charged with the same crime as the claimant but weren't.[64] Needless to say, it is hard for defendants to get that information. Yet *Armstrong* holds that they can't even obtain discovery (i.e., data about the prosecutor's past charging decisions) without it: defendants must, in effect, prove discrimination in order to get the evidence necessary to prove discrimination—a classic Catch–22. And *Armstrong* involved a claim of race discrimination, which is pre-

---

[60] Harmelin v. Michigan, 501 U.S. 957 (1991).

[61] Lockyer v. Andrade, 538 U.S. 63 (2003) (upholding consecutive sentences of 25 years to life on two theft charges); Ewing v. California, 538 U.S. 11 (2003) (upholding sentence of 25 years to life for theft of some golf clubs).

[62] Justice Department data show in excess of 900,000 felony convictions per year in state court. *See* Bureau of Justice Statistics, U.S. Dep't of Justice, Sourcebook of Criminal Justice Statistics—2002, at tbl. 5.44 (924,700 felony convictions in 2000), available on-line at http://www.albany.edu/sourcebook/ [hereinafter cited as 2002 Sourcebook]. The same source shows fewer than 60,000 felony convictions per year in federal court, *id.* at tbl. 5.18 (59,433 felony convictions in fiscal year 2001). For misdemeanors, the ratio is even more lopsided, since so few federal misdemeanor cases are filed. *See id.* (showing only 9,100 federal misdemeanor convictions in fiscal 2001).

[63] 517 U.S. 456 (1996).

[64] *Id.* at 465–70.

sumptively illegal. Arbitrariness alone is illegal too, but not the kind of illegality that courts tend to worry much about. As Judge Kozinski wrote for a Ninth Circuit panel in 1992, "the type of intense inquiry that would enable a court to evaluate whether or not a prosecutor's charging decision was made in an arbitrary fashion would destroy the very system of justice it was intended to protect."[65] In other words, the game is not worth the candle. Since courts find claims like Hayes's difficult to judge and impossible to remedy, the claims are rarely made and virtually never succeed.

A third possible argument was not raised at any point in the litigation; it seems more promising yet also more complicated. Bagby could of course threaten Hayes with a longer sentence after a trial than he could get after a guilty plea—unless *even Bagby* believed the threatened punishment was unjust. Blackmailers leverage their ability to harm their victims in order to get what they want. If Bagby thought the life sentence was excessive or unfair, if he threatened to impose it *solely* as a means of extracting a guilty plea, his offer was the functional equivalent of blackmail.[66]

There is good reason to believe Bagby did not, in fact, think the life sentence was a fair punishment for Hayes's crimes. If he had, he could not possibly have offered to let Hayes off with a five-year sentence in exchange for a plea. All plea bargains offer discounts—if the defendant pleads, his sentence will be less than if he goes to trial. But those discounts are ordinarily limited; for cases involving long prison terms, a threatened post-trial sentence that is more than twice the sentence offered with a plea is unusual.[67] In Hayes's case, the post-trial sentence could have been *ten times* Bagby's plea offer. Nor can the gap be explained by fear that Hayes might win at trial—Bagby had nothing to fear on that score. The only possible explanation is that Bagby thought five years was the right sentence, and threatened the habitual criminal charge solely in order to induce a plea. Once the threat was made, it had

---

[65] United States v. Redondo–Lemos, 955 F.2d 1296, 1300 (9th Cir. 1992).

[66] Bagby's conduct also resembles the conduct that gives rise to a successful duress claim in contracts litigation. For an extended discussion of this point, see Scott & Stuntz, *supra* note 13, at 1961–66.

[67] Until recently, the federal system operated with an automatic discount for "acceptance of responsibility" in guilty-plea cases; that discount averaged 35 percent. Today, the automatic discount is closer to 25 percent; a further discount is available on prosecutors' motion. *See* Stephanos Bibas, *Plea Bargaining Outside the Shadow of Trial*, 117 HARV. L. REV. 2463, 2488–89 & notes 101–02 (2004), and sources cited therein. In state systems, data on plea-bargained sentencing discounts is skimpy. The statement in text is a (reasonable, I hope) conjecture. Academics who propose limiting plea discounts tend to suggest limits at or below 50 percent. *See id.* at 2535–36 & note 320 (citing sources).

to be carried out. But Bagby cannot have thought life-minus-five-years was an appropriate penalty for going to trial.

It's quite possible that no one—not Bagby, not the judge who presided over the case, not even the Kentucky legislators that voted for the habitual criminal statute—believed the life sentence was fair or appropriate in Hayes's case. Bagby apparently didn't. There is no reason to believe any of the judges or Justices who considered Hayes's claim thought otherwise. As for the legislators: in 1975, they passed an amended habitual criminal law that did not apply to Hayes—a fact to which Judge McCree attached some importance.[68]

Even if Kentucky legislators had left the stronger version of the law intact, it would have been reasonable to assume that they did not intend to apply it to defendants like Hayes. In Kentucky as elsewhere, legislators understand that prosecutors have discretion, that they are never required to file charges under a given criminal statute but instead can choose when to file charges, and which charges to file, and when not to. Something very important follows from that fact. When legislators vote on a law like the habitual criminal statute at issue in *Bordenkircher*, their incentives are skewed in favor of severity. If some terrible criminal comes along who, in voters' view, deserves to spend the rest of his life in prison but doesn't because the legislature didn't pass the right statute, legislators might reasonably fear the voting public's wrath. If, on the other hand, some undeserving defendant is socked away for life by an overzealous prosecutor, those same voters are unlikely to notice. And if the voters do notice, if they object to the overly harsh punishment, the prosecutor and not the legislature will take the blame. That was clear enough even in 1978. Two decades later, Ken Starr proved it: Starr became one of the most unpopular men in America due to his pursuit of Bill Clinton for lying about his relationship with Monica Lewinsky. No one blamed Congress for passing broad perjury and obstruction-of-justice laws; voters turned on Congressional Republicans only when they assumed the prosecutor's role by impeaching Clinton. Voters understand that prosecutors have discretion, that laws like Kentucky's habitual criminal statute are not meant to be enforced against every defendant to whom those laws apply.

This political asymmetry means that such laws—criminal statutes that cover a great many more people than even the legislators themselves would think just—are likely to be common, especially in an era where crime and the public's the fear of it are high. Occasionally, a legislature may decide it had gone too far and repeal some harsh sentencing statute, as the Kentucky legislature did (too late to help

---

[68] *See* Hayes v. Cowan, 547 F.2d at 42–43 & note 1.

Hayes). But those kinds of legislative actions are rare. Easier to ratchet sentences *up*. *Those* kinds of actions are very common indeed.

All of which means that, when someone like Hayes is charged and sentenced under a law like the habitual criminal statute, the only person who must agree to the sentence is the prosecutor. The statute was not mandatory as to Bagby; he could charge Hayes under it or not, as he chose. But once he filed the charge, no one else—not the jury, not the trial judge, not any appellate court—was free to examine whether the sentence was fair.

That is not a recipe for just sentencing. American constitutional law rests on the principle that concentrated power is dangerous. And Hayes's case is entirely *about* concentrated power: the charge (and hence the sentence too) was Bagby's call, and no one could second-guess that call once it was made.

Of course, just because a prosecutor *can* overpunish a defendant doesn't mean that he *will*. Prosecutors aren't paid by the prisoner; they get no bonuses for longer sentences. In all but the rarest of cases, it seems safe to assume that prosecutors are trying to reach just results. Remember, though, what result Bagby was trying to reach: he wanted Hayes to do five years, without the trouble of a trial. The habitual-criminal charge was leverage, a threat designed to produce the result he wanted; no doubt he did believe in the justice of *that* result. Hayes turned down the deal, but after the Supreme Court's decision in *Bordenkircher*, few defendants would be so foolhardy. The next defendant—and every one to follow—would take Bagby's offer, and do so quickly. Under those circumstances, there is not much reason to assume that prosecutors believe in the justice of the sentences they threaten but need never impose.

The argument has important implications for the many cases in which defendants take the plea, rather than going to trial as did Hayes. If the threatened sentence is disproportionate—if any reasonable judge, given the authority to decide, would have declined to impose it—one should not trust the fairness of the conviction and sentence the threat produces. A simple thought experiment proves the point. Suppose Hayes had been innocent of the forged check charge. Suppose further that Bagby had only a one-in-four chance of winning a jury trial on that charge. Finally, suppose that Hayes had known up front how the Supreme Court would decide his case. How would he have responded to Bagby's offer? Hayes might well have taken the five-year sentence anyway, rather than run a one-in-four risk of dying in prison.

The conclusion is simple. Plea bargains will be fair and just if, but only if, the threats that induce them are fair and just. Given the rule established by the Court in *Bordenkircher*, there is no reason to believe that those threats *are* fair—indeed, there is good reason to believe the opposite. Prosecutors have a strong incentive to threaten charges that are excessive, even by the prosecutors' own lights.

The Court could have changed that state of affairs. Imagine an opinion that required that the government make one of two showings. First, the government could point to some reasonable number of factually similar cases in which the threatened sentence had actually been imposed, not just threatened. The number need not be large to have a substantial effect. The odds are, there were *no* cases imposing Kentucky's three-strikes law on a defendant whose third strike was a theft as petty as Hayes's. If even a handful of such cases existed, that would mean Kentucky voters had seen the law's severity—the same degree of severity that Bagby's threat embodied—in action, and had not rebelled at the sight. That fact alone would offer some protection against the worst and most disproportionate threats.

In order to show that a given sentence had been imposed for a given crime with a given fact pattern some minimum number of times, the state would have to do something that few states did in the 1970s: keep detailed state-wide records of crimes charged, fact patterns, pleas, trial convictions, and sentences. More states do it now, because many of them use written guidelines to govern criminal sentencing. The sentencing commissions that write those guidelines generally keep detailed records that allow them to predict the consequences of changes in sentencing law. As Rachel Barkow has shown, those predicted consequences—the number of new prison beds that a tough new rule would require, and the number of tax dollars it would take to pay for those beds—have a significant effect on state legislators' decisionmaking.[69] As the costs of severity become more salient, moderation becomes more politically attractive. Something similar might happen to criminal codes if states had to keep such records in order to allow prosecutors to point to precedent for the sentencing threats they use to induce guilty pleas. And prosecutors themselves might moderate their threats were they forced to examine the charging patterns of their counterparts elsewhere in the state. As data become available, courts could revise the target number as appropriate, crime by crime. If, say, a three-year period saw one thousand Kentuckians convicted and punished for stealing small-dollar checks like the one Hayes wrote to the Pic Pac Grocery, it might be reasonable to require that at least fifty of those cases receive a given sentence before a prosecutor could threaten it. For crimes that occur less frequently, the number could be smaller. And for new legislation that prosecutors had

---

[69] Rachel E. Barkow, *Administering Crime*, 52 UCLA L. REV. 715 (2005); Rachel E. Barkow, *Federalism and the Politics of Sentencing*, 105 COLUM. L. REV. 1276 (2005).

not yet enforced, the outer bounds of the sentence could be stayed, to give the government time to bring other cases on similar facts elsewhere.

Even if no such showing could be made, the government would have a second means of justifying its threat: require that the trial judge find that the sentence in question—the threatened one, not just the sentence actually imposed—was fair and proportionate given the defendant's criminal conduct. If the threat in question were neither supported by precedent nor by a judge's judgment, the threat would be improper, and any guilty plea made in response to it would be invalid. Had that rule applied in *Bordenkircher*, Bagby's threat would not have passed muster. Hayes would have ended up doing prison time for the forged check, but probably closer to two years than five. A host of other defendants would have ended up either acquitted (some defendants with strong cases plead because the threatened sentence is too high) or serving less time. And the rest of us would have ended up with a fairer, more just criminal justice system.

None of those things happened. Maybe they wouldn't have happened even if the right argument had been made; the Justices might have rejected any imaginable challenge to Bagby's plea bargaining tactics. In the twenty-seven years since *Bordenkircher*, that has been the Court's pattern. Still, there is reason to wonder. The politics of crime and punishment grew steadily more punitive in the years after *Bordenkircher*. The Court, too, grew more punitive. In 1978, it was still possible to imagine serious constitutional limits on plea bargaining. Had such limits been imposed then, the law and politics of crime might have followed a different and better path in the quarter-century since.

Vindictive prosecution was a seductive argument. It was simple and straightforward, it held out the promise of victory, and it had support in the case law. For all those reasons, it was an excellent argument to make to the trial court. But its implications were enormous, and troubling. Which made it a poor Supreme Court argument. Few lawyers know the difference—and even if they did, it wouldn't help much: the Justices generally decline to address arguments that were not raised by the litigants in lower courts, and lawyers deciding on trial tactics rarely think about which claims stand the best chance of victory if the case somehow makes it to the top of the appellate ladder. So by the time Paul Hayes *did* make it to the top of the appellate ladder, he was stuck with a simple argument that seemed legally reasonable but could not possibly prevail. The argument that might have won was much more complicated and a good deal riskier. The Court might have rejected it out of hand; the lawyer who made it could end up looking foolish. But it's at least barely possible that the Justices might have bought it, and that thousands of cases might have ended more justly as a result. We'll never know.

The Aftermath

By the time the Supreme Court handed down its decision in *Borden-kircher*, two decades had passed since crime began to rise. Before those two decades America had been a low-crime society; people walked the streets of its cities at night without fear. By 1978, America was a very high-crime society, and people walked nighttime city streets in terror, if they walked at all. That massive change in our social life, the explosion of crime and of associated fear, helped bring about the Court's decision. It also had a quite a bit to do with *Bordenkircher*'s long-term effects.

As we have already seen, higher crime meant greater docket pressure. Local district attorneys' offices did not respond right away to the crime wave of the 1960s. The prison population actually declined during that decade, for the only time in American history.[70] The pressure to "get tough" on crime and criminals thus had a long time to build. By the time the Court decided *Bordenkircher*, that pressure was intense, and seemed likely to stay that way for some years to come. Dockets and prison populations were already growing, but it was obvious that both would grow much more in the next decade or two. As they did: felony prosecutions doubled between 1978 and 1991.[71] The number of prison inmates rose even faster.[72] Local prosecutors were responding to voters' demands in the only way they could (and still keep their jobs)—by prosecuting more offenders and sending more of them to prison for longer terms.

Prosecutions take time and manpower, both of which cost money. But there was no prospect of large budget increases for district attorneys' offices. Those offices would have to manage their vastly larger dockets without vastly larger staffs. One statistic makes the point: between the mid–1970s and the early 1990s, while felony prosecutions more than doubled, the number of prosecutors nationwide rose less than twenty percent, from 17,000 to 20,000.[73]

It is helpful to understand why prosecutors' budgets did not, and could not, keep up with their dockets. In all jurisdictions, street crime (criminal violence and major theft offenses—the crimes that voters most want to see prosecuted) tends to be concentrated in poorer neighbor-

---

[70] *See* MARGARET WERNER CAHALAN, HISTORICAL CORRECTIONS STATISTICS IN THE UNITED STATES, 1850–1984, at 29 tbl. 3–2 (Bureau of Justice Statistics, 1986) (showing a 12 percent decline in the prison population from 1960 to 1970).

[71] *See* William J. Stuntz, *Plea Bargaining and Criminal Law's Disappearing Shadow*, 117 HARV. L. REV. 2548, 2555 & note 9 (2004), and sources cited therein.

[72] *See* 2002 SOURCEBOOK, *supra* note 62, at tbl. 6.1.

[73] BUREAU OF JUSTICE STATISTICS, U.S. DEP'T OF JUSTICE, PROSECUTORS IN STATE COURTS—1990, at 1–2 (1998).

hoods. It follows that criminal law enforcement is redistributive: its biggest benefits are felt by residents of poor neighborhoods, but like all government services, it is disproportionately paid for by the taxes collected from wealthier neighborhoods. In the United States—this is not true elsewhere in the developed world—criminal law enforcement is staffed and paid for by city and county governments. Those local governments are poorly positioned to fund redistributive services. If they raise taxes on wealthy residents, they risk losing their tax base; middle-and upper-income taxpayers can flee to the next town or county—where poor people are few, government services are cheap, and taxes are low. These basic truths explain why taxation is more progressive at the state and national levels than at the local level. They also explain why criminal law enforcement is bound to be seriously underfunded in times of high or rising crime, like the years leading up to and following *Bordenkircher*. Notice that the one aspect of criminal justice that saw huge budget increases during those years was prisons.[74] Prisons are paid for by state and national governments, not local ones.

So entering the 1980s, it was clear that local district attorneys would have to prosecute more cases without more money or staff. The only way to do that is to get more defendants to plead guilty, since guilty pleas cost a small fraction of the time and energy spent on criminal trials. That is exactly what we see during the 1980s and 1990s: steadily rising dockets coupled with a steadily rising guilty plea rate. As late as the mid–1970s, the felony guilty plea rate—the percentage of felony convictions obtained by guilty plea—was in the neighborhood of 80 percent.[75] By the late 1980s, it was over 90 percent.[76] Today, it stands at 95 percent.[77] In the span of three decades, the trial rate fell by three fourths. Those statistics are a natural response to the need to prosecute more defendants without hiring more prosecutors.

The easiest way to raise the guilty plea rate is to offer better deals to defendants: let the Hayeses of the world plead guilty and take two or three years in prison rather than five. But that move was out of the question in these post-*Bordenkircher* years. Voters demanded not only more prosecutions and convictions, but also tougher sentences.[78] How

---

[74] According to the Prison Policy Initiative, state spending on corrections increased, on average, a whopping 175 percent from 1985 to 2000. Data are available on-line at http://www.prisonpolicy.org/prisonindex/budgetpriorities.shtml.

[75] *See* DAVID A. JONES, CRIME WITHOUT PUNISHMENT 44 tbl. 4–1 (1979).

[76] Barbara Boland et al., *The Prosecution of Felony Arrests—1987*, at 3 (1990) (showing a felony guilty plea rate of 91 percent).

[77] 2002 SOURCEBOOK, *supra* note 62, at tbl. 5.46.

[78] The public's desire for tougher sentences probably stems from the belief that those tougher sentences deter crime. The belief may well be false: punishment may indeed deter,

could local prosecutors pull off this hat trick—prosecuting many more cases, raising the guilty plea rate substantially, *and* generating tougher sentences, all at the same time? There is only one possible answer. Prosecutors had to threaten tougher sentences in order to extract more guilty pleas without giving defendants softer deals. Behavior like Bagby's would have to become the norm, not the exception.

To do that, prosecutors needed the cooperation of legislatures. That cooperation was easy to get, for state legislators and members of Congress were eager to let voters know that they too wanted to be tough on crime. This was true of both parties. Beginning in the 1960s, Republicans had used crime as a "wedge issue" to win the votes of blue-collar Democrats; by the 1980s Democratic legislators began to respond by signaling those voters that they could out-tough the Republicans. The result was an ongoing bidding war in legislative halls to see who could propose and pass the broadest criminal liability rules and the harshest sentencing statutes. Prosecutors were not required actually to apply those harsh laws across the board. So legislators had no reason to worry about the breadth and severity of the statutes that began to fill criminal codes.

That incentive structure is terribly important. Return to the context. Twenty years of pent-up demand for politicians to do something about rising crime meant that broader criminal laws and tougher sentencing rules were inevitable. Laws like Kentucky's habitual criminal statute became common. And throughout the 1980s and 1990s, tough new sentencing provisions for drug crimes and gun crimes sailed through Congress and state legislatures. There is only one reason for legislatures to hesitate to pass such laws: cost. Sending everyone with three felony convictions—when "felony" includes things like stealing an 88–dollar check—is likely to be very expensive. The Supreme Court's decision in *Bordenkircher* made those laws much cheaper. Under that decision, there is no need to impose a life sentence on everyone, or anyone, in Hayes's shoes. Indeed, there is no requirement that everyone in Hayes's circumstances be *threatened* with a life sentence. Prosecutors are free to decide.

And by making tough sentencing rules cheaper, *Bordenkircher* also made it cheaper for legislatures to use such rules to make symbolic statements. Consider Congress's enactment of the 1986 legislation that specified the sentencing ratio for crack cocaine and cocaine powder—the weights at which the sentences for possession or distribution of the two

---

but the likelihood of punishment matters much more than its severity. *See, e.g.*, Anthony N. Doob & Cheryl Marie Webster, *Sentence Severity and Crime: Accepting the Null Hypothesis*, 30 Crime & Just. 143 (2003).

substances would be equal.[79] There was widespread agreement that crack offenses should be punished more harshly, but how tilted should the ratio be? Different Members of Congress suggested different figures. The ratio that made it into the United States Code—one hundred to one, meaning that possession of a single gram of crack was punished as severely as possession of a hundred grams of cocaine powder—was the highest anyone proposed. That could not happen in any other field of legal regulation: tougher rules would carry a substantial and predictable cost, and the cost would prompt some sort of compromise. Obviously, no one in Congress compromised when the hundred-to-one ratio was enacted. Instead of a tradeoff, we saw a legislative auction, with victory going to the most extreme position on offer.

The auction happened because members of Congress knew that only a small fraction of the nation's crack cases would end up in federal court. The price of tough state sentencing rules is higher, because the vast majority of prosecutions happen in state courts. (Unsurprisingly, state sentencing laws are nearly always more lenient than their federal counterparts.) But the basic phenomenon applies to the states as well. With few exceptions, sentencing rules need not be applied or even threatened across the board; prosecutors decide how often to invoke those rules. That makes tough sentencing rules, and broader criminal liability rules as well, cheaper. Legislatures produced more such rules than they would have if the rules had been more expensive.

As legislatures added ever more felonies to their criminal codes with ever more severe sentences attached, something else happened. These laws changed their character. Criminal liability rules ceased to define the conduct that leads to a prison term. Too much conduct is prohibited; no prosecutor could possibly enforce her state's criminal code, and no federal prosecutor can pursue more than a tiny fraction of the crimes to which the federal code applies. Likewise, criminal sentencing rules ceased to define the consequences of particular crimes. Those rules sweep too broadly; they cannot possibly be enforced in all cases to which they apply. Instead, the laws that define crimes and sentences have become a menu—a list of charging and sentencing options that prosecutors may use in order to extract the plea bargains they want from the Paul Hayeses of the world.

The *real* law, the "rules" that determine who goes to prison and for how long, is not written in code books or case reports. Prosecutors like Bagby define it by the decisions they make when ordering off the menus their states' legislatures have given them. The behavior that will lead to a stay in the local house of corrections varies from courthouse to

---

[79] For the best account, see David A. Sklansky, *Cocaine, Race, and Equal Protection*, 47 STAN. L. REV. 1283, 1296–97 (1995).

courthouse, and from prosecutor to prosecutor. So do the sentences that attach to most crimes. Law does not govern criminal justice. The menu has grown too large; prosecutors have too many options.

That is not a healthy state of affairs. We are supposed to have a system of checks and balances: legislators write the laws, police and prosecutors enforce them, and judges interpret them. Actually, power is increasingly concentrated in the hands of police and prosecutors. Especially prosecutors.

Bordenkircher is by no means solely responsible for that concentration of power. No matter what the Court's decision, the generation following 1978 would have seen a proliferation of laws like Kentucky's habitual criminal statute. Prison cells, and the prisoners who fill them, would still have multiplied. Had the Court declared *all* plea bargains "vindictive," prosecutors and defense attorneys would have found ways to bargain with winks and nods and the machinery of criminal justice would have continued to grind on, generating ever more convictions and prison sentences. Even if Hayes's lawyers had made precisely the right arguments at precisely the right times, and even if the Court had heeded those arguments, ours would still be a society where criminal punishment is a massive industry, of a size and severity unknown anywhere else in the democratic world.

But the Court's decision does bear *some* responsibility for the punitive turn America's criminal justice system has taken—for its harshness, for the sheer magnitude of our two-million-plus inmate population. Also for the inexorable rise of plea bargaining, now the means by which nearly nineteen of every twenty convicted felons reach that status. And there is another effect, more important even than the prison population and the guilty plea rate. As the prisoners have multiplied, laws have multiplied as well, adding more criminal prohibitions and harsher sentences to criminal codes. As those bodies of law have grown in size, they have shrunk in consequence. In the criminal justice system, the men and women who work in district attorneys' offices increasingly rule. The law no longer does. Anyone who wants to understand how that happened would do well to start by studying an obscure case from the 1970s in Lexington, Kentucky.

*

12

Batson v. Kentucky: The Constitutional Challenges of Peremptory Challenges

Pamela S. Karlan*

Justice Felix Frankfurter observed that "[i]t is a fair summary of history to say that the safeguards of liberty have frequently been forged in controversies involving not very nice people."[1] It is perhaps just as true to say that those safeguards have frequently been forged in cases involving not very memorable crimes. An illegal search that turned up a few smutty pamphlets, a couple of photographs, and a little pencil doodle lay behind the Supreme Court's decision in *Mapp v. Ohio*[2] to overrule *Wolf v. Colorado*[3] and extend the exclusionary rule to the states. A poolroom break-in that garnered maybe $60 in coins from a juke box and a cigarette machine led the Court in *Gideon v. Wainwright*[4] to overrule *Betts v. Brady*[5] and require states to provide counsel to all indigent defendants. And a burglary after which the thieves pawned the rings they stole for $15 each precipitated the Court's decision in *Batson v. Kentucky*[6] to overrule *Swain v. Alabama*[7] and forbid prosecutors from

---

* I thank Bob Weisberg and Viola Canales for many helpful comments and suggestions and Bridget Kerlin for valuable research assistance. I served as a law clerk to Justice Harry A. Blackmun during the Term in which Batson v. Kentucky, 476 U.S. 79 (1986), was decided and, as Justice Blackmun's papers, available at the Library of Congress reveal, I worked on the case. In writing this essay, I have relied entirely on now publicly available sources.

[1] United States v. Rabinowitz, 339 U.S. 56, 69 (1950) (dissenting opinion).

[2] 367 U.S. 643 (1961). I take the description of the allegedly offending materials from Justice Douglas's concurrence. *See id.* at 668. *Mapp* is the subject of a separate chapter in this volume.

[3] 338 U.S. 25 (1949).

[4] 372 U.S. 335 (1963). *Gideon*, along with Strickland v. Washington, 466 U.S. 668 (1984), is the subject of a separate chapter in this volume.

[5] 316 U.S. 455 (1942).

[6] 476 U.S. 79 (1986).

relying on race in the exercise of their peremptory challenges.

The twin legacies of the Warren Court were the criminal procedure revolution (that brought us, among other decisions, *Mapp* and *Gideon*) and the dismantling of Jim Crow. So *Swain* seems a particularly discordant decision. There, the Court upheld the rape conviction and death sentence of Robert Swain, a 19 year-old black man charged with assaulting a white girl in Talladega County, Alabama. No black person had served on a petit jury in the county "within the memory of persons now living"[8] and Swain was tried before an all-white jury from which the prosecutor had struck the six eligible black veniremen. Faced with this textbook example of southern justice, the Court nonetheless declined to "subject the prosecutor's challenge in any particular case to the demands and traditional standards of the Equal Protection Clause."[9] Instead, the Court drew a paradoxical distinction. It forbade prosecutors from using race to exclude black jurors "in case after case, whatever the circumstances, whatever the crime and whoever the defendant or the victim may be," because such a policy would "deny the Negro the same right and opportunity to participate in the administration of justice enjoyed by the white population," a result "the peremptory challenge is not designed to facilitate or justify."[10] But it permitted a prosecutor to take into account "group affiliations" such as race that were "normally thought irrelevant to legal proceedings or official action" when that affiliation provided "knowledge ... in the context of the case to be tried"[11]—presumably because "the case ..., the particular defendant involved and the particular crime charged"[12] meant that jurors of one race would be relatively more favorable to the prosecution. So the Court's analysis denied protection to people like Robert Swain precisely *because* prosecutors might believe that excluding blacks from juries in black-on-white rape cases might make conviction more likely. The defendants who might benefit most from a prohibition on race-based strikes were least entitled to it.

Over the next twenty years, it turned out that even the Court's proscription of wholesale racial exclusion was toothless. *Swain* itself had foreshadowed this result. Despite Swain's showing that blacks had not served on a jury in at least a dozen years, the Court held that he had not "laid the proper predicate for attacking the peremptory strikes as they

---

[7] 380 U.S. 202 (1965).

[8] *Id.* at 231 (Goldberg, J., dissenting).

[9] *Id.* at 221 (opinion of the Court).

[10] *Id.* at 223–24.

[11] *Id.* at 220–21.

[12] *Id.* at 223.

were used in [his] case" because he had failed to provide sufficient detail about "when, why and under what circumstances in cases previous to this one the prosecutor used his strikes to remove Negroes."[13] Such a requirement set an insuperable evidentiary barrier, given the implausibility of expecting any defendant (or even any defense counsel) to have detailed information regarding the pattern of prosecutorial peremptory strikes in other cases.[14]

Ironically, for all the celebration of the Warren Court's criminal procedure revolution, it was the Burger Court that turned out to be more sympathetic to Swain's plight. In 1972, in light of its decision in *Furman v. Georgia*,[15] striking down the death penalty as it was then administered, at least in part because of racial discrimination in sentencing for rape convictions,[16] the Court vacated Swain's death sentence.[17] And in 1986, in *Batson*, the Court overruled *Swain* itself, holding that a defendant could prove unconstitutional racial discrimination "in selection of the petit jury solely on evidence concerning the prosecutor's exercise of peremptory challenges at the defendant's trial."[18]

The story of *Batson* the case has very little to do with Batson the man. Nothing really distinguished Batson's case from the literally thousands of others in which defendants went to trial before all-white juries after prosecutors had peremptorily struck minority venire members. The Supreme Court's decision to overrule *Swain* and to rely on the equal protection clause to forbid peremptorily striking jurors on the basis of race was not a result that Batson's lawyers had pressed; indeed, his attorney expressly disavowed both claims at oral argument. But *Batson* is an interesting story nonetheless. The story of how the Court decided to hear this utterly mundane case opens a window into how the Court chooses "vehicles" for resolving important and recurring questions of constitutional criminal procedure. The story of how the Court decided to resolve *Batson* on fourteenth amendment rather than sixth amendment grounds sheds light on how doctrinal frameworks interact with practical concerns in shaping the Court's opinions. And the story of how *Batson*

---

[13] *Id.* at 226.

[14] Indeed, in Swain's own case on remand, the Alabama courts rejected a study that examined all of the prosecutor's strikes from 1950 to 1962 and claimed to show that the prosecutor had systematically struck blacks or entered into agreements with defense counsel to eliminate them from the venire. *See* Swain v. Alabama, 231 So.2d 737 (Ala. 1970), *vacated on other grounds*, 408 U.S. 936 (1972).

[15] 408 U.S. 238 (1972).

[16] *See id.* at 251 (Douglas, J., concurring); *id.* at 364 (Marshall, J., concurring).

[17] *See* Swain v. Alabama, 408 U.S. 936 (1972).

[18] *Batson*, 476 U.S. at 96.

has played out in the lower courts illustrates how concerns about remedies can backwash into how rights are framed in the first place.

The Road from *Swain* to *Batson*: The Search for a Vehicle

Swain placed a huge roadblock in the path of defendants who wanted to challenge the way prosecutors used their peremptory challenges, essentially foreclosing approaches based on the equal protection clause. But only a few years later, the Supreme Court began to issue a series of decisions under the sixth amendment that potentially opened a new doctrinal avenue for attacking race-based peremptories.

In contrast to the more general protections of the fourteenth amendment, which applies to a wide range of state action, the sixth amendment addresses specifically "criminal prosecutions," providing defendants with the right to speedy public trials before impartial juries, the right to confront witnesses, the right to compulsory process, and the right to the assistance of counsel. Although the Supreme Court had originally held that the sixth amendment, like the rest of the Bill of Rights, did not apply to the states (as opposed to the national government),[19] over time, the Court enforced many of the same restrictions on states, holding that the due process clause of the fourteenth amendment, which expressly applied to the states, "incorporated" many of the protections set out in the first eight amendments. In 1963, the Court held that the sixth amendment, as incorporated through the fourteenth amendment required states to provide lawyers to indigent defendants charged with felonies.[20] Less than a month after *Swain*, the Court incorporated the confrontation clause,2[21] and over the next few years, it incorporated the speedy trial and compulsory process clauses as well.[22]

Duncan, *Taylor*, and the Rise of the Sixth Amendment

Finally, in *Duncan v. Louisiana*,[23] the Court completed the project of incorporating the sixth amendment, holding that juries were so "fundamental to the American scheme of justice" that the fourteenth amendment "guarantees a right of jury trial in all criminal cases which—were they to be tried in a federal court—would come within the Sixth Amendment's guarantee."[24] That concerns with racial justice may have

---

[19] *See* Barron v. Mayor & City Council of Baltimore, 32 U.S. 243 (1833).

[20] Gideon v. Wainwright, 372 U.S. 335 (1963).

[21] Pointer v. Texas, 380 U.S. 400 (1965).

[22] *See* Klopfer v. North Carolina, 386 U.S. 213 (1967) (speedy trials); Washington v. Texas, 388 U.S. 14 (1967) (compulsory process).

[23] 391 U.S. 145 (1968). *Duncan* is the subject of a separate chapter in this volume.

[24] *Id.* at 150. In Baldwin v. New York, 399 U.S. 66 (1970), the Court held that the right to a jury trial extended to any offense for which a prison sentence of more than six months was authorized.

played some part in the Court's decision is suggested by the facts of Duncan's case.[25] Gary Duncan, like Robert Swain a 19 year-old black man, was charged with a controversial interracial crime: he allegedly slapped a white youth while intervening to protect two young relatives who had recently integrated a previously all-white school in the notorious Plaquemines Parish, Louisiana. There were no black lawyers in Plaquemines Parish, so Duncan's parents contacted lawyers at a civil rights law firm in New Orleans. Those lawyers agreed to represent Duncan because they believed that the prosecution for so minor a matter—the deputy sheriff originally called to the scene declined to arrest Duncan—was intended to retaliate against the family for its role in desegregating the local schools and to intimidate other black residents of the parish from asserting their rights. (In fact, a federal court later held that "the charge against Duncan would not have been prosecuted, and certainly not reprosecuted, were it not for the civil rights context out of which the case arose, for Duncan's selection of civil rights attorneys to represent him, and for the vigor of his defense."[26])

Duncan's request for a jury was denied and he was found guilty after a bench trial and sentenced to a short jail term. The Supreme Court reversed his conviction, concluding that the fourteenth amendment required that Duncan be given a jury trial if he requested one. The Court's description of *why* juries were so fundamental had special salience in light of the situation in Plaquemines Parish, where the monumentally racist county boss, "Judge" Leander Perez, had served as district attorney from 1924–60, and then turned the position over to his like-minded son to carry on his legacy:[27]

Those who wrote our constitutions knew from history and experience that it was necessary to protect against unfounded criminal

---

[25] These facts are set out more fully in Duncan v. Perez, 321 F. Supp. 181 (E.D. La. 1970), aff'd, 445 F.2d 557 (5th Cir.), cert. denied, 404 U.S. 940 (1971), and Sobol v. Perez, 289 F. Supp. 392 (E.D. La. 1968) (three-judge court).

[26] *Duncan*, 321 F. Supp. at 184. The district court held that the initial prosecution of Duncan had been conducted in bad faith, that there was "no legitimate state interest in the reprosecution," given the de minimis nature of the allegations, and that "reprosecution of Duncan would deter and suppress the exercise of federally secured rights by Negroes in Plaquemines Parish" because "it would constitute an unmistakable message to Negroes in Plaquemines Parish that it is unprofitable to step outside familiar patterns and to seek to rely on federal rights to oppose the policies of certain parish officials." *Duncan*, 321 F. Supp. at 184–85. Sobol concerned the trumped-up prosecution of Richard Sobol, one of Duncan's *lawyers*. The district court enjoined the prosecution, agreeing with the United States Department of Justice, which had intervened on behalf of Duncan and Sobol, that the prosecution was intended to deprive the black residents of the parish of their civil rights.

[27] For a discussion of Perez's role in the administration of justice in Plaquemines Parish, *see* Marcia Berzon, Rights and Remedies, 64 La. L. Rev. 519, 525–27 (2004).

charges brought to eliminate enemies and against judges too respon-
sive to the voice of higher authority. The framers of the constitutions strove to create an independent judiciary but insisted upon
further protection against arbitrary action. Providing an accused
with the right to be tried by a jury of his peers gave him an
inestimable safeguard against the corrupt or overzealous prosecutor
and against the compliant, biased, or eccentric judge.[28]

But juries could serve this critical function only if they really did
contain the defendant's peers: a venire handpicked by the government
would provide little safeguard. And so in *Taylor v. Louisiana*,[29] the Court
held that the requirement that a jury be a fair cross-section of the
community was an "essential" component of the sixth amendment right
to jury trial made applicable to the states in *Duncan*. Thus, the Court
reversed the defendant's conviction because Louisiana automatically
excluded women from jury service unless they requested to serve. "The
purpose of a jury," the Court declared, "is to guard against the exercise
of arbitrary power—to make available the commonsense judgment of the
community as a hedge against the overzealous or mistaken prosecutor.... This prophylactic vehicle is not provided if the jury pool is made
up of only special segments of the populace or if large, distinctive groups
are excluded from the pool."[30] *Taylor*'s reliance on earlier decisions
holding that racial exclusion from jury service was "at war with our
basic concepts of a democratic society and a representative government,"[31] meant that the sixth amendment now imposed at least some
constraint on racial exclusion of potential jurors.

Duncan and *Taylor* thus opened up a potential alternative doctrinal
route for attacking race-based prosecutorial peremptory challenges. *Taylor* distinguished the Court's earlier decision in *Hoyt v. Florida*,[32] which
had rejected a defendant's equal protection clause challenge to his
conviction by a jury selected from a males-only venire:

> It is true that [*Hoyt*] held that such a system did not deny due
> process of law or equal protection of the laws because there was a
> sufficiently rational basis for such an exemption. But *Hoyt* did not
> involve a defendant's Sixth Amendment right to a jury drawn from a
> fair cross section of the community and the prospect of depriving

---

[28] *Duncan*, 391 U.S. at 156.

[29] 419 U.S. 522 (1975).

[30] *Id.* at 530.

[31] *Id.* at 527 (quoting Smith v. Texas, 311 U.S. 128, 130 (1940)). *See also id.* at 528
(reiterating the declaration in Carter v. Jury Comm'n, 396 U.S. 320, 330 (1970), that "the
exclusion of Negroes from jury service because of their race contravenes the very idea of a
jury—a body truly representative of the community") (internal quotation marks omitted)

[32] 368 U.S. 57 (1961).

him of that right if women as a class are systematically excluded. The right to a proper jury cannot be overcome on merely rational grounds. There must be weightier reasons if a distinctive class ... is for all practical purposes to be excluded from jury service. No such basis has been tendered here.[33]

Subsequently, the Court articulated a form of heightened scrutiny for sixth amendment-based claims: a challenged practice could survive only if "a significant state interest [were] manifestly and primarily advanced by those aspects of the jury-selection process ... that result in the disproportionate exclusion of a distinctive group."[34]

Applying Fair Cross–Section Analysis to Petit Juries

The sixth amendment cases and various statutory reforms of the jury summons process meant that by the mid–1970's the traditional mechanisms that had excluded blacks from the venire altogether had largely been eliminated. The Voting Rights Act of 1965, which had dramatically increased black enfranchisement in the South, meant that blacks were now called for jury service in jurisdictions that selected the jury pool from voter registration rolls. The extension of the fair cross-section requirement to the states meant that the failure to call blacks for jury service would result in convictions being overturned if jury pools were unrepresentative of a jurisdiction's racial diversity. But although blacks were no longer being winnowed out of the venire, they were still not sitting on petit juries. The peremptory challenge now became the mechanism that excluded them. In *United States v. Carter*,[35] for example, the defendant showed that in the fifteen criminal cases with black defendants taken to trial in the Western District of Missouri in 1974, the government used its peremptory challenges to strike 57 of 70 eligible black venire members, producing all-white juries in half the cases. A prosecutor in one Louisiana parish, perhaps emboldened by *Swain*'s apparent green light for trial-related race-consciousness candidly admitted that he had consistently used his peremptory challenges to remove as many blacks as possible:

> I have found through experience, some twenty-three years in the District Attorney's office, that blacks, where you have a black defendant, will generally vote not guilty, in spite of the strength of the state's case ... I find, not without justification, particularly young blacks, they are very resentful of the white establishment.[36]

---

[33] *Taylor*, 419 U.S. at 533–34.

[34] Duren v. Missouri, 439 U.S. 357, 367–68 (1979).

[35] 528 F.2d 844, 847 (8th Cir. 1975), *cert. denied*, 425 U.S. 961 (1976).

[36] *See* State v. Washington, 375 So.2d 1162 (La. 1979); *see also* State v. Brown, 371 So.2d 751, 752 note 1 (La. 1979) (relying on this testimony in finding a violation).

In fact, that admission produced the first finding of a *Swain* violation. But in parallel cases, other courts drew exactly the *opposite* legal conclusion. For example, in *State v. Baker*,[37] the Supreme Court of Missouri rejected a defendant's *Swain* claim because of the "clear inference" from his charge that "blacks have been excluded 'particularly where the accused is a Negro,' " was that "Negroes are not excluded from juries when the defendant is not a Negro." Thus, the defendant failed to satisfy *Swain's* requirement that "the exclusion of blacks is made 'in case after case, whatever the circumstances, whatever the crime and whoever the defendant or the victim may be.' "[38] The continued immunity of peremptory challenges from constitutional scrutiny often undermined whatever inclusion sixth and fourteenth amendment constraints on the composition of the venire had accomplished.

Taylor had cautioned that the fair cross-section requirement "impose[d] no requirement that petit juries actually chosen must mirror the community and reflect the various distinctive groups in the population,"[39] suggesting that the simple absence of any blacks on a particular jury would not raise sixth amendment concerns. But although defendants were not constitutionally "entitled to a jury of any particular composition," the Court did seem to suggest that jury selection methods that produced unrepresentative juries were subject to close scrutiny.[40] After all, creating a representative venire was simply a means to an end: creating representative petit juries.

Shortly after *Taylor* had extended the fair cross-section requirement to the states, two influential state courts—the California Supreme Court in *People v. Wheeler*[41] and the Massachusetts Supreme Judicial Court in *Commonwealth v. Soares*[42]—relied on state constitutional provisions that paralleled the sixth amendment's guarantee of jury trials to forbid the use of race-based peremptory challenges.[43] Thus, they sidestepped the

---

[37] 524 S.W.2d 122 (Mo. 1975).

[38] *Id.* at 125.

[39] *Taylor*, 419 U.S. at 538.

[40] *Id.*

[41] 22 Cal. 3d 258 (1978).

[42] 377 Mass. 461, *cert. denied*, 444 U.S. 881 (1979).

[43] The California court based its decision on a provision of the California Constitution providing that "[t]rial by jury is an inviolate right and shall be secured to all," Cal. Const., art. I, § 16. It held that while a defendant did not have the right to a jury of any particular racial composition, he did have the right to a jury "that is as near an approximation of the ideal cross-section of the community as the process of a random draw permits." *Wheeler*, 22 Cal. 3d at 292. The Massachusetts court based its decision on Article 12 of the Massachusetts Constitution's Declaration of Rights, which provided in pertinent part that "no

question whether equal protection, in either its federal or state itera-
tions, limited the use of peremptories. But a number of other state
appellate courts rejected such challenges, both under their state constitutions and under the sixth amendment.

A trio of these cases reached the Supreme Court during the early
spring of 1983. The first two cases to arrive, *Miller v. Illinois* and *Perry
v. Louisiana*, involved black-on-white homicides. Like Clarence Earl
Gideon, Joseph Miller filed his petition *pro se*. He pointed out that not
only had the prosecutor used all his peremptory challenges to strike the
fourteen black members of the venire, leaving Miller to be tried and
convicted by an all-white jury, but that he had responded to a defense
objection by pointing out that the defense counsel was "excluding all
whites," thereby implicitly admitting that his own strikes were based on
the venire members' race. Miller acknowledged that *Swain* seemed to
permit this practice, but argued that *Swain*'s reasoning had been undercut by more recent cases, such as *Wheeler* and *Soares*, as well as by the
Supreme Court's own sixth amendment jurisprudence. He asked the
Court to overrule *Swain*.

Joe Lewis Perry had been convicted and sentenced to death by an
all-white jury after three black venire members had been excused for
cause due to their opposition to the death penalty and the prosecution
used its peremptory challenges to remove all the remaining black venire
members. While the Louisiana Supreme Court rejected Perry's constitutional challenge to the jury selection process, two justices dissented,
describing *Swain* as "an anachronism in the modern capital punishment
era,"[44] because permitting race-based peremptory strikes would undermine the representativeness of a sentencing jury.

The initial vote on both Miller and Perry's cases was to deny
certiorari. Justice Marshall, however, announced his intention to prepare
a dissent from the denials of certiorari. In April 1983, he circulated a
first draft. The dissent stated that "[i]n the nearly two decades since it
was decided, *Swain* has been the subject of almost universal and often
scathing criticism."[45] And it identified a way to sidestep *Swain*: treat the

---

subject shall be . . . deprived of his life, liberty, or estate, but by the judgments of his peers,
or the law of the land." Using peremptory challenges on the basis of race flouted the
principle that "[a] defendant is constitutionally entitled to a jury selection process free of
discrimination against his grouping in the community." *Soares*, 377 Mass. at 478 (quoting
Commonwealth v. Rodriquez, 364 Mass. 87, 92 (1973)).

[44] Louisiana v. Perry, 420 So.2d 139, 152 (La. 1982) (Dennis, J., dissenting).

[45] Miller v. Illinois, No. 82–5840, Justice Marshall, dissenting from the *denial of
certiorari* at 2 (April 13, 1983, circulation), available in The Papers of Harry A. Blackmun,
Container 449, Batson case file (Library of Congress) [hereinafter cited as Blackmun
Papers].

Court's intervening sixth amendment fair-cross section cases as imposing an independent constraint on peremptory challenges. The dissent did
not suggest overruling *Swain* so much as bypassing it. Almost immediately, Justice Brennan announced he was joining Justice Marshall's
dissent.

In the meantime, a third petition, in *McCray v. New York*, arrived in
the Justices' chambers, and the Court decided to hold off announcing the
denials of certiorari in *Miller* and *Perry* in order to "relist" those cases
for consideration along with *McCray*. Michael McCray was charged with
an armed robbery in New York City. McCray was black; the victim was
white. The only evidence against him was the victim's identification.
McCray's first trial ended in a hung jury, when at least two and possibly
all three minority jurors voted to acquit him.[46] At his second trial,
however, the prosecution used eight of its peremptory challenges to
remove all the black or Latino jurors, and McCray was convicted.

On appeal, McCray raised both federal and state constitutional
claims. The Brooklyn District Attorney, who had prosecuted McCray,
agreed that reliance on race in the exercise of peremptory challenges
would be unconstitutional; she argued, however, that the assistant
district attorney had not in fact violated that rule in McCray's case. By a
4–3 vote, the New York Court of Appeals rejected McCray's claim.[47] The
majority found "nothing in our State Constitution or statutes which
compel[led] a departure from" *Swain*. The dissenting justices, however,
anticipated Justice Marshall's position. They argued that because *Swain*
had been decided before *Duncan*, it did not resolve the fair cross-section
issue. And they pointed to the key problem: "the fair cross section-
impartiality requirement [would be] meaningless if in any case involving
a defendant of a given race the prosecutor can intentionally and systematically exclude all members of that race without cause."[48] In his petition
for certiorari, McCray presented both options for revisiting *Swain*: either
overruling it outright or sidestepping it by relying on the sixth amendment.

When *McCray* came before the Conference, three Justices—Brennan, Marshall, and Blackmun—voted to hear the case, but there was not
the fourth vote necessary to grant certiorari. Justice Marshall circulated
a new draft of his dissent from *Miller*, this time making *McCray* the lead
case. Once again, Justice Brennan joined his dissent.

---

[46] The facts in this paragraph are taken from the Brief Amici Curiae of Michael
McCray et al. 5–6, Batson v. Kentucky, 476 U.S. 79 (1986), reprinted in 165 Landmark
Briefs and Arguments of the Supreme Court of the United States 492 (Philip B. Kurland &
Gerhard Casper eds. 1987) (hereinafter Landmark Briefs).

[47] People v. McCray, 57 N.Y.2d 542 (1982).

[48] *Id.* at 554 (Meyer, J., dissenting); *see also id.* at 556–57 (Fuchsberg, J., dissenting).

Over the course of the next week, Justice Stevens, who had been on the fence, decided that he would vote to deny certiorari, but that he would write a rare concurrence in the denial, explaining his position. Apparently, Justice Stevens felt "that at this point, were the issue to be granted, his vote on the merits would be to reaffirm *Swain*," but because he was "deeply troubled by this," he wanted "to let the issue percolate a bit, rather than make more bad law."[49] In mid-May, Justice Stevens circulated a draft, acknowledging that the petitions raised an important issue that the Court would need ultimately to confront, but suggesting that allowing the issue to percolate further in the state and lower federal courts might assist the Court in its ultimate resolution.[50] When he got Justice Stevens's draft, Justice Blackmun switched his vote, perhaps informed by a sense that it was "the prudent thing *not* to grant cert. on this issue at this time, but to wait for another, more propitious day."[51] But both he and Justice Powell joined Justice Stevens's opinion.

Two weeks later, the Court made its decision public, denying certiorari in *McCray*, *Miller*, and *Perry*.[52] The one-sentence order, though, was accompanied by two opinions. Justices Stevens, along with Justices Blackmun and Powell, announced that although they had voted to deny certiorari, they did so because of their belief that further consideration of the issue by the lower courts "will enable use to deal with the issue more wisely at a later date."[53] They noted that there was at present no conflict among the lower federal courts and that the decisions in *Wheeler* and *Soares* had understandably given rise to litigation regarding how to address the "procedural and substantive problems associated with judicial review of peremptory challenges."5[54] Thus, in their view, "it is a sound exercise of discretion for the Court to allow the various States to serve as laboratories in which the issue receives further study before it is addressed by this Court."[55] Justices Marshall and Brennan dissented from the denial of certiorari, arguing that "it is time to reexamine

---

[49] *See* Memorandum from David Ogden to Justice Blackmun, April 28, 1983 (describing a conversation with Justice Stevens's clerk on this point), available in Blackmun Papers, *supra* note 45.

[50] *See* McCray v. New York, No. 82–1381, Opinion of Justice Stevens respecting the *denial of the petitions for writ of certiorari* at 2 (May 16, 1983, circulation), available in Blackmun Papers, *supra* note 45.

[51] *See* Memorandum from David Ogden to Justice Blackmun, May 16, 1983, at 1, available in Blackmun Papers, *supra* note 45.

[52] McCray v. New York, 461 U.S. 961 (1983).

[53] *Id*. at 962.

[54] *Id*.

[55] *Id*. at 963.

whether the rule announced in *Swain* under the Equal Protection
Clause can be reconciled with the Sixth Amendment right of every
defendant."[56] The Court had given notice that it was interested in
revisiting *Swain*.

Among others, Michael McCray took up that invitation, filing a
federal habeas petition raising his sixth amendment fair cross-section
claims. The district court concluded that "the coherence of the *Swain*
opinion depends upon . . . assumptions whose validity has at least been
diluted since 1965,"[57] and granted him relief. On December 4, 1983, the
Second Circuit affirmed, holding that the sixth amendment fair cross-
section requirement forbid prosecutors from using their peremptory
strikes in a racially discriminatory manner.[58] Now, the Supreme Court
had its circuit split, since two other courts of appeals had recently
declined to apply the sixth amendment to peremptory challenges.[59] And
of course the issue also continued to percolate in the state courts, as
defendants aware of the Supreme Court's announcement in *McCray*
continued to press the issue.

Batson's Case Rises to the Top

One case that bubbled to the surface involved James Kirkland
Batson. In September 1981, Batson and an accomplice stopped at a
house in Jefferson County (Louisville), Kentucky, snatched two purses
off the doorknob while a married couple sat in an adjacent room, and
then pawned some of the loot. The victim, a neighbor, and the pawnbro-
ker all identified Batson as one of the culprits, and he was charged with
second degree burglary, receipt of stolen property, and being a persistent
felony offender.

At Batson's trial, the prosecutor used four of his six peremptory
challenges to strike the four black members of the venire, leaving Batson
with an all-white jury. Batson's lawyer objected on both sixth amendment fair cross-section and fourteenth amendment equal protection
grounds.[60] The trial judge overruled the objection, stating that "[a]ny-
body can strike anybody they want to." Batson went to trial, was
convicted, and, because he was a persistent felony offender, was sentenced to twenty years in prison.

---

[56] *Id.* at 970.

[57] McCray v. Abrams, 576 F. Supp. 1244, 1247 (E.D.N.Y. 1983).

[58] McCray v. Abrams, 750 F.2d 1113 (2d Cir. 1984).

[59] *See* United States v. Thompson, 730 F.2d 82 (8th Cir. 1984); United States v.
Whitfield, 715 F.2d 145 (4th Cir. 1983).

[60] The relevant parts of the trial transcript are reprinted in the Joint Appendix and are
available on LEXIS in the GENFED, BRIEFS, file.

On appeal to the Kentucky Supreme Court, Batson again objected to the prosecution's use of its peremptory challenges. Acknowledging that *Swain* seemed to foreclose a straightforward equal protection claim, Batson instead urged the court "to adopt the position of other states based upon the Sixth Amendment and their own state constitutions, that preemptory [*sic*] challenges against minority groups can be unconstitutional" without regard to the prosecution's behavior in other cases.[61] The court, however, rejected that claim in a single sentence: "We have recently reaffirmed our reliance upon *Swain* in *Commonwealth v. McFerron*, Ky., [680] S.W.2d [924] (1984), holding that an allegation of the lack of a fair cross-sectional jury which does not concern a systematic exclusion from the jury drum does not rise to constitutional proportions, and we decline to adopt another rule."

The Kentucky Supreme Court had issued its opinion in Batson's case on December 20, 1984—roughly two weeks after the Second Circuit had issued its opinion in *Abrams v. McCray*—but Batson filed his cert. petition first, on February 19, 1984. The question presented by Batson's petition was somewhat prolix and fact-bound, but it clearly sounded in the sixth amendment:

> In a criminal case, does a state trial court err when, over the objection of a black defendant, it swears an all white jury constituted only after the prosecutor had exercised four of his six peremptory challenges to strike all of the black veniremen from the panel in violation of constitutional provisions guaranteeing the defendant an impartial jury and a jury composed of persons representing a fair cross section of the community?[62]

His petition essentially repeated the arguments Justice Marshall had advanced in his dissent from the denial of certiorari in *McCray*, and noted that while the state courts were failing to serve as the kind of "laboratories" that Justices Stevens, Blackmun, and Powell had anticipated, a conflict had recently emerged among the federal courts of appeals.[63]

Two weeks later, on March 4, 1984, the New York Attorney General filed *his* cert. petition in *Abrams v. McCray*. Abrams's first question presented articulated the issue somewhat more crisply:

> Whether the sixth amendment right to trial by jury, made applicable to the state through the fourteenth amendment in *Duncan v.*

---

[61] *See* Batson v. Commonwealth, No. 84–SC–733–MR (Ky.Sup.Ct.1984), available in the Joint Appendix, *supra* note 60.

[62] Pet. for Cert. i, Batson v. Kentucky, 476 U.S. 79 (1986), available in Landmark Briefs, *supra* note 46, at 274.

[63] *See id.* at 8.

Louisiana, 391 U.S. 145 (1968), prohibits the use of the peremptory challenge in a criminal case, by prosecutors or defense counsel, to exclude prospective jurors solely on the basis of race.[64]

Although the relatively mechanical process by which cert. petitions worked their way through the Court meant that Batson's petition was scheduled for decision by the Justices roughly a fortnight before Abrams's, Kent Syverud, the law clerk responsible for preparing the "pool memo" in *Batson* that would be sent to six of the Justices prior to the Conference,[65] was aware that *Abrams v. McCray* would soon be ready for decision as well. In his initial memorandum, Syverud stated that the issue "squarely presented in the [Batson petition] is obviously one on which this Court will have to grant certiorari at some point in view of the CA2's recent decision in *McCray*,"[66] and suggested that "it would be more sensible to resolve the issue in the *McCray* case itself rather than in this case," in part because "[t]he Kentucky Supreme Court opinion is nowhere near as thorough as either the majority or the dissent" in *McCray*. But two days later, after examining the petition in *McCray*, Syverud sent around a supplement to the pool memo. "On closer examination," he wrote, the petition in *McCray* was a "terrible candidate for deciding the Sixth Amendment issue," since the state conceded that the Sixth Amendment applied: "Needless to say, I doubt the Court will want to decide an important Sixth Amendment issue which has split the circuits in a case where both [petitioner] and [respondent] take the same position on the merits."

By contrast, Batson's petition cleanly presented the issue and the state clearly opposed Batson's claims. "The only drawback to a grant in this case," Syverud observed, "and it may be a significant one, is that the Court cannot expect particularly able advocacy of the State's position, judging from the [response] to the [petition]." Despite that caution, on April 22, 1984, the Court agreed to hear Batson's case. It decided to "hold" the petition in *Abrams v. McCray*[67] over the objection of three

---

[64] Pet. for Cert. i, Abrams v. McCray, No. 84–1426.

[65] Six of the Justices (Justices Brennan, Marshall, and Stevens were the exceptions) participated in a "cert. pool," in which a law clerk for one of the Justices would prepare a memorandum summarizing each petition for certiorari, analyzing the legal issues, and making a proposed recommendation.

[66] The pool memo is contained in the Blackmun Papers, *supra* note 45.

[67] For a description of the "hold" process, *see* Richard L. Revesz & Pamela S. Karlan, Nonmajority Rules and the Supreme Court, 136 U. Pa. L. Rev. 1067, 1110–31 (1988). Essentially, if three or more Justices agree that the disposition of a particular case may be affected by a case the Court has already agreed to hear, then the Court will "hold" that case pending its decision. Decisions to "hold" are never made public explicitly, but it is often easy to infer that a case is being held, given the question presented and the failure to

justices who thought the two cases should be consolidated and both set for oral argument.[68] Over the next few months, the Court was to hold at least twenty-one other petitions that raised questions regarding the use of peremptory challenges, showing that the issue was indeed percolating in the lower courts.[69]

For perhaps the first time in his life, petty career criminal Batson was in the right place at the right time. Joseph Miller, Joe Lewis Perry, and Michael McCray had paved the way for his petition. But in addition to being slightly too early—or in the case of McCray's second petition, perhaps slightly too late—each of their petitions had some feature which rendered it a less attractive "vehicle" for confronting the constitutional constraints on the use of peremptory challenges.

The decision in Miller's case had been rendered by an intermediate appellate court, rather than the state's highest court (which had denied discretionary review). And he had filed his petition at the Supreme Court pro se. Thus, there was always the risk that some procedural flaw might emerge that would make his case an inappropriate vehicle.

Joe Lewis Perry had been sentenced to death. Thus, his case was potentially complicated by the unique constitutional role played by sentencing juries in capital cases.[70]

And Michael McCray's case suffered both from a lack of real adversity on the fundamental question of law and, the second time around, from its procedural posture: McCray's case was now on habeas, rather than direct, review. The Court's soon-to-emerge retroactivity jurisprudence would show that a majority of the Justices saw the standards for relief in habeas cases as involving distinct questions absent from cases on direct review. By contrast, even though Batson's petition was inartfully drafted, and sought review of an entirely perfunctory state

---

announce any decision with respect to the petition long after the certiorari papers have been circulated to the Court.

[68] Abrams v. McCray, 471 U.S. 1097 (1985) (Brennan, Marshall, and Stevens, JJ., dissenting from denial of motion to consolidate). In *Batson*, Justice Stevens stated that the motion was denied "[p]resumably because the Court believed that Batson adequately presented the issues with which other courts had consistently grappled in considering this question." *Batson*, 476 U.S. at 111 (Stevens, J., concurring). In context, Justice Stevens's comments suggest that the Court's belief turned out to be erroneous.

[69] *See* Memorandum from Justice Powell to the Conference, June 18, 1986, summarizing the held cases, available in the Blackmun Papers, *supra* note 45.

[70] In Witherspoon v. Illinois, 391 U.S. 510, 520 (1968), the Court held that a state's policy in capital cases of excusing for cause all jurors who invariably opposed the death penalty violated the sixth amendment's fair cross-section requirement and the fourteenth amendment's due process clause because a jury composed solely of people who favored the death penalty "cannot speak for the community"—a key function of juries in capital sentencing proceedings.

court opinion, it posed none of the potential problems contained in the other petitions. Its very lack of distinction was what distinguished it.

Batson at the Court

Given the tenor of Justice Stevens' and Justice Marshall's opinions in *McCray*, Batson pitched his brief almost exclusively in terms of the sixth amendment's fair cross-section requirement. That strategic decision was hardly surprising: it avoided asking the Court to overrule *Swain* expressly, and the general wisdom among lawyers is that it's easier to persuade the Court to sidestep or ignore precedent than to reject it outright. Batson's argument was relatively straightforward: the ultimate purpose of the fair cross-section requirement was to produce representative juries, and it would be "senseless to obtain a jury panel that approximates a cross section of a community only to allow the prosecutor by means of his peremptory challenges to diminish or destroy that cross section."[71] Batson proposed evaluating defendants' claims through a process derived from the approaches taken by the California and Massachusetts courts in *Wheeler* and *Soares* for evaluating state constitutional claims. First, the defendant would have to timely object to the prosecutor's actions and show "that the excluded jurors are members of a cognizable group within the meaning of [the sixth amendment] . . . and that, under all the circumstances known in the case, there is a 'strong likelihood' that the jurors are being excluded because of their group associations rather than any specific bias.' "[72] Second, if the defendant were to satisfy this burden, the trial court would then require the prosecutor to show that his strikes were based on "matters other than the race or other group associations of the excluded jurors." Finally, if the prosecutor failed to meet his burden, the panel would be discharged and jury selection would begin anew.

Several of the amicus briefs filed in support of Batson went further, urging the Court either to overrule or to expressly modify *Swain*'s equal protection analysis. Perhaps as a propitiatory gesture, they suggested that the problems with *Swain* were not entirely the Supreme Court's fault but stemmed from how *Swain* had been read by lower courts: they claimed that *Swain* had never formally immunized peremptory challenges from the demands of the equal protection clause, but rather had erred in setting an evidentiary standard that had tacitly permitted discrimination. They pointed out that in subsequent equal protection cases, the Court had held that even isolated acts of purposeful discrimination violated the Constitution and had permitted trial courts to infer

---

[71] Brief for Petitioner 31, Batson v. Kentucky, 476 U.S. 79 (1986), available in Landmark Briefs, *supra* note 46, at 297.

[72] *Id.* at 26.

discriminatory purposes from the totality of the circumstances surrounding an official act, without requiring any particular form of evidence. Thus, to the extent that *Swain*'s equal protection analysis was inconsistent with this general approach, they suggested that *Swain* was "doctrinally unsound and must be overruled." [73]

The *amici*'s emphasis on the equal protection clause, rather than the fair cross-section requirement had an additional consequence: it brought to the forefront injuries inflicted on interests other than the defendant's. For example, the brief filed by Elizabeth Holtzman, the prosecutor in McCray's case, pointed out that excluded jurors "are as much aggrieved as those indicted and tried by juries chosen under a system of racial exclusion."[74] And beyond the juror who was a direct victim of racial discrimination, there was the public at large. Public confidence in the outcome of trials might be undermined by racial exclusion from petit juries. As Holtzman pointed out, "[t]his nation will not soon forget the spectacle of all-white juries acquitting the accused murderers of civil rights workers whether in the 1960's or the 1980's."[75] Thus, she argued that the ban on race-based peremptories should extend to defense counsel as well.

Finally, the *amici* responded to possible concerns with the administrability of judicial oversight of peremptory challenges by reiterating the successful experience in California and Massachusetts. They expressed confidence in the "the prophylactic effect of a pronouncement by this Court that the misuse of peremptory challenges violates both the Sixth and Fourteenth Amendments"; told that he cannot rely on race, even in the context of a single case, "the conscientious prosecutor will stop doing it."[76] And they predicted that because "the constitutional remedy will generally occur at the trial court level" it would "involve little more than a new beginning to jury selection"—a relatively small "transactional cos[t]" for "insuring a representative jury."[77]

---

[73] Brief for the Lawyers' Committee for Civil Rights Under Law as Amicus Curiae 4, Batson v. Kentucky, 476 U.S. 79 (1986), available in Landmark Briefs, *supra* note 46, at 461.

[74] Amicus Curiae Brief for Elizabeth Holtzman 17, Batson v. Kentucky, 476 U.S. 79 (1986), available in Landmark Briefs, *supra* note 46, at 422 (quoting Carter v. Jury Commission, 396 U.S. 320, 329 (1970)).

[75] *Id.*

[76] Brief Amici Curiae of the NAACP Legal Defense and Educational Fund, Inc., the American Jewish Committee, and the American Jewish Congress 48–49, Batson v. Kentucky, 476 U.S. 79 (1986), available in Landmark Briefs, *supra* note 46, at 567.

[77] Brief of Michael McCray, the New York Civil Liberties Union, and the American Civil Liberties Union as Amici Curiae 58, Batson v. Kentucky, 476 U.S. 79 (1986), available in Landmark Briefs, *supra* note 46, at 492.

In response, Kentucky advanced a categorical position: absent the kind of systematic evidence described in *Swain*, "prosecutors should continue to be allowed to exercise peremptory challenges without question, explanation, or judicial scrutiny."[78] It suggested that any judicial inquiry into how a prosecutor had used his peremptory strikes in a particular case would prove unworkable. The United States filed an *amicus* brief supporting Kentucky and arguing that *Swain* had "draw[n] the line in just the right place,"[79] permitting prosecutors to rely on their beliefs, "however subjective," in a particular case while condemning across-the-board "racial prejudice." And it argued that race-conscious use of peremptory challenges was unlikely to significantly undercut the representativeness of juries in any event, given that "[a] prosecutor who permits himself to act on the basis of racial prejudice is likely to forgo the most effective use of his peremptory challenges" while setting himself up for "judicial oversight under *Swain*."

Although the five Justices who had indicated their willingness in *McCray* to revisit *Swain* had invoked the sixth amendment as a basis for restricting peremptory challenges, they began to back away from that approach as they prepared for oral argument. A central problem concerned the potential sweep of the fair cross-section requirement. In *Duren v. Missouri*,[80] the Court had set out a three-part test for assessing violations that began by requiring the defendant to show "that the group alleged to be excluded is a 'distinctive' group in the community," but the Court had never clearly defined what counted as "distinctive." In *Duren* itself, the excluded group was women, and it made sense to treat women as a distinctive group, given classifications based on sex were generally subject to heightened judicial scrutiny under the equal protection clause.[81] But earlier cases might be read to embrace a very expansive definition of "distinctive groups"—treating exclusion of groups whose differential treatment did not trigger heightened judicial scrutiny elsewhere as impermissible under the sixth amendment. For example, in *Thiel v. Southern Pacific Co.*,[82] the Court had suggested that "persons who work for a daily wage"[83] might constitute a "portion of the

---

[78] Brief for Respondent 6, Batson v. Kentucky, 476 U.S. 79 (1986), available in Landmark Briefs, *supra* note 46, at 339.

[79] Brief for the United States as Amicus Curiae Supporting Affirmance 5, Batson v. Kentucky, 476 U.S. 79 (1986), available in Landmark Briefs, *supra* note 46, at 385.

[80] 439 U.S. 357 (1979).

[81] Nonetheless, even a decade after *Batson*, the Court was divided 6–3 in holding that the equal protection clause forbid litigants from using their peremptory challenges on the basis of sex. *See* J.E.B. v. Alabama, 511 U.S. 127 (1994).

[82] 328 U.S. 217 (1946).

[83] *Id*. at 221.

community . . . that cannot be intentionally and systematically excluded [from jury service] in whole or in part without doing violence to the democratic nature of the jury system."[84] In *Witherspoon v. Illinois,*[85] the Court had relied on the sixth amendment to hold that states could not exclude veniremen in capital cases because they "voiced general objections to the death penalty or expressed conscientious or religious scruples against its infliction,"[86] thus suggesting that constitutionally cognizable groups might be defined by shared attitudes as well as by shared demographic characteristics. The Justices were certainly aware that the month after oral argument in *Batson,* they would be hearing oral argument in *Lockhart v. McCree,* a case in which the Eighth Circuit, in the course of holding that the sixth amendment prohibited the exclusion for cause of so-called "*Witherspoon* excludables" (jurors who refused even to consider the death penalty in a capital case), had suggested that it "would encroach upon a party's sixth amendment right to have a cross-sectional jury" if jurors could be removed because "they were pro-ERA, pro-life, Republicans or Democrats."[87] To hold that the sixth amendment governed the exercise of peremptory challenges would thus potentially precipitate time-consuming judicial scrutiny in virtually every criminal case. If the Court's real concern were solely with race-based exclusions, the sixth amendment might prove a very unattractive device for policing the process. Ironically, relying on the equal protection clause and overruling *Swain* was coming to seem the more modest approach.

At oral argument, several of the Justices raised the possibility of overruling *Swain,* but Batson's lawyer, J. David Niehaus, stunned them by repeatedly declining their offer:

Question: Your claim here is based solely on the Sixth Amendment?

Mr. Niehaus: Yes.

. . . .

Question: You are not asking for a reconsideration of *Swain,* and you are making no equal protection claim here. Is that correct?

---

[84] *Id.* at 223.

[85] 391 U.S. 510 (1968).

[86] *Id.* at 522.

[87] Grigsby v. Mabry, 758 F.2d 226, 230 (8th Cir. 1985), rev'd sub nom. Lockhart v. McCree, 476 U.S. 162 (1986). The Court ultimately decided that the process of "death qualifying" jurors in capital cases—that is, removing for cause any juror who could not consider imposing a death sentence at the penalty phase of a capital trial—did not violate a defendant's right to an impartial jury at the guilt phase, even assuming, for the sake of argument, that social science studies had demonstrated that "death qualified" juries were more prone to convict defendants than "non-death qualified" juries. Lockhart v. McCree, 476 U.S. 162 (1986).

Mr. Niehaus: We have not made an equal protection claim

. . . .

Question: Why do you fall short of a direct attack on *Swain* on equal protection?

Mr. Niehaus: *Swain* within the conventional interpretation simply states that no attack can be made on the exercise in one particular case, and as the record in this case shows no more than what happened in this one particular case.

. . . .

Question: So I ask again, why don't you attack *Swain* head on?

Mr. Niehaus: I believe that we will be attacking it in the course of our argument, Your Honor, because I think that the bases that underlie the proof standard in *Swain* have been eroded somewhat by a reexamination of the historical—

Question: I though you just answered Justice O'Connor by saying, no, you weren't really attacking *Swain* except by implication.

Mr. Niehaus: We have not made a specific argument in the briefs . . . saying that we are attacking *Swain* as such. We have maintained that because the Sixth Amendment guarantees a right to a jury that is as representative of the community as possible, that the Court may proceed on that basis alone and may or may not have to alter its holding in *Swain* in order to achieve its desire.

. . . .

Question: So I come back again to my question why you didn't attack *Swain* head on, but I take it if the Court were to overrule *Swain*, you wouldn't like that result.

Mr. Niehaus: Simply overrule Swain without adopting the remedy [that the California and Massachusetts courts had adopted]?

Question: Yes.

Mr. Niehaus: I do not think that would give us much comfort, Your Honor, no.

Question: That is a concession.

Mr. Niehaus: Pardon?

Question: I said, that is a concession.[88]

Somewhat bizarrely, in light of Batson's apparent concession that he was not seeking that *Swain* be overruled, Rickie Pierson, the lawyer for

---

[88] Tr. of Oral Arg. at 4–5, 8, Batson v. Kentucky, 476 U.S. 79 (1986).

Kentucky (who was himself black), framed the case in exactly those terms:

Mr. Pearson: Mr. Chief Justice, and may it please the Court, the issue before this Court today is simply whether Swain versus Alabama should be reaffirmed. We believe that *Swain*—

Question: Well, now, that isn't what the other side says at all. They say the issue is one of whether the Sixth Amendment should apply.

Mr. Pearson: We believe that it is the Fourteenth Amendment that is the item that should be challenged, and presents perhaps an address to the problem. . . .[89]

And he then advanced an extraordinarily aggressive reading of *Swain*, under which an equal protection violation could never be established by a prosecutor's behavior in a single case, no matter how overt the prosecutor's discrimination might be. This exchange came after several minutes of sparring:

Question: Now, what if the prosecutor gets up and says, now, look, we don't have to wait for a period of time to rely on some inference from statistics. I am striking these blacks because I don't think they can sit fairly in this case or any other case. Now, *Swain* didn't approve that, did it?

Mr. Pearson: Yes, sir, it did.

Question: It did?

Mr. Pearson: Yes, sir.

Question: What makes you think that?

Mr. Pearson: Because the test in *Swain* is that you must show that the prosecutor did it over a period of time.[90]

Immediately after the argument, there was a flurry of activity among the clerks. Later that afternoon, Justice Blackmun's clerk (and the author of this chapter) reported to him that:

It appears, from what they've told their clerks, that Justices Brennan, White, Marshall, Stevens, and O'Connor are all prepared to address the equal protection issue. (I was unable to reach Justice Powell's clerk, but another clerk told me that Justice Powell's clerk thought he too might be willing to reach the question.) Thus, you should feel no reluctance to reach the issue, since no one seriously thinks the execrable performance by Batson's lawyer removed this issue from the case.[91]

---

[89] *Id.* at 24.

[90] *Id.* at 32–33.

[91] Memorandum from Pam Karlan to Justice Blackmun, Dec. 12, 1985, available in the Blackmun Papers, *supra* note 45.

The next day, the Justices met in conference to discuss *Batson*. Chief Justice Burger led off the discussion by asserting that Batson was asserting only a sixth amendment claim and that once there was a fair cross-section in the venire, nothing in the Constitution prohibited "hunch strikes."9[92] Justice Rehnquist agreed that peremptory challenges were, by their nature, arbitrary, and also voted to retain *Swain*.

But the other seven Justices—including Justice White, *Swain*'s author—all indicated their willingness to overrule *Swain*. And each of them squarely rejected using the sixth amendment to limit peremptory challenges. The main difference among them concerned whether the constitutional limits on the *defense*'s use of peremptory challenges should be identical to those placed on the prosecution, with Justice White arguing in favor of symmetry, Justice Marshall (who questioned whether peremptory challenges should be permitted at all) arguing against, and Justice Brennan arguing that the issue was not yet before the Court and should be postponed to a later day.

Justice Powell delivered the opinion of the Court, whose first sentence telegraphed the result, announcing that the Court had decided to "reexamine" the evidentiary burden that *Swain* had placed on defendants making equal protection claims regarding prosecutorial peremptory challenges.[93] While the Court placed substantial reliance on the post-*Swain* doctrinal developments, the cases it highlighted were not primarily the sixth amendment fair cross-section decisions involving jury selection, but rather general equal protection decisions setting out how invidious purpose was to be proven. These cases established that " 'a consistent pattern of official racial discrimination' is not 'a necessary predicate to a violation of the Equal Protection Clause. A single invidiously discriminatory governmental act' is not 'immunized by the absence of such discrimination in the making of other comparable decisions.' "[94] Thus, for evidentiary requirements such as the framework set out in *Swain* "to dictate that 'several must suffer discrimination" before one could object,' *McCray v. New York*, 461 U.S., at 965 (Marshall, J. dissenting from denial of certiorari), would be inconsistent with the promise of equal protection to all."[95] Given that "the Fourteenth Amendment protects an accused throughout the proceedings bringing him to

---

[92] This account of the Justices' discussion relies entirely on Justice Blackmun's note sheet, available in the Blackmun Papers. The Justices spoke and voted in order of seniority, beginning with Chief Justice Burger, but for expositional reasons, I have grouped their comments differently in the text.

[93] *Batson*, 476 U.S. at 82.

[94] *Id*. at 95 (quoting Village of Arlington Heights v. Metropolitan Housing Development Corp., 429 U.S. 252, 266 note 14 (1977)).

[95] *Id*. at 96.

justice, the State may not draw up its jury lists pursuant to neutral procedures but then resort to discrimination at other stages in the selection process"[96] such as its use of peremptory challenges. The problem with *Swain*, according to the Court, was that it had been read by lower courts in a fashion that "placed on defendants a crippling burden of proof," rendering prosecutorial peremptory challenges "now largely immune from constitutional scrutiny."[97]

The Court then laid out an analytic framework for conducting such scrutiny that borrowed heavily both from its own approach to disparate treatment cases involving other sorts of equal protection claims and from the California and Massachusetts courts' approach to state constitutional claims. (Ironically, the state court cases had drawn on sixth amendment principles in articulating their rules.) "[T]he defendant first must show that he is a member of a cognizable racial group and that the prosecutor has exercised peremptory challenges to remove from the venire members of the defendant's race."[98] Then he "must show that these facts and any other relevant circumstances,"such as the way the prosecutor conducted voir dire, "raise an inference that the prosecutor used that practice to exclude the veniremen from the petit jury on account of their race."[99] If the defendant satisfied this burden, then the trial judge should demand that "the State to come forward with a neutral explanation for challenging black jurors."[100] That explanation "need not rise to the level justifying exercise of a challenge for cause," but it could not rest on an assumption or intuition that the challenged jurors "would be partial to the defendant because of their shared race,"[101] a view that many lower courts had treated under *Swain* as a trial-related, non-invidious rationale. Ultimately, the trial court would have to decide whether "the defendant ha[d] established purposeful discrimination."[102]

The Court's requirement that the defendant show that he and the excluded juror were members of the same racial group seemed to suggest that the equal protection violation involved depriving the *defendant* of his right to trial by a jury of his peers. But there was another strain to the equal protection analysis as well, stemming from the Court's "recogni[tion] that a 'State's purposeful or deliberate *denial* to Negroes on

---

[96] *Id*. at 88 (internal citations and quotation marks omitted).

[97] *Id*. at 92–93.

[98] *Id*. at 96.

[99] *Id*.

[100] *Id*. at 97.

[101] *Id*.

[102] *Id*. at 98.

account of race *of participation as jurors* in the administration of justice
violates the Equal Protection Clause.' "[103] The Court emphasized that
"[t]he harm from discriminatory jury selection extends beyond that
inflicted on the defendant and the excluded juror to touch the entire
community. Selection procedures that purposefully exclude black persons
from juries undermine public confidence in the fairness of our system of
justice."[104]

As for Batson himself, the Court remanded his case for the trial
court to decide whether he satisfied the new analytic framework, stating
that "[i]f the trial court decides that the facts establish ... purposeful
discrimination and the prosecutor does not come forward with a neutral
explanation for his action, our precedents require that petitioner's conviction be reversed."[105]

While Justice Powell's opinion for the Court garnered seven votes,
there were also four concurring opinions addressing various additional
issues.[106] Justice White, who had written the Court's opinion in *Swain*,
wrote to express his agreement that *Swain* should be overruled. He
thought that *Swain* itself "should have warned prosecutors that using
peremptories to exclude blacks on the assumption that no black juror
could fairly judge a black defendant would violate the Equal Protection
Clause." But several decades' experience had shown that "that the
practice of peremptorily eliminating blacks from petit juries in cases
with black defendants remains widespread."[107] Nevertheless, although
the time had come to overrule *Swain*, both Justice White and Justice
O'Connor, in her one-sentence concurrence, indicated that they would
apply the new rule only prospectively to trials occurring after the
decision in *Batson*.

Justice Marshall's concurrence sounded a pessimistic note, predicting that the Court's decision would not "end the racial discrimination
that peremptories inject into the jury-selection process."[108] Perhaps influenced by his general view that the Court had established standards of
proof even in conventional equal protection cases that shielded all but
the most flagrant discrimination, Justice Marshall asserted that the goal

---

[103] *Id*. at 84 (emphasis added) (quoting *Swain*, 380 U.S. at 203–04).

[104] *Id*. at 87.

[105] *Id*. at 100.

[106] Justice Stevens, joined by Justice Brennan, wrote a concurrence that responded to
Chief Justice Burger's complaint in dissent that the Court should not even have addressed
the equal protection issue since Batson's lawyers failed to raise it in their briefs and
expressly disclaimed it at oral argument.

[107] *Id*. at 101 (White, J., concurring).

[108] *Id*. at 102. (Marshall, J., concurring).

of preventing discrimination in jury selection "can be accomplished only by eliminating peremptory challenges entirely."[109] Moreover, precisely because *all* peremptory challenges involved intuitive judgments, Justice Marshall worried that "[e]ven if all parties approach the Court's mandate with the best of conscious intentions, that mandate requires them to confront and overcome their own racism on all levels—a challenge I doubt all of them can meet."[110]

The two dissents, by Chief Justice Burger and Justice Rehnquist, both argued that it was entirely acceptable for prosecutors to remove jurors of a defendant's race from the jury as long as such individuals were not excluded from jury service altogether. The Chief Justice saw nothing "racially insulting" in the view that "each race may have its own special concerns, or even may tend to favor its own."[111] They embraced the implicit suggestion in *Swain* that race might well affect jurors' views and it was precisely that possibility that made prosecutorial reliance on race in exercising peremptory challenges rational.

The Road from *Batson* to *Swain?*: Problems of Rights and Remedies

The Court's decision in *Batson* raised a host of questions regarding the use of peremptory challenges. Should the Court's decision apply retroactively? Should *Batson* claims be limited to defendants of the same racial group as the excluded jurors? Should *Batson* apply symmetrically—to defense counsel as well as to prosecutors? What factors other than race were impermissible bases for exercising a peremptory challenge?

The Court resolved these issues in a series of cases stretching over much of the ensuing decade; in fact, a generation later, the Supreme Court was *still* hearing *Batson* cases, including one in which the trial had occurred before *Batson* was announced.[112] In *Allen v. Hardy*,[113]

---

[109] *Id.* at 103.

[110] *Id.* at 106. Nineteen years later, Justice Breyer was to offer a reprise of this theme in his concurrence in Miller–El v. Dretke, 125 S.Ct. 2317 (2005). *See infra* text accompanying notes 132–35.

[111] *Id.* at 123 (Burger, C.J., dissenting) (quoting United States v. Leslie, 783 F.2d 541, 554 (5th Cir. 1986) (en banc)). *See also id.* at 137–38 (Rehnquist, J., dissenting) ("In my view, there is simply nothing 'unequal' about the State's using its peremptory challenges to strike blacks from the jury in cases involving black defendants, so long as such challenges are also used to exclude whites in cases involving white defendants, Hispanics in cases involving Hispanic defendants, Asians in cases involving Asian defendants, and so on.").

[112] *See* Miller–El v. Dretke, 125 S.Ct. 2317, 2340 (2005) (holding that Miller–El was entitled to habeas relief—his case had been pending on appeal at the time *Batson* was decided, *see infra* note 116—because it "blink[ed] reality" to deny that the state struck several black jurors because of their race); *see also* Johnson v. California, 125 S.Ct. 2410 (2005) (rejecting California's requirement that defendants show, as part of the first stage of

without oral argument the Court declined to apply *Batson* to cases on habeas review—thereby stripping Michael McCray of the victory he had achieved following the Court's denial of his original petition.[114] But the next Term, in *Griffith v. Kentucky*,[115] the Court held that *Batson* would apply to all cases pending on direct review. The Court's resolution of this question set the stage for its later *Teague* jurisprudence regarding retroactivity on habeas more generally.[116] In *Powers v. Ohio*,[117] the Court held that a defendant could raise a *Batson* claim whether or not he and the excluded jurors shared the same race, stressing that *Batson* was as much about the equal protection rights of excluded jurors as it was about the trial-related interests of individual defendants. In *Georgia v. McCollum*,1[118] the Court extended *Batson* to defense counsel. And in *J.E.B. v. Alabama*,1[119] the Court held that litigants could not strike potential jurors on the basis of gender, although later that year, the Court

---

the *Batson* inquiry, that race was more likely than not the explanation for the challenged strikes).

[113] 478 U.S. 255 (1986) (per curiam).

[114] *See* Abrams v. McCray, 478 U.S. 1001 (1986) (*granting, vacating, and remanding* McCray's case in light of *Batson* and *Allen v. Hardy*).

[115] 479 U.S. 314 (1987).

[116] In Teague v. Lane, 489 U.S. 288 (1989), the Court announced that federal courts generally should not entertain claims on habeas if deciding in the prisoner's favor would require them to announce a "new" rule of constitutional criminal procedure. Concomittantly, decisions announcing "new" rules are not applied retroactively to cases on collateral review. The two exceptions to *Teague*'s nonretroactivity doctrine concern new rules that place the defendant's primary conduct beyond the power of the state to proscribe (or to punish in a particular fashion) and " 'watershed rules of criminal procedure' implicating the fundamental fairness and accuracy of the criminal proceeding." Saffle v. Parks, 494 U.S. 484, 495 (1990) (quoting Teague, 489 U.S. at 311). Clearly, *Batson* claims do not implicate the first *Teague* exception. In *Allen v. Hardy*, the Court explained that the *Batson* rule did not fall within the second category either:

> By serving a criminal defendant's interest in neutral jury selection procedures, the rule in *Batson* may have some bearing on the truthfinding function of a criminal trial. But the decision serves other values as well. Our holding ensures that States do not discriminate against citizens who are summoned to sit in judgment against a member of their own race and strengthens public confidence in the administration of justice. The rule in *Batson*, therefore, was designed "to serve multiple ends," only the first of which may have some impact on truthfinding.

478 U.S. at 259.

[117] 499 U.S. 400 (1991).

[118] 505 U.S. 42 (1992). In Edmonson v. Leesville Concrete Co., 500 U.S. 614 (1991), the Court had extended Batson to peremptory challenges exercised by private litigants in civil cases.

[119] 511 U.S. 127 (1994).

declined to address the question whether *Batson* would also forbid taking religion into account in exercising peremptory challenges.[120]

But this doctrinal elaboration has had a set of remarkably paradoxical consequences. First, of course, it has shifted attention away from the protection of minority *defendants* and toward a concern with the rights of minority *jurors*.[121] That move enabled the Court to finesse a delicate issue: whether the racial composition of a jury affects its deliberations. By focusing on potential jurors, the Court could avoid having to address whether *Batson* errors actually affect trial outcomes, since the juror's rights are entirely independent of the outcome of any trial in which she sits. If a citizen is excluded from serving on a jury because of her race, then she has been denied equal protection in the same way that she would have been denied equal protection if she were denied some other governmental position. By contrast, if the Court's extensions of the *Batson* principle in *Powers*, *Leesville*, and *McCollum* had focused on the litigants' interests, the Justices might have found themselves in the uncomfortable position of acknowledging that two ostensibly "impartial" juries—impartial because, by hypothesis, jurors incapable of impartiality had been removed for cause—could reach different results because of differences in the race of the jurors. That recognition would have undercut the Rehnquist Court's insistence in other areas of equal protection, most notably with respect to redistricting and in affirmative action, that it would be pernicious to assume that race affects individuals' outlook.[122]

But the very decision to reframe the focus on the interests of jurors had another important consequence for the elaboration of *Batson*. If the problem is a denial of the equal protection rights of jurors rather than of defendants, what should courts do when they find a violation? Given the requirement that a defendant timely object to the prosecutor's use of his peremptories, there's no real problem at the trial court level: as Michael

---

[120] *See* Davis v. Minnesota, 511 U.S. 1115 (1994) (*denying certiorari* on this question with a concurrence by Justice Ginsburg and a dissent by Justices Scalia and Thomas saying that in light of J.E.B., Batson should be extended to all suspect classifications). *See also* United States v. Brown, 352 F.3d 654, 667–69 (2d Cir. 2003) (canvassing the state of the law on this issue and noting the division among the lower courts). In Hernandez v. New York, 500 U.S. 352 (1991), a fractured Court agreed that Batson proscribed reliance on ethnicity in exercising peremptory challenges, but rejected the defendant's claim because it decided that the prosecutor's decision under the facts of the particular case to exclude bilingual jurors was not the equivalent of striking on the basis of ethnicity.

[121] *See* Pamela S. Karlan, Race Rights, and Remedies in Criminal Adjudication, 96 Mich. L. Rev. 2001, 2015 (1998); Eric L. Muller, Solving the Batson Paradox: Harmless Error, Jury Representation, and the Sixth Amendment, 106 Yale L.J. 93 (1996); Barbara D. Underwood, Ending Race Discrimination in Jury Selection: Whose Right Is It Anyway?, 92 Colum. L. Rev. 725 (1992).

[122] *See* Karlan, *supra* note 121, at 2017.

McCray's *amicus* brief pointed out, the cost of curing a *Batson* violation there is not very high: the judge either rejects the prosecution's strike, seating the challenged juror, or simply requires that voir dire and jury selection begin anew. But if the trial judge rejects the defendant's *Batson* claim and the defendant goes to trial and is convicted, what should the remedy be? Reversal of defendants' convictions will provide defendants with a windfall if they would have been convicted anyway. On the other hand, harmless error review, while it would avoid giving the clearly guilty defendant the windfall of a new trial, would force courts to decide in which cases race matters—precisely the question the Supreme Court sought to avoid by reframing *Batson* as not an entirely defendant-centered right.

But when courts can't limit a remedy in circumstances where the remedy seems to be giving undeserving defendants a windfall, they face a temptation to covertly limit the right instead.

In *Batson* cases, this dynamic has been accomplished by combining a deferential standard of appellate review—under which defendants find it well-nigh impossible to overturn a trial court's finding that no *Batson* violation occurred[123]—with a sweeping scope of permissible neutral explanations for prosecutorial strikes.[124] Lower courts have essentially abandoned any requirement that the prosecutor show any connection between the proffered reason—for example, that the juror was wearing a Malcolm X hat[125] or that the juror was a cosmetologist[126]—and some feature of the particular trial.

It seems unlikely that appellate courts, in the abstract, would find that a prosecutor who peremptorily struck all the black members of the venire because of the hats they wore had rebutted an inference that race played a role in his decisions. It's hard, after all, to hypothesize a trial-related reason, or even a hunch, why the bare-headed are more conviction-prone. (And note that prosecutors are only required to proffer a reason at all in cases where the defendant has already made a prima facie case of unconstitutional behavior.) But appeals courts are not asked to rule on *Batson* issues in a vacuum: rather, they generally confront the

---

[123] *See* Joshua E. Swift, Note, Batson's Invidious Legacy: Discriminatory Juror Exclusion and the "Intuitive" Peremptory Challenge, 78 Cornell L. Rev. 336, 358 (1993) (finding that in only 3 of 76 cases did appeals courts reverse convictions where the trial court had found that the prosecutor had offered nonracial reasons for his strikes).

[124] *See* Karlan, *supra* note 121, at 2021 (collecting cases and sources).

[125] *See* United States v. Hinton, 94 F.3d 396, 396 (7th Cir. 1996).

[126] *See, e.g.,* United States v. Alvarado–Sandoval, 997 F.2d 491, 491–92 (8th Cir. 1993) (finding the prosecution's explanation acceptable when it struck a juror because "I am going to get into an aiding and abetting type theory and just for whatever reason I did not want a cosmetologist").

question only after a presumptively impartial jury has found the defendant guilty beyond a reasonable doubt.

So here, too, there is a temptation for appellate courts to shade their decisions. In some racially charged cases, trial judges may be less likely to accept, and appellate courts less likely to affirm, implausible explanations for racially correlated strikes.[127] But in cases where the court sees no racial angle, trial judges may reject *Batson* claims out of hand, and reviewing courts will be more prone to affirm.

As I have pointed out elsewhere, "this disingenuousness has its dangers":

> First, courts may underestimate, either systematically or in particular kinds of cases, the relevance of a juror's race to his or her assessment of the evidence. They may not think, for example, that cases where the credibility of police witnesses is at issue are racially charged regardless of the particular facts; it might, however, be the case that there is in fact a deep racial divide on this issue. Ironically, then, there may be cases where the racial composition of the jury is outcome-determinative, or at least outcome-affective, that end up getting affirmed. But the existing structure of *Batson* argumentation provides no occasion for making this sort of claim: it does not readily allow for the argument that, given the facts of this particular case, an otherwise-acceptable reason ought to be reviewed more carefully.

> Second, the *Batson* rule is to a great extent hortatory . . .: much of its effectiveness in the real world depends not on judicial enforcement but on its internalization by the relevant actors. When courts accept dubious justifications for racially correlated strikes, they may send a message to prosecutors and defense counsel that the exclusion of minority jurors is generally not going to be taken very seriously or scrutinized very carefully.[128]

So in the end, *both* the optimism of the civil rights *amici* and the pessimism of Justice Marshall may have been right: *Batson* no doubt has changed the hearts and minds of many litigators regarding the propriety of relying on race to exercise peremptory challenges, but where it hasn't done so, it may continue to permit both conscious and unconscious reliance on race to go undetected and undeterred.

---

[127] For one example, consider Gamble v. State, 357 S.E.2d 792 (Ga. 1987). Gamble involved a black-on-white capital murder case in which most of the state's witnesses were white and most of the defense witnesses were black. The prosecutor used all his peremptory strikes to remove potential black jurors and he thereby obtained an all-white jury. The Georgia Supreme Court reversed the conviction, finding "suspect" the prosecutor's reasons for striking various black venire persons even though these reasons—age, church membership, attitude, occupations—have often passed muster in less racially charged cases.

[128] Karlan, *supra* note 121, at 2022–23.

In fact, nearly two decades after *Batson*, the Supreme Court was *still* overturning lower courts' pinched interpretations of *Batson*. In *Johnson v. California*,[129] the Court rejected California's requirement that defendants claim establish, as part of their prima facie case, that discriminatory intent was "more likely than not" the explanation for the prosecutor's strikes. The California rule often ended the *Batson* inquiry before the prosecution was even required to articulate an explanation for its strikes. Given that "[t]he *Batson* framework is designed to produce actual answers to suspicions and inferences that discrimination may have infected the jury selection process," it would be somewhat perverse to answer that question before asking the relevant actor for his explanation, particularly when the plausibility or implausibility of the proffered reasons is so often relevant.

And in *Miller–El v. Dretke*,[130] the Court finally granted relief to Thomas Joe Miller–El, a black defendant convicted and sentenced to death by an all-white jury six weeks before *Batson* was decided. The Court found the lower courts' treatment of the evidence of racial discrimination "unsupportable," and "strained,"[131] pointing to the fact that the prosecutor had struck ten of the eleven black venire members, including potential jurors who had indicated support for capital punishment; had questioned black and white jurors differently; had manipulated the order in which jurors were questioned; and had come from an office that had "for decades . . . followed a specific policy of systematically excluding blacks from juries."[132] In a concurring opinion, Justice Breyer reiterated Justice Marshall's suggestion that perhaps the only way to end discrimination would be to abolish peremptory challenges altogether:

> [T]his case illustrates the practical problems of proof that Justice Marshall described. As the Court's opinion makes clear, Miller–El marshaled extensive evidence of racial bias. But despite the strength of his claim, Miller–El's challenge has resulted in 17 years of largely unsuccessful and protracted litigation—including 8 different judicial proceedings and 8 different judicial opinions, and involving 23 judges, of whom 6 found the *Batson* standard violated and 16 the contrary.[133]

---

[129] 125 S.Ct. 2410 (2005).

[130] 125 S.Ct. 2317 (2005).

[131] *Id*. at 2329.

[132] *Id*. at 2338.

[133] *Id*. at 2340 (Breyer, J., concurring.)

Justice Breyer noted that despite *Batson* and its progeny, discriminatory use of peremptory challenges persisted. And he suggested that peremptory were becoming "increasingly anomalous in our judicial system:"[134]

> If used to express stereotypical judgments about race, gender, religion, or national origin, peremptory challenges betray the jury's democratic origins and undermine its representative function. The "scientific" use of peremptory challenges may also contribute to public cynicism about the fairness of the jury system and its role in American government. And, of course, the right to a jury free of discriminatory taint is constitutionally protected—the right to use peremptory challenges is not.[135]

As for James Batson himself? In October 1986, he was resentenced on the burglary charge, and over the next dozen years he bounced in and out of prison until 1999, when he was prosecuted on new theft and persistent felony offender charges, by Joe Gutmann, the same prosecutor whose peremptory challenges had started him on the road to Washington nearly twenty years before, and who had later named a dog he adopted "Batson" to commemorate his most famous case.[136] Asked whether he bore any resentment, Batson was philosophical. "He's a prosecutor and that's what he's supposed to do," said Batson. "So how can I hold that against him?' "[137]

---

[134] *Id.* at 2342.

[135] *Id.* at 2343–44.

[136] Andrew Wolfson, Profile: Joe Gutmann: Star, Louisville Courier–Journal, Jan. 24, 2000, at 1A.

[137] *Id.*

*

13

United States v. Salerno: The Constitutionality of Regulatory Detention

Daniel Richman

In the custody of United States Marshals in March 1986 after his arrest on racketeering charges, Anthony Salerno, known to his associates and a federal grand jury as "Fat Tony," did not look particularly dangerous. Indeed, even before his arrest, when holding court at the Palma Boy Social Club in East Harlem, the cigar-chomping 74–year-old "Boss" of the Genovese Family of La Cosa Nostra did not look like the kind of person one crossed the street to avoid on a dark night.[1] But under the recently enacted Bail Reform Act of 1984, federal prosecutors could seek the pretrial detention of Salerno and his long-time associate Vincent ("Fish") Cafaro on grounds of dangerousness. They did, and the district court so found. Salerno thereafter spent the rest of his life in federal custody.

Is it constitutional for the government to lock up people without waiting to convict them at trial? If it is, what are the limits on the government's power to lock up anyone it deems dangerous? These are issues raised by preventive detention provisions in bail statutes, and addressed in *United States v. Salerno*. The controversy about these bail statutes, once so hotly contested, has died down. But the broader questions about the government's power to detain suspected criminals without giving them the benefit of full criminal process remain unresolved, and have taken on a new urgency as the nation confronts an increased threat of terrorist attacks.

---

[1] I was not in court when Salerno was brought in. But I did spend a lot of time with him during trial, and I saw many of pictures of him immediately prior to his arrest. For a fuller disclosure of my connection to *United States v. Salerno*: As a summer assistant, I helped with electronic surveillance paperwork. Then, after a year of clerking for Chief Judge Wilfred Feinberg and a year clerking for Justice Thurgood Marshall—who both authored dissents in Salerno during years I was not working for them—I became an Assistant U.S. Attorney, just in time to play a small part in the Salerno trial, and quite a large part in the appeals that followed. I also dealt with Cafaro when he was a cooperating witness.

Bail Background

The origins of the institution of bail in the United States lie in medieval England. There, people accused of crimes were (in numbers and circumstances that varied over time) allowed to remain at liberty pending trial—which could be far off, depending on the arrival of a traveling judge. All it took was the promise of the accused, or that of an acceptable surety, that the accused would appear for trial. Over the centuries, the system developed into one that allowed release upon a surety's pledge of money that would be forfeit should the accused fail to appear.[2]

It could be abused however, particularly when the Crown wanted to use bail as a tool of political oppression. Indeed, among the grievances against James II listed in the 1689 Bill of Rights was that "excessive bail hath been required of persons committed in criminal cases to elude the benefit of the laws made for the liberty of the subjects." The remedy established by the new constitutional order was a guarantee against "excessive bail."[3] Many defendants still languished in Newgate and other English jails before trial even after 1689,[4] but the importance of the right (at least in principle) was thus recognized.

In the United States, the guarantee in the English Bill of Rights was echoed in the Eighth Amendment to the Constitution: "Excessive bail shall not be required, nor excessive fines imposed, nor cruel and unusual punishments inflicted." Perhaps the Framers and their English predecessors could have been somewhat clearer. This amendment barred courts from imposing "excessive" bail conditions. But is there an absolute constitutional right to bail to begin with? If there is not, as Professor Caleb Foote pointed out, Congress could render the bail clause "entirely moot by enacting legislation denying the right to bail in all cases."[5] In a 1952 case, *Carlson v. Landon,*[6] however, the Supreme Court adhered to a more literal, and limited, interpretation of the bail clause:

> "The bail clause was lifted with slight changes from the Bill of Rights Act. In England, that clause has never been thought to accord a right to bail in all cases, but merely to provide that bail

---

[2] *See* William F. Duker, The Right to Bail: A Historical Inquiry, 42 Albany L. Rev. 33 (1977); Daniel J. Freed & Patricia M. Wald, Bail in the United States: 1964, at 1–2 (1964) (prepared as a working paper for the National Conference on Bail and Criminal Justice).

[3] An Act Declaring the Rights and Liberties of the Subject and Settling the Succession of the Crown, 1 Wm. & M., Sess 2, ch.2, 10.

[4] *See* John H. Langbein, The Origins of Adversary Criminal Trial, 49–51 (2003) (discussing Eighteenth Century English pretrial detention).

[5] Caleb Foote, The Coming Constitutional Crisis in Bail, 113 U. Pa. L. Rev. 959, 969 (1965).

[6] 342 U.S. 524 (1952).

shall not be excessive in those cases where it is proper to grant bail. When this clause was carried over in our Bill of Rights, nothing was said that indicated any different concept. The Eighth Amendment has not prohibited Congress from defining the classes of cases in which bail shall be allowed in this country."[7]

An important piece of evidence favoring the Supreme Court's limited reading was that in the Judiciary Act of 1789, which Congress debated even as it considered the Bill of Rights, the right to bail was qualified: "[U]pon all arrests in criminal cases, bail shall be admitted, except where the punishment may be death, in which cases it shall not be admitted but by [judges] who shall exercise their discretion therein, regarding the nature and circumstances of the offense, and of the evidence, and the usages of law."[8] At the time, "the great majority of criminal offenses involving a threat of serious physical injury or death to the victim were punishable by death under state laws" and under federal laws, to the limited extent that federal law address these sorts of crimes.[9] Since most of the original thirteen colonies had similar provisions— constraining judicial bail decisions, but leaving the decision about which offenses were bailable to the legislature[10]—the Supreme Court's reading of the bail clause was quite defensible.

Against this constitutional backdrop, the federal government and the states had considerable latitude in how they structured their bail systems. Their general approach was to sit back and allow the market to flourish. This it did, as during the mid-nineteenth century, with increasing population mobility, commercial bail bondsmen moved in to take the place of private sureties.[11] In return for a nonrefundable money premium, these firms guaranteed a defendant's appearance at trial; if he fled, they would forfeit their bonds (although they would sometimes be able to recoup their loss from the defendant or his relatives, if those people had signed indemnification contracts).[12] This system entailed a remarkable outsourcing of criminal justice authority, without parallel outside the United States.[13] But it was comfortable for court officials, who relied on

---

[7] *Id.* at 545–46.

[8] Judiciary Act of 1789, ch. 20, § 33, 1 Stat. 91 (1789).

[9] John N. Mitchell, Bail Reform and the Constitutionality of Pretrial Detention, 55 Va. L. Rev. 1223, 1227 (1969).

[10] *See* Duker, *supra* note 2, at 82.

[11] Barry Mahoney, et al. Pretrial Services Programs: Responsibilities and Potential. National Institute of Justice, NCJ 181939, at 7 (2001).

[12] Freed & Wald, *supra* note 2, at 3.

[13] *Id.* at 22 ("A study by the United Nations recently disclosed that the United States and the Philippines are the only countries to allot a significant role to professional bail bondsmen in their systems of criminal justice.")

bail bondsmen to manage the population of arrested persons, and in turn helped ensure the profitability of selling bail bonds.[14]

In the 1950s, studies in Chicago, Philadelphia and New York conducted by Professor Foote and others highlighted the painful inadequacies of this system. They showed

> the dominating role played by bondsmen in the administration of bail, the lack of any meaningful consideration to the issue of bail by the courts, and the detention of large numbers of defendants who could and should have been released but were not because bail, even in modest amounts was beyond their means. The studies also revealed that bail was used to "punish" defendants prior to a determination of guilt or to "protect" society from anticipated future conduct, neither of which is permissible purpose of bail; that defendants detained prior to trial often spent months in jail only to be acquitted or to receive a suspended sentence after conviction; and that jails were severely overcrowded with pretrial detainees housed in conditions far worse than convicted criminals.[15]

Responding to these studies, and to high-level efforts throughout the country to put bail reform on the legislative agenda, numerous jurisdictions passed new bail statutes in the 1960s. Leading the way was the federal government—in part because of the leadership of Attorney General Robert Kennedy and Senator Sam J. Ervin, Jr.,[16] but also because criminal justice reform in the federal system is far easier than in state systems, which handle so many more defendants, and in particular defendants accused of violent crimes. The result was the federal Bail Reform Act of 1966[17] which required that every defendant—save those charged with an offense punishable by death—be released on his own recognizance (a simple promise to return to court when required) unless the court determined that "such release will not reasonably assurance the appearance of the person as required." The starting point was thus to be simple release. Bond was to be imposed only to the extent necessary to assure the defendant's return. The drafters explained the limited purpose of this regime:

---

[14] Forrest Dill, Discretion, Exchange and Social Control: Bail Bondsmen in Criminal Courts, 9 Law & Soc'y Rev. 639, 670 (1975).

[15] Wayne H. Thomas, Bail Reform in America 15 (1976); *see* John S. Goldkamp et al., Personal Liberty and Community Safety: Pretrial Release in the Criminal Court xi (1995). For an intriguing proposal, under which defendants would be compensated for pretrial detention, *see* William H. Landes, The Bail System: An Economic Approach, 2 J. Legal Stud. 79 (1973); *see also* Jeffrey Manns, Liberty Takings: A Framework for Compensating Pretrail Detainees, 26 Cardozo L. Rev. 1947 (2005).

[16] *See* 6–7; 161–64.

[17] Pub. L. No. 89–465, June 22, 1966, 80 Stat. 214, codified in part as 18 U.S.C. §§ 3141 to 3151, and subsequently repealed by Pub. L. No. 98–473, Title II, 203(a), Oct. 12, 1984, 98 Stat. 1976.

This legislation does not deal with the problem of the preventive detention of the accused because of the possibility that his liberty might endanger the public. . . . It must be remembered that under American criminal jurisprudence pretrial bail may not be used as a device to protect society from the possible commission of additional crimes by the accused.[18]

Such broad pronouncements in the legislative history of the 1966 Act did not mean that the possibility of considering a defendant's dangerousness in bail decisions had been removed from the table. Immediately upon becoming President, after a campaign in which anti-crime rhetoric had figured prominently, Richard Nixon proposed amending the Act to permit "temporary pretrial detention" of criminal defendants whose "pretrial release presents a clear danger to the community."[19] While this proposal did not make immediate headway, the administration, with important assistance from William H. Rehnquist, then the Assistant Attorney General in charge of the Justice Department's Office of Legal Counsel,[20] soon gained passage of a preventive detention statute for the District of Columbia.[21] However, while many predicted that the new D.C. statute would be used as a model for similar legislation by the states, only twelve states made moves in this direction during the 1970s.[22] One reason states may have held back was uncertainty about the constitutionality of the D.C. statute. Once that was (narrowly) upheld by the Court of Appeals of the District of Columbia in 1981,[23] many more states adopted similar provisions.[24]

---

[18] H.R. Rep. No. 1541, 89th Cong., 2d Sess. 5–6, *reprinted in* 1966 U.S. Code Cong. & Admin. News 2293, 2296; *see* John B. Howard, Jr., Note, The Trial of Pretrial Dangerousness: Preventive Detention After United States v. Salerno, 75 Va. L. Rev. 639, 643 (1989).

[19] John N. Mitchell, Bail Reform and the Constitutionality of Pretrial Detention, 55 Va. L. Rev. 1223, 1223 (1969). It should be noted that when John Mitchell was later arrested, in 1973, charged with obstructing an S.E.C. investigation of Robert Vesco, he was released on bail. *See* Photograph, Mitchell Denies Charges, N.Y. Times, May 22, 1973, at A1 (showing former Attorney General John N. Mitchell leaving federal court after pleading not guilty).

[20] Albert W. Alschuler, Preventive Pretrial Detention and the Failure of Interest–Balancing Approaches to Due Process, 85 Mich. L. Rev. 510, 512 note 3 (1986).

[21] Howard, *supra* note 18, at 645; *see* Marc Miller & Martin Guggenheim, Pretrial Detention and Punishment, 75 Minn. L. Rev. 335, 340 (1990) (noting that "pretrial detention system in the District of Columbia was the first expressly based upon the threat of criminality before trial").

[22] Barbara Gottlieb, Public Danger as a Factor in Pretrial Release: A Comparative Analysis of State Laws 19 (National Institute of Justice: July 1985).

[23] United States v. Edwards, 430 A.2d 1321 (D.C. 1981), *cert. denied*, 455 U.S. 1022 (1982).

[24] Gottlieb, *supra* note 22, at 20.

The interest of legislators around the country in preventive detention statutes was not sparked simply by developments in constitutional
law. There really *was* a crime problem: In 1960, the murder rate (per
100,000) had been 5.1. In 1980, it was 10.2. (It was back down to 5.6 in
2002). In 1960, the violent crime rate had been 1,887.2; in 1980, it was
5,950.0. (In 2002, it was 4,118.8.).[25] It was not clear how many crimes
were being committed by criminal defendants out on bail,[26] but, in this
environment, Congress was far more receptive to preventive detention
provisions. A 1984 Senate report noted that the "broad base of support
for giving judges the authority to weigh risks to community safety in
pretrial release decisions is a reflection of the deep public concern, which
the Committee shares, about the growing problem of crimes committed
by persons on release."[27]

Yet there was another factor as well, one that had as much to do
with restraining government power as with restraining dangerous defendants. Even though the 1966 Bail Reform Act did not authorize consideration of dangerousness, a Senate Report found ample evidence that
judges did so anyway when setting bail, and would regularly impose
"excessively stringent release conditions, and in particular extraordinarily high money bonds, in order to achieve detention." The fault, it was
argued, lay less with the judges than with a statute that prevented the
judges from candidly addressing a critical societal concern: "Providing
statutory authority to conduct a hearing focused on the issue of a
defendant's dangerousness and to permit an order of detention where a
defendant poses such a risk to others that no form of conditional release
is sufficient, would allow the courts to address the issue of pretrial
criminality honestly and effectively."[28] As one scholar noted: "[I]f punishment before trial is to be minimized for most felony defendants, it
may be necessary to be more candid about the uses of bail as a means of
preventive detention. This would elevate the importance of process and
how decisions are made since the rationale for preventive detention
would have to be clearly stated before taking such a step."[29]

---

[25] U.S. Census Bureau, *Statistical Abstract of the United States*, at HS–23 (2003)
("Crimes and Crime Rates by Type of Offense": 1960–2002).

[26] *See* Miller & Guggenheim, *supra* note 21, at 397–405.

[27] S. Rep. No. 225, 98th Cong., 2d. Sess., 6, *reprinted in* 1984 U.S. Code Cong. &
Admin. News, 3182, 3188.

[28] *Id.* at 11, *reprinted in* 1984 U.S. Code Cong. & Admin. News, at 3194.

[29] Roy B. Flemming, Punishment Before Trial: An Organizational Perspective of
Felony Bail Processes 155 (1982).

Out of these various currents came the Bail Reform Act of 1984, part of the Comprehensive Crime Control Act of 1984.[30] Continuing the general presumption of pretrial release from the 1966 Act, the new law nonetheless provided that if a "judicial officer" (judge or magistrate) found that "no condition or combination of conditions" would "reasonably assure" not just the "appearance of the [defendant] as required" but also the "safety of any other person and the community," the judicial officer "shall order the detention of the person before trial."[31] This detention order could be entered only after an adversarial hearing, at which, although the rules of evidence would not apply, the defendant had a right to counsel, and could call and cross-examine witnesses. The government bore the burden of showing dangerousness by "clear and convincing evidence"[32]—not "proof beyond a reasonable doubt" (the standard for convicting a defendant at trial), but more demanding than the "preponderance of evidence" standard that usually applies in pretrial factfinding, and indeed applies when the government seeks to show that a defendant should be detained as a flight risk. Still, there was a presumption (albeit a rebuttable one) that a defendant posed a risk of both flight and danger where there was "probable cause to believe" that the defendant had committed a narcotics offense for which the "maximum term of imprisonment" was ten years or more, or had used a gun in connection with a crime of violence, or under certain other circumstances, including where not more than five years had elapsed since the defendant's release from imprisonment on state or federal narcotics or violent crime charges.[33] To clear up any misperceptions, the statute noted: "Nothing in this section shall be construed as modifying or limiting the presumption of innocence."[34]

The new bail statute was immediately the subject of numerous legal challenges in the lower courts. The first case to reach the United States Supreme Court involving this or any of the other state preventive detention statutes was that of Anthony Salerno.

Salerno Case Background

No one would ever have called Anthony Salerno "the Dapper Don." An obituary writer later paid tribute to his subdued sartorial tastes: "Unlike younger Mafia leaders like John Gotti, Mr. Salerno typified a

---

[30] Pub. L. No. 98–473, 98 Stat. 1976 (codified as amended at 18 U.S.C. §§ 1, 3141–3151).

[31] 18 U.S.C. § 3142(e).

[32] 18 U.S.C. § 3142(f).

[33] 18 U.S.C. § 3142(e).

[34] 18 U.S.C. § 3142(j).

more old-fashioned gangster ethic that frowned on flamboyance that might attract attention. In sharp contrast to Mr. Gotti's $1,000 designer suits, he was known to hold counsel dressed in a fedora and T-shirt."[35] From his base in East Harlem, however, Salerno built Harlem's biggest numbers racket and solidified his place in the Genovese Family hierarchy. In 1977, alleging that his numbers operation was taking in at least $10 million annually, federal authorities brought gambling and tax charges against Salerno.[36] After two mistrials on the tax counts, however, he plead the case out and received a six month sentence.[37] But the heat would soon get more intense.

By the time Salerno, then age 74, was arrested on March 21, 1986, on the charges for which he would be detained, he probably felt rather comfortable in federal court. In fact, he was already out on bail on another federal racketeering indictment, also filed in the Southern District of New York (in Manhattan).

That prior indictment, unsealed on February 26, 1985, charged that Salerno was the boss of the Genovese Family and a member of the "commission" that "had the power to resolve disputes and to regulate relations between and among La Cosa Nostra Families."[38] Among other things, Salerno and his co-defendants (who included Gambino boss Paul Castellano until his murder on December 16, 1985, outside Spark's Steakhouse[39]) were charged with using their control over the concrete workers union to control the allocation of large concrete construction jobs in New York, and with resolving a leadership dispute within the Bonanno Family by authorizing the murder of that family's boss, Carmine Galante.

The "Commission" indictment was just one component of a broad structural attack on "traditional" organized crime in New York City— "traditional" being the way law enforcement distinguished the five Mafia families and associates from the "emerging" or "non-traditional" groups of non-Italian origins that would strut the boards by the 1990s. The statutory tool for this attack, the Racketeer Influenced and Corrupt

---

[35] James Dao, Anthony (Fat Tony) Salerno, 80, A Top Crime Boss, Dies in Prison, N.Y. Times, July 29, 1992, at D19.

[36] See Arnold H. Lubasch, Reputed Organized–Crime Figure Charged With Running a $10 Million Yearly Racket, N.Y. Times, May 4, 1977, at 29.

[37] See Arnold H. Lubasch, Salerno, 67, Given 6 Months in Prison In Gambling Case, N.Y. Times, Apr. 20, 1978, at D20.

[38] James B. Jacobs, Christopher Panarella & Jay Worthington, Busting the Mob: United States v. Cosa Nostra 95 (1994) (excerpting from indictment).

[39] John Gotti, Castellano's successor as head of the Gambino family, was later convicted for his role in the murder. United States v. Locascio, 6 F.3d 924 (2d Cir. 1993).

Organizations ("RICO") Act had been on the books since 1970. And the FBI had seriously targeted La Cosa Nostra at least since J. Edgar Hoover acknowledged its existence in the late 1950s.[40] In the early 1980s, however, the Justice Department strategy evolved from piecemeal take-downs into larger scale cases designed to dismantle whole chunks of families. This strategy predated the arrival of Rudolph W. Giuliani as U.S. Attorney the Southern District of New York in 1983, but was given new energy and focus by Giuliani's high-profile methods.[41] Salerno was certainly a conspicuous target in these efforts, having topped *Fortune Magazine*'s Fall 1986 list of the "50 Biggest Mafia Bosses."

After Salerno's arrest on the "Commission" indictment, he was released on bail, set at $2 million.[42]

In March 1986, months before trial began on the "Commission" indictment, Salerno was arrested again. This indictment that, like the prior one, charged violations of the RICO Act. While the focus of the "Commission" indictment had been horizontal—arrangements between and among Cosa Nostra families—the focus of the new indictment was vertical. The enterprise charged here was "the Genovese Organized Crime Family" and the defendants were all members or associates of that family. Salerno was, again, alleged to be the Boss of the Family, and, among the other defendants, Vincent ("Fish") Cafaro was alleged to be a "capo" (a lieutenant). The racketeering activity charged in this indictment included acts relating to the bid-rigging scheme charged in the Commission indictment; a scheme to elect and control the president of the Teamsters International; sundry acts of extortion, and illegal numbers and bookmaking operations.[43] Among the other defendants charged in the indictment were Matthew ("Matty the Horse") Ianniello, a longtime "capo" in the Genovese Family; Nicholas Auletta, whose concrete company became the largest concrete construction company in New York as a result of the illegal bid rigging scheme, and Edward ("Biff") Halloran, whose alliance with the mob allowed him to obtain a virtual monopoly over the supply of concrete in Manhattan.[44]

---

[40] *See* Tony G. Poveda, "Controversies and Issues," in Athan G. Theoharis, The FBI: A Comprehensive Reference Guide, 101, 119–20 (1999).

[41] *See* Selwyn Raab, Curbing Mob Chiefs, N.Y. Times, Feb. 27, 1985, at B2; Leslie Maitland Werner, U.S. Officials Cite Key Successes in War Against Organized Crime, N.Y. Times, Nov. 7, 1983, at A1; *see also* James B. Jacobs, *supra*.

[42] *See* Arnold H. Lubasch, U.S. Indictment Says 9 Governed New York Mafia, N.Y. Times, Feb. 27, 1985, at A1.

[43] United States v. Salerno, 631 F. Supp. 1364 (S.D.N.Y. 1986).

[44] Brief for the United States in United States v. Salerno, 88–1464 (2d Cir.), at 10–11.

At Salerno and Cafaro's arraignment, the government conceded that neither defendant posed a risk of flight, but it moved that both be detained on the ground that no bail condition or combination of bail conditions would assure the safety of the community or any person. At a detention hearing, a few days later, the government called no actual witness but "proffered"[45] evidence derived from court-ordered electronic surveillance at various locations, including the Palma Boy Social Club, the club in East Harlem where Salerno seemed to spend most of his waking hours when he was in New York City (and not at his residence in rustic Rhinebeck, N.Y.). These conversations provided graphic proof of the violence with which Cafaro, under Salerno's occasional supervision, ran the gambling operation.

More powerful, however, was the government's proffer of the prospective testimony of two mob turncoats, James ("Jimmy the Weasel") Fratianno and Angelo Lonardo, the former head of the Cleveland Family that reported to the Genovese Family in New York. Fratianno had long been a star witness in mob prosecutions.[46] As he had at a previous trial, Fratianno was prepared to testify that, back in 1976, he had attended a meeting in the back room of a store at which Salerno and other Genovese Family members had voted a "hit" on a Family loanshark, John Spencer Ullo. The district court later noted that the " 'contract' was not carried out when Ullo got wind of the plan in California and was himself able to kill the hitman."[47]

The proffer from Lonardo may well have been more significant, in part because it involved more recent murderous plotting by Salerno and in part because the lateness of Lonardo's cooperation—he had not started cooperating with the government until August 1985—gave the government a reason to explain why their position on Salerno's bail had changed since the "Commission" indictment.[48] Lonardo had told of Salerno's direct involvement in a 1980 "contract" that *was* carried out, on one John Simone, a/k/a "Johnny Keyes," and in two other murder conspiracies.

---

[45] Such proffers had previously been found an acceptable way for the government to meet its burden in detention hearings. *See* United States v. Martir, 782 F.2d 1141 (2d Cir. 1986).

[46] For more on Fratianno's checkered career as a mobster and government witness, *see* Ovid Demaris, The Last Mafioso (1986). *Also see* Michael J. Zuckerman, Vengeance Is Mine: Jimmy the Weasel Fratianno Tells How He Brought the Kiss of Death to the Mafia (1987).

[47] 631 F. Supp. at 1367.

[48] The admissibility of statements that Lonardo made to a narcotics co-conspirator before Lonardo's conviction and eventual cooperation were at issue in another Supreme Court case, decided less than a month after the Salerno bail decision. Bourjaily v. United States, 483 U.S. 171 (1987).

Salerno's ability to order "hits" was corroborated by intercepted conversations. In one, from January 1985, a Genovese loanshark asked his permission to kill a debtor. Salerno responded: "If you want to kill him, we will kill him."[49] An intercept from 1984 also caught Salerno announcing what he would say if a debtor questioned his status: "Who am I? I'm the f_____g boss."

Salerno proffered more than a dozen witnesses, ready to testify that "they had known Salerno for many years, considered him a friend, and did not consider him to be any danger to the community." He also proffered a letter from his doctor telling of "a long standing history of high blood pressure complicated by congestive heart failure."[50]

In an opinion issued April 2, 1986, Judge John M. Walker, Jr., concluded that the government had "met its burden of proof by clear and convincing evidence." The information the court had received of Salerno's danger to the community, Judge Walker noted, was "overwhelming." "By 'clear and convincing' proof, the government has established that Salerno is the head, or 'Boss,' of an organization engaged in extortion, loansharking, illegal gambling, and murder. ... The government has proffered information showing that Salerno could order a murder merely by voicing his assent with the single word 'hit.' "[51] Finding "ample information to conclude that Cafaro and others under Salerno's control [had] the means to carry out the violent acts," the court also noted that "[n]owhere does Salerno claim that his vascular condition will affect his ability to run the Genovese Family enterprise if he is released."

Judge Walker also reviewed the evidence of the violence with which Cafaro managed his gambling operation and noted:

> The activities of a criminal organization such as the Genovese Family do not cease with the arrest of its principals and their release on even the most stringent of bail conditions. The illegal businesses, in place for many years, require constant attention and protection, or they will fail. Under these circumstances, this court recognizes a strong incentive on the part of its leadership to continue business as usual. When business as usual involves threats, beatings, and murder, the present danger such people pose to the community is self-evident.[52]

The MCC

Pursuant to Judge Walker's order, Salerno and Cafaro were detained in the Metropolitan Correctional Center ("MCC") in downtown

---

[49] 631 F. Supp. at 1368.

[50] 631 F. Supp. at 1370.

[51] 631 F. Supp. at 1371.

[52] 631 F. Supp. at 1375.

Manhattan, adjacent to the federal courthouse. Despite its title, the MCC is a short-term custodial facility, designed to primarily to house pretrial detainees. In a 1979 Supreme Court case arising out of complaints that the conditions of confinement in the MCC were unconstitutional, the Court painted an almost rosy picture of the facility, built just four years earlier: "The MCC differs markedly from the familiar image of a jail; there are no barred cells, dank colorless corridors, or clanging steel gates. It was intended to include the most advanced and innovative features of modern design of detention facilities."[53]

But a jail it was. The 1979 case noted that MCC inmates were locked into their rooms at night and during "head counts"; "were not permitted to receive packages from outside the facility containing items of food or personal property, except for one package of food at Christmas," and were subject to unannounced searches of their rooms, and to visual body cavity searches after every contact visit with a person from outside. Indeed, pretrial detention facilities are often more forbidding than the prisons to which defendants are sent if they are convicted. This is less a result of legal rules than of the iron laws of real estate: Prisons can be placed in suburban or rural areas, where there is ample space for outdoor activities. Jails, at least those used for detaining defendants facing trial in metropolitan jurisdictions, cannot be too far from the courthouses they serve.[54] That puts them in areas where space is at a premium. And whatever efforts are being made to provide recreational and educational opportunities to prisoners are not likely to be focused on short-termers like those in detention facilities.

Court of Appeals

After Judge Mary Johnson Lowe, to whom the case was assigned for trial, refused to reconsider Judge Walker's detention order, Salerno and Cafaro appealed both judges' decisions to the Second Circuit Court of Appeals. There, they raised several statutory challenges, including one claiming that the evidence presented was insufficient to support Judge Walker's findings. They also raised a constitutional claim: that detaining a defendant on the ground that "his release would pose a danger to the community or any person" violated the due process clause.

A three-judge Second Circuit panel heard the case with appropriate dispatch and rendered a decision on July 3, 1986. The court made short

---

[53] Bell v. Wolfish, 441 U.S. 520, 525 (1979).

[54] When pretrial detainees are housed too far away from courthouses where they will be tried, as they all too frequently are, their lawyers are severely handicapped in preparing for trial or engaging in plea negotiations. *See* Douglas J. Klein, Note, The Pretrial Detention "Crisis": The Causes and the Cure, 52 J. Urban & Contemp. L. 281, 295–96 (1997).

work of the defendants' statutory claims and found that their detention order did not violate the Bail Reform Act. But it found the Act unconstitutional. While pretrial detention could properly be used to address a risk of flight or a danger that a defendant would "tamper with or intimidate witnesses or jurors," it could not be used as a regulatory measure to protect the community generally against future crimes. The Act's authorization of detention on this ground, Judge Amalia Kearse wrote, was "repugnant to the concept of substantive due process, which we believe prohibits the total deprivation of liberty simply as a means of preventing future crimes."

The very concept of a "substantive" procedural protection is elusive, and to its critics like Justices Antonin Scalia and Clarence Thomas and others, mis-begotten.[55] The Supreme Court, however, has long held that the due process clause "contains a substantive component that bars certain arbitrary, wrongful government actions" regardless of the fairness of the procedures used to implement them.[56] The doctrine's malleability has made it a powerful instrument of judicial power, to be used for good or ill, with the definition of "good" or "ill" often being in the mind of the beholder. Among its more notable applications have been in Lochner v. New York[57] (declaring a New York maximum-hours statute for bakers unconstitutional); Roe v. Wade[58] (striking down abortion statute), and Lawrence v. Texas[59] (striking down Texas sodomy statute).[60]

To distinguish this substantive application of the due process clause from procedural applications, Judge Kearse drew on a recent opinion by another member of the panel, Judge Jon O. Newman, in a different detention case. Judge Newman had explained:

> Incarcerating dangerous persons not accused of any crime would exceed due process limits not simply for lack of procedural protec-

---

[55] *See* Troxel v. Granville, 530 U.S. 57, 80 (2000) (Thomas, J., concurring in the judgment) (noting readiness to reconsider "our substantive due process cases" as inconsistent with "the original understanding of the Due Process Clause"); Albright v. Oliver, 510 U.S. 266, 275–76 (1994) (Scalia, J., concurring); John Hart Ely, Democracy and Distrust: A Theory of Judicial Review 18 (1980) (" 'Substantive due process' is a contradiction in terms—sort of like 'green pastel redness.' ").

[56] Zinermon v. Burch, 494 U.S. 113, 125 (1990) (quoting Daniels v. Williams, 474 U.S. 327, 331 (1986)).

[57] 198 U.S. 45 (1905).

[58] 410 U.S. 113, 155 (1973).

[59] 539 U.S. 558 (2003).

[60] *See* Laurence H. Tribe, Lawrence v. Texas: The "Fundamental Right" that Dare Not Speak Its Name, 117 Harv. L. Rev. 1893 (2004).

tions. Even if a statute provided that a person could be incarcerated for dangerousness only after a jury was persuaded that his dangerousness had been established beyond a reasonable doubt at a trial surrounded with all of the procedural guarantees applicable to determinations of guilt, the statute could not be upheld, no matter how brief the period of detention. It would be constitutionally infirm, not for lack of procedural due process, but because *the total deprivation of liberty as a means of preventing future crime exceeds the substantive limitations of the Due Process Clause.* This means of promoting public safety would be beyond the constitutional pale. The system of criminal justice contemplated by the Due Process Clause—indeed, by all of the criminal justice guarantees of the Bill of Rights—is a system of announcing in statutes of adequate clarity what conduct is prohibited and then invoking the penalties of the law against those who have committed crimes. *The liberty protected under that system is premised on the accountability of free men and women for what they have done, not for what they may do. The Due Process Clause reflects the constitutional imperative that incarceration to protect society from criminals may be accomplished only as punishment of those convicted for past crimes and not as regulation* of those feared likely to commit future crimes.[61]

Judge Kearse also offered an answer to the hypothetical offered by the third member of the panel, Chief Judge Wilfred Feinberg, who dissented from her opinion. Chief Judge Feinberg had observed: "[I]f a member of a terrorist organization is indicted for blowing up an airliner for political reasons and there is clear and persuasive evidence that the defendant will do so again if not confined, it is not self-evident to me that society must nevertheless immediately release him on bail until he is tried."[62] Judge Kearse answered:

Even the risk of some serious crime ... must, under our Constitution, be guarded against by surveillance of the suspect and prompt trial on any pending charges, and not by incarceration simply because untested evidence indicates probable cause to believe he has committed one crime and is a risk to commit another one. Surveillance would doubtless be the government's response if confidential information, not disclosable to obtain an indictment, alerted the government to such a risk by a person not charged with a crime. It should be no less effective in cases where an indictment has been returned, even assuming, which is unlikely, that a person posing

---

[61] 794 F.2d at 72 (quoting United States v. Melendez–Carrion, 790 F.2d 984, 1001 (2d Cir. 1986) (emphasis added in Salerno)).

[62] 794 F.2d at 77.

such a risk would not be detained despite a well-grounded fear that he would flee.[63]

In his dissent, Chief Judge Feinberg reviewed the due process precedents and highlighted the procedural protections of the Bail Reform Act. He concluded that "detaining indicted defendants under the Bail Reform Act for a limited time on the basis of clear and convincing evidence that nothing short of confinement will prevent them from violating the law while on release does not violate any norm of decency implicit in the concept of ordered liberty, and does not violate the Due Process Clause."[64] Having resolved that the Act was not unconstitutional on its face, Chief Judge Feinberg would also have found that the detention of Salerno and Cafaro for "a little over three months" had not, under the circumstances, "degenerated into punishment."[65]

Later in July, the government sought review of the Second Circuit's decision in the Supreme Court. On November 3, 1986, the Supreme Court agreed to hear the case because of the conflict among the Circuits. As the Court later noted, "[e]very other Court of Appeals to have considered the validity of the Bail Reform Act of 1984 has rejected the facial constitutional challenge."[66]

Meanwhile, the trial of Salerno and his co-defendants on the "Commission" indictment went forward on September 8, 1986. It ended on November 19, 1986, with a verdict of guilty on all counts and on all racketeering acts. On January 13, 1987—less than two weeks before the Supreme Court was to hear arguments regarding Salerno and Cafaro's detention—District Judge Richard Owen sentenced Salerno to 100 years' imprisonment. Judge Owen, however, took care not to render the issue of Salerno's pre-trial detention moot. The bail statute shifted the burden of proof for convicted defendants and permitted their release on bail pending appeal only where a court found "by clear and convincing evidence that the person is not likely to flee or pose a danger to the safety of any person or the community if released." Nonetheless, Judge Owen ordered that, "[i]nasmuch as defendant Anthony Salerno was not ordered detained in this case, but is presently being detained pretrial in [the Genovese Family case]," Salerno's bail status in the Commission case would "remain the same . . . pending further order of the Court."[67]

---

[63] 794 F.2d at 74.

[64] 794 F.2d at 77–78.

[65] 794 F.2d at 79.

[66] 481 U.S. at 741 (citing cases).

[67] Salerno, 481 U.S. 756 note 1 (Marshall, J., dissenting).

Although Salerno's bail status thus did not change while he awaited oral argument on his detention order before the Supreme Court, Cafaro's status decidedly did. On October 9, 1986, Judge Lowe ordered that he be released "temporarily for medical care and treatment."[68] Bail was set at a $1 million personal recognizance bond, with the government's consent.[69] Why the government had become so solicitous of Cafaro's health was not quite clear at the time. After all, Salerno's proffered medical testimony had won him only a direction from Judge Walker to the Warden of Metropolitan Correctional Center in downtown Manhattan, where Salerno was being held, "to permit Salerno to receive his regular medication and . . . use an exercise bike twice a day, every day."[70] It was only later, on March 20, 1987, after the Supreme Court had heard oral argument on the bail issue, that real reason for Cafaro's release emerged. That day, U.S. Attorney Giuliani announced that Cafaro had been cooperating with the government since the fall, and had made a controlled purchase of four pounds of high-purity heroin for $420,000 from Ralph ("the General") Tutino, whom Giuliani described as "a major Mafia drug dealer."[71] In return for Cafaro's cooperation, the government had agreed to let him plead to a single racketeering count, and to drop the charges then pending against Cafaro's son, Thomas.[72]

The risk that the government will use pretrial detention as a means of putting pressure on defendants to cooperate is a real one, and one highlighted by Justice Marshall in his Supreme Court dissent. It would be unfair to assume that this is what happened here, or even that the allure of immediate release from detention was the main factor in Cafaro's decision to break his Cosa Nostra oaths of secrecy and loyalty. The chance to obtain immunity for his son Thomas might well have played an important role. One ought not lightly to make assumptions about Cafaro's personal calculus, particularly in matters involving Thomas. According to one recent report, even after cooperating Cafaro withheld information from the FBI as part of a deal with a Genovese leader, in return for protection for Thomas from retaliation.[73]

---

[68] 481 U.S. at 757.

[69] *Id.* at 757–58.

[70] 631 F. Supp. at 1374.

[71] Arnold H. Lubasch, Major Mafia Leader Turns Informer, Secretly Recording Meeting of Mob, N.Y. Times, Mar. 21, 1987, at 31; *see* United States v. Tutino, 883 F.2d 1125 (2d Cir. 1989).

[72] United States v. Cafaro, WL 138180 (S.D.N.Y. 1988).

[73] *See* Jerry Capeci, Gangland, Feb. 6, 2003, available at <http://ganglandnews.com/column316.htm>

On April 6, 1987, the day trial began for Salerno and his ten co-defendants, the government moved to sever proceedings against Vincent and Thomas Cafaro. The trial would go on for thirteen months, ending May 4, 1988.[74]

Supreme Court

By the time Salerno's challenge to his detention reached the Supreme Court, the facts of the case had lost any legal importance. His was a facial challenge to the Bail Reform Act, one that freed his counsel (Cafaro understandably did not send a lawyer), and the Court, from any obligation to navigate the gritty realities of the New York underworld. With this freedom from ugly facts came a heavy legal burden, however—one that required him to "establish that no set of circumstances exist[ed] under which the Act would be valid."[75] Indeed, as Chief Justice Rehnquist noted at the beginning of his opinion for the Court, handed down on May 26, 1987: "The fact the [] Act might operate unconstitutionally under some conceivable set of circumstances is insufficient to render it wholly invalid," since it was only in the limited First Amendment context—where a defendant could claim that, say, his freedom of speech was being "chilled" by the mere presence of an expansive statute—that a statute could be challenged as overbroad.[76] In other words, if the Court could imagine any person under any circumstances whom it would not be unconstitutional to detain pretrial on dangerousness grounds, Salerno would lose.

One nagging factual issue Rehnquist had to deal with was the dissent's assertion that the case had been mooted out by the combination of Salerno's 100–year sentence in the "Commission" case and Cafaro's cooperation and release. Rehnquist disposed of the point in a footnote: Salerno had been released on bail in the "Commission" case and the detention order at issue remained the authority for Salerno's incarceration. "The case is therefore very much alive and is properly presented for resolution."[77]

---

[74] United States v. Salerno, 937 F.2d 797 (2d Cir. 1991).

[75] 481 U.S. at 745.

[76] *Id.; see also* Schall v. Martin, 467 U.S. 253 note 18 (1984); New York v. Ferber, 458 U.S. 747 (1982). The doctrine in this area is somewhat less than clear. *See* Michael C. Dorf, Facial Challenges to State and Federal Statutes, 46 Stan. L. Rev. 235 (1994). But the Court recently noted: "[W]e have recognized the validity of facial attacks alleging overbreadth [] in relatively few settings, and, generally, on the strength of specific reasons weighty enough to overcome our well-founded reticence." Sabri v. United States, 541 U.S. 600, 609–610 (2004).

[77] 481 U.S. at 744 note 2.

Rehnquist then turned to the merits of Salerno's constitutional challenges, starting with his substantive due process claim. The essence of this claim was that Salerno's pretrial detention constituted "punishment" and that the only way such punishment could be constitutionally inflicted was after a full-blown criminal trial. Implicit in the Court's treatment of this threshold issue was its recognition of the enormous doctrinal consequences that follow from labeling adverse treatment by the state as "punishment." For the government to "punish" a criminal defendant before he ever faced trial—and had all the benefit of trial rights like the right to a jury, to the presumption of innocence and to proof beyond a reasonable doubt—would be bad enough. To tie that punishment to future crimes he had yet to commit would be quite beyond the pale, even for those justices who have taken a dim view of substantive due process claims.[78]

But the mere fact that Salerno had lost his liberty did not mean that he had been "punished." From the Court's perspective, he simply had been the subject of a regulatory measure. In drawing this distinction between punishment and regulation, the Court did not rely solely on indications in the Bail Reform Act's legislative history that Congress had the "regulatory" purpose of preventing danger to the community. It also looked to whether the restrictions that the measure imposed were "excessive in relation to" that non-punitive purpose. And it found that they were not. The Act, Rehnquist noted, "carefully limits the circumstances under which detention may be sought to the most serious of crimes. . . . The arrestee is entitled to a prompt detention hearing [], and the maximum length of pretrial detention is limited by the stringent time limitations of the Speedy Trial Act." Moreover, detainees had to be housed "in a 'facility separate, to the extent practicable, from persons awaiting or serving sentences or being held in custody pending appeal.' "[79]

Now Rehnquist had to confront the Second Circuit's reasoning, which had not turned on the characterization of pretrial detention on dangerous grounds as "punishment" but had held such a regulatory deprivation of liberty to be "beyond the constitutional pale." But he was not long detained, for, he asserted, the lower court had misread the constitutional map: "We have repeatedly held that the Government's regulatory interest in community safety can, in appropriate circum-

---

[78] In Chavez v. Martinez, 538 U.S. 760, 775 (2003), Justice Thomas noted that while the Court had often expressed its "reluctance to expand the doctrine of substantive due process," it had also made clear that the Due Process Clause "protects certain 'fundamental liberty interests' from deprivation by the government, regardless of the procedures provided, unless the infrigement is narrowly tailored to serve a compelling state interest."

[79] 481 U.S. at 747–48 (quoting 18 U.S.C. § 3142(i)(2)).

stances, outweigh an individual's liberty interest."[80] "For example," Rehnquist went on, "in times of war or insurrection, when society's interest is at its peak, the Government may detain individuals whom the Government believes to be dangerous."[81] Rehnquist then noted that "[e]ven outside the exigencies of war, we have found that sufficiently compelling governmental interests can justify detention of dangerous person," and he cited cases involving the "mentally unstable individuals who present a danger to the public," "dangerous defendants who become incompetent to stand trial," and "juveniles [found to] present a continuing danger to the community." He concluded:

> Given the well-established authority of the government, in special circumstances, to restrain individuals' liberty prior to or even without criminal trial and conviction, we think that the present statute providing for pretrial detention on the basis of dangerousness must be evaluated in precisely the same manner that we evaluated the laws in [these other cases].[82]

The Court then did the usual balancing. On one side, it looked at the "government's interest in preventing crime by arrestees," which it found "legitimate and compelling." This was no generalized interest in public safety. What Congress had done was "narrowly focus[] on a particularly acute problem in which the Government interests are overwhelming." The Act selects out only those defendants "arrested for a specific category of extremely serious offenses." Not only must the Government have first shown there to be probable cause that a defendant has committed the charged offense, but then "[i]n a full-blown adversary hearing, the Government must convince a neutral decisionmaker by clear and convincing evidence that no conditions of release can reasonably assure the safety of the community or any person." The Court concluded: "Under these narrow circumstances, society's interest in crime prevention is at its greatest."[83]

"On the other side of the scale, of course," Rehnquist recognized "the individual's strong interest in liberty." But where "the government's interest is sufficiently weighty—as it was here, given the care with which Congress 'delineat[ed] the circumstances under which detention would be permitted'—an individual's right could be 'subordinated to the greater needs of society.' "[84]

---

[80] 481 U.S. at 748.

[81] *Id.* (citing Ludecke v. Watkins, 335 U.S. 160 (1948) (upholding the detention and deportation of a Nazi—albeit one who had fallen out with that party's leadership in 1933—interned under the Alien Enemy Act during World War II)).

[82] 481 U.S. at 749.

[83] *Id.* at 750.

[84] *Id.* at 750–51.

Rehnquist then addressed Salerno's claim that the Bail Reform Act violated the excessive bail clause. Seizing on language from a case about what it meant for bail to be "excessive,"[85] Salerno had argued that the only risk that could constitutionally be considered in a bail determination was that of flight. The Court brushed the language aside as "dicta" and concluded: "Nothing in the text of the Bail Clause limits permissible Government considerations solely to questions of flight. The only arguable substantive limitation of the Bail Clause is that the Government's proposed conditions of release or detention not be 'excessive' in light of the perceived evil."[86]

Dissents

Justice Marshall's dissent, in which he was joined by Justice William J. Brennan, opened in a tone of decided outrage:

> This case brings before the Court for the first time a statute in which Congress declares that a person innocent of any crime may be jailed indefinitely, pending the trial of allegations which are legally presumed to be untrue, if the Government shows to the satisfaction of a judge that the accused is likely to commit crimes, unrelated to the pending charges, at any time in the future. Such statutes, consistent with the usages of tyranny and the excesses of what bitter experience teaches us to call the police state, have long been thought incompatible with the fundamental human rights protected by our Constitution. Today a majority of this Court holds otherwise. Its decision disregards basic principles of justice established centuries ago and enshrined beyond the reach of governmental interference in the Bill of Rights.[87]

Marshall followed with jab at the Court for disregarding the facts that Salerno had already been sentenced to "a century of jail time in another case" and that Cafaro had been released upon signing up as a cooperator. "Only by flatly ignoring these matters is the majority able to maintain the pretense" that a live controversy existed between the parties of the sort required by Article III of the Constitution.[88]

Turning to the merits, Marshall chided the majority for the "sterile formalism" of its division of Salerno's challenge into due process and

---

[85] Stack v. Boyle, 342 U.S. 1 (1951).

[86] 481 U.S. at 754.

[87] Id. at 755–756.

[88] Id. at 716.

excessive bail components. To be sure, Marshall found fault with each aspect of Rehnquist's opinion. The majority's "cramped" substantive due process analysis, Marshall complained, gave far too much license to legislators interested in using detention to serve the "regulatory" goal of preventing danger to the community. And its bail clause analysis failed to recognize that there are limits to the kinds of interests that Congress can further through the denial of bail. Because detention on dangerousness grounds authorized by the Bail Reform Act, "bears no relation to the Government's power to try charges supported by a finding of probable cause," "the interests it serves are outside the scope of interests which may be considered in weighing the excessiveness of bail under the Eighth Amendment."[89] What most troubled Marshall, however, is the way in which pretrial detention for dangerousness undermined the presumption of innocence. A mere indictment, he argued, "has been turned into evidence, if not that the defendant is guilty of the crime charged, then that left to his own devices he soon will be guilty of something else."[90]

Justice John Paul Stevens could not join Justice Marshall's opinion. Unable to disregard Chief Justice Feinberg's airline bomber hypothetical—not very hypothetical in 1987 and certainly not today[91]—he conceded that "it is indeed difficult to accept the proposition that the Government is without power to detain a person when it is a virtual certainty that he or she would otherwise kill a group of innocent people in the immediate future." In his separate dissenting opinion, Stevens agreed with Marshall that "the fact of indictment cannot, consistent with the presumption of innocence and the Eighth Amendment's Excessive Bail Clause, be used to create a special class, the members of which are, alone, eligible for detention because of future dangerousness." But, in a move Marshall would hardly have made, Stevens went on to suggest: "If the evidence of imminent danger is strong enough to warrant emergency detention, it should support that preventive measure regardless of whether the person has been charged, convicted, or acquitted of some other offense."[92]

Critique of Decision

The main intellectual challenge Rehnquist faced in *Salerno* was to explain why a decision upholding the Bail Reform Act as an acceptable regulatory measure would not license legislatures to freely toss around

---

[89] *Id.* at 765.

[90] *Id.* at 764.

[91] *See* United States v. Yousef, 327 F.3d 56 (2d Cir. 2003) (affirming conviction for conspiracy to bomb twelve U.S. commercial airliners in Southeast Asia in 1995).

[92] 481 U.S. at 768–69.

regulatory justifications whenever they wanted to restrain or even imprison the subjects of their suspicions. The Chief Justice's success in
meeting this challenge was middling at best. As Rehnquist recognized,
reliance on legislative intent for distinguishing regulation from punishment has its limits. A court might not be able "to discern the true
intentions of a legislative body."[93] And even if they could be discerned,
"making those intentions dispositive 'encourages[s] hypocrisy and unconscious self-deception.' "[94] Particularly since the regulation here put
its subjects in facilities that looked a lot like the prisons used to punish
convicted criminals, the persuasiveness of Rehnquist's opinion turned on
the extent to which he could show that the Bail Act had been appropriately tailored to its ostensibly limited regulatory goal.

Yet Congress actually had painted with a pretty broad brush. After
all, the class of defendants whose dangerousness is presumed include all
those facing narcotics charges with more than a 10–year maximum. And
it is hard to find a federal narcotics charge that does *not* expose a
defendant to more than ten years. The street dealer who sells a glassine
of heroin, or a single vial of crack faces a *twenty*-year maximum.[95] These
cases are not usually prosecuted in federal court, but they regularly find
their way there.[96] To be sure, courts have read the presumption provision
merely to impose "the burden of production" on the defendant. The
"burden of persuasion" remains with the government. Yet "when a
defendant comes forward with no evidence, the presumption alone
supports the conclusion that no conditions of release could reasonably
assure the appearance of the defendant and the safety of the community."[97] Whether or not this creative shifting of burdens makes sense or
not is not the point, which is merely that Congress did not take great
pains in deciding which felony defendants should face preventive detention.

---

[93] Note, Prevention Versus Punishment: Toward a Principled Distinction in the
Restraint of Released Sex Offenders, 109 Harv. L. Rev. 1711, 1720 (1996); *see* Maria
Foscarinis, Note, Toward a Constitutional Definition of Punishment, 80 Colum. L. Rev.
1667, 1672 (1980).

[94] Note, *supra* note 93, Harv L. Rev., at 1720 (quoting Herbert L. Packer, The Limits
of the Criminal Sanction 33 (1968)).

[95] *See* 21 U.S.C. § 841(b)(1)(C).

[96] The U.S. Attorney's Office that prosecuted Salerno would regularly prosecute street
narcotics sales as part of its "Federal Day" program. *See* Jo Thomas, Odds Heavily Favor
Leniency for Drug Dealing in the City, N.Y.Times, June 30, 1986, at A1; United States v.
Agilar, 779 F.2d 123, 125 (2d Cir. 1985) (noting that "garden-variety state law drug
offenses" had been converted into federal offenses).

[97] Federal Judicial Center, The Bail Reform Act of 1984 19–20 (2d ed. 1993) (citing
cases).

As for the safeguards offered by the Speedy Trial Act against lengthy pretrial detention, here, too, Rehnquist may have been a bit too charitable. The Speedy Trial Act—which requires that defendants be indicted within 10 days of their arrest if they have been detained, and that trial begin within 70 days of indictment—does compel courts to move cases along.[98] But its clock can be stopped for numerous reasons, including the making and consideration of defense motions. Defendants unwilling to sacrifice these avenues of legal relief for the sake of a speedy trial may end up spending considerable time in jail. And while the Court did not preclude a successful challenge by a defendant subjected to a particularly lengthy period of pretrial detention, defendants have not met with success in this regard. In one case, the Seventh Circuit held that continued detention for two years pending trial did not amount to a due process violation, and "suggested that, absent a showing of government culpability, no amount of time in detention, by itself, can constitute a due process violation."[99] In another, the Second Circuit countenanced 30 months of pretrial detention for a narcotics kingpin on both flight and dangerous grounds, and noted that " 'the constitutional limits on a detention period based on dangerousness to the community may be looser than the limits on a detention period based solely on risk of flight. In the former case, release risks injury to others, while in the later case, releases only the loss of a conviction.' "[100]

The Chief Justice may also have been overly charitable when he envisioned a custodial scheme that kept pretrial detainees separate from convicted prisoners. That is indeed a goal of the federal scheme, but the relevant provisions demands that it be achieved only "to the extent practicable." Federal Bureau of Prisons regulations, however, currently note: "What is practicable is contingent upon the individual institution's design, structure, and operation. When it is not practicable to keep pretrial inmates separate, [] staff may permit, based on sound correctional judgment, pretrial inmates who do not present a risk to the institution's security or orderly running to have regular contact with convicted inmates."[101]

In short, very little in the majority's opinion offers doctrinal assurance that the state's compelling interest in preventing future crime will

---

[98] Speedy Trial Act, 18 U.S.C. §§ 3161–3174.

[99] Federal Judicial Center, The Bail Reform Act of 1984 (2d ed., 1993) (discussing United States v. Infelise, 934 F.2d 103 (7th Cir. 1991)).

[100] United States v. Millan, 4 F.3d 1038, 1048 (2d Cir. 1993) (quoting United States v. Orena, 986 F.2d 628, 631 (2d Cir. 1993)).

[101] Federal Bureau of Prisons, U.S. Dep't of Justice, Program Statement: Pretrial Inmates, PS 7331.04 (Jan. 31, 2003).

not, someday, be allowed to justify the *"indefinite* preventive detention of individuals acquitted or not even charged."[102]

On the other hand, Marshall had only middling success in addressing why society simply lacked the power to restrain those who had been shown to pose a danger to its members. Those accused of crimes must indeed be "presumed innocent," and at trial, that presumption can be overcome only by proof beyond a reasonable doubt. But not even Marshall would have found any inconsistency in maintaining this presumption and nonetheless considering the strength of the evidence against the defendant and his prior record when deciding whether he poses a risk of flight or a threat to witnesses, should he be released on bail. And if the possibility that a defendant has committed the crime can be considered in this regard, why cannot it also be considered as a factor in deciding whether the accused poses a threat not just to witnesses but to others? Predictions of such harm can be difficult,[103] yet is the government required to release someone in its custody who it is convinced will proceed to inflict such harms? Marshall's categorical answer to the categorical question was "no," and he had to accept Chief Judge Feinberg's imminent airplane bombing as the price of liberty.

Stevens would not accept the bombing, and was thus obliged to distinguish that case from the one before him. Yet once he accepted the general proposition of preventive detention, his critique of the Bail Act ended up being that it is too narrow, rather than too broad. A nice counterintuitive debating point,[104] but not particularly satisfying for those who believe that the government does well to legislate in reasonable increments, and can legitimately take a special interest in the risk that someone it releases from custody might go out to hurt others.

Yet, to be fair to all sides, substantive due process cases often end up being exercises in contestable, even semi-arbitrary, line-drawing and interest balancing. Just because a government measure might feel like punishment to those subjected to it does not necessarily mean that those people should get all the protections guaranteed to criminal defendants. To hold otherwise would be to require the government to produce proof beyond a reasonable doubt before it could, say, quarantine an infected individual, or detain someone found dangerously mentally ill in a civil

---

[102] Stephen J. Schulhofer, Two Systems of Social Protection: Comments on the Civil–Criminal Distinction, with Particular Reference to Sexually Violent Predator Laws, 7 J. Contemp. L. Issues 69, 86 (1996).

[103] *See* John Monahan, *Prediction of Crime and Recidivism*, in 3 Encyclopedia of Crime & Justice 1125 (2d ed. 2002); John Monahan et al., Rethinking Risk Assessment: The MacArthur Study of Mental Disorder and Violence (2001).

[104] *See also* Tribe, *supra* note 60, at 405 ("If two men appear equally likely to commit a violent crime, it is arbitrary to imprison the man who is about to be tried for the past offense while imposing no restraint on the man who is not facing trial.").

proceeding. A true legislative intent to further the general good must count for something. On the other hand, as Miller and Guggenheim have noted, if "legislative intent is the sole determinant of punishment, legislatures could circumvent rights expressly protecting the individual from government authority ... by obfuscating the real purpose of punitive regulation."[105] Enormous constitutional consequences will follow the determination of whether a measure constitutes "regulation" or "punishment," yet we lack the doctrinal tools to make such determinations rest on much more than ipse dixit or complex inquiries about whose conclusions reasonable minds can differ.[106]

Some have tried a different tack, arguing that the use of dangerousness as a basis for incarceration should be limited to those situations in which the criminal justice system *could not* punish—as would be the case for both quarantines (where there is no justification for punishment) or the detention of the dangerous mentally ill who lacking criminal culpability cannot be punished.[107] This is an utterly defensible position. Yet it does leave a contestable gap between the civil and criminal confinement systems when it comes to dangerous agents who are capable of bearing blame after the danger they pose is realized.[108] Is the domain of criminal law so exclusive that the government must always wait until after a crime (however grievous) has been committed, if the perpetrator is mentally capable of standing trial? Giving the government license to lock blameworthy dangerous people without the niceties of a full-blown criminal trial risks whole-sale circumvention of the criminal justice system. But flatly denying the government such power under all circumstances risks sacrificing innocent bystanders on the alter of legal formalism.

We will shortly explore how these unresolved questions continue to haunt the case law.

Afterward

We will look at three aspects of the legacy of *United States v. Salerno*: What happened to Salerno and Cafaro; what happened to Bail Statute, and what happened to doctrine that the Supreme Court deployed to affirm it.

---

[105] Miller & Guggenheim, *supra* note 21, at 367.

[106] *See id.* at 370–73; Carol Steiker, Punishment and Procedure: Punishment Theory and the Criminal–Civil Procedural Divide, 85 Geo. L.J. 775 (1997).

[107] *See* Paul H. Robinson, Punishing Dangerousness: Cloaking Preventive Detention as Criminal Justice, 114 Harv. L. Rev. 1429 (2001).

[108] *See* Stephen J. Morse, Uncontrollable Urges and Irrational People, 88 Va. L. Rev. 1025, 1025–26 (2002); *see also* Stephen J. Morse, Preventive Confinement of Dangerous Offenders, 32 J. L. Med. & Ethics 56 (2004); Stephen J. Morse, An Essay on Preventive Detention, 76 B.U. L. Rev. 113 (1996).

What Happened to Salerno and Cafaro

In May 1988, the trial of Salerno and his co-defendants (but not Cafaro) concluded with his conviction on RICO substantive and conspiracy charges and on numerous other counts, including mail fraud (relating to the bid rigging in the concrete superstructure industry), extortion, and running an illegal numbers business. All the other defendants standing trial were also convicted on various counts. But Salerno was not convicted on counts or specifications relating to the two murders alleged in the Government's bail proffer. The jury found the "racketeering act" alleging his involvement in John Simone's murder had not been proven. And the Government had consented to dismissal of the racketeering act charging the conspiracy to murder John Spencer Ullo "after the sole witness to the crime was unable to identify Salerno in court."[109]

In October 1988, Judge Lowe sentenced Salerno to a total of seventy years' imprisonment, to run consecutive to the 100–year sentence that Judge Owen previously had imposed on him in the Commission case. While the irrelevance of the extra time perhaps reduced Salerno's interest in challenging this new conviction, the war was waged on his behalf by co-defendants who had more at stake. And a long war it was. In June 1991, a Second Circuit panel reversed all the convictions, finding that the trial court had committed reversible error in refusing to allow the defendants to introduce certain exculpatory grand jury testimony. The panel concluded that the "spillover taint" from this error "undermined [its] confidence in the accuracy of all of the guilty verdict."[110] The Government took the case to the Supreme Court, which overturned the panel's opinion and sent the case back down.[111] But the panel again reversed the convictions.[112] So the Government sought and obtained en banc review by entire Circuit, which overturned the panel in 1993.[113] By this time, however, Salerno was no longer alive, having died on July 27, 1992, at age 80, in the Springfield, Missouri, Medical Center for Federal Prisoners.[114]

Salerno continued to play parts in federal mob trials after his death. But his role changed. In 1997, at the federal racketeering and murder

---

[109] Brief for the United States, U.S. v. Salerno, 88–1464, at 38.

[110] 937 F.2d 797 (2d Cir. 1991).

[111] 505 U.S. 317 (1992).

[112] 974 F.2d 231 (2d Cir. 1992).

[113] United States v. DiNapoli, 8 F.3d 909 (2d Cir. 1993) (en banc).

[114] James Dao, Anthony (Fat Tony) Salerno, 80, A Top Crime Boss, Dies in Prison, N.Y. Times, July 29, 1992, at D19.

trial of Vincent Gigante, the Government's theory was that sometime in the early 1980s, long before Salerno's arrest, Gigante had taken the reins as the Boss of the Genovese Family. While Salerno had been out front as the ostensible boss, Gigante, who wandered around Greenwich Village in his bathrobe, pretending to be crazy, had the real power.[115]

Cafaro, for his part, had a bumpy relationship with government following his initial decision to cooperate. Shortly before the trial of the mob heroin dealer he had set up for the government, Cafaro announced that he would no longer cooperate. When called as a witness at that trial, he asserted his Fifth Amendment privilege. But months later, without having made any new agreement with the prosecutors, he appeared as a witness before the Senate Permanent Subcommittee on Investigations.[116] Eventually, Cafaro and the government reached a new modus vivendi, and he went on to do a star turn at a number of major organized crime trials. He has since disappeared into the Witness Protection Program.[117] His son Thomas did a short stint in prison (as a result of Vincent's breach of his cooperation agreement), was released, and, in 2003 went back in, having pleaded guilty, along with co-defendant Vincent Gigante, in another Genovese racketeering case.[118]

What Happened to the Bail Statute

The Supreme Court's decision and the statute it upheld were roundly criticized by many academics[119] and editorial writers.[120] But, as Laurie Levenson recently noted: "Attitudes have changed. Following *Salerno*, the public and courts predictably moved into an era in which we are relatively comfortable with preventive detention."[121]

A government study found that the percentage of federal defendants detained jumped from 26% before the 1984 Bail Reform Act to 31% soon

---

[115] *See* Joseph P. Fried, Gigante Lawyers Say U.S. Saw Another as Genovese Boss, N.Y. Times, July 9, 1997, at B3; Patricia Hurtado, FBI Agent Asked: Who is Real Don?; Gigante, Salerno Both Cited, Newsday, July 9, 1997, at A4.

[116] United States v. Tutino, 883 F.2d at 1139.

[117] Jerry Capeci, *supra* note 73.

[118] Anthony M. DeStefano, Taking One On the "Chin"; Gigante: I Faked Mental Woes, Newsday (New York), Apr. 8, 2003, at A26.

[119] *See* Laurie L. Levenson, Detention, Material Witnesses & the War on Terrorism, 35 Loyola of L.A. L. Rev. 1217, 1218 note 4 (2002) (citing critical commentaries); Paul H. Robinson, Punishing Dangerousness: Cloaking Preventive Detention as Criminal Justice, 114 Harv. L. Rev. 1429, 1445 (2001).

[120] *Id.* at 1218–19 (citing editorial criticism in newspapers including *New York Times, Chicago Tribune, Los Angeles Times*).

[121] *Id.* at 1219.

after.[122] In 1996, ten years after Salerno was detained, of 56,982 defendants arraigned in federal court, 19,254 were ordered detained (34%). For 42.3% of these defendants, the basis for the detention order was "risk of flight." For 10%, it was danger to the community, and for 47.0% it was a combination of flight and danger.[123] Although the breakdown in the bases for detention is not available for 2002, that year detention orders were entered for about 40% of all defendants, and the average length of detention for all defendants was 110.9 days.[124]

By 1988, nineteen states had enacted or were on the verge of enacing statutes allowing for preventive detention.[125] By 2005, thirty-two states made protection of the public or danger to society an explicit part of the pretrial release calculus.[126] But the regularity with which defendants are detained on dangerousness grounds in federal court soon became part of the attraction of federal jurisdiction in the violent crime area, and was touted by federal enforcers as a reason for taking federally cases that would normally have been prosecuted in state court.[127]

Does preventive detention really make communities safer? Intuitive and anecdotal responses can vary. The lone criminal's ability to personally attack people is certainly limited by his detention. But crimes can still be planned by detainees who, like Salerno himself, have the ability to order others to act on their behalf. In June 1987, during Salerno's trial and in the very facility Salerno was being held, another detainee used his visiting and telephone privileges to tamper with witnesses and obstruct justice.[128] On the other hand, the same case provides a nice

---

[122] General Accounting Office, Criminal Bail: How Bail Reform is Working in Selected District Courts 18 (1987).

[123] John Scalia, Bureau of Justice Statistics Special Report: Federal Pretrial Release and Detention, 1996, at 4, tbl.3 (Feb. 1999) (NCJ 168635). For the final 0.6%, the basis was danger to witness or juror.

[124] Bureau of Justice Statistics, U.S. Dep't of Justice, *Compendium of Federal Justice Statistics, 2002*, tbls. 3.7 & 3.11 at 47, 50 (2004).

[125] Michael W. Youtt, Note, The Effect of *Salerno v. United States* on the Use of State Preventive Detention Legislation: A New Definition of Due Process, 22 Ga. L. Rev. 805, 805 note 3 (1988).

[126] *See* Joseph L. Lester, Presumed Innocent, Feared Dangerous: The Eighth Amendment's Right to Bail, 32 N. Ky. L. Rev., 1, 55–65 (2005).

[127] *See* Daniel C. Richman, "Project Exile" and the Allocation of Federal Law Enforcement Authority, 43 Ariz. L. Rev. 369, 379 (2001); Malcolm Russell–Einhorn. Shawn Ward & Amy Sheerman, *Federal-Local Law Enforcement Collaboration in Investigating and Prosecuting Urban Crime, 1982–1999: Drugs, Weapons, and Gangs*, 28 (2000) (Abt Associates report prepared for National Institute of Justice).

[128] *See* United States v. Willoughby, 860 F.2d 15 (2d Cir. 1988); *see also* United States v. LaFontaine, 210 F.3d 125, 127 (2d Cir. 2000) (another witness tampering effort by someone confined in the MCC).

example of how detention allows the government to monitor inmate communications and thereby detect and foil planned crimes. The bottom line is that detention allows the government to narrow the window of opportunity for committing further crimes. But the window remains open.

Precisely how much has been gained from preventive detention provisions? How many crimes have jurisdictions using such provisions been able to prevent? These questions are impossible to answer, and therein lies a problem. As Miller & Guggenheim noted: "Conducting a proper blind test of an operative pretrial detention system is difficult politically because it would involve releasing some individuals who would otherwise be detained."[129] And in the absence of such tests, or conclusive results from field studies,[130] it is all to easy to assume success: "Once the government has instituted a system of imprisonment openly calculated to prevent crimes by persons awaiting trial, the system will appear to be malfunctioning only when it releases persons who prove to be worse risks than anticipated.... [W]hen the system detains persons who could safely have been released, its errors will be invisible."[131]

What Happened to Legal Doctrine

As Rehnquist noted, *Salerno* was not the first case to uphold detention on the grounds of dangerousness. The other cases, however, involved war time or juveniles who were outside regular criminal justice system. In explicitly targeting adults who could potentially held criminally responsible for the crimes the detention was meant to prevent, the 1984 Bail Act marked an important policy shift, and the decision to uphold it entailed a doctrinal shift of great significance.

Long before the Act was passed, Laurence Tribe explained the basis of his opposition to it:

> Throughout history, governments have been tempted to establish order by identifying and imprisoning in advance all likely trouble-makers. Our society, however, has made the basic decision not to entrust such sweeping power to the state. We have relied instead upon the moral and deterrent effects of laws which define particular acts as crime and which punish all who violate their proscriptions. For those believed dangerously ill and hence incapable of controlling their behavior in response to this system of deterrents, we have

---

[129] Miller & Guggenheim at 384.

[130] *See* Thomas Bak, Pretrial Release Behavior of Defendants Whom the U.S. Attorney Wished to Detain, 30 Am. J. Crim. L. 45 (2002).

[131] Laurence H. Tribe, An Once of Detention: Preventive Justice in the World of John Mitchell, 56 Va. L. Rev. 371, 375 (1970).

devised programs of civil commitment. For the rest, we have relied on the threat of sanctions. Recognizing that this threat will not deter all those who can control their behavior, we have accepted some risk of crime as the inevitable price of a system that promises to punish no man until it is shown beyond a reasonable doubt that he has committed a specifically illegal act.[132]

Yet acceptance of Tribe's broad propositions was breaking down, even as he wrote them. It is no coincidence that, in October 1985, Surgeon General C. Everett Kopp convened a Workshop on Violence and Public Health, "which signaled public health's entry into the field of violence prevention."[133] To be sure, public health experts were not proposing the use of detention as a public health tool, and focused instead on measures to change social and physical environments and individual knowledge, skills or attitudes. But by de-emphasizing moral accountability,[134] they gave intellectual support a mix of anti-crime measures that relied less on criminal punishment and more on regulation.

The extent to which criminal procedure had become elaborately constitutionalized played a role as well. As Carol Steiker has noted, with the "revolution in criminal procedure" raising "the cost to government of using the criminal process [,] state and federal legislators and regulators have sought civil avenues to address what might be more plausibly classified as criminal conduct."[135] And the result has been the creation of what Steiker has called "the preventive state," which has deployed a panoply of "prophylactic measures," including detention, in the service of its preventive goals.[136] The 1984 Bail Act must be seen as part of this broader and continuing trend. As Steiker reports:

> [P]retrial detention of both juveniles and adults has become much more common in recent years. Many states are seeking to prevent

---

[132] Tribe, *supra* note 60, at 376; *see also* Louis Michael Seidman, Points of Intersection: Discontinuities at the Junction of Criminal Law and the Regulatory State, 7 J. Contemp. L. Issues 97 (1996) ("[E]ven someone unambiguously committed to the regulatory perspective would want to retain a social practice that effectively communicated blame. Inculcating internal moral inhibitions against antisocial conduct is probably the most cost-effective means of crime control. The criminal justice system teaches these moral lessons only if it is perceived as punishing the blameworthy and vindicating the blameless.").

[133] *See* James A. Mercy, et al., Public Health Policy for Preventing Violence, 12 Health Affairs 7, 7 (1993), available at http://content.healthaffairs.org/cgi/reprint/12/4/7.

[134] *See* Mark H. Moore, Violence Prevention: Criminal Justice or Public Health 34, 43 (1993).

[135] Steiker, 85 Geo. L.J. at 780.

[136] Carol Steiker, The Limits of the Preventive State, 88 J. Crim. L. & Crim. 771, 774–75 (1998) (hereinafter "Limits").

sexual assaults, particularly those against children, by enacting sex offender registration and/or community notification statutes and by creating or reviving "sexually violent predator" statutes that permit the indefinite civil commitment of convicted sex offenders who would otherwise be released at the end of their prison terms.[137]

In upholding these measures, courts have drawn on the public health model as well, if only by analogy, creating what Edward Richards has called a "jurisprudence of prevention" that applies "traditional public health rationales and procedures to individuals who pose a threat to society."[138] "In the prevention cases," Richards observes, "the Supreme Court has transformed the traditional police power to restrict disease carriers into a general power to restrict individuals whose criminal activity poses a threat to society."[139]

Since *Salerno*, what limits are there on when the State can use detention on a regulatory measure in the service of these preventive goals? Some answers can be found in *Foucha v. Louisiana*,[140] decided in 1992, but they are quite tentative. After Foucha was tried for violent crime and acquitted by reason of insanity, he was committed to a psychiatric hospital. Although hospital officials thereafter decided he was not insane and recommended his release, state law provided that commitment would continue, even in the absence of mental illness, unless a defendant so acquitted could prove he was not dangerous to himself or others. Hospital officials found he had an "anti-social" personality and refused to certify him as non-dangerous. So Foucha remained in detention.

The Supreme Court found that Louisiana's scheme violated Foucha's right to due process. Justice Byron White (who had voted with the majority in *Salerno*) noted:

> It was emphasized in *Salerno* that the detention we found constitutionally permissible was strictly limited in duration.... Here, in contrast, the State asserts that because Foucha once committed a criminal act and now has an antisocial personality that sometimes leads to aggressive conduct, a disorder for which there is no effective treatment, he may be held indefinitely. This rationale would permit the State to hold indefinitely any other insanity acquittee not mentally ill who could be shown to have a personality disorder that may lead to criminal conduct. The same would be true of any

---

[137] *Id.* at 777.

[138] Edward P. Richards, The Jurisprudence of Prevention: The Right of Societal Self-Defense Against Dangerous Individuals, 16 Hastings Con. L. Q. 329, 330 (1989).

[139] *Id.* at 384.

[140] 504 U.S. 71 (1992).

convicted criminal, even though he has completed his prison term. It would also be only a step away from substituting confinements for dangerousness for our present system which, with only narrow exceptions and aside from permissible confinements for mental illness, incarcerates only those who are proved beyond reasonable doubt to have violated a criminal law.[141]

The implication of this reasoning, according to Stephen Schulhofer, is "to confine *Salerno* to regimes of temporary detention pending trial and to hold indefinite confinement unconstitutional in the absence of mental illness."[142] Yet the message of *Foucha* was mixed. For one thing, it was a 5–4 decision. For another, there was Justice O'Connor's separate concurrence. While she joined the majority's opinion, O'Connor suggested that it might indeed "be permissible for Louisiana to confine the insanity acquittee who has regained sanity if, unlike the situation in this case, the nature and duration of detention were tailored to reflect pressing public safety concerns related to the acquittee's continuing dangerousness. *See United States v. Salerno . . . .*"[143]

O'Connor's concurrence in *Foucha* presaged her voting with the majority in *Kansas v. Hendricks*,[144] which involved the first use of Kansas' Sexually Violent Predator Act. That act, passed in 1994, authorizes the civil commitment of persons who, due to a "mental abnormality" or a "personality disorder," are likely to engage in "predatory acts of sexual violence." The state moved to commit Hendricks, who had a long history of sexually molesting children and who was due to be released from prison after serving time for a serious of convictions for sexual assault of minors. After a hearing at which Hendricks testified that he could not control his sexual desires for children when he got "stressed out," the jury determined that he was a sexually violent predator, and he was committed.

Upholding Hendrick's commitment, the Supreme Court concluded that civil detention of sex offenders, based on a finding of "mental abnormality," was neither "punishment" as a constitutional matter, nor, as a regulatory measure, did it amount to a substantive due process violation. Writing for the Court, and without substantial disagreement from the dissenting justices on this point,[145] Justice Thomas noted:

---

[141] 504 U.S. at 82–83.

[142] Schulhofer, *supra* note 102 (Contemp Issues) at 89.

[143] 504 U.S. at 87–88; *see* Schulhofer at 90.

[144] 521 U.S. 346 (1997).

[145] 521 U.S. at 373–78 (Breyer, J., dissenting) (agreeing that the Kansas statute does not violate substantive due process).

Although freedom from physical restraint "has always been at the core of the liberty protected by the Due Process Clause from arbitrary governmental action,".... that liberty interest is not absolute. The Court has recognized that an individual's constitutionally protected interest in avoiding physical restraint may be overridden even in the civil context.... Accordingly, States have in certain narrow circumstances provided for the forcible civil detainment of people who are unable to control their behavior and who thereby pose a danger to the public health and safety.... We have consistently upheld such involuntary commitment statutes provided the confinement takes place pursuant to proper procedures and evidentiary standards ... It thus cannot be said that the involuntary civil confinement of a limited subclass of dangerous persons is contrary to our understanding of ordered liberty.[146]

Notwithstanding the lack of controversy, the Court had indeed expanded the universe of "dangerous" individuals whom a state could choose to lock up. Previous cases had involved "mental illness," which "however defined, carries with it the legal connotation [] of the kind of mental state sufficient to impair cognition or volition so seriously as to render the individual legally irresponsible and thus not properly subject to criminal punishment."[147] "Mental abnormality" or "personality disorder" are far broader terms, and the Court's opinion left open "the degree of cognitive or volitional impairment" constitutionally necessary for indefinite confinement on dangerousness grounds to occur.[148] In 2002, in *Kansas v. Crane*,[149] the Court returned to the Kansas statute, and Justice Breyer, writing for a healthy majority, addressed the issue (still without wholly clarifying it). Although the Constitution does not require that the state show "total or complete lack of control," before it could confine someone, the Court did say it required that there be some sort of finding as to his lack of control.[150]

Incremental shifts can also be found in the Court's post-*Salerno* cases involving deportable aliens. *Zadvydas v. Davis*,[151] decided in 2001, involved a statutory provision allowing the detention of aliens whose deportation had been ordered but could not be removed, there being no country to receive them. The Court, by a 5–4 vote, interpreted the statute not to authorize indefinite confinement. Yet before reading the

---

[146] 521 U.S. at 356–57.

[147] Steiker, Limits, *supra* note 136, at 786.

[148] *Id.* at 788.

[149] 534 U.S. 407 (2002).

[150] *Id.* at 411.

[151] 533 U.S. 678 (2001).

provision to avoid a "constitutional problem,"[152] Justice Breyer, writing for the majority, explained what this problem would be. Under the Court's cases, he noted, government detention violates substantive due process

> unless the detention is ordered in a *criminal* proceeding, *see United States v. Salerno*, [] or in certain special and "narrow," non-punitive "circumstances," [citing *Foucha*], where a special justification, such as harm-threatening mental illness, outweighs the "individual's constitutionally protected interest in avoiding physical restraint." *Kansas v. Hendricks* [].[153]

And he found "no sufficiently strong special justification here for indefinite civil detention, at least as administered under this statute."[154]

Addressing a quite separate immigration detention provision in 2003, *Demore v. Kim*,[155] was not necessarily inconsistent with *Zadvydas*, but its tone and deference to legislative judgment was markedly different. The provision here legislatively *required* detention during removal proceedings for limited class of deportable aliens, including those who had previously been convicted of an aggravated felony. Focusing on the limited nature of the detention (compared to that in *Zadvydas*), the Court held that "Congress, justifiably concerned that deportable criminal aliens who are not detained continue to engage in crime and fail to appear for their removal hearings in large numbers, may require that persons such as [Kim] be detained for the brief period necessary for their removal proceedings."[156] In dissent, Justice Souter, joined by Justice Stevens and Ginsburg, made an important point, however: "Due process calls for an individual determination before someone is locked away. In none of the cases cited did we ever suggest that the government could avoid the Due Process Clause by doing what § 1226(c) does, by selecting a class of people for confinement on a categorical basis and denying members of that class any chance to dispute the necessity of putting them away...."[157]

Post 9/11

Carol Steiker observed in 1998 that "[t]he preventive state is all the

---

[152] 533 U.S. at 690.

[153] *Id.*

[154] *Id.*

[155] 538 U.S. 510 (2003).

[156] 538 U.S. at 513.

[157] *Id.* at 551–52 (Souter, J., dissenting); *see* David Cole, In Aid of Removal: Due Process Limits on Immigration Detentions, 51 Emory L.J. 1003 (2002).

rage these days,"[158] and could provide considerable evidence to support for point. By 2003, fifteen states had joined Kansas in passing laws allowing the civil commitment of sexually violent predators.[159] But, for all the controversy over the legislation reviewed in these post-*Salerno* cases, and the decisions that generally upheld these measures, the categories of people subject to preventive detention in the United States were pretty limited. Defendants facing charges for past crimes. Individuals said to be suffering from some mental abnormality. Deportable aliens. The legal reasoning upholding these measures did not so clearly cabin the State's power. But whether because of policy, fiscal restraint, or self-conscious constitutional interpretation, legislators did not slide too far down the slippery slope.[160]

Then came the coordinated al Queda terrorist attacks of September 11, 2001, and the expectation of further terrorist attacks, with the fear that they would involve weapons of mass destruction.

Faced with the catastrophic consequences of such attacks, and unwilling to rely on the deterrent effects of *ex post* prosecutions, the Department of Justice immediately used—and, in the eyes of many critics, abused—available tools for detaining people it thought might be involved in further terrorist activity. Between September and December 2001, it detained more that 600 aliens on immigration charges, and a total of 762 between September 2001 and August 2002.[161] It detained other people on material witness warrants, obtained in connection with grand jury proceedings.[162] And it brought criminal charges for offenses

---

[158] Steiker, Limits, at 774.

[159] *See* Peter C. Pfaffenroth, Note, The Need for Coherence: States' Civil Commitment of Sex Offenders in the Wake of Kansas v. Crane, 55 Stan. L. Rev. 2229, 2232 note 22 (2003) (citing statutes).

[160] Frank B. Cross, Institutions and Enforcement of the Bill of Rights, 85 Cornell L. Rev. 1529 (2000) (discussing how majoritarian politics can help protect constitutional rights); *see also* David Cole, The Priority of Morality: The Emergency Constitution's Blind Spot, 113 Yale L.J. 1753, 1787–88 (2004) (endeavoring to harmonize cases).

[161] Office of the Inspector General, Dep't of Justice, The September 11 Detainee: A Review of the Treatment of Aliens Held on Immigration Charges in Connection with the Investigation of the September 11 Attacks, at 5, 23 (Apr. 2003). As part of the USA PATRIOT Act, Pub. L. No. 107–56, 115 Stat. 272 (2001), Congress also gave the Attorney General the power to detain an alien for limited periods upon certification that he "has reasonable grounds to believe" that an alien is engaged in terrorist activity or in any other activity endangering the national security of the United States. *Id.* at § 412; *see* Developments in the Law, The Law of Prisons, Plight of the Tempest-Tost: Indefinite Detention of Deportable Aliens, 115 Harv. L. Rev. 1915 (2002); Shirin Sinnar, Note, Patriotic or Unconstitutional? The Mandatory Detention of Aliens Under the USA Patriot Act, 55 Stan. L. Rev. 1419 (2003).

[162] *See* United States v. Awadallah, 349 F.3d 42 (2d Cir. 2003); Levenson, *supra* note 119; *see also* Letter & Report of Jamie E. Brown, Asst. Atty. General, Leg. Affairs, to Hon.

that ostensibly had no terrorism connection, as a means of gaining custody over terrorism suspects.[163]

Yet questions arose, first in theory: What if the government was presented with a situation in which it believed a that person posed a grave terrorist threat and, for some reason, it could not detain the person on immigration charges or as a material witness? Would its avenues for action be restricted to those allowed by the criminal process: arrest on probable cause and then indictment? What if it lacked sufficient evidence to bring such charges but had enough to make action imperative? We thus came back to the problem posed by Chief Judge Feinberg in his *Salerno* dissent. But now presented in the wake of attacks that killed 3000 people in one day.

Then, on June 10, 2002, the hypothetical became a reality when Attorney General John Ashcroft announced that Abdullah Al Muhajir, an American citizen born "Jose Padilla," who had already been arrested and detained pursuant to a material witness warrant, had been transferred to the custody of the Defense Department for indefinite detention. Padilla, Ashcroft explained, was "a known terrorist who was exploring a plan to build and explode a radiological dispersion device, or 'dirty bomb,' in the United States." And "[t]he safety of all Americans and the national security interests of the United States" required that he be detained as "an enemy combatant."[164] He offered few details then or later.

Padilla was incarcerated in a Navy brig in South Carolina and was prevented from meeting with his lawyer until 2004. But she nonetheless challenged his detention in a case that wound its way up to the Supreme Court.[165] Shortly before the Court decided the case (but long after it was

---

F. James Sensenbrenner, Jr., Chrm., House Judiciary Committee, at 50 (noting that fewer than 50 people had been detained on material witness warrants in connection with the September 11 investigation, and that 90% of these had been detained for 90 days or less).

[163] *See* Daniel C. Richman & William J. Stuntz, Al Capone's Revenge: An Essay on the Political Economy of Pretextual Prosecution, 105 Colum. L. Rev. 583 (2005).

[164] CNN, Ashcroft Statement on "Dirty Bomb" Suspect, June 10, 2002.

[165] Padilla v. Rumsfeld, 352 F.3d 695 (2d Cir. 2003), *reversing*, 233 F. Supp.2d 564 (S.D.N.Y. 2002).

argued), the Justice Department offered a few more details about Padilla. Padilla, the department revealed, had received explosives training at an al Qaeda camp, and had proposed a plan to al Qaeda leaders involving an improvised nuclear bomb. The leaders never thought anything would come of that idea, but instead suggested that Padilla blow up high-rise apartment buildings in the U.S. Deputy Attorney General James Comey explained:

> Had we tried to make a case against Jose Padilla though our criminal justice system, something that [the U.S. Attorney's office] could not do at that time without jeopardizing intelligence sources, he would very like have followed his lawyer's advice and said nothing, which would have been his constitutional right.
>
> He would likely have ended up a free man, with our only hope being to try to follow him 24 hours a day, seven days a week, and hope—pray, really—that we didn't lose him.[166]

The Supreme Court did not reach the merits of Padilla's case, holding only that the challenge to his detention should have been filed in another district.[167] But, in another case decided the same day, *Hamdi v. Rumsfeld*,[168] the Court faced a somewhat different case—an American citizen captured in Afghanistan and detained in the United States as an

---

[166] CNN, Transcript of News Conference on Jose Padilla, June 1, 2004.

[167] Rumsfeld v. Padilla, 542 U.S. 462 (2004).

[168] 542 U.S. 507 (2004).

enemy combatant. (Had he not been a citizen, he likely would have been sent to the Guantanamo Bay, Cuba, Naval Base, where the military has been detaining foreign nationals captured abroad during hostilities.[169]). A majority of the Court upheld the government's power to detain such combatents, at least for the duration of the hostilities in Afghanistan. Justice O'Connor, joined by Chief Justice Rehnquist, and Justices Kennedy and Breyer, concluded that the Executive had been authorized by the Authorization for Use of Military Force[170] passed by Congress in the immediate wake of September 11 to detain enemy combatants, regardless of their citizenship.[171] Writing separately, Justice Thomas agreed, and went on to suggest that "the President very well may have inherent authority to detain those arrayed against our troops."[172] Justice O'Connor's plurality, joined in a separate opinion by Justices Souter and Ginsburg,[173] concluded that Hamdi had a due process right to contest the basis for his detention before a neutral decisionmaker, but the government's broad authority to detain enemy combatants during wartime was, for a majority of the court, settled.

To what extent did the broad executive authority upheld in *Hamdi* extend to Padilla, who had been detained not in Afghanistan during open hostilities, but at O'Hare International Airport, in Chicago? For the district judge hearing Padilla's habeas corpus challenge to his detention—once Padilla re-filed his petition in the right district—the two cases had little in common. Congress had authorized the President to use all "necessary and appropriate force." But Padilla's

> alleged terrorist plans were thwarted at the time of his arrest. There were no impediments whatsoever to the Government bringing charges agains him for any one or all of the array of heinous crimes that he has been effectively accused of committing. Also at the Government's disposal was the material witness warrant. [S]ince [Padilla's] alleged terrorist plans were thwarted when he was arrested on the material witness warrant, the Court finds that the President's subsequent decision to detain [Padilla] as an enemy combatant was neither necessary nor appropriate.[174]

---

[169] *See* Rasul v. Bush, 542 U.S. 466 (2004) (holding that United States courts have jurisdiction to consider challenges to legality of detentions of foreign nationals captured abroad in connection with hostilities and incarcerated at Guantanamo Bay).

[170] 115 Stat. 224.

[171] 542 U.S. at 507.

[172] 542 U.S. at 587 (Thomas, J., dissenting).

[173] *Id.* at 1660 (Souter, J., concurring).

[174] Padilla v. Hanft, 389 F.Supp. 2d 678 (D.S.C. 2005).

The district court went on to note: "Simply stated, this is a law enforcement matter, not a military matter."[175]

There is a neatness to District Judge's Henry F. Floyd's approach to Padilla's detention: For American citizens in the U.S., at least, the normal rules apply. They give the government ample authority to detain charged defendants and material grand jury witnesses, and no further authority is available or needed. Yet the neatness is illusory. Regardless of the credence one gives to the government's claims about Padilla, it hardly (and sadly) does not strain reality to think that there will be people in the United States, even citizens,[176] whom the government suspects of planning catastrophic terrorist attacks, but against whom the government lacks the ability to bring criminal charges, even ones ostensibly unrelated to terrorism. Material witness warrants can often provide a basis to detain a witness pending his appearance before a grand jury or at trial, but it far from clear that their use purely as detention devices should be condoned. And even if detention were possible, other questions would remain: Is the government bound to get the testimony immediately? If it is, it is bound to let the witness go thereafter, even though he still poses threat?

So what about Judge Feinberg's terrorist bomber? Is it so clear that our only recourse for stopping him is the criminal justice system? In that system, we take risks that we generally accept, even embrace. Perfectly effective 24–hour surveillance occurs only on television programs. Yet if the bad guy whom we do not quite have the goods on commits a crime, however heinous, while we are trying to gather admissible proof of his intentions, we sigh and say "That is the price we pay for a free society." With the new scale of the threat, the risk calculus may be changing. During oral argument in the Fourth Circuit after the government appealed Judge Floyd's decision, the Solicitor General asserted that, like Afghanistan, the United States was now "a battlefield."[177] Anyone who walked around Lower Manhattan in the weeks after September 11, 2001, or the Madrid train station after March 11, 2004, or the London Underground after July 7, 2005, might well agree. Moreover, even a skeptic or critic on this score might fairly recognize that at *some* point, the classification *would* be apt and might ask whether courts are competent to do the line-drawing.

---

[175] *Id.* at 691.

[176] *See* Glenn Frankel, Four Britons Tied to London Blasts, Wash. Post, July 12, 2005, at A1.

[177] Tom Jackson, U.S. a Battlefield, Solicitor General Tells Judges, Wash. Post., July 20, 2005, at A9.

On September 9, 2005, the Fourth Circuit reversed Judge Floyd's decision in *Padilla*.[178] Because Padilla could fairly be characterized as "an enemy combatant," the court reasoned, "his military detention as an enemy combatant by the President is unquestionably authorized by [the Authorization for Use of Military Force Joint Resolution that Congress passed on September 18, 2001] as a fundamental incident to the President's prosecution of the war against al Qaeda in Afghanistan."[179] Writing for the panel, Judge Michael Luttig went on to note that

> the availability of criminal process cannot be determinative of the power to detain, if for no other reason than that criminal prosecution may well not achieve the very purpose for which detention is authorized in the first place—the prevention of return to the field of battle.[180]

The Fourth Circuit also found that the district court had "accorded insufficient deference" to "the President's determination that Padilla's detention is necessary and appropriate in the interest of national security."[181] "To subject to such exacting scrutiny the President's determination that criminal prosecution would not adequately protect the Nation's security at a vary minimum fails to accord the President the deference that is his when he acts pursuant to a broad delegation of authority from Congress, such as the [Authorization for Use of Military Force]."[182]

Whether the Supreme Court will review the Fourth Circuit's decision upholding Padilla's detention remains to be seen. On November 22, 2005, the Justice Department unsealed a criminal indictment charging Padilla with being part of a "North American support cell" that worked to support terrorist activities in Afghanistan and elsewhere from 1993 to 2001. The indictment made no allegations with respect to a "dirty bomb" plot or to any plot to blow up apartment buildings in the United Stattes. In the wake of this indictment, officials prepared to move Padilla from military custody to Justice Department detention facilities, raising

---

[178] Padilla v. Hanft, 423 F.3d 386 (4th Cir. 2005).

[179] *Id.* at 392.

[180] *Id.* at 394.

[181] *Id.* at 395.

[182] *Id.*.

the likelihood that any challenge to the Fourth Circuit's decision would be moot.[183]

It is far too early to predict how the law will develop in this area. Yet is not too early to see how, by cutting imprisonment loose from its criminal law moorings, *United States v. Salerno* has played a pivotal role in turning what many thought to be a bedrock constitutional right into a matter of legislative or even executive policy. Even one who embraces the recognition of the state's fundamental power to protect its citizens from harm can be unsettled by this new world of few certainties.

---

[183] See Eric Lichtblau, In Legal Shift, U.S. Charges Detainee in Terrorism Case, N.Y. Times, Nov. 23, 2005, at A1.

*

14

United States v. Mistretta: The Constitution and the Sentencing Guidelines

Kate Stith

On December 10, 1987, John M. Mistretta, a young man whose previous criminal record consisted of a single misdemeanor conviction for disorderly conduct, was indicted in federal District Court in Missouri on three counts related to his sale of cocaine to an undercover agent.[1] The first count alleged a conspiracy to distribute cocaine. The second count alleged the actual distribution. The third count alleged that he used a gun "during and in relation" to the crime of drug distribution; this count carried a mandatory term five year's imprisonment, consecutive to any other prison term.[2] Shortly after he was indicted, Mistretta entered a plea of guilty before Judge Howard F. Sachs. Mistretta pled guilty only to the first count, conspiracy, on the understanding that the government would dismiss the remaining two counts. He also moved to have the federal Sentencing Guidelines, under which he would be sentenced, held unconstitutional on the ground that they violated constitutional principles relating to separation-of-powers and delegation of legislative authority.[3] This plea would eventually be heard by the United States Supreme Court.[4]

At the time, the Supreme Court did not appreciate all that was before it in *Mistretta v. United States*. By a vote of 8–1, the Court upheld the constitutionality of the United States Sentencing Commission and its authority to issue the Sentencing Guidelines. But Mistretta's challenges to this new regime of criminal sentencing were narrow. He did not directly challenge the constitutionality of Congress' decision, in the

---

[1] Petition for *Certiorari* at 16a–18a, United States v. Mistretta, 488 U.S. 361 (1989) (indictment).

[2] 18 U.S.C. § 924(c) (1984 & Supp. IV).

[3] Petition for *Certiorari*, *supra* note 1, at 23a–28a.

[4] United States v. Mistretta, 488 U.S. 361 (1989).

Sentencing Reform Act of 1984,[5] to replace the sentencing discretion of federal judges with sentencing rules that are *binding* and *mandatory,* and that punish the *"real offense."*[6] The parties and the Court in *Mistretta* barely acknowledged these critical aspects of the new order, focusing instead on a fourth hallmark of the Guidelines: they had been issued by a new administrative agency, the United States Sentencing Commission. The questions on which the Court granted *certiorari* in *Mistretta* were (1) whether it was appropriate for Congress to place the Commission "in the judicial branch," as the Act provided,[7] and (2) whether Congress had given too much power to the Commission.[8] Neither of these questions encompassed the claim that the Guidelines fundamentally altered the constitutional balance-of-powers over crime-definition, prosecution, and punishment. Justice Blackmun's opinion for the Court (with only Justice Scalia dissenting) labored mightily to make sense of the questions, but its analysis is ponderous, inconsistent, and incomplete. Even when the case was argued and decided—when the Commission was young and the Sentencing Guidelines newly minted— the questions before the Court seemed artificial and curiously beside-the-point.

Within just a few years, two more significant constitutional issues came to the fore: (1) whether the Guidelines' effective shift of sentencing authority to prosecutors was appropriate, and (2) whether subjecting defendants to binding, real-offense sentencing rules deprived them of their due process rights. Throughout most of the 1990s, the Court repeatedly refused to engage issues of due process under the Guidelines, insisting, in effect, that "sentencing" is not regulated by the Constitution. However, in a series of cases beginning in 1999 with *Jones v. United States*[9] and continuing with *Apprendi v. New Jersey*[10] and *Blakely*

---

[5] Pub. L. No. 98–473, Ch. II, 98 Stat. 1987 (codified at 8 U.S.C. § 3551 *et seq.* and 28 U.S.C. § 991 *et seq).*

[6] These are three separate and independent hallmarks of the federal Sentencing Guidelines. That the Guidelines were *binding* meant that they had the force and effect of law, and any sentence imposed in violation of the instructions in the Guidelines was unlawful. Moreover, the Guidelines instructions themselves were written in *mandatory* terms, not merely *permitting* the judge to impose a sentence within a certain range, but generally *requiring* the judge to do so. Finally, because the Guidelines set punishment according to the offender's "real offense," they effectively defined and punished criminal conduct beyond that of which the defendant had been formally charged and convicted.

[7] 28 U.S.C. § 991(a).

[8] *See* Brief for the United States at 1, United States v. Mistretta, 488 U.S. 361 (1989).

[9] 526 U.S. 227 (1999).

[10] 530 U.S. 466 (2000).

v. Washington,[11] a bare majority of the Court held that binding sentencing rules which have the effect of increasing lawful punishment are constitutionally equivalent to statutory criminal charges. Most importantly, the Court held in *Blakely* that whenever a sentencing rule increases the lawful sentence upon the finding of a particular fact, that fact must be admitted by the defendant or found by a jury beyond a reasonable doubt.[12]

Sixteen years after *Mistretta*, the Court in *United States v. Booker*[13] applied *Blakely*'s holding to the federal Sentencing Guidelines, striking them down as unconstitutional not because the Sentencing Commission is located in the wrong "branch" of government, or because of its broad mandate, but because the whole system fails to meet the Constitution's due process requirements relating to prosecution and conviction.[14] Yet the surprising remedy the Court imposed in *Booker*—to keep the Guidelines intact but to provide that judges are no longer "bound" by them[15]— actually does more to reduce the hegemony of prosecutors over sentencing than to vindicate defendants' due process rights.

But this story is primarily about the *Mistretta* case itself, both the issues it decided and the issues it did not. The first section explores the contexts in which both the Guidelines and *Mistretta* arose. The second section examines the reason that two different governmental parties appeared before the Court in *Mistretta*—the Department of Justice and the United States Sentencing Commission. In order to demonstrate all that *Mistretta* missed, the third section sets forth in some depth the Sentencing Guidelines' radical transformation of both federal sentencing law and federal criminal law and practice more generally. The fourth section explores *Mistretta*'s arguments and holdings, especially the failure of the parties or the Court to recognize, much less address, any of the transformations noted above. The story ends with a consideration of *Booker*, a case with enough twists and turns to warrant its own chapter.

The Sentencing of John Mistretta

Indictment and Plea

Had Mistretta committed his crime prior to November 1, 1987, the date the Guidelines became effective, Judge Sachs would have had authority to sentence him on the conspiracy count to a term of imprisonment of up to twenty years or to any lesser term.[16] Indeed, the judge

---

[11] 542 U.S. 296 (2004).

[12] *See id.* at 303.

[13] 125 S.Ct. 738 (2005) (the U.S. cite for *Booker* is 543 U.S. 220 (2005). As of publication of this book, the case is not yet paginated in the US Reports.)

[14] *Booker*, 125 S.Ct. at 751 (Stevens, J.).

[15] *Id.* at 767 (Breyer, J.)

[16] *See* 21 U.S.C. § 841(b)(1)(C) (providing for a prison term of up to twenty years for distribution of less than 500 grams of cocaine) (1984 & Supp. IV); 21 U.S.C. § 846

could have sentenced him to probation instead. If the judge had sentenced him to prison, Mistretta would have been eligible for release by the United States Parole Commission after serving one-third of his sentence and, assuming he earned all of his statutory good-time credits, he would have to be released after serving two-thirds of his sentence.[17]

Federal judges had exercised broad sentencing discretion, within statutory limits, since the dawn of the Republic.[18] Moreover, the federal government had provided for good-time credits since the nineteenth century and parole since 1910.[19] But by the 1970s and early 1980s, reform advocates from both sides of the political spectrum increasingly viewed the system of discretionary and indeterminate sentencing as "lawless" (because there was no law governing the exercise of broad sentencing discretion), and "dishonest" (because, with parole, the actual sentence served was significantly less than the one pronounced in court). Most importantly, sentencing reformers believed that judicial discretion led to "unwarranted disparities" in sentences. These concerns—accompanied by loss of faith in the ideal of rehabilitation and concern over rising crime rates—led Congress to enact the Sentencing Reform Act, which abolished the old system and replaced it with a new system of determinate sentencing.[20] Hallmarks of the new system included abolition of early parole release (while retaining a period of supervision after release from prison), and reduction of good-time credit to no more than fifteen percent (rather than one-third) of an offender's prison sentence.[21]

(providing that punishment for conspiracy is same as for substantive offense) (1984 & Supp. IV). Mistretta was indicted under 21 U.S.C. § 841(b)(1)(B) (1984 & Supp. IV), which at the time provided for a mandatory minimum sentence of five years and a maximum sentence of forty years.

[17] See 18 U.S.C. § 4205(a) (repealed 1984) (providing in most cases for parole eligibility after one-third of term is served); 18 U.S.C. § 4161 (repealed 1984) (providing for good-time credits up to one-third of sentence).

[18] See Kate Stith & José A. Cabranes, Fear of Judging: Sentencing Guidelines in the Federal Courts 9–10, 197–98 (1998).

[19] Parole may be considered as deriving from the President's pardon authority, U.S. Const., Art. II, Sec. 2, cl. 1, and the federal parole agency has always been part of the Department of Justice. In 1976, Congress established the United States Parole Commission as an "independent agency in the Department of Justice." 18 U.S.C. § 4202 (1976) (repealed 1984).

[20] See Kate Stith & Steve Y. Koh, The Politics of Sentencing Reform: The Legislative History of the Sentencing Guidelines, 28 Wake Forest L. Rev. 223 (1993); S. Rep. No. 98–225 at 52, 56 (1984) (Senate Report accompanying Sentencing Reform Act); Stephen Breyer, The Federal Sentencing Guidelines and the Key Compromises upon Which They Rest, 17 Hofstra L. Rev. 1, 4–6 (1988).

[21] See 18 U.S.C. § 2302(a) (prospectively abolishing parole); 18 U.S.C. § 3583 (providing for supervision after release); 18 U.S.C. § 3624(b) (reducing good-time credits).

Of greatest significance to the story of *Mistretta*, the Act also established the Sentencing Commission, which it designated an "independent commission in the judicial branch of the United States."[22] The statute provided for seven voting Commissioners, at least three of whom had to be federal judges and no more than four of whom could belong to the same political party. The Commission was given the task of writing rules to govern the realm of criminal sentencing in federal courts. Congress' vision was broad and ambitious, almost utopian. The Guidelines were to "reflect, to the extent practicable, advancement in knowledge of human behavior as it relates to the criminal justice process."[23] Congress expected that binding, detailed, and comprehensive Guidelines would ensure uniform sentences in federal courts across the nation and at the same time take into account virtually all factors relevant to sentencing—thus ensuring "individualization" of punishment, formerly the province of judicial discretion, through an essentially administrative process.

Congress did not require the Commission to specify an exact sentence for each combination of relevant sentencing factors but rather to provide judges with instructions as to the weight to be given each factor, resulting in a required Guidelines sentencing range. The top end of each sentencing range could not exceed the floor of the range by more than twenty-five percent, or six months, whichever was greater.[24] Only within this range could judges hereafter exercise full sentencing discretion. The statute anticipated a limited number of cases in which a sentence outside the Guidelines range would be appropriate but severely limited judges' authority in this regard, allowing them to depart upward or downward from the Guidelines range only as authorized by the Guidelines themselves or upon finding a circumstance "not adequately taken into consideration by the Sentencing Commission in formulating the guidelines."[25] This provision was the key to the whole Sentencing Reform Act; it both made the Guidelines binding on sentencing judges and defined the narrow scope of their authority to depart.

The formal legal mechanism that ensured the new sentencing rules were binding was the right of either party, the defendant or the government, to appeal a sentence on the ground that the sentencing judge had

---

[22] 28 U.S.C. § 991(a).

[23] 28 U.S.C. § 991(b)(1)(C).

[24] 28 U.S.C. § 994(b)(2).

[25] 18 U.S.C. § 3553(b) (excised by *Booker*, 125 S.Ct. at 756–57). A subsequent amendment to the Act required that courts defer to the Commission's judgment. *See* Pub. L. No. 99–646, § 9(b) (1986) (amending 18 U.S.C. § 3553(b)). The Guidelines list certain permissible grounds for departure, including, most significantly, for defendants who have cooperated with authorities. *See infra* note 52 and accompanying text.

miscalculated the Guidelines range, that he had impermissibly departed from the range, or that any permissible departure was "unreasonable."[26] The provision for appeal was an abrupt and significant change in federal law. Criminal sentences had historically been unappealable as long as the judge sentenced within the maximum and minimum set in the statute of conviction.[27]

The Sentencing Commission issued its first set of Guidelines in late 1987.[28] The Sentencing Reform Act provided that they would be laid before Congress for 180 days, and would thereafter become effective as amended (if at all) by Congress.[29] The rules themselves were more than 250 pages in length.[30] Some were formally denominated "Guidelines" and others were called "Policy Statements" or "Commentary," but all of these (including rules governing departure from the calculated sentencing range) were binding on sentencing judges.[31]

This was the new regime under which John Mistretta was charged and would be sentenced—and in the shadow of which he entered into a plea agreement. As became commonplace in the Guidelines regime, the plea agreement not only specified to which statutory crime the defendant would plead guilty but also stipulated the factors that would determine the Guidelines sentencing range, including the amount of cocaine involved, Mistretta's possession of a gun, and his "acceptance of responsibility."[32] The judge accepted Mistretta's plea to the conspiracy charge, and ordered that a presentence Report be prepared by the Federal Probation Office. The sentencing itself would take place after the Report was completed.

First, though, the judge had to attend to Mistretta's motion to declare the Guidelines unconstitutional on the grounds that the Commission violated constitutional separation of powers principles, and that Congress had delegated excessive power to it. As Mistretta's public defender surely knew, challenges to the new regime were being made in

---

[26] 18 U.S.C. § 3742(e)(3)(C).

[27] See Dorszynski v. United States, 418 U.S. 424, 431–32 (1974).

[28] See U.S. Sentencing Guidelines Manual pt. A (1987).

[29] See Pub. L. No. 98–473, § 235(a)(1)(B)(ii) (1984).

[30] Over the course of fifteen years the federal Sentencing Guidelines have nearly doubled in length. The first Guidelines, without appendices, were 259 pages long. U.S. Sentencing Guidelines Manual (1987). The 2004 version of the Guidelines, without appendices, is 491 pages long. U.S. Sentencing Guidelines Manual (2004).

[31] See Stinson v. United States, 508 U.S. 36 (1993) (commentary binding); Williams v. United States, 503 U.S. 193 (1992) (policy statements binding).

[32] See Petition for Certiorari, supra note 1, at 21a–22a (undated stipulation of sentencing factors).

other cases in the Western District of Missouri, and nationwide. The constitutional arguments were not fact-specific or case-specific. Rather, they objected to the very existence of both the Sentencing Commission and the Sentencing Guidelines. Between February and November 1988, at least 84 written decisions were handed down by federal district courts addressing the constitutionality of the Guidelines.[33] Fifty-two decisions concluded that both the new agency and its rules violated basic constitutional principles, while thirty-three decisions upheld them against constitutional challenge. The opinion issued by the judges of the Western District of Missouri was in the latter camp, with Judge Sachs writing for himself and three others.[34] A fifth judge dissented on the ground that only Congress, not an administrative commission, could issue sentencing rules that altered the definition of federal crimes.[35]

The Sentencing Hearing

Fifteen days after the decision, Mistretta came before Judge Sachs for sentencing. Mistretta's was among the first, and perhaps the first, sentencing that Judge Sachs conducted under the Guidelines. The transcript of Mistretta's sentencing hearing[36] records Judge Sachs' attempt to harmonize the new Guidelines system with the practices of the discretionary sentencing regime. When Judge Sachs began the sentencing hearing, he had before him the presentence Report, which (except for any specific sentencing recommendation) was by law shared with both the prosecutor and the defense counsel.[37] For decades, such Reports had contained two narrative versions of the crime—the "prosecution ver-

---

[33] Between February 18, 1988 and May 11, 1988, twenty-one district courts held upheld the Guidelines, and twenty-nine invalidated them. *See* Petition for *Certiorari, supra* note 1, at 9–10 notes 10–11. My research shows that between May 12, 1988 and the Court's decision on January 18, 1989, twenty-three more courts had invalidated the Guidelines, while eleven more upheld them,; the last decision came down on Nov. 25, 1988. During the pendency of *Mistretta*, two appellate decisions were rendered. Gubiensio–Ortiz v. Kanahele, 857 F.2d 1245 (9th Cir. 1988) (invalidating Guidelines); United States v. Frank, 864 F.2d 992 (3d Cir. 1988) (upholding Guidelines).

[34] United States v. Johnson, 682 F. Supp. 1033 (W.D. Mo. 1988).

[35] *Id.* at 1035–39 (Wright, J., dissenting). Judge Scott O. Wright, in dissent, saw, long before most judges or scholars, that the Sentencing Guidelines were, in effect, supplements to the federal criminal code—though the further question whether it is unconstitutional to promulgate these supplements by means by a Sentencing Commission is a more complicated issue, *see infra* note 115 and text accompanying note 157.

[36] The Supreme Court appears not to have examined this transcript. Had it done so, it would presumably have realized that Mistretta pleaded guilty under a different provision of the drug laws than cited in its opinion. *See supra* note 16. None of the briefs in the case quoted from or cited to the sentencing hearing, except for the proposition that Mistretta was sentenced within the range required by the Sentencing Guidelines.

[37] *See* Fed. R. Crim. P. 32 (1988).

sion" and the "defense version"—as well as a summary of the probation officer's own investigation of the social background of the defendant, and, finally, the officer's confidential sentencing recommendation,[38] to which, studies showed, judges often deferred.[39] Beginning in the 1970s, the presentence Report also contained the Parole Commission's parole-release guidelines regarding the offense in question.[40] These parole guidelines were summarized in the same kind of two dimensional matrix that the Sentencing Commission would use.[41] One axis designated the numerical severity of the offense (which the Sentencing Guidelines term the "offense level"), and the other the severity of the offender's previous criminal record (which the Sentencing Guidelines term the "criminal history category"). The box where the axes intersected provided the Parole Commission's guidelines for how much time the offender should serve.

It may seem curious that the presentence Report in John Mistretta's case included a summary of how the *Parole Commission's* guidelines would treat the defendant and his crime. After all, Mistretta had to be sentenced under the new regime. Parole was abolished. Upon reflection, however, it is entirely understandable that in this transition period, the probation officer working with Judge Sachs, and the judge himself, might have retained a great interest in the parole guidelines, since they had, until now, determined sentences with reference to these guidelines. Given federal good-time law (reducing whatever sentence a judge gave by up to one-third), and given statutory restrictions on parole release (which generally could not occur until one-third of the sentence was served), the probation officer—and the judge—could calculate the necessary nominal sentence that would result in a period of incarceration within the guidelines that the United States Parole Commission had established.

And so it was that at Mistretta's hearing, Judge Sachs began by noting that under the now-inapplicable parole guidelines, the appropri-

---

[38] *See* Sharon M. Bunzel, *The Probation Officer and the Federal Sentencing Guidelines: Strange Philosophical Bedfellows*, 104 Yale L. J. 933, 940–45 (1995).

[39] *See* John C. Coffee, Jr., *The Repressed Issues of Sentencing: Accountability, Predictability, and Equality in the Era of the Sentencing Commission*, 66 Geo. L. J. 975 (1978) (summarizing studies).

[40] In 1976, Congress required the Parole Commission to publish its release guidelines, which federal parole authorities had been doing on an experimental basis since 1973. *See* 18 U.S.C. §§ 4203(a), 4206 (1976) (repealed 1984).

[41] The Sentencing Guidelines ranges are also laid out in a two-dimension matrix, with forty-three "offense levels" along the vertical axis, and six "criminal history categories" along the horizontal axis. The box at which the defendant's offense level and criminal history category intersect provides the Guidelines sentence range, absent any basis for departure.

ate point of release would be after twelve to eighteen months of incarceration. The judge recognized that these parole calculations were no longer directly relevant, but commented that under similar circumstances in the discretionary era he would have imposed a sentence of four or five years in light of this recommendation. Indeed, the judge noted that earlier that very day he had sentenced an offender in a somewhat similar case—but in which the offense had taken place prior to November 1, 1987—and had imposed a sentence of six years in prison.[42]

While discussion of the old parole guidelines was unnecessary, the probation officer was required to include in Mistretta's presentence Report his calculations under the Sentencing Guidelines.[43] In Mistretta's case, these calculations were straightforward, for the parties had stipulated to all of the facts that the Guidelines deemed relevant. The Guidelines range for Mistretta's final offense level (14) and criminal history category (I) was fifteen to twenty-one months.[44] The judge could sentence Mistretta anywhere within this range. Neither the probation officer nor the parties noted any basis for departure.

After the judge noted the Guidelines sentencing range, Mistretta renewed his separation-of-powers objections. Moreover, at the last moment before sentence was pronounced, Mistretta's public defender made a new constitutional argument, that the Due Process Clause affords defendants a right to an "individualized" sentence.[45] Mistretta's attorney noted that his client had completed participation in a drug treatment program.[46] Yet this effort at rehabilitation was nowhere factored into the Guidelines sentencing range, which surely must have seemed odd and unfair; this was precisely the type of plea for leniency that had often been made during the discretionary era.[47] Judge Sachs rejected Mistretta's due process claim, as he had the earlier separation-of-powers challenges. It was with apparent approval and relief, however, that the judge noted the Guidelines range was close to that Mistretta would have served had the judge sentenced him in the pre-Guidelines era. While

---

[42] Petition for *Certiorari*, *supra* note 1, at 23a, 29a (transcript of sentencing hearing).

[43] *See* U.S. Sentencing Guidelines Manual § 6A1.1 (1987).

[44] *See id.* §§ 2D1.4 (equating conspiracy and actual offense for drug convictions), 2D1.1 (table enhancing offense level on basis of quantity of drugs), 2D1.1(b) (imposing a firearm upward adjustment), 3E1.1 (providing a downward adjustment for acceptance of responsibility), 4A1.1 (defining criminal history categories).

[45] *See* Petition for *Certiorari*, *supra* note 1, at 26a (citing United States v. Frank, 682 F. Supp. 815 (W.D. Pa. 1988)). The *Frank* case was subsequently reversed by the Third Circuit, *see supra* note 33.

[46] Petition for *Certiorari*, *supra* note 1, at 26a–27a.

[47] *See* Jack B. Weinstein, *A Trial Judge's Second Impression of the Federal Sentencing Guidelines*, 66 S. Cal. L. Rev. 357, 364 (1992).

Judge Sachs could have sentenced Mistretta anywhere within the Guidelines range, he decided to choose the mid-point of eighteen months—
mentioning that he was reluctant to go lower because of the similarity
between Mistretta's case and the case he had sentenced earlier in the
day, exercising pre-Guidelines discretion.[48]

The Parties and the Non-party Before the Supreme Court

The Western District of Missouri's decision would normally have
been appealed to the United States Court of Appeals for the Eighth
Circuit. Before the Eighth Circuit could grant review, however, the
Supreme Court did so, citing the exceptional circumstance of "disarray
among the Federal District Courts"[49] in their multiple and contradictory
holdings as to the constitutionality of the Sentencing Commission. Until
the Court ruled definitively on the matter, no one—not courts, not
Congress, not prosecutors, not defendants—could be certain whether the
criminal sentences being handed down were valid.

When the Supreme Court granted *certiorari* in *Mistretta v. United
States*, there were only two parties to the case. One was John Mistretta,
who would be represented in the Supreme Court by Alan B. Morrison, a
veteran Supreme Court litigator. The other party was the United States,
represented by the Office of the Solicitor General in the Department of
Justice. The Solicitor General himself—Charles Fried, on leave from his
professorship at Harvard Law School—would argue the cause for the
Government. Even though its own constitutionality was at stake, the
Sentencing Commission was not a party to the case.

The United States Department of Justice

The Department of Justice clearly had an immediate, critical interest in resolving the "disarray in the Federal District Courts" over the
constitutionality of the Sentencing Guidelines, for it was representing a

---

[48] Petition for *Certiorari, supra* note 1, at 29a–30a. We may note that upon this review
of the record, it is not clear what benefit there would have been to Mistretta in having the
Guidelines declared unconstitutional. Judge Sachs had said that in a discretionary regime,
he would have given a higher nominal sentence, but only on the expectation that under the
policies of the Parole Commission, Mistretta would serve approximately the same time in
prison as under his Guidelines sentence. *Id.* at 29a–30a. Indeed, because there remained
federal good-time (of up to fifteen percent of sentence) under the Guidelines regime,
Mistretta arguably would serve a lesser prison term under the Guidelines than under the
previous regime. The judge did note, however, that in contrast to the pre-Guidelines
sentence, a Guidelines sentence would include an additional three year term of "supervised
release." *See* 18 U.S.C. § 3583(b)(2). He thus recognized that "[f]rom a technical stand-
point, I think it can be argued for the defendant that the Guidelines are adverse to him."
Petition for *Certiorari, supra* note 1, at 30a.

[49] *Mistretta*, 488 U.S. at 371. The Supreme Court's Rule 18 lists this among the factors
warranting expedited review from a district court.

party—the United States—in every criminal case in the federal courts. It also had a duty to defend the constitutionality of the Sentencing Reform Act, a federal law.[50] Even at this early stage, lawyers in the Department of Justice surely were aware of another interest the Department had in the new regime: the Guidelines were helpful to the Department's internal "clients"—federal prosecutors in the field. Guidelines sentences were, across nearly every crime category, far greater than discretionary era sentences,[51] and judges had limited authority to depart below the calculated Guidelines range. There is no reason to suppose that prosecutors are seeking to maximize sentence severity. But the prospect of severe sentences if the Guidelines were fully applied provided new leverage for inducing defendants to plead guilty to lesser charges.

The Sentencing Reform Act provided prosecutors a second major source of leverage, as well, for it allowed sentences below the calculated Guidelines range in cases where the defendant cooperated in the prosecution of others. This departure authority—which became known as a "5K1" departure after the Guidelines subsection that authorizes it—was of critical importance to both defendants and prosecutors for two reasons. First, it was one of the few lawful bases on which a judge could issue a below-Guidelines sentence. Second, the Sentencing Commission chose to make prosecutors the gatekeepers for 5K1 departures; judges could take cooperation into account only if the prosecutor made a motion to that effect, not on the defendant's motion or on information in the presentence Report.[52]

The United States Sentencing Commission

While it is clear in retrospect that the Guidelines have conferred significant power over criminal punishment to federal prosecutors, as a formal matter the Sentencing Reform Act transferred sentencing authority from individual federal judges not to prosecutors, but to the Sentencing Commission. And it was the Sentencing Commission—not the Department of Justice or its prosecutors—whose life was on the line in *Mistretta*. One of the curiosities of the Sentencing Commission, however, is that it was not—and legally could not be—a formal party in any of the cases brewing in the federal courts. Unlike virtually every other agency

---

[50] *See* Seth P. Waxman, *Defending Congress*, 79 N.C. L. Rev. 1073 (2001); Drew S. Days III, *In Search of the Solicitor General's Clients: A Drama With Many Characters*, 83 Ky. L.J. 485 (1995).

[51] *See* Stith & Cabranes, *supra* note 18, at 59–65.

[52] *See* 28 U.S.C. § 994(n) (directing Commission to assure that Guidelines provide for lower sentence, even below statutory minimum, where defendant provides substantial assistance to law enforcement); U.S. Sentencing Guidelines Manual § 5K1.1 (1987) ("substantial assistance" departure available only upon motion by government).

in the federal government, it did not enforce its own regulations.[53] Moreover, these regulations were not subject to challenge under the Administrative Procedure Act as exceeding agency authority or for being "arbitrary and capricious."[54]

The Commission's special status meant that it would never be answerable to a court—but neither would it be a party to any suit challenging its very legality. The Commission thus filed full *amicus* briefs in several lower court cases and in the Supreme Court, urging its own constitutionality on a basis different from that argued by the Department of Justice (as explored *infra*). It also requested opportunity to participate in oral argument, which the Court granted.[55] Professor Paul Bator of Harvard Law School argued on its behalf.

The Transformation Wrought by the Sentencing Guidelines

In order to appreciate why the challenges before the Court in *Mistretta* were largely beside the point, it is important to understand the scale of change wrought by the Sentencing Reform Act of 1984. Taken together, the innovations set forth in the Act effected a sea-change in the operation of the federal criminal justice system.

The Content of the Guidelines

The *structural innovations* of the Sentencing Reform Act were manifold—including abolition of parole; allowance of appeals; creation of a new administrative agency on which Article III judges would sit; and delegation to that agency of power to promulgate rules that would bind sentencing courts. But in addition—and not commented on or perhaps even realized by the Supreme Court in *Mistretta*—the *content* of the particular Guidelines issued by the United States Sentencing Commis-

---

[53] This structural oddity led the Commission to enlist federal probation officers to ensure that federal trial judges knew how to conduct the calculations required by the Guidelines. The Commission anticipated, correctly, that sentencing judges would show deference to the analysis and calculations provided for them in presentence Reports. *See* Bunzel, *supra* note 38, at 957–60.

[54] *See* 5 U.S.C. §§ 702, 706. Because the Sentencing Reform Act located the Commission "in the judicial branch," it has been understood to be within the exception of the APA that provides that "courts" are not subject to suit. *See* 5 U.S.C. § 551 ("the courts of the United States" are not an "agency" within the meaning of the APA). Although no one believes that the Commission is a court, *see Mistretta*, 488 U.S. at 384–85, Congress appears to have intended this designation to exempt the Sentencing Guidelines from judicial review under the APA. *See* S. Rep. No. 98–225, *supra* note 20, at 180–181; United States v. Lopez, 938 F.2d 1293, 1297 (D.C. Cir. 1991). Congress did provide, however, that the standard, notice-and-comment provisions of the APA would apply to the Commission, *see* 28 U.S.C. § 994(x) (applying informal rulemaking procedures of APA, at 5 U.S.C. § 553, to the Sentencing Commission).

[55] *See Mistretta*, 488 U.S. at 362.

sion (in contradistinction to the guidelines systems adopted contemporaneously in some fifteen states)[56] represented a remarkable rejection of the factors that had influenced criminal sentencing in the previous era. The Commission decreed that most background and personal factors of the defendant—including sex, age, race, education, military or other community service, youthful disadvantage, family ties, and community ties—are either never relevant or "not ordinarily relevant" to determining the punishment to be imposed.[57]

Of even greater significance, the Sentencing Commission decided to require that sentencing ranges be based in large part on the offender's "real offense" rather than the crime for which he or she was formally convicted. Such real-offense sentencing means that before imposing a sentence, judges must engage in extended factfinding (or receive factual stipulations from the parties) which determines the severity of the sentence called for by the Guidelines; these non-conviction facts were termed by the Commission "relevant conduct."[58] Among other matters, the Guidelines' "relevant conduct" rule attributes to the defendant "all reasonably foreseeable acts and omissions of others in furtherance of the jointly undertaken criminal activity."[59] Thus, for instance, a corner drug dealer may be convicted of a single sale of a small amount of drugs to an undercover agent. But if, after conviction, additional evidence is presented that allows the judge to conclude by a preponderance of the evidence that the defendant knew his employers imported large quantities of drugs over time, all of those drug sales are attributable to the defendant, whose sentence under the Guidelines would be almost equivalent to what it would be if the defendant had been convicted of personally distributing the entire amount of drugs. Even those aspects of an offender's "relevant conduct" that had been previously or separately charged as a criminal offense, even if the defendant was *acquitted*, are taken into account in calculation of the sentencing range for the offense at hand, subject only to the limitation that the defendants sentence not exceed the statutory maximum for the offense of conviction.[60]

---

[56] *See* Kate Stith, *Sentencing Guidelines: Where We Are and How We Got there*, 44 St. Louis U. L.J. 387 (2000); Kevin R. Reitz, *Sentencing Guidelines Systems and Sentence Appeals: A Comparison of Federal and State Experiences*, 91 Nw. U. L. Rev. 1441 (1997); Richard S. Frase, *Sentencing Guidelines in the States: Lessons for State and Federal Reformers*, 6 Fed. Sent. 123 (1993).

[57] *See* U.S. Sentencing Guidelines Manual § 5H1 (2004).

[58] *Id.* § 1B1.3.

[59] *Id.* § 1B1.3 (a)(1)(B).

[60] *See id.* § 1B1.3, cmt. *See also* United States v. Watts, 519 U.S. 148 (1997) (*per curiam*); Witte v. United States, 515 U.S. 389 (1995). *Watts* and *Witte* are discussed in *infra* text accompanying notes 132–33.

Because the Guidelines were premised on the need to minimize the exercise of discretionary judgment by the sentencing judge, they specify each aggravating sentencing factor (and the few mitigating factors) with exquisite detail and precision—providing, for instance, a greater enhancement for a defendant who was "leader" of a criminal enterprise than for a "manager."[61] The Commission was also constrained by a series of directives in the Sentencing Reform Act that called for harsh punishment.[62] It has been asserted that the Guidelines were largely based on "past practice" in the federal courts,[63] and the argument persists even today that the Sentencing Guidelines simply continue, in a different structure, what federal judges have always done, taking into account what Justice Breyer in *Booker* refers to as "the manner in which an offense was committed."[64] Yet both the content of the rules and their overall degree of severity belie these claims.[65]

The Content of the Criminal Law

Of even greater moment, the Guidelines changed the content of federal criminal law itself. Prior to the advent of the Guidelines, there was a clear demarcation between "crime" and "punishment"—that is, between the adjudicatory phase of the criminal law and the sentencing phase. The Constitution speaks directly to the adjudicatory phase, requiring that "in all criminal prosecutions," the crime must be charged and proved in accordance with the requirements laid out in the Fifth, Sixth, and Fourteenth Amendments—including the right to a jury trial and proof beyond a reasonable doubt of every element of the crime.[66] The Constitution, however, says nothing about punishment beyond the prohibition in the Eighth Amendment on "cruel and unusual" punishment. Neither the Due Process Clause nor other procedural protections of the Constitution were understood to apply to sentencing.[67] Criminal law

---

[61] U.S. Sentencing Guidelines Manual § 3B1.1 (2004).

[62] 28 U.S.C. §§ 994(i), 994(m); *see also* John Lott, *Eliminating Sentencing Guidelines Would Make Penalties More Equal*, Investors' Business Daily (February 7, 2005).

[63] *See* United States Sentencing Comm'n, Supplementary Report On the Initial Sentencing Guidelines and Policy Statements 16–18 (1987); Stephen G. Breyer, *supra* note 20, at 17.

[64] 125 S.Ct. at 760 (Breyer, J.).

[65] *See* Stith & Cabranes, *supra* note 18, at 59–76.

[66] *See* In re Winship, 397 U.S. 358 (1970).

[67] *See* McMillan v. Pennsylvania, 477 U.S. 79 (1986); United States v. Grayson, 438 U.S. 41, 53–55 (1978); Williams v. New York, 337 U.S. 241, 246 (1949). *See infra* notes 135–39 and accompanying text.

theorists even posited different justifications for criminal prohibitions, on the one hand, and criminal punishments, on the other.[68]

The Guidelines obliterated this distinction between "crime" and "punishment." Binding sentencing rules that increase the lawful sentencing range on the basis of conduct outside the crime of conviction in effect "criminalize" the additional (non-conviction) conduct.[69] The astounding ambition of the Sentencing Reform Act—to at once rationalize criminal punishments and to eliminate inter-judge sentencing disparity—necessitated some form of "real offense" sentencing, as the statute recognized.[70] If it were to rationalize sentencing, the Sentencing Commission needed to group together different federal statutes, which had accumulated over the centuries, and to provide a unified set of penalty provisions to whichever statutory crime might be charged. In sum, given its mandate to eliminate sentencing "disparity," the Commission could not adopt pure "charged-offense" sentencing, where the sentencing range would depend solely on the statutory crime of which the defendant was convicted.

Congress and the Commission also had another, equally important, reason to reject a system of simple charged-offense sentencing. Prosecutors decide under which statutory provisions the defendant will be charged, and which charges will be dismissed upon a plea of guilty. If the lawful sentence were tied solely to the offense of conviction, then sentencing discretion would be transferred from individual judges not to the Sentencing Commission, as Congress sought, but to individual prosecutors. Congress and the Commission apparently believed that if sentence is based not on a defendant's charged conduct, but on his *actual* conduct (his "relevant conduct"), prosecutors would not be able to monopolize control over sentencing through charge bargaining.[71] But

---

[68] *See, e.g.*, H.L.A. Hart, *Punishment and Responsibility* (1968).

[69] This argument is pursued at length in Stith & Cabranes, *supra* note 18. Consider, for instance, the conduct of using a gun during the course of distributing narcotics. We know that Congress enacted a statute specifically criminalizing such conduct; this was the charge in the third count of Mistretta's indictment, a charge that was ultimately dropped, *see supra* note 2 and accompanying text. But Mistretta's Guidelines range was mandatorily enhanced because he stipulated that he had possessed a gun in connection with the narcotics conspiracy to which he pled guilty, *see supra* note 44; U.S. Sentencing Guidelines Manual § 2D1.1 (1987).

[70] *See* 28 U.S.C. §§ 991(b)(1)(B), 994(c); William W. Wilkins, Jr. & John R. Steer, *Relevant Conduct: The Cornerstone of the Federal Sentencing Guidelines*, 41 S. C. L. Rev. 495, 501 (1990) (noting that unlike sentencing reform bill in House of Representatives, which called for a "charged-offense" system, the Senate bill, which was ultimately enacted, "did not expressly specify, [but] seemed to lean toward a real offense system.").

[71] *See id.* at 497–99; Breyer, *supra* note 20, at 8–11; Michael Tonry & John C. Coffee, *Enforcing Sentencing Guidelines: Plea Bargaining and Review Mechanisms, in* The Sentencing Commission and its Guidelines 142, 152–54 (Andrew von Hirsch et al., eds.) (1987).

there was a fundamental problem with the idea of "real-offense" sentencing rules as an antidote to the prosecutorial control: As soon as sentencing rules are promulgated, the factors listed in those rules become, in effect, additional "charges," which can be bargained over just as statutory charges may be.[72]

Granting Judges the Power to Prosecute and Convict

The Commission was aware that prosecutorial charging and plea-bargaining power could undermine its attempts to ensure that defendants who committed the same "real offense" would be sentenced within the same Guidelines range. Thus when it announced its rules relating to "relevant conduct," the Commission took pains to ensure that judges, not prosecutors, would decide which "relevant conduct" factors are present in each case, despite prosecutors' greater and earlier familiarity with case information. The Commission instructed federal probation officers to gather evidence relating to the actual extent of the defendant's criminal activity, and proscribed judges from accepting plea-agreements that "undermine" the Guidelines or that fail to "adequately reflect the seriousness of the actual offense behavior."[73]

Probation officers thus had a new role under the Guidelines, that of criminal investigator. In addition to presenting the prosecution and defense versions of the crime, the Commission required that the presentence Report advise the judge of the "facts relevant to sentencing."[74] Trained in social work, not in criminal investigation, probation officers clearly had to obtain information about the actual "facts" from someplace, but were warned against relying on the prosecutor and defense attorney—because the parties might "by agreement" attempt to "eliminate relevant information," and officers were specifically forbidden to "withhold from the court reliable information."[75] In the early years under the Guidelines, probation officers in at least some federal judicial districts did attempt to perform the new duty thrust upon them by the Sentencing Commission, leading to heated complaints from defense

---

[72] *See* Albert W. Alschuler, *Sentencing Reform and Prosecutorial Power: A Critique of Recent Proposals for "Fixed" and "Presumptive" Sentencing*, 126 U. Pa. L. Rev. 550 (1978); Coffee, *supra* note 39. As Professor Mark Tushnet concisely explained in 1992, "[A]ll a prosecutor would need to do to defeat real-offense sentencing would be to select a charge whose maximum under the guidelines was below the minimum of the range for the real offense—in other words, choose a different 'real' offense." Mark Tushnet, *The Sentencing Commission and Constitutional Theory: Bowls and Plateaus in Separation of Powers Theory*, 66 S. Cal. L. Rev. 581, 593–94 (1992).

[73] U.S. Sentencing Guidelines Manual § 6B1.2 (2004).

[74] *Id.* § 6A1.1 (cmt).

[75] Administrative Office of the United States Courts, Division of Probation, Presentence Investigation Reports under the Sentencing Reform Act of 1984, 4–5 (1987).

attorneys that probation officers seemed to operate as a "third adversary in the courtroom."[76]

The Commission's second policy complemented the first. Once the "actual" facts were reported by the probation officer, the judge was required to act on them. The Commission stressed that a judge is not "bound" by stipulations of fact proposed by the parties and should consider not only the parties' stipulations but "the results of the presentence investigation" in determining "the factual basis for the sentence."[77] Finally, having found the "facts," judges were required to impose a sentence within the Guidelines range. As Justice Breyer, who had played a major role in drafting the initial Sentencing Guidelines,[78] would explain in *Booker*, "Congress's basic statutory goal—a system that diminishes sentencing disparity—depends for its success upon judicial efforts to determine, and to base punishment upon, the real conduct that underlies the crime of conviction."[79]

This "real offense" approach so admired by Justice Breyer is based on confidence in administrative processes and neutral expertise, but little appreciation of adversary litigation. In an adversary process, there are no "facts" except those that can be proved in court, to whatever burden of proof is required. This is a fundamentally different process from administrative or investigatory factfinding, where an expert (or at least neutral) umpire obtains information from which he constructs not evidence or proof, but factual conclusions. In seeking to turn sentencing hearings into some combination of a litigated hearing and an administrative proceeding, the Commission apparently did not consider that the Constitution's specific requirements relating to criminal cases—including accusation by a grand jury, the right of confrontation, trial to a jury and proof beyond a reasonable doubt—might apply to codified sentencing rules such as the Guidelines, as *Blakely* and *Booker* later held.

But there is another aspect of the Commission's administrative approach that is constitutionally troubling, which even *Blakely* and *Booker* do not comment upon; it allowed the judge to usurp the accusatory role of the prosecutor and the grand jury. As sentencing was envisioned by the Commission, even when the prosecutor did not charge some aggravating factor under the Guidelines—or even if the parties

---

[76] *See* Jerry D. Denzlinger & David E. Miller, *The Federal Probation Officer: Life Before and After Guideline Sentencing*, Probation 49, 50–51 (December 1991).

[77] U.S. Sentencing Guidelines Manual § 6B1.4(d) & cmt. (2004).

[78] Stephen Breyer, then a judge on the U.S. Court of Appeals for the First Circuit, had been one of the original seven commissioners and by all accounts played a large role in negotiating their language. *See generally* Stith & Cabranes, *supra* note 18, at 49–50, 55, 57–58.

[79] 125 S.Ct. at 759 (Breyer, J.).

stipulated that the factor was not present—the judge (with the help of the probation officer) had authority to "charge" the factor and to hold a hearing and call witnesses, if necessary, to "find" whether the factor existed. This is what happened in *Blakely*, when the judge took on the role of third-party prosecutor, found an applicable basis for enhancement that the prosecutor had not charged, and then proceeded to both to accuse the defendant and to find him guilty of this supplemental bad conduct.[80]

Granting the Prosecutor the Power to Sentence

As a practical matter, in very few cases did any of the participants involved—the probation officer, the prosecutor, the defendant, his counsel, or the judge—have the incentive or resources to perform their new roles. While Congress and the Commission may have been committed to "real-offense" sentencing, real prosecutors and real defense attorneys have a strong interest in settling a case. Probation officers soon learned that it is time-consuming and often unproductive to attempt to learn "facts" from sources other than the attorneys in the case, while judges generally had no interest in forcing the parties to prove or disprove "facts" that neither party wanted the sentence to be based upon.

That the Sentencing Commission only wrote the Guidelines, and was without power to enforce them directly, in the end kept the Commission's vision from being implemented. In the first year of the Guidelines, just over 85% of federal convictions were obtained by guilty plea.[81] That percentage has steadily increased. By 2002, over 97% of all convictions were obtained by guilty plea,[82] and the great majority of these were accompanied by a plea-agreement stipulating applicable Guidelines factors.[83] Implicitly recognizing the legitimacy of such agreements, the Federal Rules of Criminal Procedure were amended in 1998,

---

[80] *See* Blakely v. Washington, 542 U.S. 296, 300 (2004); State v. Blakely, 47 P.3d 149, 154 (Wash. Ct. App. 2002). *See generally* Kate Stith, *Crime and Punishment Under the Constitution*, 2004 Sup. Ct. Rev. 221 (2005).

[81] *See* Administrative Office of the U.S. Courts, Federal Offenders in the United States Courts, 1986 through 1990, at 50 (1990).

[82] United States Sentencing Commission, 2002 Sourcebook on Federal Sentencing Statistics 21 (2003).

[83] *See* Frank O. Bowman III, *Train Wreck? Or Can the Federal Sentencing System Be Saved?*, 41 Am. Crim. L. Rev. 217, 229 (2004); Joseph S. Hall, *Rule 11(e)(1)(C) and the Sentencing Guidelines: Bargaining Outside the Heartland?*, 87 Iowa L. Rev. 587, 589–90 (2002). Mistretta's case is illustrative. He was originally indicted for distributing a quantity of narcotics that mandated a minimum sentence of five years in prison, but stipulated to a lesser quantity and received a lower sentence. *See supra* note 16. *See generally* Tony Garoppolo, *Fact Bargaining: What the Sentencing Commission Hath Wrought*, 10 Crim. Prac. Man. (BNA) 405 (1996).

to make clear that prosecutors could promise not only what statutory charges would be dismissed, but also what Guidelines factors would be charged.[84] Plea-bargaining in the Guidelines era became, for all intents and purposes, sentence bargaining, and prosecutors' power over sentence provided them with considerable leverage to induce pleas of guilty. It is critical to understand, as well, that prosecutors' leverage was amplified by the lesser procedural protections afforded to defendants with respect to proof of Guidelines factors. When the defendant is charged with a statutory offense, he knows that his alternative to pleading guilty is to insist upon a jury trial where the prosecutor must prove every element of the crime beyond a reasonable doubt. But under the Guidelines, judges, not juries, find aggravating or mitigating Guidelines factors; the rules of evidence (including the hearsay rule protecting the constitutional right of confrontation of witnesses) do not apply; and the burden of proof of Guidelines factors is a "preponderance of the evidence,"[85] the more-likely-than-not burden that is used in civil cases.

Implementing binding sentencing rules as part of an administrative process, rather than as part of an adversary proceeding tightly regulated by the Constitution, surely had advantages. As Justice Breyer explains in *Booker,* "the relation between the sentence and what actually occurred is likely to be considerably more distant under a system with a jury trial requirement patched onto it."[86] In other words, it is far easier to punish for the whole crime if we apply constitutional processes only to part of the prosecution.

Mistretta in the Supreme Court

Neither the parties nor any member of the Court in *Mistretta* considered the due process implications of "real offense" sentencing. Indeed, no lower court struck down the Guidelines on the basis that mandatory punishment for non-conviction conduct violates the Fifth and Sixth Amendments.[87] Such a claim surely seemed foreclosed by the Supreme Court's prior decision in *McMillan v. Pennsylvania*, upholding a statutory sentencing enhancement upon a judicial finding that the defendant had possessed a firearm during the crime of conviction.[88] Nor

---

[84] Fed. R. Crim. P. 11(c)(1) (2004).

[85] U.S. Sentencing Guidelines Manual § 6A1.3 (cmt.) (2004).

[86] 125 S.Ct. at 761 (Breyer, J.).

[87] The opinion of Judge G. Thomas Eisele came close, but ultimately wove this concern into its holding that the Sentencing Reform Act was an excessive delegation of legislative power to define crimes. *See* United States v. Brittman, 687 F.Supp. 1329, 1335 (E.D. Ark. 1988).

[88] 477 U.S. 79 (1986). In the few cases in the early days of the Guidelines that brought a Sixth Amendment or other procedural challenge to the Guidelines, the courts generally

did the claims in *Mistretta* derive from any asserted limitations on Congress' power to define crime and to set punishment—with good reason, for the Supreme Court had struck down mandatory sentencing (and required "individualized" sentencing) only in the context of capital punishment as part of its general "death is different" jurisprudence.[89]

Rather, the arguments in *Mistretta* tracked the clear battle lines that had been drawn in scores of cases in the lower courts, including two cases in the federal Courts of Appeals:[90] Congress had delegated too much power to the Commission, and placing the Commission in the judicial branch impermissibly aggrandized the power of that branch. The challenges were based on the particular way in which Sentencing Guidelines had become law. Had Congress itself simply enacted the Commission's handiwork into statutory law (even while retaining the way the Guidelines were implemented—through judicial factfinding), Mistretta's constitutional claims would have evaporated.

Delegation of Authority to the Commission

In rejecting Mistretta's claim that Congress had delegated too much authority to the Commission, Justice Blackmun's opinion stressed the many directives and restrictions that the Sentencing Reform Act placed on the Commission. Many of the statutory directives were in fact so vague or open-ended as to be meaningless,[91] or potentially inconsistent.[92] But the question as the Court saw it was simply whether the amount of guidance was sufficient. The Court had previously upheld broad delegations of congressional lawmaking authority,[93] and the guidance and

---

relied on *McMillan* to reject the claim, *see, e.g.,* United States v. McGhee, 882 F.2d 1095, 1098 (6th Cir. 1989). *See also* Tushnet, *supra* note 72, at 590 (no serious constitutional question would have been raised had Congress simply prescribed mandatory sentences for every offense).

[89] *See, e.g.,* Gregg v. Georgia, 428 U.S. 153, 188 (1976) (joint opinion of Stewart, Powell, and Stevens, JJ.); Woodson v. North Carolina, 428 U.S. 280, 298 (1976); Lockett v. Ohio, 438 U.S. 586, 608–10 (1978).

[90] *See supra* note 33.

[91] *See, e.g.,* 28 U.S.C. § 991(b)(1)(B) (requiring that Guidelines "provide certainty and fairness in meeting the purposes of sentencing, avoiding unwarranted sentencing disparities ... while maintaining sufficient flexibility to permit individualized sentences when warranted").

[92] For instance, how could the Guidelines be "sufficient[ly] flexibil[e] to permit individualized sentences," *id.*, while at the same time reflecting the "general inappropriateness" of considering personal characteristics such as education, vocational skills, employment record, and family and community ties, 28 U.S.C. § 994(e)?

[93] *See, e.g.,* Lichter v. United States, 334 U.S. 742 (1948); Yakus v. United States, 321 U.S. 414 (1944); American Power & Light Co. v. SEC, 329 U.S. 90 (1946). However, there had been intimations from some members of the Court, especially Justice Rehnquist, that

explicit requirements in the Sentencing Reform Act were at least as great as those in earlier cases. Thus, if the Court was presented with the right question, it gave the right answer.

There is a good argument, however, that the delegation issue was simply a distraction. Far from delegating too much, Congress only *nominally* delegated to the Commission the power to answer four important questions that must be answered by any set of sentencing rules. First, how much discretion should be left to judges? Second, should sentences be based on the offense of conviction alone or on non-conviction factors as well? Third, how severe should sentences be? And finally, how much authority should prosecutors have to exempt certain defendants from the otherwise binding rules? As we have seen, the Sentencing Reform Act and its legislative history[94] were relatively clear as to the answers to each of these questions: requiring that judicial discretion be greatly reduced, that sentences be based on "real offense" considerations and the defendant's prior criminal record, that punishments be made more severe for many crimes, and that below-Guidelines sentences be permitted for defendants who cooperate with prosecutors.[95] The real question was not whether Congress delegated too much, but whether its *pretended* delegation was constitutionally appropriate.

A Commission "In the Judicial Branch of the United States"

Most of the specific challenges brought by Mistretta and addressed by the Court related to the designation of the Commission, in the statute that established it, as an "independent commission in the judicial branch of the United States," and the related requirement that at least three of the seven Commissioners be Article III judges.[96] The Court acknowledged that the Commission was "a peculiar institution within the framework of our government,"[97] because rulemaking authority was normally exercised by executive branch agencies. But, in accord with its recent separation-of-powers decisions,[98] the Court was prepared to allow Congress to innovate in developing new institutions for new or newly perceived social problems, as long as there is no "encroachment or aggrandizement of one branch at the expense of the other."[99]

---

then non-delegation doctrine might be revived. *See, e.g.*, Industrial Union Dep't v. American Petroleum Inst., 448 U.S. 607 (1980).

[94] *See* S. Rep. No. 98–225, *supra* note 20; Stith & Koh, *supra* note 20.

[95] *See supra* text accompanying notes 24–26, 57–65.

[96] 28 U.S.C. § 991(a).

[97] 488 U.S. at 384.

[98] *See* Morrison v. Olson, 487 U.S. 654 (1988); Buckley v. Valeo, 424 U.S. 1, 182 (1976). *Compare* Bowsher v. Synar, 478 U.S. 714 (1986); INS v. Chadha, 462 U.S. 919 (1983).

[99] 488 U.S. at 382, *quoting* Buckley v. Valeo, 424 U.S. 1, 182 (1976).

The major basis for the argument that the Sentencing Reform Act had *aggrandized* the judicial branch was that the Sentencing Commission was exercising legislative powers that were inappropriate for the judicial branch collectively or judges individually. The Court could have answered this argument by concluding, as the Solicitor General urged,[100] that the Sentencing Commission was exercising not judicial but executive power. Accepting that Congress has plenary authority to determine the appropriate punishments for crimes, it may do so with precision, in individual criminal statutes or in a general sentencing law. Alternatively, Congress may statutorily set only broad boundaries and grant sentencing judges discretionary authority to determine sentence within these boundaries, as it did for centuries. The third alternative is for Congress to delegate sentencing authority to an administrative agency. If Congress chooses the last of these, as it did in the Sentencing Reform Act, then the agency, like all agencies delegated legislative authority, is exercising *executive* power.

Instead of acknowledging that the Commission was exercising executive power, however, *Mistretta* repeatedly accepted, indeed acclaimed, Congress' characterization of the Commission as being in the "judicial branch." Justice Blackman concluded that the Commission was not making law, and that far from aggrandizing judicial power, the Sentencing Reform Act left the balance of power in sentencing exactly as it had found it, as the Sentencing Commission insisted in its separate brief to the Court.[101] The statute simply "acknowledged the role that the Judiciary has always played, and continued to play, in sentencing,"[102] because "[p]rior to the passage of the Act, the Judicial Branch, as an aggregate, decided precisely the questions assigned to the Commission: what sentence is appropriate to what criminal conduct under what circumstances."[103] In sum, the Guidelines "do no more than fetter the discretion of sentencing judges to do what they have done for generations—impose sentences within the broad limits established by Congress."[104]

No matter how many times the Court repeated these conclusions, they rang false. Far from leaving the balance of power in sentencing

---

[100] Brief for the United States, *supra* note 8, at 33–35.

[101] Brief of Amicus Curiae United States Sentencing Commission at 10, United States v. Mistretta, 488 U.S. 361 (1989).

[102] 488 U.S. at 390–91.

[103] *Id.* at 395.

[104] *Id.* at 396.

undisturbed or aggrandizing the judicial branch, the Sentencing Reform Act took power *away from* judges. The Sentencing Reform Act did not "fetter" the discretion of judges; it *eliminated* most of it. Moreover, the statute transferred sentencing authority, at least as a formal matter, to an administrative agency that substantively had nothing to do with "the judicial branch." The members of this new agency were appointed by the President and confirmed by the Senate, and the Sentencing Reform Act additionally granted ex officio membership on the Commission to two executive officials, including the Attorney General or his designate.[105] A majority of the Commissioners were not even Article III judges. The agency issued rules that had the force and effect of law. In sum, the only substantive connection between things "judicial" and the new agency was that the agency was exercising powers that *previously* had been judicial.[106]

We may never know why eight members of the Supreme Court insisted on such a misleading characterization of the Sentencing Commission and its Guidelines. Perhaps the Court did not fully comprehend the structure and powers of the Commission. While it recognized that the Sentencing Guidelines were binding on *judges* in exercise of their sentencing responsibilities,[107] it insisted that the Guidelines, "do not bind or regulate the primary conduct of the public or vest in the Judicial Branch the legislative responsibility for establishing minimum and maximum penalties for every crime."[108] But the Guidelines did both these things. Once the Commission decided, for instance, that obstructive

---

[105] 28 U.S.C. § 991(a). The other ex officio member is the Chairman of the U.S. Parole Commission, *id.; see also supra* note 19.

[106] The Court also dealt with three subsidiary claims of aggrandizement: (1) Article III courts have power under the Constitution only to hear "Cases" and "Controversies"; (2) Article III judges cannot be assigned additional functions related to the administration of justice in the federal courts; and (3) Article III judges cannot be assigned functions unrelated to the administration of justice in the courts. These arguments are either irrelevant or already answered by history. The first argument was irrelevant because neither the Sentencing Commission as a whole nor its judge-members were operating as an Article III court. *See* 488 U.S. at 383. The second argument was a throw-away, for the Court had approved judges' role under the Rules Enabling Act and other statutes in promulgating the Federal Rules of Civil Procedure, of Criminal Procedure, and of Evidence, *id.* at 387–98; the Court had also already accepted that the realities of the modern bureaucratic state had required that Congress be permitted to assign judges additional administrative duties relating to the administration of the courts and the federal probation service. *Mistretta* properly found more problematic the third argument relating to service on the Commission of Article III judges. But here, too, history had already decided the issue, and the Court concluded: "In other words, the Constitution . . . does not forbid judges to wear two hats; it merely forbids them to wear both hats at the same time." *Id.* at 404.

[107] *Id.* at 391.

[108] *Id.* at 396.

conduct by an offender required a higher term of imprisonment, or that acceptance of responsibility required a lower term of imprisonment, these rules were "binding" on members of the public, as indeed they had to be to have their intended deterrent effect.

Similarly, the Court had it entirely backwards when it concluded that the participation of federal judges on the Commission "does not threaten, either in fact or in appearance, the impartiality of the Judicial Branch."[109] The Court explained that it reached "this conclusion by one paramount consideration," that the work of the Commission, "does not enlist the resources or reputation of the Judicial Branch in either the legislative business of determining what conduct should be criminalized or the executive business of enforcing the law."[110] But the Guidelines *did* "criminalize" behavior. And because they were not merely *binding* on judges, but also were *mandatory*, judges were placed in the position of a supplemental prosecutor, required by the terms of the Sentencing Reform Act to apply "relevant conduct" and aggravating factors regardless of the prosecutor's wishes.

Justice Scalia's dissent clearly understood these realities. As the justice explained at the outset of his opinion, "There is no doubt that the Sentencing Commission has established significant, legally binding prescriptions governing application of governmental power against private individuals."[111] For Justice Scalia, this delegation of power to the Commission was unconstitutional for two reasons. First, he objected to delegation of bald law-making authority that was not in aid of some larger agency purpose (in contrast, for example, to the Securities and Exchange Commission), with the result that the agency "exercises no governmental power except the making of rules that have the effect of law."[112] Second, he objected that the Commission was in *no* "Branch"— not the Judicial (because neither courts nor judges control the Commission), and not the Executive (because of insufficient Presidential control), and not the Legislative (because Guidelines are not laws enacted by Congress).[113] In his view, the Sentencing Commission was "a new Branch altogether, a sort of junior-varsity Congress."[114]

While it surely would have been reasonable, and consistent with the

---

[109] *Id.* at 407.

[110] *Id.*

[111] *Id.* at 413 (Scalia, J., dissenting).

[112] *Id.* at 427 (Scalia, J., dissenting).

[113] *See id.* at 423–24 (Scalia, J., dissenting).

[114] *Id.* at 427 (Scalia, J., dissenting).

recent separation-of-powers decisions,[115] for Justice Blackmun to have rejected Justice Scalia's conclusion that a "junior-varsity Congress" is unconstitutional, it is disappointing that the majority opinion bore no trace of having even considered the premise of Justice Scalia's argument—that the Sentencing Commission was exercising law-making powers. Nor did it respond to Justice Scalia's argument that with respect to its structural features (its composition and method of appointment and removal), the Commission was not "in the judicial branch."

Because Justice Blackmun accepted the statutory fiction that the Sentencing Commission is in the judicial branch, he was forced to answer two other questions. First, if the Sentencing Reform Act truly posited substantive rulemaking authority in the judicial branch, might this encroach on the powers of the executive branch? Additionally or alternatively, could this be an impermissible co-mingling of judicial and legislative functions? In response to the first possibility, the Court noted that "the President's relationship to the Commission is functionally no different from what it would have been had Congress not located the Commission in the Judicial Branch."[116] As to the possibility that Congress impermissibly gave the judicial branch legislative responsibilities,[117] the Court explained, "[A]lthough the Commission is located in the Judicial Branch, its powers are not united with the powers of the Judiciary *in a way that has meaning for separation-of-powers analysis,*" and that the Commission "does not exercise judicial power."[118] Justice Blackmun went on to concede that the Commission was "an independent agency in every relevant sense,"[119] whose decisions could be amended by Congress at any time.

Thus, the opinion in *Mistretta* was at war with itself. To answer Mistretta's primary claim of judicial aggrandizement, the opinion argued that the Commission was properly located in the judicial branch because the Guidelines merely occupy and rationalize the same sentencing space that judges used to occupy individually. But to answer the Solicitor General's claim that placement in the judicial branch would constitute inappropriate judicial encroachment on the other branches of the federal government, the opinion simultaneously had to insist that the Commis-

---

[115] *See, e.g.,* Morrison v. Olson, 487 U.S. 654, 694 (1988): "While the Constitution diffuses power the better to secure liberty, it also contemplates that practice will integrate the dispersed powers into a workable government. It enjoins upon its branches separateness but interdependence, autonomy but reciprocity," *quoting* Youngstown Sheet & Tube Co. v. Sawyer, 343 U.S. 579, 635 (1952) (Jackson, J., concurring).

[116] 488 U.S. at 388 note 14.

[117] *Id.* at 395–96.

[118] *Id.* at 393 (emphasis added).

[119] *Id.*

sion is not really part of the judicial branch, for it "does not exercise judicial power," is "fully accountable to Congress" and is "an independent agency."

Unaddressed Separation of Powers Issues

Perhaps the reason for the inconsistency in the *Mistretta* opinion is, as previously suggested, that the Court did not fully understand the operation of the federal Sentencing Guidelines. But perhaps the Court understood more than is immediately evident.

Encroachment on Judicial Power

It is possible that the majority in *Mistretta* knew full well that the nominal designation of the Commission in the judicial branch was not directly relevant to the question of whether Congress had constitutional authority to direct the Commission to write sentencing rules. Perhaps the Court realized that the real separation-of-powers issue presented by the Sentencing Reform Act was not the *aggrandizement* of judicial power, but the *usurpation* of judicial power. As Professor Dennis Curtis has astutely observed:

> The uneasiness manifest in the *Mistretta* opinion stems from the realization—deliberately unstated—that judges could be completely removed from the [sentencing] process without raising separation of powers problems.... I believe this is the reason the Court went to such lengths to emphasize the historic role of judges and to extol their expertise, while grudgingly accepting the congressional scheme.[120]

Stated somewhat differently, the Court may have mischaracterized what Congress had wrought because what Congress had done was to shrink the judicial role, and hence greatly alter the balance of powers, in the criminal justice process—and the Court did not want to concede that Congress had evident constitutional authority to effect such a sea-change. Perhaps the Court thought it was actually saving some judicial role in sentencing beyond that provided for by Sentencing Reform Act.

Uniting Prosecutorial and Sentencing Authority

A second possibility is that the Court believed that there could be even larger constitutional difficulties if the Sentencing Commission were openly acknowledged to be exercising executive power. In a footnote the Court suggested as much, noting that conferring authority on the "Executive Branch" to write sentencing rules would raise the issue whether Congress "unconstitutionally had united the power to prosecute

---

[120] Dennis Curtis, *Mistretta and Metaphor*, 66 S. Cal. L. Rev. 607, 616–17 (1992).

and the power to sentence within one Branch."[121] This question goes not to the role of the judiciary, but to the fundamental purpose of separation-of-powers doctrine. Both Mistretta and the Sentencing Commission had intimated in their briefs that assignment of the Sentencing Commission to the "Executive Branch" would be unconstitutional,[122] with both briefs quoting a pithy statement from the House Report to the Sentencing Reform Act of 1984, "Giving such significant control over the determination of sentences to the same branch of government that is responsible for the prosecution of criminal cases is no more appropriate than granting such power to a consortium of defense attorneys."[123]

As it turns out, the Court was right in suspecting that the Sentencing Reform Act could be understood to unite prosecutorial authority with sentencing authority. But if this is a constitutional infirmity, it is not cured simply by statutory assignment of the Commission to the "judicial branch" for primarily house-keeping and administrative purposes.

Mistretta's attorneys can hardly be faulted for not having raised what has turned out to be a central truth of sentencing in the Guidelines era—that authority over sentencing has been effectively transferred not to the Sentencing Commission but to federal prosecutors. In 1988, shortly after the Guidelines went into effect, counsel for Mistretta may well have believed that the Commission's avoidance strategy—sentencing on the basis of "relevant conduct"—would prevent this from occurring.[124] As we have seen, it did not. It would not be until *Blakely* and *Booker* that the Court would finally do something about Guidelines' immense impact on separation-of-powers and the balance of power in sentencing.

Constitutional Accountability

Yet Mistretta could have made another argument that was apparent from the day the Sentencing Reform Act was enacted: The statute's characterization of the Sentencing Commission as being "in the judicial branch" was unconstitutional *because it was false* An examination of the statute and its legislative history leaves no doubt that this statutory designation, as well as the requirement that three of the seven Commissioners be federal judges[125] were fig-leaves designed to obscure the

---

[121] 488 U.S. at 361 note 17. The Court also noted another issue that would be raised were the Commission recognized as an executive agency—"whether Congress unconstitutionally had assigned judicial responsibilities to the Executive." *Id.*

[122] Brief of John M. Mistretta at 35–40, Mistretta v. United States, 488 U.S. 361 (1989); Brief of United States Sentencing Commission, *supra* note 101, at 11.

[123] H.R. Rep. No. 98–1017, at 95 (1984).

[124] *See supra* notes 71–79 and accompanying text.

[125] In 2003, Congress amended the Sentencing Reform Act to limit the role of judges even more, changing the requirement that "[a]t least three" Commissioners be judges to

usurpation of (heretofore) judicial power, to distract from the radical transformation of federal criminal law effected by the Sentencing Reform Act, to protect the Guidelines from challenge under the Administrative Procedure Act (and otherwise to insulate the Commission from oversight attending virtually every other government agency with rule-making authority), and, most importantly, to clothe the Commission with the courts' reputation for impartiality and sentencing expertise.[126]

Congress may well have constitutional authority to specify precise sentencing ranges for different variations of crimes, and for different offenders depending on their criminal records. But Congress did not, and has not, enacted the Guidelines into law. Instead it created a new independent agency, with members appointed by the President and with two representatives of the President sitting ex officio, to do its bidding. It commanded that agency to deny judges sentencing authority and to write sentencing rules that require severe sentences in most cases, sentences based in part on conduct of which the defendant was never convicted. All the while, Congress remained hidden behind the veneer of legitimacy derived from pretending that these rules are merely "Guidelines" and that the agency writing these rules is part of the same "branch" of government as the Article III judges whose sentencing authority Congress has decided to take away.

One reason for the assignment of different powers to different entities in our constitutional order, both within the federal government and between the federal government and the states, is to ensure accountability for government action. If the Guidelines are indeed in the judicial branch, then the political branches commandeered that branch,[127] obscuring who is responsible for the rules under which offenders are sentenced and who is really exercising sentencing authority in criminal cases.

A New Chapter: United States v. Booker

The Supreme Court has not directly addressed any of the separation-of-powers issues just noted—relating to the usurpation of judicial sentencing power, the melding of prosecutorial and sentencing power, and the confusion spawned by designating the Sentencing Commission

---

"[n]ot more than three." Pub. L. No. 108–21, Title IV, § 401(n)(1), 117 Stat. 676 (April 30, 2003) (popularly known as the "Feeney Amendment").

[126] See generally Stith & Koh, supra note 20.

[127] The "comandeering" idea has previously been discussed in reference to vertical, rather than horizontal, separation of powers. See Printz v. United States, 521 U.S. 898, 904–33 (1997) (invalidating gun-control statutory provision that mandated involvement of state officials); New York v. United States, 505 U.S. 144, 159–80 (1992) (invalidating environmental regulation requiring states to administer waste disposal program).

as an independent agency in the judicial branch of government. This year, however, in *United States v. Booker*, an epilogue of sorts to the *Mistretta* story, the Court held the Guidelines unconstitutional on a different ground—that as implemented they denied defendants' their constitutional rights relating to prosecution and proof.[128] Ironically, had this been the only holding in *Booker*, it is likely that Guidelines would henceforth have been implemented differently, to respect these due process rights. Below I first tell the story of how the Court went from upholding the Guidelines in *Mistretta* in 1989 to striking them down as unconstitutional in 2005. I also suggest that *Booker*'s holding of unconstitutionality, had it been the only holding in the case, would have addressed the major separation-of-powers concerns raised by the Guidelines but not addressed in *Mistretta*.

But there was a second holding in *Booker* (by a different majority, and to which I shall refer as *Booker* II), which determined that the Guidelines would be constitutional as long as they are not binding on sentencing judges.[129] Ultimately, *Booker* II may not be reconcilable with the first holding in *Booker* (*Booker* I). In undoing one of the central hallmarks of the Guidelines—their status as *law*—*Booker* II ameliorates but does not eliminate the due process concerns raised by the Guidelines. It does, however, address one of the central separation-of-power problems that arose under the Guidelines, the excessive power wielded by prosecutors over criminal sentences.

Due Process Under the Sentencing Guidelines

Since *Mistretta*, the Supreme Court has not heard any further separation-of-powers challenges to the Sentencing Commission or the Guidelines. In the decade following that case, however, it heard and rejected four due process challenges to the Guidelines. Unlike the due process claim that John Mistretta and a few other defendants raised at the dawn of the Guidelines—that they had constitutional right to an "individualized" sentence—the claims raised in the 1990s related not to rights attending *sentencing* but to rights attending *prosecution*. Whereas Mistretta's due process claim had been, essentially, that judges should be allowed to exercise discretion at sentencing, the post-*Mistretta* challenges accepted the reality that the Guidelines denied such discretion, and insisted that if discretion were to be replaced with *law*, then the procedures for implementing that law should comport with the Constitution.

---

[128] 125 S.Ct. at 746–52 (holding that judicial factfinding under the Guidelines violates the defendant's jury trial rights under the Sixth Amendment, including the right to proof beyond a reasonable doubt). (Stevens, J.).

[129] *Id.* at 764 (Breyer, J.).

In two cases, the Supreme Court rejected these claims without dissent. One of these cases held that there is no constitutional impediment to the Guidelines' mandatory enhancement for obstruction of justice,[130] and the other that the defendant's Sixth Amendment right to jury trial is not implicated where judicial factfinding does not result in a sentence higher than the statutory maximum for the crime of conviction.[131] In two other decisions, only Justice Stevens dissented on the merits. *Witte v. United States* found no double jeopardy violation in separately prosecuting a defendant for criminal conduct that has already been the basis for a Guidelines enhancement,[132] while *United States v. Watts* upheld a sentence enhancement on the basis of judicial factfinding using a preponderance standard even though the jury had acquitted the defendant of the same conduct.[133] As I have elsewhere recently described at length,[134] each of these decisions, as well as the 1986 decision in *McMillan v. Pennsylvania*,[135] ultimately rely on a hoary precedent dating from 1949, *Williams v. New York*.[136] That older case upheld the exercise of broad sentencing discretion, and specifically approved the judge's reliance on hearsay allegations in the presentence Report regarding past criminal conduct by the defendant, of which he had been neither charged nor convicted.[137]

In the decades after *Williams*, the Supreme Court reconsidered and greatly expanded the rights of criminal defendants in the investigatory and trial stages of a criminal prosecution, and in the sentencing stage as well in capital cases; these are the cases canvassed in the other stories of this volume. Yet *Williams* remained the basis for refusing to subject the sentencing stage in non-capital cases to critical procedural protections. Proof beyond a reasonable doubt, the right to a jury, the prohibition on double jeopardy, and the right to confront one's accusers simply did not

---

[130] United States v. Dunnigan, 507 U.S. 87, 92–98 (1993).

[131] Edwards v. United States, 523 U.S. 511, 516 (1998).

[132] 515 U.S. 389, 395–406 (1995); *id.* at 407–08 (Stevens, J., dissenting). Justices Scalia and Thomas concurred on the basis of their understanding that the prohibition on double jeopardy prohibits only successive prosecutions, not successive punishments, *id.* at 406–07 (Scalia, J., concurring).

[133] 519 U.S. 148, 149–57 (1997) (per curiam); *id.* at 159–70 (Stevens, J., dissenting). Justice Kennedy dissented on the ground that the Court should have set the case for full briefing and argument, *id* at 170–71 (Kennedy, J., dissenting).

[134] *See* Stith, *supra* note 80.

[135] 477 U.S. 79; *see supra* note 88 and accompanying text.

[136] 337 U.S. 241 (1949) (Black, J.)

[137] *Id.* at 247 (only limitation on judge is that punishment be "within fixed statutory or constitutional limits").

apply at sentencing. As long as the sentence was within the statutory maximum and minimum, it was lawful.[138]

Even when some states and the federal government moved, in the early 1980s, to determinate sentencing systems such as the federal Sentencing Guidelines, the Supreme Court continued to rely on *Williams* and its progeny to reject claims that due process rights should apply at sentencing as well. I have previously suggested that the Court insisted that the precedents established during the discretionary era remained applicable because it would be paradoxical to hold that a system with some "process" (the Guidelines) transgresses the Constitution, while a system with no "process" at all (*Williams*) does not. One way to resolve the paradox, of course, is to reconsider the validity of *Williams* itself.[139]

No member of the Court has taken that approach. But even as they continued to insist on the constitutionality of fully discretionary sentencing, certain members of the Court became increasingly uncomfortable with relying on the *Williams* rationale to uphold judicial factfinding in the new determinate sentencing regimes. In 1998, three justices in addition to Justice Stevens objected to judicial factfinding of a statutory factor that required a higher sentence.[140] The following year, in *Jones v. United States,* these four justices were joined by a fifth, and this new majority warned that allowing punishment to be increased upon judicial factfinding would raise "grave" constitutional concerns relating to the right to jury trial and to proof beyond a reasonable doubt.[141] The warning in *Jones* became the holding the next year in *Apprendi v. New Jersey.*[142] In an opinion by Justice Stevens—joined by Justices Scalia, Souter, Thomas, and Ginsburg—*Apprendi* struck down New Jersey's "hate crime" sentencing enhancement, holding that "[A]ny fact that increases

---

[138] *See* United States v. Grayson, 438 U.S. 41, 45–55 (1978) (sentencing judge may consider defendant's apparent perjury at trial); Williams v. Oklahoma, 358 U.S. 576, 584–85 (1959) (sentencing judge may increase sentence on basis of conduct for which defendant was separately tried and sentenced); Fed. R. Evid. 1101(d)(3) (Rules of Evidence do not apply at, inter alia, sentencing hearings) (approved by the Supreme Court in 1972). The Court did hold that the Sixth Amendment right to counsel applies at sentencing, *see* Gardner v. Florida, 430 U.S. 349, 358 (1977); Mempa v. Rhay, 389 U.S. 128, 133–34 (1967).

[139] *See* Stith, *supra* note 80.

[140] Almendarez–Torres v. United States, 523 U.S. 224, 248–71 (1998) (Scalia, J., dissenting, joined by Stevens, Souter, Ginsburg, JJ.). The majority held that the finding of prior convictions under a felony recidivist statute could be made by a judge, rather than the jury, *id.* at 235.

[141] 526 U.S. 227, 229, 251 & note 11 (1999) (Souter, J., joined by Stevens, Scalia, Thomas, Ginsburg, JJ.).

[142] 530 U.S. 466 (2000).

the penalty for a crime beyond the prescribed statutory maximum must be submitted to a jury, and proved beyond a reasonable doubt."[143]

The New Jersey enhancement was statutory, and it was possible that the *Apprendi* majority would accept judicial factfinding of enhancements specified in administrative sentencing rules. That possibility was extinguished, however, with the decision in *Blakely v. Washington*,[144] in June of 2004, in which the same five-justice majority held that:

> "[T]he 'statutory maximum' for *Apprendi* purposes" is the maximum sentence a judge may impose *solely on the basis of the facts reflected in the jury verdict or admitted by the defendant*. In other words, the relevant "statutory maximum" is not the maximum sentence a judge may impose after finding additional facts, but the maximum he may impose *without* any additional findings.[145]

Justice Scalia, writing this majority opinion, appears to have had the Sentencing Guidelines in mind.[146] The *Blakely* rule requires proof beyond a reasonable doubt and the right to a jury trial for any fact that increases not the statutory maximum, but the *lawful* maximum. The Guidelines are (or were, when *Blakely* was decided) *law*, and by the terms of the Sentencing Reform Act, judges were prohibited from imposing a higher sentence than authorized by the Guidelines, both those relating to calculation of the sentencing range and those pertaining to upward departures from this range.[147] Not surprisingly, *Blakely* sent federal prosecutors and federal courts into a tizzy,[148] and by the end of the summer of 2004 the Court accepted review in *Booker*,[149] agreeing to

---

[143] *Id*. at 490. The majority in *Apprendi* explicitly carved out an exception to this rule for proof of prior convictions, *id*. at 489–90, thereby saving *Almendarez-Torres* from being overruled, *see supra* note 140. Two years later, in Harris v. New York, 536 U.S. 545 (2002), the Court declined to extend *Apprendi* to judicial fact-finding that raises the minimum but not the maximum lawful sentence. All of the members of the *Apprendi* majority except Justice Scalia dissented, *see id*. at 572 (Thomas, J., dissenting, joined by Stevens, Souter and Gisnburg, JJ.). Although Justice Breyer voted with the majority in *Harris*, he opined that the holding he was joining could not be "easily" reconciled with *Apprendi*, from which he had dissented. *See id*. at 569 (Breyer, J., concurring).

[144] 542 U.S. 296 (2004).

[145] *Id*. at 303 (emphasis in original) (citations omitted).

[146] Because the Washington State Sentencing Guidelines were enacted into statutory law by the legislature (unlike the federal Sentencing Guidelines), the enhancement at issue in *Blakely* was unconstitutional under the precise wording of the *Apprendi* holding. Yet *Blakely* expanded the holding in *Apprendi* to encompass non-statutory law that increases the "lawful maximum," and in a footnote the *Blakely* majority expressly declined to assure that it was not aiming at the federal Sentencing Guidelines. *See id*. at 305 note 9.

[147] *See supra* note 69 and accompanying text.

[148] *See* Bowman, *supra* note 83.

[149] The Court also accepted expedited review in a companion case, United States v. Fanfan, 2004 WL 1723114 (D. Me. 2004).

decide whether the *Blakely* holding would be applied to strike down the Guidelines.[150]

Few were surprised that when *Booker* was handed down, in January of 2005, the same five-Justice majority confirmed that *Blakely* doomed the federal Sentencing Guidelines.[151] This majority includes both assertedly "conservative" and assertedly "liberal" members of the Court. But one should be wary in trying to superimpose constitutional holdings along a simple left—right spectrum. The five justices who held the Sentencing Guidelines unconstitutional might reasonably be labeled constitutional "formalists" across a wide range of criminal cases. There is no doubt that the holdings in these cases are consistent with a belief that the rights provided in the Fifth and Sixth Amendments are commands that may not be significantly diluted on the basis of pragmatic considerations. What *Apprendi*, *Blakely*, and *Booker* I hold is that neither a state legislature nor Congress can achieve an end-run around the rights the Constitution guarantees "[i]n all criminal prosecutions," in the words of the Sixth Amendment, by simply moving part of the "prosecution" from the trial phase to the sentencing phase.

The dissenters from these holdings—Chief Justice Rehnquist and Justices O'Connor, Kennedy, and Breyer—might, on the other hand, be labeled "due process pragmatists." In their dissents, they decried the inefficiency and potential sentencing disparity that would result from requiring aggravating sentencing factors to be charged and proved as though they were statutory elements of the crime.[152] In *Blakely*, Justice Breyer expressed particular concern that treating aggravating sentencing factors as elements of the crime "would likely weaken the relation between real conduct" and sentencing.[153] This complaint, at bottom, is that there is a danger that some defendants who "really" engaged in aggravating "relevant conduct" will be not be punished for this conduct if procedures laid out in the Constitution are adhered to—in particular, proof beyond a reasonable doubt and conviction by a unanimous lay jury.

Separation of Powers as a Due Process Right

Had the Court in *Booker* only held the Guidelines unconstitutional, the procedural infirmities identified in *Jones, Apprendi, Blakely*, and *Booker* would have been addressed. Federal prosecutors would presumably have continued to do what they began doing immediately after the

---

[150] 542 U.S. 956 (2004).

[151] 125 S.Ct. at 755–56 (Stevens, J.).

[152] *See, e.g.*, *Blakely*, 542 U.S. at 316, 323 (O'Connor, J., dissenting); *id.* at 328–39 (Breyer, J., dissenting).

[153] *Id.* at 338 (Breyer, J., dissenting). *See also supra* note 86 and accompanying text.

Blakely decision foreordained the unconstitutionality of the Guidelines as then implemented: They would have charged aggravating Guidelines factors as elements of the crime, of which a defendant could not be convicted unless he either admitted to the factor or was found guilty by a jury.[154]

This result would have remedied not only the due process problems identified in *Jones/Booker* line of cases, but also three critical separation-of-powers issues that, as this essay has pointed out, *Mistretta* did not contemplate: (1) the role of judges as both prosecutor and fact-finder in implementing the Guidelines, and (2) the lack of transparency and constitutional accountability stemming from the placement of the Sentencing Commission "in the judicial branch," and (3) the role of prosecutors in determining criminal sentences.

Leaving the Guidelines in place as binding, mandatory, "real offense" sentencing rules but engrafting the constitutional requirements of proof beyond a reasonable doubt and jury trial in their implementation would have vitiated the Sentencing Commission's original vision of the judge (working with the probation officer) as a fact-finder independent of the adversaries before him, with the obligation to bring accusations under the Guidelines that neither party has urged. If aggravating sentencing factors are treated as elements of the crime, then a defendant cannot be convicted of them unless they are charged by the prosecutor and grand jury, and proved as required by the Constitution. The judge would have no independent role to charge or find additional "Guidelines crimes."

Moreover, accountability for sentencing in the federal courts would clearly be laid at the feet of Congress, the Sentencing Commission, and prosecutors—rather than the judiciary acting either as individual judges or through a "judicial branch" commission. Justice Stevens' majority opinion in *Booker* completely ignores Justice Blackmun's agonized insistence in *Mistretta* that the Guidelines are not really "law" but merely judicial-branch "guidelines" that inhabit the same discretionary space that individual judges used to inhabit. And while Justice Stevens asserts at one point that "[o]ur holding today does not call into question any aspect of our decision in *Mistretta*,"[155] his opinion declines to quote any of *Mistretta*'s many claims that the Commission is in the "Judicial Branch." Instead, he quotes the portion of the *Mistretta* opinion which belies this major claim, where Justice Blackmun conceded that the Commission's "powers are not united with the powers of the Judiciary in

---

[154] *See* Memorandum from James Comey, Deputy Attorney General, to All Federal Prosecutors (July 2, 2004), reprinted at 16 Fed. Sent. Rpt. 357 (2004).

[155] 125 S.Ct. at 755 (Stevens, J.) The opinion in *Booker* II does not mention *Mistretta*.

a way that has meaning for separation-of-powers analysis."[156] Much more clearly and decisively than did *Mistretta*, Justice Stevens' decision in *Booker* rejects the separation-of-powers challenges brought in that earlier case, concluding that it is within Congress's power to take away the sentencing discretion of individual judges and replace it with "an independent agency that exercises policy-making authority delegated to it by Congress."[157]

Finally, leaving the Guidelines in place but requiring that Guidelines crimes be charged and proved in accordance with the Constitution would have addressed the transfer of sentencing authority to prosecutors. It would have done so not by putting limits on prosecutorial power to charge and negotiate Guidelines sentencing factors, but by giving defendants what the Constitution demands they be provided when charged with a crime: the right to notice, a jury trial, and proof beyond a reasonable doubt. Granting these rights would have altered the balance of power between the defendant and the prosecutor by, in effect, giving the defendant some additional "cards" to play in his plea bargaining with the prosecution. No longer could the prosecutor hold over the defendant's head the possibility of conviction at trial for some relatively easy-to-prove crime, and then punishment under the Guidelines for additional or more serious criminal conduct. When phrased as the "role of the prosecutor in determining sentence," the issue of prosecutorial power over punishment seems to be a "separation-of-powers" problem that the Constitution nowhere addresses. The insight of *Jones, Apprendi, Blakely,* and *Booker* I is that the Guidelines' transfer of significant authority over punishment to prosecutors is really a due process issue, which the Constitution does address—in the rights it guarantees in all criminal prosecutions.

The New Regime: Advisory Guidelines With Appellate Review

This is not, however, what happened. Quite deliberately, *Booker* II (regarding the proper "remedy") renders *Booker* I irrelevant by decreeing that the Guidelines system it holds unconstitutional no longer exists.

Instead, *Booker* II creates a new regime, which in many ways resembles the regime that the Stevens majority found unconstitutional. Most of the Sentencing Reform Act remains in effect; Guidelines that have already been promulgated remain in effect; the Sentencing Commission remains in existence (in whatever "branch" it may be) to promulgate additional Guidelines; and sentencing judges must consider the Guidelines in determining sentence.[158] But defendants have no right

---

[156] *Id., quoting* 488 U.S. at 393; *see supra* note 118 and accompanying text.

[157] 125 S.Ct. at 755 (Stevens, J.).

[158] *Id.* at 764, 766–67 (Breyer, J.).

to jury trial or to proof beyond a reasonable doubt with respect to factors that enhance the Guidelines sentence.[159]

There are some differences between the new regime and the regime that was before the Court in *Mistretta* and subsequent cases. Most importantly, the Guidelines are now not "binding" rules that sentencing judges must follow, but, rather, are "advisory" recommendations that judges must "consult ... and take [] into account when sentencing."[160] Moreover, no longer can a sentence be reversed on appeal simply because the sentencing judge failed to abide by the Guidelines.[161] Rather, the judge can be reversed only if, considering all the factors that the Sentencing Reform Act as rewritten in *Booker* II makes relevant, the sentence is "unreasonable."[162] Of course, one of those relevant factors is the recommended Guidelines sentence.

That Justice Breyer and the other dissenters in *Jones, Apprendi,* and *Blakely* were able to save so many aspects of the old Guidelines system is, at bottom, a testament to Justice Breyer's ingenuity and persuasiveness. Unable to forestall the holding in *Booker* I that the federal Sentencing Guidelines were unconstitutional as implemented, Justice Breyer and the other pragmatists ultimately prevailed in achieving what for them was a second-best solution: Retaining the Guidelines not as "law" but as legally relevant "advice," with no requirement of jury trial or proof beyond a reasonable doubt. Moreover, they were able to convince one of the justices who had joined with Justice Stevens— Justice Ginsburg—that the transformation of the Guidelines accomplished in *Booker* II renders the new system constitutional.

If all that *Booker* II did was make the Guidelines "advisory" (rather than binding), then the regime crafted by Justice Breyer would be compatible with the holdings in *Jones, Apprendi, Blakely*, and *Booker* I. Indeed, *Booker* I specifically concedes that: "If the Guidelines as current-

---

[159] *Id.* at 762–63, 767 (Breyer, J.).

[160] *Id.* at 757, 767 (Breyer, J.).

[161] *Id.* at 767 (Breyer, J.). *Booker* II excised the provision of the Sentencing Reform Act that required judges to impose a sentence within the Guidelines range except in extraordinary circumstances, 18 U.S.C. § 3553(b)(1), *see supra* text accompanying note 25. This leaves 18 U.S.C. § 3553(a) as the only instruction to judges. That provision requires that in deciding sentence, judges consider a variety of purposes of punishment, the need to avoid sentencing disparity, and the Guidelines' sentencing range and departure rules.

[162] 125 S.Ct. at 767 ("The courts of appeals [will hereafter] review sentencing decisions for unreasonableness.") (Breyer, J.). *Booker* II excised the appellate review provision that required the appellate court to vacate a sentence imposed in violation of the Guidelines, 18 U.S.C. § 3742(e). *See* 125 S.Ct. at 765 (Breyer, J.). Beyond the scope of this essay is the issue whether Justice Breyer's creative excising and reinterpretation of the appellate review provision of the Sentencing Reform Act is persuasive as a matter of severability jurisprudence and legislative intent.

ly written could be read as merely advisory provisions that recommended, rather than required, the selection of particular sentences in response to differing sets of facts, their use would not implicate the Sixth Amendment [right to jury trial]."[163] The only judicial factfinding that the *Jones* line of cases outlaws is that which increases the *lawful* sentence. If the Guidelines were truly advisory, then judicial factfinding would not affect the lawfulness of a sentence. The judge might take account of the facts as the Guidelines advise him to do, or he might ignore this advice just as he might take or ignore the advice that the editorial page of the *New York Times* propounds regarding a particular sentencing.

But *Booker* II does something beyond asserting that the Guidelines are now "advisory"; it establishes a system of appellate review for "reasonableness" of the sentence. Appellate review for reasonableness does not render the Guidelines *binding*, but it does render them *legally meaningful*—unlike, say, the *New York Times* editorial page. If the Guidelines were simply advisory, then any sentence within the statutory maximum and minimum would be lawful. But appellate review for reasonableness means that some sentences within the statutory range will be reversed; that is, will be unlawful. Under *Booker* II, there will still be judicial factfinding on a preponderance standard, with that factfinding necessary to support the lawfulness of a sentence, which is the very situation that the first holding in *Booker*—following *Jones*, *Apprendi*, and *Blakely*—held unconstitutional.[164]

That *Booker* II is in serious tension, if not conflict, with *Booker* I (and with the cases leading up to *Booker* I) is, as a legal matter, irrelevant. A majority of the Court has said that the regime constructed in *Booker* II is constitutional, and that is now the law of the land. But it

---

[163] *Id.* at 750 (Stevens, J.).

[164] The facts of the *Booker* case provide an example. Suppose that a case with the same facts and procedural history, *see* 125 S.Ct. at 746–47, arises after *Booker* II. The jury finds the defendant guilty of a provision of the federal narcotics laws that prohibits distributing at least fifty grams of cocaine base. While the statutory range for this crime is between ten and thirty years in prison, the now-Advisory Guidelines "recommend" a sentence of between seventeen and twenty-one years for this quantity. At the sentencing hearing, the government proves by a preponderance that the amount of cocaine base within the defendant's "relevant conduct" was not fifty grams, but more than ten times that amount—566 grams—just as the Government did in the actual *Booker* case. Suppose that in the new, Advisory Guidelines regime, the judge decides that thirty years is the appropriate sentence, giving due regard to the Guidelines and to the other factors that the Sentencing Reform Act, in 18 U.S.C. § 3553(a), states are relevant to the sentence. When the Court of Appeals decides whether this thirty year sentence is reasonable, it surely is going to consider not just the facts found by the jury, but also the facts found by the judge. Indeed, a thirty year sentence for distributing only fifty grams of cocaine base might well be *unreasonable*; what makes it potentially reasonable is the judge's finding that 566 grams were involved, and that the Guidelines recommend the maximum statutory sentence in this situation. The judge's factfinding will be critical to the lawfulness of the sentence.

does mean that the due process rights vindicated in *Booker* I are undone in *Booker* II. Whether some other institution, such as Congress or the Sentencing Commission itself, will step in and address these due process concerns remains to be seen. Nothing in the Sentencing Reform Act requires that facts greatly raising the Guidelines range be proved only to a preponderance of the evidence; the Commission could recommend a higher standard of proof.[165]

Moreover, the truth is that no member of the Supreme Court, in any of the cases cited in this essay, has acknowledged that due process issues, including the appropriate standard of proof, are raised in the context of discretionary sentencing, as well as in determinate sentencing systems such as the Sentencing Guidelines. Even the majority opinions in *Apprendi*,[166] *Blakely*,[167] and *Booker* I[168] continue to cite *Williams v. New York* as good law. Until and unless that decision is thoroughly reconsidered,[169] defendants at sentencing are entitled to no "due process" as long as sentencing itself is not encumbered by "law."

Booker II also undoes *Booker* I's resolution of various separation-of-powers concerns raised by the Guidelines. At best, *Booker* II's relaxation of the extent to which the Guidelines are "law" mutes constitutional concerns relating to (1) the role of the judge as both prosecutor and fact-finder in implementing the Guidelines, and (2) the lack of accountability deriving from the statutory placement of the Sentencing Commission "in the judicial branch."

Booker II does address, however, the constitutional discomfort caused by the uniting of prosecutorial and sentencing authority that has occurred under the Guidelines regime. This essay has suggested that the Stevens holding in *Booker* I would have addressed this imbalance of power by providing the defendant additional leverage in his negotiations with the prosecutor. Justice Breyer's solution provides a different counterbalance to prosecutorial power—not by giving the defendant the right to proof beyond a reasonable doubt and recourse to a jury, but by providing greater authority to the judge to weigh aggravating (or miti-

---

[165] Indeed, the original Guidelines did not specify a standard of proof, *compare* U.S. Sentencing Guidelines Manual § 6A1.3 (cmt.) (1987) (no mention of standard) *with* U.S. Sentencing Guidelines Manual § 6A1.3 (cmt.) (2004) ("The Commission believes that use of a preponderance of the evidence standard is appropriate").

[166] 530 U.S. at 481.

[167] 542 U.S. at 299.

[168] 125 S.Ct. at 750.

[169] *Williams v. New York, see supra* text accompanying notes 136–39, has been overruled in the specific context of capital punishment. Gardner v. Florida, 430 U.S. 349, 355–62 (1978).

gating) factors differently than do the Guidelines, and to take into account factors, such as the life history and prospects of the defendant, that were legally off-limits under the Guidelines and that prosecutors do not control.

As a matter of history if not constitutional text, Justice Breyer's approach is that which our constitutional order has relied upon as a counterbalance to Congress's nearly plenary power to criminalize, and federal prosecutors' broad discretion in charging.[170] The closer the federal Courts of Appeals come to requiring that sentencing judges hew to the Guidelines, the more the new regime looks like the one held unconstitutional in *Booker* I.[171] On the other hand, *Booker* II holds some promise that the Sentencing Guidelines henceforth will provide *guidance* to judges in their exercise of discretion, perhaps similar to the role that parole guidelines previously performed.[172] If the courts and Congress refrain from insisting that the Guidelines be treated as virtually binding, then *Booker* II will allow the judiciary again to play a significant role in sentencing. And this will be a true exercise of judicial power, by individual judges in particular cases and controversies, not feigned judicial power exercised by an administrative agency that Congress mischievously chose to label as being in the "judicial branch."

Unfortunately, present indications are that Congress, with the strong support of the Department of Justice, will attempt to return to the pre-*Booker* world of mandatory sentencing rules without accompanying due process protections. This would be accomplished by taking advantage of the curious holding of *Harris v. New York*, decided 5–4 in 2002.[173] *Harris* declined to apply the *Apprendi* rule to factors that increase the lawful minimum, as opposed to the lawful maximum, punishment. Because *Blakely* and *Booker* involved increases in the maximum (rather than the minimum) sentence, the Court in those cases had no occasion to reconsider the holding of *Harris*.[174]

If *Harris* remains good law, then Congress has constitutional authority to reinstate the full Sentencing Reform Act held unconstitutional

---

[170] *See generally* Stith & Cabranes, *supra* note 18.

[171] Of course, should the Courts of Appeals hold that *only* sentences in accordance with the Guidelines are reasonable, the resulting regime would be indistinguishable from that held unconstitutional in *Booker* I, *see* 125 U.S. at 794 (Scalia, J., dissenting in part).

[172] *See supra* text accompanying notes 40–42.

[173] 536 U.S. 545 (2002). This case is discussed in *supra* note 143.

[174] Neither *Blakely* nor *Booker* cited in *Harris*, but each carefully quoted in full the *Apprendi* holding, which by its term applied only to enhancements of the "lawful maximum" sentence, *see Blakely*, 542 U.S. at 300; *Booker*, 125 S.Ct. at 748 (Stevens, J.). Overruling *Harris* would also require overruling McMillan v. Pennsylvania, 477 U.S. 79 (1986); *see* text accompanying *supra* note 88.

in *Booker* as long as it makes one, simple change in the law. Instead of instructing the Sentencing Commission to promulgate a schedule of mandatory sentencing *ranges*, each with a minimum and a maximum term of imprisonment, the new Sentencing Reform Act would require only a schedule of mandatory *minimum* sentences. Under this system, the "lawful maximum" sentence would always be the statutory maximum for the crime of conviction, and hence would never be increased in contravention of the holdings of *Apprendi, Blakely,* and *Booker.* Yet judges would still be required to enhance punishment on the basis of factors set forth by the Sentencing Commission, for there would be no judicial discretion to sentence below the Guidelines minimum.[175]

Even though post-*Booker* sentencing data indicated virtually no increase in overall sentencing disparity since that decision,[176] Attorney General Alberto Gonzalez in the summer of 2005 announced his support for legislation taking advantage of the *Harris* loophole. He said that such a "minimum guidelines system," as he termed it, was necessary because "it is inevitable over time that, with so many different individual judges involved . . . even greater disparities among sentences will occur under a system of advisory guidelines."[177]

Hence the President and Congress seem poised to act once again on the bizarre premise underlying the original Sentencing Reform Act of 1984: that reduction of inter-judge sentencing disparity should be a primary, even the primary, object of the criminal justice system—to the exclusion of the values of individualized sentencing, proportionate sentencing, and, most importantly, checks and balances on prosecutorial authority.[178] Because any move by Congress to a minimum guidelines system would be an obvious end-run around the holding of both *Booker* I and *Booker* II (that the Sentencing Guidelines are unconstitutional unless they are rendered advisory only),[179] it is possible that the Court, especially with changed membership, will reconsider its decision in *Harris v. New York.*

---

[175] This minimum guidelines (or "topless guidelines") system is discussed in more detail in Bowman, *supra* note 83, at 262–63.

[176] *See* U.S.S.C., *Sentencing in the Aftermath of* United States v. Booker (July 12, 2005), available at http://www.ussc.gov/Blakely/PostBooker_060605Extract.pdf.

[177] *See* Prepared Remarks of Attorney General Alberto R. Gonzales at the American Bar Association House of Delegates (August 8, 2005) available at http://www.usdoj.gov/ag/speeches/2005/080805agamericanbarassoc.htm. The Attorney General had signaled his support for minimum guidelines earlier in the summer, *see* Prepared Remarks of Attorney General Alberto Gonzalez Sentencing Guidelines Speech (July 21, 2005), available at http://www.usdoj.gov/ag/speeches/2005/06212005victimsofcrime.htm.

[178] *See* text accompanying *supra* note 20; Stith & Cabranes, *supra* note 18, at 104–06.

[179] *See* 125 S.Ct. at 750 (Stevens, J.); *id.* at 757, 767 (Breyer, J.).

If *Harris* is overruled, the Congress will have a simple choice before it: Allow judges some discretion in mitigating sentence, or take away all such discretion by legislatively enacting mandatory minimum sentences for every variant of every federal crime. The result of the latter approach would be the same as the Attorney General and some members of Congress hope to achieve by transforming the present advisory Sentencing Guidelines into mandatory minimum guidelines. But at least Congress would be clearly and fully accountable for this system. It would no longer have a Sentencing Commission "in the judicial branch" to hide behind.

*

Contributors

John Q. Barrett is a Professor of Law at St. John's University in New York City and the Elizabeth S. Lenna Fellow at the Robert H. Jackson Center in Jamestown, New York. After graduating from Georgetown University and Harvard Law School, Barrett was a law clerk to Judge A. Leon Higginbotham, Jr., of the United States Court of Appeals for the Third Circuit (1986–88), Associate Counsel in the Office of Independent Counsel Lawrence E. Walsh (Iran/Contra) (1988–93), and Counselor to Inspector General Michael R. Bromwich in the U.S. Department of Justice (1994–95). In 1998, Professor Barrett was a co-organizer of St. John's comprehensive symposium on Terry v. Ohio *Thirty Years Later*, which produced dozens of important articles that are published, along with the suppression hearing and trial transcripts and other historical resources on the decision, at 72 ST. JOHN'S LAW REVIEW 721–1524 (Summer–Fall 1998). Professor Barrett's work on Justice Jackson—author of opinions in important Supreme Court criminal procedure decisions during the 1940s and 1950s—includes the discovery and editing of Jackson's previously unknown, now acclaimed memoir *That Man: An Insider's Portrait of Franklin D. Roosevelt* (Oxford University Press).

Stephanos Bibas is an Associate Professor at the University of Iowa College of Law and a Visiting Associate Professor at the University of Pennsylvania and University of Chicago Law Schools. After studying at Columbia, Oxford, and Yale Law School, he clerked for Judge Patrick Higginbotham on the U.S. Court of Appeals for the Fifth Circuit and for Justice Anthony Kennedy on the U.S. Supreme Court. He litigated a wide variety of cases in private practice and as an Assistant U.S. Attorney in the Southern District of New York. Most notably, he successfully investigated and prosecuted the world's leading expert in Tiffany stained glass for hiring a grave robber to steal priceless Tiffany windows from mausolea. He teaches and writes about criminal law, criminal procedure, and sentencing.

David Cole is a professor at Georgetown University Law Center, a volunteer staff attorney for the Center for Constitutional Rights, the legal affairs correspondent for The Nation, and a commentator on National Public Radio's All Things Considered. New York Times columnist Anthony Lewis has called him "one of the country's great legal voice for civil liberties today." He is author of No Equal Justice: Race and Class in the American Criminal Justice System (New Press, 1999), which was named Best Non–Fiction Book of 1999 by the Boston Book Review, best book on an issue of national policy in 1999 by the American Political Science Association, and Enemy Aliens: Double Standards and Constitutional Freedoms in the War on Terrorism (New Press, rev. ed. 2005), which was awarded the American Book Award and the Hefner First Amendment Prize.

Bernard E. Harcourt is professor of law and faculty director of academic affairs at the University of Chicago. Professor Harcourt's scholarship focuses on issues of crime and punishment from an empirical and social theoretic perspective. He is the author of three books, including *Language of the Gun: Youth, Crime, and Public Policy* (University of Chicago Press 2005) and *Illusion of Order: The False Promise of Broken–Windows Policing* (Harvard University Press 2001). He is also the editor of a collection of essays on *Guns, Crime and Punishment in America* (New York University Press 2003), and of the journal, *The Carceral Notebooks*.

Professor Harcourt has written extensively on racial profiling and, more broadly, on the use of actuarial methods in criminal law and justice. He has a forthcoming book on the subject titled *Against Prediction: Punishing and Policing in an Actuarial Age* (University of Chicago Press 2006). He has also addressed the issue of racial profiling in his article *Rethinking Racial Profiling: A Critique of the Economics, Civil Liberties, and Constitutional Literature, and of Criminal Profiling More Generally*, published in *The University of Chicago Law Review* (Fall 2004).

Professor Harcourt earned his bachelor's degree in political theory at Princeton University, his law degree at Harvard Law School, and a Ph.D. in political science in the Government Department at Harvard University. After law school and a federal judicial clerkship, Professor Harcourt moved to Montgomery, Alabama to represent death row inmates on direct appeal, in state post-conviction, in federal habeas corpus, and at retrial. Professor Harcourt practiced at the Equal Justice Initiative (formerly known as the Alabama Capital Representation Resource Center), and has continued to represent several death row inmates pro bono since that time. Professor Harcourt has also served on human rights missions to South Africa and Guatemala.

Yale Kamisar is currently a Professor of Law at the University of San Diego since 2002, and Clarence Darrow Distinguished University Emeritus Professor of Law at the University of Michigan where he taught from 1965–2004. He has written widely on criminal law, the administration of criminal justice, and the "politics of crime."

Kamisar is author of *Police Interrogation and Confessions* (1980) and the co-author of *Criminal Justice in Our Time* (1965). He has written the chapter on constitutional-criminal procedure for collections of essays on the Warren, Burger, and Rehnquist Courts. He also is co-author of two widely used casebooks, *Modern Criminal Procedure* (1st ed. 1965, 11th ed. 2005) and *Constitutional Law* (1st ed. 1964, 9th ed. 2001).

In four decades of law teaching Kamisar has written some fifty law review articles and some ninety op-ed pieces in most of the nation's leading newspapers. He received the American Bar Foundation's 1996 Research Award in recognition of his contributions to the law and the legal profession through his research and writing.

Pamela S. Karlan is the Kenneth and Harle Montgomery Professor of Public Interest Law at Stanford Law School, where is also co-directs the school's School Supreme Court Litigation Clinic. Karlan received her B.A., M.A. (history), and J.D. from Yale. She clerked for Judge Abraham Sofaer of S.D.N.Y. and Justice Harry Blackmun (during the Term when *Batson v. Kentucky* was decided) before serving as assistant counsel at the NAACP Legal Defense and Educational Fund. She has also served as a lecturer at the F.B.I. National Academy.

Karlan's primary scholarly interests lie in the areas of constitutional law and litigation, voting rights, and criminal procedure. She is the co-author of several leading casebooks, including *Constitutional Law* (5th ed. 2005), *The Law of Democracy: Legal Structure of the Political Process* (rev. 2nd ed. 2001), and *Civil Rights Actions: Enforcing the Constitution* (2000), as well as dozens of scholarly articles, including Convictions and Doubts: Retribution, Representation, and the Debate Over Felon Disenfranchisement, 56 Stan. L. Rev. 1147 (2004), and Race, Rights, and Remedies in Criminal Adjudication, 96 Mich. L. Rev. 2001 (1998).

Karlan also participates in extensive pro bono litigation, including cases involving fourth, fifth, and sixth amendment issues. Among her recent cases at the United States Supreme Court are *United States v. Gonzalez–Lopez*, *Georgia v. Randolph*, *Illinois v. Bartels*, and *City of Evanston v. Franklin*.

Nancy J. King is Lee S. and Charles A. Speir Professor of Law at Vanderbilt University Law School. Her research focuses on the post-investigative features of the criminal process including plea bargaining, trial, juries, sentencing, double jeopardy, appeals, and post-conviction review. She is co-author of two leading treatises on criminal procedure (Wright, King & Klein, Federal Practice and Procedure, Criminal 3d;

LaFave, Israel & King, Criminal Procedure, 2d ed.) as well as the leading criminal procedure casebook. Her work has been cited in decisions of the United States Supreme Court and lower courts. Professor King is a member of the Advisory Committee on the Federal Rules of Criminal Procedure for the U.S. Judicial Conference and a former member of Sixth Circuit Rules Advisory Committee. She has testified before the United States Sentencing Commission, and has served on the Governor's Task Force on Sentencing for Tennessee. She is frequent speaker for the federal judiciary at judicial workshops and circuit conferences.

Professor King's work on criminal juries has included such topics as jury selection, anonymous juries, nullification, and jury misconduct. A chapter on ethics for jurors after the trial is forthcoming in the volume *Jury Ethics*, and she recently published four articles examining the history, theory, and practice of jury sentencing, including: "The Origins of Felony Jury Sentencing in the United States," "Jury Sentencing in Practice—a Three–State Study," (with R. Noble) and "Jury Sentencing in Non–Capital Cases: Comparing Severity and Variance with Judicial Sentences in Two States," (with R. Noble). Her present research includes a collaborative empirical study of the processing of capital and non-capital habeas cases in US District Courts, conducted with researchers from the National Center for State Courts.

Michael J. Klarman is the James Monroe Distinguished Professor of Law and Professor of History at the University of Virginia. He received his B.A. and M.A. from the University of Pennsylvania, his J.D. from Stanford Law School, and his D. Phil. from the University of Oxford, where he was a Marshall Scholar. After law school, Professor Klarman clerked for the Honorable Ruth Bader Ginsburg. He joined the faculty at the University of Virginia School of Law in 1987 and has won numerous awards for his teaching and scholarship, which are primarily in the areas of Constitutional Law and Constitutional History. Klarman has also served as the Ralph S. Tyler, Jr., Visiting Professor at Harvard Law School, Distinguished Visiting Lee Professor of Law at the Marshall Wythe School of Law at the College of William & Mary, and as Visiting Professor at Stanford Law School. His book, From *Jim Crow to Civil Rights: The Supreme Court and the Struggle for Racial Equality*, was published by Oxford University Press in 2004 and received the 2005 Bancroft Prize in History.

Tracey Maclin is a professor of law at Boston University School of Law. He teaches Constitutional Law and Criminal Procedure. Professor Maclin has written several law review articles on the Fourth Amendment. He has also authored many amicus curiae briefs and served as counsel of record for the American Civil Liberties, the National Association Criminal Defense Lawyers and the Cato Institute in several Fourth Amendment cases in the United States Supreme Court. Prior to entering law teaching, Professor Maclin served as law clerk to Judge Boyce F. Martin, Jr., of the United States Court of Appeals for the Sixth Circuit. He was then an associate at the New York law firm of Cahill, Gordon & Reindel. Professor Maclin has taught at the University of Kentucky College of Law, Cornell Law School and Harvard Law School.

Daniel Richman is a professor at Fordham Law School, where he teaches criminal procedure, federal criminal law, and evidence. Before coming to Fordham in 1992, he was an Assistant U.S. Attorney in the Southern District of New for nearly six years, working in the narcotics, organized crime, and appellate units, and ending up as the Chief Appellate Attorney. Before becoming a federal prosecutor, he served as a law clerk to Chief Judge Wilfred Feinberg, of U.S. Court of Appeals for the Second Circuit, and Justice Thurgood Marshall of the U.S.Supreme Court. He has been a visiting professor at Columbia Law School and the University of Virginia School of Law. His most recent scholarship has focused on institutional interactions within the federal criminal justice system between prosecutors and agents, Congress and the Justice Department, and federal and local authorities.

Stephen Schulhofer is the Robert B. McKay Professor of Law at New York University. He has written more than fifty scholarly articles and six books, including a leading casebook in the field of criminal law. His recent work, focusing primarily on law enforcement responses to the attacks of September 11, 2001, includes two books, Rethinking the Patriot Act (2005) and The Enemy Within: Intelligence Gathering, Law Enforcement and Civil Liberties in the Wake of September 11 (2002), a monograph on The Secrecy Problem in Terrorism Trials (2005), as well as many articles on the nexus between liberty and national security in the struggle against terrorism. He also writes extensively on other aspects of police practices, criminal law and criminal procedure. In a different field, his book, Unwanted Sex: The Culture of Intimidation and the Failure of Law (Harvard University Press 1998), examines our laws against sexual assault and other forms of intimidation and sexual overreaching.

Before joining the NYU faculty, Professor Schulhofer was the director of the Center for Studies in Criminal Justice at the University of Chicago, where he was the Julius Kreeger Professor of Law. He completed his B.A. at Princeton and his J.D. at Harvard, both summa cum laude, and was the Developments and Supreme Court editor of the Harvard Law Review. He then clerked for two years for U.S. Supreme Court Justice Hugo Black. Before teaching, he also practiced law for three years with the firm Coudert Frres, in France.

David Alan Sklansky is Professor of Law at the University of California, Berkeley. He teaches and writes about evidence, criminal procedure, and criminal law. Professor Sklansky received his A.B. in 1981 from Berkeley, majoring in Biophysics, and his J.D. in 1984 from Harvard Law School. Following graduation he clerked for Judge Abner J. Mikva on the United States Court of Appeals for the D.C. Circuit and then for U.S. Supreme Court Justice Harry A. Blackmun. He briefly practiced labor law at the Washington, D.C., firm of Bredhoff & Kaiser and then spent seven years as an Assistant United States Attorney in Los Angeles, specializing in white collar fraud prosecutions. From 1994 to 2005 he taught at UCLA School of Law, where he won the campus-wide Distinguished Teaching Award and was twice voted the law school's professor of the year. While at UCLA, he served as special counsel to the independent review panel appointed to investigate the Los Angeles Police Department's Rampart Division scandal. Among his recent publications are *Police and Democracy,* 103 Mich. L. Rev. 1699 (2005); *Quasi-Affirmative Rights in Constitutional Criminal Procedure*, 88 Va. L. Rev. 1229 (2002); *Back to the Future:* Kyllo, Katz, *and Common Law*, 72 Miss. L.J. 143 (2002); and *The Fourth Amendment and Common Law*, 100 Colum. L. Rev. 1739 (2000). He is at work on a book on the changing ideal of democratic policing

Carol S. Steiker is Professor of Law at Harvard Law School. Professor Steiker attended Harvard–Radcliffe Colleges and Harvard Law School, where she served as president of the Harvard Law Review. After clerking for Judge J. Skelly Wright of the D.C. Circuit Court of Appeals and Justice Thurgood Marshall of the U.S. Supreme Court, she worked as a staff attorney for the Public Defender Service for the District of Columbia, where she represented indigent defendants at all stages of the criminal process. She has been a member of the Harvard Law School faculty since 1992. She served as Associate Dean for Academic Affairs from 1998–2001, and she currently serves as the Dean's Special Advisor on Public Service. Professor Steiker is the author of numerous scholarly articles in the fields of criminal law, criminal procedure, and capital punishment, and most recently served on the Board of Editors of the Encyclopedia of Crime and Justice (2nd ed. Macmillan, 2002). She is currently at work on two book-length projects, one on the changing face of capital punishment in America and one on mercy and the institutions of criminal justice. In addition to her scholarly work, Professor Steiker has served as a consultant and an expert witness on issues of criminal justice for a number of non-profit organizations and federal and state legislatures.

Kate Stith, the Lafayette S. Foster Professor of Law at Yale Law School, has written widely on criminal procedure and constitutional law and is the author of FEAR OF JUDGING: SENTENCING GUIDELINES IN THE FEDERAL COURTS (U. of Chicago, 1998) (with José A. Cabranes), an examination of the historical genesis, legislative history, structure, implementation, and consequences of the Federal Sentencing Guidelines. Prior to joining the faculty at Yale, she was an Assistant United States Attorney for the Southern District of New York, where she prosecuted white-collar and organized-crime cases. She also has served as a staff economist for the President's Council of Economic Advisers, and as a Special Assistant in the Department of Justice in Washington. A graduate of Dartmouth College, the Kennedy School of Government, and Harvard Law School, Professor Stith clerked for Judge Carl McGowan of the U.S. Court of Appeals for the District of Columbia and for Supreme Court Justice Byron R. White. She is serving or has served as an Adviser for the American Law Institute project *Model Penal Code–Sentencing*; on the Committee on Law and Justice of the National Research Council; on the Professional Ethics Committee in the State of Connecticut; as a Commissioner of the Permanent Commission on the Status of Women in Connecticut; as President of the Connecticut Bar Foundation; on the Dartmouth College Board of Trustees; as faculty sponsor and director of the Women's Campaign School at Yale; as Deputy Dean of Yale Law School; and, by appointment of the Chief Justice of the United States, on the Advisory Committee on the Federal Rules of Criminal Procedure.

Bill Stuntz is a Professor at Harvard Law School. He joined Harvard's faculty in 2000; before that, he was a professor at the University of Virginia for fourteen years. Stuntz has authored more than two dozen law review articles and essays on various aspects of the criminal justice system. His works include an economic analysis of plea bargaining, a history of the "substantive origins" of the Fourth and Fifth Amendments, an analysis of the race and class biases that afflict enforcement of America's drug laws, and an examination of the political and legal sources of overcriminalization. In all of these works, Stuntz emphasizes two connections. The first links substantive criminal law and the law of criminal procedure—the way the steady expansion of the former undermines the latter's protections of criminal defendants' rights. The second concerns the interaction of constitutional law and the politics of crime. According to Stuntz, constitutional law contributes to the very political pathologies that other scholars use to justify constitutional regulation of the criminal justice system. Healthier constitutional law, he argues, would produce more reasonable politics—and more reasonable politics would produce a more just justice system.

†

y